Hymns of the Christian Life

A book of worship in song emphasizing evangelism, missions, and the deeper life

1978 revised and enlarged edition

CHRISTIAN PUBLICATIONS
Camp Hill, Pennsylvania

ISBN 0-87509-278-0

Printed in the United States of America

PREFACE

This revised edition of *Hymns of the Christian Life* is dedicated to the praise of almighty God. In the days of the prophets and apostles God's people were called to enter His presence with singing. Song has continued to be an integral part of worship throughout the ages. The Reformation in the sixteenth century gave a new emphasis to congregational song, and each great spiritual movement in the church since that time has made its distinctive contribution to the rich heritage of Christian hymnody. "Let us offer the sacrifice of praise to God continually, that is, the fruit of our lips giving thanks to his name" (Heb. 13:15). "Whoso offereth praise glorifieth me" (Ps. 50:23).

The purpose of the hymnal committee, above all else, has been to provide an adequate collection of hymns worshipful in character and sound in doctrine. To this end each selection in the edition of 1962 was reviewed and its doctrinal, literary, musical, and hymnic values considered. Where the words *Melody by* precede the name of the composer, it may be assumed that the harmony has been somewhat altered. Deletions and additions were made in order to include within reasonable limits of space hymns to meet every occasion in church life. The hymns have been arranged in topical sequence and fully indexed.

This new edition is the seventh to bear the title, *Hymns of the Christian Life*. The first was drawn up in 1891 by Albert B. Simpson with the aid of R. Kelso Carter. It was designed especially to meet the need of congregations stressing the worldwide missionary enterprise and a deeper personal spiritual life. Every effort has been made to follow the spirit and tradition of this first edition and of those that followed it. A distinctive feature is the liberal representation of the hymns of Albert B. Simpson with their special emphasis upon the indwelling Christ and the worldwide missionary vision.

Many great Christian leaders of the past, from Augustine to the Wesleys, were profoundly concerned with the place of song in worship and with its effect upon the worshipers. Their concern was that both words and music be worthy of their high purpose: the worship of God, who is not only gracious but also holy and perfect and true. This concern the committee has sought to bear in mind while carrying out its task. The apostle Paul in two places (Col. 3:16; Eph. 5:19) specifically mentions the singing of "psalms, hymns, and spiritual songs." In the present volume a number of metrical renditions of the Psalms have been included, as well as hymns that are based on Psalms and on other passages of Scripture. A number of older hymns, rich in scriptural phraseology and doctrinal content, have been included. All these are brought together to form a part of that great heritage which links the saints of the past with the Christians of today in one fellowship of praise.

Hymns should not be regarded only as a means of public worship. They are intended to be used not only in the sanctuary, the church school, and the home, but also to be read as devotional poetry in private devotion.

NEW FEATURES

In editing the music for this new edition of *Hymns of the Christian Life,* careful consideration was given in the interest of more effective congregational participation. We have endeavored to retain the best of both the 1936 and the 1962 editions in order to produce this quality hymnal. Please remember that what we have used most closely conforms to contemporary music and yet clearly retains the best of the old. Every effort has been made to limit a hymn tune to no more than three texts. Thus it has been possible to introduce a wider selection of worthy tunes.

An outstanding new feature is a procedure for a proper musical introduction. Special markings have been added to each selection to assist the accompanist in presenting a proper introduction. These "Introduction Markings" indicate the beginning and the ending or the continuation and the ending of the introduction. Where no ending markings are indicated, the introduction follows to the end of the selection. These markings are copyrighted. Please see copyright statement.

Four-part harmony has been used with all tunes except a few which lend themselves best to unison singing. Music has been provided from a variety of tradition. The great chorales and Psalm tunes of the Reformation, the more elaborate tunes of the eighteenth century, the American and British tradition of the nineteenth century, plus several of the new and contemporary additions of the twentieth century complete this 1978 edition of *Hymns of the Christian Life*.

Your new hymnal features Scripture headings under each song title, plus a Scripture heading index, an expanded Scripture Reading section, an elaborate Topical Listing index, and a special "Aids to Worship" section. These all add the dimension of a worship tool to your fine new hymnal.

Much care and thought have been expended in the choice of material both of words and music. There is a wide selection with an appeal to a variety of tastes and backgrounds. This book is offered with a sincere desire to glorify God and aid His people in praising and glorifying Him.

ACKNOWLEDGMENT

Grateful acknowledgment is given to those who have granted permission for the use of their hymns and tunes. Every effort has been made to properly accredit these in the body of the book. If, through inadvertence, any omissions occur, upon written notification,acknowledgment will be included in future editions.

The Committee on Hymnal Revision

CONTENTS

Contents

Glory Be to God 1

. . . the Father, the Word, and the Holy Ghost: and these three are one. 1 John 5:7

REGENT SQUARE 8.7.8.7.8.7.

Horatius Bonar, 1808-1889

Henry T. Smart, 1813-1879

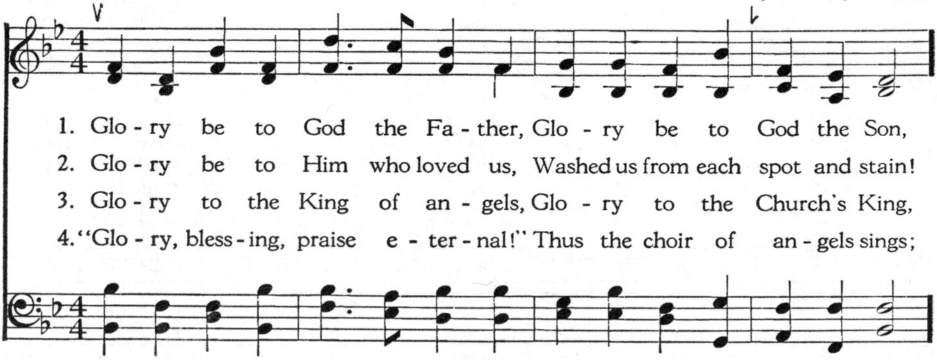
1. Glo - ry be to God the Fa - ther, Glo - ry be to God the Son,
2. Glo - ry be to Him who loved us, Washed us from each spot and stain!
3. Glo - ry to the King of an - gels, Glo - ry to the Church's King,
4. "Glo - ry, bless - ing, praise e - ter - nal!" Thus the choir of an - gels sings;

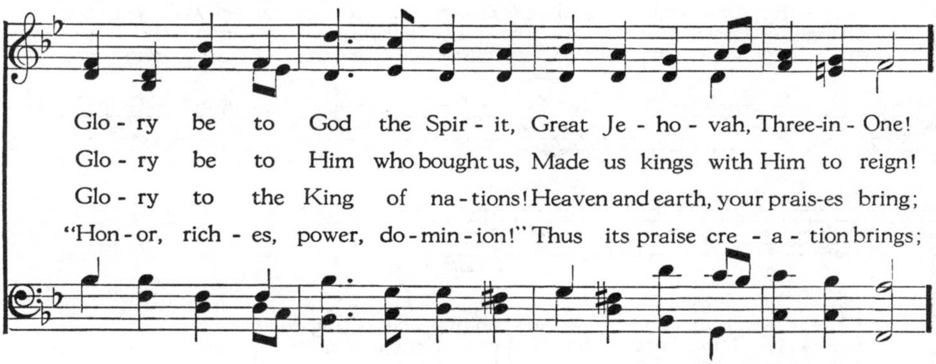
Glo - ry be to God the Spir - it, Great Je - ho - vah, Three-in - One!
Glo - ry be to Him who bought us, Made us kings with Him to reign!
Glo - ry to the King of na - tions! Heaven and earth, your prais-es bring;
"Hon - or, rich - es, power, do - min - ion!" Thus its praise cre - a - tion brings;

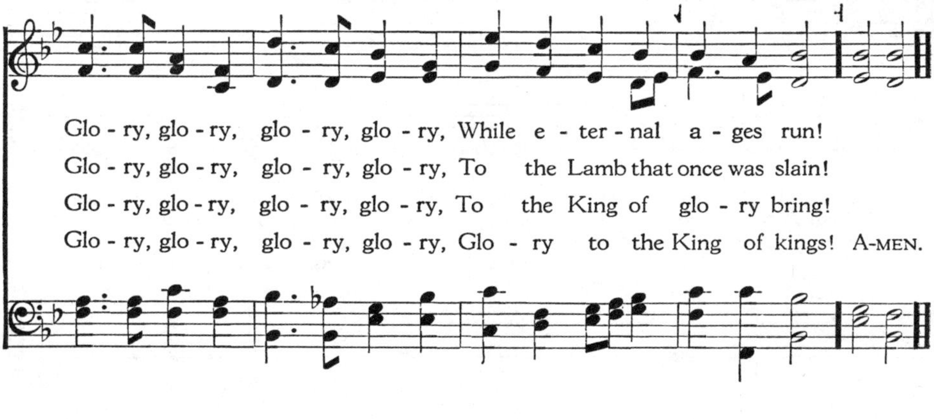
Glo - ry, glo - ry, glo - ry, glo - ry, While e - ter - nal a - ges run!
Glo - ry, glo - ry, glo - ry, glo - ry, To the Lamb that once was slain!
Glo - ry, glo - ry, glo - ry, glo - ry, To the King of glo - ry bring!
Glo - ry, glo - ry, glo - ry, glo - ry, Glo - ry to the King of kings! A-MEN.

2 Holy, Holy, Holy, Lord God Almighty

. . . which was, and is, and is to come. Rev. 4:8

NICAEA 11.12.12.10.

Reginald Heber, 1783-1826

John B. Dykes, 1823-1876

1. Ho - ly, Ho - ly, Ho - ly, Lord God Al - might - y!
2. Ho - ly, Ho - ly, Ho - ly! all the saints a - dore Thee,
3. Ho - ly, Ho - ly, Ho - ly! though the dark - ness hide Thee,
4. Ho - ly, Ho - ly, Ho - ly, Lord God Al - might - y!
Ear - ly in the morn - ing our song shall rise to Thee;
Cast - ing down their gold - en crowns a - round the glass - y sea;
Though the eye of sin - ful man Thy glo - ry may not see.
All Thy works shall praise Thy name in earth, and sky, and sea;
Ho - ly, Ho - ly, Ho - ly, mer - ci - ful and might - y!
Cher - u - bim and ser - a - phim fall - ing down be - fore Thee,
On - ly Thou art ho - ly, there is none be - side Thee,
Ho - ly, Ho - ly, Ho - ly, mer - ci - ful and might - y!
God in Three - Per - sons, bless - ed Trin - i - ty!
Which wert, and art, and ev - er - more shalt be.
Per - fect in power, in love, and pur - i - ty.
God in Three - Per - sons, bless - ed Trin - i - ty!

Come, Thou Almighty King 3

. . . Lord God Almighty; . . . thou King of saints. Rev. 15:3

Anonymous, circa 1757

ITALIAN HYMN 6.6.4.6.6.6.4.
Felice de Giardini, 1716-1796

1. Come, Thou Al - might - y King, Help us Thy
2. Come, Thou in - car - nate Word, Gird on Thy
3. Come, Ho - ly Com - fort - er, Thy sa - cred
4. To Thee, great One - in - Three, E - ter - nal
name to sing, Help us to praise. Fa - ther, all -
might - y sword, Our prayer at - tend: Come, and Thy
wit - ness bear In this glad hour: Thou who al -
prais - es be Hence ev - er - more. Thy sov - ereign
glo - ri - ous, O'er all vic - to - ri - ous,
peo - ple bless, And give Thy Word suc - cess;
might - y art, Now rule in ev - ery heart,
ma - jes - ty May we in glo - ry see,
Come, and reign o - ver us, An - cient of Days.
Spir - it of ho - li - ness, On us de - scend.
And ne'er from us de - part, Spir - it of power.
And to e - ter - ni - ty Love and a - dore.

(For different version of tune see No. 441)

4 Father of Heaven

. . . there are three that bear record in heaven . . . 1 John 5:7

HESPERUS (Quebec) L.M.

Edward Cooper, 1770-1833 | Henry Baker, 1835-1910

1. Fa - ther of heaven, whose love pro - found A ran - som
2. Al - might - y Son, in - car - nate Word, Our Proph - et,
3. E - ter - nal Spir - it, by whose breath The soul is
4. Je - ho - vah— Fa - ther, Spir - it, Son— Mys - te - rious

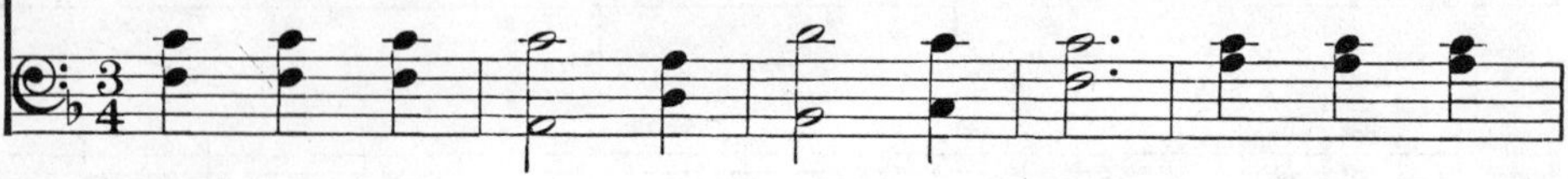

for our souls hath found, Be - fore Thy throne we
Priest, Re - deem - er, Lord, Be - fore Thy throne we
raised from sin and death, Be - fore Thy throne we
God - head, Three - in - One, Be - fore Thy throne we

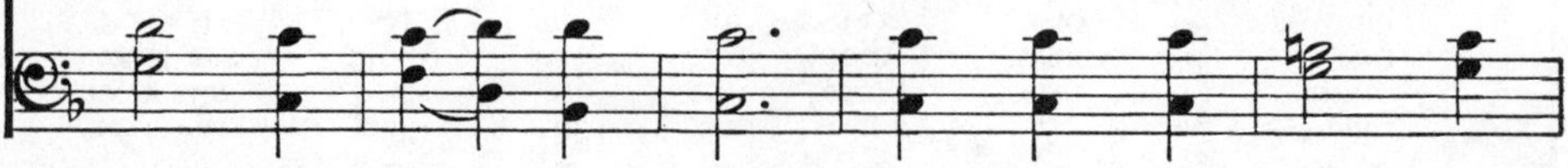

sin - ners bend; To us Thy par - doning love ex - tend.
sin - ners bend; To us Thy sav - ing grace ex - tend.
sin - ners bend; To us Thy quick - ening power ex - tend.
sin - ners bend; Grace, par - don, life to us ex - tend. A - MEN.

(For lower keys see Nos. 35 and 263)

All Glory Be to God on High 5

Glory to God in the highest . . . Luke 2:14

Metrical version of *Gloria in Excelsis*
Nikolaus Decius, circa 1490-1541
Translated by Catherine Winkworth, 1827-1878

ALLEIN GOTT IN DER HÖH' 8.7.8.7.8.8.7.
From *Lutheran Chorale,* 1524

1. All glo - ry be to God on high, Who hath our race be -
2. We praise, we wor - ship Thee, we trust, And give Thee thanks for -
3. O Je - sus Christ, our God and Lord, Son of Thy heaven-ly
4. O Ho - ly Ghost, Thou pre - cious gift, Thou Com - fort - er un -
friend - ed. To us no harm shall e'er come nigh; The strife at
ev - er, O Fa - ther that Thy rule is just, And wise, and
Fa - ther, O Thou who hast our peace re - stored, And the lost
fail - ing, O'er Sa - tan's snares our souls up - lift. And let Thy
last hath end - ed. God show - eth His good will to men, And
chang-es nev - er. Thy bound-less power o'er all things reigns, Done
sheep dost gath - er; Thou Lamb of God, to Thee on high, From
power a - vail - ing A - vert our woes, and calm our dread—For
peace shall reign on earth a - gain: Oh, thank Him for His good - ness!
is what - e'er Thy will or - dains. Blest are we that Thou reign - est!
out the depths we sin - ners cry, Have mer - cy on us, Je - sus!
us the Sav-iour's blood was shed: We trust in Thee to save us!

6 Holy God, We Praise Thy Name

. . . Holy, holy, holy, is the Lord of hosts . . . Isa. 6:3

Attributed to Ignace Franz, 1719-1790
Translated by Clarence A. Walworth, 1820-1900
From *TE DEUM,* 4th century

GROSSER GOTT, WIR LOBEN DICH 7.8.7.8.7.7.
From *Allgemeines Katholisches Gesangbuch,*
Vienna, circa 1774

1. Ho - ly God, we praise Thy name; Lord of all, we bow be - fore Thee;
2. Hark, the loud ce - les - tial hymn An - gel choirs a - bove are rais - ing;
3. Lo! the ap - os - tol - ic train Join Thy sa - cred name to hal - low;
4. Ho - ly Fa - ther, Ho - ly Son, Ho - ly Spir - it—Three we name Thee;
All on earth Thy scep - ter claim, All in heav-en a - bove a - dore Thee.
Cher - u - bim and ser - a - phim In un - ceas - ing cho - rus prais - ing,
Proph - ets swell the glad re - frain, And the white-robed mar - tyrs fol - low;
Though in es - sence on - ly one, Un - di - vid - ed God we claim Thee,
In - fi - nite Thy vast do - main, Ev - er - last - ing is Thy reign.
Fill the heavens with sweet ac - cord: Ho - ly, ho - ly, ho - ly Lord.
And from morn to set of sun, Through the church the song goes on.
And a - dor - ing bend the knee While we sing our praise to Thee. A-MEN.

7 Draw Nigh to Us, Thou Lord of Hosts

Draw nigh to God, and he will draw nigh to you. . . . James 4:8

Stanzas 1-2 by Michael Altenburg, 1584-1640
Stanza 3 from Gotha, 1651
Translated by Henry Esau, 1932

OLD HUNDREDTH L.M.
From *Genevan Psalter,* 1551
Attributed to Louis Bourgeois, circa 1510-1561

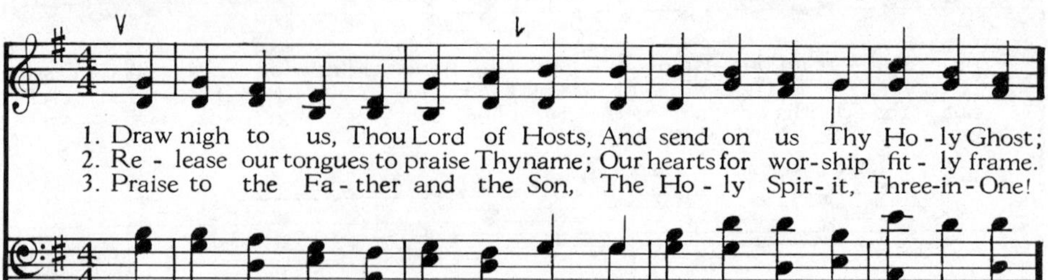
1. Draw nigh to us, Thou Lord of Hosts, And send on us Thy Ho - ly Ghost;
2. Re - lease our tongues to praise Thy name; Our hearts for wor - ship fit - ly frame.
3. Praise to the Fa - ther and the Son, The Ho - ly Spir - it, Three-in - One!

Draw Nigh to Us, Thou Lord of Hosts

With love and grace our lives com-mand, Give us Thy truths to un-der-stand.
In-crease our faith, re-new our mind; Praised be Thy name by all man-kind.
The bless-ed Trin-i-ty a-dore, At pre-sent and for-ev-er-more!

Praise Ye the Triune God 8

. . . praise thy name for thy lovingkindness . . . Psa. 138:2

Elizabeth R. Charles, 1828-1896

FLEMMING 11.11.11.5.
Friedrich F. Flemming, 1778-1813

1. Praise ye the Fa-ther for His lov-ing kind-ness, Ten-der-ly cares He for His err-ing chil-dren; Praise Him, ye an-gels, praise Him in the heav-ens, Praise ye Je-ho-vah!
2. Praise ye the Sav-iour—great is His com-pas-sion, Gra-cious-ly cares He for His cho-sen peo-ple; Young men and maid-ens, old-er men and chil-dren, Praise ye the Sav-iour!
3. Praise ye the Spir-it, Com-fort-er of Is-rael, Sent of the Fa-ther and the Son to bless us; Praise ye the Fa-ther, Son, and Ho-ly Spir-it, Praise ye the tri-une God!

9 Eternal Father, Strong to Save

O Lord God of hosts, who is a strong Lord like unto thee? . . . Psa. 89:8

Stanzas 1, 4 by William Whiting, 1825-1878 (altered)
Stanzas 2-3 by Robert N. Spencer, 1877-1961

MELITA 8.8.8.8.8.8.
John B. Dykes, 1823-1876

1. E - ter - nal Fa - ther, strong to save, Whose arm hath bound the
2. O Christ, the Lord of hill and plain O'er which our traf - fic
3. O Spir - it, whom the Fa - ther sent To spread a - broad the
4. O Trin - i - ty of love and power, Our breth - ren shield in
rest - less wave, Who bidd'st the might - y o - cean deep Its
runs a - main By moun - tain pass or val - ley low; Wher -
firm - a - ment; O Wind of heav - en, by Thy might Save
dan - ger's hour; From rock and tem - pest, fire and foe, Pro -
own ap - point - ed lim - its keep: O hear us when we
ev - er, Lord, Thy breth - ren go, Pro - tect them by Thy
all who dare the ea - gle's flight, And keep them by Thy
tect them where - so e'er they go; Thus ev - er - more shall
cry to Thee For those in per - il on the sea.
guard - ing hand From ev - ery per - il on the land.
watch - ful care From ev - ery per - il in the air.
rise to Thee Glad praise from air and land and sea. A - MEN.

(For different harmony and higher key see No. 34)

Praise to the Lord, the Almighty 10

. . . then shalt thou have thy delight in the Almighty . . . Job 22:26

Joachim Neander, 1650-1680
Translated by Catherine Winkworth, 1827-1878

LOBE DEN HERREN 14.14.4.7.8.
From *Stralsund Gesangbuch,* 1665

1. Praise to the Lord, the Al - might - y, the King of cre - a - tion!
2. Praise to the Lord, who o'er all things so won-drous-ly reign - eth,
3. Praise to the Lord, who with mar - vel - ous wis-dom hath made thee!
4. Praise to the Lord! Oh, let all that is in me a - dore Him!
O my soul, praise Him, for He is thy health and sal - va - tion!
Shel - ters thee un - der His wings, yea, so gent - ly sus - tain - eth!
Decked thee with health, and with lov - ing hand guid - ed and stayed thee;
All that hath life and breath, come now with prais - es be - fore Him!
All ye who hear, Now to His tem - ple draw near;
Hast thou not seen How thy de - sires e'er have been
How oft in grief Hath not He brought thee re - lief,
Let the A - men Sound from His peo - ple a - gain:
Join me in glad ad - o - ra - - tion!
Grant - ed in what He or - dain - - eth?
Spread - ing His wings for to shade thee!
Glad - ly for aye we a - dore Him. A - MEN.

11 A Mighty Fortress Is Our God

God is our refuge and strength . . . Psa. 46:1

EIN' FESTE BURG 8.7.8.7.6.6.6.6.7.

Martin Luther, 1483-1546
Translated by Frederick H. Hedge, 1805-1890

From a *Meistergesang* by Hans Sachs, d. 1576
Adapted by Johann Walther, 1496-1570

1. A might - y for - tress is our God, A bul-wark nev - er fail - ing;
2. Did we in our own strength con-fide, Our striv-ing would be los - ing;
3. And though this world, with dev - ils filled, Should threat-en to un - do us,
4. That Word a - bove all earth - ly powers, No thanks to them, a - bid - eth;
Our help-er He, a - mid the flood Of mor - tal ills pre - vail - ing:
Were not the right Man on our side, The Man of God's own choos - ing:
We will not fear, for God hath willed His truth to tri-umph through us:
The Spir - it and the gifts are ours Thro' Him who with us sid - eth:
For still our an - cient foe Doth seek to work us woe; His craft and power are
Dost ask who that may be? Christ Je - sus, it is He, Lord Sa - ba - oth, His
The Prince of Dark - ness grim–We trem-ble not for him; His rage we can en -
Let goods and kin - dred go, This mor - tal life al - so; The bod - y they may
great, And, armed with cru - el hate, On earth is not his e - qual.
name, From age to age the same, And He must win the bat - tle.
dure, For lo, his doom is sure, One lit - tle word shall fell him.
kill: God's truth a - bid - eth still, His king-dom is for - ev - er.

O Worship the King

. . . I will sing praise to my God . . . Psa. 104:33

Robert Grant, circa 1779-1838

LYONS 10.10.11.11.
Adapted from Johann M. Haydn, 1737-1806

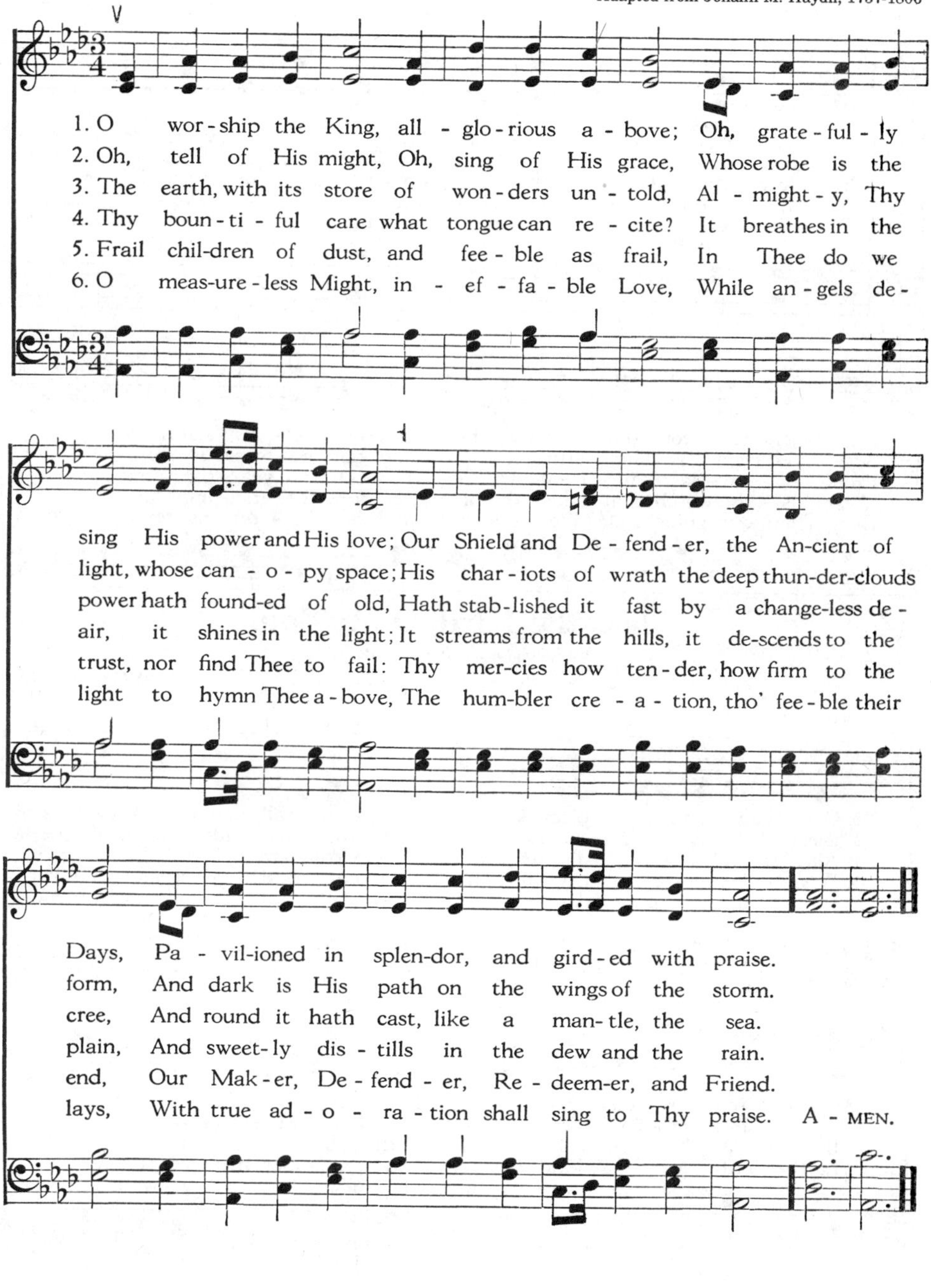
1. O wor-ship the King, all - glo-rious a - bove; Oh, grate-ful - ly
2. Oh, tell of His might, Oh, sing of His grace, Whose robe is the
3. The earth, with its store of won-ders un - told, Al - might - y, Thy
4. Thy boun - ti - ful care what tongue can re - cite? It breathes in the
5. Frail chil-dren of dust, and fee - ble as frail, In Thee do we
6. O meas-ure - less Might, in - ef - fa - ble Love, While an - gels de -
sing His power and His love; Our Shield and De - fend - er, the An-cient of
light, whose can - o - py space; His char - iots of wrath the deep thun-der-clouds
power hath found-ed of old, Hath stab-lished it fast by a change-less de -
air, it shines in the light; It streams from the hills, it de-scends to the
trust, nor find Thee to fail: Thy mer-cies how ten-der, how firm to the
light to hymn Thee a - bove, The hum-bler cre - a - tion, tho' fee - ble their
Days, Pa - vil-ioned in splen-dor, and gird - ed with praise.
form, And dark is His path on the wings of the storm.
cree, And round it hath cast, like a man-tle, the sea.
plain, And sweet-ly dis - tills in the dew and the rain.
end, Our Mak - er, De - fend - er, Re - deem-er, and Friend.
lays, With true ad - o - ra - tion shall sing to Thy praise. A - MEN.

13 O God, Our Help in Ages Past

Lord, thou hast been our dwelling place in all generations. Psa. 90:1

ST. ANNE C.M.
Supplement to the New Version, 1708
Attributed to William Croft, 1678-1727

Isaac Watts, 1674-1748

1. O God, our help in a - ges past, Our hope for years to come,
2. Un - der the shad - ow of Thy throne Still may we dwell se - cure;
3. Be - fore the hills in or - der stood, Or earth re - ceived her frame,
4. A thou - sand a - ges, in Thy sight, Are like an eve - ning gone;
5. O God, our help in a - ges past, Our hope for years to come,
Our shel - ter from the storm-y blast, And our e - ter - nal home!
Suf - fi - cient is Thine arm a - lone, And our de - fense is sure.
From ev - er - last - ing Thou art God, To end - less years the same.
Short as the watch that ends the night, Be - fore the ris - ing sun.
Be Thou our guide while life shall last, And our e - ter - nal home. A - MEN.

14 Bless the Lord, O My Soul

. . . and all that is within me . . . Psa. 103:1

MARTYRDOM C.M.
Hugh Wilson, 1764-1824

Scottish Psalter, 1650

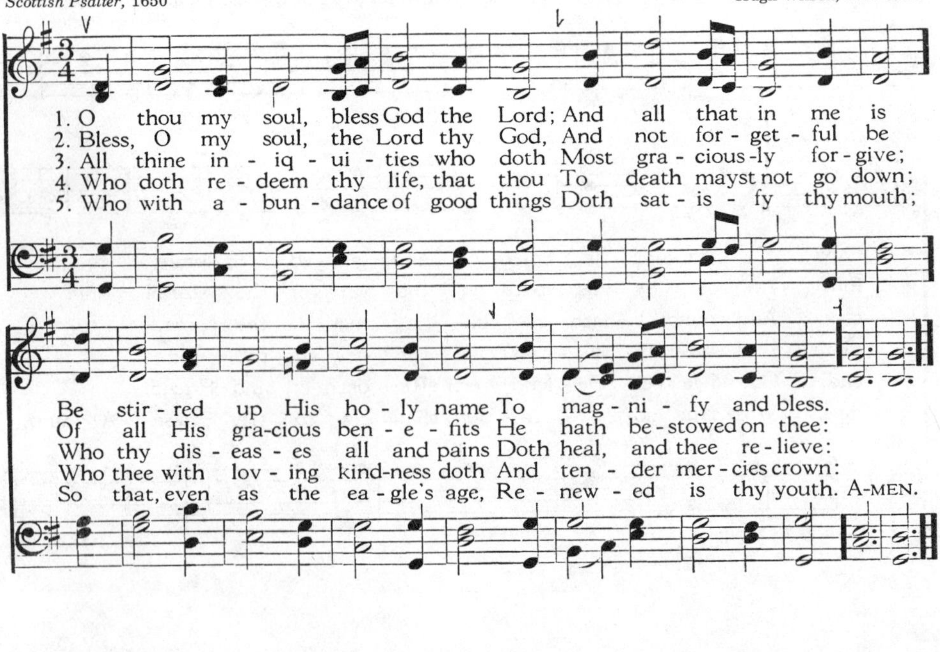
1. O thou my soul, bless God the Lord; And all that in me is
2. Bless, O my soul, the Lord thy God, And not for - get - ful be
3. All thine in - iq - ui - ties who doth Most gra - cious - ly for - give;
4. Who doth re - deem thy life, that thou To death mayst not go down;
5. Who with a - bun - dance of good things Doth sat - is - fy thy mouth;
Be stir - red up His ho - ly name To mag - ni - fy and bless.
Of all His gra - cious ben - e - fits He hath be - stowed on thee:
Who thy dis - eas - es all and pains Doth heal, and thee re - lieve:
Who thee with lov - ing kind - ness doth And ten - der mer - cies crown:
So that, even as the ea - gle's age, Re - new - ed is thy youth. A - MEN.

Immortal, Invisible, God Only Wise 15

. . . unto the King eternal, . . . be honour and glory forever and ever. . . . 1 Tim. 1:17

ST. DENIO 11.11.11.11.
Welsh melody
From John Roberts' *Caniadau y Cyssegr*, 1839

Walter C. Smith, 1824-1908

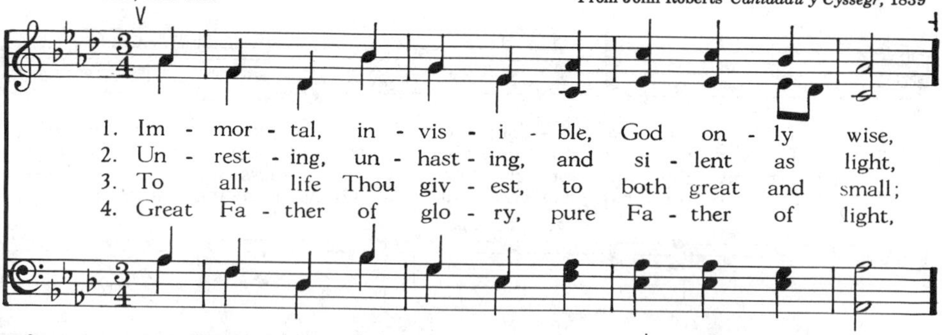
1. Im - mor - tal, in - vis - i - ble, God on - ly wise,
2. Un - rest - ing, un - hast - ing, and si - lent as light,
3. To all, life Thou giv - est, to both great and small;
4. Great Fa - ther of glo - ry, pure Fa - ther of light,

In light in - ac - ces - si - ble hid from our eyes,
Nor want - ing, nor wast - ing, Thou rul - est in might;
In all life Thou liv - est, the true life of all.
Thine an - gels a - dore Thee, all veil - ing their sight,

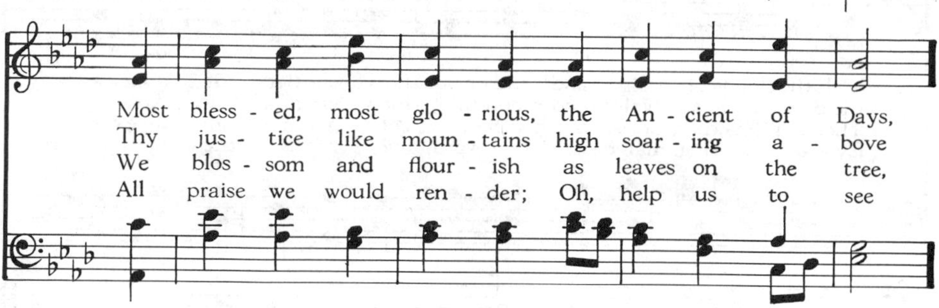
Most bless - ed, most glo - rious, the An - cient of Days,
Thy jus - tice like moun - tains high soar - ing a - bove
We blos - som and flour - ish as leaves on the tree,
All praise we would ren - der; Oh, help us to see

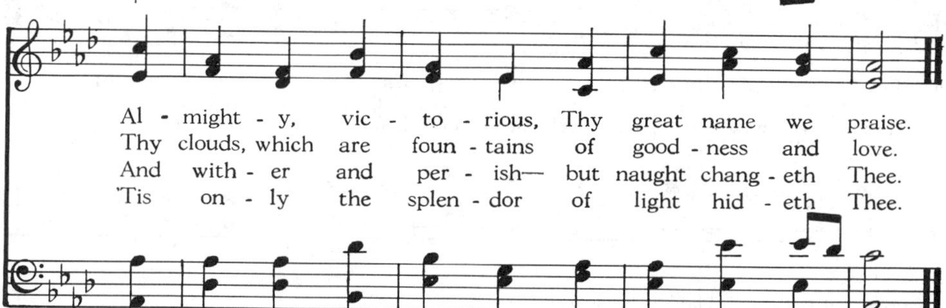
Al - might - y, vic - to - rious, Thy great name we praise.
Thy clouds, which are foun - tains of good - ness and love.
And with - er and per - ish— but naught chang - eth Thee.
'Tis on - ly the splen - dor of light hid - eth Thee.

16 Joyful, Joyful, We Adore Thee

Sing, O heavens; and be joyful, O earth; . . . Isa. 49:13

HYMN TO JOY 8.7.8.7.D.
Melody from *9th Symphony,* Ludwig van Beethoven, 1770-1827
Harmony by J. Buchanan MacMillan, b. 1915

Henry Van Dyke, 1852-1933

1. Joy - ful, joy - ful, we a - dore Thee, God of glo - ry, Lord of love;
2. All Thy works with joy sur-round Thee, Earth and heaven re - flect Thy rays,
3. Thou art giv - ing and for - giv - ing, Ev - er bless - ing, ev - er blest,
4. Mor - tals, join the hap - py cho - rus Which the morn - ing stars be - gan;
Hearts un - fold like flowers be - fore Thee, Open - ing to the sun a - bove.
Stars and an - gels sing a - round Thee, Cen - ter of un - bro - ken praise.
Well-spring of the joy of liv - ing, O - cean depth of hap - py rest!
Fa - ther love is reign-ing o'er us, Broth - er love binds man to man.
Melt the clouds of sin and sad - ness, Drive the dark of doubt a - way;
Field and for - est, vale and moun-tain, Flow - ery mead - ow, flash-ing sea,
Thou our Fa - ther, Christ our Broth - er, All who live in love are Thine;
Ev - er sing - ing, march we on - ward, Vic - tors in the midst of strife,
Giv - er of im - mor - tal glad - ness, Fill us with the light of day.
Chant - ing bird and flow - ing foun - tain, Call us to re - joice in Thee.
Teach us how to love each oth - er, Lift us to the Joy di - vine.
Joy - ful mu - sic leads us Sun - ward In the tri - umph song of life.

My God, How Wonderful Thou Art 17

Who is like unto the Lord our God . . . Psa. 113:5

WESTMINISTER C.M.

Frederick W. Faber, 1814-1863

James Turle, 1802-1882

1. My God, how won-der-ful Thou art, Thy maj-es-ty how bright!
2. How dread are Thine e-ter-nal years, O ev-er-last-ing Lord,
3. How beau-ti-ful, how beau-ti-ful The sight of Thee must be,
4. Oh, how I fear Thee, liv-ing God, With deep-est, ten-derest fears,
5. Yet I may love Thee, too, O Lord, Al-might-y as Thou art,
6. Fa-ther of Je-sus, love's re-ward, What rap-ture will it be

How beau-ti-ful Thy mer-cy seat, In depths of burn-ing light!
By pros-trate spir-its day and night In-cess-ant-ly a-dored!
Thine end-less wis-dom, bound-less power, And aw-ful pur-i-ty!
And wor-ship Thee with trem-bling hope And pen-i-ten-tial tears!
For Thou hast stooped to ask of me The love of my poor heart.
Pros-trate be-fore Thy throne to lie, And gaze and gaze on Thee! A-MEN.

God Is My Strong Salvation 18

The Lord is my light and my salvation . . . Psa. 27:1

MEIN LEBEN 7.6.7.6.

James Montgomery, 1771-1854

Melchoir Vulpius, 1560-1616

1. God is my strong sal-va-tion; What foe have I to fear?
2. Though hosts en-camp a-round me Firm to the fight I stand;
3. Place on the Lord re-li-ance, My soul, with cour-age wait;
4. His might thy heart shall strength-en, His love thy joy in-crease;

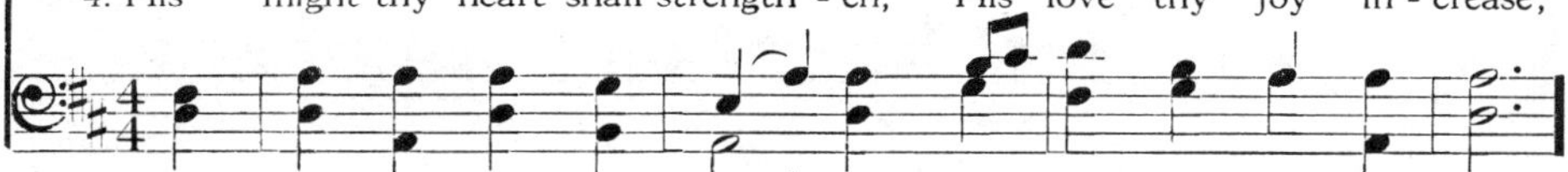

In dark-ness and temp-ta-tion My light, my help is near.
What ter-ror can con-found me, With God at my right hand?
His truth be thine af-fi-ance, When faint and des-o-late.
Mer-cy thy days shall length-en; The Lord will give thee peace. A-MEN.

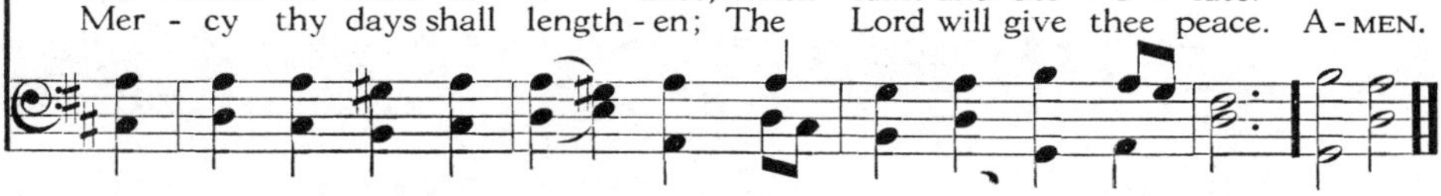

19 The Spacious Firmament on High

. . . the firmament sheweth his handywork. Psa. 19:1

CREATION L.M.D.

Joseph Addison, 1672-1719

Arrangement from Franz Joseph Haydn, 1732-1809

1. The spa - cious fir - ma - ment on high, With all the
2. Soon as the eve - ning shades pre - vail, The moon takes
3. What though in sol - emn si - lence all Move round this
blue e - the - re-al sky, And span - gled heavens, a shin - ing frame,
up the won - drous tale, And night - ly to the lis - tening earth
dark ter - res - tri-al ball? What though no re - al voice nor sound
Their great O - rig - i - nal pro - claim. Th'un-wea - ried sun, from
Re - peats the sto - ry of her birth; Whilst all the stars that
A - midst their ra-diant orbs be found? In rea - son's ear they
day to day, Does his Cre - a - tor's power dis - play, And pub - lish -
round her burn, And all the plan - ets in their turn, Con - firm the
all re - joice, And ut - ter forth a glo - rious voice; For - ev - er
es to ev - ery land The work of an al-might - y hand.
ti - dings as they roll, And spread the truth from pole to pole.
sing - ing, as they shine, "The hand that made us is di - vine." A-MEN.

All People That on Earth Do Dwell 20

. . . come before his presence with singing. Psa. 100:2

From *Scottish Psalter,* 1650
Attributed to William Kethe, 1510-1594

OLD HUNDREDTH L.M.
From *Genevan Psalter,* 1551
Attributed to Louis Bourgeois, circa 1510-1561

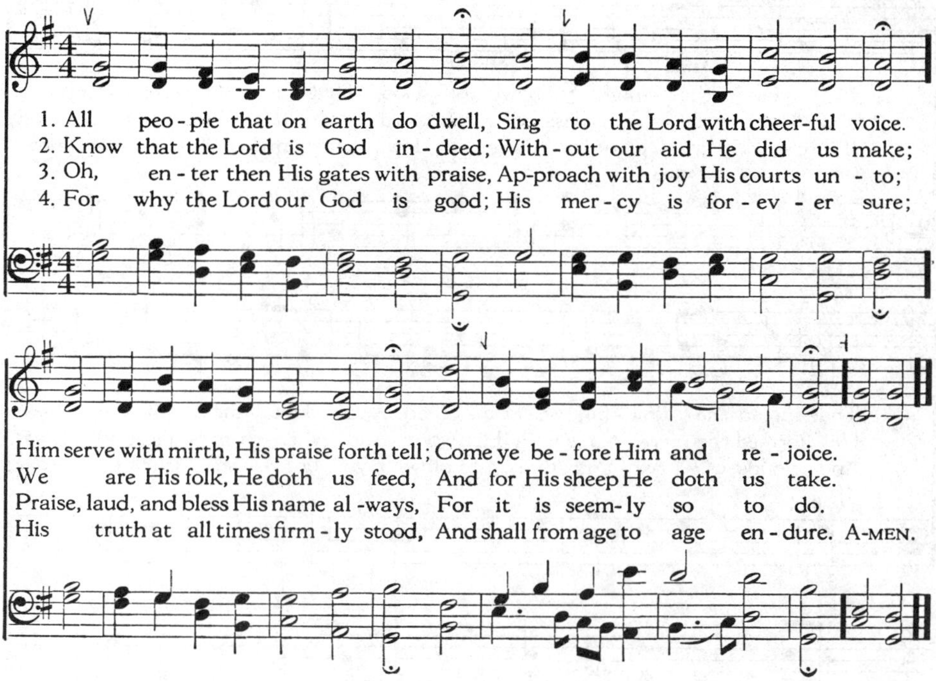
1. All people that on earth do dwell, Sing to the Lord with cheerful voice.
2. Know that the Lord is God indeed; Without our aid He did us make;
3. Oh, enter then His gates with praise, Approach with joy His courts unto;
4. For why the Lord our God is good; His mercy is forever sure;
Him serve with mirth, His praise forth tell; Come ye before Him and rejoice.
We are His folk, He doth us feed, And for His sheep He doth us take.
Praise, laud, and bless His name always, For it is seemly so to do.
His truth at all times firmly stood, And shall from age to age endure. A-MEN.

Melody in the tenor

Harmony by John Dowland, 1562-1626

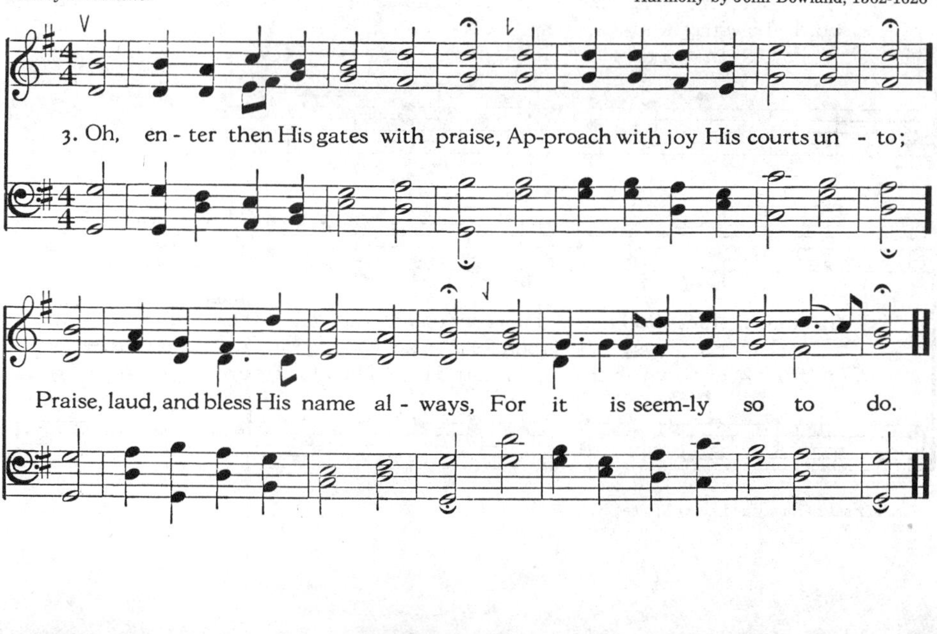
3. Oh, enter then His gates with praise, Approach with joy His courts unto;
Praise, laud, and bless His name always, For it is seemly so to do.

21 I Sing the Mighty Power of God

. . . the Lord made heaven and earth, the sea, and all that in them is . . . Exod. 20:11

ELLACOMBE C.M.D.

Isaac Watts, 1674-1748 (altered)

From *Gesangbuch der Herzogl*, Württemberg, 1784

1. I sing the might-y power of God, That made the moun-tains rise;
2. I sing the good-ness of the Lord, That filled the earth with food;
3. There's not a plant or flower be - low, But makes Thy glo - ries known;
That spread the flow - ing seas a - broad, And built the loft - y skies.
He formed the crea-tures with His word, And then pro-nounced them good.
And clouds a - rise, and tem-pests blow, By or - der from Thy throne;
I sing the wis-dom that or - dained The sun to rule the day;
Lord, how Thy won-ders are dis - played, Wher - e'er I turn my eye:
While all that bor-rows life from Thee Is ev - er in Thy care,
The moon shines full at His com-mand, And all the stars o - bey.
If I sur - vey the ground I tread, Or gaze up - on the sky!
And ev - ery - where that man can be, Thou, God, art pres - ent there.

(For different harmony and lower key see No. 447)

Praise, My Soul, the King of Heaven 22

Bless the Lord, . . . and forget not all his benefits. Psa. 103:2

BENEDIC ANIMA MEA 8.7.8.7.8.7.

Henry F. Lyte, 1793-1847

John Goss, 1800-1880

1. Praise, my soul, the King of heav - en, To His feet thy
2. Praise Him for His grace and fa - vor To our fa - thers
3. Fa - ther - like, He tends and spares us; Well our fee - ble
4. An - gels, help us to a - dore Him— Ye be - hold Him
trib - ute bring; Ran - somed, healed, re - stored, for - giv - en,
in dis - tress; Praise Him, still the same for - ev - er,
frame He knows, In His hands He gent - ly bears us,
face to face; Sun and moon, bow down be - fore Him;
Who, like me, His praise should sing? Al - le - lu - ia!
Slow to chide, and swift to bless. Al - le - lu - ia!
Res - cues us from all our foes. Al - le - lu - ia!
Dwell - ers all in time and space, Al - le - lu - ia!
Al - le - lu - ia! Praise the ev - er - last - ing King!
Al - le - lu - ia! Glo - rious in His faith - ful - ness!
Al - le - lu - ia! Wide - ly as His mer - cy flows!
Al - le - lu - ia! Praise with us the God of grace! A - MEN.

23 Unto the Hills Around Do I Lift Up

I will lift up mine eyes . . . from whence cometh my help. Psa. 121:1

SANDON 10.4.10.4.10.10.

John D.S. Campbell, 1845-1914

Charles H. Purday, 1799-1885

1. Un - to the hills a - round do I lift up My long - ing eyes:
2. He will not suf - fer that thy foot be moved: Safe shalt thou be.
3. Je - ho - vah is Him - self thy keep - er true, Thy change-less shade;
4. From ev - ery e - vil shall He keep thy soul, From ev - ery sin;
Oh, whence for me shall my sal - va - tion come, From whence a - rise?
No care - less slum - ber shall His eye - lids close, Who keep - eth thee.
Je - ho - vah thy de - fense on thy right hand Him - self hath made.
Je - ho - vah shall pre - serve Thy go - ing out, Thy com - ing in.
From God the Lord doth come my cer - tain aid,
Be - hold, He sleep - eth not, He slum - bereth ne'er,
And thee no sun by day shall ev - er smite;
A - bove thee, watch - ing, He whom we a - dore
From God the Lord who heaven and earth hath made.
Who keep - eth Is - rael in His ho - ly care.
No moon shall harm thee in the si - lent night.
Shall keep thee hence - forth, yea, for - ev - er - more.
A-MEN.

All Creatures of Our God and King 24

Let them praise the name of the Lord . . . Psa. 148:5

LASST UNS ERFREUEN 8.8.4.4.8.8. with Alleluias

St. Francis of Assisi, 1182-1226
Translated by William H. Draper, 1855-1933

From *Geistliche Kirchengesäng*, 1623
As in *The English Hymnal*, 1906

UNISON
1. All creatures of our God and King, Lift up your voice and with us
2. Thou rushing wind that art so strong, Ye clouds that sail in heaven a-
3. Dear mother earth, who day by day Unfold-est bless-ings on our
4. And all ye men of tender heart, For-giv-ing oth-ers, take your
5. Let all things their Cre-a-tor bless, And wor-ship Him in hum-ble-
Praise God from whom all bless-ings flow, Praise Him all crea-tures here be-
HARMONY
UNISON
sing, Al-le-lu-ia! Al-le-lu-ia! Thou burn-ing sun with
long, Oh, praise Him! Al-le-lu-ia! Thou ris-ing morn, in
way, Oh, praise Him! Al-le-lu-ia! The flowers and fruits that
part, Oh, sing ye! Al-le-lu-ia! Ye who long pain and
ness. Oh, praise Him! Al-le-lu-ia! Praise, praise the Fa-ther,
low, Al-le-lu-ia! Al-le-lu-ia! Praise Him a-bove, ye
HARMONY
gold-en beam, Thou sil-ver moon with soft-er gleam! Oh, praise Him,
praise re-joice, Ye lights of eve-ning, find a voice! Oh, praise Him,
in thee grow, Let them His glo-ry al-so show! Oh, praise Him,
sor-row bear, Praise God and on Him cast your care! Oh, praise Him,
praise the Son, And praise the Spir-it, Three-in-One! Oh, praise Him,
heaven-ly host, Praise Fa-ther, Son and Ho-ly Ghost, Al-le-lu-ia,
UNISON
HARMONY
Oh, praise Him, Al-le-lu-ia! Al-le-lu-ia! Al-le-lu-ia! A-MEN.
Al-le-lu-ia!

25 God Moves in a Mysterious Way

. . . I will lead them in paths that they have not known . . . Isa. 42:16

DUNDEE C.M.

William Cowper, 1731-1800 — From *Scottish Psalter,* 1615

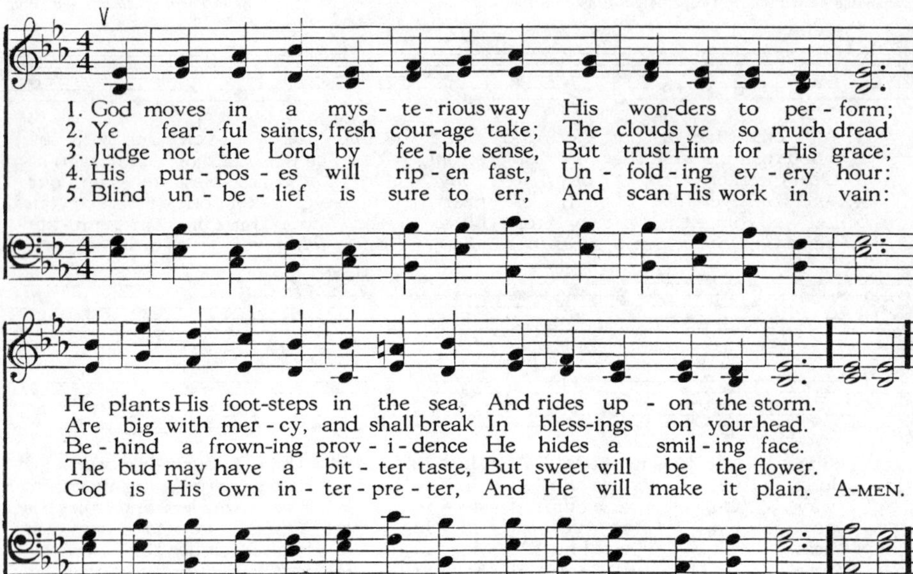
1. God moves in a mys - te - rious way His won-ders to per - form;
2. Ye fear - ful saints, fresh cour-age take; The clouds ye so much dread
3. Judge not the Lord by fee - ble sense, But trust Him for His grace;
4. His pur - pos - es will rip - en fast, Un - fold - ing ev - ery hour:
5. Blind un - be - lief is sure to err, And scan His work in vain:
He plants His foot-steps in the sea, And rides up - on the storm.
Are big with mer - cy, and shall break In bless-ings on your head.
Be - hind a frown-ing prov - i - dence He hides a smil - ing face.
The bud may have a bit - ter taste, But sweet will be the flower.
God is His own in - ter - pre - ter, And He will make it plain. A-MEN.

26 For the Beauty of the Earth

He hath made every thing beautiful . . . Eccles. 3:11

DIX 7.7.7.7.7.7.

From a chorale by Conrad Kocher, 1786-1872

Folliott S. Pierpoint, 1835-1917 — Arranged by William H. Monk, 1823-1889

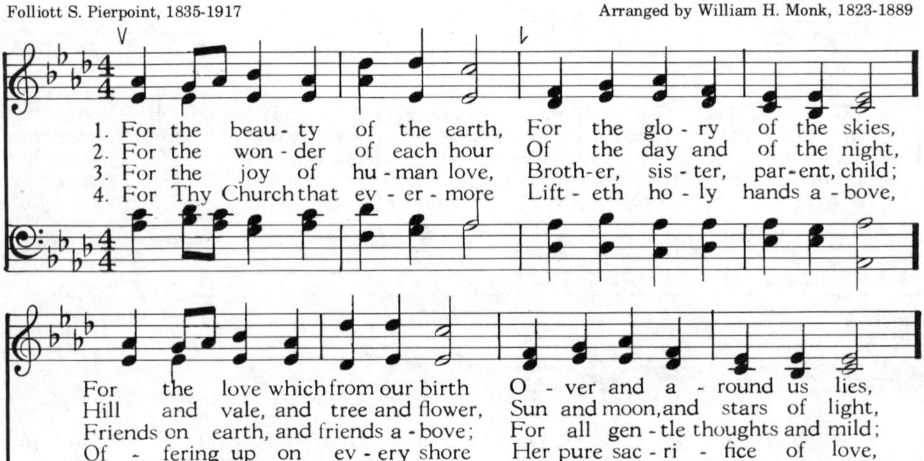
1. For the beau - ty of the earth, For the glo - ry of the skies,
2. For the won - der of each hour Of the day and of the night,
3. For the joy of hu - man love, Broth-er, sis - ter, par - ent, child;
4. For Thy Church that ev - er - more Lift - eth ho - ly hands a - bove,
For the love which from our birth O - ver and a - round us lies,
Hill and vale, and tree and flower, Sun and moon, and stars of light,
Friends on earth, and friends a - bove; For all gen - tle thoughts and mild;
Of - fering up on ev - ery shore Her pure sac - ri - fice of love,

(For lower key see No. 38)

For the Beauty of the Earth

Lord of all, to Thee we raise This our hymn of grate - ful praise.

God the Omnipotent 27

. . . All power is given unto me in heaven and in earth. Matt. 28:18

Stanzas 1-2 by Henry F. Chorley, 1808-1872 (altered)
Stanzas 3-4 by John Ellerton, 1826-1893

RUSSIAN HYMN 11.10.11.9.
Alexis Feodorovich Lvov, 1799-1870

1. God the Om - ni - po - tent! King, who or - dain - est Thun - der thy
2. God the All - mer - ci - ful! earth hath for - sak - en Thy ways all
3. God the All - right-eous One! man hath de - fied Thee, Yet to e -
4. God the All - prov - i - dent, earth by Thy chas-tening Yet shall to
cla - rion, the light-ning Thy sword; Show forth Thy pi - ty on high where Thou
ho - ly, and slight-ed Thy Word; Bid not Thy wrath in its ter - rors a -
ter - ni - ty stand-eth Thy Word; False-hood and wrong shall not tar - ry be -
free-dom and truth be re-stored; Through the thick dark-ness Thy king-dom is
reign - est: Give to us peace in our time, O Lord.
wak - en: Give to us peace in our time, O Lord.
side Thee: Give to us peace in our time, O Lord.
has - tening: Thou wilt give peace in Thy time, O Lord. A-MEN.

28 This Is My Father's World

The earth is the Lord's, . . . the world, and they that dwell therein. Psa. 24:1

TERRA BEATA S.M.D.
English melody
Adapted by Franklin L. Sheppard, 1852-1930

Malthie D. Babcock, 1858-1901 (altered)

1. This is my Fa-ther's world, And to my lis-tening ears All
2. This is my Fa-ther's world, The birds their car - ols raise, The
3. This is my Fa-ther's world, Oh, let me ne'er for - get That
na - ture sings, and round me rings The mu - sic of the spheres.
morn - ing light, the lil - y white, De - clare their Mak-er's praise.
though the wrong seems oft so strong, God is the Rul-er yet.
This is my Fa-ther's world: I rest me in the thought Of
This is my Fa-ther's world: He shines in all that's fair; In the
This is my Fa-ther's world: Why should my heart be sad? The
rocks and trees, of skies and seas—His hand the won-ders wrought.
rus - tling grass I hear Him pass, He speaks to me ev-ery-where.
Lord is King: let the heav-ens ring! God reigns: let earth be glad!

To God Be the Glory

29

Give unto the Lord the glory due unto his name . . . Psa. 29:2

TO GOD BE THE GLORY 11.11.11.11. with Refrain

Fanny J. Crosby, 1820-1915

William H. Doane, 1832-1915

1. To God be the glo-ry, great things He hath done, So loved He the world that He
2. O per - fect re-demp-tion, the pur-chase of blood, To ev - ery be - liev-er the
3. Great things He hath taught us, great things He hath done, And great our re-joic-ing thro'
gave us His Son, Who yield-ed His life an a-tone-ment for sin, And o-pened the
prom-ise of God; The vil - est of - fen-der who tru - ly believes, That moment from
Je - sus the Son; But pur - er, and high-er, and great-er will be Our won-der, our
Refrain
life - gate that all may go in.
Je - sus a par-don receives. Praise the Lord, praise the Lord, Let the earth hear His
trans-port, when Je-sus we see.
voice! Praise the Lord, praise the Lord, Let the peo-ple re-joice! O come to the
Fa-ther thro' Je - sus the Son, And give Him the glo - ry; great things He hath done.

30 The God of Abraham Praise

And God said . . . I AM THAT I AM . . . Exod. 3:14

LEONI 6.6.8.4.D.

Based on the *Yigdal* of Daniel ben Judah, circa 1400
Thomas Olivers, 1725-1799

From a Hebrew melody
Adapted by Meyer Lyon, 1751-1797

1. The God of A-braham praise, Who reigns en-throned a - bove;
2. The God of A-braham praise, At whose su - preme com - mand
3. He by Him - self hath sworn, I on His oath de - pend,
4. The whole tri - um - phant host Give thanks to God on high;
An - cient of ev - er - last - ing days, And God of love.
From earth I rise, and seek the joys At His right hand.
I shall, on ea - gles' wings up - borne, To heaven as - cend;
"Hail, Fa - ther, Son and Ho - ly Ghost!" They ev - er cry.
Je - ho - vah, great I AM, By earth and heaven con - fessed;
I all on earth for - sake, Its wis - dom, fame, and power;
I shall be - hold His face, I shall His power a - dore,
Hail, A-braham's God and mine! I join the heaven - ly lays;
I bow and bless the sa - cred name, For - ev - er blest.
And Him my on - ly por - tion make, My shield and tower.
And sing the won - ders of His grace For - ev - er - more.
All might and ma - jes - ty are Thine, And end - less praise. A-MEN.

(For different harmony and lower key see No. 450)

Oh, for a Heart to Praise My God 31

I will praise thee, O Lord, with my whole heart . . . Psa. 9:1

AZMON C.M.
Carl G. Gläser, 1784-1829
Adapted by Lowell Mason, 1792-1872

Charles Wesley, 1707-1788

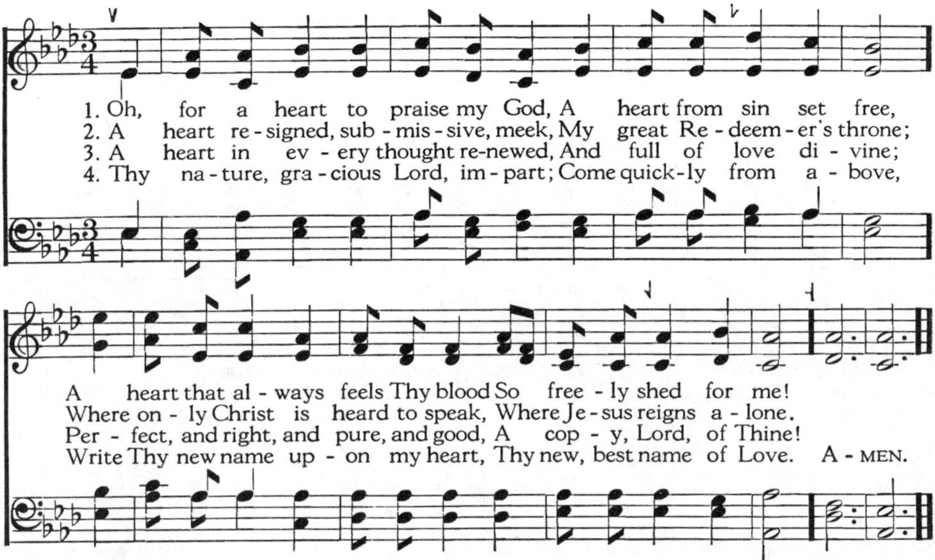
1. Oh, for a heart to praise my God, A heart from sin set free,
2. A heart re-signed, sub-mis-sive, meek, My great Re-deem-er's throne;
3. A heart in ev-ery thought re-newed, And full of love di-vine;
4. Thy na-ture, gra-cious Lord, im-part; Come quick-ly from a-bove,
A heart that al-ways feels Thy blood So free-ly shed for me!
Where on-ly Christ is heard to speak, Where Je-sus reigns a-lone.
Per-fect, and right, and pure, and good, A cop-y, Lord, of Thine!
Write Thy new name up-on my heart, Thy new, best name of Love. A-MEN.

(For lower key see No. 44)

Begin, My Tongue, Some Heavenly Theme 32

. . . *my tongue shall speak of thy righteousness* . . . Psa. 35:28

MANOAH C.M.
From Henry W. Greatorex's *Collection,* 1851

Isaac Watts, 1674-1748

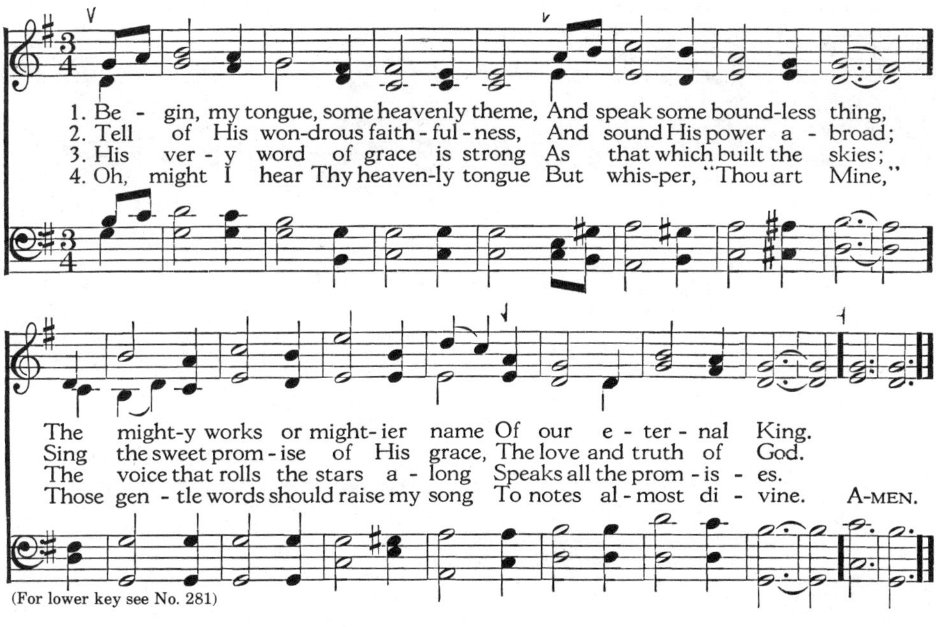
1. Be-gin, my tongue, some heavenly theme, And speak some bound-less thing,
2. Tell of His won-drous faith-ful-ness, And sound His power a-broad;
3. His ver-y word of grace is strong As that which built the skies;
4. Oh, might I hear Thy heaven-ly tongue But whis-per, "Thou art Mine,"
The might-y works or might-ier name Of our e-ter-nal King.
Sing the sweet prom-ise of His grace, The love and truth of God.
The voice that rolls the stars a-long Speaks all the prom-is-es.
Those gen-tle words should raise my song To notes al-most di-vine. A-MEN.

(For lower key see No. 281)

33

How Great Thou Art

Great is the Lord, and greatly to be praised . . . Psa. 48:1

Stuart K. Hine, b. 1899

1. O Lord, my God! When I in awe-some won-der Con-sid-er
2. When through the woods and for-est glades I wan-der And hear the
3. And when I think that God, His Son not spar-ing, Sent Him to
4. When Christ shall come with shout of ac-cla-ma-tion And take me
all the worlds* Thy hands have made, I see the stars, I hear the roll-ing*
birds sing sweet-ly in the trees; When I look down from loft-y moun-tain
die, I scarce can take it in; That on the cross, my bur-den glad-ly
home, what joys shall fill my heart! Then I shall bow in hum-ble ad-o-
thun-der, Thy power through-out the u-ni-verse dis-played.
gran-deur And hear the brook and feel the gen-tle breeze.
bear-ing, He bled and died to take a-way my sin.
ra-tion And there pro-claim, my God, how great Thou art!
Refrain
Then sings my soul, my Sav-iour God, to Thee. How great Thou art, how great Thou art! Then sings my soul, my Sav-iour God, to Thee. How great Thou art, how great Thou art!

(*Translator's original words are *works* and *mighty*.)

Our Father, Who in Heaven Art 34

. . . Hallowed be thy name. Matt. 6:9

Paraphrase of the Lord's Prayer (condensed)
By Martin Luther, 1483-1546
J. Buchanan MacMillan, b. 1915

MELITA 8.8.8.8.8.8.
John B. Dykes, 1823-1876

1. Our Father, who in heaven art, Holy art Thou—with voice and heart Thou bid'st us call upon Thy name—For ever blest, for aye the same! Oh, may Thy kingdom soon appear, Thy will be done, Thy reign be here!
2. Give us this day our daily bread; By Thee we are both clothed and fed. Forgive us, Lord, the sins we own—Contrite we bow before Thy throne–As we to men forgiveness show, And thus obey Thee here below.
3. Lead not into temptation sore; From evil shield us, we implore. Gird us with might; Thy Spirit lend. Thine is the kingdom without end! Thine all the power and glory be, Now and throughout eternity.
A-MEN.

(For different harmony and lower key see No. 9)

35 Jesus, Thou Joy of Loving Hearts

. . . that my joy might remain in you . . . John 15:11

From *Jesu dulcis memoria,* circa 1150
Translated by Ray Palmer, 1808-1887

HESPERUS (Quebec) L.M.
Henry Baker, 1835-1910

1. Je - sus, Thou Joy of lov - ing hearts, Thou Fount of
2. Thy truth un - changed hath ev - er stood; Thou sav - est
3. We taste Thee, O Thou liv - ing Bread, And long to
4. Our rest - less spir - its yearn for Thee, Wher - e'er our
5. O Je - sus, ev - er with us stay, Make all our

life, Thou Light of men, From the best bliss that
those that on Thee call; To them that seek Thee
feast up - on Thee still; We drink of Thee, the
change - ful lot is cast; Glad when Thy gra - cious
mo - ments calm and bright; Chase the dark night of

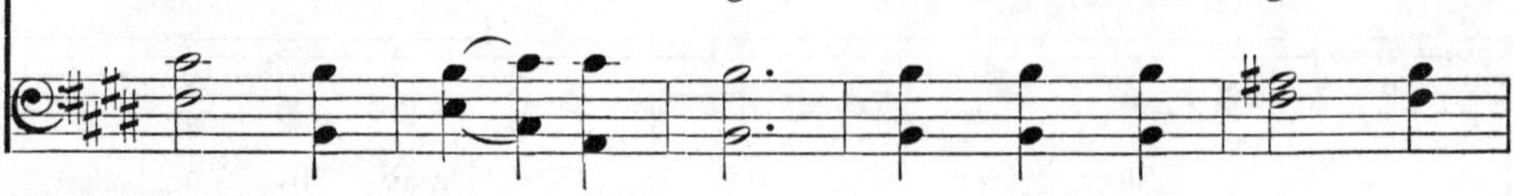

earth im - parts We turn un - filled to Thee a - gain.
Thou art good, To them that find Thee all in all.
Foun - tain - head, And thirst our souls from Thee to fill.
smile we see, Blest when our faith can hold Thee fast.
sin a - way, Shed o'er the world Thy ho - ly light. A-MEN.

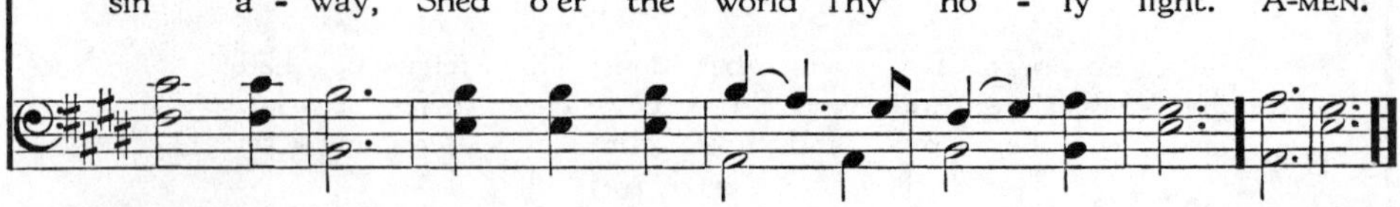

(For higher key see No. 4)

Oh, Could I Speak the Matchless Worth 36

For who in the heaven can be compared unto the Lord? . . . Psa. 89:6

ARIEL 8.8.6.8.8.6. with repeat
Attributed to Wolfgang A. Mozart, 1756-1791
Adapted by Lowell Mason, 1792-1872

Samuel Medley, 1738-1799

1. Oh, could I speak the match - less worth,
2. I'd sing the pre - cious blood He spilt,
3. I'd sing the char - ac - ters He bears,
4. Soon the de - light - ful day will come
Oh, could I sound the glo - ries forth Which in my Sav - iour shine,
My ran - som from the dread - ful guilt Of sin and wrath di - vine!
And all the forms of love He wears, Ex - alt - ed on His throne:
When my dear Lord will bring me home, And I shall see His face;
I'd soar and touch the heaven-ly strings, And vie with Ga-briel while he sings
I'd sing His glo - rious right-eous-ness, In which all per-fect heaven-ly dress
In loft-iest songs of sweet - est praise, I would to ev - er - last - ing days
Then with my Sav-iour, Broth - er, Friend, A blest e - ter - ni - ty I'll spend,
In notes al - most di - vine, In notes al - most di - vine.
My soul shall ev - er shine, My soul shall ev - er shine.
Make all His glo - ries known, Make all His glo - ries known.
Tri - um-phant in His grace, Tri - um-phant in His grace. A - MEN.

37 Awake, My Soul, to Joyful Lays

. . . praise thy name for thy lovingkindness . . . Psa. 138:2

LOVING KINDNESS L.M. with repeats

Samuel Medley, 1738-1799

William Caldwell, 19th century

1. A - wake, my soul, to joy - ful lays, And sing thy great Re -
2. He saw me ru - ined in the fall Yet loved me, not - with -
3. Though num-erous hosts of might - y foes, Though earth and hell my
4. When trou - ble, like a gloom - y cloud, Has gath - ered thick and
deem - er's praise: He just - ly claims a song from me— His
stand - ing all; He saved me from my lost es - tate— His
way op - pose, He safe - ly leads my soul a - long— His
thun - dered loud, He near my soul has al - ways stood—His
lov - ing kind - ness, oh, how free! His lov - ing kind - ness,
lov - ing kind - ness, oh, how great! His lov - ing kind - ness,
lov - ing kind - ness, oh, how strong! His lov - ing kind - ness,
lov - ing kind - ness, oh, how good! His lov - ing kind - ness,
lov - ing kind-ness, His lov - ing kind - ness, oh, how free!
lov - ing kind-ness, His lov - ing kind - ness, oh, how great!
lov - ing kind-ness, His lov - ing kind - ness, oh, how strong!
lov - ing kind-ness, His lov - ing kind - ness, oh, how good!

Christ, Whose Glory Fills the Skies 38

. . . unto you that fear my name shall the Sun of righteousness arise . . . Mal. 4:2

DIX 7.7.7.7.7.7.
From a chorale by Conrad Kocher, 1786-1872
Arranged by William H. Monk, 1823-1889

Charles Wesley, 1707-1788

1. Christ, whose glo - ry fills the skies, Christ, the true, the on - ly Light,
2. Dark and cheer - less is the morn Un - ac - com - pan - ied by Thee;
3. Vis - it then this soul of mine, Pierce the gloom of sin and grief;

Sun of right-eous - ness, a - rise, Tri - umph o'er the shades of night;
Joy - less is the day's re - turn, Till Thy mer - cy's beams I see;
Fill me, Ra - dian - cy Di - vine, Scat - ter all my un - be - lief;

Day-spring from on high, be near; Day - star, in my heart ap - pear.
Till they in - ward light im - part, Glad my eyes, and warm my heart.
More and more Thy - self dis - play, Shin - ing to the per - fect day.

(For higher key see No. 26)

39 We Come, O Christ, to Thee

. . . no man cometh unto the Father, but by me. John 14:6

DARWALL 6.6.6.6.8.8.

E. Margaret Clarkson, b. 1915

John Darwall, 1731-1789

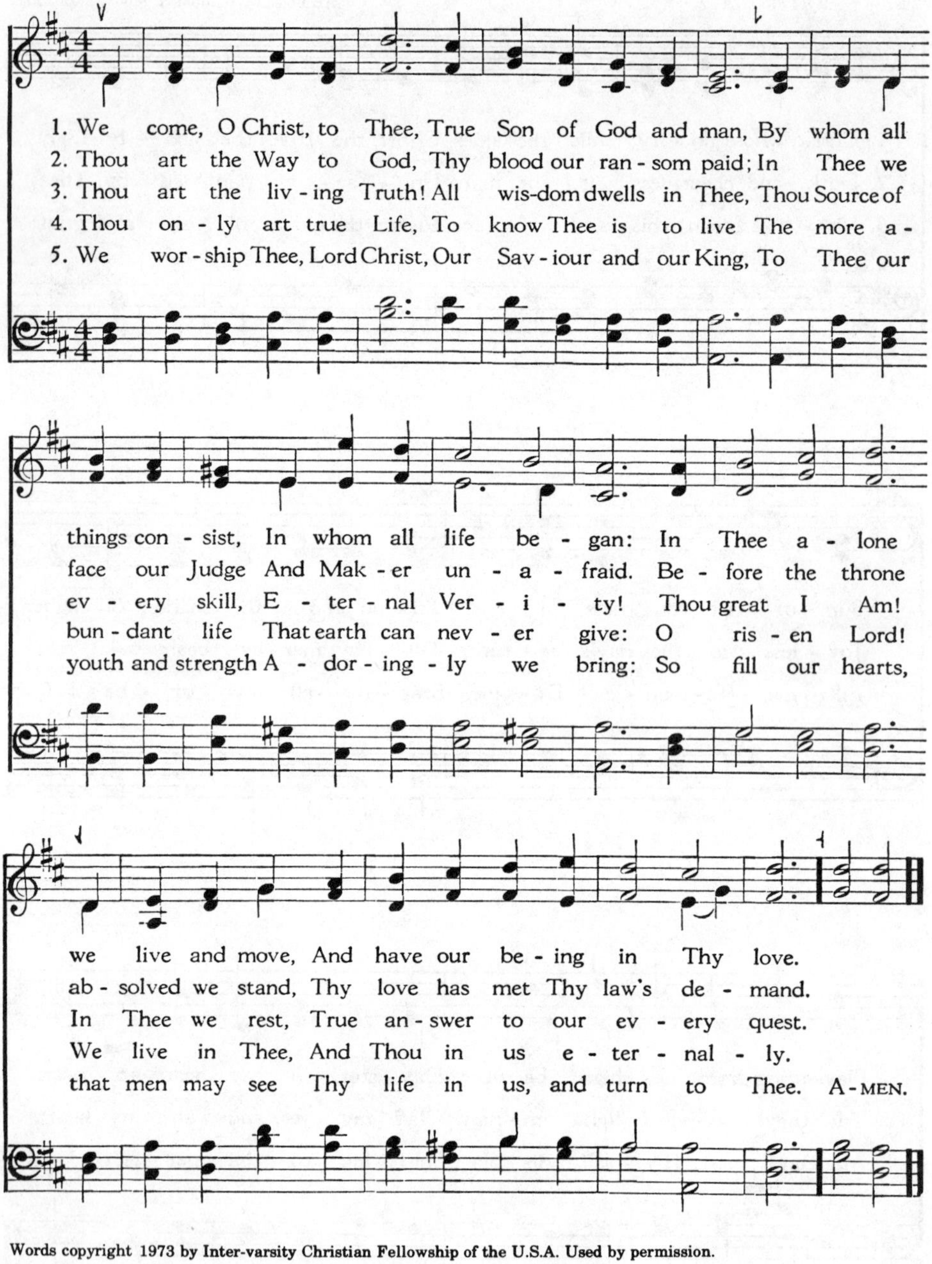
1. We come, O Christ, to Thee, True Son of God and man, By whom all
2. Thou art the Way to God, Thy blood our ran - som paid; In Thee we
3. Thou art the liv - ing Truth! All wis-dom dwells in Thee, Thou Source of
4. Thou on - ly art true Life, To know Thee is to live The more a -
5. We wor - ship Thee, Lord Christ, Our Sav - iour and our King, To Thee our
things con - sist, In whom all life be - gan: In Thee a - lone
face our Judge And Mak - er un - a - fraid. Be - fore the throne
ev - ery skill, E - ter - nal Ver - i - ty! Thou great I Am!
bun - dant life That earth can nev - er give: O ris - en Lord!
youth and strength A - dor - ing - ly we bring: So fill our hearts,
we live and move, And have our be - ing in Thy love.
ab - solved we stand, Thy love has met Thy law's de - mand.
In Thee we rest, True an - swer to our ev - ery quest.
We live in Thee, And Thou in us e - ter - nal - ly.
that men may see Thy life in us, and turn to Thee. A - MEN.

Glory Be to Him Who Loved Us

40

. . . *Blessing, and honour, and glory, and power, be unto him* . . . Rev. 5:13

STAMFORD 8.7.8.7.8.7.

Horatius Bonar, 1808-1889 (altered)

Melody by A.J. Foxwell, 19th century

1. Glo - ry be to Him who loved us, Washed us from each
2. "Glo - ry, wor - ship, laud, and bless - ing"—Thus the choir tri -
3. Glo - ry to the King of an - gels, Glo - ry to the
4. Glo - ry be to Thee, O Fa - ther, Glo - ry be to
sin - ful stain; Glo - ry be to Him who made us
um - phant sings; "Hon - or, rich - es, power, do - min - ion"—
Church - 's King, Glo - ry to the King of na - tions,
Thee, O Son, Glo - ry be to Thee, O Spir - it,
Priests and kings with Him to reign; Glo - ry, wor - ship,
Thus its praise cre - a - tion brings; Thou art wor - thy,
Heaven and earth His prais - es sing: Glo - ry ev - er
Glo - ry be to God a - lone, As it was, is
laud, and bless - ing To the Lamb who once was slain.
Thou art wor - thy, Lord of lords and King of kings.
and for - ev - er To the King of glo - ry bring.
now, and shall be While the end - less a - ges run.

41 O Jesus, Jesus

I will love thee, O Lord . . . Psa. 18:1

Frederick W. Faber, 1814-1863
Refrain by Russell K. Carter, 1849-1928

Melody adapted by Russell K. Carter, 1849-1928

1. O Jesus, Jesus, dearest Lord! Forgive me if I say,
For very love, Thy sacred name A thousand times a day.
2. I love Thee so I know not how My transports to control;
Thy love is like a burning fire Within my very soul.
3. For Thou to me art all in all, My honor and my wealth,
My heart's desire, my body's strength, My soul's eternal health.
4. Burn, burn, O love, within my heart, Burn fiercely night and day,
Till all the dross of earthly loves Is burned, and burned away.
5. O light in darkness, joy in grief, O heaven begun on earth;
Jesus, my love, my treasure, who Can tell what Thou art worth?
6. What limit is there to this love? Thy flight, where wilt Thou stay?
On, on! Our Lord is sweeter far Today than yesterday.
Refrain
O Jesus, Lord, with me abide; I rest in Thee, whate'er betide;
Thy gracious smile is my reward; I love, I love Thee, Lord!

Blessed Be the Name

. . . the Lord gave, . . . blessed be the name of the Lord. Job 1:21

BLESSED BE THE NAME C.M. with Refrain
Anonymous
Arranged by Ralph E. Hudson, 1843-1901
and William J. Kirkpatrick, 1838-1921

William H. Clark, 19th century
Refrain by Ralph E. Hudson, 1843-1901

1. All praise to Him who reigns a - bove In maj - es - ty su - preme,
2. His name a - bove all names shall stand, Ex - alt - ed more and more,
3. Re - deem er, Sav - iour, Friend of man Once ru - ined by the Fall,
4. His name shall be the Coun-sel - or, The might-y Prince of Peace,
Who gave His Son for man to die, That He might man re - deem!
At God the Fa-ther's own right hand, Where an - gel hosts a - dore.
Thou hast de - vised sal - va - tion's plan, For Thou hast died for all.
Of all earth's king-doms Con-quer - or, Whose reign shall nev - er cease.
REFRAIN
Bless-ed be the name, bless-ed be the name, Bless-ed be the name of the Lord;
Bless-ed be the name, bless - ed be the name; Bless-ed be the name of the Lord.

43 Oh, for a Thousand Tongues

(FIRST TUNE)

. . . my tongue shall speak . . . of thy praise all the day long. Psa. 35:28

LYNGHAM 8.6.6.8. with repeats

Charles Wesley, 1707-1788

Thomas Jarman, 1776-1861

1. Oh, for a thou - sand tongues to sing My great Re-deem-er's
2. My gra - cious Mas - ter and my God, As - sist me to pro-
3. Je - sus! the Name that charms our fears, That bids our sor-rows
4. He breaks the power of can - celled sin, He sets the pris-oner
praise, My great Re-deem-er's praise, The glo-ries of my
claim, As - sist me to pro - claim, To spread through all the
cease, That bids our sor - rows cease; 'Tis mu - sic in the
free, He sets the pris - oner free; His blood can make the
God and King, The tri-umphs of His grace, The
earth a - broad The hon-ors of Thy Name, The
sin - ner's ears, 'Tis life, and health, and peace; 'Tis
foul - est clean, His blood a - vailed for me, His
1. The tri-umphs of His grace, The tri-umphs of His
2. The hon-ors of Thy Name, The hon-ors of Thy
3. 'Tis life, and health, and peace; 'Tis life, and health, and
4. His blood a - vailed for me, His blood a-vailed for
tri - umphs of His grace, The tri - umphs of His grace!
hon - ors of Thy Name, The hon - ors of Thy Name.
life, and health, and peace; 'Tis life, and health, and peace.
blood a - vailed for me, His blood a - vailed for me.
grace, The tri-umphs of His grace, The tri-umphs of His grace.
Name, The hon-ors of Thy Name, The hon-ors of Thy Name.
peace; 'Tis life, and health, and peace; 'Tis life, and health, and peace.
me, His blood a-vailed for me, His blood a - vailed for me.

Oh, for a Thousand Tongues 44

(SECOND TUNE)

AZMON C.M.
Carl G. Gläser, 1784-1829
Adapted by Lowell Mason, 1792-1872

Charles Wesley, 1707-1788

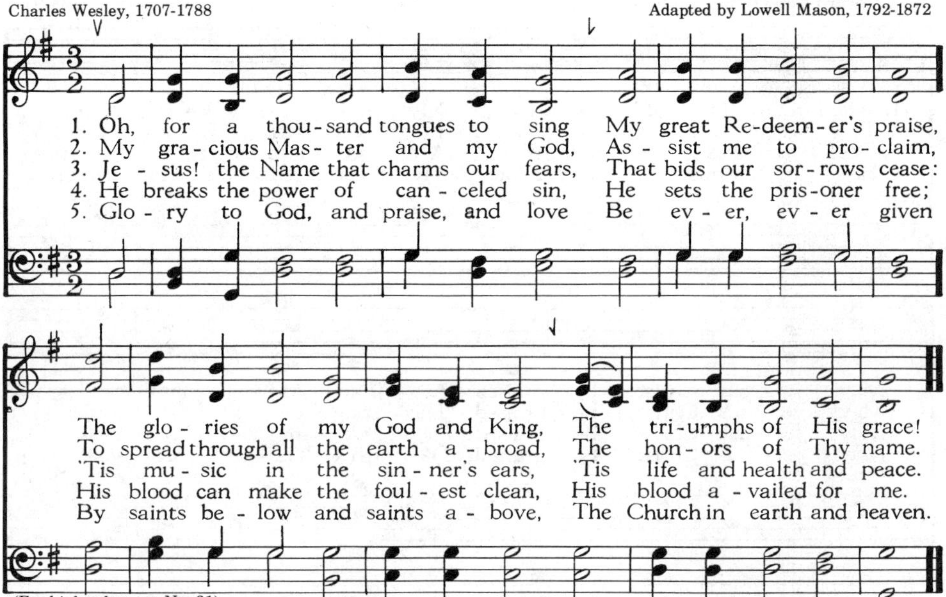
1. Oh, for a thou-sand tongues to sing My great Re-deem-er's praise,
2. My gra-cious Mas-ter and my God, As-sist me to pro-claim,
3. Je-sus! the Name that charms our fears, That bids our sor-rows cease:
4. He breaks the power of can-celed sin, He sets the pris-oner free;
5. Glo-ry to God, and praise, and love Be ev-er, ev-er given
The glo-ries of my God and King, The tri-umphs of His grace!
To spread through all the earth a-broad, The hon-ors of Thy name.
'Tis mu-sic in the sin-ner's ears, 'Tis life and health and peace.
His blood can make the foul-est clean, His blood a-vailed for me.
By saints be-low and saints a-bove, The Church in earth and heaven.

(For higher key see No. 31)

Praise the Saviour, Ye Who Know Him 45

I will praise the Lord according to his righteousness . . . Psa. 7:17

ACCLAIM 8.8.8.5.
German melody

Thomas Kelly, 1769-1854

1. Praise the Sav-iour, ye who know Him! Who can tell how much we owe Him?
2. Trust in Him, ye saints, for-ev-er; He is faith-ful, chang-ing nev-er;
3. Keep us, Lord, Oh, keep us cleav-ing To Thy self and still be-liev-ing,
4. Then we shall be where we would be, Then we shall be what we should be;
Glad-ly let us ren-der to Him All we are and have.
Nei-ther force nor guile can sev-er Those He loves from Him.
Till the hour of our re-ceiv-ing Prom-ised joys with Thee.
Things that are not now, nor could be, Soon shall be our own.

46 When Morning Gilds the Skies

... in the morning will I direct my prayer unto thee ... Psa. 5:3

German, 19th century
Translated by Edward Caswall, 1814-1878

LAUDES DOMINI 6.6.6.D.
Joseph Barnby, 1838-1896

1. When morn - ing gilds the skies, My heart a - wak - ing cries,
2. To Thee, O God a - bove, I cry with glow - ing love,
3. Does sad - ness fill my mind, A so - lace here I find;
4. Be this, while life is mine, My can - ti - cle di - vine;

May Je - sus Christ be praised: A - like at work and prayer,
May Je - sus Christ be praised: This song of sa - cred joy,
May Je - sus Christ be praised: Or fades my earth - ly bliss,
May Je - sus Christ be praised: Be this th'e - ter - nal song,

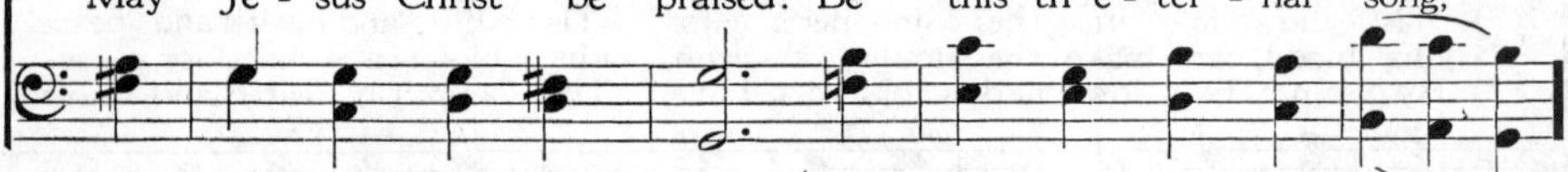

To Je - sus I re - pair; May Je - sus Christ be praised.
It nev - er seems to cloy; May Je - sus Christ be praised.
My com - fort still is this: May Je - sus Christ be praised.
Through all the a - ges long: May Je - sus Christ be praised.

47 Stand Up and Bless the Lord

... blessed be thy glorious name ... Neh. 9:5

ALTUS S.M.

James Montgomery, 1771-1854

John Willard, b. 1921

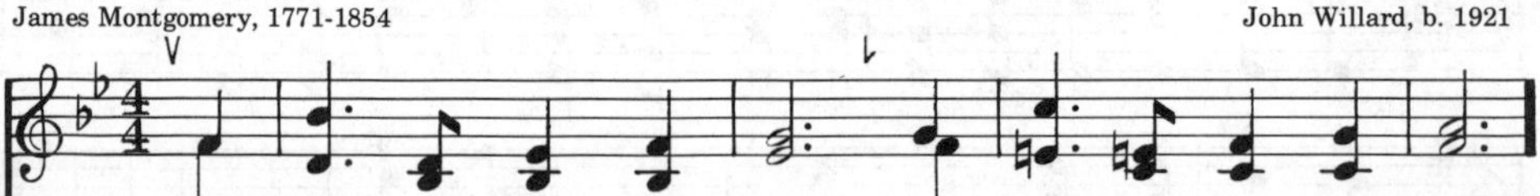

1. Stand up and bless the Lord, Ye peo - ple of His choice;
2. Though high a - bove all praise, A - bove all bless - ing high,
3. Oh, for the liv - ing flame, From His own al - tar brought,
4. God is our strength and song, And His sal - va - tion ours;
5. Stand up and bless the Lord, The Lord your God a - dore;

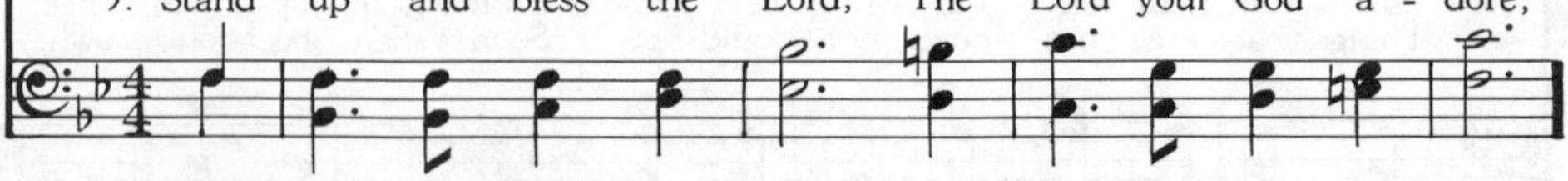

Stand Up and Bless the Lord

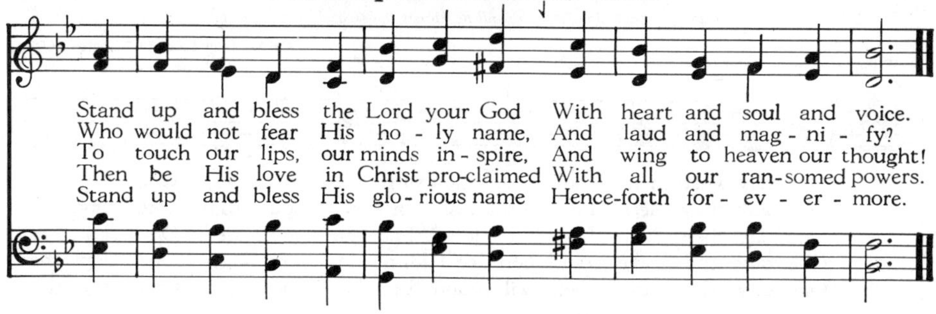
Stand up and bless the Lord your God With heart and soul and voice.
Who would not fear His ho - ly name, And laud and mag - ni - fy?
To touch our lips, our minds in - spire, And wing to heaven our thought!
Then be His love in Christ pro-claimed With all our ran-somed powers.
Stand up and bless His glo - rious name Hence-forth for - ev - er - more.

Fairest Lord Jesus 48

Thou art fairer than the children of men . . . Psa. 45:2

Stanza 1, 3 from *Gesangbuch,* Münster, 1677
Stanza 2 trans. by Heinrich von Fallersleben, 1798-1874
Stanza 4 trans. by Joseph A. Seiss, 1823-1904

CRUSADERS' HYMN P.M.
Silesian folk song
From *Schlesische Volkslieder,* 1842
Arranged by James Hopkirk, 19th century

1. Fair - est Lord Je - sus, Rul - er of all na - ture, O Thou of
2. Fair are the mead-ows, Fair - er still the wood-lands, Robed in the
3. Fair is the sun-shine, Fair - er still the moon-light, And fair the
4. All fair - est beau - ty Heav - en - ly and earth - ly, Won-drous-ly,
God and man the Son; Thee will I cher - ish,
bloom - ing garb of spring; Je - sus is fair - er,
twink - ling, star - ry host; Je - sus shines bright - er,
Je - sus, is found in Thee; None can be near - er,
Thee will I hon - or, Thou my soul's glo - ry, joy, and crown.
Je - sus is pur - er, Who makes the woe - ful heart to sing.
Je - sus shines pur - er, Than all the an - gels heaven can boast.
fair - er or dear - er, Than Thou, my Sav - iour, art to me. A-MEN.

49 One Day!

. . . unto them that look for him shall he appear the second time . . . Heb. 9:28

CHAPMAN 11.10.11.10. with Refrain

J. Wilbur Chapman, 1859-1918

Charles H. Marsh, 1886-1956

1. One day when heav - en was filled with His prais - es, One day when
2. One day they led Him up Cal - va - ry's moun - tain, One day they
3. One day they left Him a - lone in the gar - den, One day He
4. One day the grave could con - ceal Him no long - er, One day the
5. One day the trum - pet will sound for His com - ing, One day the
sin was as black as could be, Je - sus came forth to be
nailed Him to die on the tree; Suf - fer - ing an - guish, de -
rest - ed, from suf - fer - ing free; An - gels came down o'er His
stone rolled a - way from the door; Then He a - rose, o - ver
skies with His glo - ry will shine; Won - der - ful day, my be -
born of a Vir - gin, Dwelt a-mong men, my ex - am-ple is He!
spised and re - ject - ed, Bear - ing our sins, my Re-deem-er is He!
tomb to keep vig - il; Hope of the hope - less, my Sav-iour is He!
death He has con-quered; Now is as - cend - ed, my Lord ev - er - more!
lov - ed ones bring - ing; Glo - ri - ous Sav - iour, this Je - sus is mine!
REFRAIN
Liv - ing, He loved me; dy - ing, He saved me; Bur - ied, He

One Day!

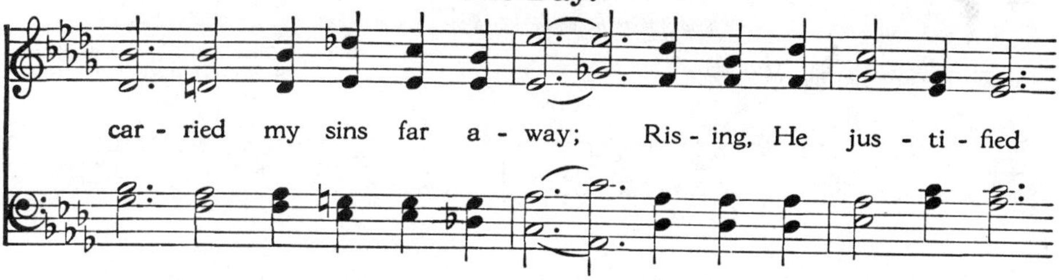
car - ried my sins far a - way; Ris - ing, He jus - ti - fied

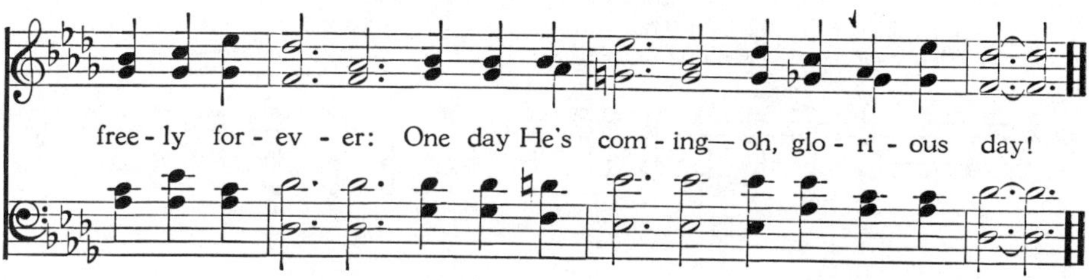
free - ly for - ev - er: One day He's com - ing— oh, glo - ri - ous day!

Jesus, the Very Thought of Thee 50

... yet believing, ye rejoice with joy unspeakable ... 1 Pet. 1:8

From *Jesu dulcis memoria,* circa 1150
Translated by Edward Caswall, 1814-1878

ST. AGNES C.M.
John B. Dykes, 1823-1876

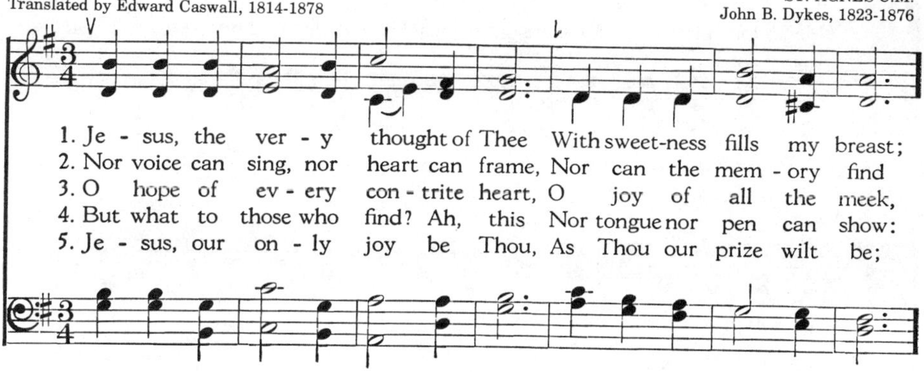
1. Je - sus, the ver - y thought of Thee With sweet-ness fills my breast;
2. Nor voice can sing, nor heart can frame, Nor can the mem - ory find
3. O hope of ev - ery con - trite heart, O joy of all the meek,
4. But what to those who find? Ah, this Nor tongue nor pen can show:
5. Je - sus, our on - ly joy be Thou, As Thou our prize wilt be;

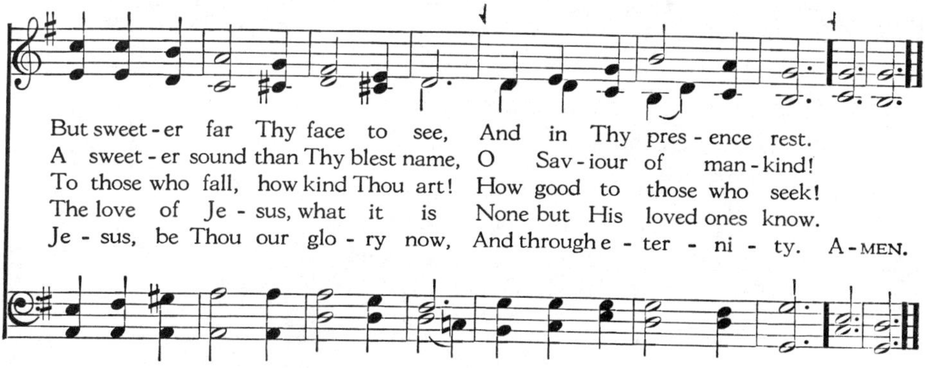
But sweet - er far Thy face to see, And in Thy pres - ence rest.
A sweet - er sound than Thy blest name, O Sav - iour of man - kind!
To those who fall, how kind Thou art! How good to those who seek!
The love of Je - sus, what it is None but His loved ones know.
Je - sus, be Thou our glo - ry now, And through e - ter - ni - ty. A - MEN.

51 I Will Praise Him

Whoso offereth praise glorifieth me . . . Psa. 50:23

I WILL PRAISE HIM 8.7.8.7. with Refrain

Margaret J. Harris, 19th century

Margaret J. Harris, 19th century

1. When I saw the cleans-ing foun-tain O - pen wide for all my sin,
2. Tho' the way seemed straight and nar-row, All I claimed was swept a - way;
3. Then God's fire up - on the al - tar Of my heart was set a - flame.
4. Bless - ed be the name of Je - sus! I'm so glad He took me in.
I o - beyed the Spir - it's woo - ing When He said, "Wilt thou be clean?"
My am - bi - tions, plans, and wish - es At my feet in ash - es lay.
I shall nev - er cease to praise Him. Glo - ry, glo - ry to His name!
He's for - giv - en my trans-gres-sions; He has cleansed my heart from sin.
REFRAIN
I will praise Him! I will praise Him! Praise the Lamb for sin-ners slain!
Give Him glo - ry, all ye peo - ple, For His blood can wash a-way each stain.

Joy to the World! 52

. . . behold, I bring you good tidings of great joy . . . Luke 2:10

Isaac Watts, 1674-1748

ANTIOCH C.M. with repeats
Adapted from George Frederick Handel, 1685-1759

1. Joy to the world! The Lord is come; Let earth re - ceive her King; Let ev - ery heart pre - pare Him room,
2. Joy to the earth! The Sav - iour reigns; Let men their songs em - ploy; While fields and floods, rocks, hills, and plains
3. No more let sins and sor - rows grow, Nor thorns in - fest the ground. He comes to make His bless - ings flow
4. He rules the earth with truth and grace, And makes the na - tions prove The glo - ries of His right - eous - ness,
And heaven and na - ture sing, And heaven and na - ture sing, And heaven, and heaven and na - ture sing.
Re - peat the sound - ing joy, Re - peat the sound - ing joy, Re - peat, re - peat the sound - ing joy.
Far as the curse is found, Far as the curse is found, Far as, far as the curse is found.
And won - ders of His love, And won - ders of His love, And won - ders, won - ders of His love.
And heaven and na - ture sing, And heaven and na-ture sing,

53 Of the Father's Love Begotten

. . . we beheld his glory, the glory as of the only begotten of the Father . . . John 1:14

DIVINUM MYSTERIUM 8.7.8.7.8.7.7.
Medieval melody
As in *Piae Cantiones,* 1582

Aurelius C. Prudentius, 348-413
Translated by John M. Neale, 1818-1866 (altered)

*
1. Of the Fa-ther's love be-got-ten, Ere the worlds be-gan to be,
2. This is He whom seers in old time Chant-ed of with one ac-cord,
3. O ye heights of heaven, a-dore Him; An-gel hosts, His prais-es sing;
4. Christ, to Thee, with God the Fa-ther, And, O Ho-ly Ghost, to Thee,
He is Al-pha and O-me-ga, He the source, the end-ing He,
Whom the voic-es of the proph-ets Prom-ised in their faith-ful word;
All do-min-ions, bow be-fore Him, And ex-tol our God and King.
Hymn and chant and high thanks-giv-ing, And un-wea-ried prais-es be;
Of the things that are and have been, And that
Now He shines, the long-ex-pect-ed; Let cre-
Let no tongue on earth be si-lent, Ev-ery
Hon-or, glo-ry, and do-min-ion, And e-
fu-ture years shall see, Ev-er-more and ev-er-more.
a-tion praise its Lord, Ev-er-more and ev-er-more.
voice in con-cert ring, Ev-er-more and ev-er-more.
ter-nal vic-to-ry, Ev-er-more and ev-er-more.

(*Performance in unison is recommended)

Away in a Manger

54

. . . she . . . wrapped him in swaddling clothes, and laid him in a manger . . . Luke 2:7

Stanzas 1-2 from *Little Children's Book,* 1885
Stanza 3 by John T. McFarland, 1851-1913

MUELLER 11.11.11.11.
James R. Murray, 1841-1905
Arranged by Donald P. Hustad, b. 1918

1. A - way in a man - ger, no crib for a bed,
2. The cat - tle are low - ing, the Ba - by a - wakes,
3. Be near me, Lord Je - sus, I ask Thee to stay
The lit - tle Lord Je - sus, laid down His sweet head;
But lit - tle Lord Je - sus, no cry - ing He makes.
Close by me for - ev - er, and love me, I pray.
The stars in the sky looked down where He lay,
I love Thee, Lord Je - sus, look down from the sky,
Bless all the dear chil - dren in Thy ten - der care,
The lit - tle Lord Je - sus a - sleep on the hay.
And stay by my cra - dle till morn - ing is nigh.
And fit us for heav - en to live with Thee there.

55 Once in Royal David's City

For unto you is born this day in the city of David a Saviour . . . Luke 2:11

IRBY 8.7.8.7.7.7.

Cecil F.H. Alexander, 1818-1895

Henry J. Gauntlett, 1805-1876

1. Once in roy - al Da - vid's cit - y Stood a low - ly cat - tle shed,
2. He came down to earth from heav-en Who is God and Lord of all,
3. And, through all His won-drous child-hood, He would hon - or and o - bey,
4. And our eyes at last shall see Him, Through His own re - deem-ing love,
5. Not in that poor low - ly sta - ble, With the ox - en stand-ing by,

Where a moth - er laid her Ba - by In a man - ger for His bed:
And His shel - ter was a sta - ble, And His cra - dle was a stall;
Love, and watch the low - ly maid - en In whose gen - tle arms He lay:
For that Child so dear and gen - tle Is our Lord in heaven a - bove;
We shall see Him; but in heav - en Set at God's right hand on high;

Ma - ry was that moth-er mild, Je - sus Christ her lit - tle Child.
With the poor, and mean, and low-ly, Lived on earth our Sav - iour ho - ly.
Chris-tian chil - dren all must be Mild, o - be - dient, good as He.
And He leads His chil-dren on To the place where He is gone.
When like stars His chil-dren crowned, All in white shall wait a - round. A-MEN.

O Come, O Come, Emmanuel

. . . they shall call his name Emmanuel . . . Matt. 1:23

Latin, circa 12th century
Translated by John M. Neale, 1818-1866 (altered)

VENI EMMANUEL 8.8.8.8.8.8.
Adapted by Thomas Helmore, 1811-1890

1. O come, O come, Em - man - u - el, And ran - som cap - tive
2. O come, Thou Rod of Jes - se, free Thine own from Sa - tan's
3. O come, Thou Day-spring, come and cheer Our spir - its by Thine
4. O come, Thou Key of Da - vid, come, And o - pen wide our
Is - ra - el, That mourns in lone - ly ex - ile here
tyr - an - ny; From depths of hell Thy peo - ple save
ad - vent here; And drive a - way the shades of night,
heaven - ly home; Make safe the way that leads on high,
Un - til the Son of God ap - pear. Re - joice! Re - joice! Em -
And give them vic - tory o'er the grave. Re - joice! Re - joice! Em -
And pierce the clouds and bring us light! Re - joice! Re - joice! Em -
And close the path to mis - er - y. Re - joice! Re - joice! Em -
man - u - el Shall come to thee, O Is - ra - el!
man - u - el Shall come to thee, O Is - ra - el!
man - u - el Shall come to thee, O Is - ra - el!
man - u - el Shall come to thee, O Is - ra - el! A-MEN.

57 Who Is He in Yonder Stall?

. . . he is Lord of lords, and King of kings . . . Rev. 17:14

RESONET IN LAUDIBUS 7.7. with Refrain
German melody, 14th century
Adapted from Johann B. König, 1691-1758

Benjamin R. Hanby, 1833-1867 (altered)

1. Who is He in yon-der stall, At whose feet the shep-herds fall?
2. Who is He in yon-der cot, Bend-ing to His toil-some lot?
3. Who is He in deep dis-tress, Fast-ing in the wil-der-ness?
4. Who is He in Cal-vary's throes, Ask-ing par-don for His foes?
5. Who is He that from the grave Comes to heal and help and save?
6. Who is He that on yon throne Rules the world of light a-lone?
Refrain
'Tis the Lord! Oh, won-drous sto-ry! 'Tis the Lord, the King of glo-ry. Je-sus Sav-iour! 'Tis the Lord, the King of glo-ry!
At His feet we hum-bly fall. 'Tis the Lord, we crown Him Lord of all.

Good Christian Men, Rejoice 58

... many shall rejoice at his birth. Luke 1:14

John M. Neale, 1818-1866

IN DULCI JUBILO Irregular
German melody, 14th century

1. Good Chris - tian men, re - joice, With heart and soul and voice;
2. Good Chris - tian men, re - joice, With heart and soul and voice;
3. Good Chris - tian men, re - joice, With heart and soul and voice!
Give ye heed to what we say: Je - sus Christ is born to - day;
Now ye hear of end - less bliss: Je - sus Christ was born for this!
Now ye need not fear the grave: Je - sus Christ was born to save!
Ox and ass be - fore Him bow, And He is in the man - ger now.
He hath oped the heaven - ly door, And man is bless - ed ev - er - more.
Calls you one and calls you all To gain His ev - er - last - ing hall.
Christ is born to - day! Christ is born to - day!
Christ was born for this! Christ was born for this!
Christ was born to save! Christ was born to save!

59 Hark, the Herald Angels Sing

Glory to God in the highest, and on earth peace . . . Luke 2:14

MENDELSSOHN 7.7.7.7.D. with Refrain
Felix Mendelssohn, 1809-1847
Adapted by William H. Cummings, 1831-1915

Charles Wesley, 1707-1788

1. Hark, the her - ald an - gels sing, "Glo - ry to the new-born King;
2. Christ, by high - est heaven a - dored; Christ, the ev - er - last - ing Lord!
3. Hail, the heaven-born Prince of Peace! Hail, the Sun of Right-eous-ness!
Peace on earth, and mer - cy mild, God and sin - ners rec - on - ciled!"
Late in time be-hold Him come, Off - spring of the Vir-gin's womb.
Light and life to all He brings, Risen with heal - ing in His wings.
Joy - ful, all ye na - tions, rise, Join the tri - umph of the skies;
Veiled in flesh the God-head see; Hail th' in - car - nate De - i - ty,
Mild He lays His glo - ry by, Born that man no more may die,
With th' an-gel - ic host pro-claim, "Christ is born in Beth - le - hem!"
Pleased as man with men to dwell, Je - sus, our Em - man - u - el!
Born to raise the sons of earth, Born to give them sec - ond birth.
Hark, the her - ald an - gels sing, "Glo - ry to the new - born King."
Organ

While Shepherds Watched Their Flocks by Night 60

... there were ... shepherds ... keeping watch over their flock by night. Luke 2:8

Nahum Tate, 1652-1715

CHRISTMAS C.M. with repeat
Adapted from George Frederick Handel, 1685-1759

1. While shep - herds watched their flocks by night,
2. "Fear not," said he— for might - y dread
3. "To you, in Da - vid's town this day,
4. "The heaven - ly Babe you there shall find
5. Thus spake the ser - aph, and forth - with
6. "All glo - ry be to God on high,

All seat - ed on the ground, The an - gel of the Lord came down,
Had seized their trou - bled mind— "Glad ti - dings of great joy I bring
Is born of Da - vid's line, A Sav - iour, who is Christ the Lord,
To hu - man view dis - played, All mean - ly wrapped in swad - dling clothes,
Ap - peared a shin - ing throng Of an - gels prais - ing God, who thus
And to the earth be peace; Good will hence - forth, from heaven to men,

And glo - ry shone a - round, And glo - ry shone a - round.
To you and all man - kind, To you and all man - kind.
And this shall be the sign, And this shall be the sign:
And in a man - ger laid, And in a man - ger laid."
Ad - dressed their joy - ful song, Ad - dressed their joy - ful song:
Be - gin and nev - er cease! Be - gin and nev - er cease!" A-MEN.

61 The First Noel

... they ... fell down, and worshipped him: and ... opened their treasures ... Matt. 2:11

THE FIRST NOEL Irregular with Refrain
From William Sandy's *Christmas Carols*, 1833

English carol, 18th century

1. The first No - el, the an - gel did say, Was to cer - tain poor
2. They look - ed up and saw a star Shin-ing in the
3. And by the light of that same star, Three wise men
4. This star drew nigh to the north-west, O'er Beth - le -
5. Then en - tered in those wise men three Full rev - erent -
6. Then let us all with one ac - cord Sing prais - es
shep-herds in fields as they lay, In fields where they lay keep-ing their
east be - yond them far, And to the earth it gave great
came from coun - try far; To seek for a king was their in -
hem it took its rest, And there it did both stop and
ly up - on their knee, And of - fered there in His pres -
to our heaven - ly Lord, That hath made heaven and earth of
Refrain
sheep, On a cold win-ter's night that was so deep.
light, And so it con - tin - ued both day and night.
tent, And to fol - low the star wher - ev - er it went. No - el, No -
stay Right o - ver the place where Je - sus lay.
ence Their gold, and myrrh, and frank - in - cense.
naught, And with His blood man - kind hath bought.
el, No - el, No - el, Born is the King of Is - ra - el! A - men.

Angels We Have Heard on High 62

Glory to God in the highest . . . Luke 2:14

GLORIA 7.7.7.7. with Refrain

Anonymous

French carol

1. An - gels we have heard on high, Sweet - ly sing - ing o'er the plains,
2. Shep-herds, why this ju - bi - lee? Why your joy - ous strains pro - long?
3. Come to Beth - le - hem and see Him whose birth the an - gels sing;
4. See with - in a man - ger laid Je - sus, Lord of heaven and earth!
And the moun-tains in re - ply Ech - o back their joy - ous strains.
Say what may the ti - dings be, Which in - spire your heaven - ly song?
Come, a - dore on bend - ed knee Christ the Lord, the new - born King.
Ma - ry, Jo - seph, lend your aid, With us sing our Sav - iour's birth.
Refrain
Glo - - - - - - - - - - - - - - ri - a
in ex - cel - sis De - o,
Glo - - - - - - - ri - a in ex - cel - sis De - o.
A-men.

63 Angels, from the Realms of Glory

... we have ... come to worship him. Matt. 2:2

REGENT SQUARE 8.7.8.7.8.7.

James Montgomery, 1771-1854

Henry T. Smart, 1813-1879

1. An - gels, from the realms of glo - ry, Wing your flight o'er
2. Shep - herds, in the fields a - bid - ing, Watch - ing o'er your
3. Sa - ges, leave your con - tem - pla - tions, Bright - er vi - sions
4. Saints, be - fore the al - tar bend - ing, Watch - ing long in
all the earth; Ye who sang cre - a - tion's sto - ry,
flocks by night, God with man is now re - sid - ing,
beam a - far; Seek the great De - sire of na - tions;
hope and fear, Sud - den - ly the Lord, de - scend - ing,
Now pro - claim Mes - si - ah's birth: Come and wor - ship,
Yon - der shines the in - fant Light: Come and wor - ship,
Ye have seen His na - tal star: Come and wor - ship,
In His tem - ple shall ap - pear: Come and wor - ship,
Come and wor - ship, Wor - ship Christ, the new - born King!
Come and wor - ship, Wor - ship Christ, the new - born King!
Come and wor - ship, Wor - ship Christ, the new - born King!
Come and wor - ship, Wor - ship Christ, the new - born King! A-men.

O Little Town of Bethlehem

. . . thou, Bethlehem . . . out of thee shall he come forth . . . Micah 5:2

ST. LOUIS 8.6.8.6.7.6.8.6.

Phillips Brooks, 1835-1893

Lewis H. Redner, 1831-1908

1. O lit - tle town of Beth - le - hem, How still we see thee lie;
2. For Christ is born of Ma - ry; And gath - ered all a - bove,
3. How si - lent - ly, how si - lent - ly The won - drous Gift is given!
4. O Ho - ly Child of Beth - le - hem! De - scend to us, we pray;
A - bove thy deep and dream-less sleep The si - lent stars go by.
While mor - tals sleep, the an - gels keep Their watch of won-dering love.
So God im - parts to hu - man hearts The bless - ings of His heaven.
Cast out our sin, and en - ter in, Be born in us to - day.
Yet in thy dark streets shin - eth The ev - er - last - ing Light;
O morn - ing stars, to - geth - er Pro - claim the ho - ly birth;
No ear may hear His com - ing, But in this world of sin,
We hear the Christ - mas an - gels The great glad ti - dings tell;
The hopes and fears of all the years Are met in thee to - night.
And prais - es sing to God the King, And peace to men on earth.
Where meek souls will re - ceive Him, still The dear Christ en - ters in.
Oh, come to us, a - bide with us, Our Lord Em - man - u - el. A-MEN.

65 There's a Song in the Air

... behold, I bring you good tidings of great joy ... Luke 2:10

Josiah G. Holland, 1819-1881 (altered)

CHRISTMAS SONG 6.6.6.6.12.12.
Karl P. Harrington, 1861-1953

1. There's a song in the air! There's a star in the sky! There's a moth-er's deep
2. There's a tu-mult of joy O'er the won-der-ful birth, For a Vir-gin's sweet
3. In the light of that star Lie the a-ges im-pearled; And that song from a-
4. We re-joice in the light, And we ech-o the song That comes down thro' the
prayer And a ba-by's low cry! And the star rains its fire while the
Boy Is the Lord of the earth. Ay! the star rains its fire while the
far Has swept o-ver the world. Ev-ery hearth is a-flame, and the
night From the heav-en-ly throng. Ay! we shout to the love-ly e-
beau-ti-ful sing, For the man-ger of Beth-le-hem cra-dles a King!
beau-ti-ful sing, For the man-ger of Beth-le-hem cra-dles a King!
beau-ti-ful sing, In the homes of the na-tions that Je-sus is King!
van-gel they bring, And we greet in His cra-dle our Sav-iour and King!

66 The People That in Darkness Sat

The people that walked in darkness have seen a great light ... Isa. 9:2

John Morison, circa 1750-1798
Scottish Paraphrase, 1781

COVENANTERS (Pisgah) C.M.
American melody

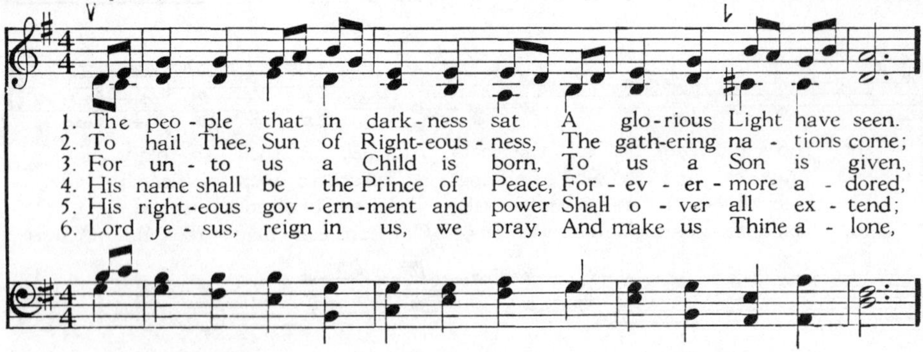
1. The peo-ple that in dark-ness sat A glo-rious Light have seen.
2. To hail Thee, Sun of Right-eous-ness, The gath-ering na-tions come;
3. For un-to us a Child is born, To us a Son is given,
4. His name shall be the Prince of Peace, For-ev-er-more a-dored,
5. His right-eous gov-ern-ment and power Shall o-ver all ex-tend;
6. Lord Je-sus, reign in us, we pray, And make us Thine a-lone,

The People That in Darkness Sat

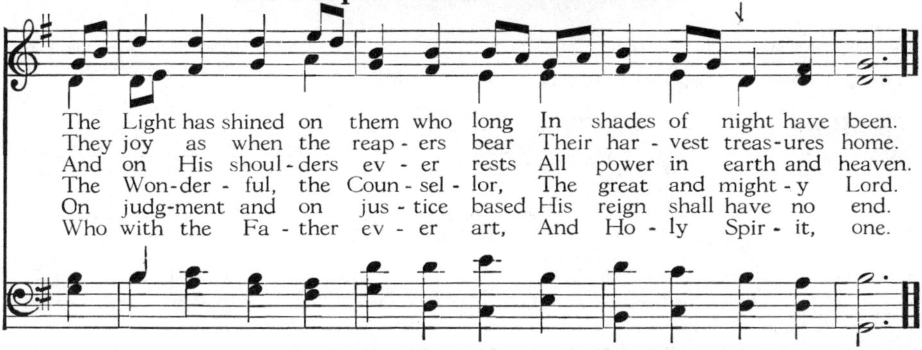
The Light has shined on them who long In shades of night have been.
They joy as when the reap - ers bear Their har - vest treas-ures home.
And on His shoul - ders ev - er rests All power in earth and heaven.
The Won-der - ful, the Coun - sel - lor, The great and might - y Lord.
On judg-ment and on jus - tice based His reign shall have no end.
Who with the Fa - ther ev - er art, And Ho - ly Spir - it, one.

As with Gladness, Men of Old 67

. . . they rejoiced with exceeding great joy. Matt. 2:10

DIX 7.7.7.7.7.7.
From a chorale by Conrad Kocher, 1786-1872
Arranged by William H. Monk, 1823-1889

William C. Dix, 1837-1898

1. As with glad-ness men of old Did the guid - ing star be - hold;
2. As with joy - ful steps they sped To that low - ly man - ger - bed,
3. As they of - fered gifts most rare At that man - ger rude and bare,
4. Ho - ly Je - sus, ev - ery day Keep us in the nar - row way;
As with joy they hailed its light, Lead - ing on - ward, beam-ing bright,
There to bend the knee be - fore Him whom heaven and earth a - dore,
So may we with ho - ly joy, Pure and free from sin's al - loy,
And, when earth - ly things are past, Bring our ran-somed souls at last
So, most gra-cious Lord, may we Ev - er-more be led to Thee.
So may we with will - ing feet Ev - er seek the mer - cy - seat.
All our cost-liest treas-ures bring, Christ, to Thee, our heaven-ly King.
Where they need no star to guide, Where no clouds Thy glo - ry hide. A-MEN.

(For lower key see No. 38)

68 O Come, All Ye Faithful

. . . Let us now go even unto Bethlehem, and see . . . Luke 2:15

Latin, circa 1740
Attributed to John F. Wade, 1711-1786
As in *Cantus Diversi,* 1751
Translated by Frederick Oakeley (and others) 1802-1880

ADESTE FIDELES Irregular with Refrain
Attributed to John F. Wade, 1711-1786
As in *Cantus Diversi,* 1751

1. O come, all ye faith - ful, Joy - ful and tri - um - phant,
2. See how the shep - herds, Sum - moned to His cra - dle,
3. Lo, *star - led chief - tains, Wise men, Christ a - dor - ing,
4. Sing, choirs of an - gels, Sing in ex - ul - ta - tion,
5. Yea, Lord, we greet Thee, Born this hap - py morn - ing;
O come ye, O come ye to Beth - le - hem;
Leav - ing their flocks draw nigh with low - ly fear.
Of - fer Him gold and frank - in - cense and myrrh;
Oh, sing, all ye cit - i - zens of heaven a - bove:
O Je - sus, to Thee be all glo - ry given;
Come and be - hold Him Born the King of an - gels.
We, too, will thith - er Bend our joy - ful foot - steps.
We to the Christ - child Bring our hearts' de - vo - tion.
"Glo - ry to God In the high - est!"
Word of the Fa - ther, Now in flesh ap - pear - ing.
REFRAIN
O come, let us a - dore Him, O come, let us a - dore Him,

(*star-led—led by a star)

O Come, All Ye Faithful

O come, let us a - dore Him, Christ the Lord.

Calm on the Listening Ear of Night 69

Glory to God in the highest, and on earth peace, good will toward men. Luke 2:14

ST. AGNES C.M.

Edmund H. Sears, 1810-1876 | John B. Dykes, 1823-1876

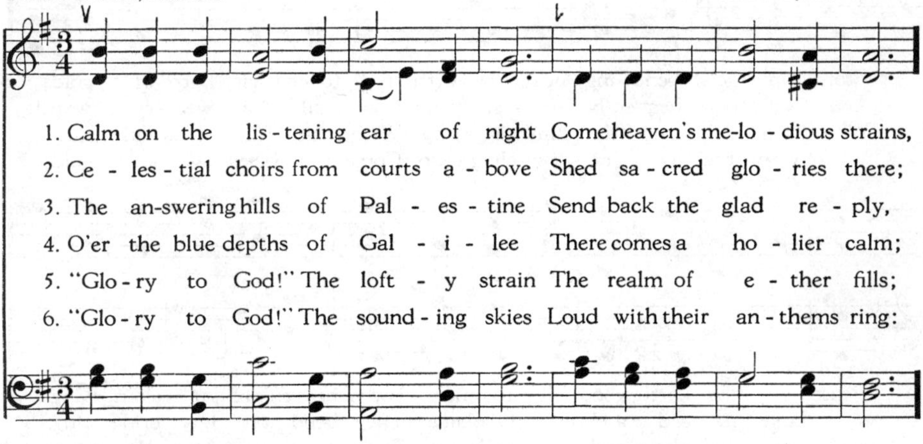
1. Calm on the lis - tening ear of night Come heaven's me-lo - dious strains,
2. Ce - les - tial choirs from courts a - bove Shed sa - cred glo - ries there;
3. The an-swering hills of Pal - es - tine Send back the glad re - ply,
4. O'er the blue depths of Gal - i - lee There comes a ho - lier calm;
5. "Glo - ry to God!" The loft - y strain The realm of e - ther fills;
6. "Glo - ry to God!" The sound - ing skies Loud with their an - thems ring:

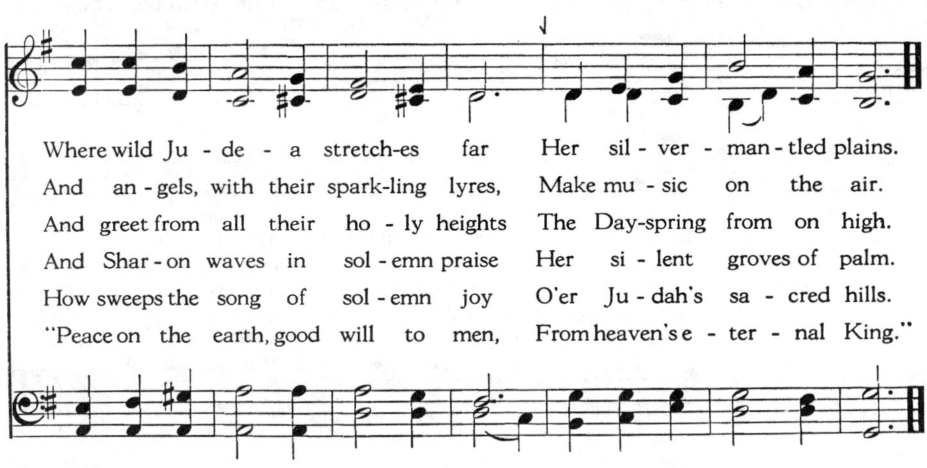
Where wild Ju - de - a stretch-es far Her sil - ver - man - tled plains.
And an - gels, with their spark-ling lyres, Make mu - sic on the air.
And greet from all their ho - ly heights The Day-spring from on high.
And Shar - on waves in sol - emn praise Her si - lent groves of palm.
How sweeps the song of sol - emn joy O'er Ju - dah's sa - cred hills.
"Peace on the earth, good will to men, From heaven's e - ter - nal King."

70 It Came upon the Midnight Clear

. . . there was . . . a multitude of the heavenly host praising God . . . Luke 2:13

CAROL C.M.D.

Edmund H. Sears, 1810-1876 — Richard S. Willis, 1819-1900

1. It came up - on the mid-night clear, That glo - rious song of old,
2. Still through the clo - ven skies they come, With peace-ful wings un - furled,
3. And ye, be - neath life's crush-ing load, Whose forms are bend-ing low,
4. For lo, the days are has-tening on, By proph-et bards fore- told,
From an - gels bend - ing near the earth, To touch their harps of gold:
And still their heaven-ly mu - sic floats O'er all the wea - ry world:
Who toil a - long the climb-ing way With pain - ful steps and slow,
When with the ev - er cir - cling years Comes round the age of gold;
"Peace on the earth, good will to men, From heaven's all-gra - cious King."
A - bove its sad and low - ly plains They bend on hov - ering wing,
Look now! For glad and gold - en hours Come swift - ly on the wing:
When peace shall o - ver all the earth Its an - cient splen-dors fling,
The world in sol-emn still - ness lay To hear the an - gels sing.
And ev - er o'er its Ba-bel sounds The bless - ed an - gels sing.
Oh, rest be - side the wea - ry road And hear the an - gels sing.
And the whole world give back the song Which now the an - gels sing. A-MEN.

Silent Night! Holy Night! 71

And they came . . . and found Mary, and Joseph, and the babe . . . Luke 2:16

Joseph Mohr, 1792-1848
Translation, anonymous

STILLE NACHT Irregular
Franz X. Grüber, 1787-1863

1. Si - lent night! Ho - ly night! All is calm, all is bright, Round yon vir - gin moth - er and Child. Ho - ly In - fant, so ten - der and mild, Sleep in heav - en - ly peace, Sleep in heav - en - ly peace.
2. Si - lent night! Ho - ly night! Shep - herds quake at the sight; Glo - ries stream from heav - en a - far, Heaven - ly hosts sing, "Al - le - lu - ia, Christ, the Sav - iour, is born! Christ, the Sav - iour, is born!"
3. Si - lent night! Ho - ly night! Son of God, love's pure light, Ra - diant beams from Thy ho - ly face, With the dawn of re - deem - ing grace, Je - sus, Lord, at Thy birth, Je - sus, Lord, at Thy birth.

72 What Child Is This, Who Laid to Rest?

. . . she had brought forth her firstborn son: and . . . called his name JESUS. Matt. 1:25

English carol
Adapted by William C. Dix, 1837-1898

GREENSLEEVES 8.7.8.7.6.8.6.7.
English melody, circa 1642
Harmony by John Stainer, 1840-1901

1. What Child is this, who, laid to rest, On Mar-y's lap is sleep-ing?
2. Why lies He in such mean es-tate Where ox and ass are feed-ing?
3. So bring Him in-cense, gold and myrrh, Come, peas-ant, king, to own Him;
Whom an-gels greet with an-thems sweet, While shep-herds watch are keep-ing?
Good Chris-tian, fear; for sin-ners here The si-lent Word is plead-ing.
The King of kings sal-va-tion brings, Let lov-ing hearts en-throne Him.
This, this is Christ the King, Whom shep-herds guard and an-gels sing:
Nails, spear, shall pierce Him through, The cross be borne for me, for you:
Raise, raise the song on high, The Vir-gin sings her lul-la-by:
Haste, haste to bring Him laud, The Babe, the Son of Mar-y!
Hail, hail the Word made flesh, The Babe, the Son of Mar-y!
Joy, joy, for Christ is born, The Babe, the Son of Mar-y!

Thou Didst Leave Thy Throne 73

. . . he was rich, yet for your sakes he became poor . . . 2 Cor. 8:9

MARGARET Irregular

Emily E.S. Elliott, 1836-1897 (altered) — Timothy R. Matthews, 1826-1910

1. Thou didst leave Thy throne and Thy king - ly crown When Thou
2. Heav - en's arch - es rang when the an - gels sang Pro -
3. The fox - es found rest, and the birds their nest In the
4. Thou cam - est, O Lord, with the liv - ing Word That should
5. When the heav - ens shall ring and the an - gels sing At Thy
cam - est to earth for me, But in Beth - le - hem's home there was
claim - ing Thy roy - al de - cree; But in low - ly birth didst Thou
shade of the for - est tree, But Thy couch was the sod, O Thou
set Thy peo - ple free, But with mock - ing scorn and with
com - ing to vic - to - ry, Let Thy voice call me home, say - ing,
found no room For Thy ho - ly na - tiv - i - ty. Oh,
come to earth, And in great hu - mil - i - ty. Oh,
Son of God, In the des - erts of Gal - i - lee. Oh,
crown of thorn They bore Thee to Cal - va - ry. Oh,
"Yet there is room, There is room at My side for thee." And my
come to my heart, Lord Je - sus: There is room in my heart for Thee!
come to my heart, Lord Je - sus: There is room in my heart for Thee!
come to my heart, Lord Je - sus: There is room in my heart for Thee!
come to my heart, Lord Je - sus: There is room in my heart for Thee!
heart shall re - joice, Lord Je - sus, When Thou com - est and call - est for me.
A-MEN.

74 Ivory Palaces

... out of the ivory palaces, whereby they have made thee glad. Psa. 45:8

MONTREAT 9.6.9.6. with Refrain

Henry Barraclough, b. 1891 | Henry Barraclough, b. 1891

1. My Lord has gar-ments so won-drous fine, And myrrh their tex-ture fills;
2. His life had al - so its sor-rows sore, For al - oes had a part;
3. His gar-ments too were in cas - sia dipped, With heal-ing in a touch;
4. In gar-ments glo - ri - ous He will come, To o - pen wide the door;
Its fra-grance reached to this heart of mine, With joy my be - ing thrills.
And when I think of the cross He bore, My eyes with tear-drops start.
Each time my feet in some sin have slipped, He took me from its clutch.
And I shall en - ter my heaven-ly home, To dwell for - ev - er - more.
REFRAIN
Out of the i - vo - ry pal - a - ces, In - to a world of woe,
On - ly His great, e - ter - nal love Made my Sav - iour go.

All Glory, Laud, and Honor 75

. . . Blessed is the King of Israel that cometh in the name of the Lord. John 12:13

Theodulph of Orleans, circa 760-821
Translated by John M. Neale, 1818-1866

ST. THEODULPH 7.6.7.6.D.
Melchoir Teschner, 1584-1635

1. All glo - ry, laud, and hon - or To Thee, Re - deem - er, King,
2. The com - pan - y of an - gels Are prais-ing Thee on high,
3. To Thee be - fore Thy pas - sion They sang their hymns of praise;
To whom the lips of chil - dren Made sweet ho - san - nas ring.
And mor - tal men and all things Cre - a - ted make re - ply.
To Thee now high ex - alt - ed Our mel - o - dy we raise.
Thou art the King of Is - rael, Thou Da-vid's roy - al Son,
The peo - ple of the He - brews With palms be - fore Thee went;
Thou didst ac - cept their prais - es, Ac - cept the prayers we bring,
Who in the Lord's name com - est, The King and bless - ed One.
Our praise and prayer and an - thems Be - fore Thee we pre - sent.
Who in all good de - light - est, Thou good and gra - cious King. A - MEN.

76 Seeking for Me!

For the Son of man is come to seek and to save that which was lost. Luke 19:10

Anonymous, 19th century

Attributed to E.E. Hasty, 19th century

1. Je - sus, my Sav - iour, to Beth - le - hem came, Born in a
2. Je - sus, my Sav - iour, on Cal - va - ry's tree, Paid the great
3. Je - sus, my Sav - iour, the same as of old, While I was
4. Je - sus, my Sav - iour, shall come from on high— Sweet is the
man - ger to sor - row and shame; Oh, it was won - der - ful—
debt and my soul He set free; Oh, it was won - der - ful—
wan - dering a - far from the fold, Gent - ly and long did He
prom - ise as wea - ry years fly; Oh, I shall see Him de -
Refrain
blest be His name! Seek - ing for me, for me! Seek - ing for
how could it be? Dy - ing for me, for me! Dy - ing for
plead with my soul, Call - ing for me, for me! Call - ing for
scend from the sky, Com - ing for me, for me! Com - ing for
me, for me! Seek - ing for me, for me! Oh, it was
me, for me! Dy - ing for me, for me! Oh, it was
me, for me! Call - ing for me, for me! Gent - ly and
me, for me! Com - ing for me, for me! Oh, I shall

Seeking for Me!

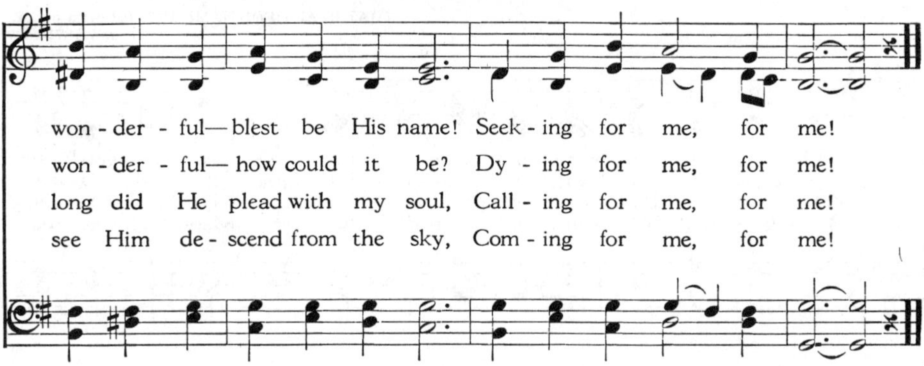
won - der - ful— blest be His name! Seek - ing for me, for me!
won - der - ful— how could it be? Dy - ing for me, for me!
long did He plead with my soul, Call - ing for me, for me!
see Him de - scend from the sky, Com - ing for me, for me!

Ride on, Ride on in Majesty 77

... thy King cometh unto thee, meek, and sitting upon an ass ... Matt. 21:5

ST. DROSTANE L.M.

Henry H. Milman, 1791-1868

John B. Dykes, 1823-1876

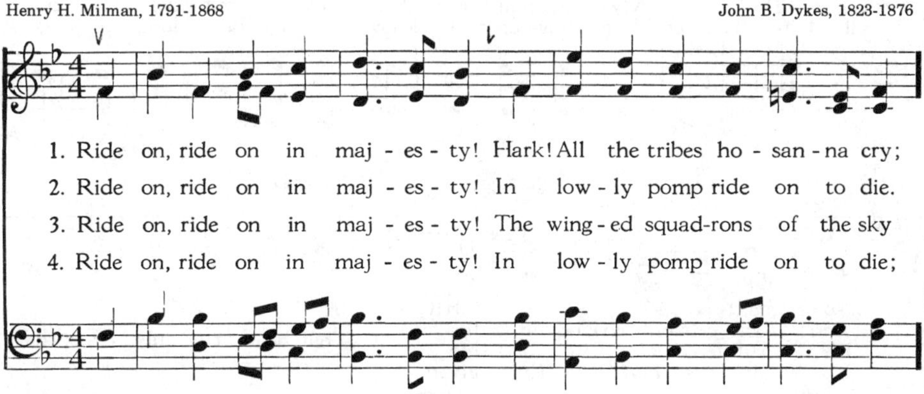
1. Ride on, ride on in maj - es - ty! Hark! All the tribes ho - san - na cry;
2. Ride on, ride on in maj - es - ty! In low - ly pomp ride on to die.
3. Ride on, ride on in maj - es - ty! The wing - ed squad-rons of the sky
4. Ride on, ride on in maj - es - ty! In low - ly pomp ride on to die;

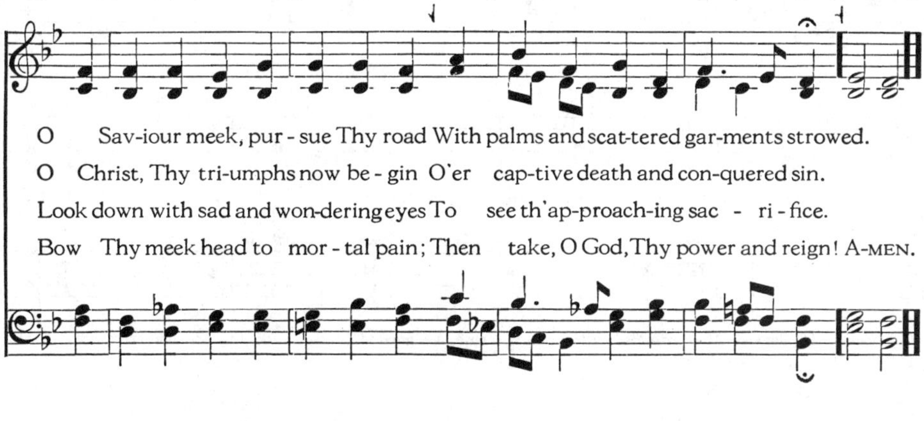
O Sav-iour meek, pur - sue Thy road With palms and scat-tered gar-ments strowed.
O Christ, Thy tri-umphs now be - gin O'er cap-tive death and con-quered sin.
Look down with sad and won-dering eyes To see th'ap-proach-ing sac - ri - fice.
Bow Thy meek head to mor - tal pain; Then take, O God, Thy power and reign! A-MEN.

78 That Beautiful Name

. . . thou shalt call his name JESUS . . . Matt. 1:21

THAT BEAUTIFUL NAME 10.7.10.7. with Refrain

Jean Perry, 1865-1935 (altered)

Mabel J. Camp, 1871-1937

3
4
1. I know of a Name, a beau - ti - ful Name, That an - gels brought
2. I know of a Name, a beau - ti - ful Name, That un - to a
3. The One of that Name, my Sav - iour be - came, My Sav - iour of
4. I love that blest Name, that won - der - ful Name, Made high - er than
down to earth; They whis-pered it low one night long a - go
Babe was giv - en; The stars glit - tered bright through - out that glad night,
Cal - va - ry; My sins nailed Him there, my bur - dens He bear;
all in heav-en; 'Twas whis-pered, I know, in my heart long a - go;
To a maid - en of low - ly birth.
And an - gels praised God in heaven.
He suf - fered all this for me.
To Je - sus my life I've given.
REFRAIN
That beau - ti - ful Name, that
beau - ti - ful Name, From sin has power to free us! That beau - ti - ful

That Beautiful Name

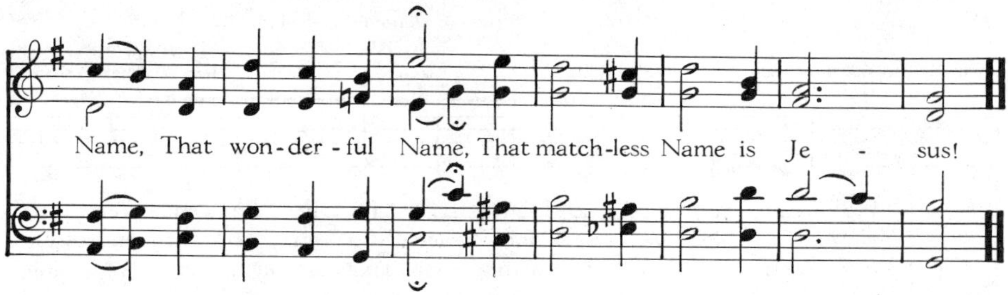
Name, That won-der-ful Name, That match-less Name is Je - sus!

O Love How Deep

79

... what is the ... depth ... to know the love of Christ ... Eph. 3:18-19

DEO GRACIAS L.M.

Latin, 15th century
Translated by Benjamin Webb, 1819-1885

The Agincourt Song, circa 1415
Harmony by Charles W. Douglas, 1867-1944

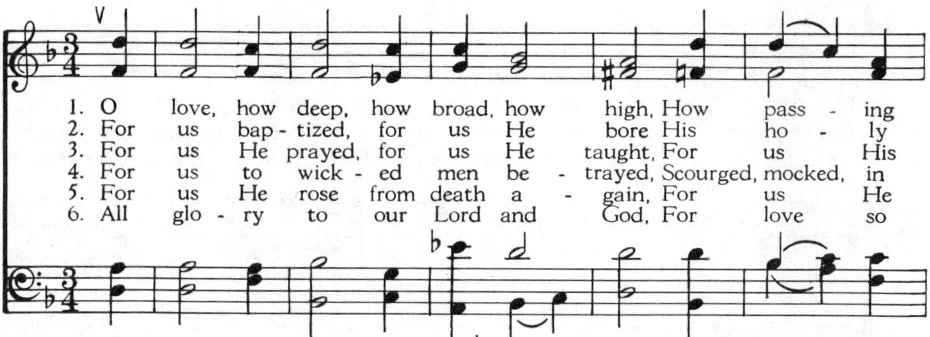

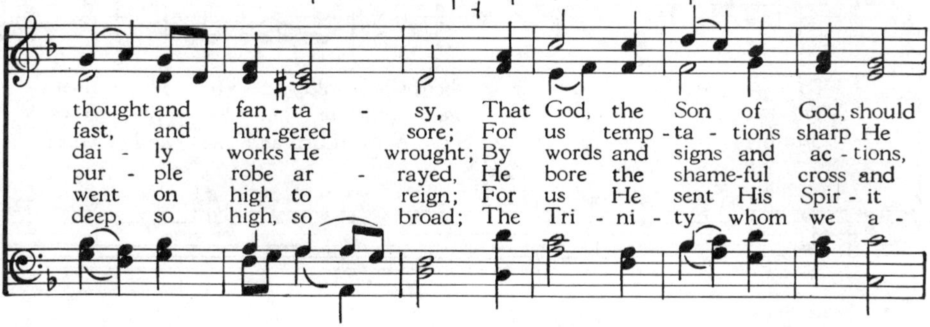

1. O love, how deep, how broad, how high, How pass-ing thought and fan-ta-sy, That God, the Son of God, should take Our mor-tal form for mor-tals' sake.
2. For us bap-tized, for us He bore His ho-ly fast, and hun-gered sore; For us temp-ta-tions sharp He knew; For us the temp-ter o-ver-threw.
3. For us He prayed, for us He taught, For us His dai-ly works He wrought; By words and signs and ac-tions, thus Still seek-ing not Him-self, but us.
4. For us to wick-ed men be-trayed, Scourged, mocked, in pur-ple robe ar-rayed, He bore the shame-ful cross and death; For us gave up His dy-ing breath.
5. For us He rose from death a-gain, For us He went on high to reign; For us He sent His Spir-it here To guide, to strength-en, and to cheer.
6. All glo-ry to our Lord and God, For love so deep, so high, so broad; The Tri-ni-ty whom we a-dore For-ev-er and for-ev-er-more. A-MEN.

80 Hosanna, Loud Hosanna

. . . they . . . went before, and . . . cried, saying, Hosanna . . . Mark 11:9

Jennette Threlfall, 1821-1880

LANCASHIRE 7.6.7.6.D.
Henry T. Smart, 1813-1879

1. Ho - san - na, loud ho - san - na, The lit - tle chil - dren sang;
2. From Ol - i - vet they fol - lowed 'Mid an ex - ult - ant crowd,
3. "Ho - san - na in the high - est!" That an - cient song we sing,
Through pil - lared court and tem - ple The love - ly an - them rang;
The vic - tor palm branch wav - ing, And chant - ing clear and loud;
For Christ is our Re - deem - er, The Lord of heaven our King.
To Je - sus, who had blessed them Close fold - ed to His breast,
The Lord of men and an - gels Rode on in low - ly state,
Oh, may we ev - er praise Him With heart and life and voice,
The chil - dren sang their prais - es, The sim - plest and the best.
Nor scorned that lit - tle chil - dren Should on His bid - ding wait.
And in His bliss - ful pres - ence E - ter - nal - ly re - joice! A-MEN.

(For lower key see No. 451)

Lead Me to Calvary

81

. . . consider him that endured such contradiction of sinners . . . Heb. 12:3

Jennie E. Hussey, 1874-1958

DUNCANNON C.M. with Refrain
William J. Kirkpatrick, 1838-1921

1. King of my life, I crown Thee now, Thine shall the glo - ry be;
2. Show me the tomb where Thou wast laid, Ten - der - ly mourned and wept;
3. Let me, like Ma - ry, through the gloom, Come with a gift to Thee;
4. May I be will - ing, Lord, to bear Dai - ly my cross for Thee;
Lest I for - get Thy thorn-crowned brow, Lead me to Cal - va - ry.
An - gels in robes of light ar - rayed Guard - ed Thee whilst Thou slept.
Show to me now the emp - ty tomb, Lead me to Cal - va - ry.
E - ven Thy cup of grief to share, Thou hast borne all for me.
REFRAIN
Lest I for - get Geth - sem - a - ne; Lest I for - get Thine ag - o - ny;
Lest I for - get Thy love for me, Lead me to Cal - va - ry.

82 When I Survey the Wondrous Cross

But what things were gain to me, those I counted loss for Christ. Phil. 3:7

HAMBURG L.M.
From *Psalm Tone I*
Adapted by Lowell Mason, 1792-1872

Isaac Watts, 1674-1748

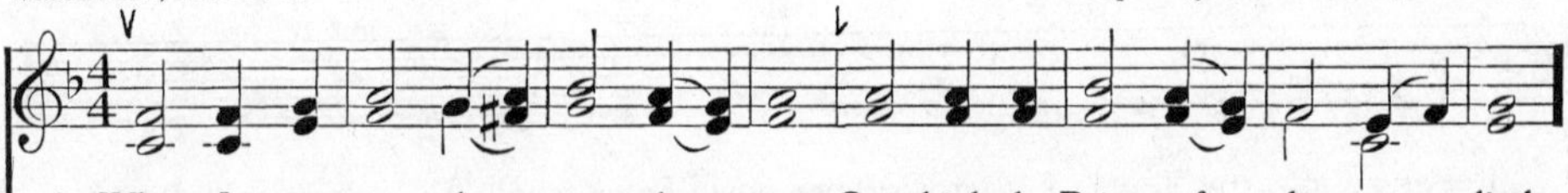

1. When I sur-vey the won - drous cross On which the Prince of glo - ry died,
2. For - bid it, Lord, that I should boast, Save in the death of Christ my God;
3. See, from His head, His hands, His feet, Sor - row and love flow min - gled down—
4. Were the whole realm of na - ture mine, That were a pres - ent far too small;

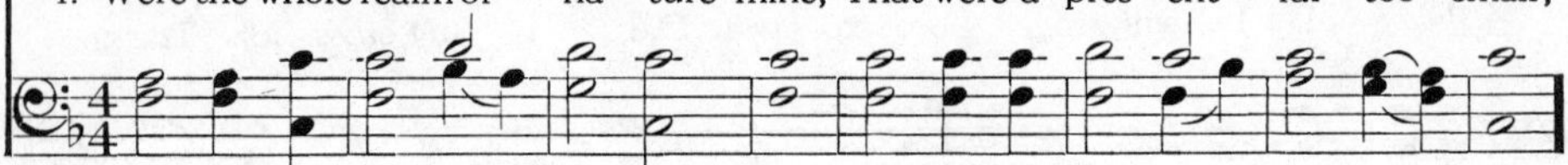

My rich-est gain I count but loss, And pour con-tempt on all my pride.
All the vain things that charm me most, I sac-ri - fice them to His blood.
Did e'er such love and sor - row meet, Or thorns com-pose so rich a crown?
Love so a-maz - ing, so di - vine, De-mands my soul, my life, my all. A-MEN.

83 In the Cross of Christ I Glory

. . . God forbid that I should glory, save in the cross of . . . Christ . . . Gal. 6:14

RATHBUN 8.7.8.7.
Ithamar Conkey, 1815-1867

John Bowring, 1792-1872

1. In the cross of Christ I glo - ry, Tower-ing o'er the wrecks of time;
2. When the woes of life o'er - take me, Hopes de - ceive, and fears an - noy,
3. When the sun of bliss is beam - ing Light and love up - on my way,
4. Bane and bless - ing, pain and pleas - ure, By the cross are sanc - ti - fied;
5. In the cross of Christ I glo - ry, Tower-ing o'er the wrecks of time;

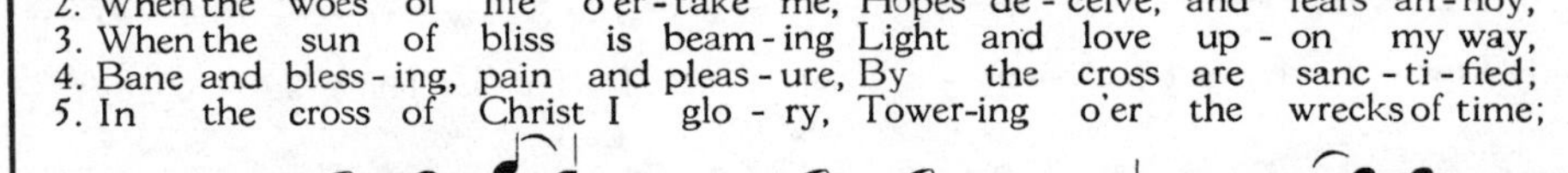

All the light of sa - cred sto - ry Gath - ers round its head sub-lime.
Nev - er shall the cross for - sake me; Lo, it glows with peace and joy.
From the cross the ra - diance stream-ing Adds more lus - ter to the day.
Peace is there that knows no meas-ure, Joys that through all time a - bide.
All the light of sa - cred sto - ry Gath - ers round its head sub-lime. A-MEN.

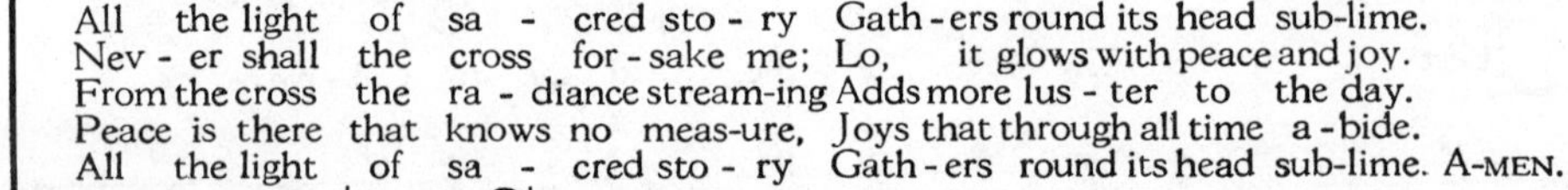

Beneath the Cross of Jesus

. . . the shadow of a great rock in a weary land. Isa. 32:2

Elizabeth C. Clephane, 1830-1869

ST. CHRISTOPHER 7.6.8.6.8.6.8.6.
Frederick C. Maker, 1844-1927

1. Be - neath the cross of Je - sus I fain would take my stand—
2. Up - on that cross of Je - sus Mine eye at times can see
3. I take, O cross, thy shad - ow For my a - bid - ing place;
The shad - ow of a might - y Rock With - in a wea - ry land;
The ver - y dy - ing form of One Who suf - fered there for me;
I ask no oth - er sun - shine than The sun - shine of His face;
A home with - in the wil - der - ness, A rest up - on the way,
And from my smit - ten heart with tears Two won - ders I con - fess—
Con - tent to let the world go by, To know no gain nor loss,
From the burn - ing of the noon - tide heat, And the bur - den of the day.
The won - ders of re - deem - ing love And my un - wor - thi - ness.
My sin - ful self my on - ly shame, My glo - ry all the cross. A-MEN.

85 At the Cross

. . . having made peace through the blood of his cross . . . Col. 1:20

Isaac Watts, 1674-1748
Refrain by Ralph E. Hudson, 1843-1901

HUDSON C.M. with Refrain
Ralph E. Hudson, 1843-1901

1. A - las! and did my Sav - iour bleed? And did my Sov-ereign die?
2. Was it for crimes that I have done He groaned up - on the tree?
3. Well might the sun in dark - ness hide And shut His glo - ries in,
4. But drops of grief can ne'er re - pay The debt of love I owe:
Would He de - vote that sa - cred head For such a worm as I?
A - maz - ing pit - y! grace un - known! And love be - yond de - gree!
When Christ, the might - y Mak - er, died For man, the crea - ture's sin.
Here, Lord, I give my - self to Thee; 'Tis all that I can do!
REFRAIN
At the cross, at the cross where I first saw the light, And the
bur - den of my heart rolled a - way, It was there by faith
I re - ceived my sight, And now I am hap - py all the day!

Not All the Blood of Beasts 86

For it is not possible that the blood of bulls . . . should take away sins. Heb. 10:4

Isaac Watts, 1674-1748

BOYLSTON S.M.
Lowell Mason, 1792-1872

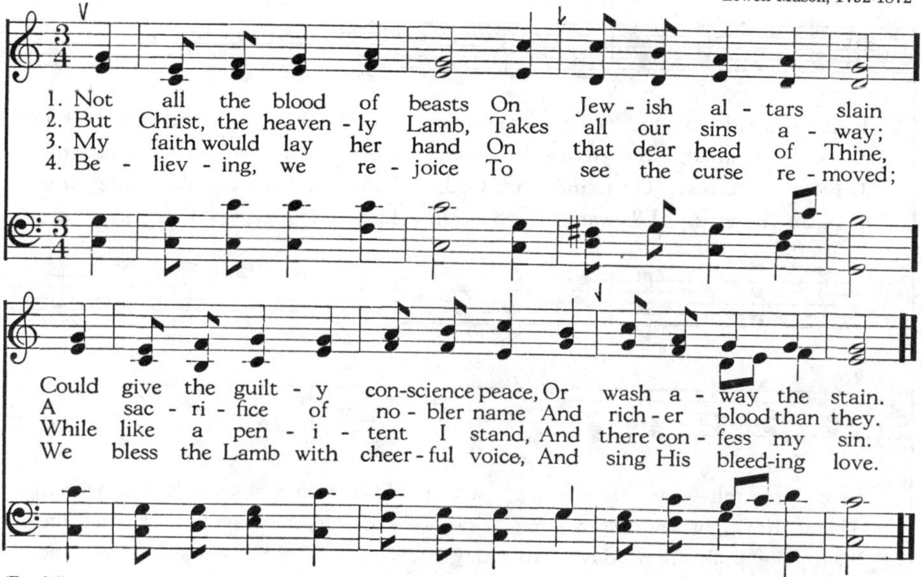
1. Not all the blood of beasts On Jew - ish al - tars slain
2. But Christ, the heaven - ly Lamb, Takes all our sins a - way;
3. My faith would lay her hand On that dear head of Thine,
4. Be - liev - ing, we re - joice To see the curse re - moved;
Could give the guilt - y con-science peace, Or wash a - way the stain.
A sac - ri - fice of no - bler name And rich - er blood than they.
While like a pen - i - tent I stand, And there con - fess my sin.
We bless the Lamb with cheer - ful voice, And sing His bleed-ing love.

(For different harmony see No. 312)

Alas, and Did My Saviour Bleed 87

. . . he was wounded for our transgressions . . . Isa. 53:5

Isaac Watts, 1674-1748

MARTYRDOM C.M.
Hugh Wilson, 1764-1824

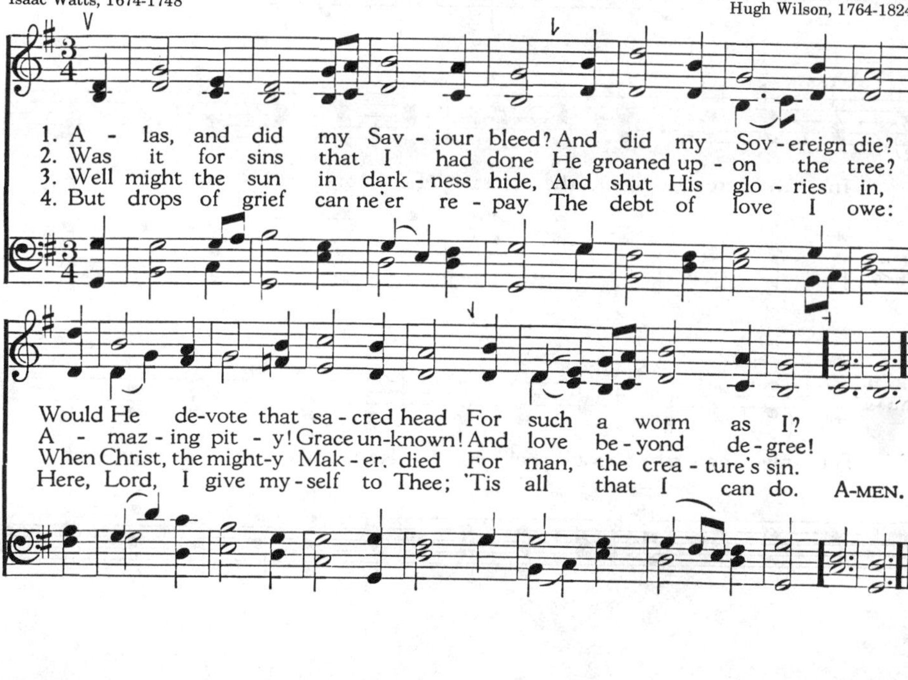
1. A - las, and did my Sav - iour bleed? And did my Sov - ereign die?
2. Was it for sins that I had done He groaned up - on the tree?
3. Well might the sun in dark - ness hide, And shut His glo - ries in,
4. But drops of grief can ne'er re - pay The debt of love I owe:
Would He de-vote that sa - cred head For such a worm as I?
A - maz - ing pit - y! Grace un-known! And love be - yond de - gree!
When Christ, the might-y Mak - er. died For man, the crea - ture's sin.
Here, Lord, I give my - self to Thee; 'Tis all that I can do. A-MEN.

88 Near the Cross

Let us draw near with a true heart . . . Heb. 10:22

NEAR THE CROSS 7.6.7.6. with Refrain

Fanny J. Crosby, 1820-1915

William H. Doane, 1832-1915

1. Je - sus, keep me near the cross, There a pre - cious foun - tain
2. Near the cross, a trem - bling soul, Love and mer - cy found me;
3. Near the cross! O Lamb of God, Bring its scenes be - fore me;
4. Near the cross I'll watch and wait, Hop - ing, trust - ing ev - er,
Free to all— a heal - ing stream Flows from Cal - vary's moun - tain.
There the Bright and Morn - ing Star Sheds its beams a - round me.
Help me walk from day to day With its shad - ows o'er me.
Till I reach the gold - en strand Just be - yond the riv - er.
REFRAIN
In the cross, in the cross, Be my glo - ry ev - er;
Till my rap - tured soul shall find Rest be - yond the riv - er.

There Is a Green Hill

... Jesus ... suffered without the gate. Heb. 13:12

Cecil F.H. Alexander, 1818-1895

GREEN HILL C.M. with Refrain
George C. Stebbins, 1846-1945

1. There is a green hill far a - way, With-out a cit - y wall,
2. We may not know, we can - not tell What pains He had to bear;
3. He died that we might be for - given, He died to make us good,
4. There was no oth - er good e - nough To pay the price of sin;
Where the dear Lord was cru - ci - fied, Who died to save us all.
But we be - lieve it was for us He hung and suf - fered there.
That we might go at last to heaven, Saved by His pre - cious blood.
He on - ly could un - lock the gate Of heaven, and let us in.
REFRAIN
Oh, dear - ly, dear - ly has He loved, And we must love Him, too;
And trust in His re - deem - ing blood, And try His works to do.

90 He Died for Me

Who his own self bare our sins in his own body on the tree . . . 1 Pet. 2:24

John Newton, 1725-1807

EXCELL C.M. with Refrain
Edwin O. Excell, 1851-1921

1. I saw One hang - ing on a tree, In ag - o - ny and blood;
2. Sure, nev - er till my lat - est breath, Can I for - get that look;
3. My con-science felt and owned the guilt, And plunged me in de - spair;
4. A sec - ond look He gave, which said, "I free - ly all for - give;
He fixed His lov - ing eyes on me, As near His cross I stood.
It seemed to charge me with His death, Though not a word He spoke.
I saw my sins His blood had spilt And helped to nail Him there.
This blood is for your ran - som paid, I die that you may live."
REFRAIN
Oh, can it be, up - on a tree The Sav - iour died for me?
My soul is thrilled, my heart is filled, To think He died for me!

O Sacred Head, Now Wounded 91

And when they had platted a crown of thorns, they put it upon his head . . . Matt. 27:29

Attrib. to Bernard of Clairvaux, 1091-1153
Trans. (Ger.) by Paul Gerhardt, 1607-1676
Trans. (Eng.) by James W. Alexander, 1804-1859

PASSION CHORALE 7.6.7.6.D.
Hans L. Hassler, 1564-1612
Harmony by Johann Sebastian Bach, 1685-1750

1. O sa - cred Head, now wound - ed, With grief and shame weighed down;
2. O Lord of life and glo - ry, What bliss till now was Thine!
3. What lan - guage shall I bor - row To thank Thee, dear - est Friend,
4. Be near when I am dy - ing, Oh, show Thy cross to me;
Now scorn - ful - ly sur - round - ed With thorns, Thine on - ly crown;
I read the won - drous sto - ry; I joy to call Thee mine.
For this Thy dy - ing sor - row, Thy pit - y with - out end?
And for my suc - cor fly - ing, Come, Lord, to set me free:
How art Thou pale with an - guish, With sore a - buse and scorn;
What Thou, my Lord, hast suf - fered Was all for sin - ners' gain;
Oh, make me Thine for - ev - er; And, should I faint - ing be,
These eyes, new faith re - ceiv - ing, From Thee shall not re - move,
How does that vis - age lan - guish, Which once was bright as morn!
Mine, mine, was the trans - gres - sion, But Thine the dead - ly pain.
Lord, let me nev - er, nev - er Out - live my love to Thee.
For he who dies be - liev - ing Dies safe - ly through Thy love. A-MEN.

92 'Tis Midnight, and on Olive's Brow

And he came out, and went, . . . to the mount of Olives . . . Luke 22:39

OLIVE'S BROW L.M.

William B. Tappan, 1794-1849 — William B. Bradbury, 1816-1868

1. 'Tis mid-night, and on O - live's brow The star is dimmed that late - ly shone;
2. 'Tis mid-night, and from all re-moved, The Sav-iour wres-tles lone with fears–
3. 'Tis mid-night, and for oth - er's guilt The Man of Sor-rows weeps in blood;
4. 'Tis mid-night, and from e - ther-plains Is borne the song that an - gels know–

'Tis mid-night in the gar-den now The suf-fering Sav-iour prays a - lone.
E'en that dis-ci-ple whom He loved Heeds not his Mas-ter's grief and tears.
Yet He that hath in an-guish knelt Is not for-sak-en by His God.
Un-heard by mor-tals are the strains That sweet-ly soothe the Sav-iour's woe.

93 Hallelujah, What a Saviour!

He is despised and rejected of men; a man of sorrows . . . Isa. 53:3

MAN OF SORROWS 7.7.7.8.

Philip P. Bliss, 1838-1876 — Philip P. Bliss, 1838-1876

1. "Man of sor-rows," what a name For the Son of God who came,
2. Bear - ing shame and scof-fing rude, In my place con-demned He stood,
3. Guilt - y, vile, and help-less we; Spot-less Lamb of God was He;
4. Lift - ed up was He to die; "It is fin-ished," was His cry,
5. When He comes, our glo-rious King, All His ran-somed home to bring,

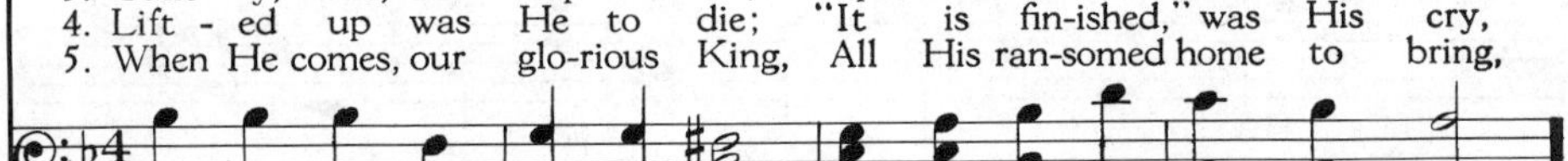

Ru - ined sin-ners to re-claim! Hal - le - lu - jah! What a Sav - iour!
Sealed my par-don with His blood; Hal - le - lu - jah! What a Sav - iour!
"Full a - tone-ment," can it be! Hal - le - lu - jah! What a Sav - iour!
Now in heaven ex - alt - ed high; Hal - le - lu - jah! What a Sav - iour!
Then a - new this song we'll sing, Hal - le - lu - jah! What a Sav - iour!

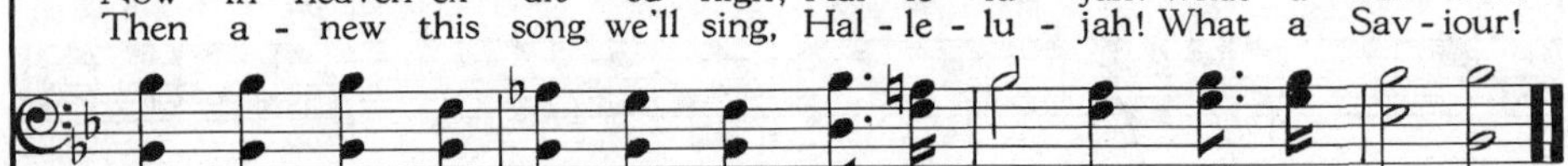

There Is a Fountain

. . . there shall be a fountain . . . for sin and for uncleanness. Zech. 13:1

CLEANSING FOUNTAIN C.M. with repeats
American melody
Arranged by Lowell Mason, 1792-1872

William Cowper, 1731-1800

1. There is a foun - tain filled with blood Drawn from Em - man - uel's veins;
2. The dy - ing thief re - joiced to see That foun - tain in his day;
3. Dear dy - ing Lamb, Thy pre - cious blood Shall nev - er lose its power,
4. E'er since by faith I saw the stream Thy flow - ing wounds sup - ply,
5. When this poor lisp - ing, stam-mering tongue Lies si - lent in the grave,
And sin - ners plunged be - neath that flood, Lose all their guilt - y stains:
And there may I, though vile as he, Wash all my sins a - way:
Till all the ran - somed Church of God Be saved, to sin no more:
Re - deem - ing love has been my theme, And shall be till I die:
Then in a no - bler, sweet - er song I'll sing Thy power to save:
Lose all their guilt - y stains, Lose all their guilt - y stains;
Wash all my sins a - way, Wash all my sins a - way;
Be saved, to sin no more, Be saved, to sin no more;
And shall be till I die, And shall be till I die;
I'll sing Thy power to save, I'll sing Thy power to save;
And sin - ners plunged be - neath that flood, Lose all their guilt - y stains.
And there may I, though vile as he, Wash all my sins a - way.
Till all the ran-somed Church of God Be saved, to sin no more.
Re - deem - ing love has been my theme, And shall be till I die.
Then in a no - bler, sweet - er song I'll sing Thy power to save.

95 Blessed Be the Fountain

. . . wash me, and I shall be whiter than snow. Psa. 51:7

BLESSED FOUNTAIN L.M.D. with Refrain

Eden R. Latta, b. 1839

Henry S. Perkins, 1833-1914

1. Bless-ed be the Foun-tain of blood To a world of sin-ners re-vealed;
2. Thorn-y was the crown that He wore, And the cross His bod-y o'er-came;
3. Fa-ther, I have wan-dered from Thee, Oft-en has my heart gone a-stray;
Bless-ed be the dear Son of God, On-ly by His stripes we are healed.
Griev-ous were the sor-rows He bore, But He suf-fered thus not in vain.
Crim-son do my sins seem to me, Wa-ter can-not wash them a-way.
Though I've wan-dered far from His fold, Bring-ing to my heart pain and woe,
May I to that Foun-tain be led, Made to cleanse my sins here be-low;
Je-sus, to that Foun-tain of Thine, Lean-ing on Thy prom-ise, I go;
Wash me in the blood of the Lamb, And I shall be whit-er than snow.
Wash me in the blood that He shed, And I shall be whit-er than snow.
Cleanse me by Thy wash-ing di-vine, And I shall be whit-er than snow.
REFRAIN
Whit-er than the snow, Whit-er than the snow;
Whit-er than the snow, Whit-er than the snow;

Blessed Be the Fountain

Wash me in the blood of the Lamb, And I shall be whit-er than snow.

Go to Dark Gethsemane

96

Then cometh Jesus with them unto a place called Gethsemane . . . Matt. 26:36

GETHSEMANE 7.7.7.7.7.7.

James Montgomery, 1771-1854

Richard Redhead, 1820-1901

1. Go to dark Geth-sem-a-ne, Ye that feel the tempt-er's power;
2. Fol-low to the judg-ment hall; View the Lord of life ar-raigned.
3. Cal-vary's mourn-ful moun-tain climb; There, a-dor-ing at His feet,
4. Ear-ly has-ten to the tomb Where they laid His breath-less clay;
Your Re-deem-er's con-flict see; Watch with Him one bit-ter hour;
Oh, the worm-wood and the gall! Oh, the pangs His soul sus-tained!
Mark that mir-a-cle of time, God's own sac-ri-fice com-plete:
All is sol-i-tude and gloom. Who hath tak-en Him a-way?
Turn not from His griefs a-way; Learn of Je-sus Christ to pray.
Shun not suf-fering, shame, or loss; Learn of Him to bear the cross.
"It is fin-ished!" hear the cry; Learn of Je-sus Christ to die.
Christ is risen! He meets our eyes. Sav-iour, teach us so to rise. A-MEN.

97 Welcome, Happy Morning!

. . . thanks be to God, which giveth us the victory . . . 1 Cor. 15:57

Venantius H.C. Fortunatus, 530-609
Translated by John Ellerton, 1826-1893

HERMAS 6.5.6.5.D. with Refrain
Frances R. Havergal, 1836-1879

1. "Wel-come, hap-py morn-ing!" age to age shall say; "Hell to - day is
2. Earth with joy con - fess - es, cloth-ing her for spring, All good gifts re -
3. Mak - er and Re-deem - er, life and health of all, Thou from heaven be -
van-quished! Heaven is won to - day!" Lo! The dead is liv - ing,
turn with her re-turn-ing King; Bloom in ev - ery mea - dow,
hold - ing hu - man na-ture's fall, Of th'e - ter - nal Fa - ther
God for - ev - er - more, Him, their true Cre - a - tor, all His works a - dore;
leaves on ev - ery bough, Speak His sor-rows end-ed, hail His tri-umph now:
true and on - ly Son, Man-hood to de - liv - er, man-hood didst put on:
Refrain
"Wel-come, hap - py morn - ing!" age to age shall say;
"Hell to - day is van-quished! Heaven is won to - day!" A - men.

(For different harmony and higher key see No. 109)

The Day of Resurrection! 98

. . . said Jesus unto them, . . . go tell my brethren . . . there shall they see me. Matt. 28:10

ELLACOMBE 7.6.7.6.D.

John of Damascus, circa 700-754
Translated by John M. Neale, 1818-1866

German melody, 18th century
From *Hymns Ancient and Modern,* 1868

1. The day of res - ur - rec - tion! Earth, tell it out a - broad;
2. Our hearts be pure from e - vil, That we may see a - right
3. Now let the heavens be joy - ful, Let earth her song be - gin;
The pass - o - ver of glad - ness, The pass - o - ver of God!
The Lord in rays e - ter - nal Of res - ur - rec - tion light,
Let the round world keep tri - umph And all that is there - in;
From death to life e - ter - nal, From earth un - to the sky,
And, lis - tening to His ac - cents, May hear, so calm and plain,
In - vis - i - ble and vis - i - ble, Their notes let all things blend,
Our Christ hath brought us o - ver With hymns of vic - to - ry.
His own "All Hail!" and, hear - ing, May raise the vic - tor strain.
For Christ the Lord hath ris - en, Our joy that hath no end. A-MEN.

(For different harmony and lower key see No. 447)

99 Christ the Lord Is Risen Today

. . . now is Christ risen from the dead . . . 1 Cor. 15:20

EASTER HYMN 7.4.7.4.D.
Lyra Davidica, 1708
From *Compleat Psalmodist,* 1749 (altered)

Charles Wesley, 1707-1788

1. "Christ the Lord is risen to - day," Al - - - - le - lu - ia!
2. Love's re - deem - ing work is done, Al - - - - le - lu - ia!
3. Lives a - gain our glo - rious King; Al - - - - le - lu - ia!
4. Soar we now where Christ has led, Al - - - - le - lu - ia!
Sons of men and an - gels say. Al - - - - le - lu - ia!
Fought the fight, the bat - tle won; Al - - - - le - lu - ia!
Where, O death, is now thy sting? Al - - - - le - lu - ia!
Fol - lowing our ex - alt - ed Head; Al - - - - le - lu - ia!
Raise your joys and tri - umphs high; Al - - - - le - lu - ia!
Death in vain for - bids Him rise, Al - - - - le - lu - ia!
Dy - ing once, He all doth save: Al - - - - le - lu - ia!
Made like Him, like Him we rise; Al - - - - le - lu - ia!
Sing, ye heavens, and earth re - ply: Al - - - - le - lu - ia!
Christ has o - pened Par - a - dise. Al - - - - le - lu - ia!
Where's thy vic - to - ry, O grave? Al - - - - le - lu - ia!
Ours the cross, the grave, the skies. Al - - - - le - lu - ia! A-MEN.

Christ Arose **100**

. . . the angel of the Lord . . . came and rolled back the stone . . . Matt. 28:2

Robert Lowry, 1826-1899

CHRIST AROSE 6.5.6.4. with Refrain
Robert Lowry, 1826-1899

1. Low in the grave He lay— Je - sus, my Sav - iour! Wait - ing the
2. Vain - ly they watch His bed— Je - sus, my Sav - iour! Vain - ly they
3. Death can - not keep his prey— Je - sus, my Sav - iour! He tore the
com - ing day— Je - sus, my Lord!
seal the dead— Je - sus, my Lord!
bars a - way— Je - sus, my Lord!
Refrain
Up from the grave He a - rose,
He a-rose,
With a might - y tri - umph o'er His foes;
He a - rose!
He a - rose a
vic - tor from the dark do-main, And He lives for - ev - er with His saints to reign.
He a - rose! He a - rose! Hal - le - lu - jah! Christ a - rose!
He a - rose! He a - rose!

101 The Strife Is O'er

. . . *Death is swallowed up in victory.* 1 Cor. 15:54

VICTORY 8.8.8.4.

Latin, Cologne, circa 1695
Translated by Francis Pott, 1832-1909

Giovanni P. da Palestrina, 1525-1594
Adapted by William H. Monk, 1823-1889

Al - le - lu - ia! Al - le - lu - ia! Al - le - lu - ia!
Organ
1. The strife is o'er, the bat - tle done; The vic - to - ry of life is won; The song of tri - umph has be - gun. Al - le - lu - ia!
2. The powers of death have done their worst, But Christ their le - gions hath dis - persed: Let shouts of ho - ly joy out - burst. Al - le - lu - ia!
3. The three sad days have quick - ly sped; He ris - es glo - rious from the dead: All glo - ry to our ris - en Head! Al - le - lu - ia!
4. He closed the yawn - ing gates of hell; The bars from heaven's high por - tals fell: Let hymns of praise His tri - umphs tell. Al - le - lu - ia!
5. Lord, by the stripes which wound - ed Thee, From death's dread sting Thy ser - vants free, That we may live and sing to Thee. Al - le - lu - ia! A - MEN.
D. S.
Organ

The Lord Is Risen Indeed 102

. . . and hath appeared to Simon. Luke 24:34

FRANCONIA S.M.
Harmonischer Liedershatz, 1738
Thomas Kelly, 1769-1854 Adapted by William H. Havergal, 1793-1870

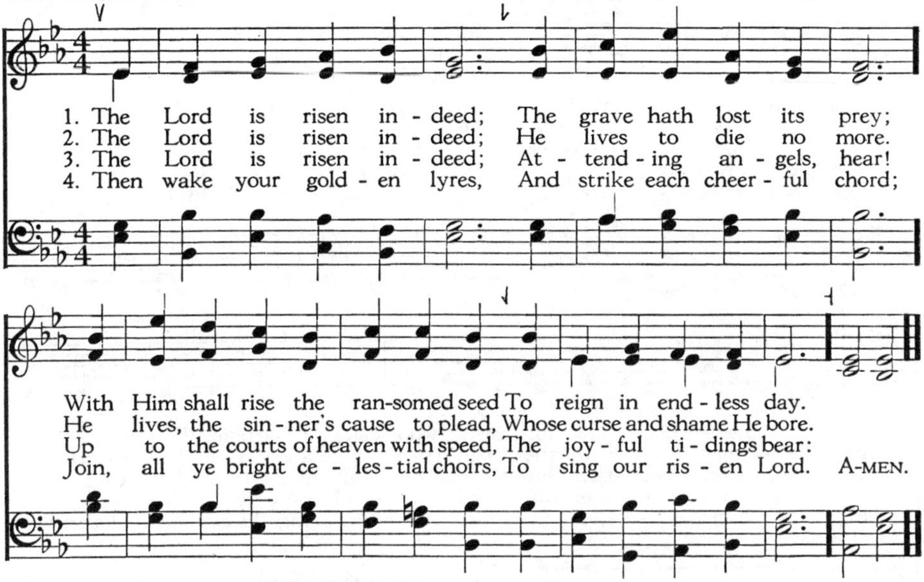
1. The Lord is risen in - deed; The grave hath lost its prey;
2. The Lord is risen in - deed; He lives to die no more.
3. The Lord is risen in - deed; At - tend - ing an - gels, hear!
4. Then wake your gold - en lyres, And strike each cheer - ful chord;
With Him shall rise the ran-somed seed To reign in end - less day.
He lives, the sin - ner's cause to plead, Whose curse and shame He bore.
Up to the courts of heaven with speed, The joy - ful ti - dings bear:
Join, all ye bright ce - les - tial choirs, To sing our ris - en Lord.
A-MEN.

Lift Up, Lift Up Your Voices Now 103

He will swallow up death in victory . . . Isa. 25:8

WALTHAM L.M.
John M. Neale, 1818-1866 John B. Calkin, 1827-1905

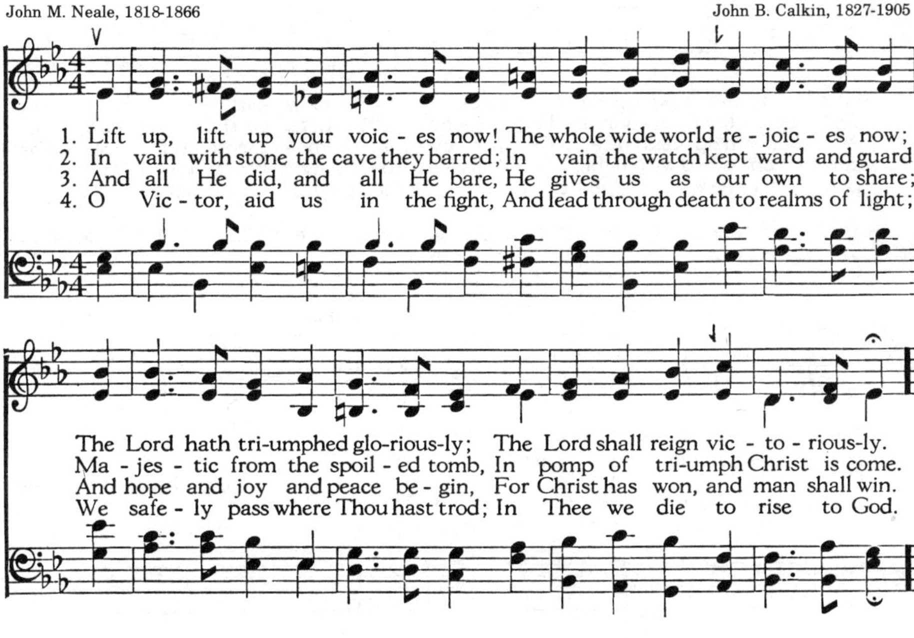
1. Lift up, lift up your voic - es now! The whole wide world re - joic - es now;
2. In vain with stone the cave they barred; In vain the watch kept ward and guard;
3. And all He did, and all He bare, He gives us as our own to share;
4. O Vic - tor, aid us in the fight, And lead through death to realms of light;
The Lord hath tri-umphed glo-rious-ly; The Lord shall reign vic - to - rious-ly.
Ma - jes - tic from the spoil - ed tomb, In pomp of tri-umph Christ is come.
And hope and joy and peace be - gin, For Christ has won, and man shall win.
We safe - ly pass where Thou hast trod; In Thee we die to rise to God.

104 And Can It Be That I Should Gain

. . . while we were yet sinners, Christ died for us. Rom. 5:8

SAGINA 8.8.8.8.8.8. with Refrain

Charles Wesley, 1707-1788

Thomas Campbell, 1777-1844

1. And can it be that I should gain An in - terest in the
2. 'Tis mys - tery all! Th' Im - mor - tal dies! Who can ex - plore His
3. He left His Fa - ther's throne a - bove, So free, so in - fi -
4. Long my im - pris - oned spir - it lay Fast - bound in sin and
5. No con - dem - na - tion now I dread; Je - sus, and all in
Sav - iour's blood? Died He for me, who caused His pain, For me, who
strange de - sign? In vain the first - born ser - aph tries To sound the
nite His grace; Emp - tied Him - self of all but love, And bled for
na - ture's night; Thine eye dif - fused a quick - ening ray. I woke, the
Him, is mine! A - live in Him, my liv - ing Head, And clothed in
Him to death pur - sued? A - maz - ing love! How can it be That
depths of love di - vine! 'Tis mer - cy all! Let earth a - dore; Let
A - dam's help - less race. 'Tis mer - cy all, im - mense and free! For,
dun - geon flamed with light; My chains fell off, my heart was free; I
right - eous - ness di - vine, Bold I ap - proach th' e - ter - nal throne, And
Thou, my God, shouldst die for me?
an - gel minds in - quire no more.
O my God, it found out me.
rose, went forth, and fol - lowed Thee.
claim the crown through Christ, my own.
REFRAIN
A - maz - ing love! How
A - maz - ing love!

And Can It Be That I Should Gain

can it be That Thou, my God, shouldst die for me! A-MEN.
How can it be That Thou, my God, shouldst die for me!

I Know That My Redeemer Lives 105

. . . and that he shall stand at the latter day upon the earth. Job 19:25

MESSIAH C.M.

Charles Wesley, 1707-1788

Arrangement from *The Messiah,* George Frederick Handel, 1685-1759

1. I know that my Re - deem - er lives And ev - er prays for me;
2. I find Him lift - ing up my head; He brings sal - va - tion near;
3. He wills that I should ho - ly be: What can with - stand His will?
4. Je - sus, I hang up - on Thy Word: I stead - fast - ly be - lieve

A to - ken of His love He gives, A pledge of lib - er - ty.
His pres - ence makes me free in - deed, And He will soon ap-pear.
The coun - sel of His grace in me He sure - ly shall ful - fill.
Thou wilt re - turn and claim me, Lord, And to Thy - self re-ceive.

106 Thine Is the Glory

O death, where is thy sting? O grave, where is thy victory? 1 Cor. 15:55

Edmond L. Budry, 1854-1932
Translated by Richard B. Hoyle, 1875-1939

JUDAS MACCABEUS 10.11.11.11. with Refrain
George Frederick Handel, 1685-1759

1. Thine is the glo - ry, Ris - en, con-quering Son; End - less is the
2. Lo! Je - sus meets us, Ris - en from the tomb; Lov - ing - ly He
3. No more we doubt Thee, Glo - rious Prince of life! Life is naught with-
vic - tory Thou o'er death hast won. An - gels in bright rai - ment
greets us, Scat - ters fear and gloom; Let His church with glad - ness
out Thee; Aid us in our strife; Make us more than con-querors,
Rolled the stone a - way, Kept the fold - ed grave - clothes
Hymns of tri - umph sing, For her Lord now liv - eth;
Through Thy death - less love; Bring us safe through Jor - dan
Where Thy bod - y lay.
Death hath lost its sting.
To Thy home a - bove.
REFRAIN
Thine is the glo - ry, Ris - en, con-quering Son;

Thine Is the Glory

End - less is the vic - tory Thou o'er death hast won. A - MEN.

Rejoice, the Lord Is King

107

. . . himself purged our sins, sat down on the right hand of the Majesty on high . . . Heb. 1:3

Charles Wesley, 1707-1788

DARWALL 6.6.6.6.8.8.
John Darwall, 1731-1789

1. Re - joice, the Lord is King; Your Lord and King a - dore! Re - joice, give
2. Je - sus, the Sav - iour, reigns, The God of truth and love; When He had
3. His king-dom can - not fail; He rules o'er earth and heaven; The keys of
4. Re - joice in glo - rious hope! Our Lord, the Judge, shall come, And take His

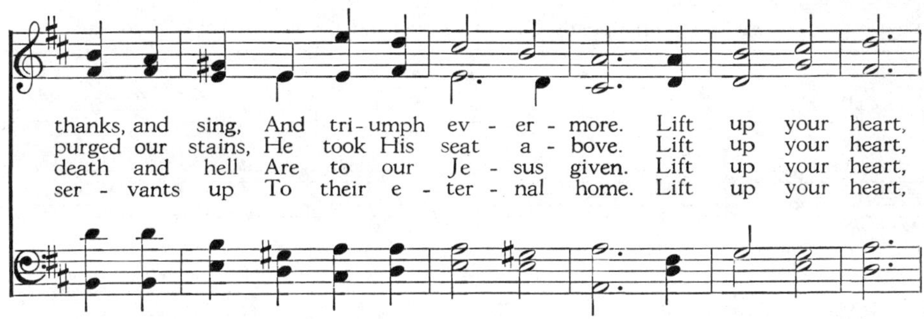
thanks, and sing, And tri - umph ev - er - more. Lift up your heart,
purged our stains, He took His seat a - bove. Lift up your heart,
death and hell Are to our Je - sus given. Lift up your heart,
ser - vants up To their e - ter - nal home. Lift up your heart,

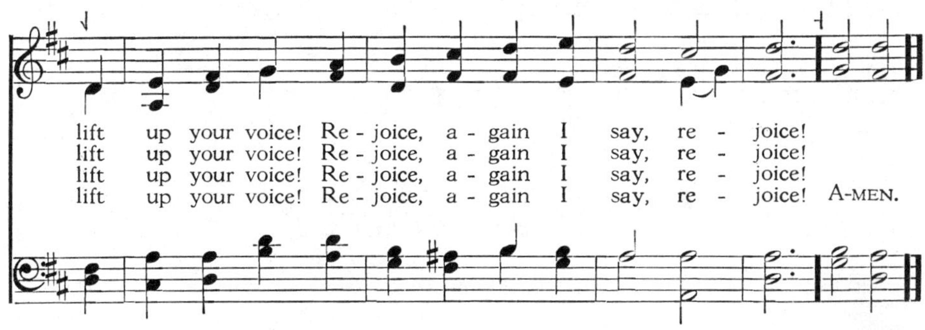
lift up your voice! Re - joice, a - gain I say, re - joice!
lift up your voice! Re - joice, a - gain I say, re - joice!
lift up your voice! Re - joice, a - gain I say, re - joice!
lift up your voice! Re - joice, a - gain I say, re - joice! A-MEN.

108 He Rose Triumphantly

... Death is swallowed up in victory. 1 Cor. 15:54

Oswald J. Smith, b. 1890

Bentley D. Ackley, 1872-1958

1. Our bless - ed Lord was slain, The Christ who came to reign,
was slain, to reign,
2. They sor - rowed when He died, Nor sought their tears to hide;
He died, to hide;
3. The stone was rolled a - way, For Christ was raised that day;
a - way, that day;
And in a grave He lay, To wait the com - ing day.
But soon their bit - ter pain Was turned to joy a - gain.
And now He lives a - bove To man - i - fest His love.
REFRAIN
He rose tri - um - phant - ly, In power and maj - es - ty, The Sav - iour
rose no more to die; Oh, let us now pro - claim
The glo - ry of His name, And tell to all, He lives to - day.

Golden Harps Are Sounding

109

. . . I have finished the work which thou gavest me to do. John 17:4

HERMAS 6.5.6.5.D. with Refrain

Frances R. Havergal, 1836-1879 | Frances R. Havergal, 1836-1879

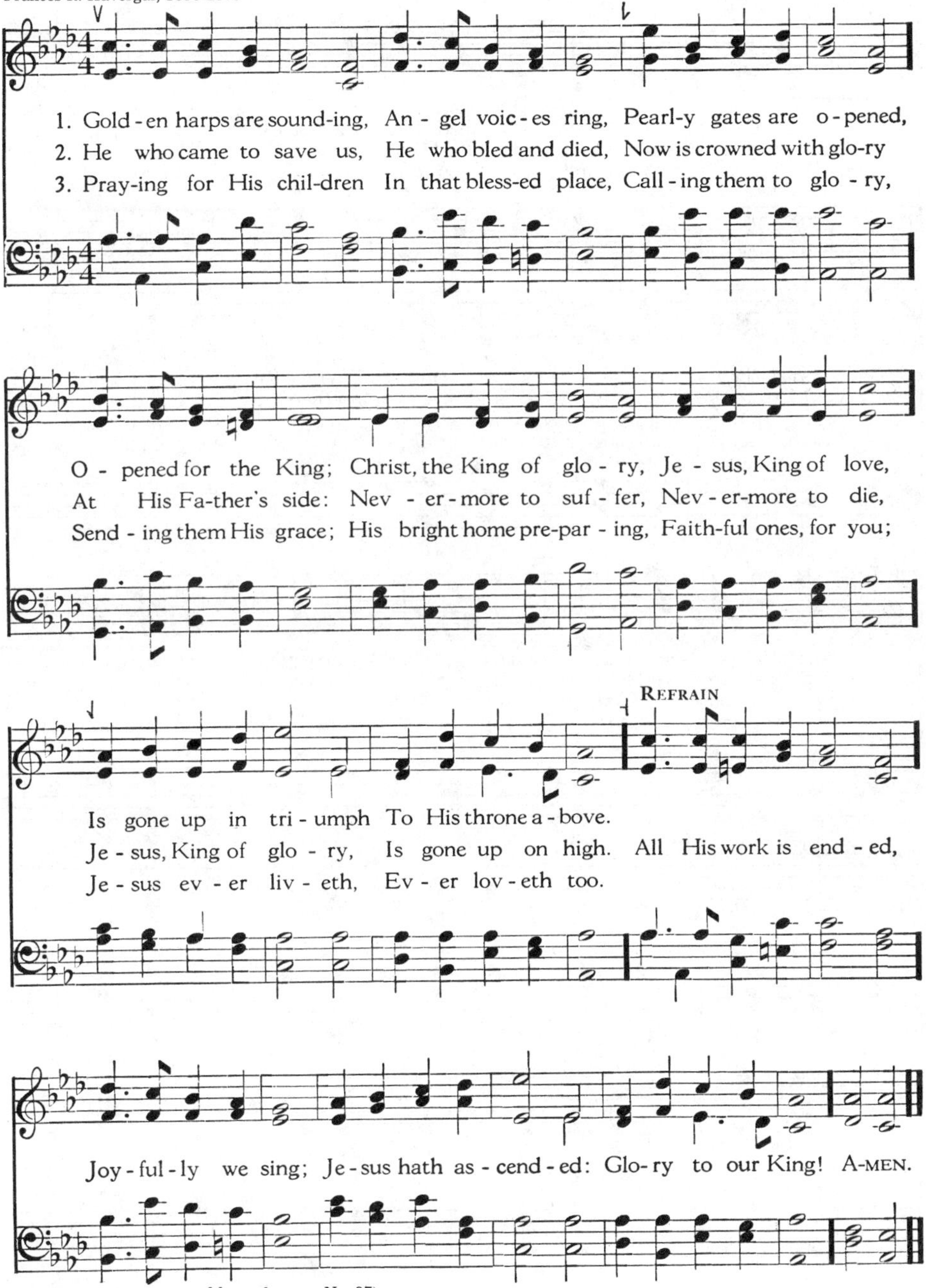
1. Gold - en harps are sound-ing, An - gel voic - es ring, Pearl-y gates are o - pened,
2. He who came to save us, He who bled and died, Now is crowned with glo-ry
3. Pray-ing for His chil-dren In that bless-ed place, Call - ing them to glo - ry,
O - pened for the King; Christ, the King of glo - ry, Je - sus, King of love,
At His Fa-ther's side: Nev - er-more to suf - fer, Nev - er-more to die,
Send - ing them His grace; His bright home pre-par - ing, Faith-ful ones, for you;
Is gone up in tri - umph To His throne a - bove.
Je - sus, King of glo - ry, Is gone up on high.
Je - sus ev - er liv - eth, Ev - er lov - eth too.
REFRAIN
All His work is end - ed,
Joy - ful - ly we sing; Je - sus hath as - cend - ed: Glo - ry to our King! A-MEN.

(For different harmony and lower key see No. 97)

110 Worthy Is the Lamb

. . . that was slain to receive . . . honour, and glory, and blessing. Rev. 5:12

Johnson Oatman, Jr., 1856-1926

George C. Hugg, 1848-1907

1. "Wor-thy is the Lamb," the hosts of heav-en sing, As be-fore the
2. Wor-thy is the Lamb, who shed His pre-cious blood To re-store a
3. Wor-thy is the Lamb, the bleed-ing sac-ri-fice, Who for A-dam's
4. "Wor-thy is the Lamb," let men and an-gels sing; "Wor-thy is the
throne they make His prais-es ring; "Wor-thy is the Lamb the
world to hap-pi-ness and God; When no eye could pit-y
race paid such a fear-ful price; Wor-thy is the Lamb, the
Lamb," let hal-le-lu-jahs ring; And when life is past, up-
book to o-pen wide; Wor-thy is the Lamb who once was cru-ci-fied."
and no arm could save, Je-sus, for our ran-som, Him-self free-ly gave.
pas-chal Lamb of God, For the world re-ceived re-demp-tion through His blood.
on the gold-en shore, "Wor-thy is the Lamb," we'll shout for-ev-er-more.
REFRAIN
Oh, this bleed-ing Lamb, oh, this bleed-ing Lamb, Oh, this dy-ing
Lamb, He was found wor-thy; Oh, this bleed-ing Lamb, oh, this

Worthy Is the Lamb

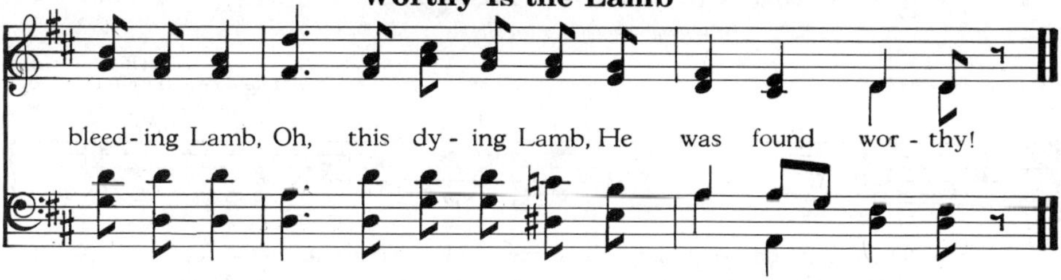
bleed - ing Lamb, Oh, this dy - ing Lamb, He was found wor - thy!

Majestic Sweetness Sits Enthroned 111

... we see Jesus, ... crowned with glory and honour ... Heb. 2:9

ORTONVILLE C.M. with repeat
Melody by Thomas Hastings, 1784-1872
Harmony by J. Buchanan MacMillan, b. 1915

Samuel Stennett, 1727-1795

1. Ma - jes - tic sweet - ness sits en - throned Up - on the Sav - iour's brow; His head with ra - diant glo - ries crowned, His lips with grace o'er - flow, His lips with grace o'er - flow.
2. No mor - tal can with Him com - pare A - mong the sons of men; Fair - er is He than all the fair That fill the heaven - ly train, That fill the heaven - ly train.
3. To Him I owe my life and breath, And all the joys I have; He makes me tri - umph o - ver death, And saves me from the grave, And saves me from the grave.
4. To heaven, the place of His a - bode, He brings my wea - ry feet; Shows me the glo - ries of my God, And makes my joys com - plete, And makes my joys com - plete.
5. Since from His boun - ty I re - ceive Such proofs of love di - vine; Had I a thou - sand hearts to give, Lord, they should all be Thine, Lord, they should all be Thine.

(For different harmony see No. 195)

112 Hail, Thou Once Despised Jesus

He is despised and rejected of men . . . Isa. 53:3

AUSTRIA 8.7.8.7.D.

John Bakewell, 1721-1819

Franz Joseph Haydn, 1732-1809

1. Hail, Thou once de - spis - ed Je - sus, Hail, Thou Gal - i - le - an King!
2. Pas - chal Lamb, by God ap - point-ed, All our sins on Thee were laid;
3. Je - sus, hail! En-throned in glo - ry, There for - ev - er to a - bide,
Thou didst suf - fer to re - deem us, Thou didst free sal - va - tion bring.
By al-might - y love a - noint-ed, Thou hast full a - tone - ment made.
All the heaven-ly hosts a - dore Thee, Seat-ed at Thy Fa - ther's side.
Hail, Thou un - i - ver - sal Sav-iour, Bear - er of our sin and shame,
All Thy peo - ple are for - giv - en Through the vir - tue of Thy blood;
Wor - ship, hon - or, power, and bless-ing Thou art wor - thy to re-ceive;
By Thy mer-its we find fa - vor; Life is giv - en through Thy name.
O - pened is the gate of heav-en, Peace is made 'twixt man and God.
Loud - est prais-es, with-out ceas-ing, Meet it is for us to give. A-MEN.

See the Conqueror Mount in Triumph 113

Thou hast ascended on high . . . Psa. 68:18

HYMN TO JOY 8.7.8.7.D.
Melody from *9th Symphony,* Ludwig van Beethoven, 1770-1827
Harmony by J. Buchanan MacMillan, b. 1915

Christopher Wordsworth, 1807-1885

1. See the Con-queror mount in tri-umph, See the King in roy - al state
2. Who is this that comes in glo - ry, With the trump of ju - bi - lee?
3. While He lifts His hands in bless - ing, He is part - ed from His friends;
4. Now our heaven-ly Aa - ron en - ters, With His blood, with - in the veil;
5. He has raised our hu - man na - ture On the clouds to God's right hand;
Rid - ing on the clouds His char - iot To His heaven-ly pal - ace gate;
Lord of bat - tles, God of ar-mies, He has gained the vic - to - ry;
While their ea - ger eyes be - hold Him, He up - on the clouds as - cends;
Josh - ua now is come to Can-aan, And the kings be - fore Him quail;
There we sit in heaven-ly plac - es, There with Him in glo - ry stand.
Hark! The choirs of an - gel voic - es Joy - ful al - le - lu - ias sing,
He who on the cross did suf - fer, He who from the grave a - rose,
He who walked with God and pleased Him, Preach-ing truth and doom to come,
Now He plants the tribes of Is - rael In their prom-ised rest - ing - place;
Je - sus reigns, a - dored by an-gels; Man with God is on the throne;
And the por - tals high are lift - ed To re - ceive their heaven-ly King.
He has van-quished sin and Sa - tan, He by death has spoiled His foes.
He, our E - noch, is trans - lat - ed To His ev - er - last - ing home.
Now our great E - li - jah of - fers Dou - ble por - tion of His grace.
Might-y Lord, in Thine as - cen - sion We by faith be - hold our own.

114 All Hail the Power of Jesus' Name

(FIRST TUNE)

. . . *God . . . exalted him, and given him a name which is above every name.* Phil. 2:9

Edward Perronet, 1726-1792
Stanza 4 by John Rippon, 1751-1836

DIADEM 8.6.6.8. with repeats
James Ellor, 1819-1899

1. All hail the power of Je - sus' name! Let an - gels pros-trate
2. Ye cho - sen seed of Is - rael's race, Ye ran-somed from the
3. Let ev - ery kin - dred, ev - ery tribe, On this ter - res - trial
4. Oh, that with yon - der sa - cred throng We at His feet may
fall, Let an - gels pros - trate fall; Bring forth the roy - al
fall, Ye ran - somed from the fall, Hail Him who saves you
ball, On this ter - res - trial ball, To Him all maj - es -
fall, We at His feet may fall! We'll join the ev - er -
And crown.. Him,
di - a - dem,
by His grace, And crown Him, crown Him, crown Him, crown Him, And
ty as - cribe,
last - ing song, And crown.. Him,
And crown Him, crown Him, crown Him, crown......
crown Him, crown Him, crown Him,
crown Him Lord of all, crown Him, And crown Him Lord of all!
crown Him, crown............ Him,
...................................Him, And crown Him Lord of all!

All Hail the Power of Jesus' Name 115

(SECOND TUNE)

Edward Perronet, 1726-1792

CORONATION C.M. with repeat
Oliver Holden, 1765-1844

1. All hail the power of Je - sus' name! Let an - gels pros-trate fall;
2. Ye cho - sen seed of Is - rael's race, Ye ran-somed from the fall,
3. Let ev - ery kin - dred, ev - ery tribe, On this ter - res - trial ball,
Bring forth the roy - al di - a - dem, And crown Him Lord of all;
Hail Him who saves you by His grace, And crown Him Lord of all;
To Him all maj - es - ty as - cribe, And crown Him Lord of all;
Bring forth the roy - al di - a - dem, And crown Him Lord of all!
Hail Him who saves you by His grace, And crown Him Lord of all!
To Him all maj - es - ty as - cribe, And crown Him Lord of all! A-MEN.

All Hail the Power of Jesus' Name 116

(THIRD TUNE)

Edward Perronet, 1726-1792

MILES LANE 8.6.8.7.5.
William Shrubsole, 1760-1806

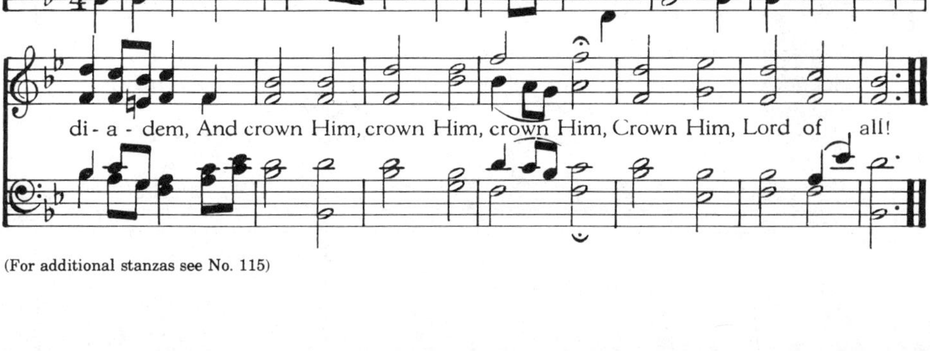
All hail the power of Je-sus' name! Let an-gels pros-trate fall; Bring forth the roy-al
di - a - dem, And crown Him, crown Him, crown Him, Crown Him, Lord of all!

(For additional stanzas see No. 115)

117 Crown Him with Many Crowns

. . . on his head were many crowns . . . Rev. 19:12

DIADEMATA S.M.D.

Matthew Bridges, 1800-1894

George J. Elvey, 1816-1893

1. Crown Him with man - y crowns, The Lamb up - on His throne;
2. Crown Him the Lord of love; Be - hold His hands and side,
3. Crown Him the Lord of peace, Whose power a scep - ter sways
4. Crown Him the Lord of years, The Po - ten - tate of time,
Hark! How the heaven-ly an - them drowns All mu - sic but its own.
Those wounds yet vis - i - ble a - bove In beau - ty glo - ri - fied.
From pole to pole, that wars may cease, And all be prayer and praise.
Cre - a - tor of the roll - ing spheres, In - ef - fa - bly sub - lime.
A - wake, my soul, and sing Of Him who died for thee,
No an - gel in the sky Can ful - ly bear that sight,
His reign shall know no end And round His pierc - ed feet
All hail! Re - deem - er, hail! For Thou hast died for me;
And hail Him as thy match-less King Through all e - ter - ni - ty.
But down-ward bends his burn - ing eye At mys - ter - ies so bright.
Fair flowers of Par - a - dise ex - tend Their fra-grance ev - er sweet.
Thy praise shall nev - er, nev - er fail Through-out e - ter - ni - ty. A-MEN.

Hark! Ten Thousand Harps and Voices 118

. . . I heard the voice of many angels round about the throne . . . Rev. 5:11

HARWELL 8.7.8.7.7.7. with Refrain
Melody by Lowell Mason, 1792-1872
Harmony by J. Buchanan MacMillan, b. 1915

Thomas Kelly, 1769-1854

1. Hark! Ten thou - sand harps and voic - es Sound the note of praise a - bove;
2. Sing how Je - sus came from heav - en, How He bore the cross be - low,
3. Je - sus, hail! Thy glo - ry bright - ens All a - bove and gives it worth;
4. King of glo - ry, reign for - ev - er! Thine an ev - er - last - ing crown.
5. Sav - iour, has - ten Thine ap - pear - ing; Bring, oh, bring the glo-rious day,
Je - sus reigns and heaven re - joic - es, Je - sus reigns, the God of love.
How all power to Him is giv - en, How He reigns in glo - ry now.
Lord of life, Thy smile en - light - ens, Cheers, and charms Thy saints on earth.
Noth-ing from Thy love shall sev - er Those whom Thou hast made Thine own:
When, the aw - ful sum-mons hear - ing, Heaven and earth shall pass a - way.
See, He sits on yon - der throne; Je - sus rules the world a - lone.
'Tis a great and end - less theme— Oh, 'tis sweet to sing of Him.
When we think of love like Thine, Lord, we own it love di - vine.
Hap - py ob - jects of Thy grace, Des - tined to be - hold Thy face.
Then with gold - en harps we'll sing, "Glo - ry, glo - ry to our King!"
REFRAIN
Hal - le - lu - jah, Hal - le - lu - jah, Hal - le - lu - jah, A - men.

119 Yesterday, Today, Forever

Jesus Christ the same yesterday, and today, and forever. Heb. 13:8

Albert B. Simpson, 1843-1919 | J.H. Burke, 19th century

1. Oh, how sweet the glo - rious mes - sage Sim - ple faith may claim;
2. He, who was the friend of sin - ners, Seeks thee, lost one, now;
3. Oft on earth He healed the suf - ferer By His might - y hand;
4. As of old He walked t'Em - ma - us, With them to a - bide;
Yes - ter - day, to - day, for - ev - er, Je - sus is the same.
Sin - ner, come, and at His foot - stool Pen - i - tent - ly bow.
Still our sick - ness - es and sor - rows Go at His com - mand.
So, through all life's way He walk - eth, Ev - er near our side.
Still He loves to save the sin - ful, Heal the sick and lame,
He who said, "I'll not con - demn thee; Go and sin no more,"
He who gave His heal - ing vir - tue To a wo - man's touch,
Soon a - gain we shall be - hold Him— Has - ten, Lord, the day!
Cheer the mourn - er, still the tem - pest— Glo - ry to His name!
Speaks to thee that word of par - don As in days of yore.
To the faith that claims His full - ness Still will give as much.
But 'twill still be "this same Je - sus," As He went a - way.
REFRAIN
Yes - ter - day, to - day, for - ev - er, Je - sus is the same;

Yesterday, Today, Forever

All may change, but Je - sus nev - er! Glo - ry to His name!
Glo - ry to His name; Glo - ry to His name;
All may change, but Jesus never! Glo - ry to His name.

The Head That Once Was Crowned with Thorns 120

... we see Jesus, ... crowned with glory and honour ... Heb. 2:9

Thomas Kelly, 1769-1854

ST. MAGNUS C.M.
Jeremiah Clark, 1670-1707

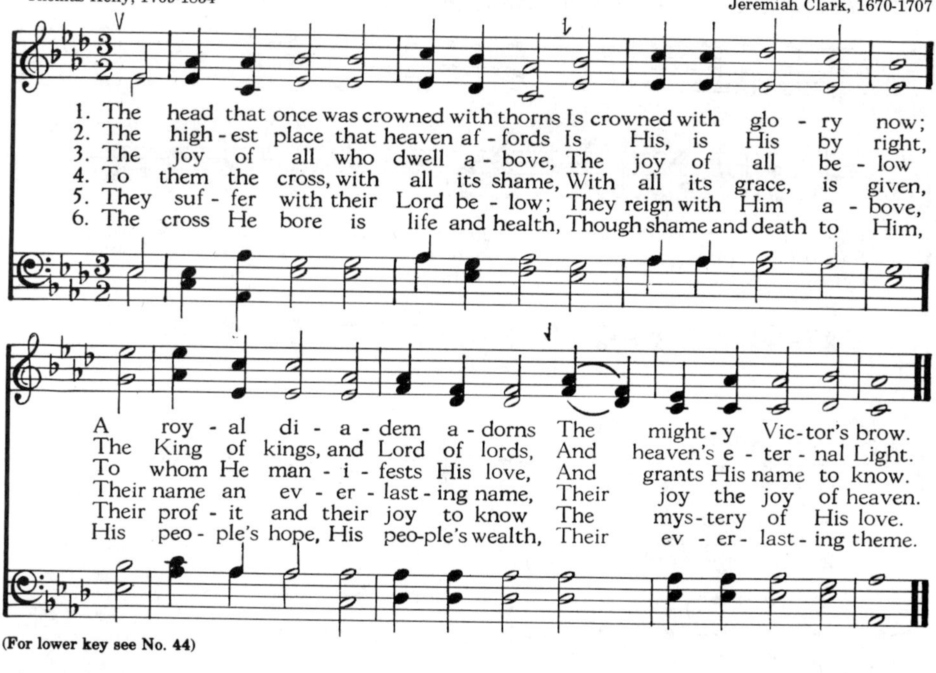
1. The head that once was crowned with thorns Is crowned with glo - ry now;
2. The high - est place that heaven af - fords Is His, is His by right,
3. The joy of all who dwell a - bove, The joy of all be - low
4. To them the cross, with all its shame, With all its grace, is given,
5. They suf - fer with their Lord be - low; They reign with Him a - bove,
6. The cross He bore is life and health, Though shame and death to Him,
A roy - al di - a - dem a - dorns The might - y Vic - tor's brow.
The King of kings, and Lord of lords, And heaven's e - ter - nal Light.
To whom He man - i - fests His love, And grants His name to know.
Their name an ev - er - last - ing name, Their joy the joy of heaven.
Their prof - it and their joy to know The mys - tery of His love.
His peo - ple's hope, His peo - ple's wealth, Their ev - er - last - ing theme.

(For lower key see No. 44)

121 Praise Him! Praise Him!

. . . praise him according to his excellent greatness. Psa. 150:2

Fanny J. Crosby, 1820-1915

JOYFUL SONG Irregular with Refrain
Chester G. Allen, 1838-1878

1. Praise Him! Praise Him! Je - sus, our bless - ed Re - deem - er! Sing, O
2. Praise Him! Praise Him! Je - sus, our bless - ed Re - deem - er! For our
3. Praise Him! Praise Him! Je - sus, our bless - ed Re - deem - er! Heaven-ly
earth; His won - der - ful love pro - claim! Hail Him! Hail Him! High-est arch-
sins He suf - fered, and bled, and died; He our rock, our hope of e -
por - tals loud with ho - san - nas ring. Je - sus, Sav - iour, reign-eth for -
an - gels in glo - ry; Strength and hon - or give to His ho - ly name!
ter - nal sal - va - tion; Hail Him! Hail Him! Je - sus, the cru - ci - fied.
ev - er and ev - er; Crown Him! Crown Him! Proph-et, and Priest, and King!
Like a shep-herd Je - sus will guard His chil - dren; In His arms He
Sound His prais - es— Je - sus who bore our sor - rows; Love un - bound - ed,
Christ is com - ing, o - ver the world vic - to - rious; Power and glo - ry
car - ries them all day long.
won - der - ful, deep, and strong!
un - to the Lord be - long.
Refrain
Praise Him! Praise Him! Tell of His

Praise Him! Praise Him!

ex - cel-lent great-ness; Praise Him! Praise Him, ev - er in joy - ful song!

Arise, My Soul, Arise! 122

. . . seeing he ever liveth to make intercession for them. Heb. 7:25

Charles Wesley, 1707-1788

LENOX (Trumpet) 6.6.6.6.8.8.8.
Melody by Lewis Edson, 1748-1820

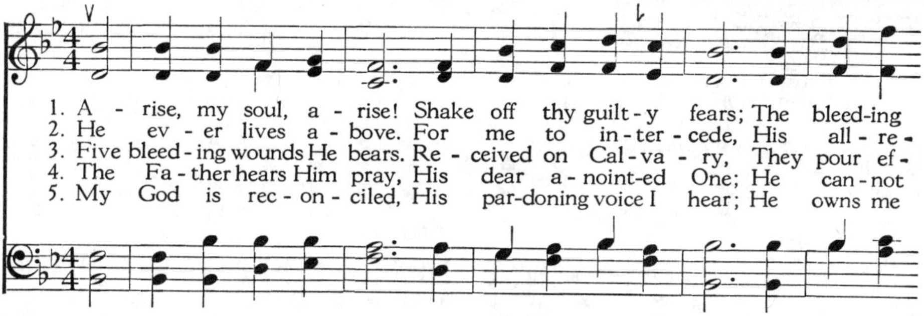
1. A - rise, my soul, a - rise! Shake off thy guilt - y fears; The bleed-ing
2. He ev - er lives a - bove. For me to in - ter - cede, His all - re -
3. Five bleed - ing wounds He bears. Re - ceived on Cal - va - ry, They pour ef -
4. The Fa - ther hears Him pray, His dear a - noint-ed One; He can - not
5. My God is rec - on - ciled, His par-doning voice I hear; He owns me

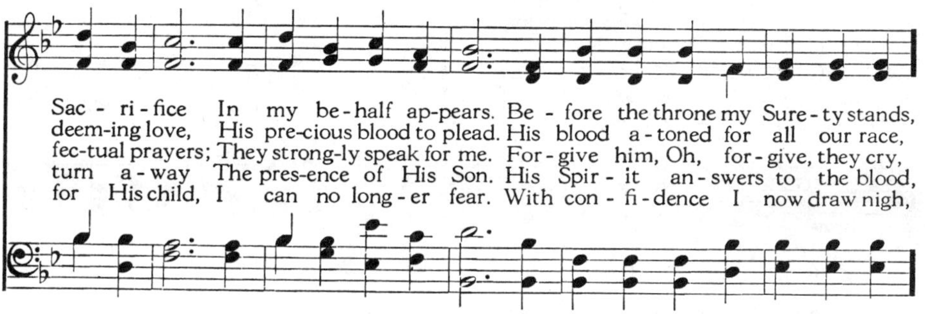
Sac - ri - fice In my be - half ap-pears. Be - fore the throne my Sure - ty stands,
deem-ing love, His pre-cious blood to plead. His blood a - toned for all our race,
fec-tual prayers; They strong-ly speak for me. For - give him, Oh, for - give, they cry,
turn a - way The pres-ence of His Son. His Spir - it an - swers to the blood,
for His child, I can no long - er fear. With con - fi - dence I now draw nigh,

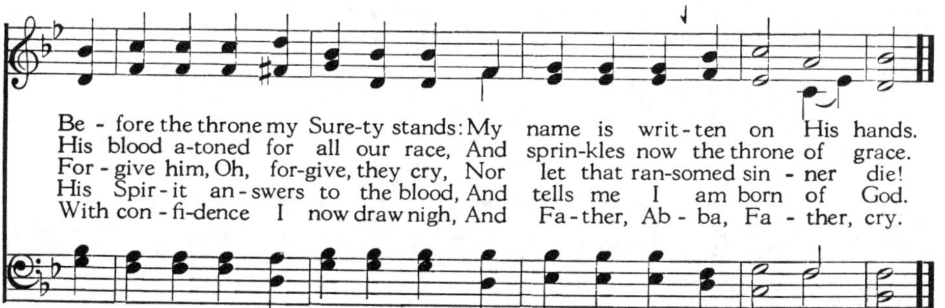
Be - fore the throne my Sure-ty stands: My name is writ - ten on His hands.
His blood a-toned for all our race, And sprin-kles now the throne of grace.
For - give him, Oh, for-give, they cry, Nor let that ran-somed sin - ner die!
His Spir - it an - swers to the blood, And tells me I am born of God.
With con - fi-dence I now draw nigh, And Fa-ther, Ab - ba, Fa - ther, cry.

123 Be Thou Exalted

. . . Lord, . . . so will we sing and praise thy power. Psa. 21:13

Fanny J. Crosby, 1820-1915
Adapted by Alfred B. Smith, b. 1916

Alfred B. Smith, b. 1916

1. Be Thou ex-alt-ed for-ev- er and ev - er, God of e - ter-ni-ty, The An-cient of
2. Be Thou ex-alt-ed O Son of the High-est, Gra-cious Re-deem - er, Our Sav-iour and
3. Be Thou ex-alt-ed O Spir-it e - ter - nal! Dwell in our hearts, keep us ho- ly with-
Days! Won-drous in maj-es - ty, so might-y in wis-dom, Per-fect in
King! One with the Fa - ther, co - e - qual in glo - ry, Here at Thy
in; Feed us each day with Thy heav-en - ly man-na. Heal-er of
ho - li-ness and wor-thy of praise.
foot - stool our hom-age we bring.
wound-ed hearts, Thy prais-es we sing.
Refrain
Be Thou ex - alt-ed by ser-aphs and
an - gels, Be Thou ex - alt - ed with harp and with song;
Saints in their an-thems of rap-ture a - dore Thee, Thine be the glo-ry for-ev-er, A - men!

Thou Art Coming, O My Saviour

124

Behold, he cometh with clouds . . . Rev. 1:7

Frances R. Havergal, 1836-1879

BEVERLEY P.M.
William H. Monk, 1823-1889

1. Thou art com - ing, O my Sav - iour, Thou art com-ing, O my King, In Thy
2. Thou art com - ing, Thou art com - ing– We shall meet Thee on Thy way, We shall
3. Thou art com - ing—at Thy ta - ble We are wit - ness-es for this; While re -
4. Thou art com - ing—we are wait - ing With a hope that can - not fail, Ask - ing
5. Oh, the joy to see Thee reign-ing– Thee, my own be - lov - ed Lord! Ev - ery
beau - ty all - re - splen-dent, In Thy glo - ry all - tran - scend-ent; Well may
see Thee, we shall know Thee, We shall bless Thee, we shall show Thee All our
mem-bering hearts Thou meet-est In com - mun - ion clear-est, sweet - est, Ear - nest
not the day or hour, Rest - ing on Thy Word of pow - er, An - chored
tongue Thy name con - fess - ing; Wor-ship, hon - or, glo - ry, bless - ing Brought to
we re - joice and sing; Com - ing in the o-pening east Her - ald brightness slow-ly
hearts could nev-er say. What an an-them that will be, Ring - ing out our love to
of our com-ing bliss; Show-ing not Thy death a - lone, And Thy love ex - ceed-ing
safe with - in the veil. Time ap-point - ed may be long, But the vi - sion must be
Thee with one ac - cord–Thee, my Mas - ter and my Friend, Vin - di - cat - ed and en -
swells; Com - ing— O my glo-rious Priest, Hear we not Thy gold - en bells?
Thee, Pour - ing out our rap - ture sweet At Thine own all - glo-rious feet.
great, But Thy com-ing, and Thy throne–All for which we long and wait.
sure; Cer - tain - ty shall make us strong; Joy - ful pa-tience can en - dure.
throned, Un - to earth's re - mot - est end Glo - ri - fied, a-dored, and owned! A-MEN.

125 Jesus Is Coming Again

. . . ye know neither the day nor the hour wherein the Son of man cometh. Matt. 25:13

John W. Peterson, b. 1921

COMING AGAIN 7.7.7.7. with Refrain
John W. Peterson, b. 1921

1. Mar-vel-ous mes-sage we bring, Glo-ri-ous car-ol we sing,
2. For-est and flow-er ex-claim, Moun-tain and mead-ow the same,
3. Stand-ing be-fore Him at last, Tri-al and trou-ble all past,
Won-der-ful word of the King— Je-sus is com-ing a-gain! (a-gain!)
All earth and heav-en pro-claim— Je-sus is com-ing a-gain! (a-gain!)
Crowns at His feet we will cast— Je-sus is com-ing a-gain! (a-gain!)
REFRAIN - UNISON
Com-ing a-gain, Com-ing a-gain;
May-be morn-ing, may-be noon, May-be eve-ning and may-be soon!
Com-ing a-gain, Com-ing a-gain;

Jesus Is Coming Again

HARMONY

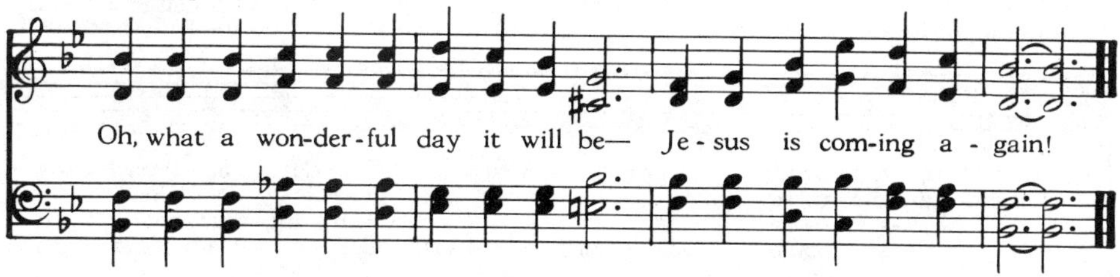
Oh, what a won-der-ful day it will be— Je-sus is com-ing a-gain!

The Coming of His Feet

126

And his feet shall stand in that day upon the mount of Olives . . . Zech. 14:4

S. Whitney Allen, 19th century

George C. Stebbins, 1846-1945

1. In the crim-son of the morn-ing, In the white-ness of the noon, In the
2. I have heard His wea-ry foot-steps By the Gal-i-le-an sea, On the
3. Down the min-ster aisles of splen-dor, From be-tween the Cher-u-bim, Thro' the
4. Comes He san-daled not with sil-ver, Gild-ed not with wov-en gold, Weight-ed
5. He is com-ing, O my spir-it, With His ev-er-last-ing peace, With His
am-ber glo-ry of the day's re-treat; In the mid-night robed in dark-ness,
tem-ple's mar-ble pave-ment, on the street; Worn with weight of sor-row fal-tering
won-dering throngs with mo-tion strong and fleet, Sounds His vic-tor tread, with mu-sic
not with shim-mering gems and o-dors sweet; But white-winged and shod with glo-ry,
bless-ed-ness im-mor-tal and com-plete; He is com-ing, O my spir-it,
Or the gleam-ing of the moon—I lis-ten for the com-ing of His feet.
Up the slopes of Cal-va-ry— The sor-row of the com-ing of His feet.
Of re-demp-tion's cho-ral hymn—The mu-sic of the com-ing of His feet.
In the Ta-bor light of old— The glo-ry of the com-ing of His feet.
And His com-ing brings re-lease— I lis-ten for the com-ing of His feet.

127 He Is Coming Again

. . . see the Son of man coming in a cloud with power and great glory. Luke 21:27

CAMP Irregular with Refrain

Mabel J. Camp, 1871-1937 | Mabel J. Camp, 1871-1937

1. Lift up your heads, Pil - grims a - wea - ry; See day's ap - proach Now
2. Dark was the night, Sin warred a - gainst us; Heav - y the load Of
3. O bless - ed hope! O bliss - ful prom - ise! Fill - ing our hearts With
4. E - ven so, come, Pre - cious Lord Je - sus; Cre - a - tion waits re -
crim - son the sky; Night shad - ows flee, And your Be - lov - ed, A -
sor - row we bore; But now we see Signs of His com - ing; Our
rap - ture di - vine; O day of days! Hail Thy ap - pear - ing! Thy
demp - tion to see; Caught up in clouds, Soon we shall meet Thee; O
wait - ed with long - ing, At last draw - eth nigh.
hearts glow with - in us, Joy's cup run - neth o'er!
tran - scend - ent glo - ry For - ev - er shall shine.
bless - ed as - sur - ance, For - ev - er with Thee!
REFRAIN
He is com - ing a - gain, He is com - ing a - gain, The ver - y same Je - sus, Re -
ject - ed of men; He is com - ing a - gain, He is com - ing a - gain;

He Is Coming Again

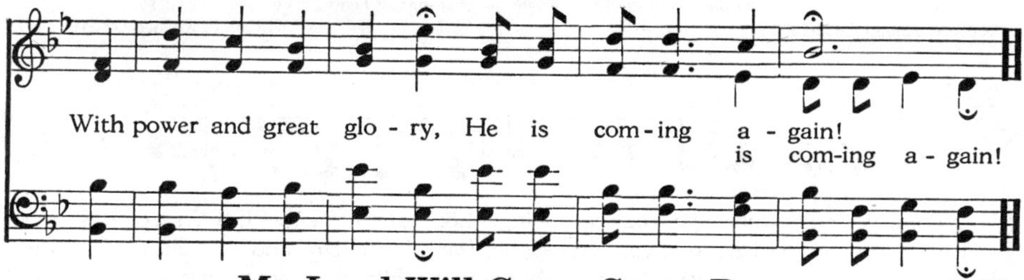
With power and great glo - ry, He is com - ing a - gain!
is com-ing a - gain!

My Lord Will Come Some Day 128

. . . and every eye shall see him . . . Rev. 1:7

Alice S. MacMillan, b. 1900

C. Austin Miles, 1868-1946

1. When dark the night and bur - dens press, When steep and rough the way,
2. I lis - ten for His bless - ed voice, I seek to watch and pray;
3. At ear - ly dawn I watch for Him, I watch for Him at noon;
4. As eve-ning shad - ows gath - er 'round And dark - en all the sky,
This hope o'er-floods my soul with joy: My Lord will come some day.
I trust His pre - cious prom - ise true, My Lord will come some day.
My heart sings o'er the sweet re - frain, "My Lord is com - ing soon."
I lift my head, I cry with joy, "His com - ing draw - eth nigh."
REFRAIN
Some day, Some day,
Some day, some day, My Lord will come some day.
Through His won-drous grace I shall see His face; My Lord will come some day.

129 Lo, Jesus Comes!

. . . for the day of the Lord cometh, for it is nigh at hand . . . Joel 2:1

Phoebe P. Knapp, 1839-1908

William J. Kirkpatrick, 1838-1921

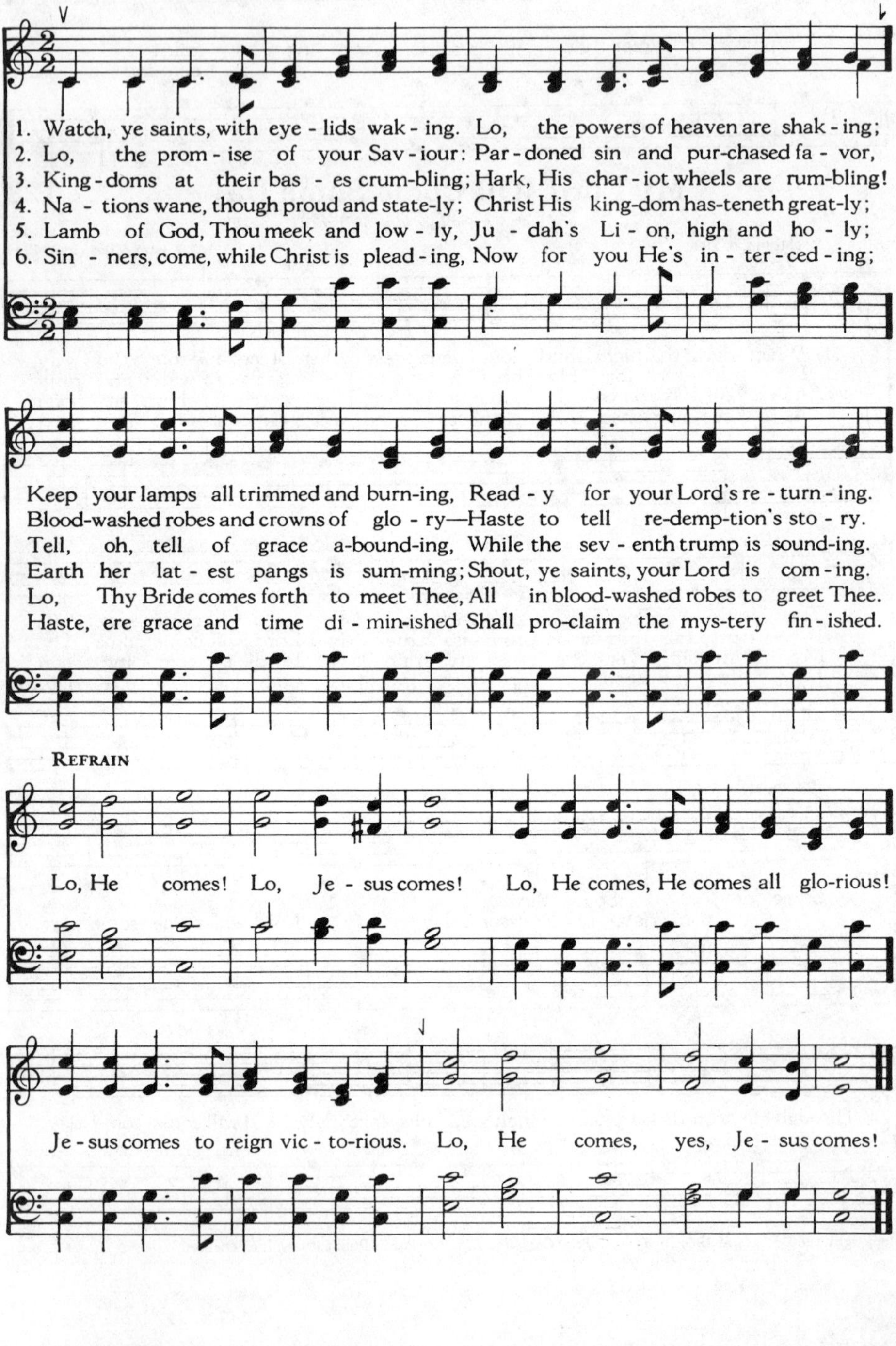
1. Watch, ye saints, with eye - lids wak - ing. Lo, the powers of heaven are shak - ing;
2. Lo, the prom - ise of your Sav - iour: Par - doned sin and pur-chased fa - vor,
3. King - doms at their bas - es crum-bling; Hark, His char - iot wheels are rum-bling!
4. Na - tions wane, though proud and state-ly; Christ His king-dom has-teneth great-ly;
5. Lamb of God, Thou meek and low - ly, Ju - dah's Li - on, high and ho - ly;
6. Sin - ners, come, while Christ is plead - ing, Now for you He's in - ter - ced - ing;
Keep your lamps all trimmed and burn-ing, Read - y for your Lord's re - turn - ing.
Blood-washed robes and crowns of glo - ry—Haste to tell re-demp-tion's sto - ry.
Tell, oh, tell of grace a-bound-ing, While the sev - enth trump is sound-ing.
Earth her lat - est pangs is sum-ming; Shout, ye saints, your Lord is com - ing.
Lo, Thy Bride comes forth to meet Thee, All in blood-washed robes to greet Thee.
Haste, ere grace and time di - min-ished Shall pro-claim the mys-tery fin - ished.
REFRAIN
Lo, He comes! Lo, Je - sus comes! Lo, He comes, He comes all glo-rious!
Je - sus comes to reign vic - to-rious. Lo, He comes, yes, Je - sus comes!

Christ Is Coming 130

. . . for the coming of the Lord draweth nigh. James 5:8

MACOMBER 8.7.8.7.D. with repeat

Winfield Macomber, 1865-1896 | Winfield Macomber, 1865-1896

1. In the glow of ear - ly morn-ing, In the sol - emn hush of night,
2. Oft me - thinks I hear His foot-steps Steal-ing down the paths of time;
3. Long we've wait - ed, blest Re-deem - er, Wait - ed for the first bright ray
Down from heav - en's o - pen por - tals Steals a mes - sen - ger of light,
And the fu - ture, dark with shad - ows, Bright-ens with this hope sub-lime.
Of the morn when sin and sor - row At Thy pres - ence flee a - way.
Whis-pering sweet - ly to my spir - it, While the hosts of heav - en sing:
Sound the soul - in - spir - ing an - them; An - gel hosts, your harps at - tune;
But our vig - il's near - ly o - ver; Hope of heaven, O price-less boon!
This the won-drous thrill-ing sto - ry—Christ is com - ing, Christ my King.
Earth's long night is al - most o - ver—Christ is com - ing, com - ing soon.
In the east the glow ap - pear-ing—Christ is com - ing, com - ing soon.
This the won-drous thrill-ing sto - ry—Christ is com - ing, Christ my King.
Earth's long night is al - most o - ver—Christ is com - ing, com - ing soon.
In the east the glow ap - pear - ing—Christ is com - ing, com - ing soon.

131 The Bridegroom Cometh

. . . in such an hour as ye think not the Son of man cometh. Matt. 24:44

C. Austin Miles, 1868-1946

A.A. Payn, 20th century

Arranged by Helen I. Young, b. 1931

1. Who can tell how soon the Bride may hear the cry, "Be-hold, the Bride-groom com - eth!" Hear the shout of tri - umph ring - ing in the sky, "Be - hold, the Bride-groom com-eth!"
2. Who will have his lamps all trimmed and burn-ing bright? "Be-hold, the Bride-groom com - eth!" Read - y be to meet Him should he hear to - night, "Be - hold, the Bride-groom com-eth!"
3. Hark! From far a - way I seem to hear Him say, "Be-hold, the Bride-groom com - eth!" Oh, my soul, be read - y! This may be the day, "Be - hold, the Bride-groom com-eth!"
REFRAIN
Al - most I can see His glo - ry in the sky;
Can it be the dawn-ing of that day is nigh? How my heart would leap if
I should hear the cry, "Be - hold, the Bride-groom com - eth!"

Christ Returneth

132

. . . ye shall see the Son of man . . . coming in the clouds of heaven. Mark 14:62

H.L. Turner, 19th century

James McGranahan, 1840-1907

1. It may be at morn, when the day is a-wak-ing, When sun-light through
2. It may be at mid - day, it may be at twi-light, It may be, per -
3. While its hosts cry ho - san - na, from heav - en de - scend-ing, With glo - ri - fied
4. O joy, O de - light, should we go with - out dy - ing! No sick-ness, no
dark - ness and shad - ow is break - ing, That Je - sus will come in the
chance, that the black-ness of mid - night Will burst in - to light in the
saints and the an - gels at - tend - ing, With grace on His brow, like a
sad - ness, no dread - ing, no cry - ing! Caught up through the clouds with our
full - ness of glo - ry To re - ceive from the world His own.
blaze of His glo - ry, When Je - sus re - ceives His own.
ha - lo of glo - ry, Will Je - sus re - ceive His own.
Lord in - to glo - ry, When Je - sus re - ceives His own.
REFRAIN
O Lord Je - sus, how long, how long Ere we shout the glad song? Christ re -
turn-eth– Hal - le - lu - jah! Hal - le - lu - jah! A - men. Hal - le - lu - jah! A - men.

133 When the Mists Have Rolled Away

. . . we see through a glass, darkly; but then face to face . . . 1 Cor. 13:12

Anonymous
Arranged by Annie Herbert, 19th century

Ira D. Sankey, 1840-1908
Refrain arranged by Helen I. Young, b. 1931

1. When the mists have rolled in splen-dor From the beau-ty of the hills,
2. Oft we tread the path be-fore us With a wea-ry bur-dened heart;
3. We shall come with joy and glad-ness, We shall gath-er round the throne;
And the sun-light falls in glad-ness On the riv-er and the rills,
Oft we toil a-mid the shad-ows, And our fields are far a-part;
Face to face with those that love us, We shall know as we are known:
We re-call our Fa-ther's prom-ise In the rain-bow of the spray:
But the Sav-iour's "Come, ye bless-ed" All our la-bor will re-pay.
And the song of our re-demp-tion Shall re-sound through end-less day
We shall know each oth-er bet-ter When the mists have rolled a-way.
When we gath-er in the morn-ing Where the mists have rolled a-way.
When the shad-ows have de-part-ed, And the mists have rolled a-way.
REFRAIN
We shall know as we are known, Nev-er more to walk a-lone,

When the Mists Have Rolled Away

In the dawn-ing of the morn-ing Of that bright and hap-py day,
We shall know each oth-er bet-ter When the mists have rolled a-way.

When He Shall Come 134

. . . I will come again, and receive you unto myself . . . John 14:3

Almeda J. Pearce, b. 1893

PEARCE 11.10.11.10.
Almeda J. Pearce, b. 1893

1. When He shall come, re-splend-ent in His glo-ry, To take His own from out this vale of night, Oh, may I know the joy at His ap-pear-ing, On-ly at morn to walk with Him in white!
2. When I shall stand with-in the court of heav-en Where white-robed pil-grims pass be-fore my sight— Earth's mar-tyred saints and blood-washed o-ver-com-ers— These then are they who walk with Him in white!
3. When He shall call, from earth's re-mot-est cor-ners, All who have stood tri-um-phant in His might, Oh, to be wor-thy then to stand be-side them, And in that morn to walk with Him in white!

135 What If It Were Today?

For the Lord himself shall descend from heaven with a shout . . . 1 Thess. 4:16

SECOND COMING Irregular with Refrain

Lelia N. Morris, 1862-1929 | Lelia N. Morris, 1862-1929

1. Je - sus is com - ing to earth a - gain; What if it
2. Sa - tan's do - min - ion will then be o'er. Oh, that it
3. Faith - ful and true would He find us here If He should
were to - day? Com - ing in pow - er and love to reign;
were to - day! Sor - row and sigh - ing shall be no more.
come to - day? Watch-ing in glad - ness and not in fear,
What if it were to - day? Com - ing to claim His cho - sen Bride,
Oh, that it were to - day! Then shall the dead in Christ a - rise,
If He should come to - day? Signs of His com - ing mul - ti - ply;
All the re - deemed and pu - ri - fied, O - ver this whole earth
Caught up to meet Him in the skies. When shall these glo - ries
Morn - ing light breaks in east - ern sky; Watch, for the time is

What If It Were Today?

scat - tered wide.
meet our eyes? What if it were to - day?
draw - ing nigh!
Refrain
Glo - ry! Glo - ry! Joy to my heart 'twill bring:
Joy to my heart 'twill bring:
Glo - ry! Glo - ry! When we shall crown Him King;
When we shall crown Him King;
Glo - ry! Glo - ry! Haste to pre-pare the way!
Haste to pre-pare the way!
Glo - ry! Glo - ry! Je - sus will come some day!

136 Is It the Crowning Day?

And when the chief Shepherd shall appear, ye shall receive a crown . . . 1 Pet. 5:4

CROWNING DAY Irregular with Refrain

George W. Whitcomb, 19th century

Charles H. Marsh, 1886-1956

1. Je - sus may come to - day, Glad day! Glad day! And I would
2. I may go home to - day, Glad day! Glad day! Seem - eth I
3. Why should I anx - ious be? Glad day! Glad day! Lights ap - pear
4. Faith - ful I'll be to - day, Glad day! Glad day! And I will
see my Friend; Dan - gers and trou - bles would end If
hear their song; Hail to the ra - di - ant throng! If
on the shore, Storms will af - fright nev - er - more, For
free - ly tell Why I should love Him so well, For
REFRAIN
Je - sus should come to - day.
I should go home to - day. Glad day! Glad day! Is it the crown-ing
He is "at hand" to - day.
He is my all to - day.
day? I'll live for to - day, nor anx - ious be, Je - sus, my Lord, I
soon shall see; Glad day! Glad day! Is it the crown - ing day?

Spirit of God, Descend upon My Heart 137

... the Comforter, ... shall teach you all things ... John 14:26

MORECAMBE 10.10.10.10.

George Croly, 1780-1860

Frederick C. Atkinson, 1841-1897

1. Spir - it of God, de - scend up - on my heart;
2. I ask no dream, no proph - et ec - sta - sies,
3. Hast Thou not bid us love Thee, God and King?
4. Teach me to feel that Thou art al - ways nigh;
5. Teach me to love Thee as Thine an - gels love,
Wean it from earth, through all its puls - es move;
No sud - den rend - ing of the veil of clay,
All, all Thine own— soul, heart and strength and mind.
Teach me the strug - gles of the soul to bear,
One ho - ly pas - sion fill - ing all my frame;
Stoop to my weak - ness, might - y as Thou art,
No an - gel vis - it - ant, no o - pening skies;
I see Thy cross— there teach my heart to cling.
To check the ris - ing doubt, the reb - el sigh;
The bap - tism of the heaven - de - scend - ed Dove;
And make me love Thee as I ought to love.
But take the dim - ness of my soul a - way.
Oh, let me seek Thee, and, oh, let me find.
Teach me the pa - tience of un - an - swered prayer.
My heart an al - tar, and Thy love the flame. A - MEN.

138 Come, Sevenfold Holy Spirit

. . . shall your heavenly Father give the Holy Spirit to them that ask him? Luke 11:13

Albert B. Simpson, 1843-1919

Melody by Albert B. Simpson, 1843-1919
Harmony by J. Buchanan MacMillan, b. 1915

1. Come, bless-ed, ho - ly, heaven-ly Dove, Spir - it of light and life and love,
2. Spir - it of life, the dead a - wake. The slum-ber-ing sin-ner's fet - ters break,
3. Ce - les - tial Dove of peace and rest, Hide us be - neath Thy brood-ing breast,
Re - vive our souls we pray! Come with the power of Pen - te - cost,
And set the cap - tive free! Speak with the gos - pel's an - cient power,
Thine o - ver - shad-owing wing! Bid all our doubts and cares to cease,
Come as the seven-fold Ho - ly Ghost, And fill our hearts to - day.
And let us all this sa - cred hour Thy great sal - va - tion see.
And keep our hearts in per - fect peace And ev - er - last - ing spring.
REFRAIN
Come with the power of Pen - te - cost, Come as the seven - fold Ho - ly Ghost,

Come, Sevenfold Holy Spirit

Come save us to the ut - ter-most, And fill our hearts to - day.

Breathe on Me, Breath of God

139

. . . he breathed on them, and saith . . . Receive ye the Holy Ghost. John 20:22

Edwin Hatch, 1835-1889

BOYLSTON S.M.
Lowell Mason, 1792-1872

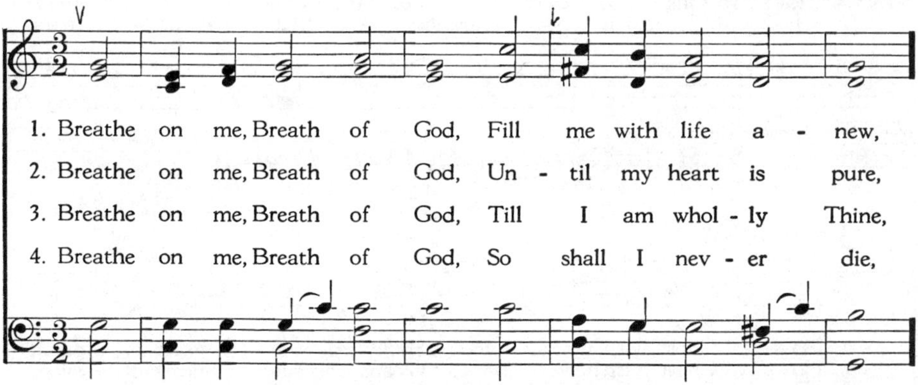
1. Breathe on me, Breath of God, Fill me with life a - new,
2. Breathe on me, Breath of God, Un - til my heart is pure,
3. Breathe on me, Breath of God, Till I am whol - ly Thine,
4. Breathe on me, Breath of God, So shall I nev - er die,

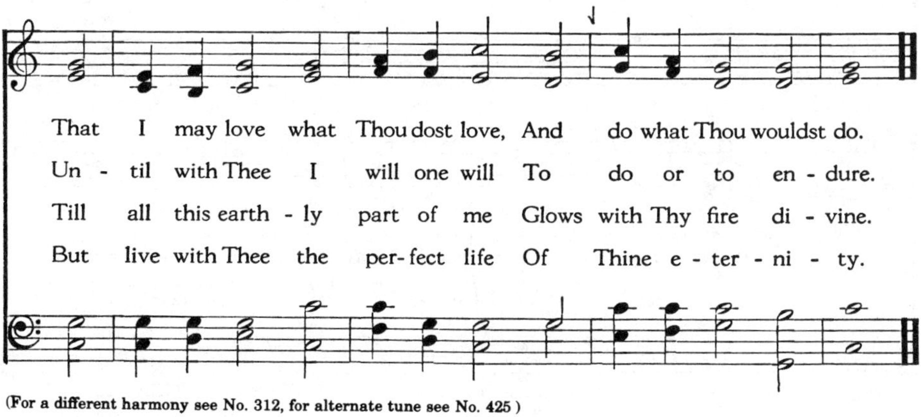
That I may love what Thou dost love, And do what Thou wouldst do.
Un - til with Thee I will one will To do or to en - dure.
Till all this earth - ly part of me Glows with Thy fire di - vine.
But live with Thee the per - fect life Of Thine e - ter - ni - ty.

(For a different harmony see No. 312, for alternate tune see No. 425)

140 Come, Holy Spirit, Heavenly Dove

. . . the love of God is shed abroad in our hearts by the Holy Ghost . . . Rom. 5:5

STEPHENS (Newington) C.M.

Isaac Watts, 1674-1748

William Jones, 1726-1800

1. Come, Ho - ly Spir - it, heaven-ly Dove, With all Thy quicken-ing powers;
2. In vain we tune our for - mal songs, In vain we strive to rise;
3. Dear Lord, and shall we ev - er live At this poor, dy - ing rate?
4. Come, Ho - ly Spir - it, heaven-ly Dove, With all Thy quicken-ing powers;
Kin - dle a flame of sa - cred love In these cold hearts of ours.
Ho - san - nas lan - guish on our tongues, And our de - vo - tion dies.
Our love so faint, so cold, to Thee, And Thine to us so great?
Come, shed a - broad a Sav - iour's love; And that shall kin - dle ours.

(For different harmony and higher key see No. 416)

141 Holy Ghost, with Light Divine

. . . Christ . . . shall also quicken your mortal bodies by his Spirit . . . Rom. 8:11

LAST HOPE 7.7.7.7.

Andrew Reed, 1787-1862

Louis M. Gottschalk, 1829-1869

Arranged by Edwin P. Parker, 1836-1925

1. Ho - ly Ghost, with light di - vine, Shine up - on this heart of mine;
2. Ho - ly Ghost, with power di - vine, Cleanse this guilt - y heart of mine;
3. Ho - ly Ghost, with joy di - vine, Cheer this sad-dened heart of mine;
4. Ho - ly Spir - it, all di - vine, Dwell with - in this heart of mine;
Chase the shades of night a - way; Turn my dark-ness in - to day.
Long hath sin, with - out con - trol, Held do - min - ion o'er my soul.
Bid my man - y woes de - part; Heal my wounded, bleed - ing heart.
Cast down ev - ery i - dol throne; Reign su - preme–and reign a - lone.

O Comforter, Gentle and Tender 142

. . . he dwelleth with you, and shall be in you. John 14:17

Albert B. Simpson, 1843-1919 — Albert B. Simpson, 1843-1919

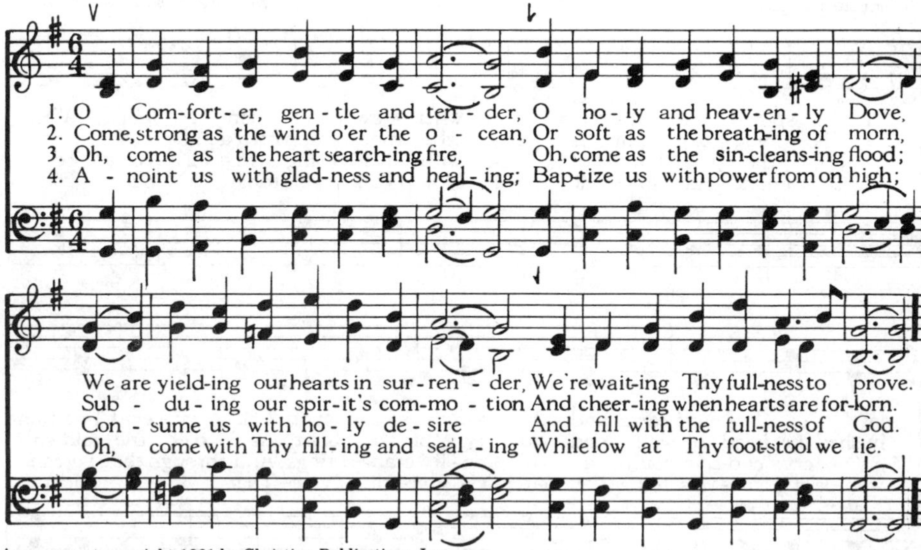

1. O Com-fort-er, gen-tle and ten-der, O ho-ly and heav-en-ly Dove,
2. Come, strong as the wind o'er the o-cean, Or soft as the breath-ing of morn,
3. Oh, come as the heart search-ing fire, Oh, come as the sin-cleans-ing flood;
4. A-noint us with glad-ness and heal-ing; Bap-tize us with power from on high;

We are yield-ing our hearts in sur-ren-der, We're wait-ing Thy full-ness to prove.
Sub-du-ing our spir-it's com-mo-tion And cheer-ing when hearts are for-lorn.
Con-sume us with ho-ly de-sire And fill with the full-ness of God.
Oh, come with Thy fill-ing and seal-ing While low at Thy foot-stool we lie.

Gracious Spirit, Holy Ghost 143

. . . faith, hope, charity, . . . the greatest of these is charity. 1 Cor. 13:13

CHARITY 7.7.7.5.

Christopher Wordsworth, 1807-1885 — John Stainer, 1840-1901

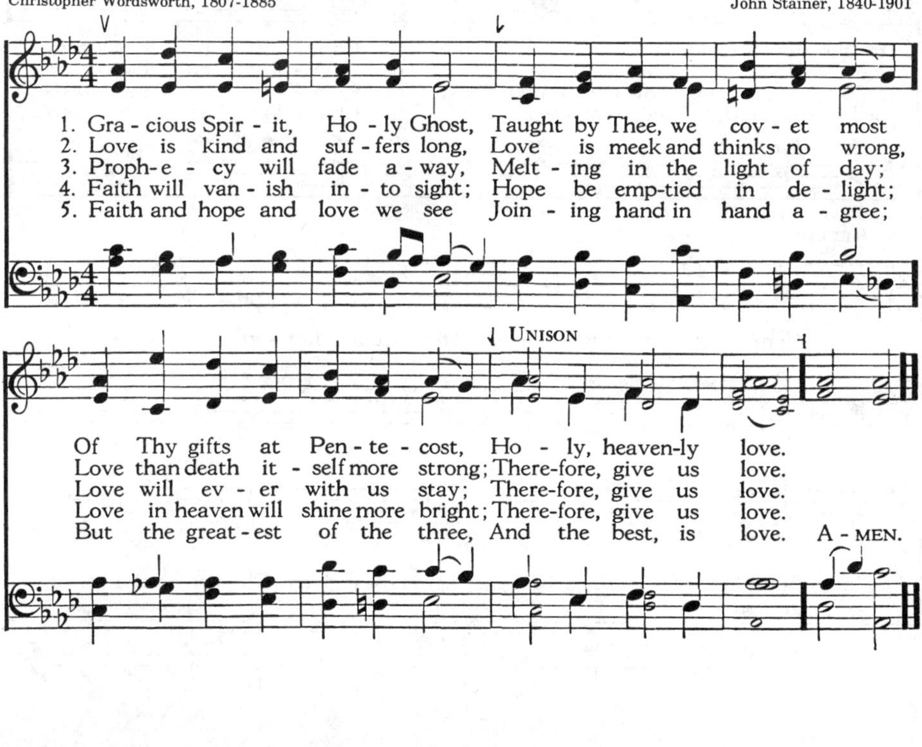

1. Gra-cious Spir-it, Ho-ly Ghost, Taught by Thee, we cov-et most
2. Love is kind and suf-fers long, Love is meek and thinks no wrong,
3. Proph-e-cy will fade a-way, Melt-ing in the light of day;
4. Faith will van-ish in-to sight; Hope be emp-tied in de-light;
5. Faith and hope and love we see Join-ing hand in hand a-gree;

UNISON

Of Thy gifts at Pen-te-cost, Ho-ly, heaven-ly love.
Love than death it-self more strong; There-fore, give us love.
Love will ev-er with us stay; There-fore, give us love.
Love in heaven will shine more bright; There-fore, give us love.
But the great-est of the three, And the best, is love. A-MEN.

144 The Comforter Has Come

. . . he shall give you another Comforter, . . . John 14:16

COMFORTER 12.12.12.6. with Refrain

Frank Bottome, 1823-1894

William J. Kirkpatrick, 1838-1921

1. Oh, spread the ti - dings 'round wher - ev - er man is found, Wher -
2. The long, long night is past, the morn - ing breaks at last, And
3. Lo, the great King of kings, with heal - ing in His wings, To
4. O bound - less love di - vine! How shall this tongue of mine To
ev - er hu-man hearts and hu - man woes a - bound; Let ev - ery Chris-tian
hushed the dread-ful wail and fu - ry of the blast, As o'er the gold-en
ev - ery cap-tive soul a full de - liv-erance brings; And through the va-cant
won-dering mor - tals tell the match-less grace di - vine— That I, a child of
tongue pro - claim the joy - ful sound: The Com - fort - er has come!
hills the day ad - vanc - es fast! The Com - fort - er has come!
cells the song of tri - umph rings; The Com - fort - er has come!
hell, should in His im - age shine! The Com - fort - er has come!
REFRAIN
The Com - fort - er has come, The Com - fort - er has come! The
Ho - ly Ghost from Heaven, The Fa-ther's prom-ise given; Oh, spread the ti - dings

The Comforter Has Come

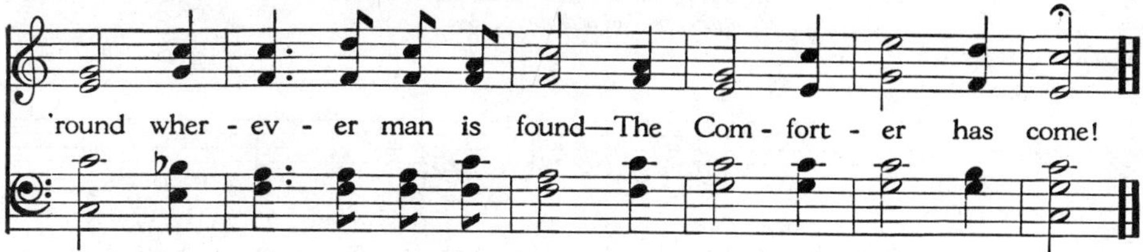
'round wher - ev - er man is found—The Com - fort - er has come!

145

Old Time Power

... he shall baptize you with the Holy Ghost, and with fire. Matt. 3:11

TABERNACLE 8.7.8.7. with Refrain

Paul Rader, 1879-1938

Paul Rader, 1879-1938

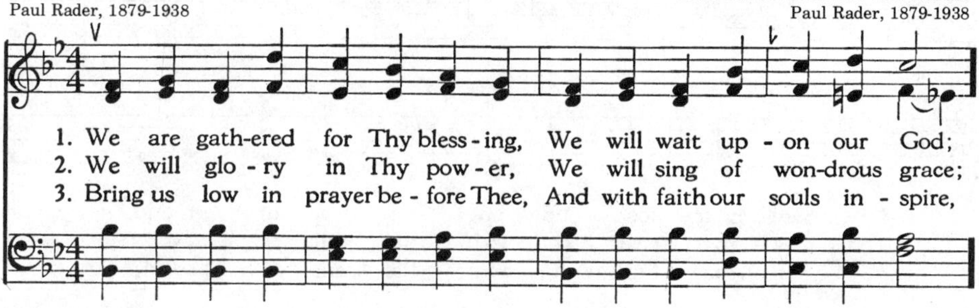
1. We are gath-ered for Thy bless - ing, We will wait up - on our God;
2. We will glo - ry in Thy pow - er, We will sing of won-drous grace;
3. Bring us low in prayer be - fore Thee, And with faith our souls in - spire,

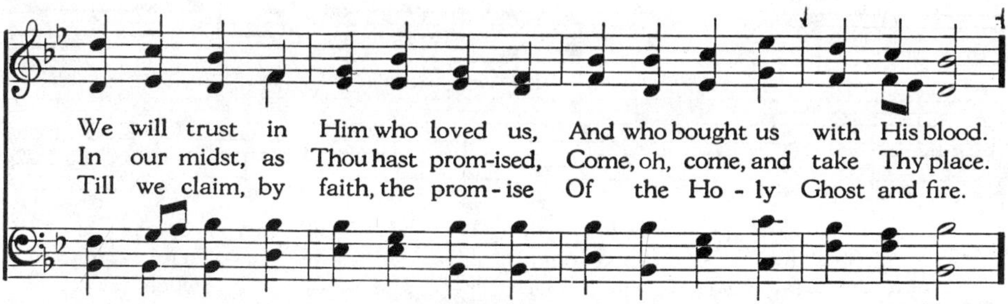
We will trust in Him who loved us, And who bought us with His blood.
In our midst, as Thou hast prom-ised, Come, oh, come, and take Thy place.
Till we claim, by faith, the prom - ise Of the Ho - ly Ghost and fire.

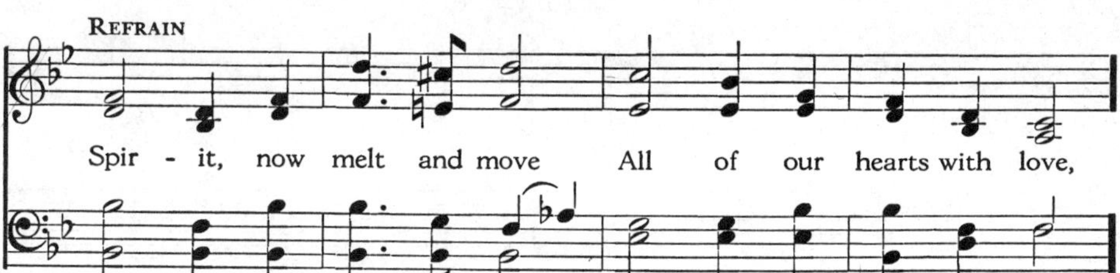
REFRAIN
Spir - it, now melt and move All of our hearts with love,

Breathe on us from a - bove With old - time power.

146 I Will Pour Water

. . . upon him that is thirsty . . . Isa. 44:3

Dwight Hall, b. 1923 | Dwight Hall, b. 1923

1. "I will pour wa - ter on him that is thirst - y;
2. Gent - ly the flow of the Spir - it de - scend - ing;
3. Lord, send Thy Spir - it, con - vict - ing the sin - ful;
I will pour floods up - on all the dry ground.
Touch - es my heart, and with life all a - new.
Fill - ing the faith - ful with life and with power.
Up - on thy seed will I pour of my Spir - it;
Chang - es my dross for gold's val - ue un - end - ing;
Work - ing with - in us the plan of Thy whole will;
And of my bless - ing up - on their own."
Cleans - ing and wash - ing me all the way through.
Blest Ho - ly Spir - it, de - scend yet this hour!

Holy Spirit, Faithful Guide 147

. . . the Spirit . . . will guide you into all truth . . . John 16:13

Marcus M. Wells, 1815-1895

FAITHFUL GUIDE 7.7.7.7.D.
Marcus M. Wells, 1815-1895

1. Ho - ly Spir - it, faith - ful Guide, Ev - er near the Chris - tian's side,
2. Ev - er pres - ent, tru - est Friend, Ev - er near Thine aid to lend,
3. When our days of toil shall cease, Wait - ing still for sweet re - lease,
Gent - ly lead us by the hand—Pil - grims in a des - ert land.
Leave us not to doubt and fear, Grop - ing on in dark - ness drear.
Noth - ing left but heaven and prayer, Won-dering if our names are there;
Wea - ry souls for - e'er re - joice, While they hear that sweet - est voice,
When the storms are rag - ing sore, Hearts grow faint, and hopes give o'er;
Wad - ing deep the dis - mal flood, Plead - ing nought but Je - sus' blood,
Whis-pering soft - ly, "Wan-derer, come, Fol - low Me, I'll guide thee home."
Whis-pering soft - ly, "Wan-derer, come, Fol - low Me, I'll guide thee home."
Whis-pering soft - ly, "Wan-derer, come, Fol - low Me, I'll guide thee home." A-MEN.

148 Come Unto Me, Ye Weary

... and I will give you rest. Matt. 11:28

AURELIA 7.6.7.6.D.

William C. Dix, 1837-1898

Samuel S. Wesley, 1810-1876

1. "Come un - to Me, ye wea - ry, And I will give you rest."
2. "Come un - to Me, ye wan - derers, And I will give you light."
3. "Come un - to Me, ye faint - ing, And I will give you life."
4. "And who - so - ev - er com - eth I will not cast him out."
O bless - ed voice of Je - sus, Which comes to hearts op - pressed!
O lov - ing voice of Je - sus, Which comes to cheer the night!
O cheer - ing voice of Je - sus, Which comes to aid our strife!
O wel - come voice of Je - sus, Which drives a - way our doubt,
It tells of ben - e - dic - tion, Of par - don, grace, and peace,
Our hearts were filled with sad - ness, And we had lost our way;
The foe is stern and ea - ger, The fight is fierce and long;
Which calls us, ver - y sin - ners, Un - wor - thy though we be
Of joy that hath no end - ing, Of love which can - not cease.
But morn - ing brings us glad - ness, And songs the break of day.
But Thou hast made us might - y, And strong - er than the strong.
Of love so free and bound - less, To come, dear Lord, to Thee!

I Am Coming, Lord 149

If we confess our sins, he is faithful and just to forgive us our sins . . . 1 John 1:9

Lewis Hartsough, 1828-1919

WELCOME VOICE S.M. with Refrain
Melody by Lewis Hartsough, 1828-1919

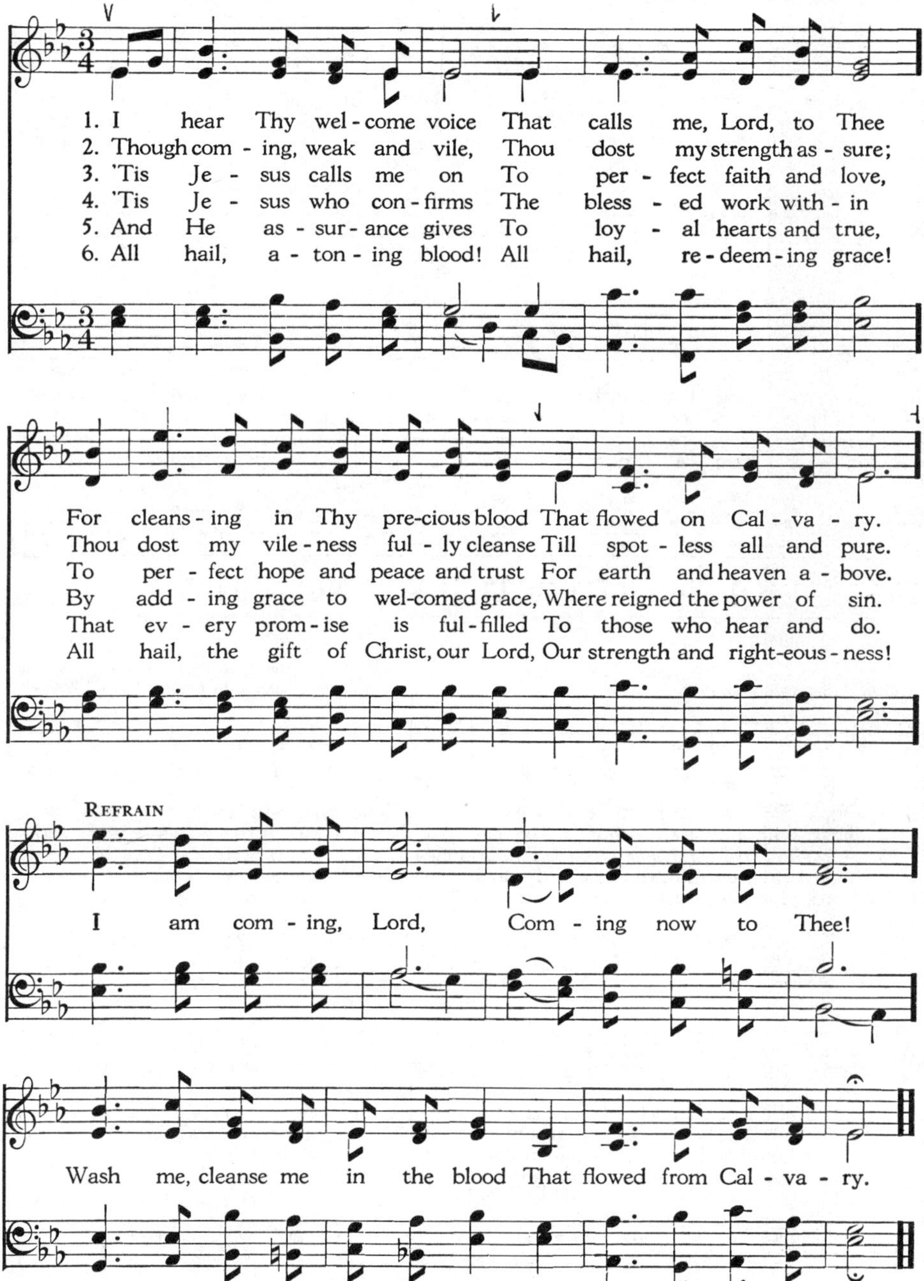
1. I hear Thy wel-come voice That calls me, Lord, to Thee
2. Though com-ing, weak and vile, Thou dost my strength as-sure;
3. 'Tis Je-sus calls me on To per-fect faith and love,
4. 'Tis Je-sus who con-firms The bless-ed work with-in
5. And He as-sur-ance gives To loy-al hearts and true,
6. All hail, a-ton-ing blood! All hail, re-deem-ing grace!
For cleans-ing in Thy pre-cious blood That flowed on Cal-va-ry.
Thou dost my vile-ness ful-ly cleanse Till spot-less all and pure.
To per-fect hope and peace and trust For earth and heaven a-bove.
By add-ing grace to wel-comed grace, Where reigned the power of sin.
That ev-ery prom-ise is ful-filled To those who hear and do.
All hail, the gift of Christ, our Lord, Our strength and right-eous-ness!
REFRAIN
I am com-ing, Lord, Com-ing now to Thee!
Wash me, cleanse me in the blood That flowed from Cal-va-ry.

150 Depth of Mercy! Can There Be

For thy mercy is great above the heavens . . . Psa. 108:4

WEBER 7.7.7.7.

Charles Wesley, 1707-1788

Adapted from Carl M. von Weber, 1786-1826

1. Depth of mer - cy! Can there be Mer - cy still re - served for me?
2. I have long with - stood His grace, Long pro - voked Him to His face,
3. Lord, in - cline me to re - pent; Let me now my fall la - ment,
4. Still for me the Sav - iour stands, Shows His wounds, and spreads His hands;

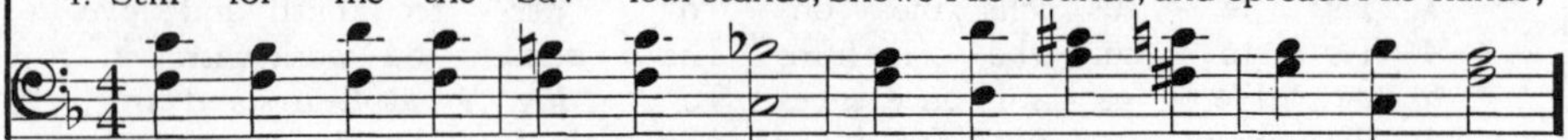

Can my God His wrath for - bear? Me, the chief of sin - ners spare?
Would not heark - en to His calls, Grieved Him by a thou-sand falls.
Deep - ly my re - volt de - plore, Weep, be - lieve, and sin no more.
God is love, I know, I feel. Je - sus weeps, and loves me still.

151 Oh, for a Faith That Will Not Shrink

. . . Lord, Increase our faith. Luke 17:5

AZMON C.M.

Melody by Carl G. Gläser, 1784-1829

William H. Bathurst, 1796-1877

Adapted by Lowell Mason, 1792-1872

1. Oh, for a faith that will not shrink, Though pressed by man - y a foe,
2. That will not mur - mur or com-plain Be - neath the chas-tening rod,
3. A faith that shines more bright and clear When tem-pests rage with - out;
4. That bears, un-moved, the world's dread frown, Nor heeds its scorn - ful smile;
5. Lord, give us such a faith as this; And then, what -e'er may come,

That will not trem - ble on the brink Of an - y earth-ly woe;
But, in the hour of grief or pain, Will lean up - on its God;
That when in dan - ger knows no fear, In dark-ness feels no doubt;
That seas of trou - ble can-not drown, Nor Sa-tan's arts be - guile.
We'll taste, e'en here, the hal-lowed bliss Of an e - ter - nal home. A-MEN.

(For higher key see No. 31)

There's a Wideness in God's Mercy 152

But thou, O Lord, art a God . . . plenteous in mercy . . . Psa. 86:15

WELLESLEY 8.7.8.7.

Frederick W. Faber, 1814-1863

Melody by Lizzie S. Tourjée, 1858-1913

1. There's a wide - ness in God's mer - cy, Like the
2. There is wel - come for the sin - ner, And more
3. For the love of God is broad - er Than the
4. There is plen - ti - ful re - demp - tion In the
5. Pin - ing souls, come near - er Je - sus, And, oh,
6. If our love were but more sim - ple, We should
wide - ness of the sea; There's a kind - ness in His
grac - es for the good; There is mer - cy with the
meas - ures of man's mind, And the heart of the E -
blood that has been shed; There is joy for all the
come not doubt - ing thus; But with faith that trusts more
take Him at His word; And our lives would be all
jus - tice, Which is more than lib - er - ty.
Sav - iour; There is heal - ing in His blood.
ter - nal Is most won - der - ful - ly kind.
mem - bers In the sor - rows of the Head.
brave - ly His vast ten - der - ness for us.
sun - shine In the sweet - ness of our Lord.
A - MEN.

153 O Jesus, Thou Art Standing

Behold, I stand at the door, and knock . . . Rev. 3:20

ST. HILDA 7.6.7.6.D.

William W. How, 1823-1897

Edward Husband, 1843-1908

1. O Je - sus, Thou art stand-ing Out - side the fast-closed door,
2. O Je - sus, Thou art knock-ing; And lo, that hand is scarred,
3. O Je - sus, Thou art plead-ing In ac - cents meek and low,
In low - ly pa - tience wait - ing To pass the thresh - old o'er.
And thorns Thy brow en - cir - cle, And tears Thy face have marred.
"I died for you, my chil - dren, And will ye treat Me so?"
Shame on us, Chris - tian broth - ers, His name and sign who bear,
O love that pass - eth knowl - edge, So pa - tient - ly to wait!
O Lord, with shame and sor - row We o - pen now the door;
Oh, shame, thrice shame up - on us, To keep Him stand - ing there!
O sin that hath no e - qual, So fast to bar the gate!
Dear Sav - iour, en - ter, en - ter, And leave us nev - er - more.

Dear Lord and Father of Mankind 154

In whose hand is . . . the breath of all mankind. Job 12:10

John G. Whittier, 1807-1892

REST (Whittier) 8.6.8.8.6.
Frederick C. Maker, 1844-1927

1. Dear Lord and Fa - ther of man - kind, For - give our fool - ish
2. In sim - ple trust like theirs who heard, Be - side the Syr - ian
3. O sab - bath rest by Gal - i - lee! O calm of hills a -
4. With that deep hush sub - du - ing all Our words and works that
5. Drop Thy still dews of qui - et - ness Till all our striv - ings
6. Breathe through the heats of our de - sire Thy cool - ness and Thy
ways; Re - clothe us in our right - ful mind; In pur - er
sea, The gra - cious call - ing of the Lord, Let us, like
bove, Where Je - sus knelt to share with Thee The si - lence
drown The ten - der whis - per of Thy call; As noise - less
cease; Take from our souls the strain and stress, And let our
balm; Let sense be dumb, let flesh re - tire; Speak through the
lives Thy serv - ice find, In deep - er rev - erence, praise.
them, with - out a word Rise up and fol - low Thee.
of e - ter - ni - ty, In - ter - pret - ed by love!
let Thy bless - ing fall As fell Thy man - na down.
or - dered lives con - fess The beau - ty of Thy peace.
earth-quake, wind, and fire, O still small voice of calm! A - MEN.

155 Oh, the Bitter Shame and Sorrow

For to me to live is Christ, and to die is gain. Phil. 1:21

MACMILLAN 8.7.8.8.7.

Theodore Monod, 1836-1921

Harold M. Best, b. 1931

1. Oh, the bit - ter shame and sor - row That a time could
2. Yet He found me; I be - held Him Bleed - ing on the ac -
3. Day by day His ten - der mer - cy, Heal - ing, help - ing,
4. High - er than the high - est heav - en, Deep - er than the

ev - er be, When I let the Sav - iour's pit - y Plead
curs - ed tree, Heard Him pray, "For - give them, Fa - ther." And
full and free, Sweet and strong—and ah, so ten - der— Brought
deep - est sea, Lord, Thy love at last hath con - quered, Grant

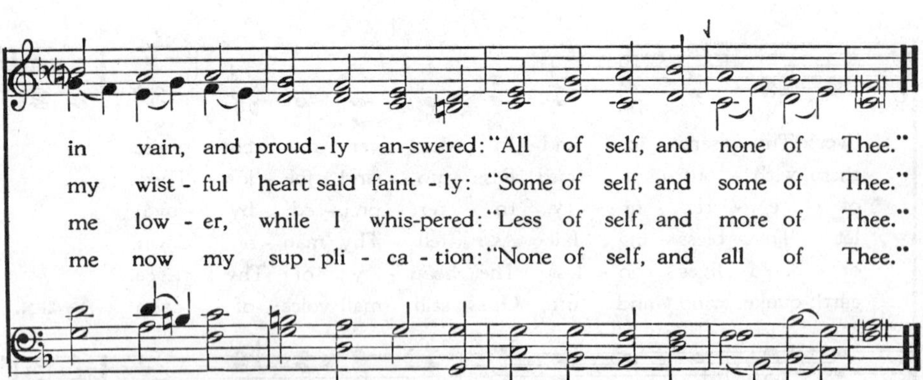
in vain, and proud - ly an-swered: "All of self, and none of Thee."
my wist - ful heart said faint - ly: "Some of self, and some of Thee."
me low - er, while I whis-pered: "Less of self, and more of Thee."
me now my sup - pli - ca - tion: "None of self, and all of Thee."

Jesus, and Shall It Ever Be 156

For whosoever shall be ashamed of me . . . of him shall the Son of man be ashamed . . . Luke 9:26

Joseph Grigg, circa 1720-1738
Altered by Benjamin Francis, circa 1734-1799

FEDERAL STREET L.M.
Henry K. Oliver, 1800-1885

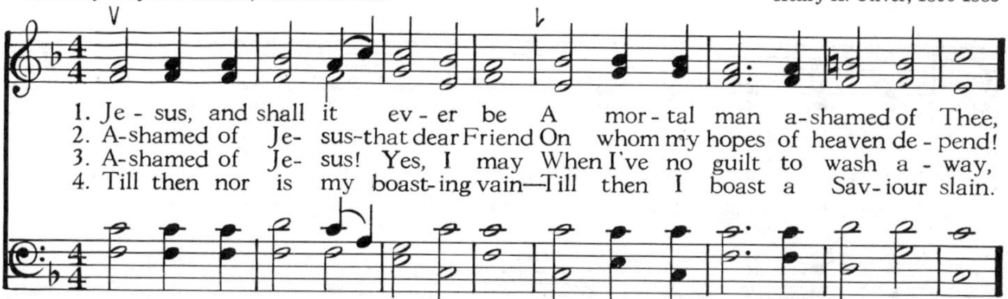
1. Je - sus, and shall it ev - er be A mor - tal man a - shamed of Thee,
2. A - shamed of Je - sus - that dear Friend On whom my hopes of heaven de - pend!
3. A - shamed of Je - sus! Yes, I may When I've no guilt to wash a - way,
4. Till then nor is my boast - ing vain— Till then I boast a Sav - iour slain.

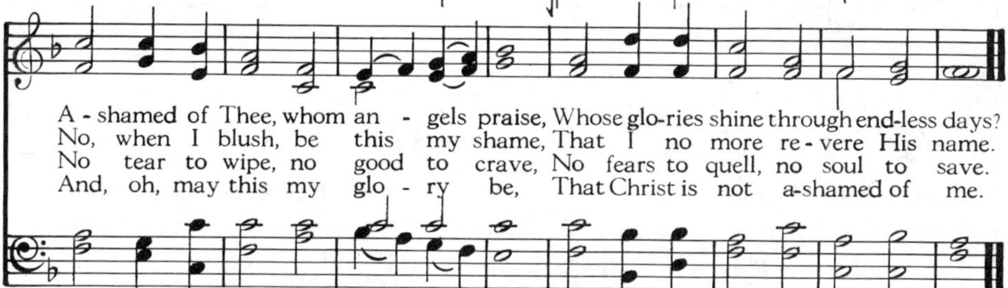
A - shamed of Thee, whom an - gels praise, Whose glo - ries shine through end - less days?
No, when I blush, be this my shame, That I no more re - vere His name.
No tear to wipe, no good to crave, No fears to quell, no soul to save.
And, oh, may this my glo - ry be, That Christ is not a - shamed of me.

Jesus, Thy Blood and Righteousness 157

. . . he hath clothed me with the garments of salvation . . . Isa. 61:10

Nicolaus L. von Zinzendorf, 1700-1760
Translated by John Wesley, 1703-1791

WALTON L.M.
From William Gardiner's *Sacred Melodies,* 1815

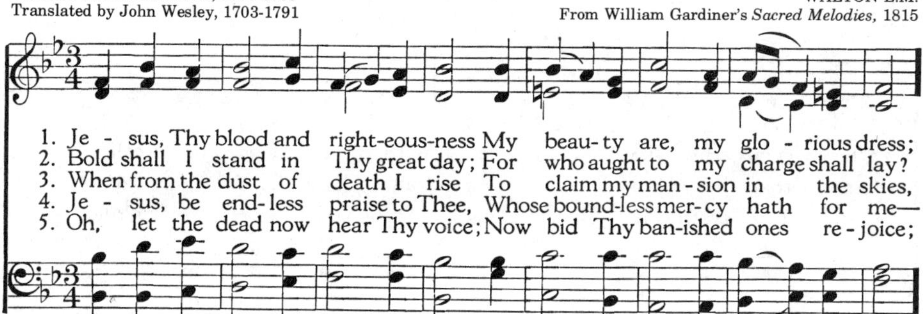
1. Je - sus, Thy blood and right - eous - ness My beau - ty are, my glo - rious dress;
2. Bold shall I stand in Thy great day; For who aught to my charge shall lay?
3. When from the dust of death I rise To claim my man - sion in the skies,
4. Je - sus, be end - less praise to Thee, Whose bound - less mer - cy hath for me—
5. Oh, let the dead now hear Thy voice; Now bid Thy ban - ished ones re - joice;

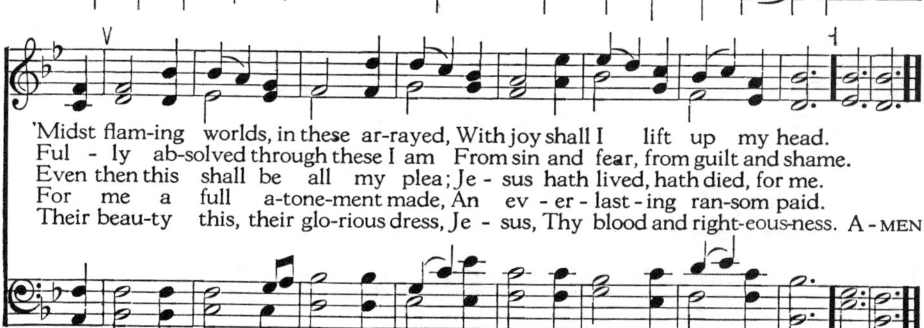
'Midst flam - ing worlds, in these ar - rayed, With joy shall I lift up my head.
Ful - ly ab - solved through these I am From sin and fear, from guilt and shame.
Even then this shall be all my plea; Je - sus hath lived, hath died, for me.
For me a full a - tone - ment made, An ev - er - last - ing ran - som paid.
Their beau - ty this, their glo - rious dress, Je - sus, Thy blood and right - eous - ness. A - MEN.

(For different harmony see No. 374)

158 In the Hour of Trial

. . . God is faithful, who will not suffer you to be tempted above that ye are able . . . 1 Cor. 10:13

PENITENCE 6.5.6.5.D.

James Montgomery, 1771-1854

Spencer Lane, 1843-1903

1. In the hour of tri - al, Je - sus, plead for me,
2. Should Thy mer - cy send me Sor - row, toil, or woe;
3. When in dust and ash - es To the grave I sink,
Lest, by base de - ni - al, I de - part from Thee.
Or should pain at - tend me On my path be - low;
While heaven's glo - ry flash - es O'er the shelv - ing brink,
When Thou seest me wav - er, With a look re - call;
Grant that I may nev - er Fail Thy hand to see;
On Thy truth re - ly - ing Through that mor - tal strife,
Nor for fear or fa - vor, Suf - fer me to fall.
Grant that I may ev - er Cast my care on Thee.
Lord, re - ceive me, dy - ing, To e - ter - nal life.

I Need Thee Every Hour

Bow down thine ear, O Lord, . . . I am poor and needy. Psa. 86:1

Stanzas by Annie S. Hawks, 1835-1918
Refrain by Robert Lowry, 1826-1899

NEED 6.4.6.4. with Refrain
Robert Lowry, 1826-1899

1. I need Thee ev - ery hour, Most gra - cious Lord;
2. I need Thee ev - ery hour, Stay Thou near by;
3. I need Thee ev - ery hour, In joy or pain;
4. I need Thee ev - ery hour, Most ho - ly One;
No ten - der voice like Thine Can peace af - ford.
Temp - ta - tions lose their power When Thou art nigh.
Come quick - ly and a - bide, Or life is vain.
Oh, make me Thine in - deed, Thou bless - ed Son!
REFRAIN
I need Thee, oh, I need Thee; Ev - ery hour I need Thee!
Oh, bless me now, my Sav - iour, I come to Thee!

160 I Lay My Sins on Jesus

Who his own self bare our sins in his own body . . . 1 Pet. 2:24

RUTHERFORD 7.6.7.6.D.
Chrétien Urhan, 1790-1845
Horatius Bonar, 1808-1889
Arranged by Edward F. Rimbault, 1816-1876

1. I lay my sins on Je - sus, The spot - less Lamb of God;
2. I lay my wants on Je - sus; All full - ness dwells in Him.
3. I rest my soul on Je - sus, This wea - ry soul of mine;
4. I long to be like Je - sus– Meek, lov - ing, low - ly, mild;
He bears them all, and frees us From the ac - curs - ed load.
He heals all my dis - eas - es; He doth my soul re - deem.
His right hand me em - brac - es, I on His breast re - cline.
I long to be, like Je - sus, The Fa - ther's ho - ly child.
I bring my guilt to Je - sus To wash my crim - son stains
I lay my griefs on Je - sus, My bur - dens, and my cares—
I love the name of Je - sus, Em - man - uel, Christ, the Lord;
I long to be with Je - sus A - mid the heaven - ly throng,
White in His blood most pre - cious, Till not a spot re - mains.
He from them all re - leas - es; He all my sor - rows shares.
Like fra - grance on the breez - es, His name a - broad is poured.
To sing with saints His prais - es, To learn the an - gels' song. A-MEN.

Only Believe

. . . all things are possible to him that believeth. Mark 9:23

Paul Rader, 1879-1938 Paul Rader, 1879-1938

1. Fear not, lit - tle flock, from the cross to the throne, From death in - to
2. Fear not, lit - tle flock, He go - eth a - head, Your Shep - herd se -
3. Fear not, lit - tle flock, what - ev - er your lot; He en - ters all
life He went for His own; All pow - er in earth, all pow-er a-bove,
lect - eth the path you must tread; The wa-ters of Ma-rah He'll sweet-en for thee—
rooms, "the doors be - ing shut." He nev - er for-sakes, He nev-er is gone—
Is giv - en to Him for the flock of His love.
He drank all the bit - ter in Geth-sem - a - ne.
So count on His pres - ence in dark-ness and dawn.
REFRAIN
On - ly be-lieve,
on - ly be - lieve; All things are pos - si - ble, on - ly be - lieve;
On - ly be - lieve, on - ly be - lieve; All things are pos-si-ble, on-ly be-lieve.

162 Whiter Than Snow

. . . wash me, and I shall be whiter than snow. Psa. 51:7

FISCHER 11.11.11.11. with Refrain

James L. Nicholson, circa 1828-1896

William G. Fischer, 1835-1912

1. Lord Je - sus, I long to be per - fect - ly whole; I want Thee for -
2. Lord Je - sus, look down from Thy throne in the skies, And help me to
3. Lord Je - sus, for this I most hum - bly en - treat; I wait, bless - ed
4. Lord Je - sus, Thou see - st I pa - tient - ly wait; Come now, and with -
ev - er to live in my soul. Break down ev - ery i - dol, cast
make a com - plete sac - ri - fice. I give up my - self, and what -
Lord, at Thy cru - ci - fied feet; By faith, for my cleans - ing, I
in me a new heart cre - ate. To those who have sought Thee, Thou
out ev - ery foe; Now wash me, and I shall be whit - er than snow.
ev - er I know—Now wash me, and I shall be whit - er than snow.
see Thy blood flow—Now wash me, and I shall be whit - er than snow.
nev - er saidst "No." Now wash me, and I shall be whit - er than snow.
REFRAIN
Whit - er than snow, yes, whit - er than snow;
Now wash me, and I shall be whit - er than snow.

Come, Thou Fount 163

. . . there shall be a fountain opened . . . for sin and for uncleanness. Zech. 13:1

NETTLETON 8.7.8.7.D.
American melody
From John Wyeth's *Repository of Sacred Music,* 1813

Robert Robinson, 1735-1790

1. Come, Thou Fount of ev - ery bless - ing, Tune my heart to sing Thy grace;
2. Hith - er - to Thy love has blest me; Thou hast brought me to this place;
3. Oh, to grace how great a debt - or, Dai - ly I'm con-strained to be!
Streams of mer - cy nev - er ceas - ing, Call for songs of loud-est praise.
And I know Thy hand will bring me Safe - ly home by Thy good grace.
Let Thy good - ness, as a fet - ter, Bind my wan-dering heart to Thee;
Teach me some me - lo-dious son - net, Sung by flam - ing tongues a - bove.
Je - sus sought me when a stran - ger, Wan-dering from the fold of God;
Prone to wan - der, Lord, I feel it, Prone to leave the God I love;
Praise the mount—I'm fixed up - on it— Mount of Thy re - deem-ing love.
He, to res - cue me from dan - ger Bought me with His pre - cious blood.
Here's my heart, oh, take and seal it— Seal it for Thy courts a - bove.

164 Where Jesus Is, 'Tis Heaven

. . . we shall also bear the image of the heavenly. 1 Cor. 15:49

C.F. Butler, 19th century

Melody by James M. Black, 1856-1938

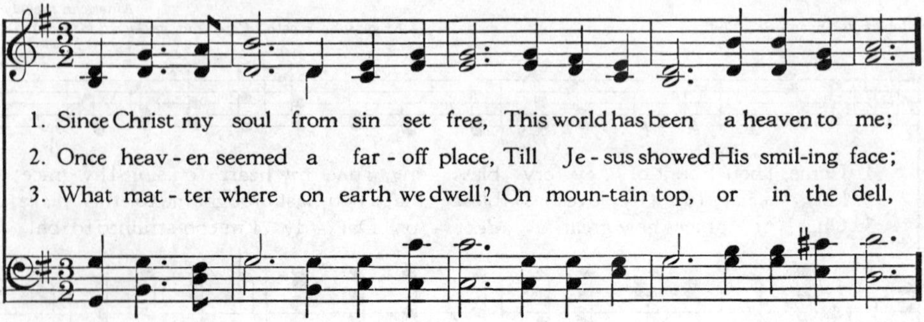
1. Since Christ my soul from sin set free, This world has been a heaven to me;
2. Once heav-en seemed a far-off place, Till Je-sus showed His smil-ing face;
3. What mat-ter where on earth we dwell? On moun-tain top, or in the dell,

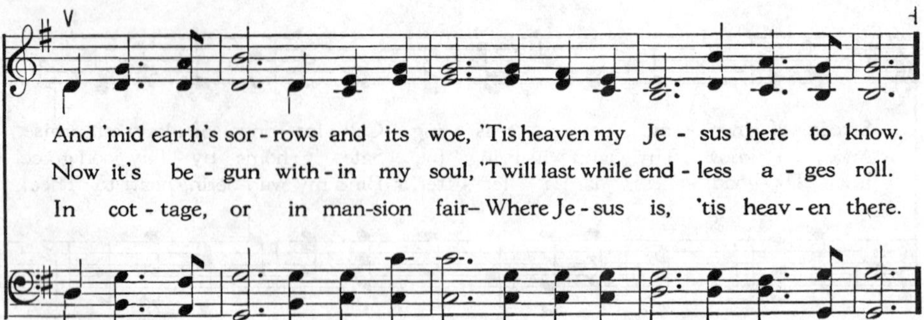
And 'mid earth's sor-rows and its woe, 'Tis heaven my Je-sus here to know.
Now it's be-gun with-in my soul, 'Twill last while end-less a-ges roll.
In cot-tage, or in man-sion fair– Where Je-sus is, 'tis heav-en there.

REFRAIN
Oh, hal-le-lu-jah, yes, 'tis heaven! 'Tis heaven to know my sins for-given;

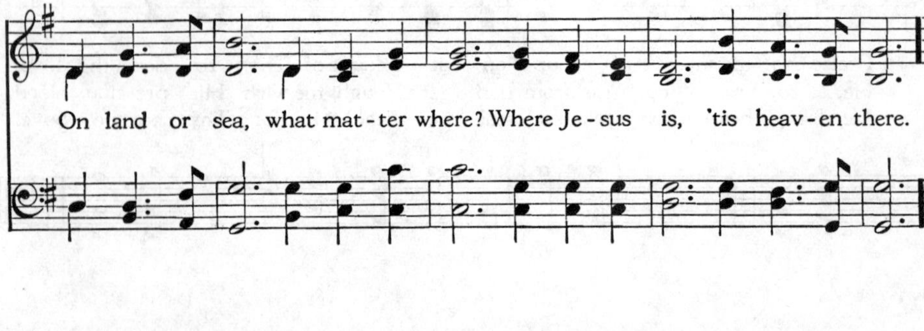
On land or sea, what mat-ter where? Where Je-sus is, 'tis heav-en there.

O Boundless Salvation 165

. . . it is the power of God unto salvation to every one that believeth . . . Rom. 1:16

William Booth, 1829-1912

BOOTH 11.11.11.12.11.
Attributed to J. Ellis, 19th century

1. O bound-less sal - va - tion, deep o - cean of love! O full - ness of
2. My sins, they are man - y, their stains are so deep, And bit - ter the
3. The tide now is flow - ing; I'm touch-ing the wave, I hear the loud
4. And now, hal - le - lu - jah! The rest of my days Shall glad - ly be
mer - cy Christ brought from a - bove, The whole world re - deem - ing, so
tears of re - morse that I weep; But weep - ing is use - less– thou
call of "the Might-y to save." My faith's grow-ing bold - er— de -
spent in pro - mot - ing His praise, Who o - pened His bos - om to
rich and so free, Now flow - ing for all men, Now flow - ing for
great crim - son sea, Thy wa - ters can cleanse me, Thy wa - ters can
liv - ered I'll be! I plunge 'neath the wa - ters, I plunge 'neath the
pour out this sea Of bound-less sal - va - tion, Of bound-less sal -
all men, Now flow - ing for all men–Come, roll o - ver me!
cleanse me, Thy wa - ters can cleanse me– Come, roll o - ver me!
wa - ters, I plunge 'neath the wa - ters– They roll o - ver me!
va - tion, Of bound - less sal - va - tion, For you and for me!

166 Christ in Me

. . . *Christ in you, the hope of glory.* Col. 1:27

Albert B. Simpson, 1843-1919 — Albert B. Simpson, 1843-1919

1. This is my won-der-ful sto - ry—Christ to my heart has come;
2. Was there e'er sto - ry so mov-ing, Sto - ry of love and pain;
3. I am so glad I re - ceived Him, Je - sus, my heart's dear King;
4. How can I ev - er be lone - ly, How can I ev - er fall;
5. Now in His bos - om con - fid - ing, This my glad song shall be:
Je - sus, the King of glo - ry, Finds in my heart a home.
Was there e'er Bride-groom so lov - ing, Seek - ing our hearts to gain?
I who so of - ten have grieved Him, All to His feet would bring.
What can I want, if on - ly Christ is my all in all?
I am in Je - sus a - bid - ing, Je - sus a - bides in me.
REFRAIN
Christ in me, Christ in me, Christ in me—Oh, won-der-ful sto - ry;
Christ in me, Christ in me, Christ in me, the hope of glo - ry.

He Included Me 167

For whosoever shall call upon the name of the Lord shall be saved. Rom 10:13

Johnson Oatman, Jr., 1856-1926

Hampton H. Sewell, 1874-1937

1. I am so hap-py in Christ to-day, That I go sing-ing a-long my way;
2. Glad-ly I read, "Who-so-ev-er may Come to the foun-tain of life to-day;"
3. Ev-er God's Spir-it is say-ing, "Come!" Hear the Bride say-ing, "No long-er roam"
4. "Free-ly come, drink," words the soul to thrill! Oh, with what joy they my heart do fill!
Yes, I'm so hap-py to know and say, "Je-sus in-clud-ed me too."
But when I read it I al-ways say, "Je-sus in-clud-ed me too."
But I am sure while they're call-ing home, Je-sus in-clud-ed me too.
For when He said, "Who-so-ev-er will," Je-sus in-clud-ed me too.
REFRAIN
Je-sus in-clud-ed me, Yes, He in-clud-ed me, When the Lord said
"Who-so-ev-er," He in-clud-ed me; Je-sus in-clud-ed me, Yes, He in-
clud-ed me, When the Lord said "Who-so-ev-er," He in-clud-ed me.

168 Constantly Abiding

. . . *I will never leave thee, nor forsake thee.* Heb. 13:5

CONSTANTLY ABIDING 12.8.12.9. with Refrain

Anne S. Murphy, d. 1942

Anne S. Murphy, d. 1942

1. There's a peace in my heart that the world nev - er gave, A peace it can
2. All the world seemed to sing of a Sav-iour and King, When peace sweet-ly
3. This treas-ure I have in a tem-ple of clay, While here on His
not take a - way; Though the tri-als of life may sur-round like a cloud,
came to my heart; Trou - bles all fled a - way and my night turned to day,
foot-stool I roam; But He's com-ing to take me some glo-ri-ous day,
I've a peace that has come there to stay!
Bless-ed Je - sus, how glo-rious Thou art!
O - ver there to my heav-en-ly home!
REFRAIN
Con - stant-ly a-
Con-stant-ly a-bid - ing,
bid - ing, Je - sus is mine;
con-stant-ly a - bid-ing, Je - sus is mine, yes, Je - sus is mine;
Con - stant-ly a-bid - ing, rap - ture di-
Con-stant-ly a - bid - ing, con-stant-ly a - bid-ing, rap-ture di-vine, oh,

Constantly Abiding

vine; He nev - er leaves me lone - ly, whis-pers,
rap-ture di-vine; He nev-er leaves me, nev-er leaves me lone-ly, whis-pers,
oh, so kind— "I will nev-er leave thee," Je - sus is mine.
whis-pers, oh, so kind:— nev-er leave thee," Je-sus, Je-sus is mine.

Content 169

. . . in whatsoever state I am, therewith to be content. Phil. 4:11

Jeanne M. Guyon, 1648-1717 — Mabel J. Camp, 1871-1937

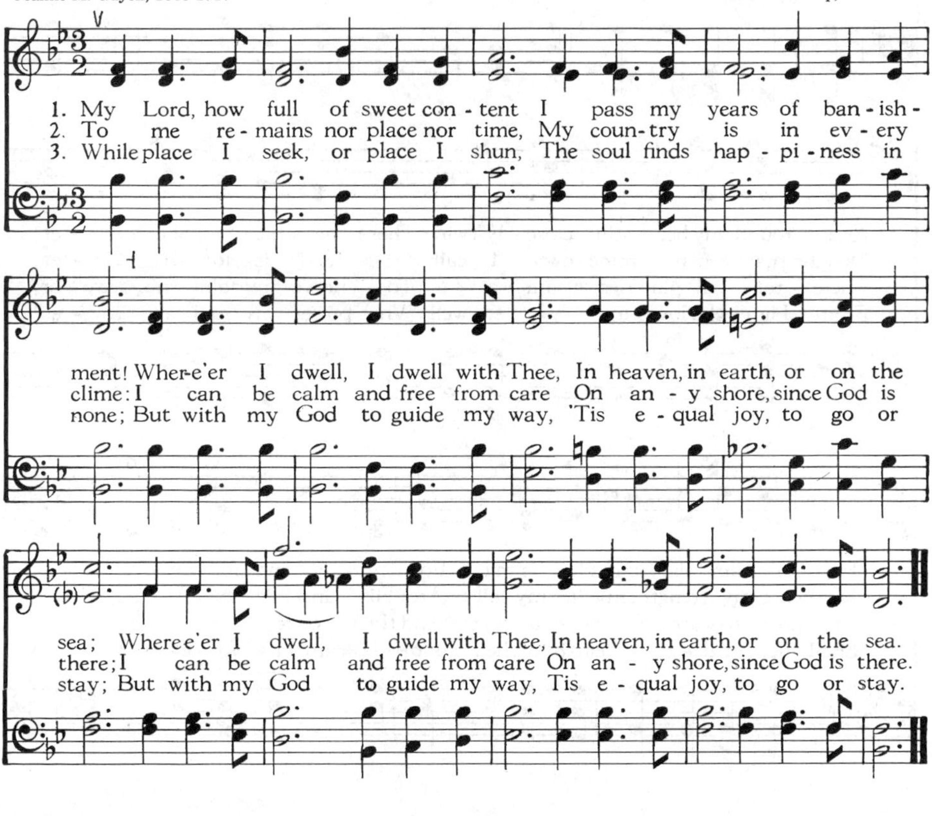
1. My Lord, how full of sweet con - tent I pass my years of ban - ish -
2. To me re - mains nor place nor time, My coun-try is in ev - ery
3. While place I seek, or place I shun, The soul finds hap - pi - ness in
ment! Wher-e'er I dwell, I dwell with Thee, In heaven, in earth, or on the
clime: I can be calm and free from care On an - y shore, since God is
none; But with my God to guide my way, 'Tis e - qual joy, to go or
sea; Wheree'er I dwell, I dwell with Thee, In heaven, in earth, or on the sea.
there; I can be calm and free from care On an - y shore, since God is there.
stay; But with my God to guide my way, 'Tis e - qual joy, to go or stay.

170 I've Found a Friend, Oh, Such a Friend

. . . I have called you friends . . . John 15:15

I'VE FOUND A FRIEND 8.7.8.7.D.

James G. Small, 1817-1888

George C. Stebbins, 1846-1945

1. I've found a Friend, oh, such a Friend! He loved me ere I knew Him;
2. I've found a Friend, oh, such a Friend! He bled, He died to save me;
3. I've found a Friend, oh, such a Friend! All power to Him is giv - en,
4. I've found a Friend, oh, such a Friend! So kind, and true, and ten - der,
He drew me with the cords of love, And thus He bound me to Him.
And not a - lone the gift of life, But His own self He gave me.
To guard me on my on-ward course, And bring me safe to heav - en.
So wise a Coun - sel - lor and Guide, So might - y a De - fend - er.
And round my heart still close - ly twine Those ties which nought can sev - er;
Nought that I have mine own I call, I hold it for the Giv - er;
The e - ter - nal glo - ries gleam a - far To nerve my faint en - deav - or;
From Him who loves me now so well What power my soul can sev - er?
For I am His, and He is mine, For - ev - er and for - ev - er.
My heart, my strength, my life, my all Are His, and His for - ev - er.
So now to watch, to work, to war; And then to rest for - ev - er.
Shall life, or death, or earth, or hell? No— I am His for - ev - er. A-MEN.

In My Heart There Rings a Melody 171

... singing and making melody in your heart to the Lord. Eph. 5:19

HEART MELODY Irregular with Refrain

Elton M. Roth, 1891-1951

Elton M. Roth, 1891-1951

1. I have a song that Je - sus gave me, It was sent from heaven a - bove;
2. I love the Christ who died on Cal-vary, For He washed my sins a - way;
3. 'Twill be my end- less theme in glo - ry, With the an-gels I will sing;
There nev-er was a sweet-er mel - o - dy, 'Tis a mel - o - dy of love.
He put with - in my heart a mel - o - dy, And I know it's there to stay.
'Twill be a song with glo-rious har - mo - ny, When the courts of heav-en ring.
REFRAIN
In my heart there rings a mel - o - dy, There
rings a mel - o - dy with heav- en's har - mo - ny;
In my heart there rings a mel - o - dy, There rings a mel - o - dy of love.

172 If You Want Joy

Now the God of hope fill you with all joy and peace in believing . . . Rom 15:13

Joseph D. Carlson, b. 1915

Joseph D. Carlson, b. 1915
Harmony by Helen I. Young, b. 1931

I walked a - long life's earth - ly road Seek - ing for peace and joy,
Wan - der - ing friend, I plead with you, Come to the crim - son fount,
Then I found Je - sus as Sa - viour and Lord, Now I have peace and joy.
Just as you are, re - pent, and be - lieve; He'll nev - er cast you out.
REFRAIN
3
If you want joy, real joy, won - der - ful joy, Let Je - sus come
in - to your heart, If you want joy, real joy, won - der - ful joy, Let
Je - sus come in - to your heart, Your sin He'll wash a - way, Your

If You Want Joy

bur-den roll a - way, Your life He'll make it o - ver a - new, If you want
joy, real joy, won-der - ful joy, Let Je - sus come in - to your heart.

We Bless Thee for Thy Peace 173

. . . the Lord will bless his people with peace. Psa. 29:11

Anonymous

BEATITUDO C.M.
John B. Dykes, 1823-1876

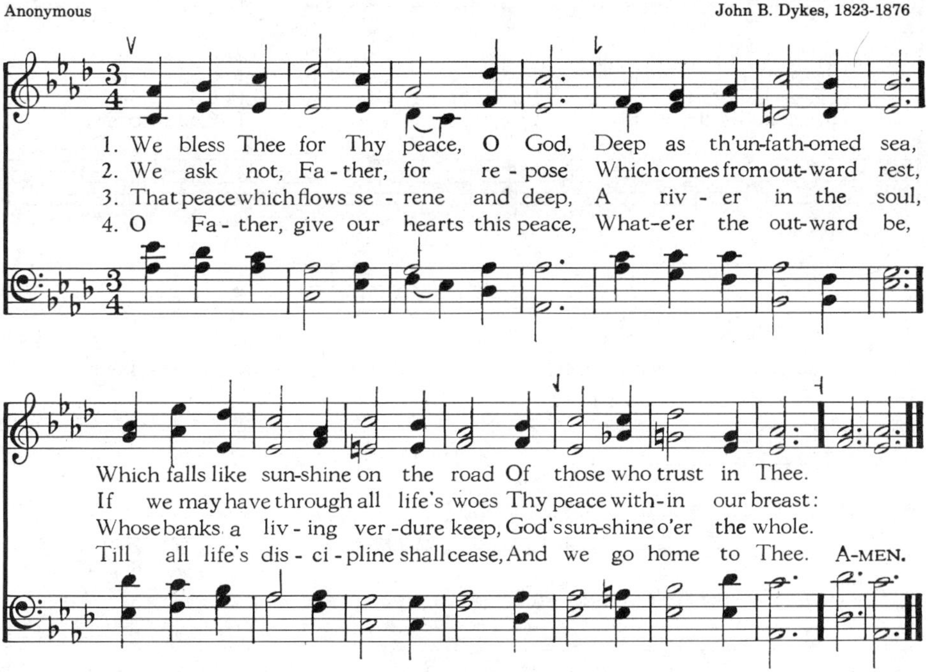
1. We bless Thee for Thy peace, O God, Deep as th'un-fath-omed sea,
2. We ask not, Fa - ther, for re - pose Which comes from out-ward rest,
3. That peace which flows se - rene and deep, A riv - er in the soul,
4. O Fa - ther, give our hearts this peace, What-e'er the out-ward be,
Which falls like sun-shine on the road Of those who trust in Thee.
If we may have through all life's woes Thy peace with-in our breast:
Whose banks a liv - ing ver - dure keep, God's sun-shine o'er the whole.
Till all life's dis - ci - pline shall cease, And we go home to Thee.
A-MEN.

174 Sweet Peace, the Gift of God's Love

. . . my peace I give unto you . . . John 14:27

Peter P. Bilhorn, 1861-1936

SWEET PEACE 8.8.8.7. with Refrain
Melody by Peter P. Bilhorn, 1861-1936

1. There comes to my heart one sweet strain, A glad and a joy - ous re - frain; I sing it a - gain and a - gain: Sweet peace, the gift of God's love.
2. By Christ on the cross peace was made, My debt by His death was all paid; No oth - er foun - da - tion is laid For peace, the gift of God's love.
3. When Je - sus as Lord I had crowned, My heart with this peace did a - bound; In Him the rich bless - ing I found, Sweet peace, the gift of God's love.
4. In Je - sus for peace I a - bide; And as I keep close to His side, There's noth - ing but peace doth be - tide— Sweet peace, the gift of God's love.
Refrain
Peace, peace, sweet peace, Won - der - ful gift from a - bove;
Oh, won - der - ful, won - der - ful peace, Sweet peace, the gift of God's love.

Wonderful Peace

175

. . . we have peace with God through our Lord Jesus Christ. Rom. 5:1

W.D. Cornell, 19th century (altered)

Melody by W.G. Cooper, 19th century

1. Far a - way in the depths of my spir - it to - night Rings a
2. I am rest - ing to - night in this won - der - ful peace, Rest - ing
3. And I think when I rise to that cit - y of peace, Where the
4. O dear soul, are you here with-out com - fort and rest, March-ing
mel - o - dy sweet - er than psalm; And in heav - en - ly strains it un -
sweet - ly in Je - sus' con - trol; For I'm kept from all dan - ger by
Au - thor of peace I shall see, That one strain of the song which the
down the rough path-way of time? Make Je - sus your friend ere the
ceas - ing - ly falls O'er my soul like an in - fi - nite calm.
night and by day, And His glo - ry is flood - ing my soul!
ran - somed will sing In that heav - en - ly king - dom will be:
shad - ows grow dark; Oh, ac - cept now this peace so sub - lime!
REFRAIN
Peace, peace, won - der - ful peace, Com - ing down from the Fa - ther a - bove, Sweep
o - ver my spir - it for - ev - er, I pray, In fath - om - less bil - lows of love!

176 Thou Wilt Keep Him in Perfect Peace

. . . whose mind is stayed on thee. Isa. 26:3

PERFECT PEACE 8.6.9.6. with Refrain

Stanza 1 by Vivian K. Amsler, 20th century
Stanzas 2-3 by Floyd W. Hawkins, b. 1904

Vivian K. Amsler, 20th century
Arranged by Floyd W. Hawkins, b. 1904

1. "Thou wilt keep him in per-fect peace, Whose mind is stayed on Thee."
2. In the shad-ow of the might-y Rock I lay me down to sleep;
3. 'Tis the prom-ise of the Ho-ly One, "My peace I give to thee."
When the shad-ows come and dark-ness falls, He giv-eth in-ward peace.
He who watch-es o-ver Is-ra-el So faith-ful-ly will keep.
Though the storm of life in fu-ry rage, Thy ref-uge sure is He.
Refrain
Oh, He is the on-ly per-fect rest-ing place! He
giv-eth per-fect peace.
"Thou wilt keep him in
per-fect peace, whose mind is stayed on Thee."
stayed on Thee."
1-2
3.

Oh, the Deep, Deep Love of Jesus 177

... he loved them unto the end. John 13:1

EBENEZER 8.7.8.7.D.

Samuel T. Francis, 1834-1925 — Thomas J. Williams, 1869-1944

1. Oh, the deep, deep love of Je - sus, Vast, un - measured, bound-less free;
2. Oh, the deep, deep love of Je - sus, Spread His praise from shore to shore;
3. Oh, the deep, deep love of Je - sus, Love of ev - ery love the best;
Roll - ing as a might-y o - cean In its full - ness o - ver me.
How He lov - eth, ev - er lov - eth, Chang-eth nev - er, nev - er more;
'Tis an o - cean vast of bless-ing, 'Tis a ha - ven sweet of rest.
Un - der - neath me, all a - round me, Is the cur-rent of Thy love;
How He watch-eth o'er His loved ones, Died to call them all His own;
Oh, the deep, deep love of Je - sus, 'Tis a heaven of heavens to me;
Lead-ing on-ward, lead-ing home-ward, To my glo-rious rest a-bove.
How for them He in - ter - ced-eth, Watch-eth o'er them from the throne.
And it lifts me up to glo - ry, For it lifts me up to Thee. A-MEN.

178 The King of Love My Shepherd Is

The Lord is my shepherd; I shall not want. Psa. 23:1

DOMINUS REGIT ME 8.7.8.7.

Henry W. Baker, 1821-1877

John B. Dykes, 1823-1876

1. The King of love my Shep - herd is,
2. Where streams of liv - ing wa - ter flow
3. Per - verse and fool - ish oft I strayed;
4. In death's dark vale I fear no ill
5. Thou spreadst a ta - ble in my sight;
6. And so through all the length of days
Whose good - ness fail - eth nev - er; I noth - ing lack if
My ran - somed soul He lead - eth, And where the ver - dant
But yet in love He sought me, And on His shoul - der
With Thee, dear Lord, be - side me; Thy rod and staff my
Thy unc - tion grace be - stow - eth; And, oh, what trans - port
Thy good - ness fail - eth nev - er: Good Shep - herd, may I
I am His And He is mine for - ev - er.
pas - tures grow, With food ce - les - tial feed - eth.
gent - ly laid, And home, re - joic - ing, brought me.
com - fort still, Thy cross be - fore to guide me.
of de - light From Thy pure chal - ice flow - eth.
sing Thy praise With - in Thy house for - ev - er. A - MEN.

O Love Divine 179

. . . faith, hope, charity, . . . but the greatest of these is charity. 1 Cor. 13:13

Albert B. Simpson, 1843-1919

May A. Stephens, 1865-1935

1. O Love that gave it - self for me, Help me to love and
2. Set all my ran - somed powers on fire, Give me the love that
3. O Ho - ly Ghost, for Thee I cry; Bap - tize with pow - er
4. Help me to pray till all my soul Shall move and bend at
live like Thee, And kin - dle in this heart of mine The
naught can tire, And kin - dle in this heart of mine The
from on high, And kin - dle in this heart of mine The
Thy con - trol, And kin - dle in this heart of mine The
REFRAIN
pas - sion fire of love di - vine.
liv - ing fire of zeal di - vine.
liv - ing fire of power di - vine.
liv - ing fire of prayer di - vine.
O Love di - vine, O
Love di - vine, Re - vive this long - ing heart of mine, And
kin - dle in me from a - bove The liv - ing fire of heav - en - ly love.

180 Love Divine, All Loves Excelling

. . . charity, which is the bond of perfectness. Col. 3:14

BEECHER 8.7.8.7.D.

Charles Wesley, 1707-1788

John Zundel, 1815-1882

1. Love di - vine, all loves ex - cell - ing, Joy of heaven, to earth come down;
2. Breathe, oh, breathe Thy lov - ing Spir - it In - to ev - ery trou - bled breast;
3. Come, Al - might - y, to de - liv - er, Let us all Thy life re - ceive;
4. Fin - ish, then, Thy new cre - a - tion, Pure and spot - less let us be;
Fix in us Thy hum - ble dwell - ing, All Thy faith - ful mer - cies crown.
Let us all in Thee in - her - it, Let us find the prom - ised rest;
Sud - den - ly re - turn, and nev - er, Nev - er - more Thy tem - ples leave.
Let us see Thy great sal - va - tion Per - fect - ly re-stored in Thee;
Je - sus, Thou art all com - pas - sion, Pure, un - bound-ed love Thou art—
Take a - way the love of sin - ning; Al - pha and O - me - ga be;
Thee we would be al - ways bless - ing, Serve Thee as Thy hosts a - bove,
Changed from glo - ry in - to glo - ry Till in heaven we take our place,
Vis - it us with Thy sal - va - tion, En - ter ev - ery trem-bling heart.
End of faith, as its be - gin-ning, Set our hearts at lib - er - ty.
Pray, and praise Thee with-out ceas-ing, Glo - ry in Thy per-fect love.
Till we cast our crowns be - fore Thee, Lost in won-der, love, and praise. A-MEN.

O Love That Wilt Not Let Me Go 181

. . . I have loved thee with an everlasting love . . . Jer. 31:3

George Matheson, 1842-1906

ST. MARGARET 8.8.8.8.6.
Albert L. Peace, 1844-1912

1. O Love that wilt not let me go,
2. O Light that fol - lowest all my way,
3. O Joy that seek - est me through pain,
4. O Cross that lift - est up my head,
I rest my wea - ry soul in Thee;
I yield my flick - ering torch to Thee;
I can - not close my heart to Thee;
I dare not ask to fly from Thee;
I give Thee back the life I owe, That in Thine
My heart re - stores its bor - rowed ray, That in Thy
I trace the rain - bow through the rain, And feel the
I lay in dust life's glo - ry dead, And from the
o - cean depths its flow May rich - er, full - er be.
sun - shine's blaze its day May bright - er, fair - er be.
prom - ise is not vain That morn shall tear - less be.
ground there blos - soms red Life that shall end - less be.
A-MEN.

182 Wonderful Love of Jesus

But God, who is rich in mercy, for his great love wherewith he loved us. Eph. 2:4

Cora R. Turnbull, 1879-1928

Elton M. Roth, 1891-1951
Refrain arranged by Helen I. Young, b. 1931

1. Won-der - ful love of Je - sus, Sav - ing my soul from sin,
2. Won-der - ful love of Je - sus, Keep-ing me day and night,
3. Won-der - ful love of Je - sus, Choos-ing a life so small,
4. Won-der - ful love of Je - sus, Com - ing a - gain some day,
Lift - ing me from its shad - ows, Giv - ing me peace with - in.
When I dis - cern no dan - ger, When all my skies are bright.
Us - ing it for Thy glo - ry, Be - ing its all in all.
Com - ing per - haps at mid - night, Or when the dawn is gray!
Crown-ing my life with glad - ness, Flood-ing with joy my way;
Keep - ing 'mid tem-pest's fu - ry When I can scarce-ly stand,
Won - der - ful love of Je - sus, Pass - ing the an - gels by,
Ev - en so, come, Lord Je - sus, It can - not be too soon,
How can I keep from sing - ing! Heav - en has come to stay.
Keep - ing, se - cure - ly keep - ing! Safe in my Fa - ther's hand.
Lost in trans-port - ing rap - ture I can but won - der why!
Come at the gold - en sun - set Or at the wea - ry noon.

Wonderful Love of Jesus

Refrain
Oh, what won - der - ful love! Oh, what won - der - ful love!
'Tis a debt I can nev - er pay.
Lord, I fall at Thy feet, With my of - fering com - plete,
All I have shall be Thine own to - day.

183 Jesus Loves Even Me

... Christ Jesus came ... to save sinners; of whom I am chief. 1 Tim. 1:15

GLADNESS 10.10.10.10. with Refrain

Philip P. Bliss, 1838-1876 | Philip P. Bliss, 1838-1876

1. I am so glad that our Fa - ther in heaven Tells of His love in the Book He has given. Won - der - ful things in the Bi - ble I see; This is the dear - est, that Je - sus loves me.
2. Tho' I for - get Him and wan - der a - way, Still He doth love me wher - ev - er I stray. Back to His dear, lov - ing arms would I flee When I re - mem - ber that Je - sus loves me.
3. Oh, if there's on - ly one song I can sing When in His beau - ty I see the great King. This shall my song in e - ter - ni - ty be: "Oh, what a won - der that Je - sus loves me!"
Refrain
I am so glad that Je - sus loves me, Je - sus loves me, Je - sus loves me!
I am so glad that Je - sus loves me, Je - sus loves e - ven me!

More Love to Thee 184

And this I pray, that your love may abound yet more and more . . . Phil. 1:9

MORE LOVE TO THEE 6.4.6.4.6.6.4.4.
Elizabeth P. Prentiss, 1818-1878 — William H. Doane, 1832-1915

1. More love to Thee, O Christ, More love to Thee!
2. Once earth - ly joy I craved, Sought peace and rest;
3. Let sor - row do its work, Send grief and pain;
4. Then shall my lat - est breath Whis - per Thy praise;
Hear Thou the prayer I make On bend - ed knee;
Now Thee a - lone I seek, Give what is best;
Sweet are Thy mes - sen - gers, Sweet their re - frain,
This be the part - ing cry My heart shall raise;
This is my ear - nest plea: More love, O Christ, to Thee,
This all my prayer shall be: More love, O Christ, to Thee,
When they can sing with me: More love, O Christ, to Thee,
This still its prayer shall be: More love, O Christ, to Thee,
More love to Thee, More love to Thee! A - MEN.

185 Since the Fullness of His Love Came In

And to know the love of Christ, which passeth knowledge . . . Eph. 3:19

Eliza E. Hewitt, 1851-1920

Bentley D. Ackley, 1872-1958

1. Once my way was dark and drear - y, For my heart was full of sin,
2. There is grace for all the low - ly, Grace to keep the trust - ing soul,
3. Let me spread a - broad the sto - ry, Oth - er souls to Je - sus win;
But the sky is bright and cheer - y, Since the full-ness of His love came in.
Power to cleanse and make me ho - ly; Je - sus shall my yield-ed life con - trol.
For the cross is now my glo - ry, Since the full-ness of His love came in.
REFRAIN
I can nev - er tell how much I love Him, I can nev - er tell His love for me;
For it pass-eth hu-man meas-ure Like a deep, un-fath-omed sea;
deep, un-fath-omed sea;
'Tis re-deem-ing love in Christ my Sav-iour, In my soul the heaven-ly joys be-gin;

Since the Fullness of His Love Came In

And I live for Je - sus on - ly, Since the full-ness of His love came in.

How Can I Help but Love Him? 186

For God so loved the world, that he gave his only begotten Son . . . John 3:16

Elton M. Roth, 1891-1951 — Elton M. Roth, 1891-1951

1. Down from His splen-dor in glo - ry He came In - to a world of woe,
2. I am un - wor - thy to take of His grace, Won-der-ful grace so free;
3. He is the fair - est of thou-sands to me, His love is sweet and true;
Took on Him - self all my guilt and my shame– Why should He love me so?
Yet Je - sus suf-fered and died in my place, E'en for a soul like me.
Won - der - ful beau - ty in Him I now see, More than I ev - er knew.
REFRAIN
How can I help but love Him When He loved me so?
How can I help but love Him When He loved me so?

187 My Jesus, I Love Thee

We love him, because he first loved us. 1 John 4:19

GORDON 11.11.11.11.

William R. Featherstone, 1846-1873

Adoniram J. Gordon, 1836-1895

1. My Jesus, I love Thee, I know Thou art mine,
For Thee all the follies of sin I resign;
My gracious Redeemer, my Saviour art Thou,
If ever I loved Thee, my Jesus, 'tis now.
2. I love Thee because Thou hast first loved me,
And purchased my pardon on Calvary's tree;
I love Thee for wearing the thorns on Thy brow;
If ever I loved Thee, my Jesus, 'tis now.
3. I'll love Thee in life, I will love Thee in death,
And praise Thee as long as Thou lendest me breath;
And say, when the death-dew lies cold on my brow,
If ever I loved Thee, my Jesus, 'tis now.
4. In mansions of glory and endless delight,
I'll ever adore Thee in heaven so bright;
I'll sing with the glittering crown on my brow,
If ever I loved Thee, my Jesus, 'tis now.

I Love Thee, I Love Thee 188

I will love thee, O Lord, my strength. Psa. 18:1

I LOVE THEE 11.11.11.11.

Anonymous

From Jeremiah Ingall's *Christian Harmony,* 1805

1. I love Thee, I love Thee, I love Thee, my Lord;
2. I'm hap - py, I'm hap - py, Oh, won - drous ac - count!
3. O Je - sus, my Sav - iour, with Thee I am blest,
4. Oh, who's like my Sav - iour? He's Sa - lem's bright King;
I love Thee, my Sav - iour, I love Thee, my God;
My joys are im - mor - tal, I stand on the mount;
My life and sal - va - tion, my joy and my rest;
He smiles and He loves me and helps me to sing;
I love Thee, I love Thee, and that Thou dost know;
I gaze on my treas - ure and long to be there,
Thy name be my theme, and Thy love be my song;
I'll praise Him, I'll praise Him with notes loud and clear,
But how much I love Thee my ac - tions will show.
With Je - sus and an - gels and kin - dred so dear.
Thy grace shall in - spire both my heart and my tongue.
While riv - ers of pleas - ure my spir - it shall cheer.

189 I Know I Love Thee Better, Lord

... thy lovingkindness is better than life, my lips shall praise thee. Psa. 63:3

Frances R. Havergal, 1836-1879 | Ralph E. Hudson, 1843-1901

1. I know I love Thee bet - ter, Lord, Than an - y earth - ly joy;
2. I know that Thou art near - er still Than an - y earth - ly throng;
3. Thou hast put glad-ness in my heart; Then may I well be glad!
4. O Sav - iour, pre-cious Sav - iour mine! What will Thy pres - ence be,
For Thou hast giv - en me the peace Which noth - ing can de - stroy.
And sweet - er is the thought of Thee Than an - y love - ly song.
With - out the se - cret of Thy love I could not but be sad.
If such a life of joy can crown Our walk on earth with Thee?
REFRAIN
The half has nev - er yet been told Of love so full and free!
The half has nev - er yet been told— The blood it cleans-eth me!

He Keeps Me Singing

. . . singing and making melody in your heart to the Lord. Eph. 5:19

SWEETEST NAME 9.7.9.7. with Refrain

Luther B. Bridgers, 1884-1948 | Luther B. Bridgers, 1884-1948

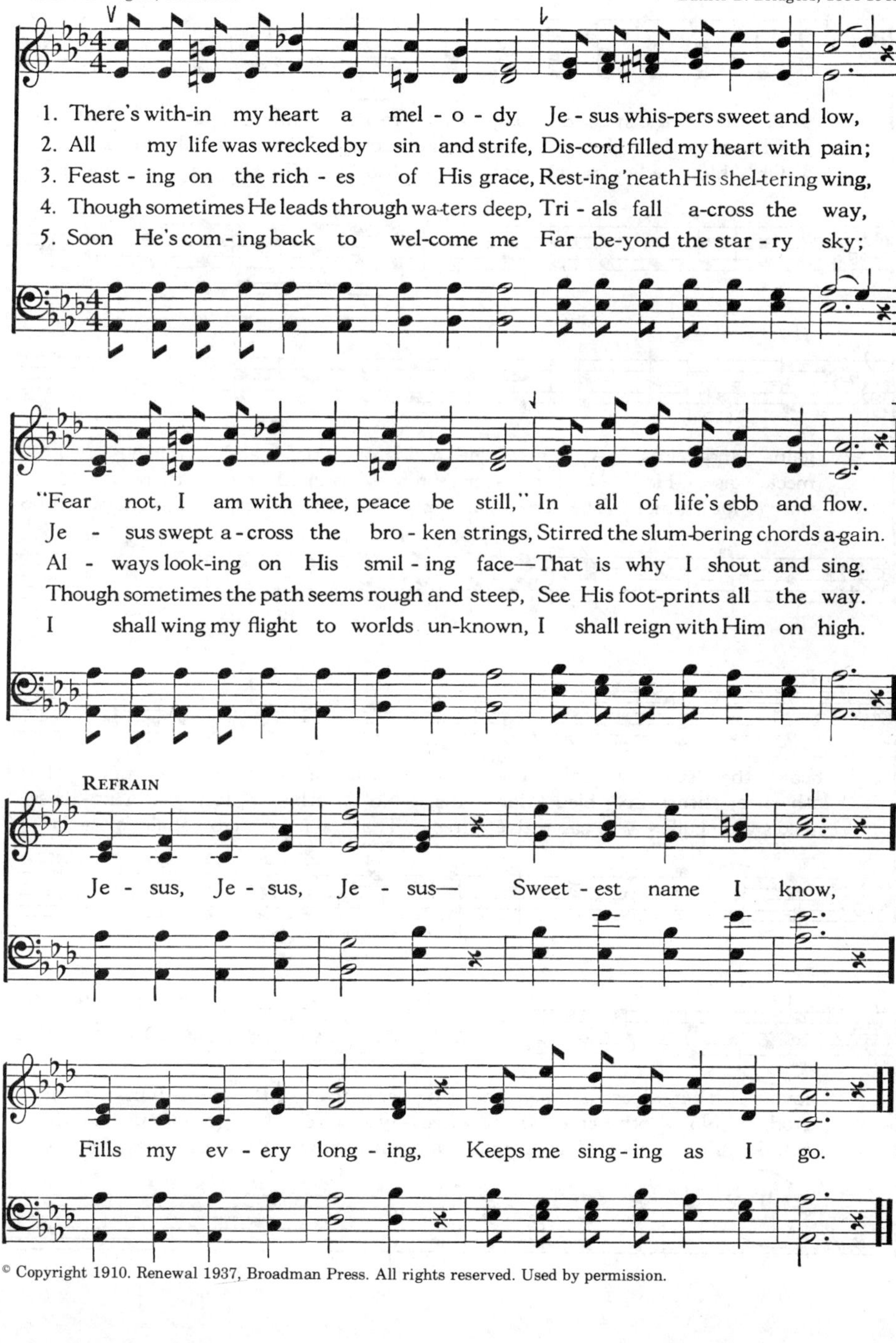
1. There's with-in my heart a mel - o - dy Je - sus whis-pers sweet and low,
2. All my life was wrecked by sin and strife, Dis-cord filled my heart with pain;
3. Feast - ing on the rich - es of His grace, Rest-ing 'neath His shel-tering wing,
4. Though sometimes He leads through wa-ters deep, Tri - als fall a-cross the way,
5. Soon He's com-ing back to wel-come me Far be-yond the star - ry sky;
"Fear not, I am with thee, peace be still," In all of life's ebb and flow.
Je - sus swept a - cross the bro - ken strings, Stirred the slum-bering chords a-gain.
Al - ways look-ing on His smil - ing face—That is why I shout and sing.
Though sometimes the path seems rough and steep, See His foot-prints all the way.
I shall wing my flight to worlds un-known, I shall reign with Him on high.
REFRAIN
Je - sus, Je - sus, Je - sus— Sweet - est name I know,
Fills my ev - ery long - ing, Keeps me sing - ing as I go.

191 The Story of the Cross

. . . *God forbid that I should glory, save in the cross of . . . Christ* . . . Gal. 6:14

Carrie E. Breck, 1855-1934 George C. Stebbins, 1846-1945

1. A - bove the sweet-est songs of earth, Through all the strife of
2. Oh, none but Je - sus bore such scorn, No strick - en lamb so
3. Oh, bless - ed cross of sac - ri - fice, Where Je - sus died for
gain and loss, A - bove the sounds of grief and mirth I
meek as He, No oth - er brow so bruised by thorn, No
me, for me! The cross of my Re - deem - er, Christ, Who
hear the sto - ry of the cross. That sto - ry is a tale of
oth - er heart so bled for me, No oth - er feet the wine - press
makes the guilt - y cap - tive free! That shin - ing cross shall ev - er
love That wipes a - way the sin - ner's tears; It makes him heir of
trod, No oth - er hand so free - ly gave, No Sav - iour like the
stand For all of love that man can know; Yet none may ful - ly

The Story of the Cross

heaven a - bove, And gives him joy through end - less years.
Son of God, No love like His to reach and save!
un - der - stand The love that God a - lone can show.
Refrain
'Tis the old, old sto - ry, 'Tis the old, old sto - ry of the cross;
old, the old,
When e - ter - ni - ty is hoar - y, Pre - cious still will be the sto - ry
Of re - demp - tion by the cross, Of re - demp - tion by the cross.

192 The Old Rugged Cross

. . . who for the joy . . . endured the cross, despising the shame . . . Heb. 12:2

OLD RUGGED CROSS Irregular with Refrain

George Bennard, 1873-1958 George Bennard, 1873-1958

1. On a hill far a - way stood an old rug - ged cross, The em-blem of
2. Oh, that old rug-ged cross, so de-spised by the world, Has a won-drous at -
3. In the old rug-ged cross, stained with blood so di - vine, A won - drous
4. To the old rug-ged cross I will ev - er be true, Its shame and re -
suf - fering and shame; And I love that old cross where the dear - est and best
trac - tion for me; For the dear Lamb of God left His glo - ry a - bove
beau - ty I see; For 'twas on that old cross Je - sus suf - fered and died
proach glad-ly bear; Then He'll call me some day to my home far a - way,
For a world of lost sin - ners was slain.
To bear it to dark Cal - va - ry.
To par - don and sanc - ti - fy me.
Where His glo - ry for - ev - er I'll share.
Refrain
So I'll cher - ish the old rug-ged cross, the old rug-ged cross,
cross,
Till my tro - phies at last I lay down; I will cling to the

The Old Rugged Cross

old rug-ged cross, And ex - change it some day for a crown.
cross, the old rug-ged cross,

Jesus Loves Me 193

... Suffer the little children to come unto me, and forbid them not ... Mark 10:14

JESUS LOVES ME 7.7.7.7. with Refrain

Anna B. Warner, 1820-1915

William B. Bradbury, 1816-1868

1. Je - sus loves me! this I know, For the Bi - ble tells me so.
2. Je - sus loves me! He who died Heav-en's gates to o - pen wide.
3. Je - sus loves me! He will stay Close be - side me all the way;
Lit - tle ones to Him be - long; They are weak but He is strong.
He will wash a - way my sin, Let His lit - tle child come in.
Thou hast bled and died for me; I will hence-forth live for Thee.
REFRAIN
Yes, Je-sus
loves me. Yes, Je-sus loves me. Yes, Je-sus loves me. The Bi-ble tells me so.

194 He Giveth More Grace

. . . every one . . . is given grace according to the measure of the gift of Christ. Eph. 4:7

HE GIVETH MORE GRACE 12.11.12.11. with Refrain

Annie J. Flint, 1862-1932

Hubert Mitchell, 20th century

1. He giv - eth more grace when the bur-dens grow great-er; He send - eth more strength when the la - bors in - crease, To add - ed af - flic - tion He add - eth His mer - cy; To mul - ti - plied tri - als, His mul - ti - plied peace.
2. When we have ex - haust - ed our store of en - dur-ance, When our strength has failed ere the day is half done, When we reach the end of our hoard-ed re - sourc - es, Our Fa - ther's full giv - ing is on - ly be - gun.
REFRAIN
His love has no lim - it; His grace has no meas - ure; His power has no boun - da - ry known un - to men. For out of His in - fi - nite

He Giveth More Grace

rich - es in Je - sus, He giv - eth, and giv - eth, and giv - eth a - gain!

Jesus, Thine All-Victorious Love 195

Behold, what manner of love the Father hath bestowed upon us . . . 1 John 3:1

Charles Wesley, 1707-1788

ORTONVILLE C.M. with repeat
Melody by Thomas Hastings, 1784-1872

1. Je - sus, Thine all vic - to - rious love Shed in my
2. Re - fin - ing fire, go through my heart, Il - lu - min -
3. No long - er then my heart shall mourn, While, pur - i -
4. My stead - fast soul, from fall - ing free, Shall then no
heart a - broad: Then shall my feet no long - er rove, Root -
ate my soul; Scat - ter Thy life through ev - ery part, And
fied by grace, I on - ly for His glo - ry burn, And
long - er move, While Christ is all the world to me, And
ed and fixed in God, Root - ed and fixed in God.
sanc - ti - fy the whole, And sanc - ti - fy the whole.
al - ways see His face, And al - ways see His face.
all my heart is love, And all my heart is love.

(For different harmony see No. 111)

196 Wonderful Grace of Jesus

. . . where sin abounded, grace did much more abound. Rom. 5:20

WONDERFUL GRACE Irregular with Refrain

Haldor Lillenas, 1885-1959 | Haldor Lillenas, 1885-1959

1. Won - der - ful grace of Je - sus, Great - er than all my sin—
2. Won - der - ful grace of Je - sus, Reach - ing to all the lost—
3. Won - der - ful grace of Je - sus, Reach - ing the most de - filed—
How shall my tongue des - cribe it, Where shall its praise be - gin?
By it I have been par - doned, Saved to the ut - ter - most;
By its trans-form - ing pow - er, Mak - ing him God's dear child,
Tak - ing a - way my bur - den, Set - ting my spir - it free;
Chains have been torn a - sun - der, Giv - ing me lib - er - ty;
Pur - chas - ing peace and heav - en, For all e - ter - ni - ty;
For the won - der - ful grace of Je - sus reach - es me.
For the won - der - ful grace of Je - sus reach - es me.
And the won - der - ful grace of Je - sus reach - es me.
Refrain
the match-less grace of Je - sus,
Won-der - ful the match-less grace of Je - - sus, Deep - er than the

Wonderful Grace of Jesus

the roll - ing sea; Won - - der - ful
might - y roll - ing sea; High - er than the moun - tain,
grace, all - suf - fi - cient for
spark - ling like a foun - tain, All - suf - fi - cient grace for e - ven
me, for e - ven me, Broad - er than the scope of my trans -
me, trans -
gres - sions, Great - er far than all my sin and shame,
gres - sions, sing it! my sin and shame,
Oh, mag - ni - fy the pre - cious name of Je - sus, Praise His name!

196

197 Amazing Grace

And God is able to make all grace abound toward you . . . 2 Cor. 9:8

AMAZING GRACE C.M.
American melody
Carrell and Clayton's *Virginia Harmony,* 1831
Arranged by Edwin O. Excell, 1851-1921

John Newton, 1725-1807
Stanza 6 by John P. Rees, circa b. 1859

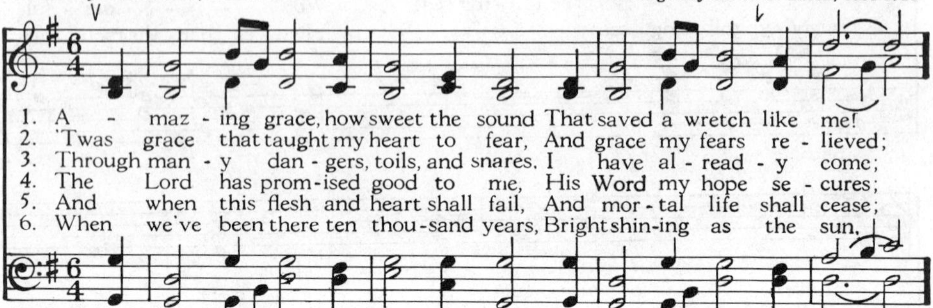
1. A - maz - ing grace, how sweet the sound That saved a wretch like me!
2. 'Twas grace that taught my heart to fear, And grace my fears re - lieved;
3. Through man - y dan - gers, toils, and snares, I have al - read - y come;
4. The Lord has prom - ised good to me, His Word my hope se - cures;
5. And when this flesh and heart shall fail, And mor - tal life shall cease;
6. When we've been there ten thou - sand years, Bright shin - ing as the sun,

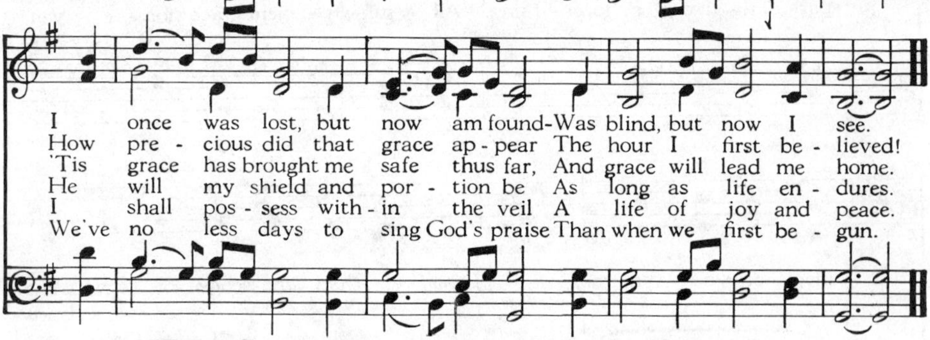
I once was lost, but now am found - Was blind, but now I see.
How pre - cious did that grace ap - pear The hour I first be - lieved!
'Tis grace has brought me safe thus far, And grace will lead me home.
He will my shield and por - tion be As long as life en - dures.
I shall pos - sess with - in the veil A life of joy and peace.
We've no less days to sing God's praise Than when we first be - gun.

198 How Sweet the Name of Jesus Sounds

. . . he hath by inheritance obtained a more excellent name . . . Heb. 1:4

ST. PETER C.M.
Alexander R. Reinagle, 1799-1877

John Newton, 1725-1807

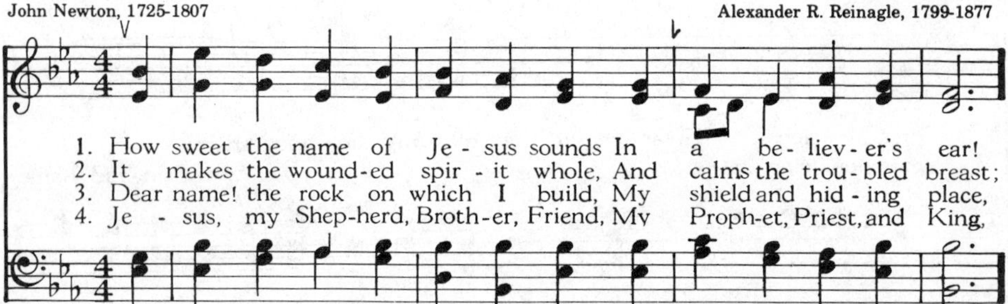
1. How sweet the name of Je - sus sounds In a be - liev - er's ear!
2. It makes the wound - ed spir - it whole, And calms the trou - bled breast;
3. Dear name! the rock on which I build, My shield and hid - ing place,
4. Je - sus, my Shep - herd, Broth - er, Friend, My Proph - et, Priest, and King,

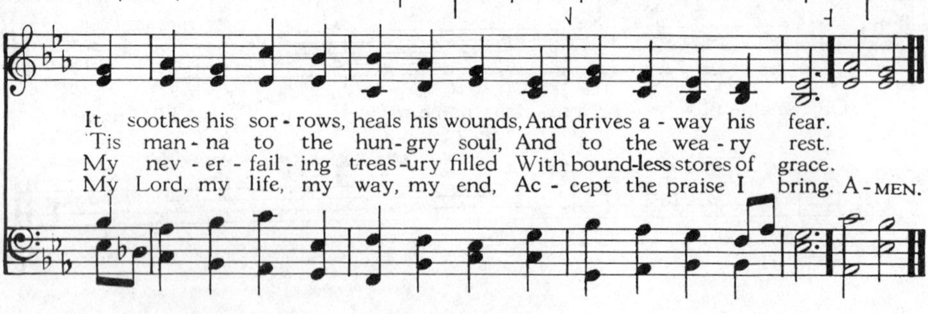
It soothes his sor - rows, heals his wounds, And drives a - way his fear.
'Tis man - na to the hun - gry soul, And to the wea - ry rest.
My nev - er - fail - ing treas - ury filled With bound - less stores of grace.
My Lord, my life, my way, my end, Ac - cept the praise I bring. A - MEN.

I Am His, and He Is Mine 199

. . . neither death, nor life, . . . shall be able to separate us from the love of God . . . Rom. 8:38-39

EVERLASTING LOVE 7.7.7.7.D.

George W. Robinson, 1838-1877

James Mountain, 1843-1933

1. Loved with ev - er - last - ing love, Led by grace that love to know;
2. Heaven a - bove is soft - er blue, Earth a - round is sweet - er green—
3. Things that once were wild a - larms Can - not now dis - turb my rest,
4. His for - ev - er, on - ly His; Who the Lord and me shall part?
Spir - it, breath - ing from a - bove, Thou hast taught me it is so!
Some-thing lives in ev - ery hue, Christ-less eyes have nev - er seen.
Closed in ev - er - last - ing arms, Pil - lowed on the lov - ing breast.
Ah, with what a rest of bliss, Christ can fill the lov - ing heart!
Oh, this full and per - fect peace! Oh, this trans - port all di - vine!
Birds with glad - der songs o'er - flow, Flowers with deep - er beau-ties shine,
Oh, to lie for - ev - er here, Doubt and care and self re - sign,
Heaven and earth may fade and flee, First - born light in gloom de - cline;
In a love which can - not cease, I am His, and He is mine.
Since I know, as now I know, I am His, and He is mine.
While He whis - pers in my ear— I am His, and He is mine.
But while God and I shall be, I am His, and He is mine.

200 Count Your Blessings

Many, . . . are thy wonderful works . . . more than can be numbered. Psa. 40:5

BLESSINGS 11.11.11.11. with Refrain

Johnson Oatman, Jr., 1856-1926

Edwin O. Excell, 1851-1921

1. When up - on life's bil - lows you are tem - pest-tossed, When you are dis -
2. Are you ev - er bur-dened with a load of care? Does the cross seem
3. When you look at oth - ers with their lands and gold, Think that Christ has
4. So, a - mid the con - flict, wheth-er great or small, Do not be dis -
cour-aged, think-ing all is lost, Count your man - y bless-ings, name them
heav - y you are called to bear? Count your man - y bless-ings, ev - ery
prom-ised you His wealth un - told; Count your man - y bless-ings, wealth can
heart-ened–God is o - ver all; Count your man - y bless-ings, an - gels
one by one, And it will sur - prise you what the Lord hath done.
doubt will fly, And you will keep sing - ing as the days go by.
nev - er buy Your re - ward in heav - en, nor your home on high.
will at - tend, Help and com - fort give you to your jour - ney's end.
Refrain
Count your bless-ings, name them one by one; Count your
Count your man-y bless-ings, name them one by one; Count your man-y
bless-ings, see what God hath done! Count your bless-ings,
bless-ings, see what God hath done! Count your man-y bless-ings,

Count Your Blessings

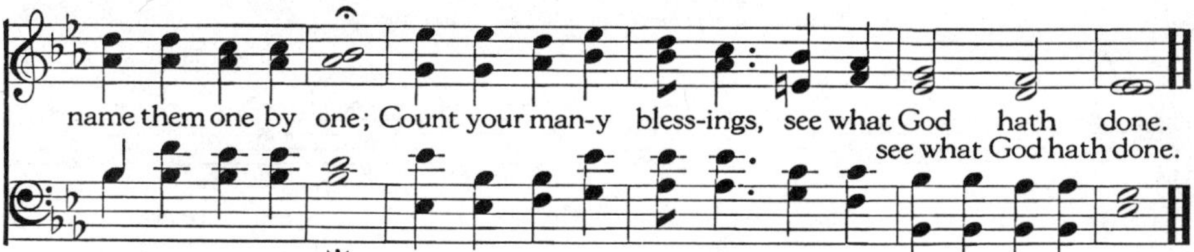
name them one by one; Count your man-y bless-ings, see what God hath done.
see what God hath done.

Jesus for Me 201

. . . If God be for us, who can be against us? Rom. 8:31

William J. Kirkpatrick, 1838-1921 — William J. Kirkpatrick, 1838-1921

1. Je - sus, my Sav - iour, is all things to me, Oh, what a won - der - ful
2. Je - sus in sick - ness, and Je - sus in health, Je - sus in pov - er - ty,
3. He is my ref - uge, my rock, and my tower, He is my fort - ress, my
4. He is my Proph - et, my Priest, and my King, He is my Bread of life,
5. Je - sus in sor - row, in joy, or in pain, Je - sus, my treas-ure in
Sav - iour is He; Guid - ing, pro - tect - ing, o'er life's roll - ing sea,
com - fort, or wealth; Sun - shine or tem - pest, what - ev - er it be,
strength, and my power; Life ev - er - last - ing, my days - man is He,
foun - tain, and spring; Bright Sun of right-eous - ness, day - star is He,
loss or in gain; Con - stant com - pan - ion, wher - e'er I may be,
Might - y de - liv - erer— Je - sus for me.
He is my safe - ty— Je - sus for me.
Bless - ed Re - deem - er— Je - sus for me.
Horn of sal - va - tion— Je - sus for me.
Liv - ing or dy - ing— Je - sus for me.
REFRAIN
Je - sus for me,
Je - sus for me, All the time, ev - ery-where, Je - sus for me!

202 Still Sweeter Every Day

My meditation of him shall be sweet . . . Psa. 104:34

W.C. Martin, 19th century

C. Austin Miles, 1868-1946

1. To Je - sus ev - ery day I find my heart is
2. His glo - ry broke up - on me when I saw Him
3. My heart is some - times heav - y, but He comes with
clos - er drawn; He's fair - er than the glo - ry of the
from a - far; He's fair - er than the lil - y, bright - er
sweet re - lief; He folds me to His bos - om when I
gold and pur - ple dawn; He's all my fan - cy pic - tures
than the morn - ing star; He fills and sat - is - fies my
droop with blight - ing grief; I love the Christ who all my
in its fair - est dreams, and more; Each day He grows still
long - ing spir - it o'er and o'er; Each day He grows still
bur - dens in His bod - y bore; Each day He grows still

Still Sweeter Every Day

Refrain
sweet - er than He was the day be - fore. The half
sweet - er than He was the day be - fore.
sweet - er than He was the day be - fore. The half can-not be fan -
can - not be fan - cied this side
cied on this side the gold - en shore, The half can - not be fan -
the gold - en shore;
Oh, there
cied on this side the gold - en shore; Oh, there He'll be still sweet -
He'll be still sweet - er than He ev - er was be - fore.
er than He ev - er was be - fore, than He ev - er was be - fore.

202

203 Jesus Is All the World to Me

. . . I count all things but loss for the excellency of the knowledge of Christ . . . Phil. 3:8

ELIZABETH Irregular

Will L. Thompson, 1847-1909 | Will L. Thompson, 1847-1909

1. Je - sus is all the world to me, My life, my joy, my all;
2. Je - sus is all the world to me, My friend in tri - als sore;
3. Je - sus is all the world to me, And true to Him I'll be;
4. Je - sus is all the world to me, I want no bet - ter friend;
He is my strength from day to day, With - out Him I would fall.
I go to Him for bless - ings and He gives them o'er and o'er.
Oh, how could I this friend de - ny When He's so true to me?
I trust Him now, I'll trust Him when Life's fleet - ing days shall end.
When I am sad, to Him I go, No oth - er one can cheer me so;
He sends the sun-shine and the rain, He sends the har - vest's gold - en grain;
Fol - low - ing Him I know I'm right, He watch - es o'er me day and night;
Beau - ti - ful life with such a friend, Beau - ti - ful life that has no end;
When I am sad He makes me glad— He's my friend.
Sun - shine and rain, har - vest of grain— He's my friend.
Fol - low - ing Him by day and night— He's my friend.
E - ter - nal life, e - ter - nal joy! He's my friend!

What a Friend We Have in Jesus 204

. . . let your requests be made known unto God. Phil. 4:6

FRIENDSHIP 8.7.8.7.D.

Joseph M. Scriven, 1819-1886

Charles C. Converse, 1832-1918

1. What a friend we have in Je - sus, All our sins and griefs to bear!
2. Have we tri - als and temp - ta - tions? Is there trou - ble an - y - where?
3. Are we weak and heav - y - la - den, Cum-bered with a load of care?
What a priv - i - lege to car - ry Ev - ery-thing to God in prayer!
We should nev - er be dis - cour - aged—Take it to the Lord in prayer.
Pre - cious Sav-iour, still our ref - uge— Take it to the Lord in prayer.
Oh, what peace we oft - en for - feit, Oh, what need-less pain we bear,
Can we find a friend so faith - ful Who will all our sor - rows share?
Do thy friends de-spise, for - sake thee? Take it to the Lord in prayer;
All be-cause we do not car - ry Ev - ery-thing to God in prayer!
Je - sus knows our ev - ery weak - ness—Take it to the Lord in prayer.
In His arms He'll take and shield thee; Thou wilt find a sol - ace there.

205 Speak, Lord, in the Stillness

I will hear what God the Lord will speak . . . Psa. 85:8

QUIETUDE 6.5.6.5.

E. May Grimes, 1868-1927

Harold Green, 1871-1931

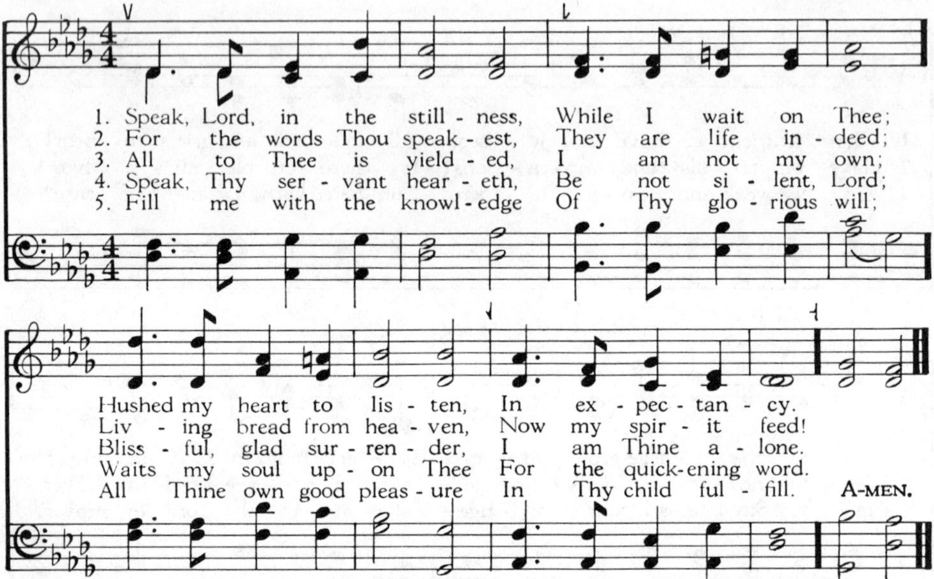
1. Speak, Lord, in the still - ness, While I wait on Thee; Hushed my heart to lis - ten, In ex - pec - tan - cy.
2. For the words Thou speak - est, They are life in - deed; Liv - ing bread from hea - ven, Now my spir - it feed!
3. All to Thee is yield - ed, I am not my own; Bliss - ful, glad sur - ren - der, I am Thine a - lone.
4. Speak, Thy ser - vant hear - eth, Be not si - lent, Lord; Waits my soul up - on Thee For the quick-ening word.
5. Fill me with the knowl - edge Of Thy glo - rious will; All Thine own good pleas - ure In Thy child ful - fill.
A-MEN.

206 Approach, My Soul, the Mercy Seat

. . . come boldly unto the throne of grace, that we may obtain mercy . . . Heb. 4:16

COVENANTERS (Pisgah) C.M.

John Newton, 1725-1807

American melody

1. Ap - proach, my soul, the mer - cy seat, Where Je - sus an - swers prayer; There hum - bly fall be - fore His feet, For none can per - ish there.
2. Thy prom - ise is my on - ly plea, With this I ven - ture nigh; Thou call - est bur - dened souls to Thee, And such, O Lord, am I.
3. Bowed down be - neath a load of sin, By Sa - tan sore - ly pressed, By war with - out and fears with - in, I come to Thee for rest.
4. O won - drous Love to bleed and die, To bear the cross and shame, That guilt - y sin - ners, such as I, Might plead Thy gra - cious name!

Send Refreshing

207

That he might sanctify and cleanse it with the washing of water by the word. Eph. 5:26

Daniel W. Whittle, 1840-1901

Arthur B. Hunt, 1890-1971

1. Heaven-ly Fa - ther, we Thy chil - dren, Gath-ered round our ris - en Lord,
2. Gra - cious gales of heaven-ly bless - ing In Thy love to us af - ford;
3. Weak and wea - ry in the con - flict, Wres-tling "not with flesh and blood,"
4. With Thy strength, O Mas - ter, gird us; Be our guide and be our guard;
Lift our hearts in ear - nest plead - ing— Oh, re - vive us by Thy Word!
Let us feel Thy Spir - it's pres - ence—Oh, re - vive us by Thy Word!
Help us, Lord, as faint we fal - ter— Oh, re - vive us by Thy Word!
Fill us with Thy Ho - ly Spir - it— Oh, re - vive us by Thy Word!
REFRAIN
Send re - fresh - ing, send re - fresh - ing From Thy pres-ence, gra - cious Lord!
Send re - fresh - ing, send re - fresh-ing And re - vive us by Thy Word!

208 Lord, I Have Shut the Door

. . . when thou hast shut thy door, pray to thy Father . . . Matt. 6:6

SANCTUARY 6.4.6.4.D.

William M. Runyan, 1870-1957 | William M. Runyan, 1870-1957

1. Lord, I have shut the door, Speak now the word Which in the din and throng Could not be heard; Hushed now my in - ner heart, Whis - per Thy will, While I have come a - part, While all is still.
2. Lord, I have shut the door, Here do I bow; Speak, for my soul at - tent Turns to Thee now. Re - buke Thou what is vain, Coun - sel my soul, Thy ho - ly will re - veal, My will con - trol.
3. In this blest qui - et - ness Clam - or - ings cease; Here in Thy pres - ence dwells In - fi - nite peace; Yon - der the strife and cry, Yon - der, the sin. Lord, I have shut the door, Thou art with - in!
4. Lord, I have shut the door, Strength-en my heart; Yon - der a - waits the task— I share a part. On - ly through grace be-stowed May I be true; Here, while a - lone with Thee, My strength re - new.

Sweet Hour of Prayer

209

. . . Peter and John went . . . into the temple at the hour of prayer . . . Acts 3:1

HOUR OF PRAYER L.M.D.

William W. Walford, 1772-1850

William B. Bradbury, 1816-1868

1. Sweet hour of prayer, sweet hour of prayer That calls me from a world of care,
2. Sweet hour of prayer, sweet hour of prayer, Thy wings shall my pe - ti - tion bear
3. Sweet hour of prayer, sweet hour of prayer, May I thy con - so - la - tion share
And bids me at my Fa-ther's throne, Make all my wants and wish - es known.
To Him whose truth and faith - ful - ness En - gage the wait - ing soul to bless.
Till, from Mount Pis-gah's loft - y height, I view my home and take my flight.
In sea - sons of dis - tress and grief, My soul has oft - en found re - lief,
And since He bids me seek His face, Be - lieve His Word, and trust His grace,
This robe of flesh I'll drop, and rise To seize the ev - er - last - ing prize,
And oft es-caped the tempt-er's snare, By thy re - turn, sweet hour of prayer!
I'll cast on Him my ev - ery care And wait for thee, sweet hour of prayer!
And shout, while pass-ing through the air, "Fare-well, fare-well, sweet hour of prayer!"

210 Prayer Is the Soul's Sincere Desire

Praying always with all prayer . . . in the Spirit . . . Eph. 6:18

EVAN C.M.

James Montgomery, 1771-1854 — William H. Havergal, 1793-1870

1. Prayer is the soul's sin - cere de - sire, Un - ut - tered or ex - pressed;
2. Prayer is the bur - den of a sigh, The fall - ing of a tear.
3. Prayer is the Chris-tian's vi - tal breath, The Chris-tian's na - tive air,
4. Prayer is the con - trite sin - ner's voice Re - turn - ing from his ways,
5. O Thou, by whom we come to God, The Life, the Truth, the Way,

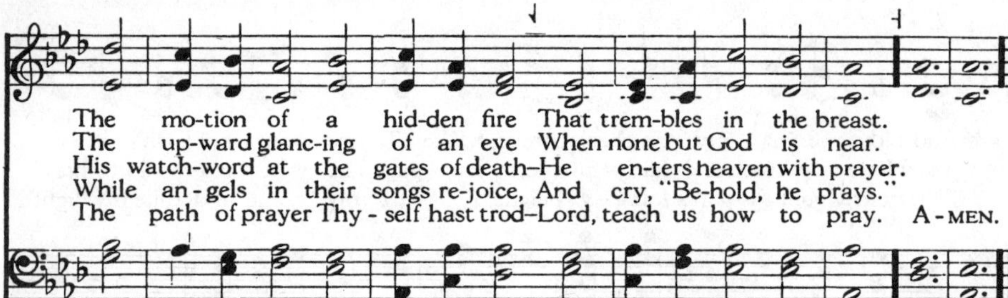
The mo-tion of a hid-den fire That trem-bles in the breast.
The up-ward glanc-ing of an eye When none but God is near.
His watch-word at the gates of death–He en-ters heaven with prayer.
While an - gels in their songs re-joice, And cry, "Be-hold, he prays."
The path of prayer Thy - self hast trod–Lord, teach us how to pray. A-MEN.

211 From Every Stormy Wind That Blows

. . . I will commune with thee from above the mercy seat . . . Exod. 25:22

RETREAT L.M.

Hugh Stowell, 1799-1865 — Melody by Thomas Hastings, 1784-1872

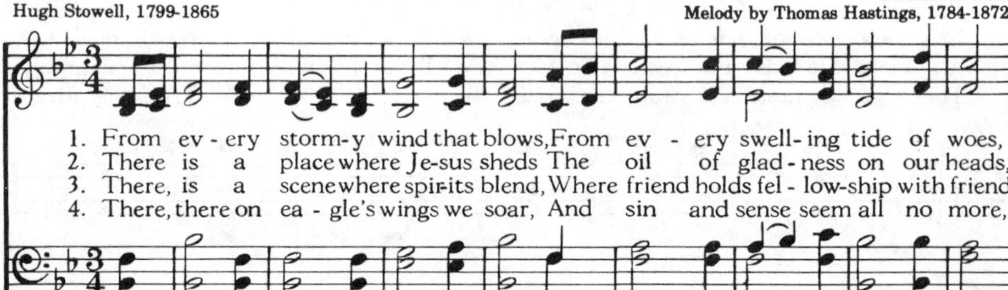
1. From ev - ery storm-y wind that blows, From ev - ery swell- ing tide of woes,
2. There is a place where Je-sus sheds The oil of glad - ness on our heads,
3. There, is a scene where spir-its blend, Where friend holds fel - low-ship with friend;
4. There, there on ea - gle's wings we soar, And sin and sense seem all no more,

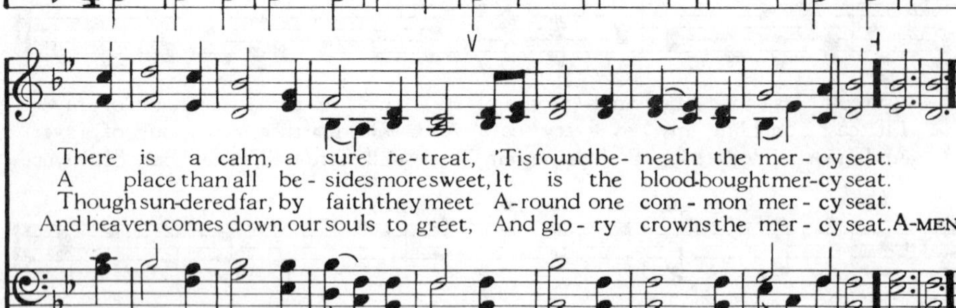
There is a calm, a sure re - treat, 'Tis found be - neath the mer - cy seat.
A place than all be - sides more sweet, It is the blood-bought mer - cy seat.
Though sun-dered far, by faith they meet A-round one com - mon mer - cy seat.
And heaven comes down our souls to greet, And glo - ry crowns the mer - cy seat. A-MEN.

(For different harmony see No. 426)

Take Time to Be Holy

Follow peace with all men, and holiness . . . Heb. 12:14

William D. Longstaff, 1822-1894

HOLINESS 6.5.6.5.D.
George C. Stebbins, 1846-1945

1. Take time to be ho - ly— Speak oft with thy Lord;
2. Take time to be ho - ly— The world rush - es on;
3. Take time to be ho - ly— Let Him be thy guide,
4. Take time to be ho - ly— Be calm in thy soul,
A - bide in Him al - ways, And feed on His Word.
Spend much time in se - cret With Je - sus a - lone.
And run not be - fore Him What - ev - er be - tide.
Each thought and each mo - tive Be - neath His con - trol.
Make friends of God's chil - dren; Help those who are weak,
By look - ing to Je - sus, Like Him thou shalt be;
In joy or in sor - row, Still fol - low thy Lord;
Thus, led by His Spir - it To foun - tains of love,
For - get - ting in noth - ing His bless - ing to seek.
Thy friends in thy con - duct His like - ness shall see.
And, look - ing to Je - sus, Still trust in His Word.
Thou soon shalt be fit - ted For serv - ice a - bove.

213 Is Your All on the Altar?

I beseech you . . . that ye present your bodies a living sacrifice . . . Rom. 12:1

Elisha A. Hoffman, 1839-1929 | Elisha A. Hoffman, 1839-1929

1. You have longed for sweet peace, and for faith to in - crease, And have
2. Would you walk with the Lord in the light of His Word, And have
3. Oh, we nev - er can know what the Lord will be - stow Of the
4. Who can tell all the love He will send from a - bove! Oh, how
ear - nest - ly, fer - vent - ly prayed; But you can - not have rest, or be
peace and con - tent - ment al - way? You must do His sweet will to be
bless - ings for which we have prayed, Till our bod - y and soul He doth
hap - py our hearts will be made! Oh, what fel - low - ship sweet we shall
per - fect - ly blest, Un - til all on the al - tar is laid.
free from all ill; On the al - tar your all you must lay.
ful - ly con - trol, And our all on the al - tar is laid.
share at His feet, When our all on the al - tar is laid!
REFRAIN
Is your all on the al - tar of sac - ri - fice laid? Your heart, does the
Spir - it con - trol? You can on - ly be blest and have

Is Your All on the Altar?

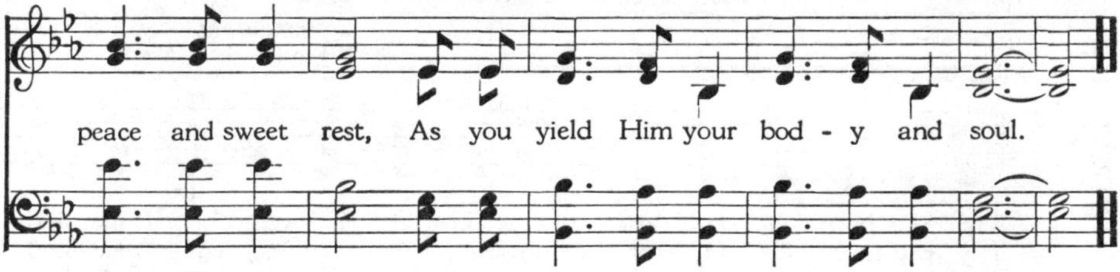
peace and sweet rest, As you yield Him your bod - y and soul.

I Choose Thee, Blessed Will of God 214

I delight to do thy will, O my God . . . Psa. 40:8

May A. Stephens, 1865-1935

Kenneth Mackenzie, 1853-1943
Harmony adapted

1. I choose Thee, bless-ed will of God! In Thee a - lone my heart can rest;
2. I choose Thee, bless-ed will of God! No long - er shall this will of mine,
3. I choose Thee, bless-ed will of God! For in the cir-cling of Thine arms,
The cur - rent of Thy love, I know, Can on - ly bear me to Thy breast.
In self - ish blind-ness to Thy love, Its hate - ful choice and strength com-bine.
The glad - dest spring of joy I find; Out - side Thee fears and strange a - larms.
REFRAIN
I choose Thee, bless-ed will of God! In Thee a - lone my heart can rest.

215 Sweet Will of God

. . . he that doeth the will of God abideth forever. 1 John 2:17

SPRING HILL C.M. with Refrain
Melody by Lelia N. Morris, 1862-1929
Stanza Harmony by J. Buchanan MacMillan, b. 1915

Lelia N. Morris, 1862-1929

1. My stub-born will at last has yield - ed; I would be Thine, and Thine a - lone; And this the prayer my lips are bring - ing, "Lord, let in me Thy will be done."
2. Thy pre-cious will, O con - quering Sav - iour, Doth now em - brace and com - pass me; All dis - cords hushed, my peace a riv - er, My soul a pris-oned bird set free.
3. Shut in with Thee, O Lord, for - ev - er, My way-ward feet no more to roam; What power from Thee my soul can sev - er? The cen - ter of God's will my home.
REFRAIN
Sweet will of God, still fold me clos - er Till I am whol - ly lost in Thee; Sweet will of God, still fold me clos-er Till I am whol - ly lost in Thee.

I Surrender All

. . . Lo, we have left all, and have followed thee. Mark 10:28

Judson W. Van De Venter, 1855-1939

SURRENDER 8.7.8.7. with Refrain
Winfield S. Weeden, 1847-1908

1. All to Je - sus I sur - ren - der; All to Him I free - ly give.
2. All to Je - sus I sur - ren - der; Hum - bly at His feet I bow,
3. All to Je - sus I sur - ren - der; Make me, Sav - iour, whol - ly Thine;
4. All to Je - sus I sur - ren - der; Lord, I give my - self to Thee.
5. All to Je - sus I sur - ren - der; Now I feel the sa - cred flame.
I will ev - er love and trust Him, In His pres - ence dai - ly live.
World - ly pleas - ures all for - sak - en. Take me, Je - sus, take me now.
Let me feel the Ho - ly Spir - it, Tru - ly know that Thou art mine.
Fill me with Thy love and pow - er; Let Thy bless - ing fall on me.
Oh, the joy of full sal - va - tion! Glo - ry, glo - ry to His name!
Refrain
I sur - ren - der all. I sur - ren - der all.
All to Thee, my bless - ed Sav - iour, I sur - ren - der all.

217 I Will Say "Yes" to Jesus

. . . doing the will of God from the heart. Eph. 6:6

Albert B. Simpson, 1843-1919

J.H. Burke, 19th century

1. I will say "Yes" to Je - sus; Oft it was "No" be - fore, As He
2. I will say "Yes" to Je - sus. His prom - is - es I'll claim, And on
3. I will say "Yes" to Je - sus, To all that He com - mands, I will
4. I will say "Yes" to Je - sus, What-e'er His hands may bring; And, though
knocked at my heart's proud en - trance, And I firm - ly barred the door; But I've
ev - ery check He en - dors - es I'll dare to write my name; I will
has - ten to do His bid - ding With will - ing heart and hands; I will
clouds hang o-ver my path - way, My trust - ing heart will sing. I will
made a com-plete sur - ren - der, And given Him right of way; And
put my "A - men" wher - ev - er My God has put His "Yea," And
lis - ten to hear His whis - pers, And learn His will each day, And
fol - low wher-e'er He lead - eth; My Shep-herd knows the way, And
hence-forth it is al - ways "Yes," What - ev - er He may say.
ev - er bold - ly an - swer "Yes," What - ev - er He may say.
al - ways glad - ly an - swer "Yes," What - ev - er He may say.
while I live I'll an - swer "Yes," What - ev - er He may say.
REFRAIN
I will say "Yes" to Je - sus, "Yes, Lord, for - ev - er yes.

I Will Say "Yes" to Jesus

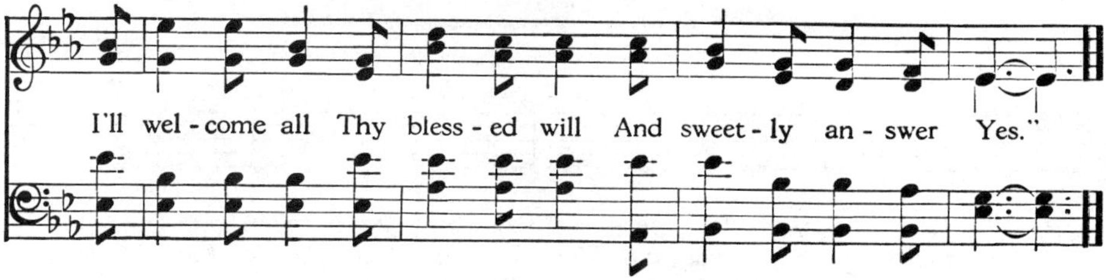
I'll wel - come all Thy bless - ed will And sweet - ly an - swer Yes."

Fully Surrendered 218

. . . yield your members servants to righteousness unto holiness. Rom. 6:19

Alfred C. Snead, 1884-1961 | George C. Stebbins, 1846-1945

1. Ful - ly sur - ren - dered, Lord, I would be, Ful - ly sur - ren - dered,
2. Ful - ly sur - ren - dered— life, time, and all, All Thou hast given me
3. Ful - ly sur - ren - dered— sil - ver and gold, His, who hath given me
4. Ful - ly sur - ren - dered— Lord, I am Thine; Ful - ly sur - ren - dered,
dear Lord, to Thee. All on the al - tar laid, Sur - ren - der
held at Thy call. Speak but the word to me, Glad - ly I'll
rich - es un - told. All, all be - long to Thee, For Thou didst
Sav - iour di - vine! Live Thou Thy life in me; All full - ness
ful - ly made, Thou hast my ran - som paid; I yield to Thee.
fol - low Thee, Now and e - ter - nal - ly O - bey my Lord.
pur - chase me, Thine ev - er - more to be, Je - sus, my Lord.
dwells in Thee; Not I, but Christ in me, Christ all in all.

219 All for Jesus

(FIRST TUNE)

. . . bringing into captivity every thought to the obedience of Christ. 2 Cor. 10:5

CONSTANCY 8.7.8.7. with Refrain

Mary D. James, 1810-1883

Anonymous

1. All for Je - sus, all for Je - sus! All my be - ing's ran - somed powers,
2. Let my hands per - form His bid - ding, Let my feet run in His ways,
3. Since my eyes were fixed on Je - sus, I've lost sight of all be - side,
4. Oh, what won - der! How a - maz - ing! Je - sus, glo - rious King of kings,
All my thoughts and words and do - ings, All my days and all my hours.
Let my eyes see Je - sus on - ly, Let my lips speak forth His praise.
So en - chained my spir - it's vi - sion, Look - ing at the Cru - ci - fied.
Deigns to call me His be - lov - ed, Lets me rest be - neath His wings.
Refrain
All for Je - sus, all for Je - sus! All my days and all my hours;
All for Je - sus, all for Je - sus! Let my lips speak forth His praise;
All for Je - sus, all for Je - sus! Look - ing at the Cru - ci - fied;
All for Je - sus, all for Je - sus! Rest - ing now be - neath His wings;
All for Je - sus, all for Je - sus! All my days and all my hours.
All for Je - sus, all for Je - sus! Let my lips speak forth His praise.
All for Je - sus, all for Je - sus! Look - ing at the Cru - ci - fied.
All for Je - sus, all for Je - sus! Rest - ing now be - neath His wings.

All for Jesus 220

(SECOND TUNE)

WYCLIFF 8.7.8.7.

Mary D. James, 1810-1883

John Stainer, 1840-1901

1. All for Je - sus, all for Je - sus! All my be - ing's ran-somed powers,
All my thoughts and words and do - ings, All my days and all my hours.

(Omit Refrain when this tune is used)

Jesus Calls Us 221

And he said unto them, Follow me . . . Matt. 4:19

GALILEE 8.7.8.7.

Cecil F.H. Alexander, 1818-1895

William H. Jude, 1852-1922

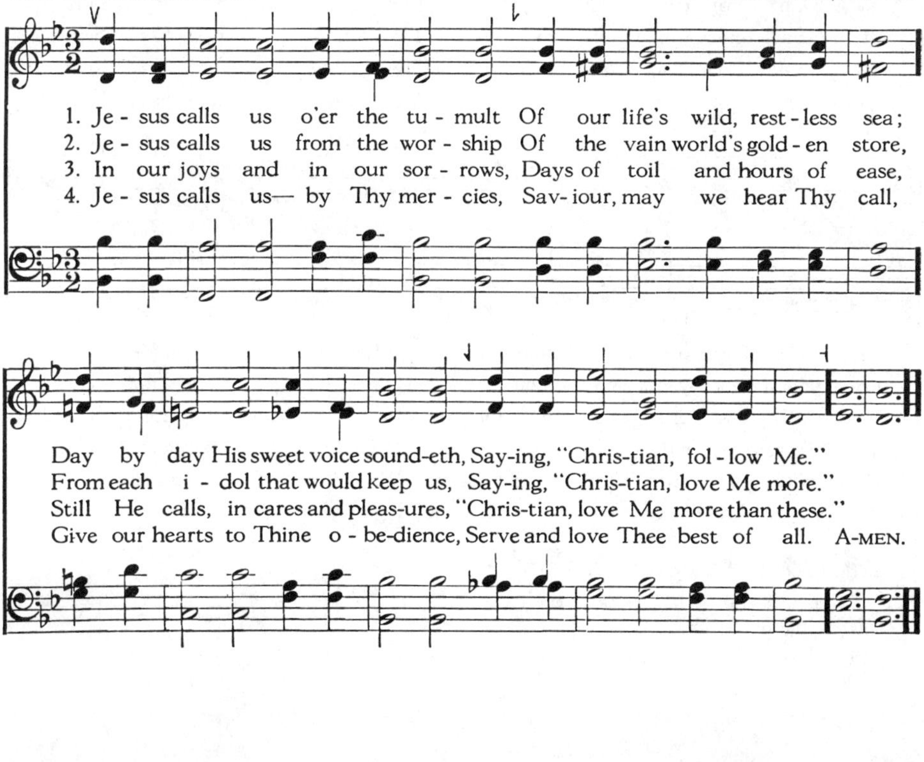
1. Je - sus calls us o'er the tu - mult Of our life's wild, rest - less sea;
2. Je - sus calls us from the wor - ship Of the vain world's gold - en store,
3. In our joys and in our sor - rows, Days of toil and hours of ease,
4. Je - sus calls us— by Thy mer - cies, Sav- iour, may we hear Thy call,
Day by day His sweet voice sound-eth, Say-ing, "Chris-tian, fol - low Me."
From each i - dol that would keep us, Say-ing, "Chris-tian, love Me more."
Still He calls, in cares and pleas-ures, "Chris-tian, love Me more than these."
Give our hearts to Thine o - be-dience, Serve and love Thee best of all. A-MEN.

222 Thy Life Was Given for Me

. . . he died for all, that they which live should . . . live . . . unto him . . . 2 Cor. 5:15

Frances R. Havergal, 1836-1879
Adapted in *Church Hymns*

KENOSIS 6.6.6.6.8.6.8.6.
Melody by Philip P. Bliss, 1838-1876

1. Thy life was given for me; Thy blood, O Lord, was shed,
2. Long years were spent for me In wea - ri - ness and woe,
3. Thy Fa - ther's throne of light, Thy rain - bow - cir - cled throne,
4. Thou, Lord, hast borne for me More than my tongue can tell
5. And Thou hast brought to me Down from Thy home a - bove
6. Oh, let my life be given, My years for Thee be spent,

That I might ran - somed be And quick - ened from the dead.
That through e - ter - ni - ty Thy glo - ry I might know.
Were left for earth - ly night, For wan-derings sad and lone;
Of bit - terest ag - o - ny To res - cue me from hell.
Sal - va - tion full and free, Thy par - don, and Thy love.
World fet - ters all be riven, And joy with suf - fering blent.

Thy life, Thy life was given for me—What have I given for Thee?
Long years, long years were spent for me—Have I spent one for Thee?
Yes, all, yes, all was left for me—Have I left aught for Thee?
Thou suf-feredst, suf - feredst all for me—What have I borne for Thee?
Great gifts, great gifts Thou brought-est me—What have I brought to Thee?
Thou gavest, Thou gavest Thy - self for me; I give my - self to Thee.

Thy Life Was Given for Me

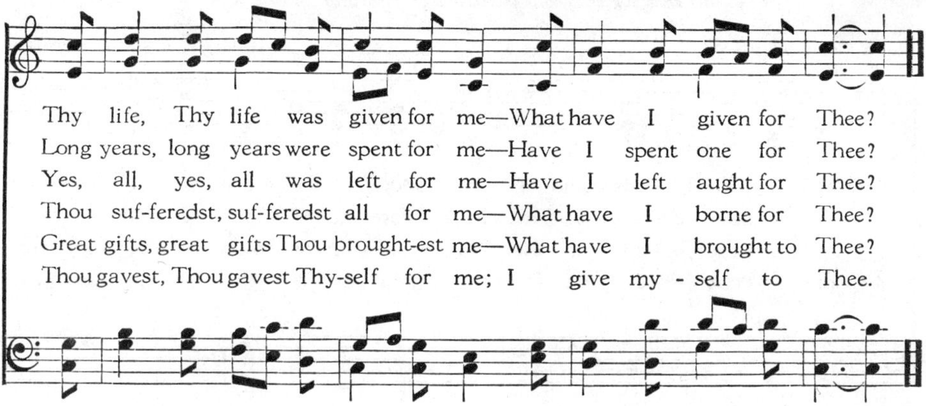
Thy life, Thy life was given for me—What have I given for Thee?
Long years, long years were spent for me—Have I spent one for Thee?
Yes, all, yes, all was left for me—Have I left aught for Thee?
Thou suf-feredst, suf-feredst all for me—What have I borne for Thee?
Great gifts, great gifts Thou brought-est me—What have I brought to Thee?
Thou gavest, Thou gavest Thy-self for me; I give my - self to Thee.

We Give Thee But Thine Own 223

. . . of thine own have we given thee. 1 Chron. 29:14

FRANCONIA S.M.
From *Harmonischer Liederschatz,* 1738
Adapted by William H. Havergal, 1793-1870

William W. How, 1823-1897

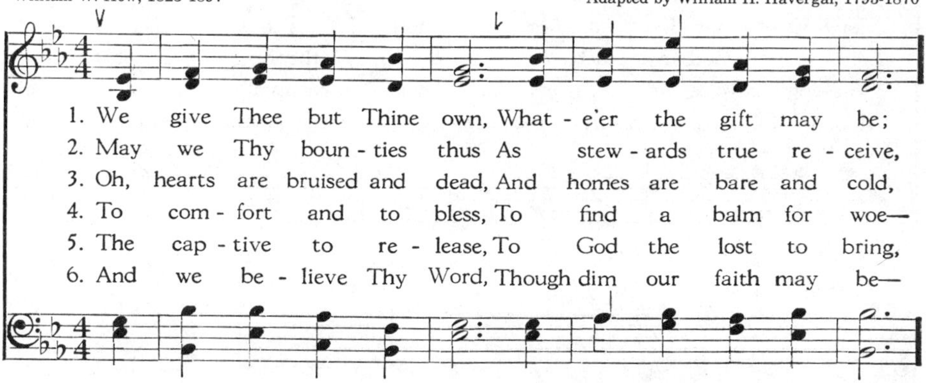
1. We give Thee but Thine own, What - e'er the gift may be;
2. May we Thy boun - ties thus As stew - ards true re - ceive,
3. Oh, hearts are bruised and dead, And homes are bare and cold,
4. To com - fort and to bless, To find a balm for woe—
5. The cap - tive to re - lease, To God the lost to bring,
6. And we be - lieve Thy Word, Though dim our faith may be—

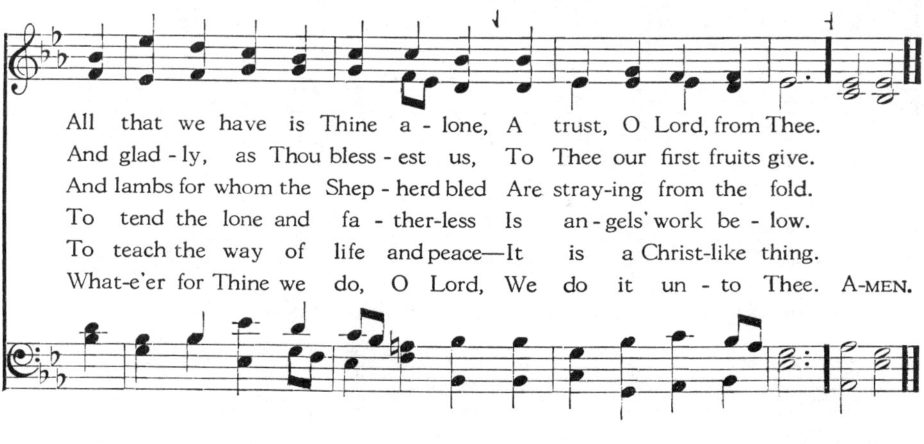
All that we have is Thine a - lone, A trust, O Lord, from Thee.
And glad - ly, as Thou bless - est us, To Thee our first fruits give.
And lambs for whom the Shep - herd bled Are stray-ing from the fold.
To tend the lone and fa - ther-less Is an - gels' work be - low.
To teach the way of life and peace—It is a Christ-like thing.
What-e'er for Thine we do, O Lord, We do it un - to Thee. A-MEN.

224 More about Jesus

But grow in grace, and in the knowledge of our Lord . . . 2 Pet. 3:18

SWENEY L.M. with Refrain

Eliza E. Hewitt, 1851-1920

Melody by John R. Sweney, 1837-1899

1. More a-bout Je-sus would I know, More of His grace to oth-ers show,
More of His sav-ing full-ness see, More of His love who died for me.
2. More a-bout Je-sus let me learn, More of His ho-ly will dis-cern;
Spir-it of God, my teach-er be, Show-ing the things of Christ to me.
3. More a-bout Je-sus in His Word–Hold-ing com-mun-ion with my Lord,'
Hear-ing His voice in ev-ery line, Mak-ing each faith-ful say-ing mine.
4. More a-bout Je-sus on His throne, Rich-es in glo-ry all His own;
More of His king-dom's sure in-crease; More of His com-ing, Prince of Peace.
REFRAIN
More, more a-bout Je-sus, More, more a-bout Je-sus!
More of His sav-ing full-ness see, More of His love who died for me!

Take My Life, and Let It Be 225

. . . yield your members servants to righteousness unto holiness. Rom. 6:19

HENDON 7.7.7.7. with repeat

Frances R. Havergal, 1836-1879

Melody by Henri A.C. Malan, 1787-1864

1. Take my life, and let it be Con - se - crat - ed, Lord, to Thee. Take my mo - ments and my days, Let them flow in cease - less praise, Let them flow in cease - less praise.
2. Take my hands, and let them move At the im - pulse of Thy love. Take my feet, and let them be Swift and beau - ti - ful for Thee, Swift and beau - ti - ful for Thee.
3. Take my voice, and let me sing Al - ways, on - ly for my King. Take my lips, and let them be Filled with mes - sag - es from Thee, Filled with mes - sag - es from Thee.
4. Take my sil - ver and my gold, Not a mite would I with - hold. Take my in - tel - lect, and use Ev - ery power as Thou shalt choose, Ev - ery power as Thou shalt choose.
5. Take my will, and make it Thine; It shall be no long - er mine. Take my heart; it is Thine own; It shall be Thy roy - al throne, It shall be Thy roy - al throne.
6. Take my love; my Lord, I pour At Thy feet its treas - ure store. Take my - self, and I will be Ev - er, on - ly, all for Thee, Ev - er, on - ly, all for Thee.

226 Have Thine Own Way, Lord!

... as the clay is in the potter's hand, so are ye in mine hand ... Jer. 18:6

ADELAIDE 5.4.5.4.D.

Adelaide A. Pollard, 1862-1934

George C. Stebbins, 1846-1945

1. Have Thine own way, Lord! Have Thine own way! Thou art the
2. Have Thine own way, Lord! Have Thine own way! Search me and
3. Have Thine own way, Lord! Have Thine own way! Wound-ed and
4. Have Thine own way, Lord! Have Thine own way! Hold o'er my
Pot - ter, I am the clay. Mold me and make me
try me, Mas - ter, to - day! Whit - er than snow, Lord,
wea - ry, Help me I pray! Pow - er— all pow - er—
be - ing Ab - so - lute sway! Fill with Thy Spir - it
Aft - er Thy will, While I am wait - ing Yield - ed and still.
Wash me just now, As in Thy pres - ence Hum - bly I bow.
Sure - ly is Thine! Touch me and heal me, Sav - iour di - vine!
Till all shall see Christ on - ly, al - ways, Liv - ing in me!

I Would Be Like Jesus

. . . we all, . . . are changed into the same image from glory to glory . . . 2 Cor. 3:18

James Rowe, 1865-1933

Bentley D. Ackley, 1872-1958

1. Earth - ly pleas - ures vain - ly call me, I would be like Je - sus;
2. He has bro - ken ev - ery fet - ter, I would be like Je - sus;
3. All the way from earth to glo - ry, I would be like Je - sus;
4. That in heav - en He may meet me, I would be like Je - sus;
would be like Je - sus;
Noth - ing world - ly shall en-thrall me, I would be like Je - sus.
That my soul may serve Him bet - ter, I would be like Je - sus.
Tell - ing o'er and o'er the sto - ry, I would be like Je - sus.
That His words, "Well done," may greet me, I would be like Je - sus.
would be like Je - sus.
REFRAIN
Be like Je - sus, this my song, In the home and in the throng;
Be like Je - sus all day long! I would be like Je - sus.

228 Let Me Come Closer to Thee, Jesus

Let us draw near with a true heart . . . Heb. 10:22

J.L. Lyne, 19th century

LLANTHONY ABBEY 9.6.9.6.
From *Llanthony Abbey Hymns*

1. Let me come clos - er to Thee, Je - sus, Oh, clos-er day by day;
2. Let me show forth Thy beau - ty, Je - sus, Like sun-shine on the hills;
3. Yes, like a foun - tain, pre - cious Je - sus, Make me and let it be;
4. In all my heart and will, O Je - sus, Be al - to - geth - er King;
5. Thirst-ing and hung - ering for Thee, Je - sus, With bless-ed hun - ger here,

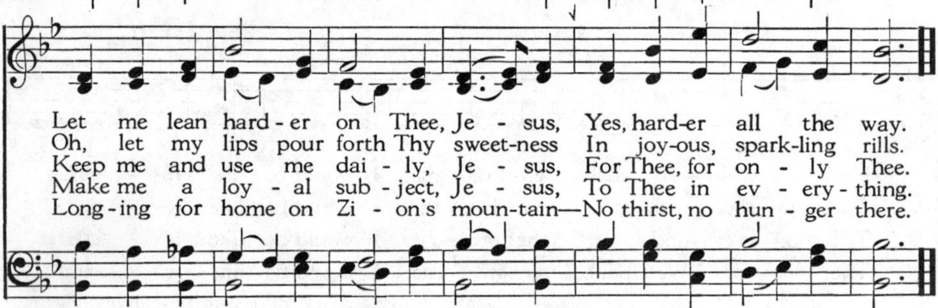
Let me lean hard - er on Thee, Je - sus, Yes, hard-er all the way.
Oh, let my lips pour forth Thy sweet-ness In joy-ous, spark-ling rills.
Keep me and use me dai - ly, Je - sus, For Thee, for on - ly Thee.
Make me a loy - al sub - ject, Je - sus, To Thee in ev - ery - thing.
Long - ing for home on Zi - on's moun-tain—No thirst, no hun - ger there.

229 I'll Live for Him

For to me to live is Christ, and to die is gain. Phil. 1:21

Ralph E. Hudson, 1843-1901

DUNBAR 8.8.8.9. with Refrain
C.R. Dunbar, 19th century

1. My life, my love I give to Thee, Thou Lamb of God, who died for me;
2. I now be - lieve Thou dost re - ceive, For Thou hast died that I may live:
3. O Thou, who died on Cal - va - ry To save my soul and make me free,
REFRAIN
I'll live for Him who died for me; How hap - py then my soul shall be!

D. C. for Refrain
Oh, may I ev - er faith-ful be, My Sav - iour and my God!
And now hence-forth I'll trust in Thee, My Sav - iour and my God!
I con - se - crate my - self to Thee, My Sav - iour and my God!
I'll live for Him who died for me, My Sav - iour and my God!

Close to Thee

230

He that saith, he abideth in him ought himself also so to walk . . . 1 John 2:6

Fanny J. Crosby, 1820-1915

Silas J. Vail, 1818-1884

231 Oh, to Be Like Thee, Blessed Redeemer

. . . to be conformed to the image of his Son . . . Rom 8:29

Thomas O. Chisholm, 1866-1960

CHRISTLIKE 10.9.10.9. with Refrain
William J. Kirkpatrick, 1838-1921

Deeper and Deeper

232

O the depth of the riches both of the wisdom and knowledge of God! . . . Rom. 11:33

Oswald J. Smith, b. 1890 — Oswald J. Smith, b. 1890

233 My Spirit, Soul, and Body

. . . I pray God your whole spirit and soul and body be preserved blameless . . . 1 Thess. 5:23

MUNICH 7.6.7.6.D.
From *Neuvermehrtes Meiningisches Gesangbuch,* 1693
Attributed to Mary D. James, 1810-1883
Harmony by Felix Mendelssohn, 1809-1847

(For different harmony see No. 423)

Jesus, Master, Whose I Am 234

. . . and whom I serve. Acts 27:23

ST. PETERSBURG 7.7.7.7.7.7.

Frances R. Havergal, 1836-1879

Dimitri S. Bortnianski, 1751-1825

235 I Want to Be Holy

Sanctify yourselves therefore, and be ye holy . . . Lev. 20:7

Albert B. Simpson, 1843-1919 — George C. Stebbins, 1846-1945

I Want to Be Holy

REFRAIN
I long, oh, I long to be ho - ly, Con-formed to His will and His Word;
I want to be gen - tle and Christ-like, I want to be just like my Lord.

Use Me Today

236

... serve him with a perfect heart ... 1 Chron. 28:9

Gertrude R. Dugan, 1873-1948

George C. Stebbins, 1846-1945

1. Use me to - day, O Sav - iour di - vine! Cleanse and re - new this ser - vant of Thine. Lord, with Thy Spir - it fill me, I pray; Then, in Thy serv - ice, use me to - day.
2. Use me to - day, Lord, use e - ven me— Use me to lead some lost one to Thee. Lead where Thou wilt, Lord; o - pen the way, And to Thy glo - ry, use me to - day.
3. Use me to - day to scat - ter the seed, Bring - ing the bless - ing some - one may need. Wheth - er I toil or qui - et - ly pray, Bless - ed Lord Je - sus, use me to - day.

237 More Holiness Give Me

For God hath not called us unto uncleanness, but unto holiness. 1 Thess. 4:7

MY PRAYER 6.5.6.5.D.

Philip P. Bliss, 1838-1876

Melody by Philip P. Bliss, 1838-1876

1. More ho - li - ness give me, More striv - ings with - in,
2. More grat - i - tude give me, More trust in the Lord,
3. More pu - ri - ty give me, More strength to o'er - come;
More pa - tience in suf - fering, More sor - row for sin,
More pride in His glo - ry, More hope in His Word;
More free - dom from earth - stains, More long - ings for home;
More faith in my Sav - iour, More sense of His care,
More tears for His sor - rows, More pain at His grief;
More fit for the king - dom, More used would I be;
More joy in His serv - ice, More pur - pose in prayer.
More meek - ness in tri - al, More praise for re - lief.
More bless - ed and ho - ly— More, Sav - iour, like Thee.

Make Me a Captive, Lord

238

Being then made free from sin, ye became the servants of righteousness. Rom. 6:18

LEOMINSTER S.M.D.
George W. Martin, 1828-1881
Arranged by Arthur S. Sullivan, 1842-1900

George Matheson, 1842-1906

1. Make me a cap - tive, Lord, And then I shall be free;
2. My heart is weak and poor Un - til its mas - ter find;
3. My power is faint and low Till I have learned to serve;
4. My will is not my own Till Thou hast made it Thine;
Force me to ren - der up my sword, And I shall con-queror be.
It has no spring of ac - tion sure— It var - ies with the wind.
It wants the need - ed fire to glow, It wants the breeze to nerve;
If it would reach a mon-arch's throne, It must its crown re - sign;
I sink in life's a - larms When by my - self I stand;
It can - not free - ly move Till Thou hast wrought its chain;
It can - not drive the world Un - til it - self be driven;
It on - ly stands un - bent A - mid the clash - ing strife,
Im - pris - on me with - in Thine arms, And strong shall be my hand.
En - slave it with Thy match-less love, And death - less it shall reign.
Its flag can on - ly be un-furled When Thou shalt breathe from heaven.
When on Thy bos - om it has leant And found in Thee its life. A-MEN.

239 Search Me, O God

. . . and know my heart: try me, and know my thoughts. Psa. 139:23

Albert B. Simpson, 1843-1919 | Melody by Albert B. Simpson, 1843-1919

1. Search me, O God, search me and know my heart; Try me and prove me
2. Thou art the same to - day and yes - ter - day: Oh, make Thy life in
3. Take my poor heart and on - ly let me love The things that al - ways
4. Help me to lay my treas-ures up on high; Teach me to seek my
5. Oh, let my work a - bide the test - ing day That shall con - sume the
in the hid - den part; Cleanse me and make me ho - ly, as Thou
me the same al - way. Take from my heart the things that pass a -
shall a - bid - ing prove. Bind all my heart-strings to the world a -
fu - ture in the sky; Give me my por - tion yon - der by and
stub-ble and the hay; Oh, build my house up - on the Rock I
art, And lead me in the way ev - er - last - ing.
way; Lead, lead me in the way ev - er - last - ing.
bove, And lead me in the way ev - er - last - ing.
by— And lead me in the way ev - er - last - ing.
pray— And lead me in the way ev - er - last - ing.
REFRAIN
Lead me, lead me, lead me in the way ev - er - last - ing; Keep me from the
things that with - er and de - cay; Give to me the things that

Search Me, O God

can - not pass a - way— And lead me in the way ev - er - last - ing.

Thy Holy Spirit, Lord, Alone 240

. . . the Spirit is life because of righteousness. Rom. 8:10

Henrietta E. Blair, 19th century | William J. Kirkpatrick, 1838-1921

1. Thy Ho - ly Spir - it, Lord, a - lone Can turn our hearts from sin;
2. Thy Ho - ly Spir - it, Lord, a - lone Can deep - er love in - spire;
3. Thy Ho - ly Spir - it, Lord, can bring The gifts we seek in prayer;
4. Thy Ho - ly Spir - it, Lord, can give The grace we need this hour;
His power a - lone can sanc - ti - fy And keep us pure with - in.
His power a - lone with - in our souls Can light the sa - cred fire.
His voice can words of com - fort speak And still each wave of care.
And while we wait, O Spir - it, come In sanc - ti - fy - ing power.
Refrain
1-3. O Spir - it of faith and love, Come in our midst, we pray,
4. O Spir - it of love, de - scend; Come in our midst, we pray,
And pu - ri - fy each wait - ing heart; Bap - tize us with power to - day.
And like a rush - ing, might - y wind Sweep o - ver our souls to - day.

241 Draw Me Nearer

But it is good for me to draw near to God . . . Psa. 73:28

I AM THINE 10.7.10.7. with Refrain

Fanny J. Crosby, 1820-1915

William H. Doane, 1832-1915

1. I am Thine, O Lord, I have heard Thy voice, And it
2. Con - se - crate me now to Thy serv - ice, Lord, By the
3. Oh, the pure de - light of a sin - gle hour That be -
4. There are depths of love that I can - not know Till I
told Thy love to me; But I long to rise in the arms of faith
power of grace di - vine; Let my soul look up with a stead-fast hope,
fore Thy throne I spend, When I kneel in prayer, and with Thee, my God,
cross the nar - row sea; There are heights of joy that I may not reach
REFRAIN
And be clos - er drawn to Thee.
And my will be lost in Thine. Draw me near - er,
I com - mune as friend with friend!
Till I rest in peace with Thee.
near - er, bless - ed Lord, To the cross where Thou hast died; Draw me
near - er, near - er, near - er, bless - ed Lord, To Thy pre-cious, bleed - ing side.

Jesus, I Would Faithful Be 242

. . . cause me to know the way wherein I should walk . . . Psa. 143:8

J.O. Hillyer, 19th century

Melody by J.O. Hillyer, 19th century

1. Je - sus, I would faith - ful be— Give me the power, Give me the power.
2. Je - sus, I would talk with Thee While in the way, While in the way;
3. Give me, Lord, Thy burn - ing heart To dwell with - in, To dwell with - in;
4. Thus my dai - ly walk shall be In Thy sweet will, In Thy sweet will;
Je - sus, I would walk with Thee Each pass - ing hour, Each pass - ing hour.
Joy - ful, while Thy smile I see Each hap - py day, Each hap - py day.
Thine own na - ture, Lord, im - part To free from sin, To free from sin.
Je - sus on - ly, on - ly Thee, My heart can fill, My heart can fill.
REFRAIN
In Thy foot-steps place my feet, As Thou dost will, As Thou dost will;
And if thorns my path - way meet, Bid me be still, be still.

243 Ho, Everyone That Is Thirsty

For I will pour water upon him that is thirsty . . . Isa. 44:3

Lucy J. Rider, 19th century

Melody by Lucy J. Rider, 19th century

1. Ho, ev - ery - one that is thirst - y in spir - it! Ho, ev - ery - one that is wea - ry and sad! Come to the foun - tain; there's full - ness in Je - sus—All that you're long-ing for; come and be glad.
2. Child of the world, are you tired of your bond - age? Wea - ry of earth-joys, so false, so un - true; Thirst - ing for God, and His full - ness of bless - ing? List to the prom-ise— a mes - sage for you.
3. Child of the king - dom, be filled with the Spir - it. Noth - ing but full - ness thy long - ing can meet; 'Tis the en - due - ment for life and for serv - ice—Thine is the prom-ise, so cer - tain, so sweet.
Refrain
"I will pour wa - ter on him who is thirst - y, I will pour

Ho, Everyone That Is Thirsty

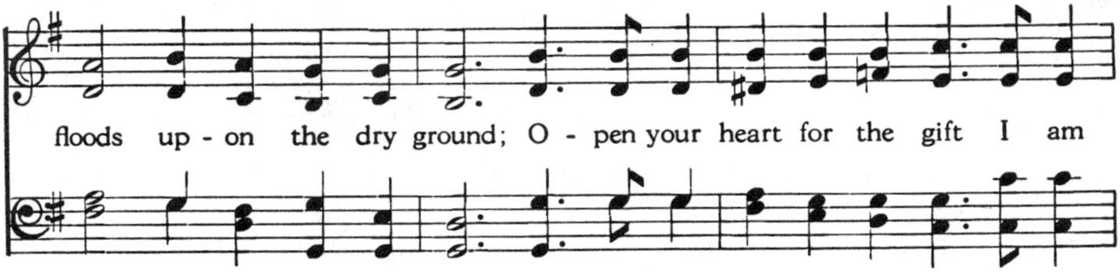
floods up - on the dry ground; O - pen your heart for the gift I am

bring - ing. While ye are seek - ing me, I will be found."

There's a Secret 244

... his secret is with the righteous. Prov. 3:32

SARDIS 8.7.8.7.

Albert B. Simpson, 1843-1919

Adapted from Ludwig van Beethoven, 1770-1827

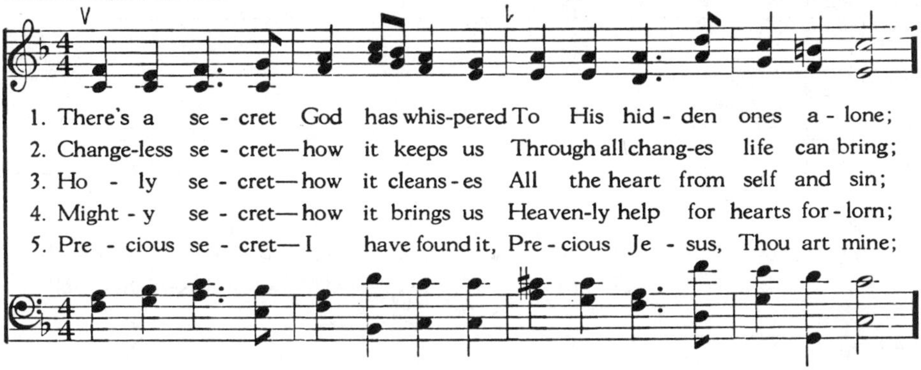
1. There's a se - cret God has whis-pered To His hid - den ones a - lone;
2. Change-less se - cret—how it keeps us Through all chang-es life can bring;
3. Ho - ly se - cret—how it cleans - es All the heart from self and sin;
4. Might - y se - cret—how it brings us Heaven-ly help for hearts for - lorn;
5. Pre - cious se - cret—I have found it, Pre - cious Je - sus, Thou art mine;

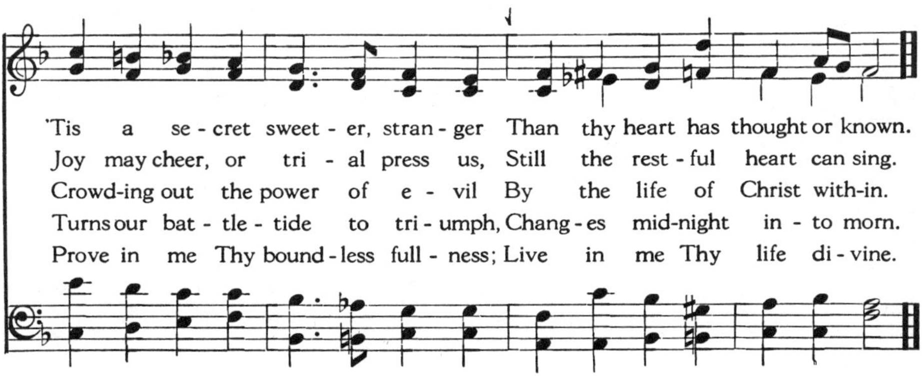
'Tis a se - cret sweet - er, stran - ger Than thy heart has thought or known.
Joy may cheer, or tri - al press us, Still the rest - ful heart can sing.
Crowd-ing out the power of e - vil By the life of Christ with-in.
Turns our bat - tle - tide to tri - umph, Chang - es mid-night in - to morn.
Prove in me Thy bound - less full - ness; Live in me Thy life di - vine.

245 'Tis Burning in My Soul

... the love of God is shed abroad in our hearts by the Holy Ghost ... Rom. 5:5

Delia T. White, 19th century — William J. Kirkpatrick, 1838-1921

1. God sent His might - y power To this poor, sin - ful heart,
2. Be - fore the cross I bow, Up - on the al - tar lay
3. No good that I have done— His prom - ise I em - brace.
To keep me ev - ery hour, And need - ful grace im - part;
A will - ing of - fering now, My all from day to day.
Ac - cept - ed in the Son— He saves me by His grace.
And since His Spir - it came To take su - preme con - trol,
My Sav - iour paid the price, My name He sweet - ly calls;
All glo - ry be to God! Let hal - le - lu - jahs roll!
The love - en - kin - dled flame Is burn - ing in my soul.
Up - on the sac - ri - fice The fire from heav - en falls.
His love is shed a - broad. The fire is in my soul.

'Tis Burning in My Soul

REFRAIN
'Tis burn-ing in my soul, 'Tis burn-ing in my soul,
The fire of heaven-ly love is burn-ing in my soul.
The Ho-ly Spir-it came, All glo-ry to His name!
The fire of heaven-ly love is burn-ing in my soul.

246 Burn On!

. . . he is like a refiner's fire . . . Mal. 3:2

Albert B. Simpson, 1843-1919 | Albert B. Simpson, 1843-1919

1. O fire of God, be-gin in me; Burn out the dross of self and sin,
2. Bap-tize with fire this soul of mine; En-due me with Thy Spir-it's might
3. Burn in, O fire of God, burn in Till all my soul Christ's im-age bears,
4. Burn on, O fire of God, burn on Till all my dross is burned a-way,
Burn off my fet-ters, set me free, And make my heart a heaven with-in.
And make me by Thy power di-vine A burn-ing and a shin-ing light.
And ev-ery power and pulse with-in His ho-ly, heaven-ly na-ture wears.
Till earth and sin and self are gone, And I can stand the test-ing day.
REFRAIN
Burn on! O fire of God, burn on Till all my dross is burned a-way!
Burn on!
Burn on!
Burn on! Burn on! Pre-pare me for the test-ing day.

The Fire Is Burning 247

... the goodness of God endureth continually. Psa. 52:1

Johnson Oatman, Jr., 1856-1926

Melody by George C. Hugg, 1848-1907

1. I've been on Mount Pis-gah's lof - ty height, And I've sat - is - fied my long-ing
2. I will walk with Je - sus, bless His name, And to be like Him I ev - ery
3. I my all up - on the al - tar lay As I to my clos - et lov - ing -
4. By faith's eye I scan the o - cean's foam, And be - yond I see the ha - ven
heart's de - sire; For I caught a glimpse of glo - ry bright, And my soul is
day as - pire; For His love is like a heaven-ly flame, And my soul is
ly re - tire; And the flame con - sumes while there I pray, And my soul is
I de - sire; There I view the bea - con light of home, And my soul is
burn - ing with the fire.
Refrain
Oh, the fire is burn-ing, yes, 'tis bright-ly burn-ing,
Oh, 'tis burn - ing, burn - ing in my soul; Oh, the fire is burn-ing,
yes, 'tis bright-ly burn - ing, Oh, 'tis burn-ing, burn - ing in my soul.

248 Himself

. . . *Christ is all, and in all.* Col. 3:11

Albert B. Simpson, 1843-1919 — Albert B. Simpson, 1843-1919

1. Once it was the bless - ing, Now it is the Lord; Once it was the feel-ing,
2. Once 'twas pain-ful try - ing, Now 'tis per-fect trust; Once a half sal - va-tion,
3. Once 'twas bus - y plan-ning, Now 'tis trust-ful prayer; Once 'twas anxious car-ing,
4. Once it was my work - ing, His it hence shall be; Once I tried to use Him,
5. Once I hoped in Je - sus, Now I know He's mine; Once my lamps were dy-ing,
Now it is His Word; Once His gift I want - ed, Now the Giv - er own;
Now the ut - ter - most! Once 'twas cease-less hold-ing, Now He holds me fast;
Now He has the care; Once 'twas what I want - ed, Now what Je - sus says;
Now He us - es me; Once the power I want - ed, Now the Might-y One;
Now they bright-ly shine; Once for death I wait - ed, Now His com - ing hail;
REFRAIN
Once I sought for heal - ing, Now Him-self a - lone.
Once 'twas con-stant drift-ing, Now my an-chor's cast.
Once 'twas con-stant ask - ing, Now 'tis cease-less praise. All in all for - ev - er,
Once for self I la - bored, Now for Him a - lone.
And my hopes are an-chored Safe with-in the vail.
Je - sus will I sing; Ev-ery-thing in Je - sus, And Je - sus ev-ery-thing.

Power from on High 249

. . . tarry . . . until ye be endued with power from on high. Luke 24:49

Albert B. Simpson, 1843-1919 — Albert B. Simpson, 1843-1919

1. Gra - cious Heaven-ly Fa - ther, Hear Thy peo - ple's cry; See us!
2. Oh, how long we strug - gle! Oh, how hard we try! Help-less-
3. Send di - vine con - vic - tion, Bring sal - va - tion nigh; Cru - ci-
4. As the heaven - ly sun - shine Bring - ing sum - mer nigh, As the
How we lan - guish! Help us ere we die! Send us by Thy
ly we la - bor, Help - less - ly we sigh Till Thy Spir - it
fy and quick - en, Save and sanc - ti - fy. Bless - ed Spir - it,
showers that wa - ter Des - erts parched and dry, Quick-ening Spir - it,
Spir - it Pow - er from on high.
gives us Pow - er from on high.
bring us Pow - er from on high.
bring us Pow - er from on high.
REFRAIN
Pow - er, pow - er, pow - er
from on high, Send us by Thy Spir - it Pow - er from on high.

250 Breathe upon Us

. . . he breathed on them, . . . Receive ye the Holy Ghost. John 20:22

Russell K. Carter, 1849-1928

Melody by Russell K. Carter, 1849-1928
Harmony by J. Buchanan MacMillan, b. 1915

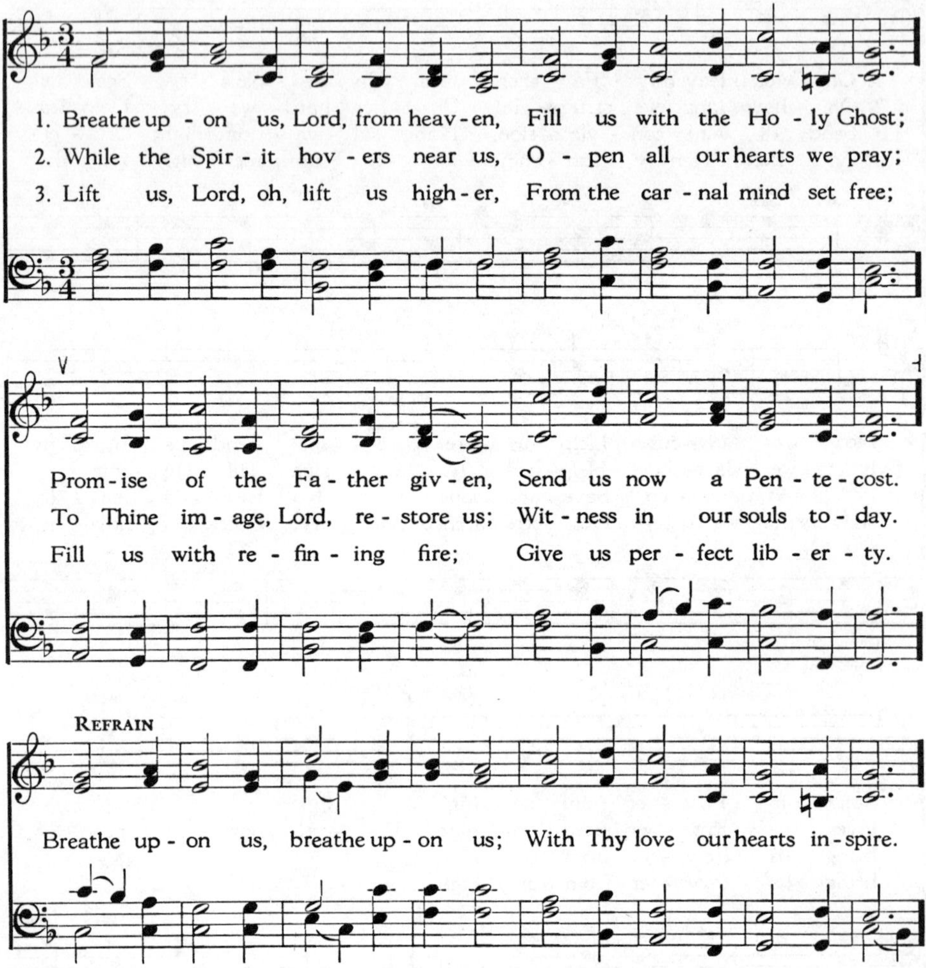
3
4
1. Breathe up - on us, Lord, from heav - en, Fill us with the Ho - ly Ghost;
2. While the Spir - it hov - ers near us, O - pen all our hearts we pray;
3. Lift us, Lord, oh, lift us high - er, From the car - nal mind set free;
Prom - ise of the Fa - ther giv - en, Send us now a Pen - te - cost.
To Thine im - age, Lord, re - store us; Wit - ness in our souls to - day.
Fill us with re - fin - ing fire; Give us per - fect lib - er - ty.
REFRAIN
Breathe up - on us, breathe up - on us; With Thy love our hearts in - spire.
Breathe up - on us, breathe up - on us; Lord, bap - tize us now with fire.

Breathing Out and Breathing In

. . . they . . . sought him with their whole desire; and he was found of them . . . 2 Chron. 15:15

Albert B. Simpson, 1843-1919

HOLY MANNA 8.7.8.7.D.
William Moore, 19th century

1. Je - sus, breathe Thy Spir-it on me, Teach me how to breathe Thee in,
2. Breath-ing out my sin-ful na - ture, Thou hast borne it all for me;
3. I am breath-ing out my long-ings, In Thy list-'ning lov-ing ear,
Help me pour in - to Thy bos - om All my life of self and sin.
Breath-ing in Thy cleans-ing full - ness, Find-ing all my life in Thee.
I am breath-ing in Thy an - swers, Still-ing ev-ery doubt and fear.
I am breath-ing out my own life, That I may be filled with Thine;
I am breath-ing out my sor-row, On Thy kind and gen-tle breast;
I am breath-ing ev - ery mo-ment, Draw-ing all my life from Thee;
Let - ting go my strength and weak-ness, Breath-ing in Thy life di-vine.
Breath-ing in Thy joy and com-fort, Breath-ing in Thy peace and rest.
Breath by breath I live up - on Thee, Bless-ed Spir-it, breathe in me.

252 Fill Me Now

. . . be filled with the Spirit. Eph. 5:18

FILL ME NOW 8.7.8.7. with Refrain

Elwood H. Stokes, 1815-1895

John R. Sweney, 1837-1899

1. Hov - er o'er me, Ho - ly Spir - it, Bathe my trem-bling heart and brow;
2. Thou canst fill me, gra - cious Spir - it, Though I can - not tell Thee how;
3. I am weak-ness, full of weak - ness– At Thy sa - cred feet I bow:
4. Cleanse and com-fort, bless and save me; Bathe, oh, bathe my heart and brow;
Fill me with Thy hal-lowed pres - ence; Come, oh, come and fill me now.
But I need Thee, great - ly need Thee; Come, oh, come and fill me now.
Blest, di - vine, e - ter - nal Spir - it, Fill with power, and fill me now.
Thou art com - fort - ing and sav - ing, Thou art sweet - ly fill - ing now.
REFRAIN
Fill me now, fill me now, Je - sus, come and fill me now.
Fill me with Thy hal - lowed pres-ence; Come, oh, come and fill me now.

Blessed Quietness 253

. . . he may abide with you for ever. John 14:16

Manie P. Ferguson, 19th century

BLESSED QUIETNESS 8.7.8.7. with Refrain
Melody by W.S. Marshall, 19th century
Adapted by James M. Kirk, 1854-1945

1. Joys are flow - ing like a riv - er, Since the Com - fort - er has come;
2. Bring-ing life and health and glad-ness All a - round, this heaven-ly Guest
3. Like the rain that falls from heav - en, Like the sun - light from the sky,
4. See a fruit - ful field is grow-ing Bless - ed fruits of right-eous-ness,
5. What a won - der - ful sal - va - tion Where we al - ways see His face!
He a - bides with us for - ev - er, Makes the trust - ing heart His home.
Ban-ished un - be - lief and sad - ness, Changed our wea - ri - ness to rest.
So the Ho - ly Ghost is giv - en, Com - ing on us from on high.
And the streams of life are flow - ing In the lone - ly wil - der - ness.
What a per - fect hab - i - ta - tion! What a qui - et rest - ing place!
REFRAIN
Bless - ed qui - et - ness, ho - ly qui - et - ness— What as -
sur - ance in my soul! On the storm - y sea He speaks
peace to me. How the bil - lows cease to roll!

254 Be Thou My Vision

. . . thou mayest be to us instead of eyes. Num. 10:31

Irish Hymn, circa 8th century
Translated by Mary E. Byrne, 1880-1931
Adapted by Eleanor H. Hull, 1860-1935

SLANE 10.10.9.10.
Irish melody
Arranged by Norman Johnson, b. 1928

1. Be Thou my Vi - sion, O Lord of my heart,
2. Be Thou my Wis - dom and Thou my true Word,
3. Rich - es I heed not, nor man's emp - ty praise,
4. High King of heav - en, my vic - to - ry won,
Nought be all else to me, save that Thou art;
I ev - er with Thee and Thou with me, Lord;
Thou mine In - her - it - ance now and al - ways;
May I reach heav - en's joys, O bright heaven's Sun!
Thou my best thought by day or by night,
Thou my great Fa - ther, I Thy true son,
Thou and Thou on - ly, first in my heart,
Heart of my own heart, what - ev - er be - fall,
Wak - ing or sleep - ing, Thy pres - ence my light.
Thou in me dwell - ing, and I with Thee one.
High King of heav - en, my Treas - ure Thou art.
Still be my Vi - sion, O Rul - er of all.

Open My Eyes That I May See 255

. . . that I may behold wondrous things . . . Psa. 119:18

Clara H. Scott, 1841-1897 (altered)

SCOTT Irregular
Clara H. Scott, 1841-1897

1. O - pen my eyes that I may see Glimp-ses of truth Thou hast for me;
2. O - pen my mind that I may read More of Thy love in word and deed.
3. O - pen my way that I may bring Tro - phies of grace to Christ, my King;

Place in my hands the won-der - ful key That shall un-clasp and set me free.
What shall I fear while yet Thou dost lead? On - ly for light from Thee I plead.
Ech - oed in love Thy Word shall out-ring, Sweet as the note that an - gels sing.

Si - lent - ly now I wait for Thee, Read - y, my God, Thy will to see;
Si - lent - ly now I wait for Thee, Read - y, my God, Thy will to see;
Si - lent - ly now I wait for Thee, Read - y, my God, Thy will to see;

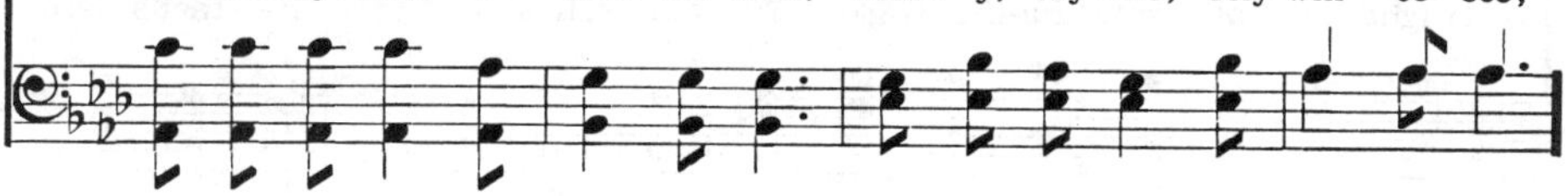

O - pen my eyes, il - lu - mine me, Spir - it di - vine!
O - pen my mind, il - lu - mine me, Spir - it di - vine!
O - pen my way, il - lu - mine me, Spir - it di - vine!

256 Jesus, I Am Resting, Resting

. . . ye shall find rest for your souls. . . . Jer. 6:16

TRANQUILITY 8.7.8.5.D. with Refrain

Jean S. Pigott, 1845-1882

James Mountain, 1843-1933

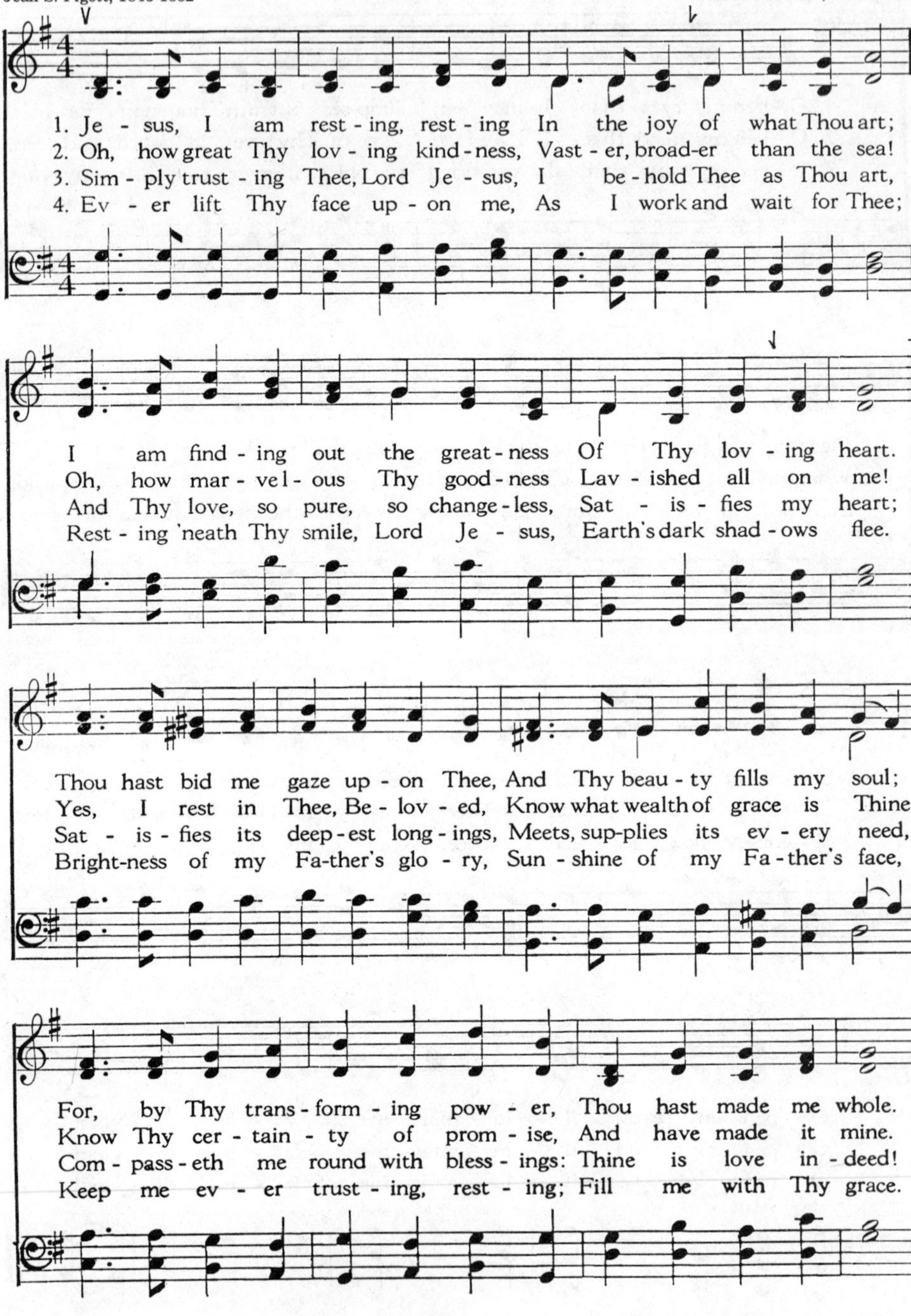
1. Je - sus, I am rest - ing, rest - ing In the joy of what Thou art;
2. Oh, how great Thy lov - ing kind - ness, Vast - er, broad - er than the sea!
3. Sim - ply trust - ing Thee, Lord Je - sus, I be - hold Thee as Thou art,
4. Ev - er lift Thy face up - on me, As I work and wait for Thee;
I am find - ing out the great - ness Of Thy lov - ing heart.
Oh, how mar - vel - ous Thy good - ness Lav - ished all on me!
And Thy love, so pure, so change - less, Sat - is - fies my heart;
Rest - ing 'neath Thy smile, Lord Je - sus, Earth's dark shad - ows flee.
Thou hast bid me gaze up - on Thee, And Thy beau - ty fills my soul;
Yes, I rest in Thee, Be - lov - ed, Know what wealth of grace is Thine,
Sat - is - fies its deep - est long - ings, Meets, sup - plies its ev - ery need,
Bright - ness of my Fa - ther's glo - ry, Sun - shine of my Fa - ther's face,
For, by Thy trans - form - ing pow - er, Thou hast made me whole.
Know Thy cer - tain - ty of prom - ise, And have made it mine.
Com - pass - eth me round with bless - ings: Thine is love in - deed!
Keep me ev - er trust - ing, rest - ing; Fill me with Thy grace.

Jesus, I Am Resting, Resting

REFRAIN
Je - sus, I am rest - ing, rest - ing In the joy of what Thou art;
I am find - ing out the great - ness Of Thy lov - ing heart.

May the Mind of Christ, My Saviour 257

Let this mind be in you, which was also in Christ Jesus. Phil. 2:5

Kate B. Wilkinson, 1859-1928

ST. LEONARDS 8.7.8.5.
Arthur C. Barham-Gould, 1891-1953

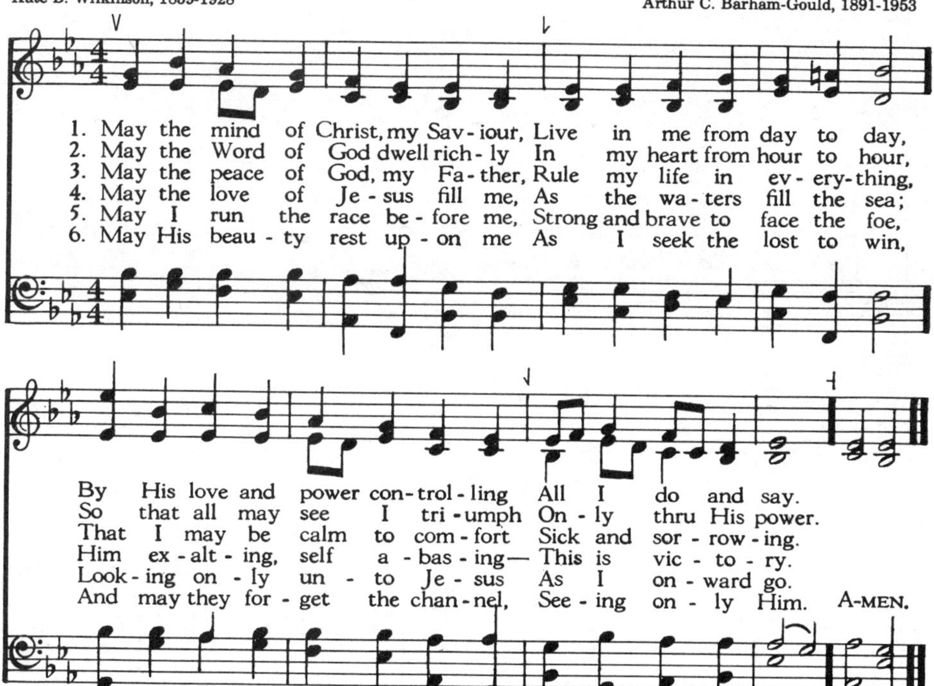
1. May the mind of Christ, my Sav - iour, Live in me from day to day, By His love and power con - trol - ling All I do and say.
2. May the Word of God dwell rich - ly In my heart from hour to hour, So that all may see I tri - umph On - ly thru His power.
3. May the peace of God, my Fa - ther, Rule my life in ev - ery - thing, That I may be calm to com - fort Sick and sor - row - ing.
4. May the love of Je - sus fill me, As the wa - ters fill the sea; Him ex - alt - ing, self a - bas - ing— This is vic - to - ry.
5. May I run the race be - fore me, Strong and brave to face the foe, Look - ing on - ly un - to Je - sus As I on - ward go.
6. May His beau - ty rest up - on me As I seek the lost to win, And may they for - get the chan - nel, See - ing on - ly Him.
A - MEN.

258 Bring Your Vessels, Not a Few

... borrow ... empty vessels; borrow not a few. 2 Kings 4:3

Lelia N. Morris, 1862-1929 | Lelia N. Morris, 1862-1929

1. Are you long - ing for the full - ness of the bless - ing
2. Bring your emp - ty earth - en ves - sels, clean through Je - sus'
3. Like the cruse of oil un - fail - ing is His grace for -
of the Lord In your heart and life to - day? Claim the
pre - cious blood. Come, ye need - y, one and all; And in
ev - er - more, And His love un - chang - ing still; And ac -
prom - ise of your Fa - ther, come ac - cord - ing to His Word
hum - ble con - se - cra - tion wait be - fore the throne of God
cord - ing to His prom - ise with the Ho - ly Ghost and power,
In the bless - ed old - time way.
Till the Ho - ly Ghost shall fall.
He will ev - ery ves - sel fill.
REFRAIN
He will fill your
He will fill

Bring Your Vessels, Not a Few

heart to - day to o - ver - flow - ing,
your heart to o - ver - flow - ing,
As the Lord com - mand - eth you, "Bring your ves - sels,
not a few"; He will fill your heart to - day to o - ver -
He will fill your
flow - ing With the Ho - ly Ghost and power.
heart to o - ver - flow - ing

259 Launch Out

. . . thou, Lord, art . . . plenteous in mercy unto all them that call upon thee. Psa. 86:5

Albert B. Simpson, 1843-1919 — Melody by Russell K. Carter, 1849-1928

1. The mer - cy of God is an o - cean di - vine, A bound-less and fath - om - less flood; Launch out in the deep, cut a - way the shore-line, And be lost in the mer - cy of God.
2. But man - y, a - las, on - ly stand on the shore And gaze on the o - cean so wide; They nev - er have ven - tured its depths to ex-plore, Or to launch on the fath - om - less tide.
3. Oh, let us launch out on this o - cean so broad, Where floods of sal - va - tion e'er flow; Oh, let us be lost in the mer - cy of God, Till the depths of His full - ness we know.
REFRAIN
Launch out in - to the deep, Oh, let the shore - line go; Launch out, launch out in the o - cean di - vine, Out where the full tides flow.
Launch out

Jesus, I My Cross Have Taken 260

. . . come, take up the cross, and follow me. Mark 10:21

DISCIPLE (Ellesdie) 8.7.8.7.D.
Attributed to Wolfgang A. Mozart, 1756-1791
From Joshua Leavitt's *The Christian Lyre,* 1831
Arranged by Hubert P. Main, 1839-1925

Henry F. Lyte, 1793-1847

1. Je - sus, I my cross have tak - en, All to leave, and fol - low Thee;
2. Let the world de - spise and leave me—They have left my Sav - iour, too;
3. Man may trou-ble and dis - tress me—'Twill but drive me to Thy breast.
4. Go then, earth-ly fame and treas-ure! Come, dis - as - ter, scorn, and pain!
Des - ti - tute, de - spised, for - sak - en, Thou from hence my all shalt be.
Hu - man hearts and looks de - ceive me—Thou art not, like man, un - true;
Life with tri - als hard may press me; Heaven will bring me sweet - er rest.
In Thy serv - ice pain is pleas-ure; With Thy fa - vor loss is gain.
Per - ish ev - ery fond am - bi - tion, All I've sought, and hoped, or known;
And while Thou shalt smile up - on me, God of wis - dom, love, and might,
Oh, 'tis not in grief to harm me, While Thy love is left to me;
I have called Thee, Ab - ba, Fa - ther, I have stayed my heart on Thee;
Yet, how rich is my con - di - tion! God and heaven are still my own.
Foes may hate, and friends may shun me; Show Thy face and all is bright.
Oh, 'twere not in joy to charm me, Were that joy un-mixed with Thee.
Storms may howl and clouds may gath - er; All must work for good to me.

261 Wherever He Leads I'll Go

. . . I am the Lord thy God which . . . leadeth thee . . . Isa. 48:17

FALLS CREEK 8.6.8.7. with Refrain

Baylus B. McKinney, 1886-1952 | Baylus B. McKinney, 1886-1952

1. "Take up thy cross and fol - low Me," I heard my Mas - ter say.
2. He drew me clos - er to His side. I sought His will to know,
3. It may be through the shad - ows dim, Or o'er the storm - y sea.
4. My heart, my life, my all I bring To Christ, who loves me so.
"I gave My life to ran - som thee; Sur - ren - der your all to - day."
And in that will I now a - bide; Wher - ev - er He leads I'll go.
I take my cross and fol - low Him, Wher - ev - er He lead - eth me.
He is my Mas - ter, Lord, and King; Wher - ev - er He leads I'll go.
REFRAIN
Wher - ev - er He leads I'll go; Wher - ev - er He leads I'll go.
I'll fol - low my Christ, who loves me so. Wher - ev - er He leads I'll go.

Where He Leads Me 262

. . . leaving us an example, that ye should follow his steps. 1 Pet. 2:21

E.W. Blandy, 19th century

NORRIS 8.8.8.9. with Refrain
John S. Norris, 1844-1907

1. I can hear my Sav - iour call - ing, I can hear my Sav - iour call - ing,
2. I'll go with Him through the gar - den, I'll go with Him through the gar - den,
3. I'll go with Him through the judg-ment, I'll go with Him through the judg-ment,
4. He will give me grace and glo - ry, He will give me grace and glo - ry,

Refrain
Where He leads me I will fol - low, Where He leads me I will fol - low,

D. C. for Refrain

I can hear my Sav - iour call - ing, "Take thy cross and fol - low, fol - low Me."
I'll go with Him through the gar - den; I'll go with Him, with Him all the way.
I'll go with Him through the judg-ment; I'll go with Him, with Him all the way.
He will give me grace and glo - ry And go with me, with me all the way.
Where He leads me I will fol - low, I'll go with Him, with Him all the way.

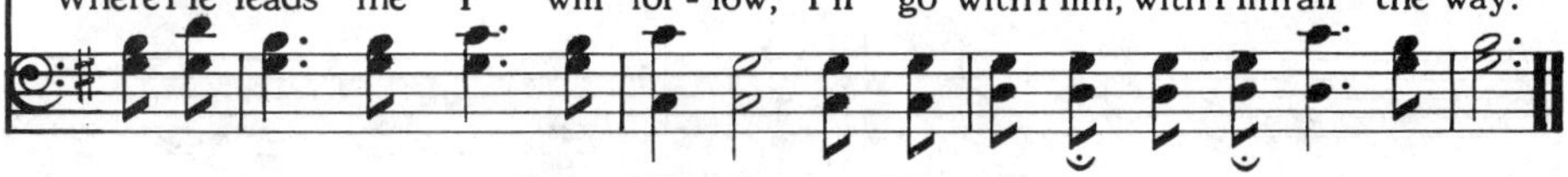

My Glorious Victor 263

. . . I love my master, . . . I will not go out free. Exod. 21:5

Handley C.G. Moule, 1841-1920

HESPERUS (Quebec) L.M.
Henry Baker, 1835-1910

1. My glo-rious Vic - tor, Prince di - vine, Clasp these sur-ren-dered hands in Thine;
2. My Mas-ter, lead me to Thy door; Pierce this now will - ing ear once more;
3. Yes, ear and hand, and thought, and will– Use all in Thy dear slav - ery still!
4. Tread them still down; and then, I know, These hands shall with Thy gifts o'er-flow;

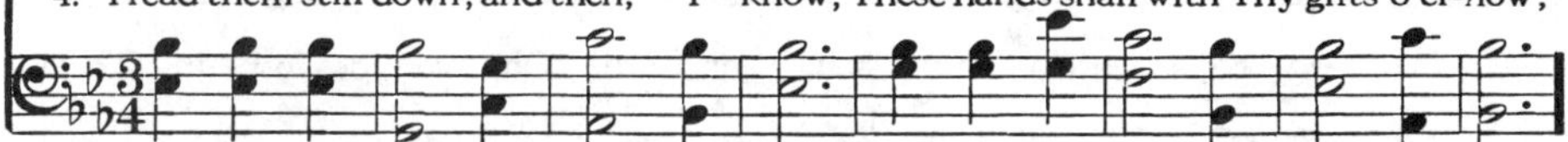

At length my will is all Thine own, Glad vas - sal of a Sav-iour's throne.
Thy bonds are free-dom; let me stay With Thee to toil, en - dure, o - bey.
Self's wea - ry lib - er - ties I cast Be-neath Thy feet; there keep them fast.
And pierc-ed ears shall hear the tone Which tells me Thou and I are one.

(For higher keys see Nos. 4 and 35)

264 Not I, But Christ

. . . yet not I, but Christ liveth in me . . . Gal. 2:20

Mrs. A.A. Whiddington, 19th century

Albert B. Simpson, 1843-1919

1. Not I but Christ be hon - ored, loved, ex - alt - ed; Not I but
2. Not I but Christ to gent - ly soothe in sor - row; Not I but
3. Christ, on - ly Christ, no i - dle word e'er fall - ing; Christ, on - ly
4. Not I but Christ my ev - ery need sup - ply - ing; Not I but
5. Christ, on - ly Christ ere long will fill my vi - sion; Glo - ry ex -
Christ be seen, be known, be heard; Not I but Christ in ev - ery
Christ to wipe the fall - ing tear: Not I but Christ to lift the
Christ, no need - less bust - ling sound; Christ, on - ly Christ, no self - im -
Christ my strength and health to be; Christ, on - ly Christ for bod - y,
cell - ing soon, full soon I'll see— Christ, on - ly Christ my ev - ery
look and ac - tion; Not I but Christ in ev - ery thought and word.
wea - ry bur - den; Not I but Christ to hush a - way all fear.
port - ant bear - ing; Christ, on - ly Christ, no trace of "I" be found.
soul, and spir - it; Christ, on - ly Christ, live then Thy life in me.
wish ful - fill - ing— Christ, on - ly Christ my all and all to be.
REFRAIN
Oh, to be saved from my - self, dear Lord! Oh, to be lost in Thee!
Oh, that it might be no more I, but Christ that lives in me!

My Goal Is God Himself

265

. . . that God may be all in all. 1 Cor. 15:28

F. Brook, 19th century

EVENTIDE 10.10.10.10.
William H. Monk, 1823-1889

1. My goal is God Him - self— not joy, nor peace,
2. So faith bounds for - ward to its goal in God,
3. No mat - ter if the way be some - times dark,
4. One thing I know, I can - not say Him nay;
Nor e - ven bless - ing, but Him - self, my God.
And love can trust her Lord to lead her there;
No mat - ter though the cost be oft - times great,
One thing I do, I press to - wards my Lord;
'Tis His to lead me there, not mine, but His—
Up - held by Him, my soul is fol - lowing hard,
He know - eth how I best shall reach the mark—
My God my glo - ry here from day to day,
"At an - y cost, dear Lord, by an - y road!"
Till God hath full ful - filled my deep - est prayer.
The way that leads to Him must needs be strait.
And in the glo - ry there my Great Re - ward.

266 Come, All Christians, Be Committed

. . . brethren, . . . present your bodies a living sacrifice . . . Rom. 12:1

BEACH SPRING 8.7.8.7.D.
American melody
From J.T. White's *The Sacred Harp*, 1844
Arranged by James H. Wood, b. 1921

Eva B. Lloyd, b. 1912

1. Come, all Chris-tians, be com - mit - ted To the serv - ice of the
2. Of your time and tal - ents give ye, They are gifts from God a -
3. God's com - mand to love each oth - er Is re - quired of ev - ery
4. Come in praise and ad - o - ra - tion, All who on Christ's name be -
Lord. Make your lives for Him more fit - ted, Tune your hearts with one ac -
bove, To be used by Chris-tians free - ly To pro - claim His won-drous
man. Show - ing mer - cy to a broth-er Mir - rors His re - demp-tive
lieve. Wor - ship Him with con - se - cra - tion, Grace and love will you re -
cord. Come in - to His courts with glad - ness, Each His sa - cred vows re -
love. Come a - gain to serve the Sav - iour, Tithes and of - ferings with you
plan. In com - pas - sion He has giv - en Of His love that is di -
ceive. For His grace give Him the glo - ry, For the Spir - it and the
new, Turn a - way from sin and sad - ness, Be trans-formed with life a - new.
bring. In your work, with Him find fa - vor, And with joy His prais-es sing.
vine; On the cross sins were for - giv - en; Joy and peace are ful - ly thine.
Word, And re - peat the gos - pel sto - ry Till all men His name have heard.

Lord, Thou Lovest the Cheerful Giver 267

. . . God loveth a cheerful giver. 2 Cor. 9:7

Robert Murray, 1832-1910

BEECHER 8.7.8.7.D.
John Zundel, 1815-1882

1. Lord, thou lov'st the cheer-ful giv - er, Who with o - pen heart and hand
2. We are Thine, Thy mer - cy sought us, Found us in death's dread-ful way,
3. Blest by Thee with gifts and grac - es, May we heed Thy church-'s call;
4. Sav - iour, Thou hast free - ly giv - en All the bless-ings we en - joy.
Bless - es free - ly, as a riv - er That re - fresh - es all the land.
To the fold in safe - ty brought us, Nev - er - more from Thee to stray.
Glad - ly in all times and plac - es Give to Thee who giv - est all.
Earth - ly store and bread of heav - en, Love and peace with - out al - loy;
Grant us then the grace of giv - ing With a spir - it large and free,
Thine own life Thou free - ly gav - est As an of - fering on the cross
Thou hast bought us, and no long - er Can we claim to be our own;
Hum - bly now we bow be - fore Thee, And our all to Thee re - sign;
That our life and all our liv - ing We may con - se - crate to Thee.
For each sin - ner whom Thou sav - est From e - ter - nal shame and loss.
Ev - er free and ev - er strong - er, We shall serve Thee, Lord, a - lone.
For the king-dom, power, and glo - ry Are, O Lord, for - ev - er Thine!

268 The Healer

. . . he was wounded for our transgressions, he was bruised for our iniquities . . . Isa. 53:5

Lois Irwin, 20th century | Lois Irwin, 20th century

1. On the cross cru - ci - fied, in great sor - row He died, The
2. Price for heal - ing was paid as those cruel stripes were made With-
3. Came the lep - er to Christ, say - ing, "Sure - ly I know That
4. He has healed my sick soul, made me ev - ery whit whole, And
Giv - er of life was He; Yet my Lord was des - pised
in Pi - late's judg - ment hall; Now His suf - fering af - fords
Thou, Lord, canst make me whole." When his great faith was seen
He'll do the same for you; He's the same yes - ter - day
and re - ject - ed of men, This Je - sus of Cal - va - ry.
per - fect heal - ing for all, This won - der - ful Heal - er's mine.
Je - sus said, "Yes, I will," And touched him and made him clean.
and to - day and for aye, This Heal - er of men to - day.
REFRAIN
He was wound - ed for our trans - gres - sions, He was
bruised for our in - iq - ui - ties; Sure - ly He

The Healer

bore our sor - rows, And by His stripes we are healed.

The Great Healer

269

Who forgiveth all thine iniquities; who healeth all thy diseases. Psa. 103:3

HEBRON L.M.

Thomas C. Upham, 1799-1872 (altered)

Lowell Mason, 1792-1872

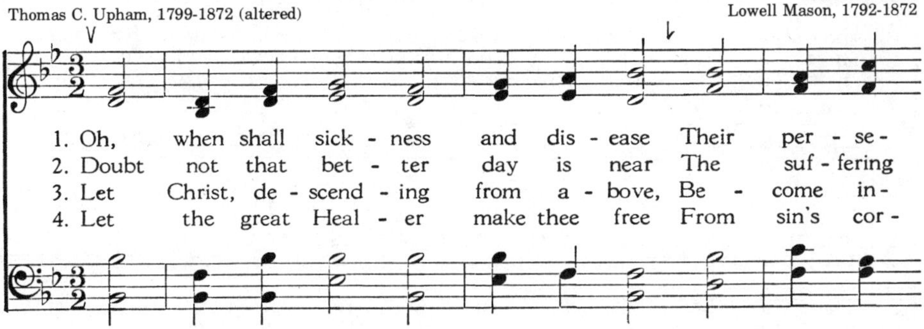
1. Oh, when shall sick - ness and dis - ease Their per - se -
2. Doubt not that bet - ter day is near The suf - fering
3. Let Christ, de - scend - ing from a - bove, Be - come in -
4. Let the great Heal - er make thee free From sin's cor -

cut - ing war - fare cease; And weak - ness die, and
sons of earth to hear; Dis - ease and pain are
car - nate in thy love; The in - ward ills and
rod - ing mal - a - dy; And then His life with -

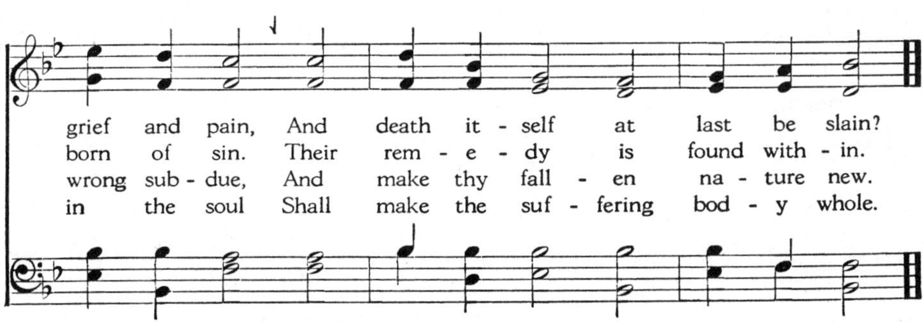
grief and pain, And death it - self at last be slain?
born of sin. Their rem - e - dy is found with - in.
wrong sub - due, And make thy fall - en na - ture new.
in the soul Shall make the suf - fering bod - y whole.

270 Healing in Jesus

. . . he . . . healed them that had need of healing. Luke 9:11

Albert B. Simpson, 1843-1919

George C. Stebbins, 1846-1945

1. There is cleans - ing in Je - sus for guilt and for sin;
2. There is heal - ing in Je - sus, the same as of old;
3. There is glad - ness in Je - sus that nev - er grows old;
There's a foun - tain that wash - es us whit - er than snow.
There is heal - ing for all who be - lieve and o - bey;
There's a sun - shine that shall nev - er van - ish a - way.
There's a Spir - it that's will - ing to fill us with - in
For the love and com - pas - sion that nev - er grow cold
Oh, the rest and the sweet - ness can nev - er be told
Till the depths of our be - ing His cleans - ing shall know.
Are as a - ble and will - ing to help us to - day.
Of the hearts that have learned to be - lieve and o - bey.
REFRAIN
There is heal - ing in Je - sus, heal - ing for thee, Heal - ing for

Healing in Jesus

all who be - lieve and o - bey; There is heal - ing in Je - sus,
heal - ing for me— Je - sus, I take Thee for heal - ing to - day.

Healing in His Wings 271

. . . shall the Sun of righteousness arise with healing in his wings . . . Mal. 4:2

Albert B. Simpson, 1843-1919

BAYVIEW 8.8.8.6.
J. Buchanan MacMillan, b. 1915

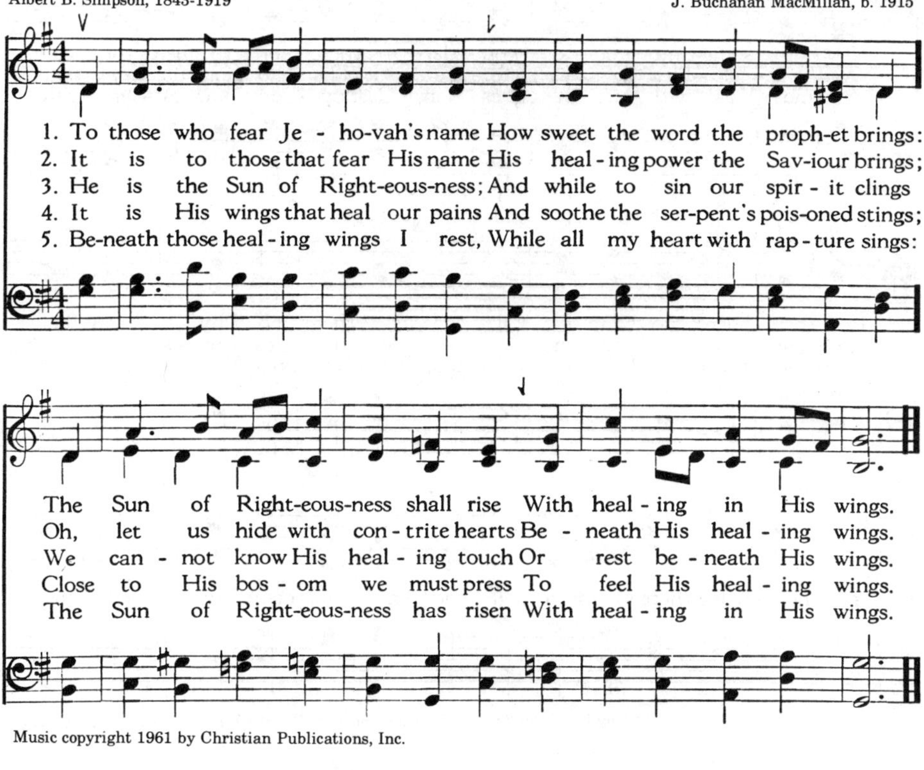
1. To those who fear Je - ho-vah's name How sweet the word the proph-et brings:
2. It is to those that fear His name His heal - ing power the Sav-iour brings;
3. He is the Sun of Right-eous-ness; And while to sin our spir - it clings
4. It is His wings that heal our pains And soothe the ser-pent's pois-oned stings;
5. Be-neath those heal - ing wings I rest, While all my heart with rap - ture sings:
The Sun of Right-eous-ness shall rise With heal - ing in His wings.
Oh, let us hide with con - trite hearts Be - neath His heal - ing wings.
We can - not know His heal - ing touch Or rest be - neath His wings.
Close to His bos - om we must press To feel His heal - ing wings.
The Sun of Right-eous-ness has risen With heal - ing in His wings.

272 Balm in Gilead

Is there no balm in Gilead; is there no physician there? . . . Jer. 8:22

Albert B. Simpson, 1843-1919 (adapted)

Melody by George C. Stebbins, 1846-1945 (adapted)

1. As I sad - ly look a - round me O'er a world of grief and woe—
2. There is heal - ing in the prom - ise, There is heal - ing in the blood,
3. Would you prove this great Phy - si - cian? You must do what He com-mands,
Oh, the hearts that break with an - guish, Oh, the bit - ter tears that flow—
There is strength for all our weak - ness In the ris - en Son of God;
Care - ful - ly o - bey His or - ders, Lie sub - mis-sive in His hands.
I am some-times prone to won - der If there's none to help or care.
And the fee - blest of His chil - dren All His glo - rious life may share.
You must trust with - out a ques - tion, Cast up - on Him ev - ery care—
Is there, then, no balm in Gil - ead? Is there no Phy - si - cian there?
He has bet - ter balm in Gil - ead, He, the great Phy - si - cian there!
Then you'll find there's balm in Gil - ead, There's a great Phy - si - cian there.
REFRAIN
Yes, there's balm, there's balm in Gil - ead; There's a great Phy - si - cian there!

Balm in Gilead

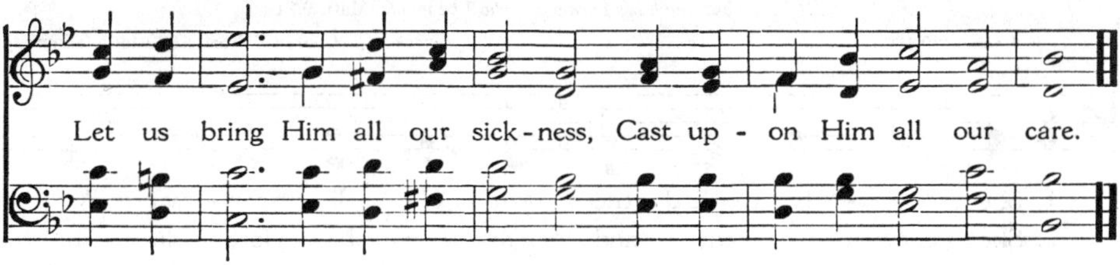
Let us bring Him all our sick - ness, Cast up - on Him all our care.

At Even Ere the Sun Was Set 273

... they brought unto him all that were diseased ... Mark 1:32

Henry Twells, 1823-1900

ANGELUS L.M.
Cantica Spiritualia, 1847
From *Hymns Ancient and Modern,* 1868

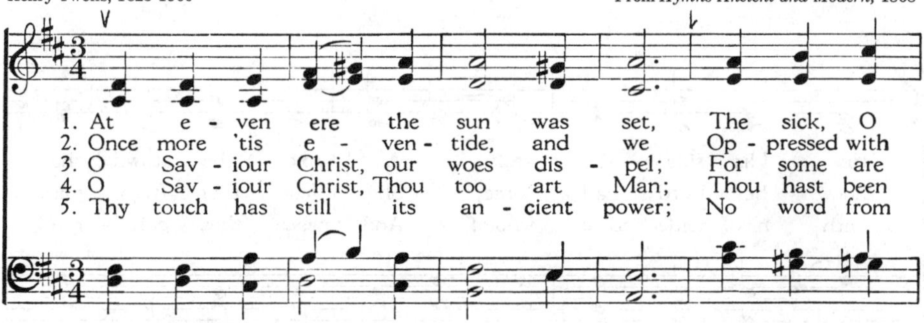
1. At e - ven ere the sun was set, The sick, O
2. Once more 'tis e - ven - tide, and we Op - pressed with
3. O Sav - iour Christ, our woes dis - pel; For some are
4. O Sav - iour Christ, Thou too art Man; Thou hast been
5. Thy touch has still its an - cient power; No word from

Lord, a - round Thee lay. Oh, in what di - vers
va - rious ills draw near. What if Thy form we
sick, and some are sad, And some have nev - er
trou - bled, tempt - ed, tried; Thy kind but search - ing
Thee can fruit - less fall; Hear, in this sol - emn

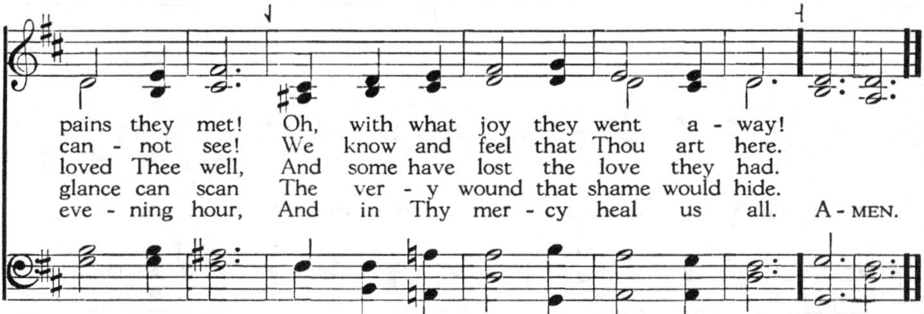
pains they met! Oh, with what joy they went a - way!
can - not see! We know and feel that Thou art here.
loved Thee well, And some have lost the love they had.
glance can scan The ver - y wound that shame would hide.
eve - ning hour, And in Thy mer - cy heal us all. A - MEN.

274 She Only Touched the Hem of His Garment

. . . If I may but touch his garment, I shall be whole. Matt. 9:21

George F. Root, 1820-1895 | George F. Root, 1820-1895 (adapted)

1. She on - ly touched the hem of His gar - ment, As
2. She came in fear and trem - bling be - fore Him; She
3. He turned with "Daugh - ter, be of good com - fort, Thy
to His side she stole A - mid the crowd that
knew her Lord had come; She felt that from Him
faith has made thee whole!" And peace that pass - eth
gath - ered a - round Him, And straight - way she was whole.
vir - tue had healed her– The might - y deed was done.
all un - der - stand - ing With glad - ness filled her soul.
REFRAIN
Oh, touch the hem of His gar - ment! And thou, too, shalt be free!

She Only Touched the Hem of His Garment

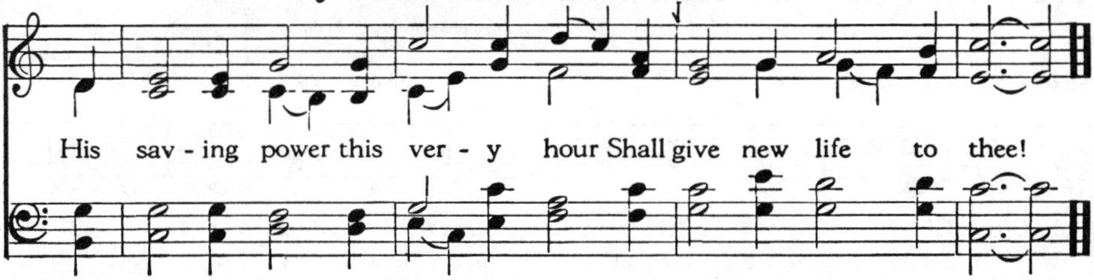
His sav - ing power this ver - y hour Shall give new life to thee!

The Branch of Healing 275

. . . for I am the Lord that healeth thee. Exod. 15:26

RETREAT L.M.

Albert B. Simpson, 1843-1919

Melody by Thomas Hastings, 1784-1872

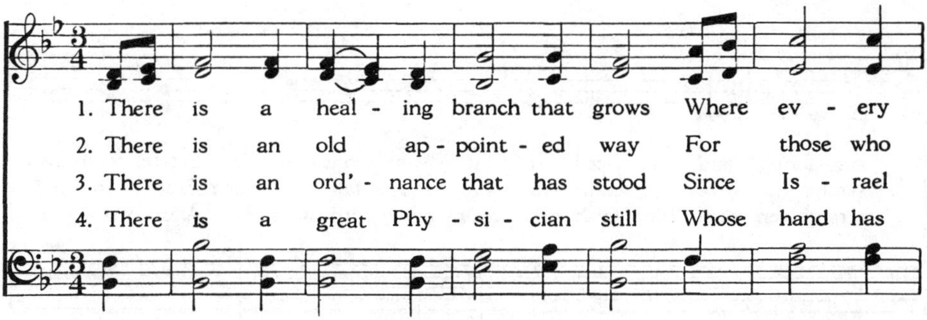
1. There is a heal - ing branch that grows Where ev - ery
2. There is an old ap - point - ed way For those who
3. There is an ord' - nance that has stood Since Is - rael
4. There is a great Phy - si - cian still Whose hand has

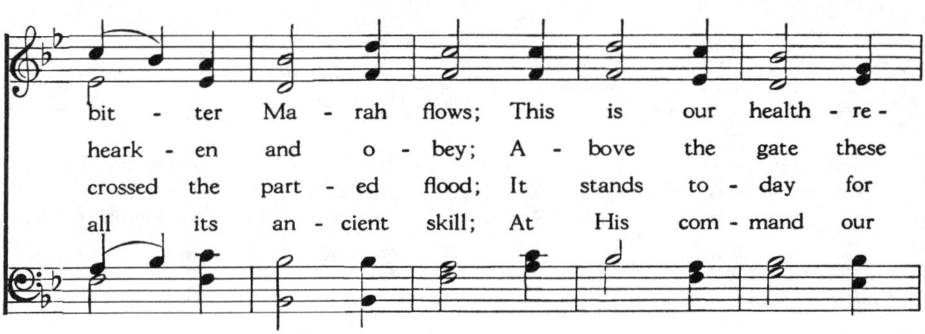
bit - ter Ma - rah flows; This is our health - re -
heark - en and o - bey; A - bove the gate these
crossed the part - ed flood; It stands to - day for
all its an - cient skill; At His com - mand our

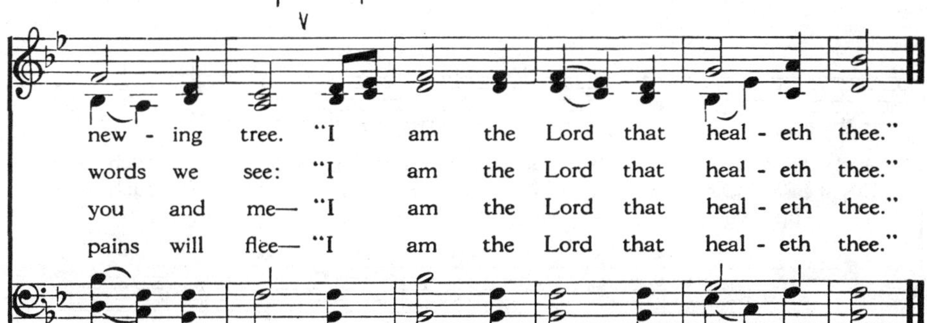
new - ing tree. "I am the Lord that heal - eth thee."
words we see: "I am the Lord that heal - eth thee."
you and me— "I am the Lord that heal - eth thee."
pains will flee— "I am the Lord that heal - eth thee."

(For different harmony see No. 426)

276 Stretch Forth Thy Hand

. . . And he stretched it forth; and it was restored whole . . . Matt. 12:13

Albert B. Simpson, 1843-1919

Melody by Albert B. Simpson, 1843-1919
Adapted by J. Buchanan MacMillan, b. 1915

1. When Christ of old with heal - ing power Went forth through all the
2. That change - less Christ is still as near And just as kind and
3. What though you feel so weak and faint? He can your will with
suf - fering land, His word so oft was wont to be, "Stretch forth thy
strong to save; He came to lift our fall - en race From sin and
strength en - due, New faith and cour - age breathe with - in And work in
hand, stretch forth thy hand!" And though the pal - sied arm might shrink
sick - ness and the grave. As in the days of Gal - i - lee,
you to will and do. Reach out to meet His quick-ening touch;
And trem - ble at the strange com - mand, The heal - ing touch was
Dis - ease still flees at His com - mand; But ere His touch your
Take up your bed, a - rise and stand; And press - ing through to

Stretch Forth Thy Hand

on - ly felt While stretch - ing forth the with - ered hand.
frame can feel, You, too, must still stretch forth your hand.
meet your Lord, Stretch forth your hand, stretch forth your hand.
Refrain
O suf - fering one, stretch forth your hand, Up - on His
prom - ise take your stand. At His com - mand stretch
forth your hand, And Christ shall make you whole.

276

277 Wilt Thou Be Made Whole?

. . . thy faith hath made thee whole . . . Mark 5:34

William J. Kirkpatrick, 1838-1921 — William J. Kirkpatrick, 1838-1921

1. Hear the foot-steps of Je-sus— He is now pass-ing by,
2. 'Tis the voice of that Sav-iour, Whose mer-ci-ful call
3. Are you halt-ing and strug-gling, O-ver-powered by your sin,
4. Bless-ed Sav-iour, as-sist us To rest on Thy Word;
Bear-ing balm for the wound-ed, Heal-ing all who ap-ply;
Free-ly of-fers sal-va-tion To one and to all;
While the wa-ters are trou-bled Can you not en-ter in?
Let the soul-heal-ing pow-er On us now be out-poured;
As He spake to the suf-ferer Who lay at the pool,
He is now beck-oning to Him Each sin-taint-ed soul
Lo, the Sav-iour stands wait-ing To strength-en your soul;
Wash a-way ev-ery sin spot, Take per-fect con-trol,
He is say-ing this mo-ment, "Wilt thou be made whole?"
And lov-ing-ly ask-ing, "Wilt thou be made whole?"
He is ear-nest-ly plead-ing, "Wilt thou be made whole?"
Say to each trust-ing spir-it, "Thy faith makes thee whole."

Wilt Thou Be Made Whole?

Refrain
Wilt thou be made whole? Wilt thou be made whole?
Oh, come, wea - ry suf - ferer, Oh, come, sin - sick soul;
See the life - stream is flow - ing, See the cleans - ing waves roll;
Step in - to the cur - rent and thou shalt be whole.

278 Blessed Be the Glorious Tidings

. . . with his stripes we are healed. Isa. 53:5

Albert B. Simpson, 1843-1919

A. Verne Westlake, 1884-1939

1. Bless-ed be the glo-rious tid-ings To a suf-fering world re-vealed.
2. Je-sus ev-er wel-comed sin-ners To His mer-cy who ap-pealed;
3. Sa-cred is the best a-noint-ing By the Ho-ly Spir-it sealed.
4. Je-sus, to Thy glo-ry ev-er All our mem-bers we would yield.
Christ has made a full a-tone-ment; By His stripes we may be healed.
Still He of-fers us sal-va-tion; By His stripes we may be healed.
Je-sus, lay Thy hands up-on us; By Thy stripes we may be healed.
Grant that al-ways we re-mem-ber— By Thy stripes we may be healed.
REFRAIN
Bless-ed be the great a-tone-ment To a suf-fering world re-vealed;
Bless-ed be this great sal-va-tion— By His stripes we may be healed.

Higher Ground 279

I press toward the mark for the . . . high calling of God . . . Phil. 3:14

Johnson Oatman, Jr., 1856-1926

HIGHER GROUND L.M. with Refrain
Charles H. Gabriel, 1856-1932

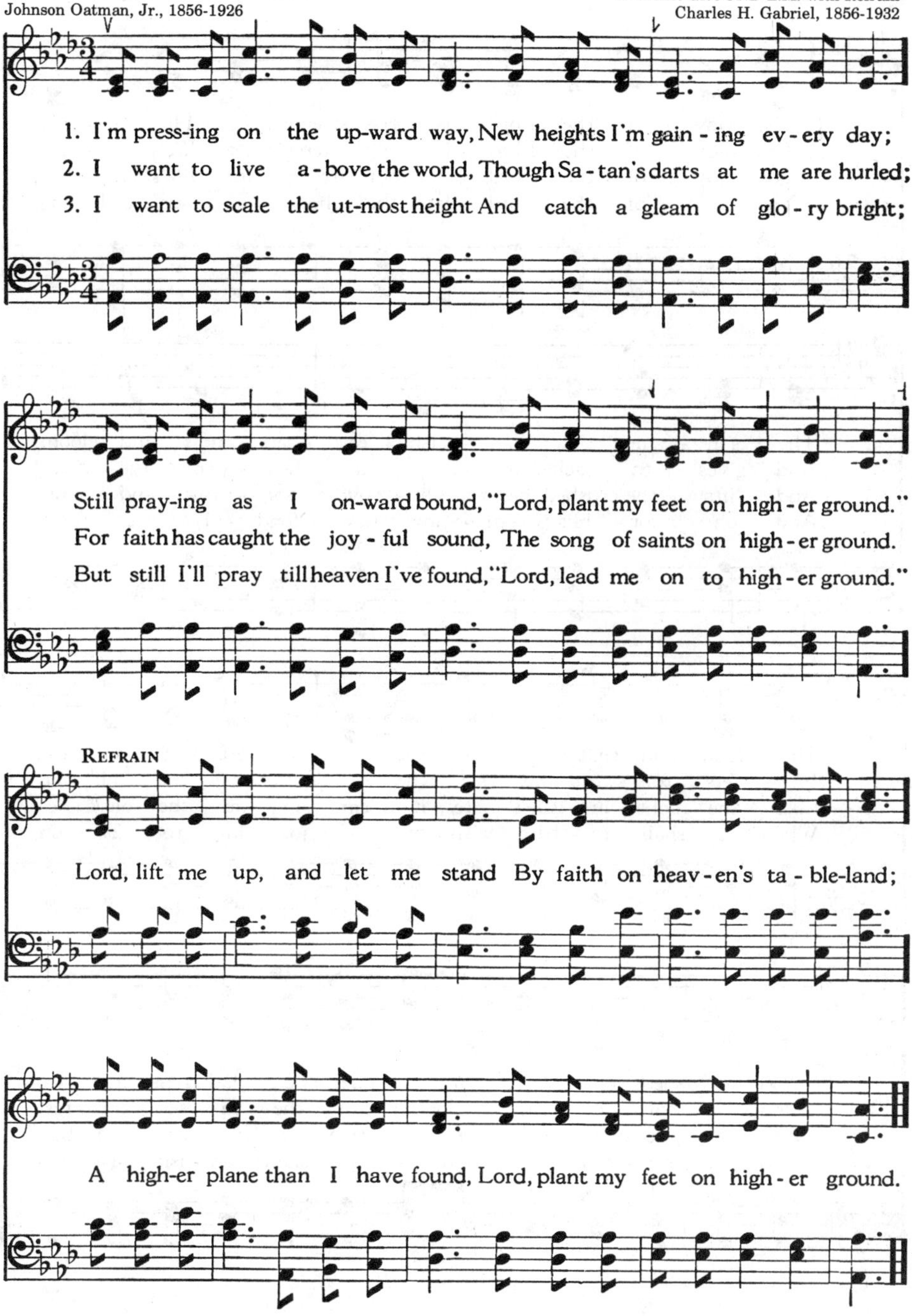
1. I'm press-ing on the up-ward way, New heights I'm gain - ing ev - ery day;
2. I want to live a - bove the world, Though Sa - tan's darts at me are hurled;
3. I want to scale the ut-most height And catch a gleam of glo - ry bright;
Still pray-ing as I on-ward bound, "Lord, plant my feet on high - er ground."
For faith has caught the joy - ful sound, The song of saints on high - er ground.
But still I'll pray till heaven I've found, "Lord, lead me on to high - er ground."
Refrain
Lord, lift me up, and let me stand By faith on heav - en's ta - ble-land;
A high-er plane than I have found, Lord, plant my feet on high - er ground.

280 The Joy of the Lord

. . . the joy of the Lord is your strength. Neh. 8:10

Albert B. Simpson, 1843-1919

Melody by Albert B. Simpson, 1843-1919

1. The joy of the Lord is the strength of His peo - ple,
2. The joy of the Lord is our strength for life's bur - dens,
3. The joy of the Lord is our strength for life's tri - als,
4. The joy of the Lord is the hope of our call - ing,
The sun - shine that ban - ish - es sad - ness and gloom;
And gives to each du - ty a heav - en - ly zest;
And lifts the crushed heart a - bove sor - row and care;
And, oh, for His com - ing how fond - ly we pray!
The foun - tain that bursts in the des - ert of sor - row,
It sets to sweet mu - sic the task of the toil - er,
Like the night - in - gale's notes, it can sing in the dark - ness,
When we shall re - turn with re - joic - ing to Zi - on,
And sheds o'er the wil - der - ness glad - ness and bloom.
And soft - ens the couch of the la - bor - er's rest.
And re - joice when the fig tree is fruit - less and bare.
And sor - row and sigh - ing shall van - ish a - way.

The Joy of the Lord

REFRAIN
Oh, the joy of the Lord is our strength and our song;
Our sor - row and sigh - ing are o'er; We'll re - joice in the Lord,
We'll re - joice in the Lord, We'll re - joice in the Lord ev - er - more.

Walk in the Light! 281

... walk in the light, as he is in the light ... 1 John 1:7

Bernard Barton, 1784-1849

MANOAH C.M.
From Henry W. Greatorex's *Collection,* 1851

1. Walk in the light! and you shall know That fel - low - ship of love,
2. Walk in the light! and you shall find Your heart made tru - ly His,
3. Walk in the light! and you shall see Your dark - ness pass a - way,
4. Walk in the light! and you shall share Your path, though thorn - y, bright;
His Spir - it on - ly can be - stow Who reigns in light a - bove.
Who dwells in cloud - less light en - shrined, In whom no dark - ness is.
Be - cause the Light has come to be, In which is per - fect day.
For God in grace walks with you there, And God Him - self is light.

(For higher key see No. 32)

282 Yielded to God

. . . yield yourselves unto God . . . Rom. 6:13

James M. Kirk, 1854-1945

Melody by James M. Kirk, 1854-1945

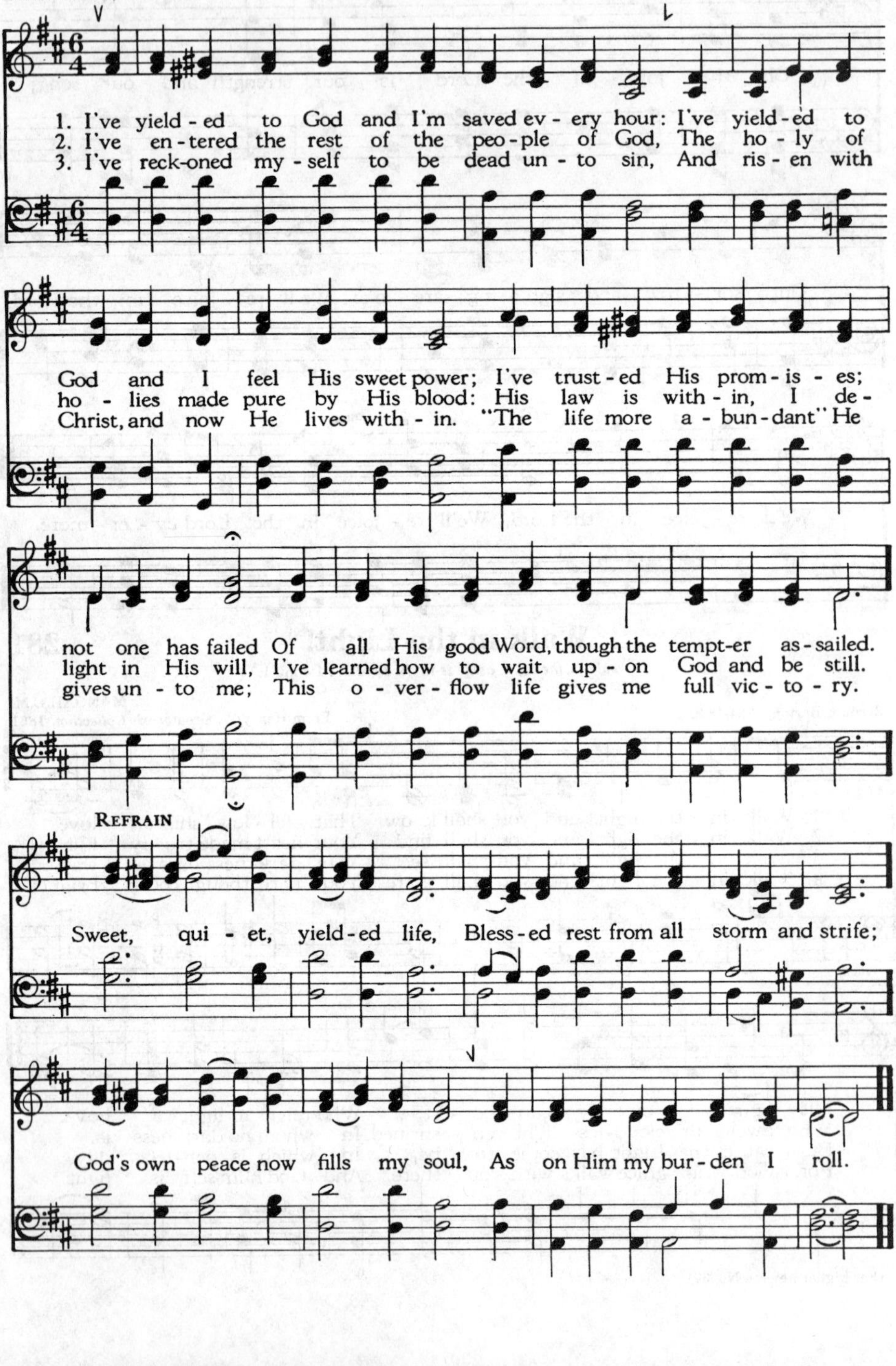
1. I've yield - ed to God and I'm saved ev - ery hour: I've yield - ed to
2. I've en - tered the rest of the peo - ple of God, The ho - ly of
3. I've reck-oned my - self to be dead un - to sin, And ris - en with
God and I feel His sweet power; I've trust - ed His prom - is - es;
ho - lies made pure by His blood: His law is with - in, I de -
Christ, and now He lives with - in. "The life more a - bun - dant" He
not one has failed Of all His good Word, though the tempt - er as - sailed.
light in His will, I've learned how to wait up - on God and be still.
gives un - to me; This o - ver - flow life gives me full vic - to - ry.
REFRAIN
Sweet, qui - et, yield - ed life, Bless - ed rest from all storm and strife;
God's own peace now fills my soul, As on Him my bur - den I roll.

My Grace Is Sufficient for Thee 283

. . . for my strength is made perfect in weakness. . . . 2 Cor. 12:9

Albert B. Simpson, 1843-1919 Albert B. Simpson, 1843-1919

1. I'll sing of the won-der-ful prom-ise That Je-sus has giv-en to me:
2. His grace is suf-fi-cient to save me And cleanse me from guilt and from sin,
3. His grace is suf-fi-cient for sick-ness, Sus-tain-ing and mak-ing me whole;
4. His grace is suf-fi-cient to live by; And should we be sum-moned to die,
"My strength is made per-fect in weak-ness, My grace is suf-fi-cient for thee."
Suf-fi-cient to sanc-ti-fy whol-ly And give me His Spir-it with-in.
His grace is suf-fi-cient when sor-rows Like bil-lows roll o-ver my soul.
'Twill light up the val-ley of shad-ows And bear us a-way to the sky.
And lest my poor heart should for-get it, Or ev-er for-get-ful should be,
His grace is suf-fi-cient for tri-als, No mat-ter how hard they may be;
His grace is suf-fi-cient for serv-ice: It sets us from self-ish-ness free
And when we shall stand with the ran-somed And Christ in His glo-ry shall see,
He still keeps re-peat-ing the prom-ise–"My grace is suf-fi-cient for thee."
This prom-ise stands o-ver a-gainst them–"My grace is suf-fi-cient for thee."
And sends us to tell to the tried ones–"His grace is suf-fi-cient for thee."
We'll fall at His foot-stool con-fess-ing–"Thy grace was suf-fi-cient for me."

284 Abiding and Confiding

Abide in me, and I in you. . . . John 15:4

Albert B. Simpson, 1843-1919

J.H. Burke, 19th century

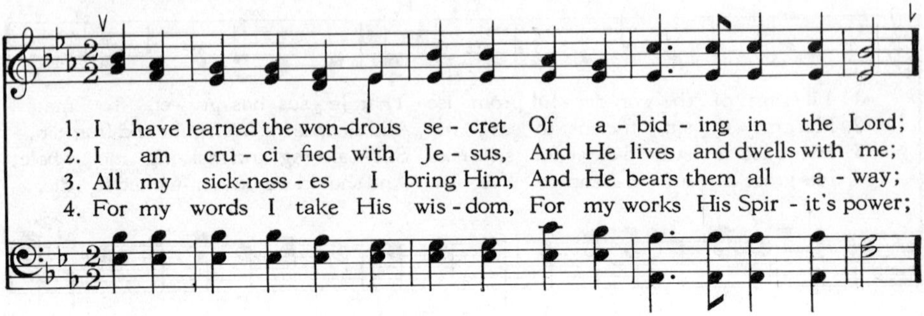
1. I have learned the won-drous se - cret Of a - bid - ing in the Lord;
2. I am cru - ci - fied with Je - sus, And He lives and dwells with me;
3. All my sick-ness - es I bring Him, And He bears them all a - way;
4. For my words I take His wis - dom, For my works His Spir - it's power;

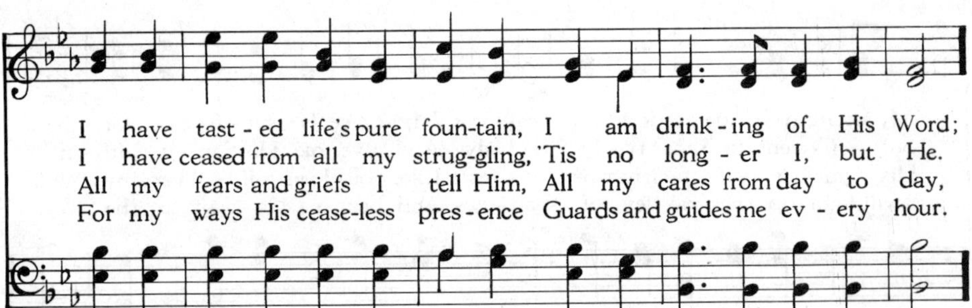
I have tast - ed life's pure foun-tain, I am drink - ing of His Word;
I have ceased from all my strug-gling, 'Tis no long - er I, but He.
All my fears and griefs I tell Him, All my cares from day to day,
For my ways His cease-less pres - ence Guards and guides me ev - ery hour.

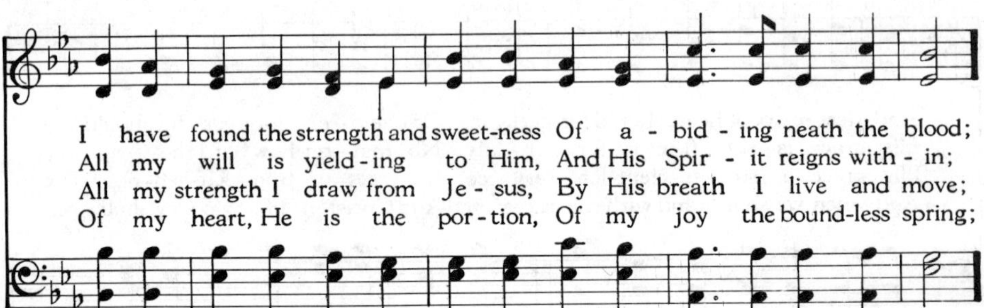
I have found the strength and sweet-ness Of a - bid - ing 'neath the blood;
All my will is yield - ing to Him, And His Spir - it reigns with - in;
All my strength I draw from Je - sus, By His breath I live and move;
Of my heart, He is the por - tion, Of my joy the bound-less spring;

I have lost my - self in Je - sus, I am sink - ing in - to God.
And His pre-cious blood each mo-ment Keeps me cleansed and free from sin.
E'en His ver - y mind He gives me, And His faith, and life, and love.
Sav-iour, Sanc - ti - fi - er, Heal - er, Glo - rious Lord, and com - ing King.

Is Not This the Land of Beulah? 285

. . . for the Lord delighteth in thee . . . Isa. 62:4

Harriet W. Re Qua, 19th century

J.W. Dadman, 19th century

1. I am dwell - ing on the moun-tain Where the gold - en sun-light gleams
2. I can see far down the moun-tain Where I wan-dered wea - ry years,
3. I am drink - ing at the foun-tain Where I ev - er would a - bide;
4. Tell me not of heav - y cross - es, Nor the bur - dens hard to bear,
O'er a land of won-drous beau-ty Far ex - ceeds my fond - est dreams;
Oft - en hin - dered in my jour-ney By the ghosts of doubts and fears;
For I've tast - ed life's pure riv - er, And my soul is sat - is - fied;
For I've found this great sal - va - tion Makes this bur - den light ap - pear;
Where the air is pure, e - the - real, La - den with the breath of flowers,
Bro - ken vows and dis - ap-point-ments Thick-ly sprin - kled all the way,
There's no thirst-ing for life's pleas-ures Nor a - dorn - ing rich and gay,
And I love to fol - low Je - sus, Glad - ly count - ing all but dross,
REFRAIN
Is not this the land of Beu - lah? Bless - ed, bless - ed land of light
D. S. for Refrain
They are bloom - ing by the foun-tain, 'Neath the am - a - ran-thine bowers.
But the Spir - it led, un - err - ing, To the land I hold to - day.
For I've found a rich - er treas-ure, One that fad - eth not a - way.
World - ly hon - ors all for - sak - ing For the glo - ry of the cross.
Where the flow - ers bloom for - ev - er, And the sun is al - ways bright.

286 Living in the Glory

... an entrance shall be ministered unto you ... into the everlasting kingdom ... 2 Pet. 1:11

Albert B. Simpson, 1843-1919 | May A. Stephens, 1865-1935

1. I have found a heaven be - low, I am liv - ing in the glo - ry;
2. Storms of sor - row 'round me fall, But I'm liv - ing in the glo - ry;
3. Sa - tan can - not touch my heart While I'm liv - ing in the glo - ry;
4. I can tri - umph o - ver pain While I'm liv - ing in the glo - ry;
5. I am poor and lit - tle known, But I'm liv - ing in the glo - ry;
6. Soon the King will come for me To be with Him in the glo - ry;
Oh, the joy and strength I know, Liv - ing in the glo - ry of the Lord.
I can sing a - bove them all, Liv - ing in the glo - ry of the Lord.
This dis - arms each fier - y dart, Liv - ing in the glo - ry of the Lord.
I can count each loss a gain, Liv - ing in the glo - ry of the Lord.
And I'm wait - ing for a throne, Liv - ing in the glo - ry of the Lord.
Then my song shall sweet - er be, Reign - ing in the glo - ry of the Lord.
REFRAIN
Yes, I'm liv - ing in the glo - ry As He prom - ised in His Word;
I am dwell - ing in the heaven - lies, Liv - ing in the glo - ry of the Lord.

Abundant Life

287

. . . I am come that they might have life, and . . . have it more abundantly. John 10:10

W. Leslie, 19th century

Melody by Stephen C. Foster, 1826-1864

1. Un - der the bur-dens of guilt and care, Man - y a spir - it is griev-ing, Who in the joy of the Lord might share, Life ev - er-last - ing re - ceiv - ing.
2. Bur-dened one, why will you long - er bear Sor - rows from which He re - leas - es? O - pen your heart and re - joic - ing share Life more a - bun - dant in Je - sus!
3. Oh, for the showers on the thirst - y land! Oh, for a might - y re - vi - val! Oh, for a sanc - ti - fied, fear - less band Read - y to hail His ar - ri - val!
REFRAIN
Life, life, e - ter - nal life! Je - sus a - lone is the giv - er! Life, life, a - bun - dant life! Glo - ry to Je - sus for - ev - er!

288 Even as He

... when he shall appear, we shall be like him ... 1 John 3:2

Albert B. Simpson, 1843-1919

Melody by Albert B. Simpson, 1843-1919
Harmony by J. Buchanan MacMillan, b. 1915

1. Oh, what a won - der - ful place Je - sus has
2. One in His death on the tree, One as He
3. One in His mer - its I stand, One as I
giv - en to me! Saved by His glo - ri - ous grace, I may be
rose from the dead; I from the curse am as free E'en as my
pray in His name; All that His worth can com - mand, I can with
e - ven as He. When with my Lord I ap - pear Like Him I
glo - ri - ous head. One on the throne by His side, One in His
con - fi - dence claim. One in His faith and His love, One in His
know I shall be; But while I walk with Him here,
son - ship di - vine; One as the bride-groom and bride,
life I may be. Sealed by the heav - en - ly Dove,

Even as He

REFRAIN
I may be e - ven as He.
One as the branch and the vine.
I may be ho - ly as He.
E - ven as He,
E - ven as He,
E - ven as He,
E - ven as He, Won - der - ful words that
e - ven we, Saved by His mar - vel - ous grace may be
One with the Sav - iour, E - ven as He.

289 Near to the Heart of God

Draw nigh to God, and he will draw nigh to you. . . . James 4:8

Cleland B. McAfee, 1866-1944

MCAFEE C.M. with Refrain
Cleland B. McAfee, 1866-1944

1. There is a place of qui - et rest Near to the heart of God,
2. There is a place of com - fort sweet Near to the heart of God,
3. There is a place of full re - lease Near to the heart of God,
A place where sin can - not mo - lest, Near to the heart of God.
A place where we our Sav - iour meet, Near to the heart of God.
A place where all is joy and peace, Near to the heart of God.
REFRAIN
O Je - sus, blest Re - deem - er, Sent from the heart of God,
Hold us, who wait be - fore Thee, Near to the heart of God.

I Take, He Undertakes

I can do all things through Christ which strengtheneth me. Phil. 4:13

Albert B. Simpson, 1843-1919

Melody by Albert B. Simpson, 1843-1919

1. I clasp the hand of Love di - vine, I claim the gra-cious prom - ise mine,
2. I take sal - va - tion full and free Through Him who gave His life for me;
3. I take Him as my ho - li - ness, My spir - it's, spot-less, heaven-ly dress,
4. I take the prom-ised Ho - ly Ghost, I take the power of Pen - te-cost
5. I take Him for this mor - tal frame, I take my heal-ing through His name,
6. I sim - ply take Him at His word, I praise Him that my prayer is heard,
And this e - ter - nal coun - ter - sign— I take, He un - der - takes.
He un - der-takes my all to be— I take, He un - der - takes.
I take the Lord, my right - eous - ness— I take, He un - der - takes.
To fill me to the ut - ter - most—I take, He un - der - takes.
And all His ris - en life I claim—I take, He un - der - takes.
And claim my an - swer from the Lord—I take, He un - der - takes.
REFRAIN
I take Thee, bless - ed Lord, I give my - self to Thee;
And Thou, ac - cord - ing to Thy Word, Dost un - der - take for me.

291 'Tis So Sweet to Trust in Jesus

It is better to trust in the Lord than to put confidence in man. Psa. 118:8

Louisa M.R. Stead, circa 1850-1917 — Melody by William J. Kirkpatrick, 1838-1921

1. 'Tis so sweet to trust in Je - sus, Just to take Him at His word,
2. Oh, how sweet to trust in Je - sus, Just to trust His cleans-ing blood,
3. Yes, 'tis sweet to trust in Je - sus, Just from sin and self to cease,
4. I'm so glad I learned to trust Thee, Pre - cious Je - sus, Sav-iour, Friend;
Just to rest up - on His prom - ise, Just to know, "Thus saith the Lord."
Just in sim - ple faith to plunge me 'Neath the heal - ing, cleans-ing flood.
Just from Je - sus sim - ply tak - ing Life, and rest, and joy, and peace.
And I know that Thou art with me, Will be with me to the end.
REFRAIN
1-3. Je - sus, Je - sus, how I trust Him, How I've proved Him o'er and o'er;
4. Je - sus, Je - sus, how I trust Thee, How I've proved Thee o'er and o'er;
Je - sus, Je - sus, pre - cious Je - sus! Oh, for grace to trust Him more.
Je - sus, Je - sus, pre - cious Je - sus! Oh, for grace to trust Thee more.

Nearer the Cross 292

Let us draw near with a true heart in full assurance of faith . . . Heb. 10:22

Fanny J. Crosby, 1820-1915 | Phoebe P. Knapp, 1839-1908

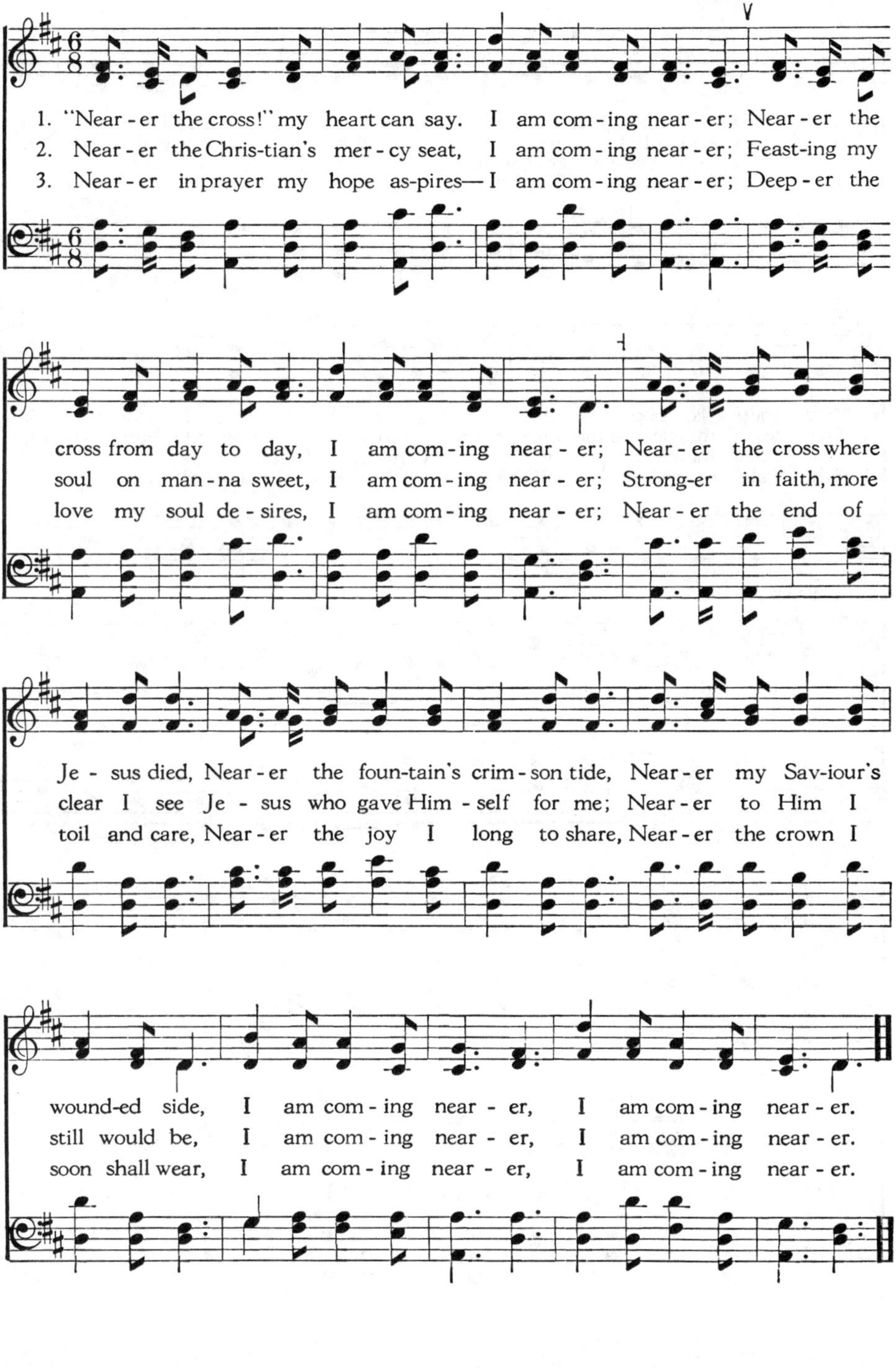
6
8
1. "Near - er the cross!" my heart can say. I am com - ing near - er; Near - er the
2. Near - er the Chris-tian's mer - cy seat, I am com - ing near - er; Feast-ing my
3. Near - er in prayer my hope as-pires— I am com - ing near - er; Deep - er the
cross from day to day, I am com - ing near - er; Near - er the cross where
soul on man - na sweet, I am com - ing near - er; Strong-er in faith, more
love my soul de - sires, I am com - ing near - er; Near - er the end of
Je - sus died, Near - er the foun-tain's crim - son tide, Near - er my Sav-iour's
clear I see Je - sus who gave Him - self for me; Near - er to Him I
toil and care, Near - er the joy I long to share, Near - er the crown I
wound-ed side, I am com - ing near - er, I am com - ing near - er.
still would be, I am com - ing near - er, I am com - ing near - er.
soon shall wear, I am com - ing near - er, I am com - ing near - er.

293 At the Cross I'll Abide

Wash me throughly from mine iniquity, and cleanse me from my sin. Psa. 51:2

Isaiah Baltzell, 1832-1893 | Isaiah Baltzell, 1832-1893

1. O Je - sus, Sav - iour, I long to rest Near the cross where Thou hast died;
2. My dy - ing Je - sus, my Sav-iour, God, Who hast borne my guilt and sin,
3. O Je - sus, Sav-iour, now make me Thine, Nev - er let me stray from Thee;
4. The cleans-ing power of Thy blood ap - ply, All my guilt and sin re - move;
For there is hope for the ach - ing breast; At the cross I will a - bide.
Now wash me, cleanse me with Thine own blood; Ev - er keep me pure and clean.
Oh, wash me, cleanse me, for Thou art mine, And Thy love is full and free.
Oh, help me, while at Thy cross I lie, Fill my soul with per - fect love.
REFRAIN
At the cross I'll a - bide, At the cross I'll a - bide; At the cross I'll a - bide, There His blood is ap - plied; At the cross I am sat - is - fied.

Saviour, More Than Life to Me **294**

But cleave unto the Lord your God . . . Josh. 23:8

EVERY DAY AND HOUR 7.9.7.9. with Refrain

Fanny J. Crosby, 1820-1915

William H. Doane, 1832-1915

1. Sav - iour, more than life to me, I am cling-ing, cling-ing close to Thee;
2. Through this chang-ing world be - low, Lead me gent - ly, gent - ly as I go;
3. Let me love Thee more and more Till this fleet-ing, fleet-ing life is o'er,

Let Thy pre - cious blood ap - plied Keep me ev - er, ev - er near Thy side.
Trust - ing Thee, I can - not stray, I can nev - er, nev - er lose my way.
Till my soul is lost in love In a bright-er, bright-er world a - bove.

REFRAIN

Ev - ery day, ev - ery hour, Let me feel Thy cleans-ing power;

May Thy ten - der love to me Bind me clos - er, clos-er, Lord, to Thee.

295 Nearer, Still Nearer

. . . let not any iniquity have dominion over me. Psa. 119:133

Lelia N. Morris, 1862-1929

MORRIS 9.10.9.10. with repeat
Lelia N. Morris, 1862-1929

1. Near - er, still near - er, close to Thy heart, Draw me, my
2. Near - er, still near - er— noth - ing I bring, Naught as an
3. Near - er, still near - er, Lord, to be Thine; Sin, with its
4. Near - er, still near - er, while life shall last, Till safe in
Sav - iour, so pre - cious Thou art; Fold me, oh, fold me
of - fering to Je - sus my King— On - ly my sin - ful,
fol - lies, I glad - ly re - sign, All of its pleas - ures,
glo - ry my an - chor is cast, Through end - less a - ges
close to Thy breast, Shel - ter me safe in that ha - ven of
now con - trite heart. Grant me the cleans - ing Thy blood doth im -
pomp, and its pride. Give me but Je - sus, my Lord cru - ci -
ev - er to be Near - er, my Sav - iour, still near - er to
rest, Shel - ter me safe in that ha - ven of rest.
part, Grant me the cleans - ing Thy blood doth im - part.
fied, Give me but Je - sus, my Lord cru - ci - fied.
Thee, Near - er, my Sav - iour, still near - er to Thee.

Come, Ye Disconsolate 296

Let us therefore come boldly . . . and find grace to help in time of need. Heb. 4:16

Thomas Moore, 1779-1852
Altered by Thomas Hastings, 1784-1872

CONSOLATION 11.10.11.10.
Samuel Webbe, Sr., 1740-1816

1. Come, ye dis - con - so - late, wher - e'er ye lan - guish,
2. Joy of the des - o - late, light of the stray - ing,
3. Here see the Bread of Life; see wa - ters flow - ing
Come to the mer - cy seat, fer - vent - ly kneel;
Hope of the pen - i - tent, fade - less and pure!
Forth from the throne of God, pure from a - bove:
Here bring your wound - ed hearts, here tell your an - guish;
Here speaks the Com - fort - er, ten - der - ly say - ing,
Come to the feast of love; come, ev - er know - ing
Earth has no sor - rows that heaven can - not heal.
"Earth has no sor - rows that heaven can - not cure."
Earth has no sor - rows but heaven can re - move. A-MEN.

297 Hiding in Thee

. . . God is the rock of my refuge. Psa. 94:22

HIDING IN THEE 11.11.11.11. with Refrain

William O. Cushing, 1823-1902

Ira D. Sankey, 1840-1908

1. Oh, safe to the Rock that is high - er than I My
2. In the calm of the noon - tide, in sor - row's lone hour, In
3. How oft in the con - flict, when pressed by the foe, I have
soul in its con - flicts and sor - rows would fly. So sin - ful, so
times when temp - ta - tion casts o'er me its power; In the tem - pests of
fled to my Ref - uge and breathed out my woe; How oft - en, when
wea - ry, Thine, Thine would I be! Thou blest Rock of
life, on its wide, heav - ing sea, Thou blest Rock of
tri - als like sea bil - lows roll, Have I hid - den in
A - ges, I'm hid - ing in Thee.
A - ges, I'm hid - ing in Thee.
Thee, O Thou Rock of my soul.
Refrain
Hid - ing in Thee, Hid - ing in
Thee, Thou blest Rock of A - ges, I'm hid - ing in Thee.

Under His Wings 298

He shall cover thee with his feathers, and under his wings shalt thou trust . . . Psa. 91:4

HINGHAM 11.10.11.10. with Refrain

William O. Cushing, 1823-1902

Ira D. Sankey, 1840-1908

1. Un - der His wings I am safe - ly a - bid - ing; Though the night
2. Un - der His wings—what a ref - uge in sor - row! How the heart
3. Un - der His wings— oh, what pre - cious en - joy-ment! There will I
deep - ens and tem - pests are wild, Still I can trust Him, I
yearn - ing - ly turns to His rest! Oft - en when earth has no
hide till life's tri - als are o'er; Shel - tered, pro - tect - ed, no
know He will keep me; He has re-deemed me, and I am His child.
balm for my heal - ing, There I find com - fort, and there I am blest.
e - vil can harm me; Rest - ing in Je - sus I'm safe ev - er - more.
REFRAIN
Un - der His wings, un - der His wings, Who from His love can sev - er?
Un - der His wings my soul shall a - bide, Safe-ly a - bide for - ev - er.

299 Blessed Assurance

. . . he hath given assurance unto all men . . . Acts 17:31

ASSURANCE 9.10.9.9. with Refrain

Fanny J. Crosby, 1820-1915

Phoebe P. Knapp, 1839-1908

1. Bless-ed as - sur - ance, Je - sus is mine! Oh, what a fore - taste of
2. Per - fect sub - mis - sion, per-fect de - light, Vi - sions of rap - ture now
3. Per - fect sub - mis - sion, all is at rest; I in my Sav - iour am
glo - ry di - vine! Heir of sal - va - tion, pur-chase of God, Born of His
burst on my sight. An - gels de - scend - ing, bring from a - bove Ech - oes of
hap - py and blest, Watch-ing and wait - ing, look - ing a - bove, Filled with His
Spir - it, washed in His blood.
mer - cy, whis-pers of love.
good-ness, lost in His love.
REFRAIN
This is my sto - ry, this is my
song: Prais - ing my Sav - iour all the day long. This is my
sto - ry, this is my song: Prais-ing my Sav - iour all the day long.

It Is Well with My Soul

300

And the peace of God, . . . shall keep your hearts and minds through Christ Jesus. Phil. 4:7

VILLE DU HAVRE 11.8.11.9. with Refrain

Horatio G. Spafford, 1828-1888

Philip P. Bliss, 1838-1876

1. When peace like a riv - er at - tend - eth my way, When
2. Though Sa - tan should buf - fet, though tri - als should come, Let
3. My sin— oh, the bliss of this glo - ri - ous thought–My
4. And, Lord, haste the day when the faith shall be sight, The
sor - rows like sea bil - lows roll, What - ev - er my lot, Thou hast
this blest as - sur - ance con - trol, That Christ hath re - gard - ed my
sin, not in part but the whole, Is nailed to His cross and I
clouds be rolled back as a scroll, The trump shall re - sound, and the
taught me to say, "It is well, it is well with my soul."
help - less es - tate, And hath shed His own blood for my soul.
bear it no more! Praise the Lord, praise the Lord, O my soul!
Lord shall de - scend! E - ven so— it is well with my soul!
Refrain
It is well with my soul; it is well, it is well with my soul!
It is well with my soul;

301 Jesus, Lover of My Soul

(FIRST TUNE)

For thou hast been a . . . refuge from the storm . . . Isa. 25:4

ABERYSTWYTH 7.7.7.7.D.

Charles Wesley, 1707-1788 — Joseph Parry, 1841-1903

1. Je - sus, Lov - er of my soul, Let me to Thy bos - om fly
2. Oth - er ref - uge have I none; Hangs my help-less soul on Thee.
3. Thou, O Christ, art all I want; More than all in Thee I find;
4. Plen - teous grace with Thee is found, Grace to cov - er all my sin;
While the near - er wa - ters roll, While the tem-pest still is high.
Leave, ah, leave me not a - lone; Still sup - port and com-fort me.
Raise the fall - en, cheer the faint, Heal the sick, and lead the blind.
Let the heal - ing streams a - bound; Make and keep me pure with - in.
Hide me, O my Sav - iour, hide Till the storm of life is past;
All my trust on Thee is stayed, All my help from Thee I bring;
Just and ho - ly is Thy name; I am all un - right - eous-ness.
Thou of life the Foun - tain art, Free - ly let me take of Thee;
Safe in - to the ha - ven guide; Oh, re - ceive my soul at last!
Cov - er my de - fense-less head With the shad - ow of Thy wing.
False and full of sin I am; Thou art full of truth and grace.
Spring Thou up with - in my heart, Rise to all e - ter - ni - ty. A-MEN.

Jesus, Lover of My Soul

(SECOND TUNE)

MARTYN 7.7.7.7.D.

Charles Wesley, 1707-1788

Melody by Simon B. Marsh, 1798-1875

1. Je - sus, Lov - er of my soul, Let me to Thy bos - om fly
2. Oth - er ref - uge have I none; Hangs my help - less soul on Thee.
3. Thou, O Christ, art all I want; More than all in Thee I find;
4. Plen-teous grace with Thee is found, Grace to cov - er all my sin;
While the near - er wa - ters roll, While the tem - pest still is high.
Leave, ah, leave me not a - lone; Still sup - port and com-fort me.
Raise the fall - en, cheer the faint, Heal the sick, and lead the blind.
Let the heal - ing streams a-bound; Make and keep me pure with - in.
Hide me, O my Sav - iour, hide Till the storm of life is past;
All my trust on Thee is stayed, All my help from Thee I bring;
Just and ho - ly is Thy name; I am all un - right - eous - ness.
Thou of life the Foun - tain art, Free - ly let me take of Thee;
Safe in - to the ha - ven guide; Oh, re - ceive my soul at last!
Cov - er my de - fense-less head With the shad-ow of Thy wing.
False and full of sin I am; Thou art full of truth and grace.
Spring Thou up with - in my heart, Rise to all e - ter - ni - ty.

303 In Heavenly Love Abiding

If ye keep my commandments, ye shall abide in my love . . . John 15:10

SEDGWICK 7.6.7.6.D.

Anna L. Waring, 1823-1910

Lee H. Bristol, Jr., b. 1923

1. In heaven-ly love a - bid - ing, No change my heart shall fear;
2. Wher - ev - er He may guide me, No want shall turn me back;
3. Green pas - tures are be - fore me, Which yet I have not seen;
And safe is such con - fid - ing, For noth - ing chang - es here:
My Shep - herd is be - side me, And noth - ing can I lack:
Bright skies will soon be o'er me Where dark - est clouds have been:
The storm may roar with - out me, My heart may low be laid;
His wis - dom ev - er wak - eth; His sight is nev - er dim;
My hope I can - not meas - ure; My path to life is free;
But God is round a - bout me, And can I be dis - mayed?
He knows the way He tak - eth, And I will walk with Him.
My Sav - iour has my treas - ure, And He will walk with me. A - MEN.

Like a River Glorious 304

. . . I will extend peace to her like a river . . . Isa. 66:12

WYE VALLEY 6.5.6.5.D. with Refrain

Frances R. Havergal, 1836-1879

James Mountain, 1843-1933

1. Like a riv - er glo - rious Is God's per - fect peace, O - ver
2. Hid - den in the hol - low Of His bless - ed hand, Nev - er
3. Ev - ery joy or tri - al Fall - eth from a - bove, Traced up -
all vic - to - rious In its bright in - crease; Per - fect, yet it
foe can fol - low, Nev - er trai - tor stand. Not a surge of
on our di - al By the Sun of love. We may trust Him
flow - eth Full - er ev - ery day; Per - fect, yet it grow - eth
wor - ry, Not a shade of care, Not a blast of hur - ry
ful - ly— All for us to do; They who trust Him whol - ly
REFRAIN
Deep - er all the way.
Touch the spir - it there. Stayed up - on Je - ho - vah Hearts are
Find Him whol - ly true.
ful - ly blest, Find - ing, as He prom - ised, Per - fect peace and rest.

305 Lord, I Hear of Showers of Blessing

He shall come down like rain upon the mown grass . . . Psa. 72:6

EVEN ME 8.7.8.7.6.7.

Elizabeth Codner, 1824-1919

Melody by William B. Bradbury, 1816-1868

1. Lord, I hear of showers of bless-ing Thou art scat-tering full and free—
2. Pass me not, O gra - cious Fa-ther, Sin - ful though my heart may be,
3. Pass me not, O ten - der Sav-iour, Let me love and cling to Thee.
4. Pass me not, O might - y Spir - it; Thou canst make the blind to see.
5. Love of God, so pure and change-less; Blood of Christ, so rich and free;

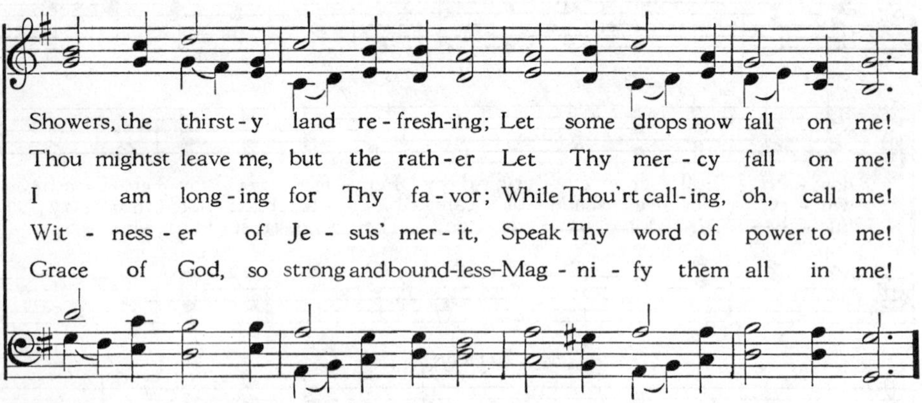
Showers, the thirst - y land re - fresh-ing; Let some drops now fall on me!
Thou mightst leave me, but the rath - er Let Thy mer - cy fall on me!
I am long - ing for Thy fa - vor; While Thou'rt call - ing, oh, call me!
Wit - ness - er of Je - sus' mer - it, Speak Thy word of power to me!
Grace of God, so strong and bound-less–Mag - ni - fy them all in me!

E - ven me, e - ven me! Let some drops now fall on me!
E - ven me, e - ven me! Let Thy mer - cy fall on me!
E - ven me, e - ven me! While Thou'rt call - ing, oh, call me!
E - ven me, e - ven me! Speak Thy word of power to me!
E - ven me, e - ven me! Mag - ni - fy them all in me!

My Hope Is Built on Nothing Less 306

He . . . set my feet upon a rock, and established my goings. Psa. 40:2

SOLID ROCK L.M. with Refrain

Edward Mote, 1797-1874

William B. Bradbury, 1816-1868

1. My hope is built on noth - ing less Than Je - sus' blood and
2. When dark-ness veils His love - ly face, I rest on His un -
3. His oath, His cov - e - nant, His blood Sup - port me in the
4. When He shall come with trum - pet sound, Oh, may I then in
right - eous - ness; I dare not trust the sweet - est frame But
chang - ing grace; In ev - ery high and storm - y gale My
whelm - ing flood; When all a - round my soul gives way, He
Him be found, Dressed in His right - eous - ness a - lone, Fault -
whol - ly lean on Je - sus' name.
an - chor holds with - in the veil.
then is all my hope and stay.
less to stand be - fore the throne!
Refrain
On Christ, the sol - id rock I stand;
All oth - er ground is sink-ing sand, All oth - er ground is sink - ing sand.

307 My Faith Looks Up to Thee

Looking unto Jesus the author and finisher of our faith . . . Heb. 12:2

OLIVET 6.6.4.6.6.6.4.

Ray Palmer, 1808-1887

Melody by Lowell Mason, 1792-1872

1. My faith looks up to Thee, Thou Lamb of
2. May Thy rich grace im - part Strength to my
3. While life's dark maze I tread And griefs a -
4. When ends life's tran - sient dream, When death's cold,
Cal - va - ry, Sav - iour di - vine; Now hear me
faint - ing heart, My zeal in - spire; As Thou hast
round me spread, Be Thou my guide; Bid dark - ness
sul - len stream Shall o'er me roll, Blest Sav - iour,
while I pray, Take all my guilt a - way;
died for me, Oh, may my love to Thee
turn to day, Wipe sor - row's tears a - way,
then, in love, Fear and dis - trust re - move;
Oh, let me from this day Be whol - ly Thine!
Pure, warm, and change - less be, A liv - ing fire!
Nor let me ev - er stray From Thee a - side.
Oh, bear me safe a - bove, A ran - somed soul! A-MEN.

Still, Still with Thee

308

. . . when I awake, I am still with thee. Psa. 139:18

Harriet B. Stowe, 1812-1896

CONSOLATION (Mendelssohn) 11.10.11.10.
Adapted from Felix Mendelssohn, 1809-1847

1. Still, still with Thee, when pur - ple morn - ing break - eth,
2. A - lone with Thee, a - mid the mys - tic shad - ows,
3. When sinks the soul, sub - dued by toil, to slum - ber,
4. So shall it be at last, in that bright morn - ing
When the bird wak - eth and the shad - ows flee;
The sol - emn hush of na - ture new - ly born;
Its clos - ing eyes look up to Thee in prayer;
When the soul wak - eth and life's shad - ows flee;
Fair - er than morn - ing, love - lier than the day - light,
A - lone with Thee in breath - less ad - o - ra - tion,
Sweet the re - pose be - neath Thy wings o'er - shad - ing,
Oh, in that hour, fair - er than day - light dawn - ing,
Dawns the sweet con - scious - ness, I am with Thee.
In the calm dew and fresh - ness of the morn.
But sweet - er still to wake and find Thee there.
Shall rise the glo - rious thought—I am with Thee. A - MEN.

(For different harmony see No. 436)

309 Be Still, My Soul

Be still, and know that I am God . . . Psa. 46:10

FINLANDIA 10.10.10.10.10.10.
Katharina A.D. von Schlegel, b. 1697 — From Jean Sibelius' *Finlandia*, 1899
Translated by Jane L. Borthwick, 1813-1897 — Arranged for *The Hymnal*, 1933

1. Be still, my soul, the Lord is on thy side; Bear pa-tient-ly the
2. Be still, my soul, thy God doth un-der-take To guide the fu-ture
3. Be still, my soul, the hour is has-tening on When we shall be for-

cross of grief or pain; Leave to thy God to or-der or pro-vide;
as He has the past. Thy hope, thy con-fi-dence let noth-ing shake;
ev-er with the Lord, When dis-ap-point-ment, grief, and fear are gone,

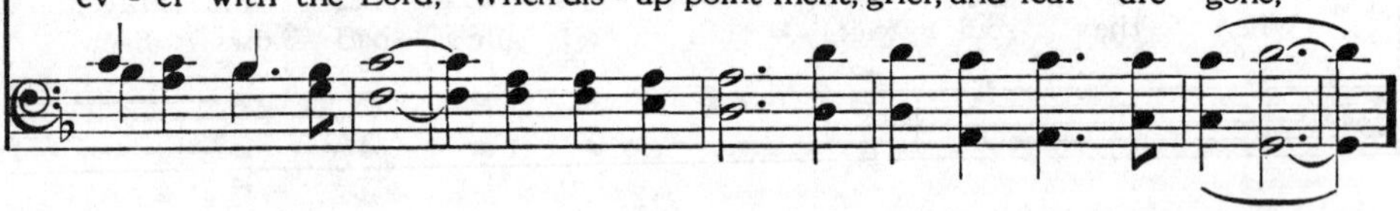

In ev-ery change He faith-ful will re-main. Be still, my soul, thy
All now mys-te-rious shall be bright at last. Be still, my soul, the
Sor-row for-got, love's pur-est joys re-stored. Be still, my soul, when

best, thy heaven-ly Friend Through thorn-y ways leads to a joy-ful end.
waves and winds still know His voice who ruled them while He dwelt be-low.
change and tears are past, All safe and bless-ed we shall meet at last. A-MEN.

I Am Trusting Thee, Lord Jesus 310

. . . his heart is fixed, trusting in the Lord. Psa. 112:7

BULLINGER 8.5.8.3.

Frances R. Havergal, 1836-1879

Ethelbert W. Bullinger, 1837-1913

1. I am trust - ing Thee, Lord Je - sus,
2. I am trust - ing Thee for par - don;
3. I am trust - ing Thee for cleans - ing
4. I am trust - ing Thee to guide me;
5. I am trust - ing Thee for pow - er;
6. I am trust - ing Thee, Lord Je - sus,
Trust - ing on - ly Thee! Trust - ing Thee for
At Thy feet I bow; For Thy grace and
In the crim - son flood; Trust - ing Thee to
Thou a - lone shalt lead, Ev - ery day and
Thine can nev - er fail; Words which Thou Thy -
Nev - er let me fall; I am trust - ing
full sal - va - tion, Great and free.
ten - der mer - cy, Trust - ing now.
make me ho - ly By Thy blood.
hour sup - ply - ing All my need.
self shalt give me Must pre - vail.
Thee for - ev - er And for all.

311 My Anchor Holds

. . . we have . . . an anchor of the soul, both sure and stedfast . . . Heb. 6:19

MY ANCHOR HOLDS 7.7.7.7. with Refrain

W.C. Martin, 19th century

Daniel B. Towner, 1850-1919

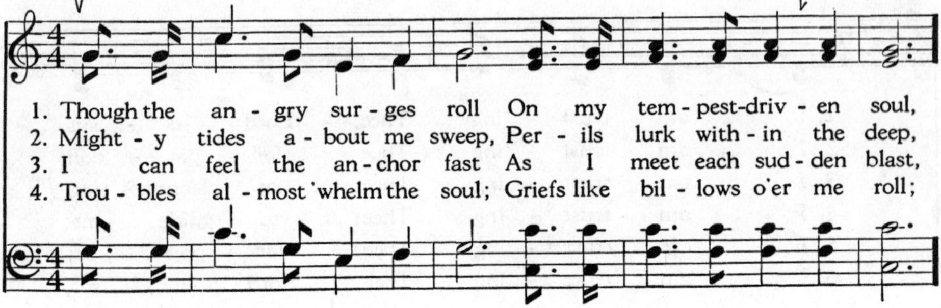
1. Though the an - gry sur - ges roll On my tem - pest-driv - en soul,
2. Might - y tides a - bout me sweep, Per - ils lurk with - in the deep,
3. I can feel the an - chor fast As I meet each sud - den blast,
4. Trou - bles al - most 'whelm the soul; Griefs like bil - lows o'er me roll;

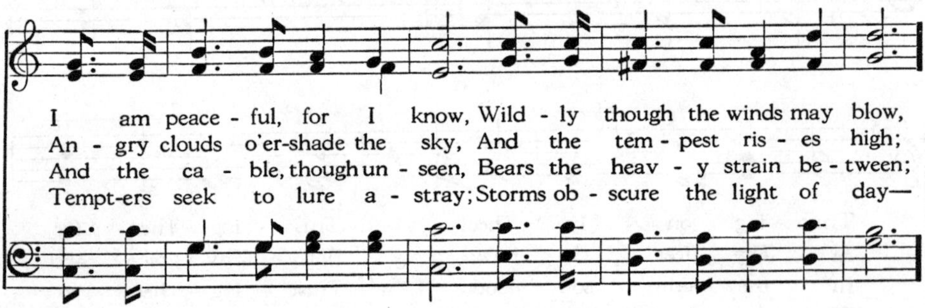
I am peace - ful, for I know, Wild - ly though the winds may blow,
An - gry clouds o'er-shade the sky, And the tem - pest ris - es high;
And the ca - ble, though un - seen, Bears the heav - y strain be - tween;
Tempt-ers seek to lure a - stray; Storms ob - scure the light of day—

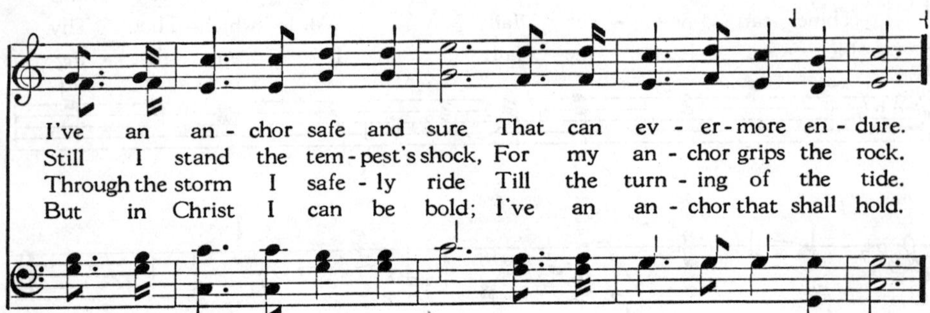
I've an an - chor safe and sure That can ev - er-more en - dure.
Still I stand the tem - pest's shock, For my an - chor grips the rock.
Through the storm I safe - ly ride Till the turn - ing of the tide.
But in Christ I can be bold; I've an an - chor that shall hold.

REFRAIN

And it holds, my an - chor holds; Blow your wild - est, then, O
And it holds, my an - chor holds; Blow your wild - - est,

My Anchor Holds

gale, On my bark so small and frail; By His grace I shall not
gale, O gale,
fail, For my an - chor holds, my an - chor holds.
For my an - chor holds, it firm - ly holds,

My Times Are in Thy Hand 312

. . . deliver me from the hand of mine enemies . . . Psa. 31:15

William F. Lloyd, 1791-1853

BOYLSTON S.M.
Melody by Lowell Mason, 1792-1872

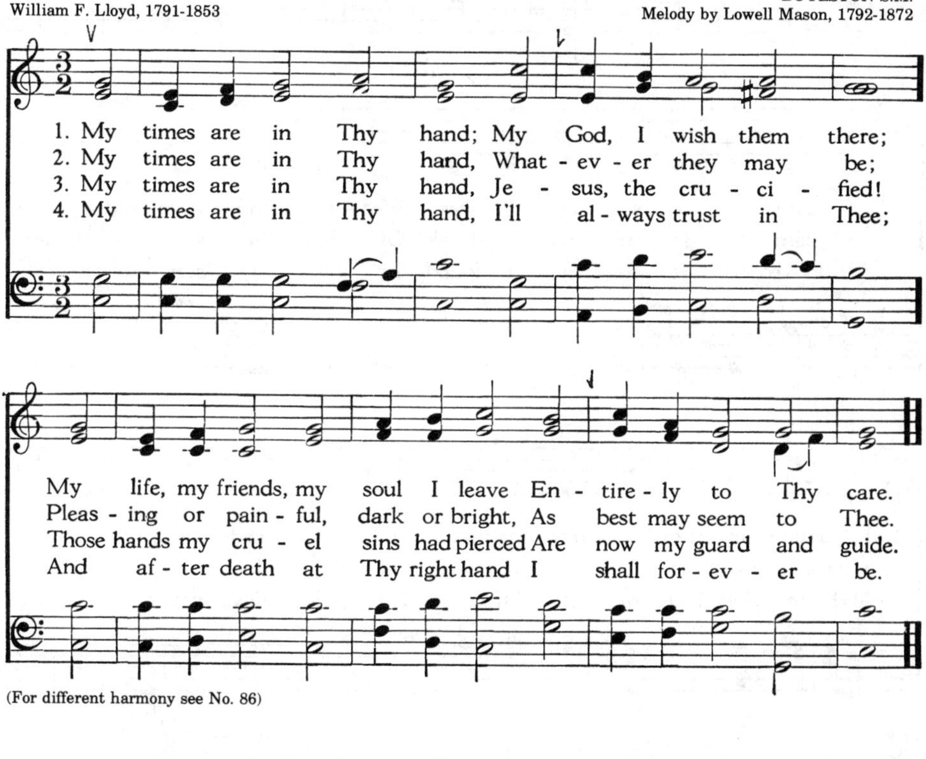
1. My times are in Thy hand; My God, I wish them there;
2. My times are in Thy hand, What - ev - er they may be;
3. My times are in Thy hand, Je - sus, the cru - ci - fied!
4. My times are in Thy hand, I'll al - ways trust in Thee;
My life, my friends, my soul I leave En - tire - ly to Thy care.
Pleas - ing or pain - ful, dark or bright, As best may seem to Thee.
Those hands my cru - el sins had pierced Are now my guard and guide.
And af - ter death at Thy right hand I shall for - ev - er be.

(For different harmony see No. 86)

313 I Heard the Voice of Jesus Say

Come unto me, . . . and . . . rest. Matt. 11:28

VOX DILECTI C.M.D.

Horatius Bonar, 1808-1889

John B. Dykes, 1823-1876

1. I heard the voice of Je - sus say, "Come un - to Me and rest;
2. I heard the voice of Je - sus say, "Be - hold, I free - ly give
3. I heard the voice of Je - sus say, "I am this dark world's light;

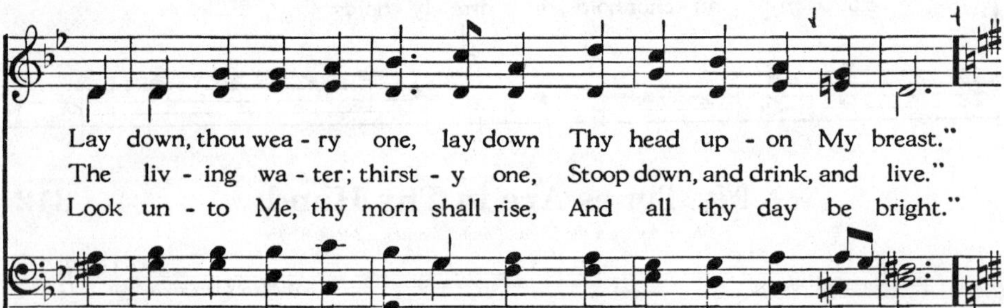
Lay down, thou wea - ry one, lay down Thy head up - on My breast."
The liv - ing wa - ter; thirst - y one, Stoop down, and drink, and live."
Look un - to Me, thy morn shall rise, And all thy day be bright."

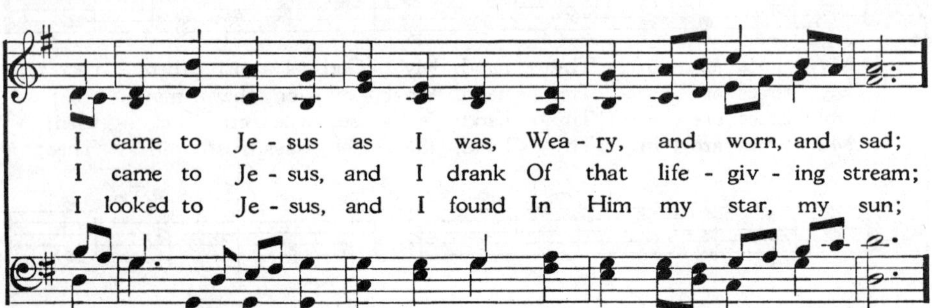
I came to Je - sus as I was, Wea - ry, and worn, and sad;
I came to Je - sus, and I drank Of that life - giv - ing stream;
I looked to Je - sus, and I found In Him my star, my sun;

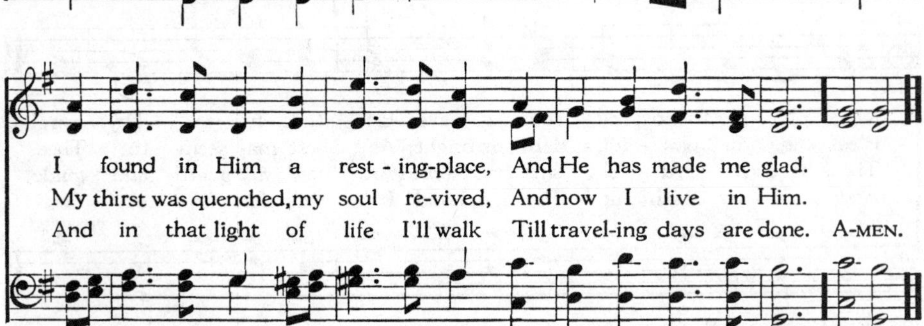
I found in Him a rest - ing-place, And He has made me glad.
My thirst was quenched, my soul re-vived, And now I live in Him.
And in that light of life I'll walk Till travel-ing days are done. A-MEN.

Does Jesus Care?

Casting all your care upon him; for he careth for you. 1 Pet. 5:7

MY SAVIOUR CARES Irregular with Refrain

Frank E. Graeff, 1860-1919

J. Lincoln Hall, 1866-1930

1. Does Je - sus care when my heart is pained Too deep - ly for
2. Does Je - sus care when my way is dark With a name - less
3. Does Je - sus care when I've tried and failed To re - sist some temp -
4. Does Je - sus care when I've said good - by To the dear - est on
mirth and song; As the bur - dens press, and the cares dis - tress,
dread and fear? As the day - light fades in - to deep night shades,
ta - tion strong; When for my deep grief I find no re - lief,
earth to me, And my sad heart aches till it near - ly breaks—
And the way grows wea - ry and long?
Does He care e - nough to be near?
Though my tears flow all the night long?
Is it aught to Him? Does He see?
REFRAIN
Oh, yes, He cares; I
know He cares, His heart is touched with my grief; When the
days are wea - ry, the long nights drear - y, I know my Sav - iour cares.

315 Would You Live for Jesus?

For to me to live is Christ, and to die is gain. Phil. 1:21

Cyrus S. Nusbaum, 1861-1937 | Cyrus S. Nusbaum, 1861-1937

1. Would you live for Je - sus and be al - ways pure and good?
2. Would you have Him make you free and fol - low at His call?
3. Would you in His king - dom find a place of con - stant rest?
Would you walk with Him with - in the nar - row road? Would you
Would you know the peace that comes by giv - ing all? Would you
Would you prove Him true in prov - i - den - tial test? Would you
have Him bear your bur - den, car - ry all your load? Let Him
have Him save you so that you need nev - er fall? Let Him
in His serv - ice la - bor al - ways at your best? Let Him
have His way with thee.
REFRAIN
His power can make you what you ought to be; His

Would You Live for Jesus?

blood can cleanse your heart and make you free; His love can fill your
soul and you will see 'Twas best for Him to have His way with thee.

Must Jesus Bear the Cross Alone? 316

. . . let him deny himself, and take up his cross, and follow me. Matt. 16:24

Thomas Shepherd, 1665-1739

MAITLAND C.M.
George N. Allen, 1812-1877

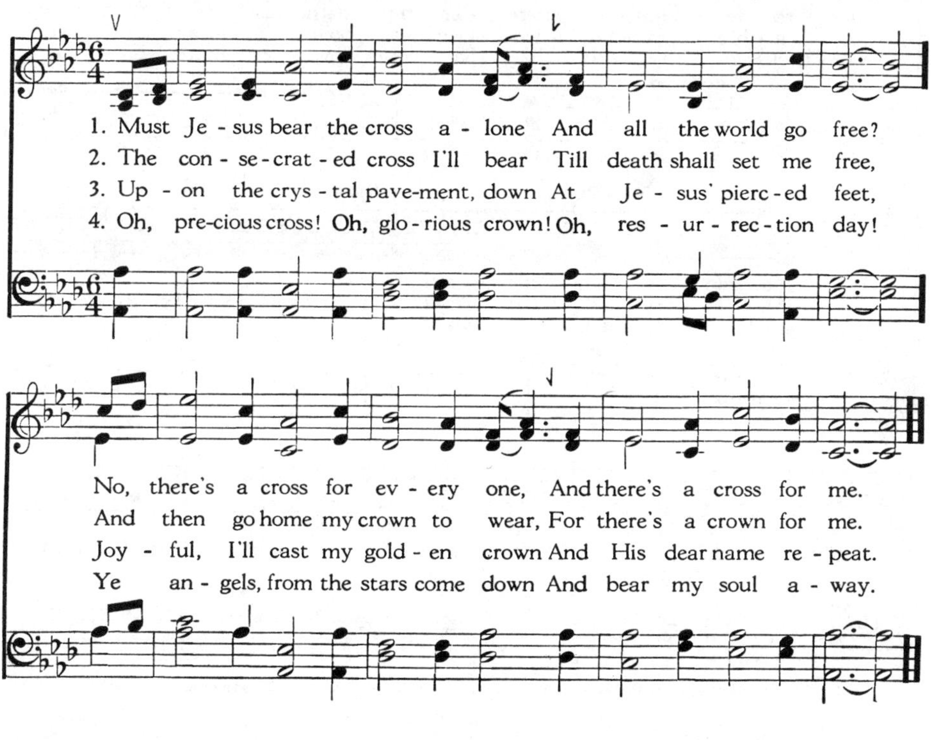
1. Must Je - sus bear the cross a - lone And all the world go free?
2. The con - se - crat - ed cross I'll bear Till death shall set me free,
3. Up - on the crys - tal pave-ment, down At Je - sus' pierc - ed feet,
4. Oh, pre-cious cross! Oh, glo - rious crown! Oh, res - ur - rec - tion day!
No, there's a cross for ev - ery one, And there's a cross for me.
And then go home my crown to wear, For there's a crown for me.
Joy - ful, I'll cast my gold - en crown And His dear name re - peat.
Ye an - gels, from the stars come down And bear my soul a - way.

317 It Is Glory Just to Walk with Him

. . . as . . . we have fellowship one with another . . . 1 John 1:7

Avis M.B. Christiansen, 1895-1966 | Haldor Lillenas, 1885-1959

1. It is glo - ry just to walk with Him whose blood has ran-somed me;
2. It is glo - ry when the shad - ows fall to know that He is near;
3. 'Twill be glo - ry when I walk with Him on heav - en's gold - en shore,
It is rap - ture for my soul each day. It is joy di -
Oh, what joy to sim - ply trust and pray! It is glo - ry
Nev - er from His side a - gain to stray. 'Twill be glo - ry,
vine to feel Him near where - e'er my path may be; Bless the
to a - bide in Him when skies a - bove are clear; Yes, with
won - drous glo - ry with the Sav - iour ev - er - more, Ev - er -
Lord, it's glo - ry all the way!
Him, it's glo - ry all the way!
last - ing glo - ry all the way!
REFRAIN
It is glo - ry just to
walk with Him, It is glo - ry just to walk with
walk with Him,

It Is Glory Just to Walk with Him

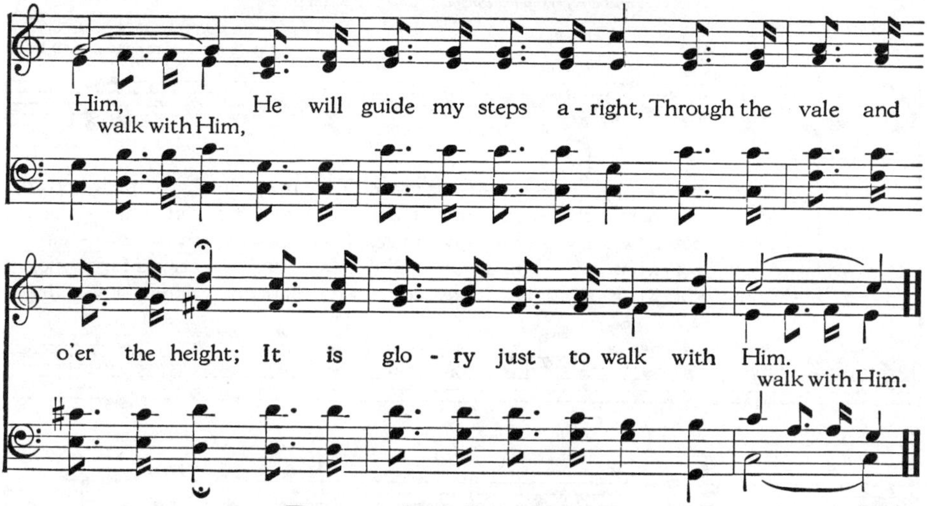
Him, He will guide my steps a - right, Through the vale and
walk with Him,
o'er the height; It is glo - ry just to walk with Him.
walk with Him.

Peace, Perfect Peace 318

Peace . . . not as the world giveth, give I unto you. . . . John 14:27

PAX TECUM 10.10.
George T. Caldbeck, 1852-circa 1918
Arranged by Charles J. Vincent, 1852-1934

Edward H. Bickersteth, 1825-1906

1. Peace, per - fect peace, in this dark world of sin?
2. Peace, per - fect peace, by throng - ing du - ties pressed?
3. Peace, per - fect peace, with sor - rows surg - ing round?
4. Peace, per - fect peace, with loved ones far a - way?
5. Peace, per - fect peace, our fu - ture all un - known?
6. Peace, per - fect peace, death shad - owing us and ours?
7. It is e - nough: earth's strug - gles soon shall cease,
The blood of Je - sus whis - pers peace with - in.
To do the will of Je - sus— this is rest.
On Je - sus' bos - om naught but calm is found.
In Je - sus' keep - ing we are safe, and they.
Je - sus we know, and He is on the throne.
Je - sus has van - quished death and all its powers.
And Je - sus, call us to heaven's per - fect peace.

319 I Know Whom I Have Believed

. . . and am persuaded that he is able . . . 2 Tim. 1:12

EL NATHAN C.M. with Refrain

Daniel W. Whittle, 1840-1901

James McGranahan, 1840-1907

1. I know not why God's won-drous grace To me He hath made known,
2. I know not how this sav-ing faith To me He did im-part,
3. I know not how the Spir-it moves, Con-vinc-ing men of sin,
4. I know not what of good or ill May be re-served for me,
5. I know not when my Lord may come, At night or noon-day fair,
Nor why—un-wor-thy—Christ in love Re-deemed me for His own.
Nor how be-liev-ing in His Word Wrought peace with-in my heart.
Re-veal-ing Je-sus through the Word, Cre-a-ting faith in Him.
Of wea-ry ways or gold-en days, Be-fore His face I see.
Nor if I walk the vale with Him Or meet Him in the air.
REFRAIN
But "I know whom I have be-liev-ed, And am per-suad-ed that He is
a-ble To keep that which I've com-mit-ted Un-to Him a-gainst that day."

Nothing Is Too Hard for Jesus 320

Ah Lord God! . . . there is nothing too hard for thee. Jer. 32:17

Albert B. Simpson, 1843-1919 | Albert B. Simpson, 1843-1919

1. Oft there comes a won-drous mes-sage When my hopes are grow-ing dim,
2. When my frame is worn with sick-ness And with tears my eye-lids swim,
3. When my way is closed in dark-ness And my foes are fierce and grim,
4. When my heart is crushed with an-guish And the wa-ters reach the brim,
5. Let us claim the might-y prom-ise, Let us light the torch-es dim.
I can hear it through the dark-ness Like some sweet and far-off hymn.
I can hear the prom-ise ring-ing Like some sweet and heaven-ly hymn.
Still it sings a-bove the con-flict Like some glad, vic-to-rious hymn.
Faith can hear the might-y cho-rus Like some might-y bat-tle hymn.
Let us join the might-y cho-rus, Let us swell the glo-rious hymn.
REFRAIN
Noth-ing is too hard for Je-sus, No man can work like Him;
Noth-ing is too hard for Je-sus, No man can work like Him.

321 Held in His Mighty Arms

Thou hast a mighty arm . . . Psa. 89:13

Winfield Macomber, 1865-1896 — Winfield Macomber, 1865-1896

1. Safe is my ref - uge, sweet is my rest, Ill can-not harm me, nor
2. Press - ing my tear-stained cheek to His own, Hush - ing my grief with His
3. Tem - pests may rage, sin's sur - ges may beat, Ne'er can they reach my
foes e'er mo - lest; Je - sus my spir - it so ten - der - ly calms,
sweet, gen - tle tone, Touch-ing my heart with His heal - ing balms,
shel - tered re - treat; Free from all dan - ger, from dread a - larms,
Hold - ing me close in His might-y arms.
Hold - ing me still in His might-y arms.
Rest - ing quite safe in His might-y arms.
Refrain
Oh, what won - der - ful,
won - der - ful rest! Trust - ing com-plete - ly in Je - sus I'm blest; Sweet - ly He
com-forts and shields from a - larms, Hold-ing me safe in His might-y arms.

Leaning on the Everlasting Arms 322

The eternal God is thy refuge, and underneath are the everlasting arms . . . Deut. 33:27

SHOWALTER 10.9.10.9. with Refrain

Elisha A. Hoffman, 1839-1929

Anthony J. Showalter, 1858-1924

1. What a fel-low-ship, what a joy di-vine, Lean-ing on the ev-er-
2. Oh, how sweet to walk in this pil-grim way, Lean-ing on the ev-er-
3. What have I to dread, what have I to fear, Lean-ing on the ev-er-
last-ing arms; What a bless-ed-ness, what a peace is mine,
last-ing arms; Oh, how bright the path grows from day to day,
last-ing arms; I have bless-ed peace with my Lord so near,
Lean-ing on the ev-er-last-ing arms.
REFRAIN
Lean - - ing,
Lean-ing on Je-sus,
lean - - ing, Safe and se-cure from all a-larms; Lean - -
lean-ing on Je-sus, Lean-ing on
ing, lean - - ing, Lean-ing on the ev-er-last-ing arms.
Je-sus, lean-ing on Je-sus,

323 The Everlasting Arms

The eternal God is thy refuge . . . Deut. 33:27

Albert B. Simpson, 1843-1919

Melody by Albert B. Simpson, 1843-1919

1. Art thou sunk in depths of sor - row Where no arm can reach so low?
2. Oth - er arms grow faint and wea - ry, These can nev - er faint nor fail;
3. Un - der - neath us— oh, how eas - y! We have not to mount on high,
4. Arms of Je - sus, fold me clos - er To Thy strong and lov - ing breast,
There is One whose arms al - might - y Reach be - yond thy deep - est woe.
Oth - ers reach our mounts of bless - ing, These our low - est, lone - liest vale.
But to sink in - to His full - ness And in trust - ful weak-ness lie.
Till my spir - it on Thy bos - om Finds its ev - er - last - ing rest;
God th'E - ter - nal is thy ref - uge, Let it still thy wild a - larms;
Oh, that all might know His friend - ship! Oh, that all might see His charms!
And we find our hum-bling fail - ures Save us from the strength that harms;
And when time's last sands are sink - ing, Shield my heart from all a - larms,
Un - der - neath thy deep - est sor - row Are the ev - er - last - ing arms.
Oh, that all might have be - neath them Je - sus' ev - er - last - ing arms.
We may fail, but un - der - neath us Are the ev - er - last - ing arms.
Soft - ly whis-pering, "Un-der - neath thee Are the ev - er - last - ing arms."
REFRAIN
Un - der - neath thee, un - der - neath thee Are the ev - er - last - ing arms,

The Everlasting Arms

Ev - er - last - ing, ev - er - last - ing, Are the ev - er - last - ing arms.

O Thou, in Whose Presence 324

. . . in thy presence is fulness of joy . . . Psa. 16:11

MEDITATION 11.8.11.8.

Joseph Swain, 1761-1796 — Freeman Lewis, 1780-1859

1. O Thou, in whose pres - ence my soul takes de - light, On
2. Where dost Thou, dear Shep - herd, re - sort with Thy sheep, To
3. Oh, why should I wan - der, an al - ien from Thee, Or
4. He looks! And ten thou - sands of an - gels re - joice, And
5. Dear Shep - herd, I hear and will fol - low Thy call; I
whom in af - flic - tion I call, My com - fort by day and my
feed them in pas - tures of love? Say, why in the val - ley of
cry in the des - ert for bread? Thy foes will re - joice when my
myr - i - ads wait for His word; He speaks! And e - ter - ni - ty,
know the sweet sound of Thy voice; Re - store and de - fend me, for
song in the night, My hope, my sal - va - tion, my all!
death should I weep, Or a - lone in this wil - der - ness rove?
sor - rows they see, And smile at the tears I have shed.
filled with His voice, Re - ech - oes the praise of the Lord.
Thou art my all; And in Thee I will ev - er re - joice. A-MEN.

325 A Shelter in the Time of Storm

... an hiding place from the wind, and a covert from the tempest ... Isa. 32:2

Vernon J. Charlesworth, b. 1839
Adapted by Ira D. Sankey, 1840-1908

SHELTER L.M. with Refrain
Ira D. Sankey, 1840-1908

1. The Lord's our rock, in Him we hide, A shel - ter in the time of storm;
2. A shade by day, de - fense by night, A shel - ter in the time of storm;
3. The rag - ing storms may round us beat, A shel - ter in the time of storm;
4. O Rock di - vine, O Ref - uge dear, A shel - ter in the time of storm;
Se - cure what - ev - er ill be - tide, A shel - ter in the time of storm.
No fears a - larm, no fears af - fright, A shel - ter in the time of storm.
We'll nev - er leave our safe re - treat, A shel - ter in the time of storm.
Be Thou our help - er ev - er near, A shel - ter in the time of storm.
Refrain
Oh, Je - sus is a rock in a wea - ry land, A
wea - ry land, a wea - ry land; Oh, Je - sus is a rock
in a wea - ry land, A shel - ter in the time of storm.

Moment by Moment

326

Who are kept by the power of God through faith . . . 1 Pet. 1:5

WHITTLE 10.10.10.10. with Refrain

Daniel W. Whittle, 1840-1901

May W. Moody, 1870-1963

1. Dy - ing with Je - sus, by death reck-oned mine; Liv - ing with Je - sus, a
2. Nev - er a tri - al that He is not there, Nev - er a bur - den that
3. Nev - er a heart-ache and nev - er a groan, Nev - er a tear-drop and
4. Nev - er a weak-ness that He doth not feel, Nev - er a sick-ness that
new life di - vine; Look - ing to Je - sus till glo - ry doth shine, Mo-ment by
He doth not bear, Nev - er a sor - row that He doth not share, Mo-ment by
nev - er a moan, Nev - er a dan - ger but there on the throne, Mo-ment by
He can - not heal; Mo - ment by mo-ment, in woe or in weal, Je - sus, my
REFRAIN
mo - ment, O Lord, I am Thine.
mo - ment I'm un - der His care. Mo-ment by mo-ment I'm kept in His love;
mo - ment He thinks of His own.
Sav - iour, a - bides with me still.
Mo-ment by mo-ment I've life from a - bove; Look-ing to Je - sus till
glo - ry doth shine; Mo - ment by mo - ment, O Lord, I am Thine.

327 Only Wait

Rejoicing in hope; patient in tribulation . . . Rom. 12:12

Albert B. Simpson, 1843-1919
Refrain by L.B. Haines, 20th century

Dwight Hall, b. 1923

1. Oft I hear a gen-tle whis-per o'er me steal-ing, When my
2. When I can-not un-der-stand my Fa-ther's lead-ing, And it
3. When the prom-ise seems to lin-ger, long de-lay-ing, And I
4. When I see the wick-ed pros-per in their sin-ning, And the
tri-als and my bur-dens seem too great; Like the chim-ing bells of
seems to be but hard and cru-el fate, Still I hear that gen-tle
trem-ble, lest per-haps it comes too late, Still I hear that sweet-voiced
right-eous pressed by man-y-a cru-el strait, I re-mem-ber this is
eve-ning soft-ly peal-ing, It is say-ing to my spir-it, "On-ly wait."
whis-per ev-er plead-ing, God is work-ing, God is faith-ful, on-ly wait!
an-gel ev-er say-ing, "Though it tar-ry, it is com-ing; on-ly wait."
on-ly the be-gin-ning, And I whis-per to my spir-it, "On-ly wait!"
REFRAIN
On-ly wait! A-gain I hear that whis-per. On-ly
wait! 'Twill not be ver-y long; Ev-en now the Fa-ther's hand is

Only Wait

lead - ing; Soon with Je - sus, we will sing the vic - tor's song.

Rock of Ages

328

. . . I will put thee in a clift of the rock . . . Exod. 33:22

TOPLADY 7.7.7.7.7.7.

Augustus M. Toplady, 1740-1778

Thomas Hastings, 1784-1872

1. Rock of A - ges, cleft for me, Let me hide my - self in Thee;
2. Not the la - bors of my hands Can ful - fill Thy laws de - mands.
3. Noth - ing in my hand I bring, Sim - ply to Thy cross I cling;
4. While I draw this fleet - ing breath, When mine eyes shall close in death,

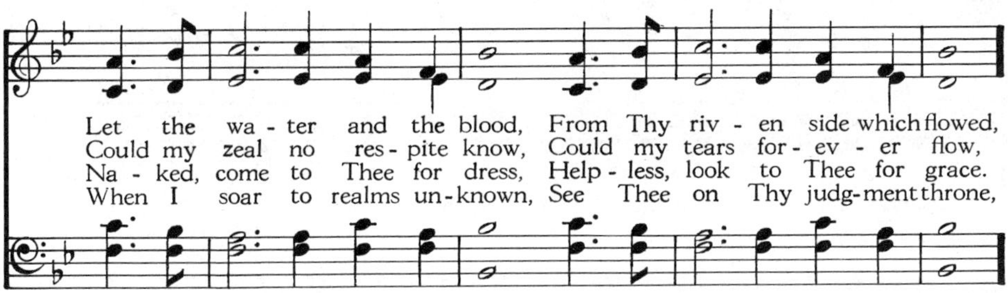
Let the wa - ter and the blood, From Thy riv - en side which flowed,
Could my zeal no res - pite know, Could my tears for - ev - er flow,
Na - ked, come to Thee for dress, Help - less, look to Thee for grace.
When I soar to realms un - known, See Thee on Thy judg - ment throne,

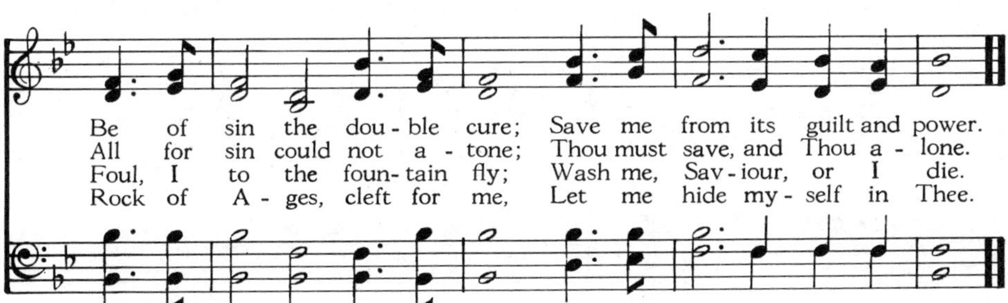
Be of sin the dou - ble cure; Save me from its guilt and power.
All for sin could not a - tone; Thou must save, and Thou a - lone.
Foul, I to the foun - tain fly; Wash me, Sav - iour, or I die.
Rock of A - ges, cleft for me, Let me hide my - self in Thee.

329 Standing on the Promises

Whereby are given unto us exceeding great and precious promises . . . 2 Pet. 1:4

Russell K. Carter, 1849-1928 | Russell K. Carter, 1849-1928

1. Stand-ing on the prom - is - es of Christ, my King, Through e - ter - nal a - ges
2. Stand-ing on the prom - is - es that can - not fail, When the howl-ing storms of
3. Stand-ing on the prom - is - es of Christ the Lord, Bound to Him e - ter - nal -
4. Stand-ing on the prom - is - es I can - not fall, Lis - tening ev - ery mo-ment
let His prais - es ring; Glo - ry in the high - est, I will shout and sing,
doubt and fear as - sail, By the liv - ing Word of God I shall pre - vail,
ly by love's strong cord, O - ver-com - ing dai - ly with the Spir - it's sword,
to the Spir - it's call, Rest - ing in my Sav - iour as my all in all,
Stand-ing on the prom-is - es of God.
REFRAIN
Stand - ing, stand - ing,
Stand-ing on the prom-is-es, stand-ing on the promises,
Stand-ing on the prom - is - es of God, my Sav - iour; Stand - ing,
Stand-ing on the prom-is-es,
stand - ing, I'm stand - ing on the prom - is - es of God.
stand-ing on the prom-is - es,

My Jesus, As Thou Wilt! 330

. . . nevertheless not as I will, but as thou wilt. Matt. 26:39

JEWETT 6.6.6.6.D.

Benjamin Schmolck, 1672-1737
Translated by Jane L. Borthwick, 1813-1897

Carl M. von Weber, 1786-1826
Adapted by Joseph P. Holbrook, 1822-1888

1. My Je - sus, as Thou wilt! Oh, may Thy will be mine!
2. My Je - sus, as Thou wilt! Though seen through man - y a tear,
3. My Je - sus, as Thou wilt! All shall be well for me;
In - to Thy hand of love I would my all re - sign.
Let not my star of hope Grow dim or dis - ap - pear.
Each chang - ing fu - ture scene I glad - ly trust with Thee.
Through sor - row or through joy, Con - duct me as Thine own;
Since Thou on earth hast wept, And sor - rowed oft a - lone,
Straight to my home a - bove I trav - el calm - ly on,
And help me still to say, "My Lord, Thy will be done."
If I must weep with Thee, "My Lord, Thy will be done."
And sing, in life or death, "My Lord, Thy will be done." A-MEN.

331 Children of the Heavenly Father

Like as a father pitieth his children, so the Lord pitieth them that fear him. Psa. 103:13

Carolina V.S. Berg, 1832-1903
Translated by Ernest W. Olson, 1870-1958

TRYGARRE KAN INGEN VARA L.M.
Swedish melody

1. Chil - dren of the heaven - ly Fa - ther Safe - ly
2. God His own doth tend and nour - ish: In His
3. Nei - ther life nor death shall ev - er From the
4. Praise the Lord in joy - ful num - bers: Your pro -
5. Though He giv - eth or He tak - eth, God His
in His bos - om gath - er; Nest - ling bird nor star in
ho - ly courts they flour - ish. From all e - vil things He
Lord His chil - dren sev - er; Un - to them His grace He
tect - or nev - er slum - bers. At the will of your de -
chil - dren ne'er for - sak - eth, His the lov - ing pur - pose
heav - en Such a ref - uge e'er was giv - en.
spares them, In His might - y arms He bears them.
show - eth, And their sor - rows all He know - eth.
fend - er, Ev - ery foe— man must sur - ren - der.
sole - ly To pre - serve them pure and ho - ly.

Turn Your Eyes upon Jesus

. . . from whence cometh my help. Psa. 121:1

LEMMEL 9.8.9.8. with Refrain

Helen H. Lemmel, 1864-1961 | Helen H. Lemmel, 1864-1961

1. Oh, soul, are you wea-ry, and trou - bled? No light in the
2. Through death in - to life ev - er - last - ing He passed, and we
3. His Word shall not fail you—He prom - ised; Be - lieve Him and
dark-ness you see? There's light for a look at the Sav - iour,
fol - low Him there; O - ver us sin no more hath do - min - ion—
all will be well: Then go to a world that is dy - ing,
And life more a - bun-dant and free!
For more than con-qu'rors we are!
His per-fect sal - va - tion to tell!
REFRAIN
Turn your eyes up - on Je - sus, Look full in His won - der - ful face;
And the things of earth will grow strange-ly dim In the light of His glo - ry and grace.

333 He Hideth My Soul

. . . I have covered thee in the shadow of mine hand . . . Isa. 51:16

Fanny J. Crosby, 1820-1915

KIRKPATRICK 11.8.11.8. with Refrain
William J. Kirkpatrick, 1838-1921

1. A won - der - ful Sav - iour is Je - sus, my Lord, A won - der -
2. A won - der - ful Sav - iour is Je - sus, my Lord, He tak - eth
3. With num - ber - less bless - ings each mo - ment He crowns, And, filled with
4. When clothed in His bright - ness, trans - port - ed I rise To meet Him
ful Sav - iour to me; He hid - eth my soul in the cleft of
my bur - den a - way; He hold - eth me up, and I shall not
His full - ness di - vine, I sing in my rap - ture, oh, glo - ry
in clouds of the sky, His per - fect sal - va - tion, His won - der -
the rock Where riv - ers of pleas - ure I see.
be moved; He giv - eth me strength as my day.
to God For such a Re - deem - er as mine!
ful love I'll shout with the mil - lions on high.
REFRAIN
He hid - eth my
soul in the cleft of the rock That shad - ows a dry, thirst - y

He Hideth My Soul

land; He hid - eth my life in the depths of His love, And

cov - ers me there with His hand, And cov - ers me there with His hand.

Lord Jesus, Think on Me 334

. . . according to thy mercy remember thou me . . . Psa. 25:7

DENNIS S.M.

Synesius of Cyrene, 375-430
Translated by Allen W. Chatfield, 1808-1896

Johann H.G. Nageli, 1768-1836
Arranged by Lowell Mason, 1792-1872

1. Lord Je - sus, think on me And purge a - way my sin; From
2. Lord Je - sus, think on me, With care and woe op-pressed; Let
3. Lord Je - sus, think on me A - mid the bat-tle's strife; In
4. Lord Je - sus, think on me Nor let me go a - stray; Through
5. Lord Je - sus, think on me When flows the tem-pest high; When
6. Lord Je - sus, think on me That, when the flood is past, I

earth-born pas-sions set me free And make me pure with-in.
me Thy lov - ing ser-vant be And taste Thy prom-ised rest.
all my pain and mis - er - y Be Thou my health and life.
dark-ness and per - plex - i - ty Point Thou my heaven-ly way.
on doth rush the en - e - my, O Sav - iour, be Thou nigh.
may th'e - ter - nal bright-ness see And share Thy joy at last. A - MEN.

335 Our Great Saviour

. . . a friend of publicans and sinners! Luke 7:34

HYFRYDOL 8.7.8.7. with Refrain
Melody by Rowland H. Prichard, 1811-1887
Arranged by Robert Harkness, 1880-1961

J. Wilbur Chapman, 1859-1918

1. Je - sus, what a friend for sin - ners! Je - sus! Lov - er of my soul;
2. Je - sus, what a strength in weak-ness! Let me hide my - self in Him;
3. Je - sus, what a help in sor - row! While the bil - lows o'er me roll,
4. Je - sus, what a guide and keep - er! While the tem - pest still is high,
5. Je - sus! I do now re - ceive Him, More than all in Him I find;
Friends may fail me, foes as - sail me, He, my Sav - iour, makes me whole.
Tempt - ed, tried, and some - times fail - ing, He, my strength, my vic - tory wins.
E - ven when my heart is break-ing, He, my com - fort, helps my soul.
Storms a - bout me, night o'er - takes me, He, my pi - lot, hears my cry.
He hath grant - ed me for - give - ness, I am His, and He is mine.
Refrain
Hal - le - lu - jah! What a Sav - iour! Hal - le - lu - jah! What a friend!
Sav - ing, help - ing, keep - ing, lov - ing, He is with me to the end.

(For different harmony and lower key see No. 442)

The Cross Is Not Greater

. . . we are more than conquerors through him that loved us. Rom. 8:37

Ballington Booth, 1859-1940 — Ballington Booth, 1859-1940

1. The cross that He gave may be heav - y, But it ne'er out-weighs His grace,
2. The thorns in my path are not sharp - er Than com-posed His crown for me,
3. The light of His love shin-eth bright - er, As it falls on paths of woe,
4. His will I have joy in ful - fill - ing, As I'm walk - ing in His sight,
The storm that I feared may sur-round me, But it ne'er ex-cludes His face.
The cup that I drink not more bit - ter Than He drank in Geth-sem-a - ne.
The toil of my work grow-eth light - er, As I stoop to raise the low.
My all to the blood I am bring - ing, It a - lone can keep me right.
REFRAIN
The cross is not great - er than His grace, The storm can - not
hide His bless - ed face; I am sat - is - fied to know
That with Je - sus here be - low, I can con - quer ev - ery foe.

337 Faith Is the Victory

... this is the victory that overcometh the world, even our faith. 1 John 5:4

John H. Yates, 1837-1900

SANKEY C.M.D. with Refrain
Ira D. Sankey, 1840-1908

1. En - camped a - long the hills of light, Ye Chris - tian sol - diers, rise,
2. His ban - ner o - ver us is love, Our sword the Word of God;
3. On ev - ery hand the foe we find Drawn up in dread ar - ray;
4. To him that o - ver - comes the foe White rai - ment shall be given;
And press the bat - tle ere the night Shall veil the glow - ing skies.
We tread the road the saints a - bove With shouts of tri - umph trod.
Let tents of ease be left be - hind, And on - ward to the fray;
Be - fore the an - gels he shall know His name con - fessed in heaven.
A - gainst the foe in vales be - low, Let all our strength be hurled;
By faith they, like a whirl - wind's breath, Swept on o'er ev - ery field;
Sal - va - tion's hel - met on each head, With truth all girt a - bout,
Then on - ward from the hills of light, Our hearts with love a - flame,
Faith is the vic - to - ry, we know, That o - ver - comes the world.
The faith by which they con - quered death Is still our shin - ing shield.
The earth shall trem - ble 'neath our tread And ech - o with our shout.
We'll van - quish all the hosts of night In Je - sus' con - quering name.
REFRAIN
Faith is the vic - to - ry! Faith is the vic - to - ry!

Faith Is the Victory

Oh, glo - ri - ous vic - to - ry That o - ver-comes the world.

Fade, Fade, Each Earthly Joy 338

I in them, and thou in me ... John 17:23

LUNDIE 6.4.6.4.6.6.6.4.

Jane C. Bonar, 1821-1884

Theodore E. Perkins, 1831-1912

1. Fade, fade, each earth - ly joy; Je - sus is mine. Break ev - ery
2. Tempt not my soul a - way; Je - sus is mine. Here would I
3. Fare - well, ye dreams of night; Je - sus is mine. Lost in this
4. Fare - well, mor - tal - i - ty; Je - sus is mine. Wel - come, e -

ten - der tie; Je - sus is mine. Dark is the wil - der - ness,
ev - er stay; Je - sus is mine. Per - ish - ing things of clay,
dawn - ing bright, Je - sus is mine. All that my soul has tried
ter - ni - ty; Je - sus is mine. Wel - come, O loved and blest,

Earth has no rest-ing-place, Je - sus a - lone can bless; Je - sus is mine.
Born but for one brief day, Pass from my heart a - way; Je - sus is mine.
Left but a dis-mal void; Je - sus has sat - is - fied; Je - sus is mine.
Wel-come sweet scenes of rest, Wel-come, my Sav-iour's breast; Je - sus is mine.

339 The Redeemed of the Lord

. . . Arise ye, and let us go up to Zion . . . Jer. 31:6

Frances V. Hubbard, 19th century | Melody by George C. Stebbins, 1846-1945

1. The re - deemed of the Lord shall re - turn To Zi - on with
2. The re - deemed of the Lord shall re - turn From lands where, as
3. The re - deemed of the Lord shall re - turn With sing - ing for
mu - sic and song; And dai - ly sweet les - sons of
cap - tives, they sighed; With love and de - vo - tion their
Zi - on's bright day; Far, far on the hill - tops their
mer - cy will learn As they jour - ney the path - way a - long.
spir - its shall burn As they sing of the Once - cru - ci - fied.
glad eyes dis - cern, And sor - row and fear flee a - way.
Refrain
With joy and with sing - ing, Thanks - giv - ing and praise, Their
sweet voi - ces ring - ing In tri - um - phant lays; His mer -

The Redeemed of the Lord

cy and good - ness Shall still be their song, As
home - ward to Zi - on they jour - ney a - long.

As Pants the Hart for Cooling Streams 340

. . . so panteth my soul after thee, O God. Psa. 42:1

SPOHR C.M.

From *The New Version of the Psalms,* 1696 — Adapted from Ludwig Spohr, 1784-1859

1. As pants the hart for cool - ing streams When heat - ed in the chase,
2. For Thee, my God, the liv - ing God, My thirst - y soul doth pine;
3. Why rest - less, why cast down, my soul? Trust God, who will em - ploy
4. God of my strength, how long shall I Like one for - got - ten mourn,
5. Why rest - less, why cast down, my soul? Hope still, and thou shalt sing
So longs my soul, O God, for Thee And Thy re - fresh - ing grace.
Oh, when shall I be - hold Thy face, Thou Ma - jes - ty di - vine?
His aid to thee and change these sighs To thank-ful hymns of joy.
For - lorn, for - sak - en, and ex-posed To my op-press-or's scorn?
The praise of Him who is thy God, Thy health's e - ter - nal spring. A-MEN.

341 Come, Come, Ye Saints

. . . all things work together for good to them that love God . . . Rom. 8:28

William Clayton, 1814-1879
Adapted by Avis M.B. Christiansen, 1895-1966

ALL IS WELL 10.6.10.6.8.8.8.6.
English melody
Adapted from J.T. White's *The Sacred Harp*, 1844

1. Come, come, ye saints, no toil or la - bor fear, But with joy wend your way;
2. What though the path you tread be rough and steep? Have no fear, He is near!
3. God hath pre-pared a glo-rious home a - bove Round His throne for His own,
4. With long-ing hearts we wait the prom-ised day When the trump we shall hear,
Though hard to you life's jour-ney may ap-pear, Grace shall be as your day.
His might-y arm un - to the end will keep; Soon His call you shall hear.
Where they may rest for - ev - er in His love, Toil and tears all un-known.
That sum-mons us from earth-ly cares a - way, At His side to ap - pear!
God's hand of love shall be your guide, And all your need He will pro-vide;
Then fol-low on, fresh cour-age take, For God His own will ne'er for-sake
There they shall sing e - ter-nal praise To Him who saved them by His grace.
But un-til then we'll la-bor on In pa-tience till our course is run,
His power shall ev - ery foe dis-pel, All is well, All is well!
Till in His pres - ence they shall dwell. All is well, All is well!
Through heav-en's courts the song shall swell, All is well, All is well!
Al - though the hour we may not tell, All is well, All is well!

Guide Me, O Thou Great Jehovah 342

. . . he will be our guide even unto death. Psa. 48:14

From the Welsh of William Williams, 1717-1791
Stanza 1 Trans. by Peter Williams, 1722-1796
Stanzas 2-3 Trans. by William Williams, 1717-1791

CWM RHONDDA 8.7.8.7.8.7. with repeat
John Hughes, 1873-1932

1. Guide me, O Thou great Je - ho - vah, Pil - grim through this
2. O - pen now the crys - tal foun - tain, Whence the heal - ing
3. When I tread the verge of Jor - dan, Bid my anx - ious
bar - ren land; I am weak, but Thou art might - y; Hold me with Thy
stream doth flow; Let the fire and cloud - y pil - lar Lead me all my
fears sub-side; Death of death, and hell's de - struc-tion, Land me safe on
power - ful hand; Bread of heav - en, Bread of heav - en,
jour - ney through; Strong De - liv - erer, strong De - liv - erer,
Ca - naan's side; Songs of prais - es, songs of prais - es
Feed me till I want no more, Feed me till I want no more.
Be Thou still my strength and shield, Be Thou still my strength and shield.
I will ev - er give to Thee, I will ev - er give to Thee. A-MEN.

343 Jesus, Saviour, Pilot Me

When thou passest through the waters, I will be with thee . . . Isa. 43:2

PILOT 7.7.7.7.7.7.

Edward Hopper, 1816-1888 | John E. Gould, 1822-1875

1. Je - sus, Sav - iour, pi - lot me O - ver life's tem - pes - tuous sea; Un - known waves be - fore me roll, Hid - ing rock and treach-erous shoal; Chart and com - pass came from Thee; Je - sus, Sav - iour, pi - lot me.
2. As a moth - er stills her child, Thou canst hush the o - cean wild; Bois - terous waves o - bey Thy will When Thou say'st to them, "Be still!" Won - drous sov - ereign of the sea, Je - sus, Sav - iour, pi - lot me.
3. When at last I near the shore, And the fear - ful break - ers roar 'Twixt me and the peace-ful rest, Then, while lean - ing on Thy breast, May I hear Thee say to me, "Fear not, I will pi - lot thee." A - MEN.

Saviour, Like a Shepherd, Lead Us 344

I am the good shepherd, and know my sheep . . . John 10:14

From *Hymns for the Young,* 1836
Attributed to Dorothy A. Thrupp, 1779-1847

PLEASANT PASTURES 8.7.8.7.8.7. with repeat
Melody by William B. Bradbury, 1816-1868

1. Sav - iour, like a shep-herd, lead us, Much we need Thy ten-derest care;
2. We are Thine; do Thou be - friend us, Be the guard-ian of our way;
3. Thou hast prom-ised to re - ceive us, Poor and sin - ful though we be;
4. Ear - ly let us seek Thy fa - vor, Ear - ly let us do Thy will;
In Thy pleas-ant pas-tures feed us, For our use Thy folds pre - pare;
Keep Thy flock, from sin de - fend us, Seek us if we go a - stray;
Thou hast mer - cy to re - lieve us, Grace to cleanse and power to free;
Bless - ed Lord and on - ly Sav - iour, With Thy love our bos - oms fill;
Bless - ed Je - sus, bless - ed Je - sus, Thou hast bought us, Thine we are;
Bless - ed Je - sus, bless - ed Je - sus, Hear, oh, hear us when we pray;
Bless - ed Je - sus, bless - ed Je - sus, Ear - ly let us turn to Thee;
Bless - ed Je - sus, bless - ed Je - sus, Thou hast loved us, love us still;
Bless - ed Je - sus, bless - ed Je - sus, Thou hast bought us, Thine we are.
Bless - ed Je - sus, bless - ed Je - sus, Hear, oh, hear us when we pray.
Bless - ed Je - sus, bless - ed Je - sus, Ear - ly let us turn to Thee.
Bless - ed Je - sus, bless - ed Je - sus, Thou hast loved us, love us still.

345 Surely Goodness and Mercy

... shall follow me all the days of my life ... Psa. 23:6

John W. Peterson, b. 1921
and Alfred B. Smith, b. 1916

SURELY GOODNESS AND MERCY Irregular with Refrain
John W. Peterson, b. 1921
and Alfred B. Smith, b. 1916

1. A pilgrim was I and a-wan-dering, In the cold night of sin I did roam, When Je-sus the kind Shep-herd found me, And now I am on my way home.
2. He re-stor-eth my soul when I'm wea-ry, He giv-eth me strength day by day; He leads me be-side the still wa-ters, He guards me each step of the way.
3. When I walk through the dark lone-some val-ley, My Saviour will walk with me there; And safe-ly His great hand will lead me To the man-sions He's gone to pre-pare.
REFRAIN
Sure-ly good-ness and mer-cy shall fol-low me All the days, all the days of my life; Sure-ly good-ness and mer-cy shall fol-low me All the days, all the days of my life.

Surely Goodness and Mercy

CODA
3
And I shall dwell in the house of the Lord for - ev - er, And I shall feast at the
ta - ble spread for me; Sure - ly good - ness and mer - cy shall fol - low me
All the days, all the days of my life, All the days, all the days of my life.

The Lord's My Shepherd 346

. . . I shall not want. **Psa. 23:1**

From *The Scottish Psalter,* 1650

CRIMOND C.M.
Jessie S. Irvine, 1836-1887

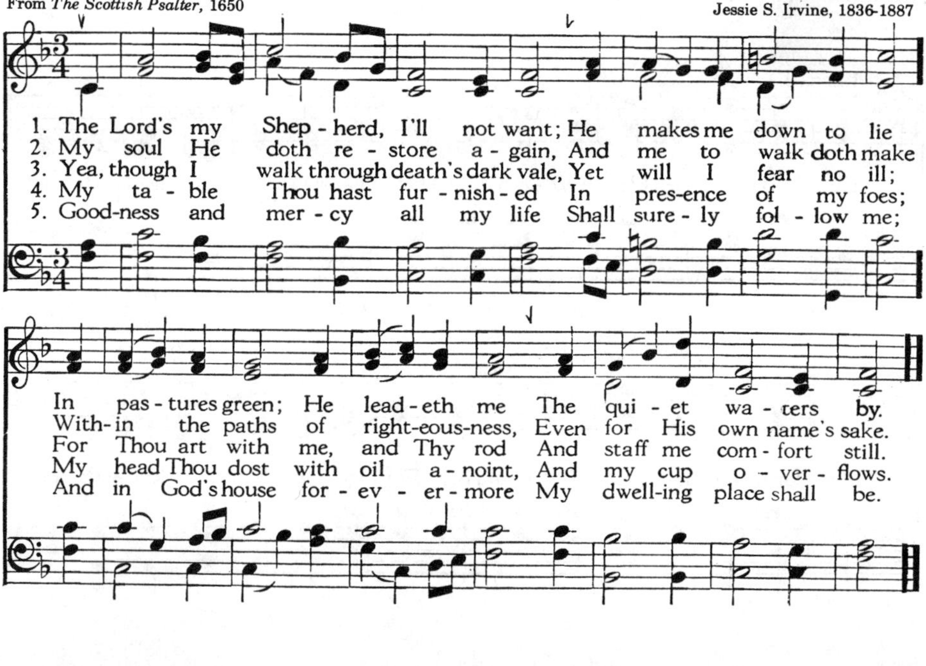
1. The Lord's my Shep - herd, I'll not want; He makes me down to lie
2. My soul He doth re - store a - gain, And me to walk doth make
3. Yea, though I walk through death's dark vale, Yet will I fear no ill;
4. My ta - ble Thou hast fur - nish - ed In pres-ence of my foes;
5. Good-ness and mer - cy all my life Shall sure - ly fol - low me;
In pas - tures green; He lead - eth me The qui - et wa - ters by.
With-in the paths of right-eous-ness, Even for His own name's sake.
For Thou art with me, and Thy rod And staff me com - fort still.
My head Thou dost with oil a - noint, And my cup o - ver - flows.
And in God's house for - ev - er - more My dwell-ing place shall be.

347 He Leadeth Me

. . . in the paths of righteousness for his name's sake. Psa. 23:3

Joseph H. Gilmore, 1834-1918
Refrain added

HE LEADETH ME L.M. with Refrain
William B. Bradbury, 1816-1868

1. He lead - eth me– Oh, bless-ed thought! Oh, words with heaven-ly com-fort fraught!
2. Some-times 'mid scenes of deep-est gloom, Some-times where E - den's bow-ers bloom,
3. Lord, I would clasp Thy hand in mine, Nor ev - er mur - mur nor re - pine;
4. And when my task on earth is done, When, by Thy grace, the vic-tory's won,
What - e'er I do, wher-e'er I be, Still 'tis God's hand that lead-eth me.
By wa - ters calm, o'er trou-bled sea, Still 'tis His hand that lead-eth me.
Con - tent, what - ev - er lot I see, Since 'tis my God that lead-eth me.
E'en death's cold wave I will not flee, Since God through Jor - dan lead-eth me.
REFRAIN
He lead - eth me, He lead - eth me; By His own hand He lead - eth me;
His faith - ful fol-lower I would be, For by His hand He lead - eth me.

Teach Me Thy Way, O Lord 348

. . . I will walk in thy truth . . . Psa. 86:11

Benjamin M. Ramsey, 1849-1923

CAMACHA 6.4.6.4.6.6.6.4.
Benjamin M. Ramsey, 1849-1923

3/4
1. Teach me Thy way, O Lord, Teach me Thy way!
2. When I am sad at heart, Teach me Thy way!
3. When doubts and fears a - rise, Teach me Thy way!
4. Long as my life shall last, Teach me Thy way!
Thy guid - ing grace af - ford—Teach me Thy way!
When earth - ly joys de - part, Teach me Thy way!
When storms o'er - spread the skies, Teach me Thy way!
Wher - e'er my lot be cast, Teach me Thy way!
Help me to walk a - right, More by faith, less by sight;
In hours of lone - li - ness, In times of dire dis - tress,
Shine through the cloud and rain, Through sor - row, toil and pain;
Un - til the race is run, Un - til the jour - ney's done,
Lead me with heaven - ly light, Teach me Thy way!
In fail - ure or suc - cess, Teach me Thy way!
Make Thou my path - way plain, Teach me Thy way!
Un - til the crown is won, Teach me Thy way! A - MEN.

349 Step by Step

For we walk by faith, not by sight. 2 Cor. 5:7

Albert B. Simpson, 1843-1919 | Albert B. Simpson, 1843-1919

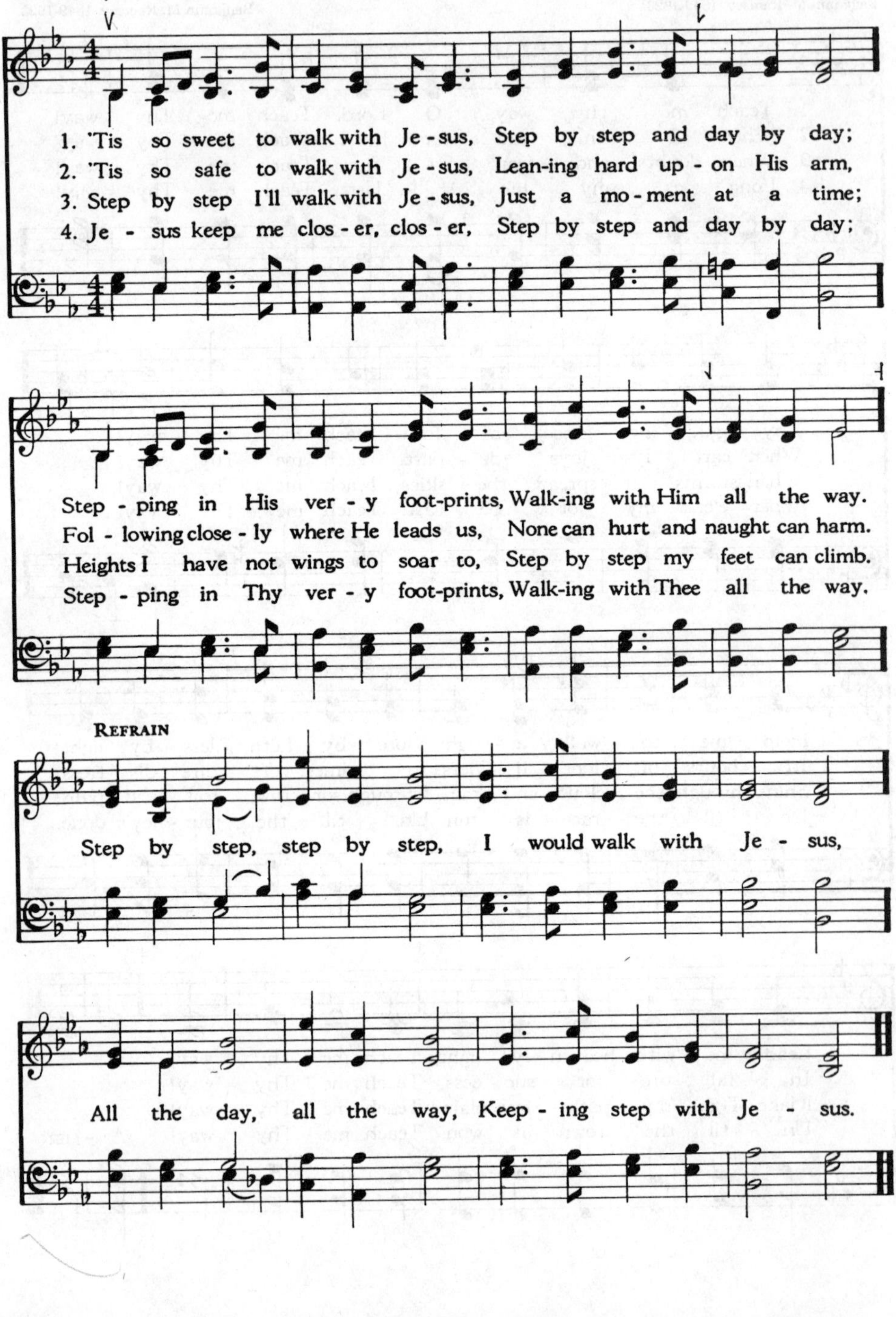
1. 'Tis so sweet to walk with Je - sus, Step by step and day by day;
2. 'Tis so safe to walk with Je - sus, Lean-ing hard up - on His arm,
3. Step by step I'll walk with Je - sus, Just a mo - ment at a time;
4. Je - sus keep me clos - er, clos - er, Step by step and day by day;
Step - ping in His ver - y foot-prints, Walk-ing with Him all the way.
Fol - lowing close - ly where He leads us, None can hurt and naught can harm.
Heights I have not wings to soar to, Step by step my feet can climb.
Step - ping in Thy ver - y foot-prints, Walk-ing with Thee all the way.
REFRAIN
Step by step, step by step, I would walk with Je - sus,
All the day, all the way, Keep - ing step with Je - sus.

Anywhere with Jesus

. . . lo, I am with you alway . . . Matt. 28:20

Stanzas 1-2 by Jessie B. Pounds, 1861-1921
Stanzas 3-4-5 by Helen C.A. Dixon, 1877-1969

SECURITY 11.11.11.11. with Refrain
Daniel B. Towner, 1850-1919

1. An - y - where with Je - sus I can safe - ly go; An - y - where He
2. An - y - where with Je - sus I need fear no ill, Though temp-ta-tions
3. An - y - where with Je - sus I am not a - lone; Oth - er friends may
4. An - y - where with Je - sus o - ver land and sea, Tell - ing souls in
5. An - y - where with Je - sus I can go to sleep, When the dark-ening
leads me in this world be - low; An - y - where with-out Him dear - est
gath - er round my path - way still; He Him - self was tempt-ed that He
fail me, He is still my own; Though His hand may lead me o - ver
dark-ness of sal - va - tion free; Read - y as He sum-mons me to
shad-ows round a - bout me creep; Know - ing I shall wak - en, nev - er
joys would fade; An - y - where with Je - sus I am not a - fraid.
might help me; An - y - where with Je - sus I may vic - tor be.
drear - y ways; An - y - where with Je - sus is a house of praise.
go or stay, An - y - where with Je - sus when He points the way.
more to roam, An - y - where with Je - sus will be home, sweet home.
REFRAIN
An - y - where! An - y - where! Fear I can - not know;
An - y - where with Je - sus I can safe - ly go.

351 If Jesus Goes with Me

. . . the Lord thy God is with thee whithersoever thou goest. Josh. 1:9

C. Austin Miles, 1868-1946 C. Austin Miles, 1868-1946

1. It may be in the val - ley where count - less dan - gers hide;
2. It may be I must car - ry the bless - ed Word of life
3. But if it be my por - tion to bear my cross at home,
4. It is not mine to ques - tion the judg - ment of my Lord;
It may be in the sun - shine that I in peace a - bide;
A - cross the burn - ing des - erts to those in sin - ful strife;
While oth - ers bear their bur - dens be - yond the bil - lows foam,
It is but mine to fol - low the lead - ings of His Word;
But this one thing I know— if it be dark or fair,
And though it be my lot to bear my col - ors there,
I'll prove my faith in Him— con - fess His judg - ments fair,
But if to go or stay, or wheth - er here or there,
If Je - sus is with me, I'll go an - y - where!
If Je - sus goes with me, I'll go an - y - where!
And, if He stays with me, I'll stay an - y - where!
I'll be, with my Sav - iour, con - tent an - y - where!

If Jesus Goes with Me

REFRAIN
If Je - sus goes with me, I'll go An - y - where! 'Tis
heav - en to me Wher - e'er I may be, If He is there!
I count it a priv - i - lege here His cross to bear;
If Je - sus goes with me I'll go an - y - where.

352 God Will Take Care of You

Cast thy burden upon the Lord, and he shall sustain thee . . . Psa. 55:22

GOD CARES C.M. with Refrain

Civilla D. Martin, 1869-1948

Walter S. Martin, 1862-1935

1. Be not dis - mayed what-e'er be - tide, God will take care of you;
2. Through days of toil when heart doth fail, God will take care of you;
3. All you may need He will pro - vide, God will take care of you;
4. No mat - ter what may be the test, God will take care of you;
Be - neath His wings of love a - bide, God will take care of you.
When dan - gers fierce your path as - sail, God will take care of you.
Noth - ing you ask will be de - nied, God will take care of you.
Lean, wea - ry one, up - on His breast, God will take care of you.
Refrain
God will take care of you Through ev - ery day, O'er all the way;
He will take care of you; God will take care of you.

We're Marching to Zion 353

. . . let the children of Zion be joyful in their King. Psa. 149:2

Isaac Watts, 1674-1748
Refrain by Robert Lowry, 1826-1899

MARCHING TO ZION 6.6.8.8.6.6. with Refrain
Robert Lowry, 1826-1899

1. Come, we that love the Lord, And let our joys be known; Join
2. Let those re - fuse to sing Who nev - er knew our God; But
3. The hill of Zi - on yields A thou - sand sa - cred sweets, Be -
4. Then let our songs a - bound And ev - ery tear be dry; We're
in a song with sweet ac - cord, Join in a song with sweet ac - cord,
chil - dren of the heaven - ly King, But chil - dren of the heaven - ly King
fore we reach the heaven - ly fields, Be - fore we reach the heaven - ly fields,
march - ing through Em - man - uel's ground, We're march - ing through Em - man - uel's ground
And thus sur - round the throne, And thus sur - round the throne.
May speak their joys a - broad, May speak their joys a - broad.
Or walk the gold - en streets, Or walk the gold - en streets.
To fair - er worlds on high, To fair - er worlds on high.
REFRAIN
We're march - ing to Zi - on, Beau - ti - ful, beau - ti - ful Zi - on; We're
march - ing up - ward to Zi - on, The beau - ti - ful cit - y of God.

354 Jesus Giveth Us the Victory

... thanks be to God ... 1 Cor. 15:57

Albert B. Simpson, 1843-1919 — Melody by Albert B. Simpson, 1843-1919

1. There's a bat - tle rag - ing in the heaven-ly plac - es, Sin and
2. Faith can hear our Cap - tain call - ing from the heav - ens, "Cour - age,
3. We are led by One who nev - er lost a bat - tle, And our
4. Let us take the vic - tory o - ver Sa - tan's king - dom, O - ver
death and sick - ness with Sa - tan lead - ing on; With the hosts of
broth - er, I have o - ver-come for you; Fear not, I am
ad - ver - sar - y is a con-quered foe; We are more than
sick - ness, sor - row, self, and sin; Let us bear the
earth and hell ar-rayed a - gainst us, How in all our weak-ness
with you, I will nev - er fail you; Trust - ing in My prom - ise,
con-querors through our Cap-tain's tri - umph; Let us shout the vic - tory
ban - ner o'er the lands of dark - ness, Till the foes' last strong-hold
shall the fight be won?
you shall con - quer too."
as we on - ward go.
we for Christ shall win.
REFRAIN
Je - sus giv - eth us the vic - to - ry.
He, who o - ver-came on Cal - va - ry, O-ver-comes a - gain in

Jesus Giveth Us the Victory

you and me. Hal - le - lu - jah! Je - sus gives the vic - to - ry!

Dare to Be a Daniel 355

Watch ye, stand fast in the faith . . . 1 Cor. 16:13

Philip P. Bliss, 1838-1876

Melody by Philip P. Bliss, 1838-1876

1. Stand - ing by a pur - pose true, Heed - ing God's com - mand,
2. Man - y might - y men are lost, Dar - ing not to stand,
3. Man - y gi - ants, great and tall, Stalk - ing through the land,
4. Hold the gos - pel ban - ner high On to vic - tory grand!
Hon - or them, the faith - ful few! All hail to Dan - iel's band!
Who for God had been a host By join - ing Dan - iel's band!
Head - long to the earth would fall If met by Dan - iel's band!
Sa - tan and his host de - fy And shout for Dan - iel's band!
Refrain
Dare to be a Dan - iel, Dare to stand a - lone;
Dare to have a pur - pose firm, Dare to make it known!

356 Victory through Grace

. . . and he went forth conquering and to conquer. Rev. 6:2

Fanny J. Crosby, 1820-1915 | John R. Sweney, 1837-1899

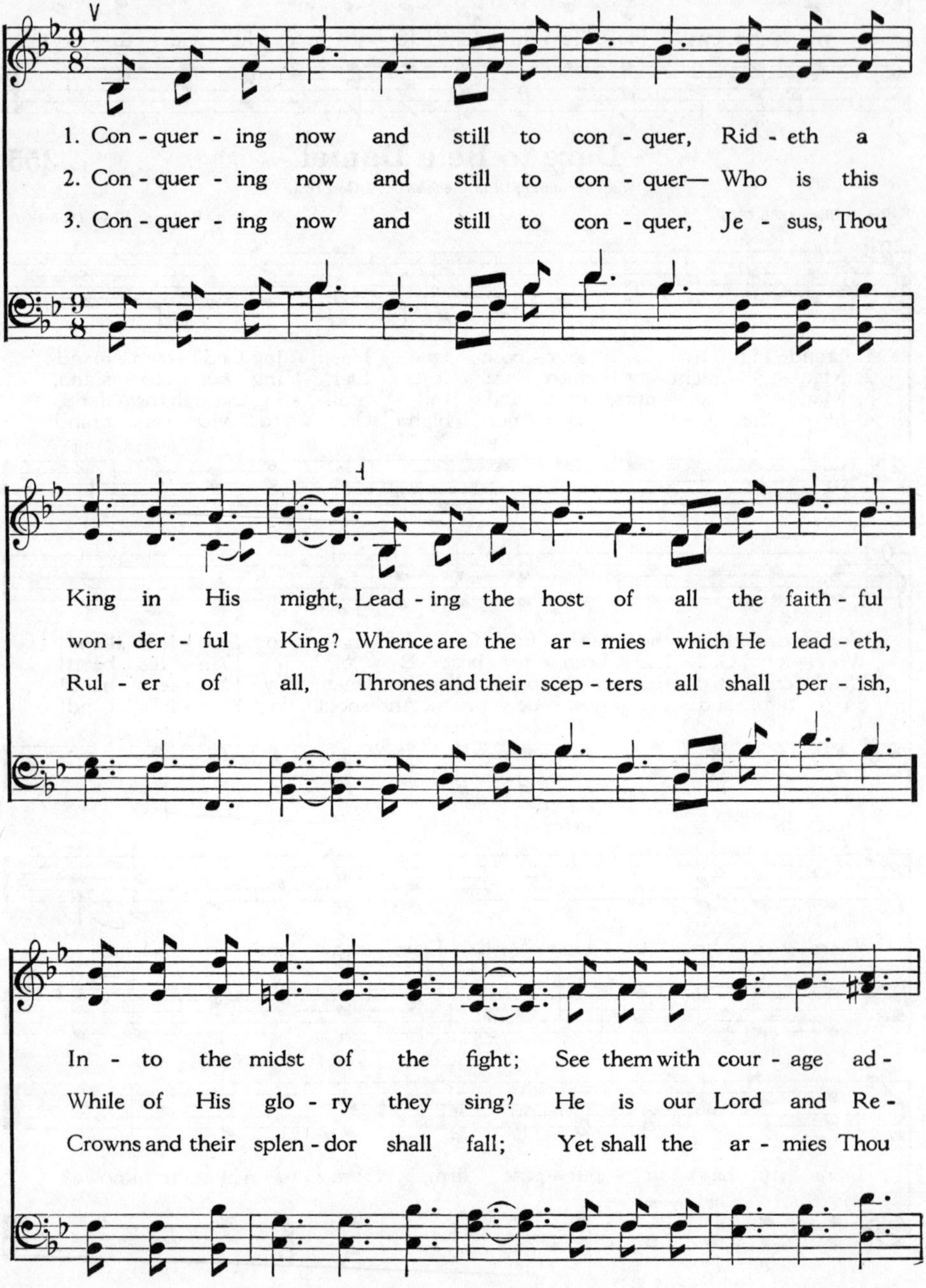
1. Con - quer - ing now and still to con - quer, Rid - eth a
2. Con - quer - ing now and still to con - quer— Who is this
3. Con - quer - ing now and still to con - quer, Je - sus, Thou
King in His might, Lead - ing the host of all the faith - ful
won - der - ful King? Whence are the ar - mies which He lead - eth,
Rul - er of all, Thrones and their scep - ters all shall per - ish,
In - to the midst of the fight;
See them with cour - age ad -
While of His glo - ry they sing?
He is our Lord and Re -
Crowns and their splen - dor shall fall;
Yet shall the ar - mies Thou

Victory through Grace

vanc - ing, Clad in their bril - liant ar - ray, Shout - ing the
deem - er, Sav - iour and Mon - arch di - vine; They are the
lead - est, Faith - ful and true to the last, Find in Thy
name of their Lead - er, Hear them ex - ult - ing - ly say:
stars that for - ev - er Bright in His king - dom will shine.
man - sions e - ter - nal Rest, when their war - fare is past.
Refrain
Not to the strong is the bat - tle, Not to the swift is the race,
Yet to the true and the faith - ful Vic-tory is prom-ised through grace.

357 On to Victory

Put on the whole armour of God . . . Eph. 6:11

Elisha A. Hoffman, 1839-1929

Melody by Elisha A. Hoffman, 1839-1929

1. Chris - tian, gird the ar - mor on, There's a vic - tory to be won
2. Let His ban - ner be un - furled Till it waves o'er all the world,
3. When the bat - tle shall be done And the vic - to - ry be won,
4. That will be an hour of joy; Praise shall then our tongues em - ploy
For the Lord, for the Lord; Take the hel - met, sword, and shield
Sea to sea, shore to shore; Till the na - tions all shall own
Con - flict past, con - flict past, In the new Je - ru - sa - lem
More and more, more and more; We shall stand be - fore the King
Forth un - to the bat - tle - field At His word, at His word.
He is King, and He a - lone, Ev - er - more, ev - er - more.
We shall wear a di - a - dem At the last, at the last.
And the song of tri - umph sing Ev - er - more, ev - er - more.
REFRAIN
On we'll march to vic - to - ry! Je - sus will our lead - er
On we'll march

On to Victory

be, Je - sus will our lead - er be! On we'll march to vic - to -
ry, To a fin - al and a glo - rious vic - to - ry!

A Charge to Keep I Have 358

So then every one of us shall give account of himself to God. Rom. 14:12

Charles Wesley, 1707-1788

LABAN S.M.
Lowell Mason, 1792-1872

1. A charge to keep I have, A God to glo - ri - fy;
2. To serve the pres - ent age, My call - ing to ful - fill—
3. Arm me with jeal - ous care, As in Thy sight to live;
4. Help me to watch and pray, And on Thy - self re - ly,
A nev - er - dy - ing soul to save And fit it for the sky;
Oh, may it all my powers en - gage To do my Mas-ter's will.
And, oh, Thy ser - vant, Lord, pre - pare A strict ac - count to give.
As - sured, if I my trust be - tray, I shall for - ev - er die.

(For different harmony see No. 368)

359 Who Is on the Lord's Side?

. . . let him come unto me. . . . Exod. 32:26

ARMAGEDDON 6.5.6.5.D. with Refrain
C. Luise Reichardt, circa 1780-1826
Arranged by John Goss, 1800-1880

Frances R. Havergal, 1836-1879

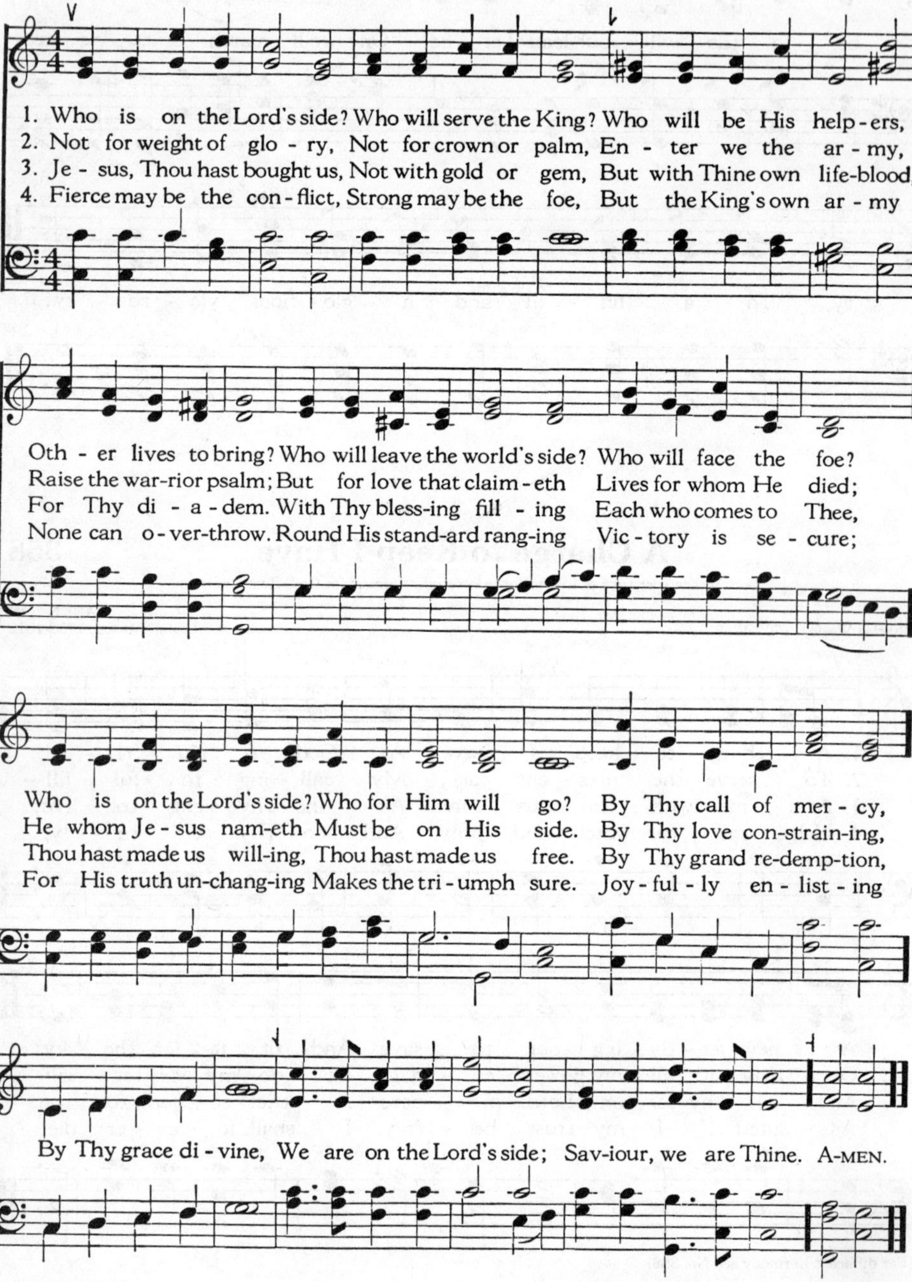
1. Who is on the Lord's side? Who will serve the King? Who will be His help-ers,
2. Not for weight of glo - ry, Not for crown or palm, En - ter we the ar - my,
3. Je - sus, Thou hast bought us, Not with gold or gem, But with Thine own life-blood,
4. Fierce may be the con - flict, Strong may be the foe, But the King's own ar - my
Oth - er lives to bring? Who will leave the world's side? Who will face the foe?
Raise the war-rior psalm; But for love that claim - eth Lives for whom He died;
For Thy di - a - dem. With Thy bless-ing fill - ing Each who comes to Thee,
None can o - ver-throw. Round His stand-ard rang-ing Vic - tory is se - cure;
Who is on the Lord's side? Who for Him will go? By Thy call of mer - cy,
He whom Je - sus nam-eth Must be on His side. By Thy love con-strain-ing,
Thou hast made us will-ing, Thou hast made us free. By Thy grand re-demp-tion,
For His truth un-chang-ing Makes the tri - umph sure. Joy - ful - ly en - list - ing
By Thy grace di - vine, We are on the Lord's side; Sav-iour, we are Thine. A-MEN.

Yield Not to Temptation 360

Watch and pray, that ye enter not into temptation . . . Matt. 26:41

PALMER 6.5.6.5.6.5.6.6.

Horatio R. Palmer, 1834-1907

Melody by Horatio R. Palmer, 1834-1907

1. Yield not to temp-ta-tion, For yield-ing is sin— Each vic-tory will
2. Shun e-vil com-pan-ions, Bad lan-guage dis-dain, God's name hold in
3. To him that o'er-com-eth God giv-eth a crown; Through faith we shall
help you Some oth-er to win; Fight man-ful-ly on-ward,
rev-erence, Nor take it in vain; Be thought-ful and ear-nest,
con-quer Though of-ten cast down; He, who is our Sav-iour,
Dark pas-sions sub-due; Look ev-er to Je-sus, He will car-ry you through.
Kind-heart-ed and true; Look ev-er to Je-sus, He will car-ry you through.
Our strength will re-new; Look ev-er to Je-sus, He will car-ry you through.
REFRAIN
Ask the Sav-iour to help you, Com-fort, strength-en, and keep you;
He is will-ing to aid you, He will car-ry you through.

361 I Have Overcome

. . . but be of good cheer; I have overcome the world. John 16:33

Albert B. Simpson, 1843-1919

Melody by Albert B. Simpson, 1843-1919

1. Faint - ing sol - dier of the Lord, Hear His sweet in - spir - ing word—
2. Fear not, though thy foes be strong; Faint not, though the strife be long;
3. Soon the con - flict will be done, Soon the bat - tle will be won,
"I have con - quered all thy foes, I have suf - fered all thy woes;
Trust thy glo - rious Cap - tain's power, Watch with Him one lit - tle hour;
Soon shall wave the vic - tor's palm, Soon shall ring th'e - ter - nal psalm—
Strug - gling sol - dier, trust in Me, I have o - ver - come for thee."
Hear Him call - ing, "Fol - low Me, I have o - ver - come for thee."
Then our joy - ful song shall be, "I have o - ver - come for thee."
REFRAIN
"I have o - ver-come, o - ver - come, O - ver-come for thee;
Thou shall o - ver-come, o - ver - come, O - ver-come through Me."

Caleb Saw the Lord 362

How should one chase a thousand . . . Deut. 32:30

Anna E. Richards, 19th century
Refrain by Mabel J. Camp, 1871-1937

Mabel J. Camp, 1871-1937

1. Oth- ers saw the gi - ants, Ca- leb saw the Lord; They were sore dis -
2. Oh, to fol - low ful - ly like this one of old; Oh, to be like
3. If we are half-heart-ed, we'll not taste God's best; Those who fol - low
4. Oh, to have one Mas- ter, on - ly One to please; Oh, to have one
heart-ened, he be - lieved God's word; And that word he ful - ly,
Ca - leb, do - ing what is told; Then the Lord's rich bless-ing
whol - ly will be whol - ly blest, Blest in soul and spir - it,
pur - pose, not our will or ease; Press - ing ev - er on-ward
fear-less - ly, o - beyed—Was it not suf - fi- cient that the Lord hath said?
will be ours to - day, He will pros-per ev - er those who Him o - bey.
bod - y, mind, and heart, Rich in heaven-ly treas-ure, which He will im - part.
to the goal be - fore, Serv-ing glad - ly, whol - ly, Him whom we a - dore.
REFRAIN
I will nev - er leave thee; Go in this Thy might;
One shall chase a thou - sand, Two put ten to flight.

363 Sound the Battle Cry!

. . . be strong in the Lord, and in the power of his might. Eph. 6:10

William F. Sherwin, 1826-1888 — Melody by William F. Sherwin, 1826-1888

1. Sound the bat - tle cry! See, the foe is nigh; Raise the stand - ard high
2. Strong to meet the foe, March-ing on we go, While our cause we know
3. O Thou God of all, Hear us when we call; Help us one and all
For the Lord! Gird your ar - mor on, Stand firm ev - ery one,
Must pre - vail; Shield and ban - ner bright Gleam - ing in the light,
By Thy grace; When the bat - tle's done And the vic - tory won,
REFRAIN
Rest your cause up - on His ho - ly Word!
Bat - tling for the right We ne'er can fail! Rouse then, sol-diers, ral - ly
May we wear the crown Be - fore Thy face!
round the ban - ner! Read - y, stead - y, pass the word a - long; On-ward!
For-ward! Shout a - loud Ho-san - na! Christ is Cap-tain of the might-y throng!

Onward, Christian Soldiers 364

. . . endure hardness, as a good soldier of Jesus Christ. 2 Tim. 2:3

ST. GERTRUDE 6.5.6.5.D. with Refrain

Sabine Baring-Gould, 1834-1924

Arthur S. Sullivan, 1842-1900

1. On - ward, Chris-tian sol - diers, March-ing as to war, With the cross of Je - sus
2. Like a might-y ar - my Moves the Church of God; Broth-ers, we are tread - ing
3. Crowns and thrones may per-ish, King-doms rise and wane, But the Church of Je - sus
4. On - ward, then, ye peo - ple, Join our hap-py throng, Blend with ours your voic-es
Go - ing on be-fore: Christ, the roy - al Mas - ter, Leads a - gainst the foe;
Where the saints have trod; We are not di - vid - ed, All one bod - y we,
Con - stant will re-main; Gates of hell can nev - er 'Gainst that Church pre-vail;
In the tri-umph song; Glo - ry, laud, and hon - or Un - to Christ the King;
REFRAIN
For - ward in - to bat - tle, See His ban-ners go.
One in hope and doc - trine, One in char - i - ty. On-ward, Chris-tian sol - diers,
We have Christ's own prom-ise, And that can - not fail.
This through countless a - ges Men and an - gels sing.
March-ing as to war, With the cross of Je - sus Go - ing on be - fore.

365 Cross of Christ, Lead Onward

. . . we are more than conquerors through him that loved us. Rom. 8:37

Russell K. Carter, 1849-1928 — Russell K. Carter, 1849-1928

1. Cross of Christ, lead on-ward Through the ho - ly war; In this sign we
2. Not with pomp and pa-geant, Not in earth - ly pride; We must fight our
3. Pan - o - plied in grac - es, Bold, yet hum-bly meek; Rest - ing while we're
4. By a cloud en-com-passed, Wit - ness - es a - bove; Saints, a - pos - tles,
5. March-ing in the path-way That the Mas - ter trod, Walks One dai - ly
con - quer Now and ev - er - more. Not of man the pow - er, Not to
bat - tles Like the Cru - ci - fied. O - ver - come by suf-fering, Con - quer
work - ing; Strong, but ev - er weak. Tim - id, though cou - ra-geous, Gain - ing
proph-ets, Pre - cious ones we love; While "Ad-vance!" is sound-ing, Mounts the
with us Like the Son of God. To the end en - dur - ing, Ar - mor
man the fame; We are vic - tors on - ly In our Lead - er's name.
through de - feat; Tried and test - ed dai - ly In the fur - nace heat.
as we give; Cru - ci - fied with Je - sus, Yet, in Him, we live.
bat - tle thrill. Cross of Christ, lead on - ward Where the Cap - tain will.
ne'er laid down Till the cross leads up - ward To the blood-bought crown.
REFRAIN
Cross of Christ, lead on - ward, Through the ho - ly war;
In this sign we con - quer Now and ev - er - more.

The Banner of the Cross

Thou hast given a banner to them . . . that it may be displayed . . . Psa. 60:4

Daniel W. Whittle, 1840-1901

James McGranahan, 1840-1907

1. There's a roy - al ban - ner giv - en for dis - play
2. Though the foe may rage and gath - er as the flood,
3. O - ver land and sea, wher - ev - er man may dwell,
4. When the glo - ry dawns—'tis draw - ing ver - y near;
To the sol - diers of the King. As an en - sign fair we
Let the stand - ard be dis - played! And be - neath its folds, as
Make the glo - rious ti - dings known; Of the crim - son ban - ner
It is hast - ening day by day— Then be - fore our King the
lift it up to - day, While as ran - somed ones we sing:
sol - diers of the Lord, For the truth be not dis - mayed!
now the sto - ry tell, While the Lord shall claim His own!
foe shall dis - ap - pear, And the cross the world shall sway!
REFRAIN
March - ing on, march - ing on! For Christ count ev - ery-thing but loss;
And to crown Him King, toil and sing 'Neath the ban - ner of the cross!

367 Am I a Soldier of the Cross?

. . . quit you like men, be strong. 1 Cor. 16:13

Isaac Watts, 1674-1748

ARLINGTON C.M.
Adapted from Thomas A. Arne, 1710-1778

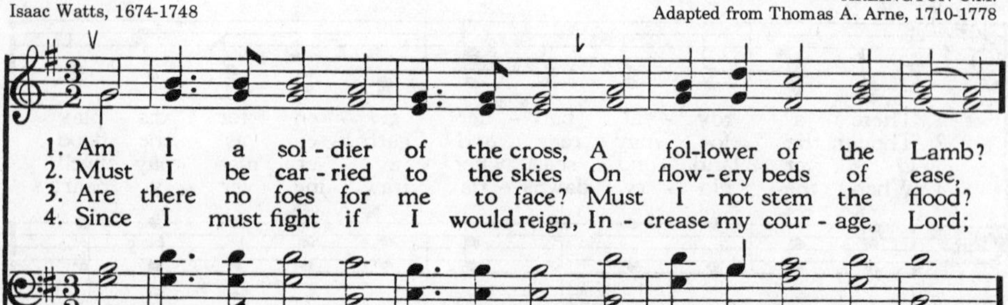
1. Am I a sol - dier of the cross, A fol-lower of the Lamb?
2. Must I be car - ried to the skies On flow - ery beds of ease,
3. Are there no foes for me to face? Must I not stem the flood?
4. Since I must fight if I would reign, In - crease my cour - age, Lord;

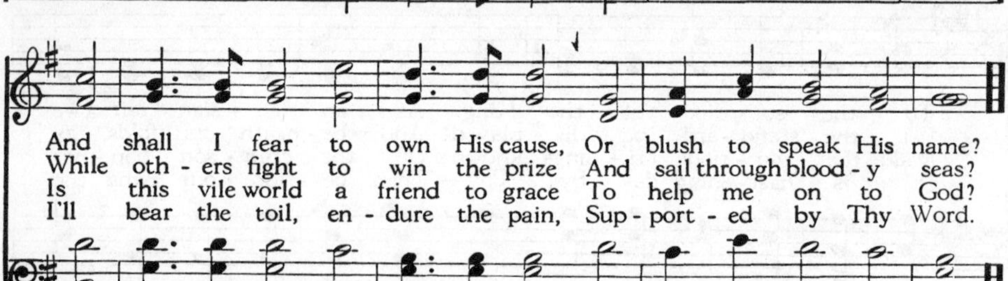
And shall I fear to own His cause, Or blush to speak His name?
While oth - ers fight to win the prize And sail through blood - y seas?
Is this vile world a friend to grace To help me on to God?
I'll bear the toil, en - dure the pain, Sup - port - ed by Thy Word.

368 My Soul, Be on Thy Guard

Be sober, be vigilant . . . 1 Pet. 5:8

George Heath, 1750-1822

LABAN S.M.
Lowell Mason, 1792-1872

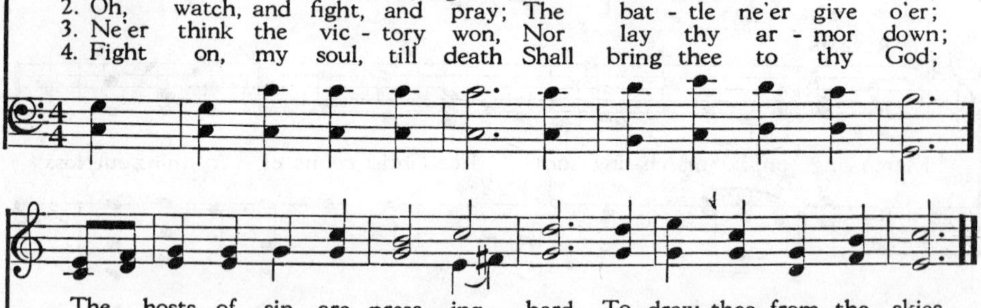
1. My soul, be on thy guard; Ten thou - sand foes a - rise;
2. Oh, watch, and fight, and pray; The bat - tle ne'er give o'er;
3. Ne'er think the vic - tory won, Nor lay thy ar - mor down;
4. Fight on, my soul, till death Shall bring thee to thy God;

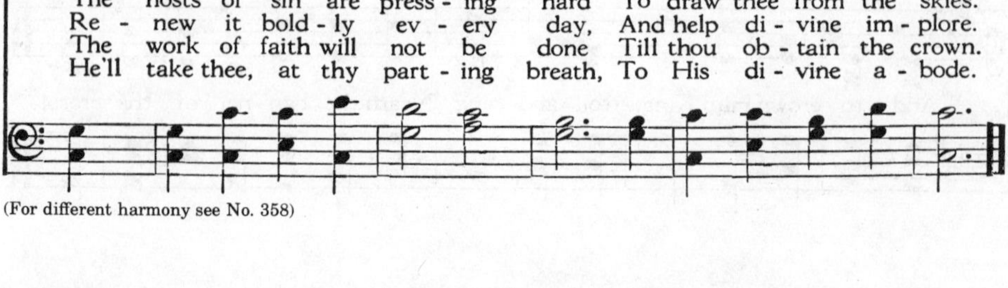
The hosts of sin are press - ing hard To draw thee from the skies.
Re - new it bold - ly ev - ery day, And help di - vine im - plore.
The work of faith will not be done Till thou ob - tain the crown.
He'll take thee, at thy part - ing breath, To His di - vine a - bode.

(For different harmony see No. 358)

Stand Up, Stand Up for Jesus

369

. . . endure hardness, as a good soldier of Jesus Christ. 2 Tim. 2:3

WEBB (Morning Light) 7.6.7.6.D.

George Duffield, 1818-1888

George J. Webb, 1803-1887

1. Stand up, stand up for Je - sus, Ye sol - diers of the cross;
2. Stand up, stand up for Je - sus, The trum - pet call o - bey;
3. Stand up, stand up for Je - sus, Stand in His strength a - lone;
4. Stand up, stand up for Je - sus— The strife will not be long;
Lift high His roy - al ban - ner, It must not suf - fer loss.
Forth to the might - y con - flict, In this His glo - rious day!
The arm of flesh will fail you, Ye dare not trust your own.
This day the noise of bat - tle, The next the vic - tor's song.
From vic - tory un - to vic - tory His ar - my shall He lead,
Ye that are men, now serve Him A - gainst un - num-bered foes;
Put on the gos - pel ar - mor, Each piece put on with prayer;
To him that o - ver - com - eth A crown of life shall be;
Till ev - ery foe is van-quished And Christ is Lord in - deed.
Let cour - age rise with dan - ger And strength to strength op-pose.
Where du - ty calls, or dan - ger, Be nev - er want-ing there.
He with the King of glo - ry Shall reign e - ter - nal - ly. A-MEN.

370 Faith of Our Fathers

. . . earnestly contend for the faith which was once delivered unto the saints. Jude 3

ST. CATHERINE L.M. with Refrain
Melody by Henri F. Hemy, 1818-1888
Adapted by James G. Walton, 1821-1905

Frederick W. Faber, 1814-1863 (altered)

1. Faith of our fa - thers, liv - ing still In spite of dun - geon,
2. Our fa - thers, chained in pris - on dark, Were still in heart and
3. Faith of our fa - thers, we will strive To win all na - tions
4. Faith of our fa - thers! We will love Both friend and foe in
fire, and sword! Oh, how our hearts beat high with joy
con - science free. Lord, grant their chil - dren strength and love,
un - to Thee; And through the truth that comes from God
all our strife; And preach thee, too, as love knows how
When - e'er we hear that glo - rious word:
Like them, to live and die for Thee.
Man - kind shall then in - deed be free.
By kind - ly words and vir - tuous life.
Refrain
Faith of our fa - thers,
ho - ly faith! We will be true to thee till death.

We Rest on Thee 371

. . . and in thy name we go . . . 2 Chron. 14:11

FINLANDIA 11.10.11.10. with repeat
From Jean Sibelius' *Finlandia*, 1899
Arranged for *The Hymnal*, 1933

Edith G. Cherry, 1872-1897

1. "We rest on Thee" our Shield and our De - fend-er! We go not forth a-
2. Yea, "in Thy Name," O Cap-tain of sal - va - tion! In Thy dear Name, all
3. "We go" in faith, our own great weak- ness feel-ing, And need-ing more each
4. "We rest on Thee" our Shield and our De - fend-er! Thine is the bat - tle,
lone a-gainst the foe; Strong in Thy strength, safe in Thy keep-ing ten - der,
oth - er names a - bove: Je - sus our Right - eous-ness, our sure foun-da - tion,
day Thy grace to know: Yet from our hearts a song of tri-umph peal - ing;
Thine shall be the praise When pass-ing through the gates of pearl - y splen-dor,
"We rest on Thee, and in Thy Name we go," Strong in Thy strength, safe
Our Prince of glo - ry and our King of love, Je - sus our Right- eous-
"We rest on Thee, and in Thy Name we go," Yet from our hearts a
Vic - tors—we rest with Thee, through end-less days, When pass-ing through the
in Thy keep-ing ten - der, "We rest on Thee, and in Thy Name we go."
ness our sure foun-da - tion, Our Prince of glo - ry and our King of love.
song of tri-umph peal-ing; "We rest on Thee, and in Thy Name we go."
gates of pearl - y splen-dor, Vic - tors—we rest with Thee, through end-less days.

372 Speak, My Lord

. . . for thy servant heareth. . . . 1 Sam. 3:9

George Bennard, 1873-1958 — George Bennard, 1873-1958

1. Hear the Lord of har - vest sweet - ly call - ing, "Who will go and
2. When the coal of fire touched the proph - et, Mak - ing him as
3. Mil - lions now in sin and shame are dy - ing, Lis - ten to their
4. Soon the time for reap - ing will be o - ver; Soon we'll gath - er
work for Me to - day? Who will bring to Me the lost and dy - ing?
pure, as pure can be, When the voice of God said, "Who'll go for us?"
sad and bit - ter cry; Has - ten, broth - er, has - ten to the res - cue;
for the har - vest home; May the Lord of har - vest smile up - on us,
Who will point them to the nar - row way?"
Then he an-swered, "Here I am, send me."
Quick - ly an-swer, "Mas - ter, here am I."
May we hear His bless-ed, "Child, well done."
REFRAIN
Speak, my Lord, speak, my
Speak, my Lord,
Lord, Speak, and I'll be quick to an - swer Thee; Speak, my
Speak, my Lord, to an-swer Thee;
Lord, speak, my Lord, Speak, and I will an-swer, "Lord, send me."
Speak, my Lord, "Lord, send me."

A Worker's Prayer 373

And the things that thou hast heard . . . commit thou to faithful men . . . 2 Tim. 2:2

CANONBURY L.M.

Frances R. Havergal, 1836-1879

Melody adapted from Robert A. Schumann, 1810-1856

4
4
1. Lord, speak to me, that I may speak In
2. Oh, lead me, Lord, that I may lead The
3. Oh, strength - en me, that while I stand Firm
4. Oh, teach me, Lord, that I may teach The
5. Oh, fill me with Thy full - ness, Lord, Un -
6. Oh, use me, Lord, use e - ven me Just
liv - ing ech - oes of Thy tone; As Thou hast sought, so
wan-dering and the wav - ering feet; Oh, feed me, Lord, that
on the rock and strong in Thee, I may stretch out a
pre - cious things Thou dost im - part; And wing my words, that
til my ver - y heart o'er - flow In kin - dling thought and
as Thou wilt, and when, and where; Un - til Thy bless - ed
let me seek Thy err - ing chil - dren, lost and lone.
I may feed Thy hun - gering ones with man - na sweet.
lov - ing hand To wrest - lers with the trou - bled sea.
they may reach The hid - den depths of many a heart.
glow - ing word, Thy love to tell, Thy praise to show.
face I see, Thy rest, Thy joy, Thy glo - ry share. A - MEN.

374 Where Cross the Crowded Ways of Life

Multitudes, multitudes in the valley of decision . . . Joel 3:14

WALTON L.M.

Frank M. North, 1850-1935

From William Gardiner's *Sacred Melodies*, 1815

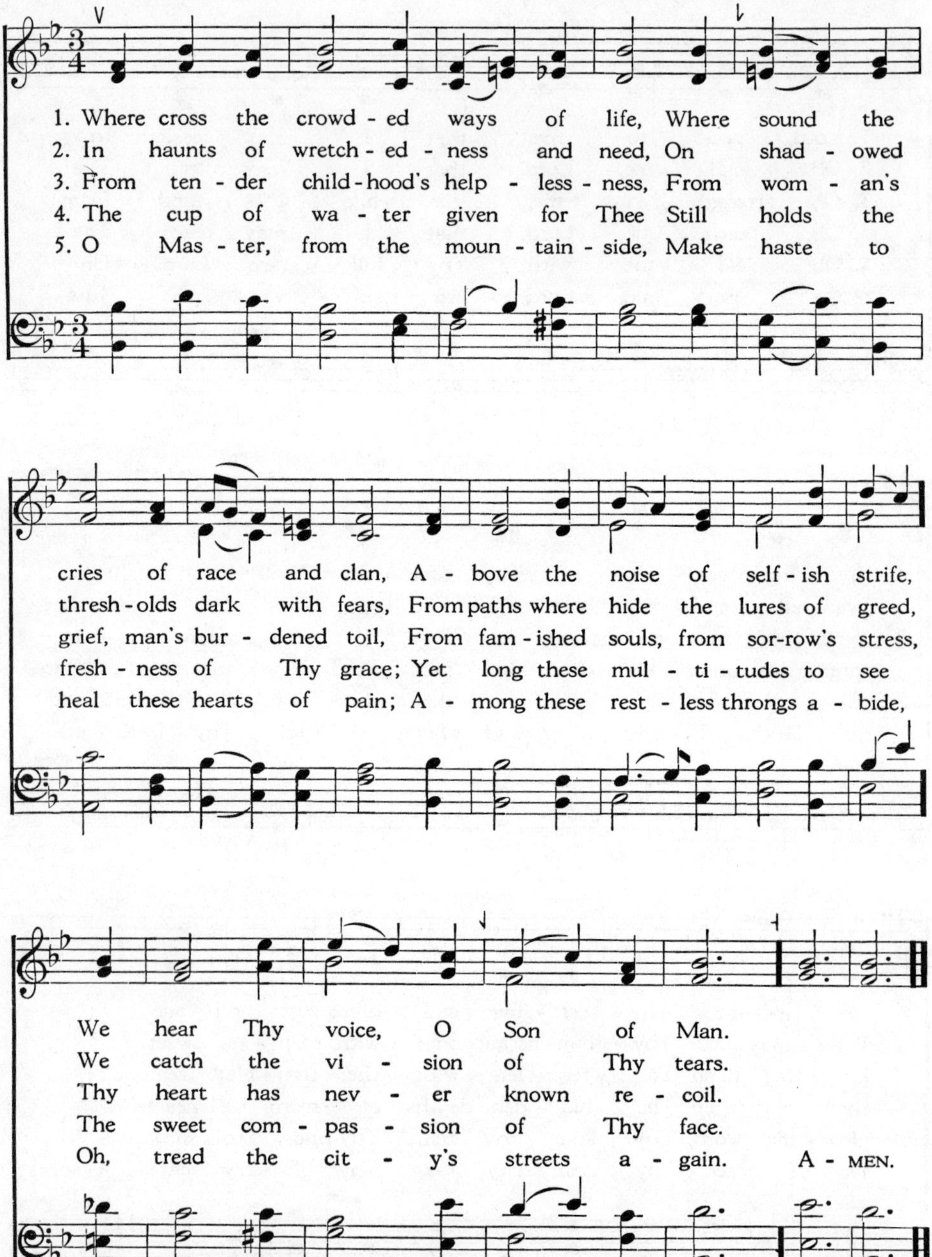
1. Where cross the crowd - ed ways of life, Where sound the
2. In haunts of wretch - ed - ness and need, On shad - owed
3. From ten - der child - hood's help - less - ness, From wom - an's
4. The cup of wa - ter given for Thee Still holds the
5. O Mas - ter, from the moun - tain - side, Make haste to
cries of race and clan, A - bove the noise of self - ish strife,
thresh - olds dark with fears, From paths where hide the lures of greed,
grief, man's bur - dened toil, From fam - ished souls, from sor - row's stress,
fresh - ness of Thy grace; Yet long these mul - ti - tudes to see
heal these hearts of pain; A - mong these rest - less throngs a - bide,
We hear Thy voice, O Son of Man.
We catch the vi - sion of Thy tears.
Thy heart has nev - er known re - coil.
The sweet com - pas - sion of Thy face.
Oh, tread the cit - y's streets a - gain. A - MEN.

(For different harmony see No. 157)

Channels Only

375

. . . he shall be a vessel . . . meet for the master's use . . . 2 Tim. 2:21

Mary E. Maxwell, 20th century

CHANNELS 8.7.8.7. with Refrain
Ada R. Gibbs, 1865-1905

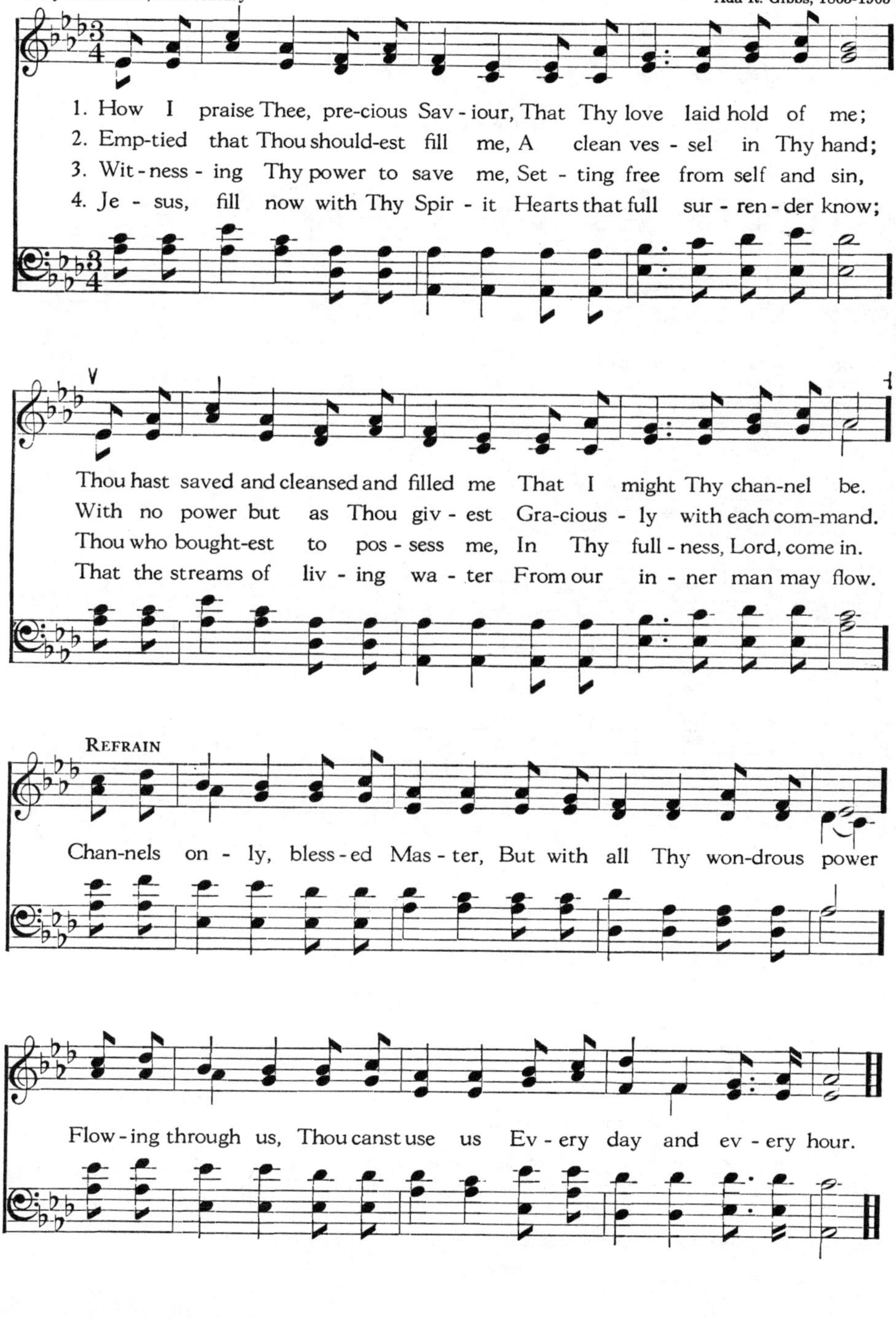
1. How I praise Thee, pre-cious Sav - iour, That Thy love laid hold of me;
2. Emp-tied that Thou should-est fill me, A clean ves - sel in Thy hand;
3. Wit - ness - ing Thy power to save me, Set - ting free from self and sin,
4. Je - sus, fill now with Thy Spir - it Hearts that full sur - ren - der know;
Thou hast saved and cleansed and filled me That I might Thy chan-nel be.
With no power but as Thou giv - est Gra-cious - ly with each com-mand.
Thou who bought-est to pos - sess me, In Thy full - ness, Lord, come in.
That the streams of liv - ing wa - ter From our in - ner man may flow.
Refrain
Chan-nels on - ly, bless-ed Mas - ter, But with all Thy won-drous power
Flow - ing through us, Thou canst use us Ev - ery day and ev - ery hour.

376 Make Me a Blessing

And I will make them . . . a blessing . . . Ezek. 34:26

Ira B. Wilson, 1880-1950

SCHULER 10.7.10.7. with Refrain
George S. Schuler, 1882-1973

1. Out in the high-ways and by-ways of life, Man-y are wea-ry
2. Tell the sweet sto-ry of Christ and His love, Tell of His power to
3. Give as 'twas giv-en to you in your need, Love as the Mas-ter
and sad; Car-ry the sun-shine where dark-ness is rife,
are wea-ry and sad;
for-give; Oth-ers will trust Him If on-ly you prove
His power to for-give;
loved you; Be to the help-less a help-er in-deed,
the Mas-ter loved you.
Mak-ing the sor-row-ing glad.
True, ev-ery mo-ment you live.
Un-to your mis-sion be true.
REFRAIN
Make me a bless-ing, Make me a bless-ing,
Out of my life. May Je-sus shine; Make me a bless-ing, O
out of my life
Sav-iour, I pray, Make me a bless-ing to some-one to-day.
Thee, my Sav-iour,

Thou Who the Night in Prayer Didst Spend 377

. . . it is required in stewards, that a man be found faithful. 1 Cor. 4:2

Anonymous

MELITA 8.8.8.8.8.8.
John B. Dykes, 1823-1876

1. Thou who the night in prayer didst spend, And then Thy twelve a - pos - tles send; And bidd'st us pray the har - vest's Lord To send forth sow - ers of Thy Word, Hear, and Thy cho - sen ser - vants bless With sev - en - fold gifts of ho - li - ness.
2. Oh, may Thy pas - tors faith - ful be, Not la - boring for them - selves, but Thee; Give grace to feed with whole - some food The sheep and lambs bought by Thy blood; To tend Thy flock, and thus to prove How dear - ly they the Shep - herd love!
3. Oh, may Thy peo - ple faith - ful be, And in Thy pas - tors hon - or Thee And with them work, and for them pray, And glad - ly Thee in them o - bey; Re - ceive the proph - et of the Lord, And gain the proph - et's own re - ward!
4. So may we, when our work is done, To - geth - er stand be - fore the throne; And joy - ful hearts and voic - es raise In one u - nit - ed song of praise, With all the bright ce - les - tial host, To Fa - ther, Son, and Ho - ly Ghost.
A-MEN.

(For different harmony and higher key see No. 34)

378 They That Wait upon the Lord

... shall renew their strength ... Isa. 40:31

Anonymous

Melody by James McGranahan, 1840-1907

1. Ho! Reap - ers in the whit-ened har - vest, Oft fee - ble, faint and few,
2. Too oft a - wea - ry and dis - cour - aged, We pour a sad com - plaint;
3. Re - joice, for He is with us al - way, Lo, e - ven to the end!
Come wait up - on the bless - ed Mas - ter; Our strength He will re - new.
Be - liev - ing in a liv - ing Sav - iour, Why should we ev - er faint?
Look up, take cour-age, and go for - ward; All need - ed grace He'll send.
REFRAIN
For they that wait up - on the Lord shall re - new
their strength, They shall mount up with wings, they shall

They That Wait upon the Lord

mount up with wings as ea - gles; They shall run and not be
wea - ry, they shall walk and not faint; They shall
run and not be wea - ry, they shall walk and not
faint; They shall run and not be wea - ry, shall walk and not faint.

379 I'll Go Where You Want Me to Go

. . . Here am I; send me. Isa. 6:8

Stanza 1 by Mary A. Brown, 19th century
Stanzas 2-3 by Charles E. Prior, 1856-1927

MANCHESTER Irregular with Refrain
Carrie E. Rounsefell, 1861-1930

1. It may not be on the moun-tain's height Or o - ver the storm-y sea;
2. Per - haps to - day there are lov - ing words Which Je-sus would have me speak;
3. There's sure - ly some-where a low - ly place In earth's har-vest fields so wide,
It may not be at the bat - tle's front My Lord will have need of me;
There may be now, in the paths of sin, Some wan-derer whom I should seek.
Where I may la - bor through life's short day For Je - sus, the Cru - ci - fied.
But if by a still, small voice He calls To paths I do not know,
O Sav - iour, if Thou will be my Guide, Though dark and rug-ged the way,
So, trust - ing my all un - to Thy care, I know Thou lov - est me!
I'll an-swer, dear Lord, with my hand in Thine, I'll go where you want me to go.
My voice shall ech - o the mes-sage sweet– I'll say what you want me to say.
I'll do Thy will with a heart sin-cere, I ll be what you want me to be.

I'll Go Where You Want Me to Go

REFRAIN

I'll go where you want me to go, dear Lord, O'er moun-tain, or plain, or sea;
I'll say what you want me to say, dear Lord, I'll be what you want me to be.

O Master, Let Me Walk with Thee 380

. . . let us walk in the light of the Lord. Isa. 2:5

Washington Gladden, 1836-1918

MARYTON L.M.
Henry P. Smith, 1825-1898

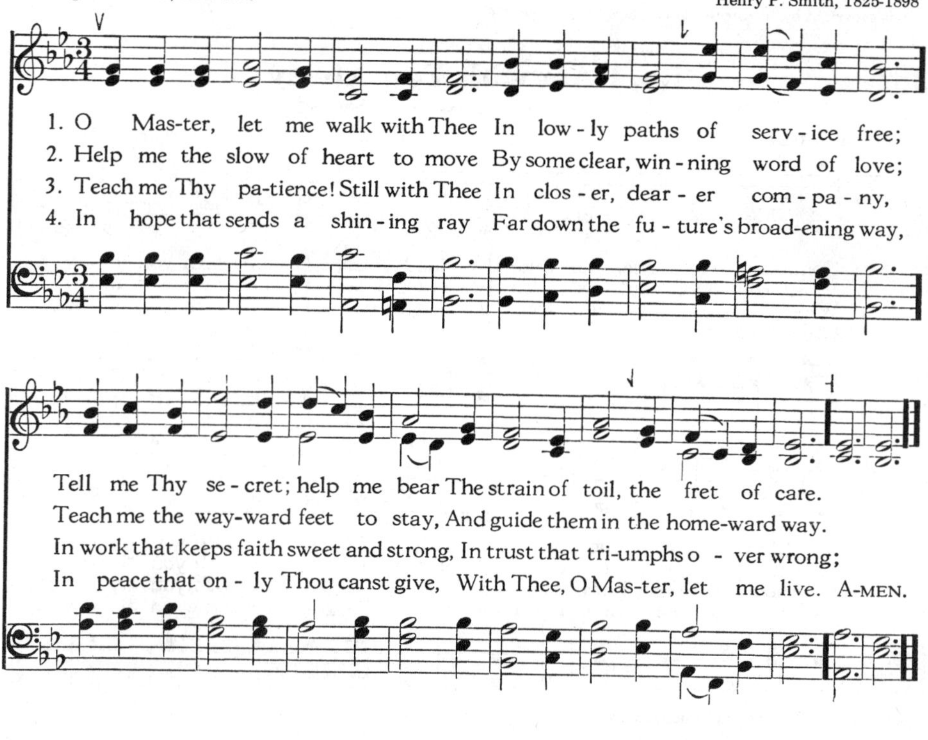
1. O Mas-ter, let me walk with Thee In low-ly paths of serv-ice free;
2. Help me the slow of heart to move By some clear, win-ning word of love;
3. Teach me Thy pa-tience! Still with Thee In clos-er, dear-er com-pa-ny,
4. In hope that sends a shin-ing ray Far down the fu-ture's broad-ening way,
Tell me Thy se-cret; help me bear The strain of toil, the fret of care.
Teach me the way-ward feet to stay, And guide them in the home-ward way.
In work that keeps faith sweet and strong, In trust that tri-umphs o-ver wrong;
In peace that on-ly Thou canst give, With Thee, O Mas-ter, let me live. A-MEN.

381 Rise Up, O Men of God

. . . serve him with all your heart and with all your soul. Deut. 11:13

FESTAL SONG S.M.

William P. Merrill, 1867-1954 | William H. Walter, 1825-1893

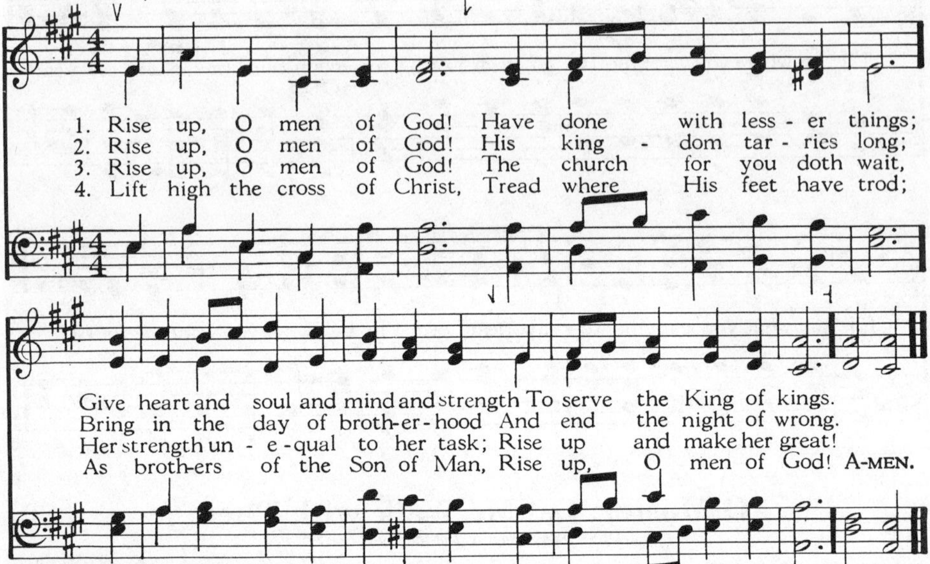
1. Rise up, O men of God! Have done with less - er things;
2. Rise up, O men of God! His king - dom tar - ries long;
3. Rise up, O men of God! The church for you doth wait,
4. Lift high the cross of Christ, Tread where His feet have trod;
Give heart and soul and mind and strength To serve the King of kings.
Bring in the day of broth-er-hood And end the night of wrong.
Her strength un - e - qual to her task; Rise up and make her great!
As broth-ers of the Son of Man, Rise up, O men of God! A-MEN.

(For higher key see No. 413)

382 Lo, I Am with You Alway

. . . even unto the end of the world. . . . Matt. 28:20

Dwight Hall, b. 1923 | Dwight Hall, b. 1923

1. Come un - to Me, I'll take thy load; "Lo, I am with you al - way."
2. When thy poor soul is deep - ly vexed; "Lo, I am with you al - way."
3. When thou art anx - ious, sore dis-tressed; "Lo, I am with you al - way."
4. Oh, wea - ried soul, for - sake thy sin; "Lo, I am with you al - way."
Let Me come in and make a - bode; "Lo, I am with you al - way."
And when thy mind is oft per - plexed; "Lo, I am with you al - way."
Lean thou up - on Him, take thy rest; "Lo, I am with you al - way."
O - pen your heart's door; Let Him in To guide you on-ward al - way.

Oh, That Will Be Glory 383

. . . we shall see him as he is. 1 John 3:2

Charles H. Gabriel, 1856-1932

GLORY SONG 10.10.10.10. with Refrain
Charles H. Gabriel, 1856-1932

1. When all my la-bors and tri-als are o'er And I am safe on that
2. When, by the gift of His in-fi-nite grace, I am ac-cord-ed in
3. Friends will be there I have loved long a-go; Joy like a riv-er a-
beau-ti-ful shore, Just to be near the dear Lord I a-dore
heav-en a place, Just to be there and to look on His face
round me will flow; Yet, just a smile from my Sav-iour, I know,
Will through the a-ges be glo-ry for me.
REFRAIN
Oh, that will be
Oh, that will
glo-ry for me, Glo-ry for me, glo-ry for me, When by His grace
be glo-ry for me, Glo-ry for me, glo-ry for me,
I shall look on His face, That will be glo-ry, be glo-ry for me.

384 When the Roll Is Called Up Yonder

. . . so shall we ever be with the Lord. 1 Thess. 4:17

THE ROLL 15.11.15.11. with Refrain

James M. Black, 1856-1938 James M. Black, 1856-1938

1. When the trum-pet of the Lord shall sound and time shall be no more, And the
2. On that bright and cloud-less morn-ing when the dead in Christ shall rise, And the
3. Let us la - bor for the Mas-ter from the dawn to set - ting sun, Let us
morn-ing breaks e - ter - nal, bright and fair; When the saved of earth shall gath-er
glo - ry of His res - ur - rec-tion share; When His cho-sen ones shall gath-er
talk of all His won-drous love and care; Then when all of life is o - ver,
o - ver on the oth - er shore, And the roll is called up yon-der, I'll be there.
to their home be-yond the skies, And the roll is called up yon-der, I'll be there.
and our work on earth is done, And the roll is called up yon-der, We'll be there.
Refrain
When the roll is called up yon - der, When the
When the roll is called up yon - der, I'll be there,
roll is called up yon - der, When the roll is
When the roll is called up yon-der, I'll be there, When the roll is

When the Roll Is Called Up Yonder

called up yon - der, When the roll is called up yon- der, I'll be there.

When This Passing World Is Done 385

Therefore, brethren, we are debtors . . . Rom. 8:12

Robert M. McCheyne, 1813-1843

GETHSEMANE 7.7.7.7.7.7.
Richard Redhead, 1820-1901

1. When this pass - ing world is done, When has sunk yon glar - ing sun,
2. When I stand be - fore the throne, Dressed in beau - ty not my own,
3. When the praise of heaven I hear, Loud as thun- ders to the ear,
4. Even on earth, as through a glass, Dark- ly, let Thy glo - ry pass;
When I stand with Christ in glo-ry, Look- ing o'er life's fin - ished sto-ry
When I see Thee as Thou art, Love Thee with un - sin - ning heart
Loud as man - y wa - ters' noise, Sweet as harp's me - lo - dious voice
Make for- give - ness feel so sweet; Make Thy Spir- it's help so meet
Then, Lord, shall I ful - ly know, Not till then, how much I owe.
Then, Lord, shall I ful - ly know, Not till then, how much I owe.
Then, Lord, shall I ful - ly know, Not till then, how much I owe.
Even on earth, Lord, make me know Some-thing of how much I owe. A-MEN.

386 Saved by Grace

For by grace are ye saved through faith . . . Eph. 2:8

Fanny J. Crosby, 1820-1915

Melody by George C. Stebbins, 1846-1945

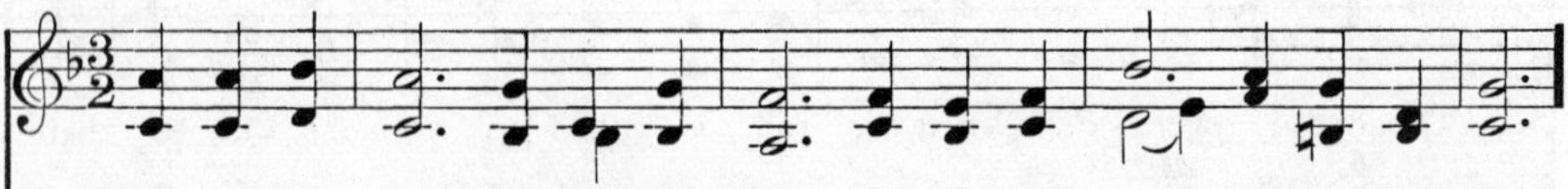

1. Some day the sil - ver cord will break, And I no more as now shall sing;
2. Some day my earth - ly house will fall—I can-not tell how soon 'twill be;
3. Some day, when fades the gold - en sun Be - neath the ros - y - tint - ed west,
4. Some day–till then I'll watch and wait, My lamp all trimmed and burn-ing bright,

But, oh, the joy when I shall wake With-in the pal - ace of the King!
But this I know—my All in All Has now a place in heaven for me.
My bless-ed Lord will say, "Well done!" And I shall en - ter in - to rest.
That when my Sav - iour opes the gate, My soul to Him may take its flight.

REFRAIN

And I shall see Him face to face And tell the sto - ry—saved by grace:

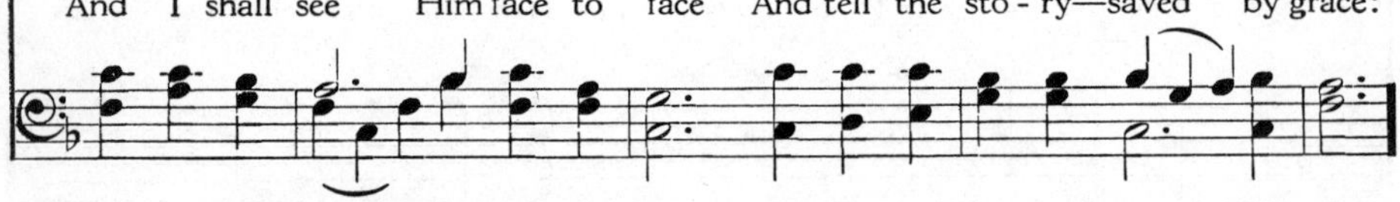

And I shall see Him face to face And tell the sto - ry— saved by grace.

Face to Face

. . . now I know in part; but then shall I know . . . 1 Cor. 13:12

FACE TO FACE 8.7.8.7. with Refrain

Carrie E. Breck, 1855-1934

Grant Colfax Tullar, 1869-1950

1. Face to face with Christ, my Sav - iour, Face to face–what will it be—
2. On - ly faint - ly now I see Him, With the dark-ling veil be-tween;
3. What re - joic - ing in His pres - ence When are ban-ished grief and pain,
4. Face to face! Oh, bliss - ful mo - ment! Face to face— to see and know!
When with rap - ture I be - hold Him, Je - sus Christ, who died for me?
But a bless - ed day is com - ing When His glo - ry shall be seen.
When the crook - ed ways are straight-ened, And the dark things shall be plain!
Face to face with my Re - deem - er, Je - sus Christ, who loves me so!
REFRAIN
Face to face shall I be - hold Him, Far be - yond the star - ry sky;
Face to face in all His glo - ry, I shall see Him by and by!

388 Safe in the Arms of Jesus

. . . whoso putteth his trust in the Lord shall be safe. Prov. 29:25

Fanny J. Crosby, 1820-1915 — William H. Doane, 1832-1915

1. Safe in the arms of Je - sus, Safe on His gen-tle breast, There, by His love o'er - shad - ed, Sweet-ly my soul shall rest. Hark! 'Tis the voice of an - gels Borne in a song to me O - ver the fields of glo - ry, O - ver the jas - per sea.
2. Safe in the arms of Je - sus, Safe from cor-rod-ing care, Safe from the world's temp-ta - tions—Sin can-not harm me there. Free from the blight of sor - row, Free from my doubts and fears; On - ly a few more tri - als, On - ly a few more tears!
3. Je - sus, my heart's dear ref - uge, Je - sus has died for me; Firm on the Rock of A - ges Ev - er my trust shall be. Here let me wait with pa - tience, Wait till the night is o'er, Wait till I see the morn - ing Break on the gold - en shore.
REFRAIN
Safe in the arms of Je - sus, Safe on His gen - tle breast, There, by His love o er - shad - ed, Sweet-ly my soul shall rest. A-MEN.

Jerusalem, the Golden 389

. . . the city was pure gold . . . Rev. 21:18

EWING 7.6.7.6.D.

Bernard of Cluny, circa 1140
Translated by John M. Neale, 1818-1866

Melody by Alexander Ewing, 1830-1895
From *Hymns Ancient and Modern,* 1861

1. Je - ru - sa - lem, the gold - en, With milk and hon - ey blest!
2. They stand, those halls of Zi - on, All ju - bi - lant with song,
3. There is the throne of Da - vid; And there, from care re - leased,
4. Oh, sweet and bless - ed coun - try, The home of God's e - lect!
Be - neath thy con - tem - pla - tion Sink heart and voice op - pressed;
And bright with many an an - gel, And all the mar - tyr throng;
The song of them that tri - umph, The shout of them that feast;
Oh, sweet and bless - ed coun - try That ea - ger hearts ex - pect!
I know not, oh, I know not What joys a - wait us there;
The Prince is ev - er in them; The day - light is se - rene,
And they, who with their Lead - er, Have con - quered in the fight,
Je - sus, in mer - cy bring us To that dear land of rest,
What ra - dian - cy of glo - ry, What bliss be - yond com - pare.
The pas - tures of the bless - ed Are decked in glo - rious sheen.
For - ev - er and for - ev - er Are clad in robes of white.
Who art, with God, the Fa - ther And Spir - it, ev - er blest. A-MEN.

390 The Sands of Time Are Sinking

. . . the glory of God did lighten it . . . Rev. 21:23

RUTHERFORD 7.6.7.6.7.6.7.5.

From *The Last Sayings of Samuel Rutherford,* 1600-1661
Adapted by Anne R. Cousin, 1824-1906

Chrétien Urhan, 1790-1845
Arranged by Edward F. Rimbault, 1816-1876

1. The sands of time are sink - ing; The dawn of heav - en breaks;
2. O Christ! He is the foun - tain, The deep, sweet well of love;
3. With mer - cy and with judg - ment My web of time He wove,
4. I've wres - tled on towards heav - en, 'Gainst storm and wind and tide;
The sum - mer morn I've sighed for, The fair, sweet morn a - wakes.
The streams on earth I've tast - ed, More deep I'll drink a - bove:
And aye the dews of sor - row Were lus - tered by His love;
Now, like a wea - ry trav - eler That lean - eth on his guide,
Dark, dark hath been the mid - night, But day - spring is at hand,
There to an o - cean full - ness His mer - cy doth ex - pand,
I'll bless the hand that guid - ed, I'll bless the heart that planned,
A - mid the shades of eve - ning, While sinks life's lin - gering sand,
And glo - ry, glo - ry dwell - eth In Em - man - uel's land.
And glo - ry, glo - ry dwell - eth In Em - man - uel's land.
When throned where glo - ry dwell - eth In Em - man - uel's land.
I hail the glo - ry dawn - ing From Em - man - uel's land. A-MEN.

No Night There

. . . they need no candle, neither light of the sun . . . Rev. 22:5

John R. Clements, 1868-1946

Melody by Hart P. Danks, 1834-1903

1. In the land of fade - less day Lies the cit - y four - square;
2. All the gates of pearl are made In the cit - y four - square,
3. And the gates shall nev - er close Of the cit - y four - square:
4. There they need no sun-shine bright In that cit - y four - square,
It shall nev - er pass a - way— And there is no night there.
All the streets with gold are laid, And there is no night there.
There life's crys - tal riv - er flows, And there is no night there.
For the Lamb is all the light, And there is no night there.
Refrain
God shall wipe a - way all tears; There's no death, no pain, no fears;
And they count not time by years, For there is no night there.

392 The King in His Beauty

Thine eyes shall see the king in his beauty . . . Isa. 33:17

Adoniram J. Gordon, 1836-1895

Melody by Adoniram J. Gordon, 1836-1895

1. I shall see the King in His beau - ty In the
2. To be - hold the Chief of ten thou - sand— Ah, my
3. Who can tell the rap - tur - ous meet - ing, When the
4. Oh, to none will the King be a stran - ger Of the
5. I shall see Him, I shall be like Him, By one

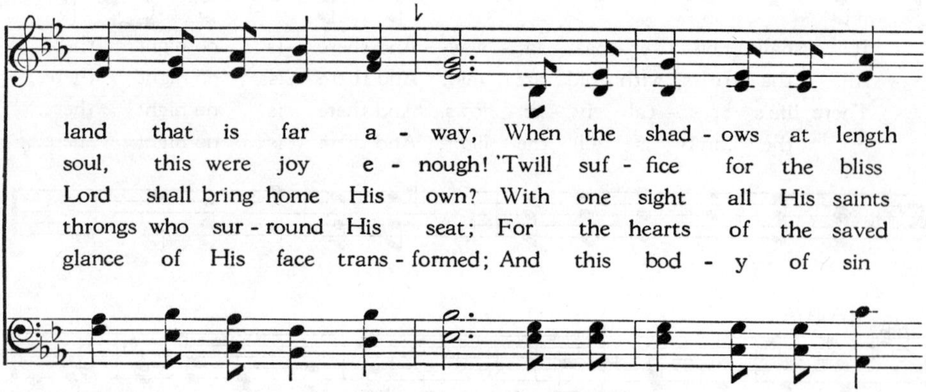
land that is far a - way, When the shad - ows at length
soul, this were joy e - nough! 'Twill suf - fice for the bliss
Lord shall bring home His own? With one sight all His saints
throngs who sur - round His seat; For the hearts of the saved
glance of His face trans - formed; And this bod - y of sin

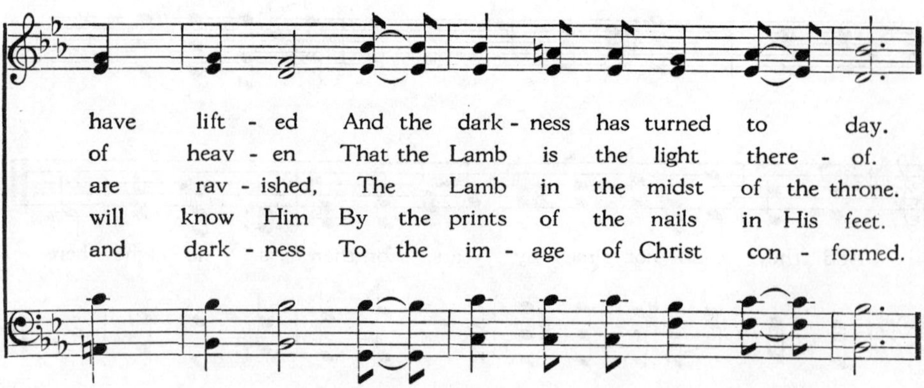
have lift - ed And the dark - ness has turned to day.
of heav - en That the Lamb is the light there - of.
are rav - ished, The Lamb in the midst of the throne.
will know Him By the prints of the nails in His feet.
and dark - ness To the im - age of Christ con - formed.

The King in His Beauty

Refrain
I shall see Him in the glo - ry, The Lamb that once was slain; How I'll then re - sound the sto - ry With all the ran - somed train! Hal - le - lu - jah, Hal - le - lu - jah, To the Lamb that once was slain! Hal - le - lu - jah, Hal - le - lu - jah, Hal - le - lu - jah, A - men!

393 My Saviour First of All

. . . blessed are they that have not seen, and yet have believed. John 20:29

Fanny J. Crosby, 1820-1915

Melody by John R. Sweney, 1837-1899

1. When my life work is end - ed and I cross the swell - ing tide,
2. Oh, the soul - thrill - ing rap - ture when I view His bless - ed face
3. Oh, the dear ones in glo - ry, how they beck - on me to come,
4. Through the gates to the cit - y in a robe of spot - less white,
When the bright and glo - rious morn - ing I shall see; I shall
And the lus - tre of His kind - ly beam - ing eye; How my
And our part - ing at the riv - er I re - call; To the
He will lead me where no tears shall ev - er fall; In the
know my Re - deem - er when I reach the oth - er side, And His
full heart will praise Him for the mer - cy, love, and grace That pre -
sweet vales of E - den they will sing my wel - come home, But I
glad song of a - ges I shall min - gle with de - light; But I
smile will be the first to wel - come me.
pares for me a man - sion in the sky.
long to meet my Sav - iour first of all.
long to meet my Sav - iour first of all.
Refrain
I shall know
I shall know
Him, I shall know Him, When re - deemed by His side I shall stand; I shall

My Saviour First of All

know Him, I shall know Him By the print of the nails in His hand.

He the Pearly Gates Will Open 394

. . . that they may . . . enter . . . Rev. 22:14

Frederick A. Blom, 1867-1927
Translated by Nathaniel Carlson, 1879-1957

PEARLY GATES 8.7.8.7. with Refrain
Elsie Ahlwen, b. 1905

1. Love di-vine, so great and won-drous, Deep and might-y, pure, sub-lime;
2. Like a dove when hunt-ed, fright-ened, As a wound-ed fawn was I;
3. Love di-vine, so great and won-drous- All my sins He then for-gave.
4. In life's e-ven-tide, at twi-light, At His door I'll knock and wait;
Com-ing from the heart of Je-sus— Just the same through tests of time.
Bro-ken-heart-ed, yet He healed me— He will heed the sin-ner's cry.
I will sing His praise for-ev-er For His blood, His power to save.
By the pre-cious love of Je-sus, I shall en-ter heav-en's gate.
Refrain
He the pear-ly gates will o-pen So that I may en-ter in;
For He pur-chased my re-demp-tion And for-gave me all my sin.

395 The Church's One Foundation

For other foundation can no man lay than that is laid, which is Jesus Christ. 1 Cor. 3:11

AURELIA 7.6.7.6.D.

Samuel J. Stone, 1839-1900

Samuel S. Wesley, 1810-1876

1. The Church-'s one Foun - da - tion Is Je - sus Christ her Lord;
2. E - lect from ev - ery na - tion Yet one o'er all the earth,
3. Though with a scorn - ful won - der Men see her sore op - pressed,
4. 'Mid toil and trib - u - la - tion And tu - mult of her war,
5. Yet she on earth hath un - ion With God the Three - in - One,
She is His new cre - a - tion By wa - ter and the Word:
Her char - ter of sal - va - tion, One Lord, one faith, one birth;
By schis-ms rent a - sun - der, By her - e - sies dis - tressed,
She waits the con - sum - ma - tion Of peace for - ev - er - more;
And mys - tic sweet com - mun - ion With those whose rest is won.
From heaven He came and sought her To be His ho - ly bride;
One ho - ly name she bless - es, Par - takes one ho - ly food,
Yet saints their watch are keep - ing; Their cry goes up– "How long?"
Till with the vi - sion glo - rious Her long - ing eyes are blest,
Oh, hap - py ones and ho - ly! Lord, give us grace that we,
With His own blood He bought her, And for her life He died.
And to one hope she press - es, With ev - ery grace en - dued.
But soon the night of weep - ing Shall be the morn of song.
And the great Church vic - to - rious Shall be the Church at rest.
Like them, the meek and low - ly, On high may dwell with Thee. A-MEN.

Christ Is Made the Sure Foundation 396

. . . Behold, I lay in Zion . . . a sure foundation . . . Isa. 28:16

Latin, 7th century
Translated by John M. Neale, 1818-1866

REGENT SQUARE 8.7.8.7.8.7.
Henry T. Smart, 1813-1879

1. Christ is made the sure foun - da - tion, Christ, the head and
2. To this tem - ple, where we call Thee, Come, O Lord of
3. Here vouch - safe to all Thy ser - vants What they ask of
4. Laud and hon - or to the Fa - ther, Laud and hon - or
cor - ner - stone, Cho - sen of the Lord and pre - cious,
hosts, to - day. With Thy wont - ed lov - ing - kind - ness
Thee to gain; What they gain from Thee for - ev - er
to the Son, Laud and hon - or to the Spir - it—
Bind - ing all the Church in one; Ho - ly Zi - on's
Hear Thy peo - ple as they pray; And Thy full - est
With the bless - ed to re - tain, And here - af - ter
Ev - er Three and ev - er One, One in might and
help for - ev - er, And her con - fi - dence a - lone.
ben - e - dic - tion Shed with - in its walls al - way.
in Thy glo - ry Ev - er - more with Thee to reign.
One in glo - ry, While un - end - ing a - ges run! A-MEN.

397 Glorious Things of Thee Are Spoken

Glorious things are spoken of thee, O city of God. . . . Psa. 87:3

AUSTRIA 8.7.8.7.D.

John Newton, 1725-1807 — Franz Joseph Haydn, 1732-1809

1. Glo - rious things of thee are spo-ken, Zi - on, cit - y of our God;
2. See, the streams of liv - ing wa - ters, Spring-ing from e - ter - nal love,
3. Round each hab - i - ta - tion hov-ering, See the cloud and fire ap - pear
4. Blest in - hab - i - tants of Zi - on, Washed in the Re - deem - er's blood;
5. Sav - iour, if of Zi - on's cit - y I, through grace, a mem - ber am,

He whose word can - not be bro - ken Formed thee for His own a - bode:
Well sup - ply thy sons and daugh - ters, And all fear of want re - move:
For a glo - ry and a cov-ering, Show - ing that the Lord is near;
Je - sus, whom their souls re - ly on, Makes them kings and priests to God.
Let the world de - ride or pi - ty—I will glo - ry in Thy name.

On the Rock of A - ges found-ed, What can shake thy sure re - pose?
Who can faint, when such a riv - er Ev - er flows their thirst t' as-suage;
Thus de - riv - ing from their ban - ner Light by night, and shade by day,
'Tis His love His peo - ple rais - es O - ver self to reign as kings;
Fad - ing is the world-ling's pleas-ure, All his boast - ed pomp and show;

With sal - va - tion's walls sur - round-ed, Thou may'st smile at all thy foes.
Grace, which like the Lord, the giv - er, Nev - er fails from age to age.
Safe they feed up - on the man - na Which He gives them when they pray.
And as priests, His sol - emn prais - es, Each for a thank-of-fering brings.
Sol - id joys and last - ing treas - ure None but Zi - on's chil - dren know.

398

Jesus Only

. . . they saw no man, save Jesus only. Matt. 17:8

Albert B. Simpson, 1843-1919

J.H. Burke, 19th century

1. Je - sus on - ly is our mes - sage, Je - sus all our theme shall be;
2. Je - sus on - ly is our Sav - iour, All our guilt He bore a - way,
3. Je - sus is our Sanc-ti - fi - er, Cleans-ing us from self and sin,
4. Je - sus on - ly is our Heal - er, All our sick-ness - es He bear,
5. Je - sus on - ly is our pow - er, He the gift of Pen - te - cost;
6. And for Je - sus we are wait - ing, Lis-tening for the ad - vent call;
We will lift up Je - sus ev - er, Je - sus on - ly will we see.
All our right-eous - ness He gives us, All our strength from day to day.
And with all His Spir-it's full-ness, Fill-ing all our hearts with-in.
And His ris - en life and full-ness All His mem - bers still may share.
Je - sus, breathe Thy power up-on us, Fill us with the Ho - ly Ghost.
But 'twill still be Je - sus on - ly, Je - sus ev - er, all in all.
Refrain
Je - sus on - ly, Je - sus ev - er, Je - sus all in all we sing,
Sav-iour, Sanc - ti - fi - er, and Heal - er, Glo-rious Lord and com-ing King.

399 Renew Thy Church

. . . repent, and do the first works . . . Rev. 2:5

ALL IS WELL 10.6.10.6.8.8.8.6.
English melody

Kenneth L. Cober, b. 1902

From J.T. White's *The Sacred Harp,* 1844

1. Re - new Thy Church, her min-is - tries re - store: Both to serve and a - dore.
2. Teach us Thy Word, re - veal its truth di - vine, On our path let it shine;
3. Teach us to pray, for Thou art ev - er near, Thy still voice let us hear.
4. Teach us to love, with strength of heart and mind, Ev - ery - one, all man-kind,
Make her a - gain as salt through-out the land, And as light from a stand.
Tell of Thy works, Thy might-y acts of grace, From each page show Thy face.
Our souls are rest-less till they rest in Thee, This our glad des - ti - ny.
Break down old walls of prej - u - dice and hate, Leave us not to our fate.
'Mid som - ber shad-ows of the night, Where greed and ha - treds spread their blight,
As Thou hast loved us, sent Thy Son, And our sal - va - tion now is won,
Be - fore Thy pres-ence keep us still That we may find for us Thy will,
As Thou hast loved and given Thy life To end hos - til - i - ty and strife,
Oh, send us forth with power en - dued, Help us, Lord, be re-newed.
Oh, let our hearts with love be stirred, Help us, Lord, know Thy Word.
And seek Thy guid-ance ev - ery day, Teach us, Lord, how to pray.
Oh, share Thy grace from heaven a - bove, Teach us, Lord, how to love. A-MEN.

I Love Thy Kingdom, Lord

400

... the place where thine honour dwelleth. Psa. 26:8

ST. THOMAS S.M.

Timothy Dwight, 1752-1817

From Aaron Williams' *Psalmody*, 1770

1. I love Thy king - dom, Lord, The house of Thine a - bode,
2. I love the Church, O God! Her walls be - fore Thee stand,
3. For her my tears shall fall, For her my prayers as - cend;
4. Be - yond my high - est joy I prize her heaven-ly ways,
5. Sure as Thy truth shall last, To Zi - on shall be given
The Church our blest Re - deem - er saved With His own pre - cious blood.
Dear as the ap - ple of Thine eye, And grav - en on Thy hand.
To her my cares and toils be given Till toils and cares shall end.
Her sweet com - mun - ion, sol - emn vows, Her hymns of love and praise.
The bright - est glo - ries earth can yield, And bright - er bliss of heaven.

Blest Be the Tie That Binds

401

... ye are all one in Christ Jesus. Gal. 3:28

DENNIS S.M.

John Fawcett, 1740-1817

Adapted from Johann H.G. Nageli, 1768-1836

1. Blest be the tie that binds Our hearts in Chris - tian love; The
2. Be - fore our Fa - ther's throne We pour our ar - dent prayers; Our
3. We share our mu - tual woes, Our mu - tual bur - dens bear; And
4. When we a - sun - der part It gives us in - ward pain; But
fel - low - ship of kin - dred minds Is like to that a - bove.
fears, our hopes, our aims are one, Our com - forts and our cares.
oft - en for each oth - er flows The sym - pa - thiz - ing tear.
we shall still be joined in heart And hope to meet a - gain.

402 For All the Saints

. . . they may rest from their labours . . . Rev. 14:13

SINE NOMINE 10.10.10.4.4.

William W. How, 1823-1897

Ralph V. Williams, 1872-1958

UNISON (stanzas 1, 2, and 6, 7)
1. For all the saints who from their la - bors rest,
2. Thou wast their rock, their for - tress, and their might;
6. But lo! There breaks a yet more glo - rious day;
7. From earth's wide bounds, from o - cean's far - thest coast,
Who Thee by faith be - fore the world con - fessed,
Thou, Lord, their cap - tain in the well - fought fight;
The saints tri - um - phant rise in bright ar - ray;
Through gates of pearl stream in the count - less host,
Thy name, O Je - sus, be for - ev - er blest.
Thou, in the dark - ness drear, their one true light.
The King of glo - ry pass - es on His way.
Sing - ing to Fa - ther, Son, and Ho - ly Ghost.
(after stanza 7)
Al - le - lu - ia! Al - le - lu - ia! A - MEN.

For All the Saints

HARMONY (stanzas 3, 4, 5)

3. O blest com - mun - ion, fel - low - ship di - vine!
4. And when the strife is fierce, the war - fare long,
5. The gold - en eve - ning bright - ens in the west;
We fee - bly strug - gle; they in glo - ry shine.
Steals on the ear the dis - tant tri - umph song;
Soon, soon to faith - ful war - riors com - eth rest;
Yet all are one in Thee, for all are Thine.
And hearts are brave a - gain and arms are strong.
And sweet the calm of Par - a - dise, the blest.
(Sop.) Al - le - lu - ia!
D.C. stanzas 6 and 7
Al - le - lu - ia! Al - le - lu - ia!

403 Ten Thousand Times Ten Thousand

. . . I heard the voice of many angels round about the throne . . . Rev. 5:11

ALFORD 7.6.8.6.D.

Henry Alford, 1810-1871 — John B. Dykes, 1823-1876

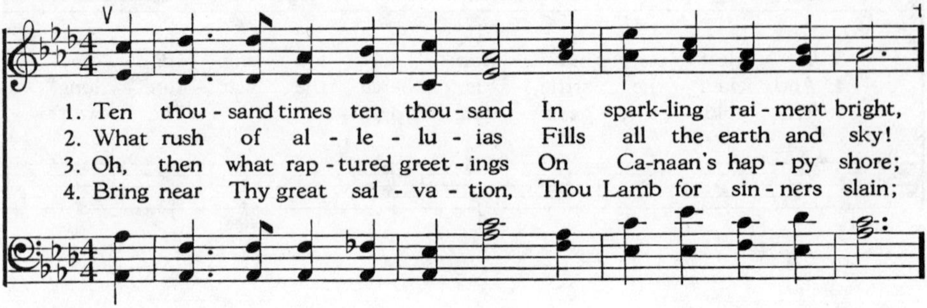
1. Ten thou - sand times ten thou - sand In spark-ling rai - ment bright,
2. What rush of al - le - lu - ias Fills all the earth and sky!
3. Oh, then what rap - tured greet - ings On Ca-naan's hap - py shore;
4. Bring near Thy great sal - va - tion, Thou Lamb for sin - ners slain;

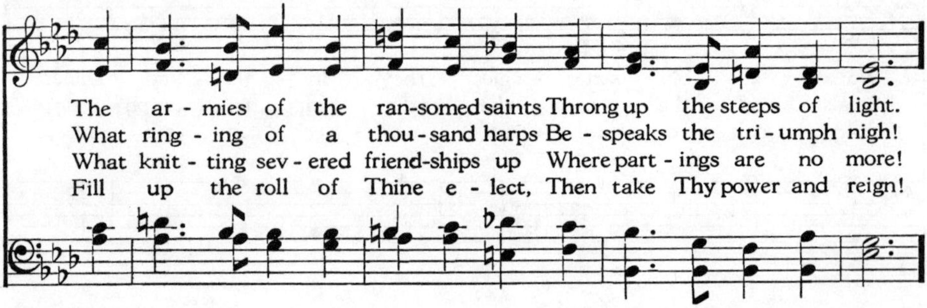
The ar - mies of the ran-somed saints Throng up the steeps of light.
What ring - ing of a thou - sand harps Be - speaks the tri - umph nigh!
What knit - ting sev - ered friend-ships up Where part - ings are no more!
Fill up the roll of Thine e - lect, Then take Thy power and reign!

'Tis fin - ished, all is fin - ished! Their fight with death and sin;
O day for which cre - a - tion And all its tribes were made;
Then eyes with joy shall spar - kle That brimmed with tears of late!
Ap - pear, De - sire of na - tions, Thine ex - iles long for home;

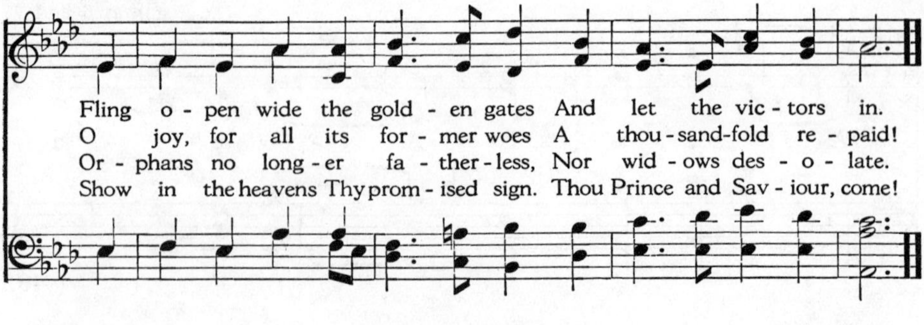
Fling o - pen wide the gold - en gates And let the vic - tors in.
O joy, for all its for - mer woes A thou - sand-fold re - paid!
Or - phans no long - er fa - ther - less, Nor wid - ows des - o - late.
Show in the heavens Thy prom - ised sign. Thou Prince and Sav - iour, come!

O Word of God Incarnate 404

The entrance of thy words giveth light . . . Psa. 119:130

MUNICH 7.6.7.6.D.
Neuvermehrtes Meiningisches Gesangbuch, 1693
Harmony by Felix Mendelssohn, 1809-1847

William W. How, 1823-1897

1. O Word of God in - car - nate, O Wis - dom from on high,
2. The Church from her dear Mas - ter Re - ceived the gift di - vine,
3. It float - eth like a ban - ner Be - fore God's host un - furled;
4. Oh, make Thy Church, dear Sav - iour, A lamp of pur - est gold,
O Truth un-changed, un-chang - ing, O Light of our dark sky;
And still that light she lift - eth O'er all the earth to shine.
It shin - eth like a bea - con A - bove the dark - ling world.
To bear be - fore the na - tions Thy true light, as of old.
We praise Thee for the ra - diance That from the hal - lowed page,
It is the gold - en cas - ket Where gems of truth are stored;
It is the chart and com - pass That o'er life's surg - ing sea,
Oh, teach Thy wan-dering pil - grims By this their path to trace,
A lan - tern to our foot - steps, Shines on from age to age.
It is the heaven - drawn pic-ture Of Christ, the liv - ing Word.
'Mid mists and rocks and quick-sands Still guides, O Christ, to Thee.
Till, clouds and dark - ness end - ed, They see Thee face to face. A-MEN.

(For different harmony see No. 423; for alternate tune see No. 395)

405 How Firm a Foundation

(FIRST TUNE)

. . . *the word of the Lord endureth for ever.* . . . 1 Pet. 1:25

From John Rippon's *Selection of Hymns*, "K", 1787

ADESTE FIDELES 11.11.11.11. with repeat
Attributed to John F. Wade, circa 1711-1786
As in *Cantus Diversi*, 1751

1. How firm a foun - da - tion, ye saints of the Lord, Is
2. "Fear not, I am with thee, Oh, be not dis - mayed, For
3. "When through the deep wa - ters I call thee to go, The
4. "When through fi - ery tri - als thy path - way shall lie, My
5. "The soul that on Je - sus hath leaned for re - pose, I
laid for your faith in His ex - cel - lent Word! What more can He
I am thy God, I will still give thee aid; I'll strength-en thee,
riv - ers of sor - row shall not o - ver - flow, For I will be
grace all - suf - fi - cient shall be thy sup - ply; The flame shall not
will not, I will not de - sert to his foes; That soul, though all
say than to you He hath said, To you who for ref - uge to
help thee, and cause thee to stand, Up - held by My gra - cious, om -
with thee, thy tri - als to bless, And sanc - ti - fy to thee thy
hurt thee; I on - ly de - sign Thy dross to con - sume and thy
hell should en - deav - or to shake, I'll nev - er, no nev - er, no
Je - sus have fled, To you who for ref - uge to Je - sus have fled?
nip - o - tent hand, Up - held by My gra - cious, om-nip - o - tent hand.
deep - est dis - tress, And sanc - ti - fy to thee thy deep - est dis-tress.
gold to re - fine, Thy dross to con - sume and thy gold to re - fine.
nev - er for - sake! I'll nev - er, no nev - er, no nev - er for - sake!"

How Firm a Foundation

406

(SECOND TUNE)

FOUNDATION (Bellevue) 11.11.11.11.
American melody
From Mercer's *Cluster of Spiritual Songs,* 1817

From John Rippon's *Selection of Hymns,* "K", 1787

1. How firm a foun - da - tion, ye saints of the Lord,
2. "Fear not, I am with thee, Oh, be not dis - mayed,
3. "When through the deep wa - ters I call thee to go,
4. "When through fi - ery tri - als thy path - way shall lie,
5. "The soul that on Je - sus hath leaned for re - pose,
Is laid for your faith in His ex - cel - lent Word!
For I am thy God, I will still give thee aid;
The riv - ers of sor - row shall not o - ver - flow,
My grace all - suf - fi - cient shall be thy sup - ply;
I will not, I will not de - sert to his foes;
What more can He say than to you He hath said,
I'll strength - en thee, help thee, and cause thee to stand,
For I will be with thee, thy tri - als to bless,
The flame shall not hurt thee; I on - ly de - sign
That soul, though all hell should en - deav - or to shake,
To you who for ref - uge to Je - sus have fled?
Up - held by My gra - cious, om - nip - o - tent hand.
And sanc - ti - fy to thee thy deep - est dis - tress.
Thy dross to con - sume and thy gold to re - fine.
I'll nev - er, no nev - er, no nev - er for - sake!"

407 How Precious Is the Book Divine

Thy word is a lamp unto my feet . . . Psa. 119:105

MARTYRDOM C.M.
John Fawcett, 1740-1817 — Hugh Wilson, 1764-1824

1. How pre-cious is the Book di-vine, By in - spi - ra - tion given!
2. Its light, de - scend - ing from a - bove Our gloom - y world to cheer,
3. It shows to man his wan-dering ways, Where err - ing feet have trod;
4. It sweet - ly cheers our droop - ing hearts In this dark vale of tears;
5. This lamp through all the ted - ious night Of life shall guide our way,

Bright as a lamp its doc - trines shine To guide our souls to heaven.
Dis - plays a Sav-iour's bound-less love And brings His glo - ries near.
It brings to view the match - less grace Of a for - giv - ing God.
Life, light, and joy it still im - parts And quells our ris - ing fears.
Till we be - hold the clear - er light Of an e - ter - nal day. A - MEN.

(For different harmony and higher key see No. 432)

408 Holy Bible, Book Divine

. . . *it is my meditation all the day.* Psa. 119:97

ALETTA 7.7.7.7.
John Burton, Sr., 1773-1822 — William B. Bradbury, 1816-1868

1. Ho - ly Bi - ble, Book di - vine, Pre - cious treas - ure, thou art mine;
2. Mine to chide me when I rove; Mine to show a Sav-iour's love;
3. Mine to com - fort in dis - tress, Suf - fering in this wil - der - ness;
4. Mine to tell of joys to come And the re - bel's sin - ner's doom;

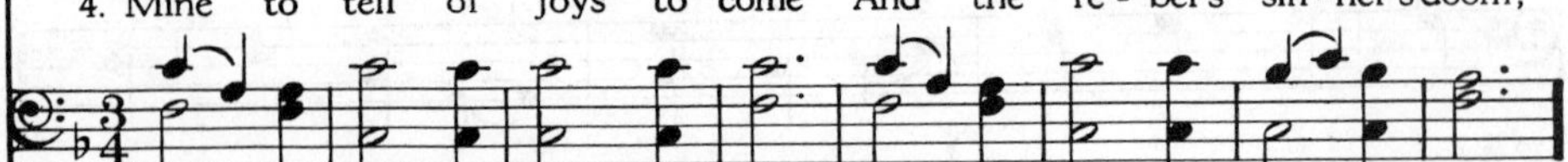

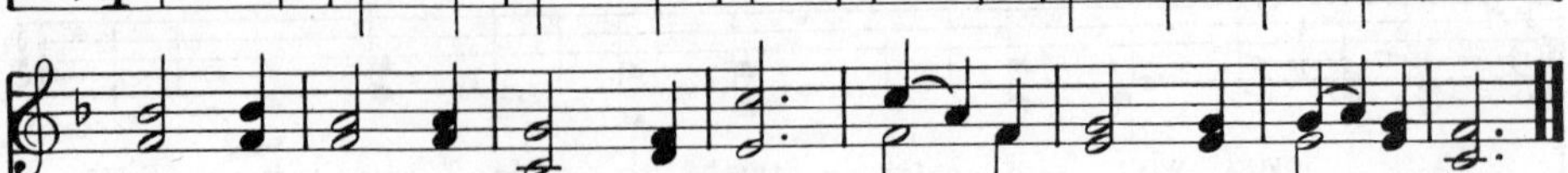

Mine to tell me whence I came, Mine to teach me what I am,
Mine thou art to guide and guard; Mine to pun - ish or re - ward;
Mine to show by liv - ing faith Man can tri - umph o - ver death;
Oh, thou ho - ly Book di - vine, Pre - cious treas - ure, thou art mine.

The Light and Glory of the Word 409

The Lord gave the word . . . Psa. 68:11

BELMONT C.M.

William Cowper, 1731-1800

From William Gardiner's *Sacred Melodies,* 1812

1. The Spir - it breathes up - on the Word And
2. What glo - ry gilds the sa - cred page, Ma -
3. The hand that gave it still sup - plies His
4. Let ev - er - last - ing thanks be Thine For
5. My soul re - joic - es to pur - sue The
brings the truth to sight; Pre - cepts and prom - is -
jes - tic, like the sun! It gives a light to
gra - cious light and heat, His truths up - on the
such a bright dis - play As makes the world of
paths of truth and love, Till glo - ry breaks up -
es af - ford A sanc - ti - fy - ing light.
ev - ery age; It gives, but bor - rows none.
na - tions rise; They rise, but nev - er set.
dark - ness shine With beams of heaven - ly day.
on my view In bright - er worlds a - bove.

410 Thy Word Is Like a Garden, Lord

How sweet are thy words unto my taste! . . . Psa. 119:103

BETHLEHEM (Seraph) C.M.D.
Gottfried W. Fink, 1783-1846

Edwin Hodder, 1837-1904

1. Thy Word is like a gar - den, Lord, With flow - ers bright and fair;
2. Thy Word is like a star - ry host: A thou - sand rays of light
3. Oh, may I love Thy pre - cious Word, May I ex - plore the mine,
And ev - ery one who seeks may pluck A love - ly clus - ter there.
Are seen to guide the trav - el - er, And make his path - way bright.
May I its fra - grant flow - ers glean, May light up - on me shine.
Thy Word is like a deep, deep mine; And jew - els rich and rare
Thy Word is like an ar - mor - y, Where sol - diers may re - pair,
Oh, may I find my ar - mor there, Thy Word my trust - y sword;
Are hid - den in its might - y depths For ev - ery search - er there.
And find, for life's long bat - tle day, All need - ful weap - ons there.
I'll learn to fight with ev - ery foe The bat - tle of the Lord!

Break Thou the Bread of Life

Then opened he their understanding . . . Luke 24:45

Stanzas 1-2 by Mary A. Lathbury, 1841-1913
Stanzas 3-4 by Alexander Groves, 1843-1909

LATHBURY 6.4.6.4.D
William F. Sherwin, 1826-1888

1. Break Thou the bread of life, Dear Lord, to me,
2. Bless Thou the truth, dear Lord, To me, to me,
3. Thou art the bread of life, O Lord, to me,
4. Oh, send Thy Spir - it, Lord, Now un - to me,
As Thou didst break the loaves Be - side the sea;
As Thou didst bless the bread By Gal - i - lee;
Thy ho - ly Word, the truth That sav - eth me;
That He may touch my eyes And make me see;
Be - yond the sa - cred page I seek Thee, Lord;
Then shall all bond - age cease, All fet - ters fall,
Give me to eat and live With Thee a - bove,
Show me the truth con - cealed With - in Thy Word,
My spir - it pants for Thee, O liv - ing Word.
And I shall find my peace, My all in all.
Teach me to love Thy truth For Thou art love.
And in Thy Book re - vealed, I see Thee, Lord.

412 Safely through Another Week

. . . one sabbath to another, shall all flesh come to worship . . . Isa. 66:23

John Newton, 1725-1807

SABBATH 7.7.7.7.7.7. with repeat
Melody by Lowell Mason, 1792-1872

1. Safe - ly through an - oth - er week God has brought us on our way;
2. While we seek sup - plies of grace Through the blest Re - deem - er's name,
3. Here we come, Thy name to praise: Let us feel Thy pres - ence near;
4. May the gos - pel's joy - ful sound Con - quer sin - ners, com - fort saints;
Let us each a bless - ing seek, Wait - ing in His courts to - day;
Show Thy rec - on - cil - ing face, Take a - way our sin and shame;
May Thy glo - ry meet our eyes While we in Thy house ap - pear;
Make the fruits of grace a - bound, Bring re - lief to all com - plaints;
Day of all the week the best, Em - blem of e - ter - nal rest,
From our world - ly care set free, May we rest this day in Thee,
Here af - ford us, Lord, a taste Of our ev - er - last - ing rest,
Thus let all our wor - ship prove Till we join Thy courts a - bove,
Day of all the week the best, Em - blem of e - ter - nal rest.
From our world - ly care set free, May we rest this day in Thee.
Here af - ford us, Lord, a taste Of our ev - er - last - ing rest.
Thus let all our wor - ship prove Till we join Thy courts a - bove.

This Is the Day of Light 413

. . . *the dayspring . . . hath visited us, To give light* . . . Luke 1:78-79

John Ellerton, 1826-1893

FESTAL SONG S.M.
William H. Walter, 1825-1893

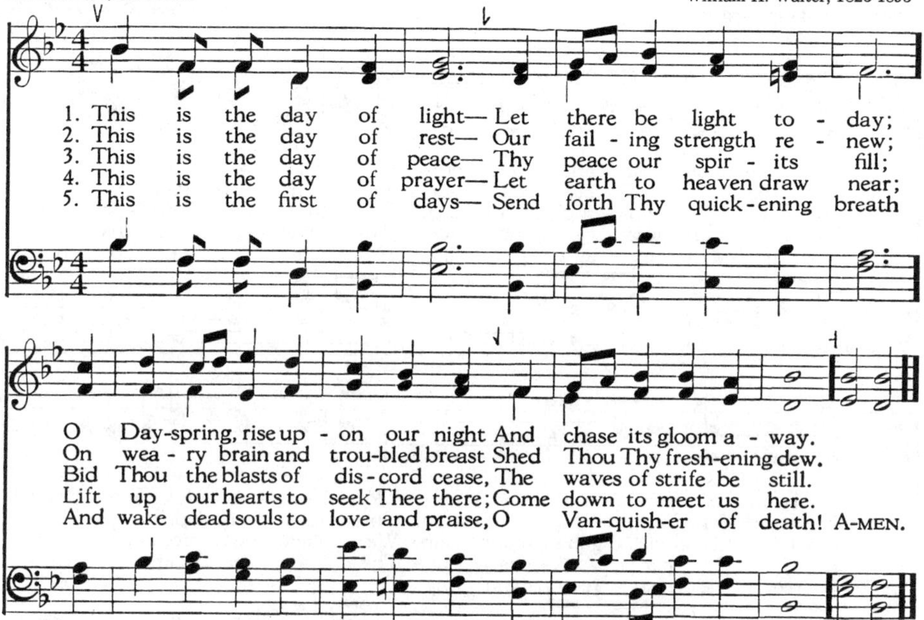
1. This is the day of light— Let there be light to - day;
2. This is the day of rest— Our fail - ing strength re - new;
3. This is the day of peace— Thy peace our spir - its fill;
4. This is the day of prayer— Let earth to heaven draw near;
5. This is the first of days— Send forth Thy quick - ening breath
O Day-spring, rise up - on our night And chase its gloom a - way.
On wea - ry brain and trou-bled breast Shed Thou Thy fresh-ening dew.
Bid Thou the blasts of dis - cord cease, The waves of strife be still.
Lift up our hearts to seek Thee there; Come down to meet us here.
And wake dead souls to love and praise, O Van-quish-er of death! A-MEN.

(For lower key see No. 381)

This Is the Day the Lord Hath Made 414

. . . *we will rejoice and be glad in it.* Psa. 118:24

Isaac Watts, 1674-1748

WINCHESTER OLD C.M.
From Thomas Este's *Psalter,* 1592

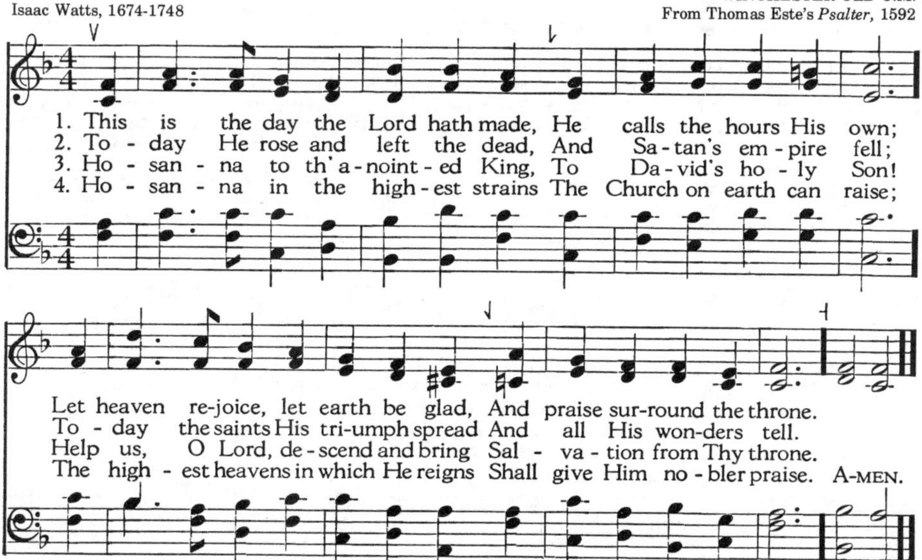
1. This is the day the Lord hath made, He calls the hours His own;
2. To - day He rose and left the dead, And Sa - tan's em - pire fell;
3. Ho - san - na to th' a - noint - ed King, To Da - vid's ho - ly Son!
4. Ho - san - na in the high - est strains The Church on earth can raise;
Let heaven re - joice, let earth be glad, And praise sur-round the throne.
To - day the saints His tri-umph spread And all His won-ders tell.
Help us, O Lord, de - scend and bring Sal - va - tion from Thy throne.
The high - est heavens in which He reigns Shall give Him no - bler praise. A-MEN.

415 O Day of Rest and Gladness

. . . call the sabbath a delight . . . Isa. 58:13

MENDEBRAS 7.6.7.6.D.
German melody
Arranged by Lowell Mason, 1792-1872

Christopher Wordsworth, 1807-1885
From *Hymns Ancient and Modern*

1. O day of rest and glad - ness, O day of joy and light,
2. On thee, at the cre - a - tion, The light first had its birth;
3. Thou art a cool - ing foun - tain In life's dry drear - y sand;
4. To - day on wea - ry na - tions The heaven - ly man - na falls;
5. New grac - es ev - er gain - ing From this our day of rest,
O balm of care and sad - ness, Most beau - ti - ful, most bright!
On thee, for our sal - va - tion, Christ rose from depths of earth;
From thee, like Pis - gah's moun - tain, We view our prom - ised land.
To ho - ly con - vo - ca - tions The sil - ver trum - pet calls
We reach the rest re - main - ing To spir - its of the blest.
On thee the high and low - ly Be - fore th'e - ter - nal throne
On thee our Lord vic - to - rious The Spir - it sent from heaven:
A day of sweet re - fec - tion, A day of ho - ly love,
Where gos - pel light is glow - ing With pure and ra - diant beams,
To Ho - ly Ghost be prais - es, To Fa - ther, and to Son;
Sing, "Ho - ly, ho - ly, ho - ly!" To the great Three-in - One.
And thus on thee most glo - rious A tri - ple light was given.
A day of res - ur - rec - tion From earth to things a - bove.
And liv - ing wa - ter flow - ing With soul - re - fresh - ing streams.
The Church her voice up - rais - es To Thee, blest Three-in - One.
A-MEN.

With Joy We Hail the Sacred Day 416

I was glad when they said unto me, Let us go into the house of the Lord. Psa. 122:1

Harriet Auber, 1773-1862

STEPHENS (Newington) C.M.
William Jones, 1726-1800

1. With joy we hail the sa - cred day Which
2. Thy cho - sen tem - ple, Lord, how fair! As
3. Spir - it of grace, O deign to dwell With -
4. Let peace with - in her walls be found; Let
5. Great God, we hail the sa - cred day Which
God hath called His own; With joy the sum - mons
here Thy ser - vants throng To breathe the hum - ble,
in Thy Church be - low; Make her in ho - li -
all her sons u - nite To spread with ho - ly
Thou hast called Thine own; With joy the sum - mons
we o - bey To wor - ship at His throne.
fer - vent prayer And pour the cho - ral song.
ness ex - cel, With pure de - vo - tion glow.
zeal a - round Her clear and shin - ing light.
we o - bey To wor - ship at Thy throne. A - MEN.

(For different harmony and lower key see No. 140)

417 Friend of the Home

Then were there brought unto him little children . . . Matt. 19:13

ELLERS 10.10.10.10.

Howell E. Lewis, 1860-1953

Edward J. Hopkins, 1818-1901

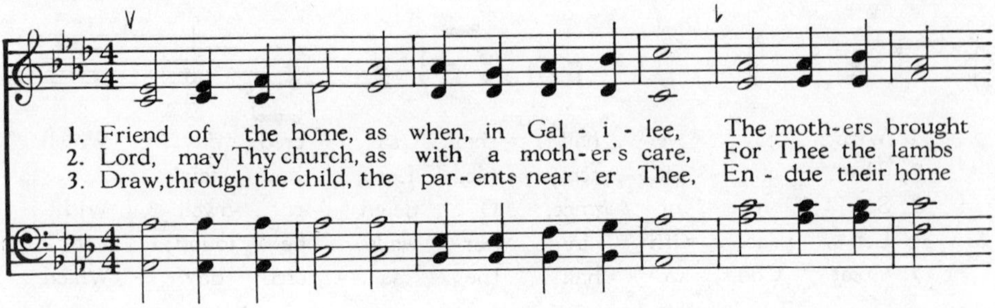
1. Friend of the home, as when, in Gal - i - lee, The moth-ers brought
2. Lord, may Thy church, as with a moth-er's care, For Thee the lambs
3. Draw, through the child, the par-ents near-er Thee, En - due their home

their lit - tle ones to Thee, So we, dear Lord, would now the
with - in her bos - om bear; And grant, as morn - ing grows to
with grow - ing sanc - ti - ty; And gath - er all, by earth - ly

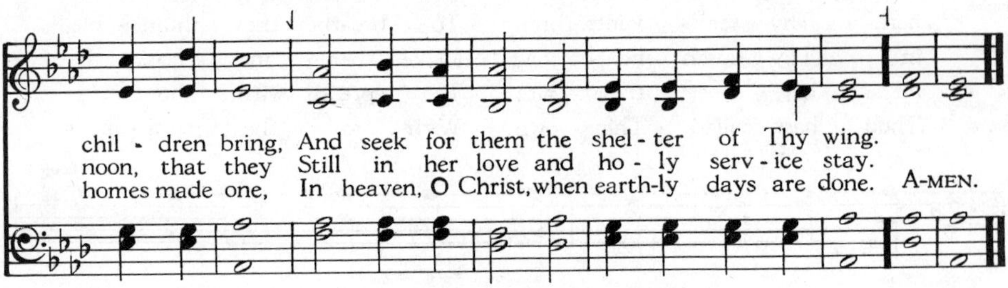
chil - dren bring, And seek for them the shel - ter of Thy wing.
noon, that they Still in her love and ho - ly serv - ice stay.
homes made one, In heaven, O Christ, when earth-ly days are done. A-MEN.

418 See Israel's Gentle Shepherd Stand

. . . Suffer the little children to come unto me . . . Mark 10:14

SERENITY C.M.

Philip Doddridge, 1702-1751

William V. Wallace, 1814-1865

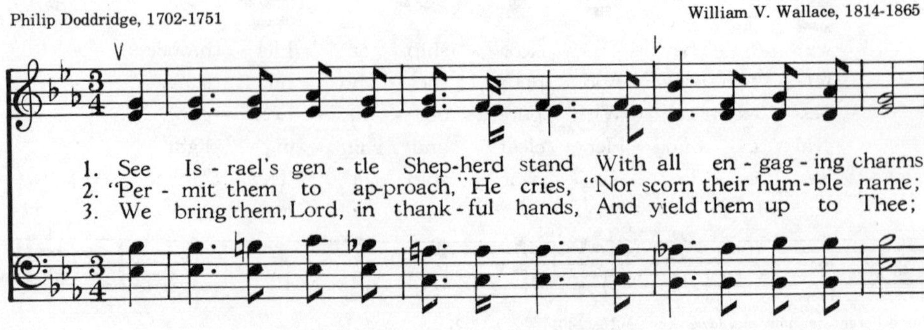
1. See Is - rael's gen - tle Shep-herd stand With all en - gag - ing charms;
2. "Per - mit them to ap-proach," He cries, "Nor scorn their hum - ble name;
3. We bring them, Lord, in thank - ful hands, And yield them up to Thee;

See Israel's Gentle Shepherd Stand

Hark, how He calls the ten-der lambs, And folds them in His arms!
For 'twas to bless such souls as these The Lord of an-gels came."
Joy - ful that we our-selves are Thine, Thine let our off-spring be.
A-MEN.

This Child We Dedicate to Thee 419

For this child I prayed . . . I have lent him to the Lord . . . 1 Sam. 1:27-28

Anonymous, German
Translated by Samuel Gilman, 1791-1858 (altered)

FEDERAL STREET L.M.
Henry K. Oliver, 1800-1885

1. This child we ded - i - cate to Thee, O God of grace and pu - ri - ty! In Thy great love its life pro - long, Shield it, we pray, from sin and wrong.
2. O may Thy Spir - it gent - ly draw Its will - ing soul to keep Thy law; May vir - tue, pi - e - ty, and truth Dawn e - ven with its dawn - ing youth.
A - MEN.

420 When He Cometh

. . . when I make up my jewels; and I will spare them . . . Mal. 3:17

JEWELS 8.6.8.5. with Refrain

William O. Cushing, 1823-1902

George F. Root, 1820-1895

1. When He com - eth, when He com - eth To make up His jew - els,
2. He will gath - er, He will gath - er The gems for His king-dom;
3. Lit - tle chil - dren, lit - tle chil - dren, Who love their Re - deem - er,
All His jew - els, pre - cious jew - els, His loved and His own:
All the pure ones, all the bright ones, His loved and His own.
Are the jew - els, pre - cious jew - els, His loved and His own.
Refrain
Like the stars of the morn - ing, His bright crown a - dorn - ing,
They shall shine in their beau - ty— Bright gems for His crown.

Buried in Baptism with Our Lord 421

. . . we are buried with him by baptism into death . . . Rom. 6:4

WARD L.M.

Anonymous — Lowell Mason, 1792-1872

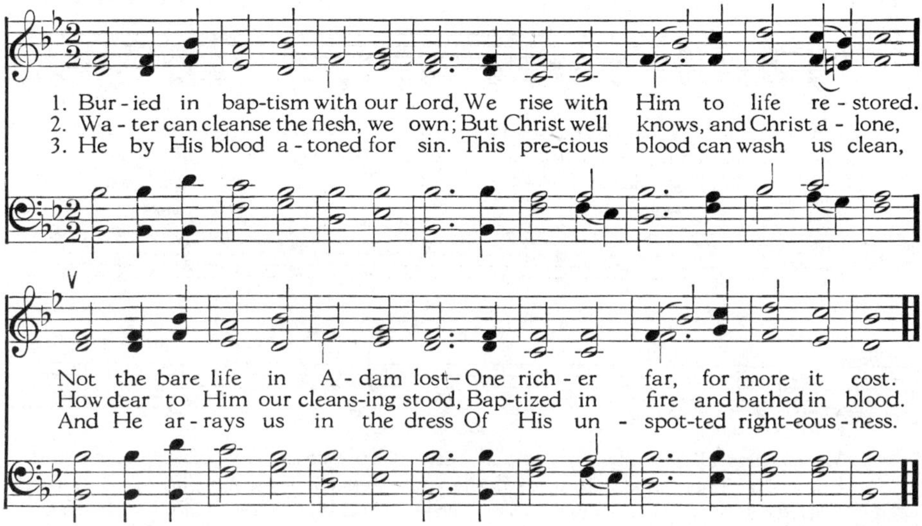
1. Bur-ied in bap-tism with our Lord, We rise with Him to life re-stored.
2. Wa-ter can cleanse the flesh, we own; But Christ well knows, and Christ a-lone,
3. He by His blood a-toned for sin. This pre-cious blood can wash us clean,
Not the bare life in A-dam lost– One rich-er far, for more it cost.
How dear to Him our cleans-ing stood, Bap-tized in fire and bathed in blood.
And He ar-rays us in the dress Of His un-spot-ted right-eous-ness.

O Happy Day, That Fixed My Choice 422

. . . I will rejoice in thy salvation. Psa. 9:14

HAMBURG L.M.
From *Psalm Tone I*

Philip Doddridge, 1702-1751 — Adapted by Lowell Mason, 1792-1872

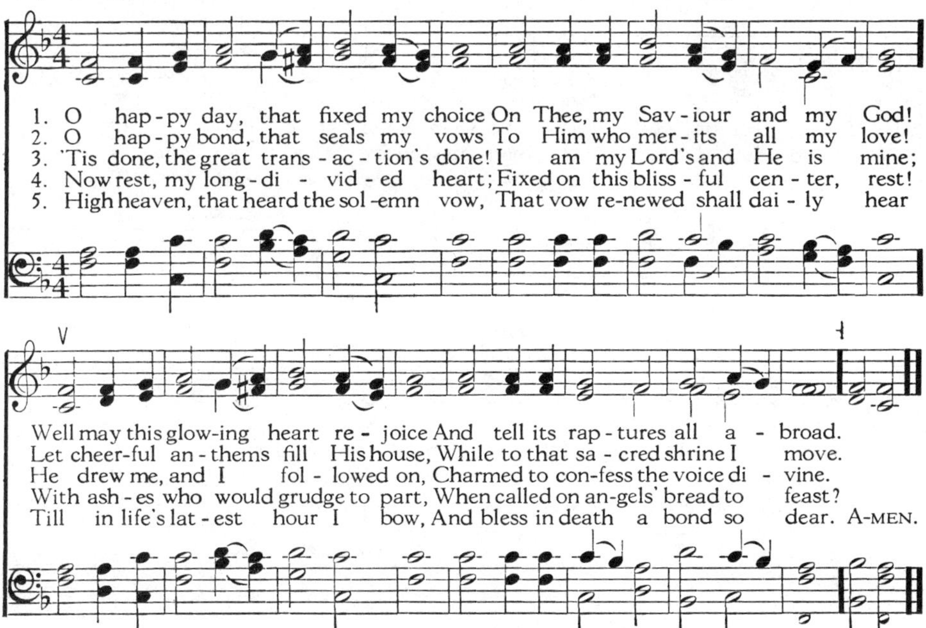
1. O hap-py day, that fixed my choice On Thee, my Sav-iour and my God!
2. O hap-py bond, that seals my vows To Him who mer-its all my love!
3. 'Tis done, the great trans-ac-tion's done! I am my Lord's and He is mine;
4. Now rest, my long-di-vid-ed heart; Fixed on this bliss-ful cen-ter, rest!
5. High heaven, that heard the sol-emn vow, That vow re-newed shall dai-ly hear
Well may this glow-ing heart re-joice And tell its rap-tures all a-broad.
Let cheer-ful an-thems fill His house, While to that sa-cred shrine I move.
He drew me, and I fol-lowed on, Charmed to con-fess the voice di-vine.
With ash-es who would grudge to part, When called on an-gels' bread to feast?
Till in life's lat-est hour I bow, And bless in death a bond so dear. A-MEN.

423 Baptized into His Death

Know ye not, that so many of us . . . were baptized into his death? Rom. 6:3

MUNICH 7.6.7.6.D.
From *Neuvermehrtes Meiningisches Gesangbuch,* 1693
Harmony by Felix Mendelssohn, 1809-1847

James G. Deck, 1802-1884 (altered)

1. A - round Thy grave, Lord Je - sus, Thine emp - ty grave, we stand,
2. O Lord, Thou now art ris - en, Thy trav - ail all is o'er;
3. In - to Thy death bap - tiz - ed, To sin with Thee we died,
With hearts all full of prais - es, To keep Thy blest com-mand;
For sin Thou once hast suf - fered, Thou liv'st to die no more.
With Thee, our Life, are ris - en— And shall be glo - ri - fied.
By faith our souls, re - joic - ing, Do trace Thy path of love
Sin, death and hell are van - quished By Thee, Thy church-'s Head;
From sin, the world, and Sa - tan, Now ran - somed by Thy blood,
Through death's dark, an-gry bil - lows Up to the throne a - bove.
And lo, we share Thy tri - umph, Thou first-born from the dead!
We walk on earth as stran - gers A - live with Thee, to God.
A-MEN.

(For different harmony see No. 404)

Baptized into Our Saviour's Death 424

Buried with him in baptism . . . risen with him through . . . faith . . . Col. 2:12

EVAN C.M.

Philip Doddridge, 1702-1751

William H. Havergal, 1793-1870

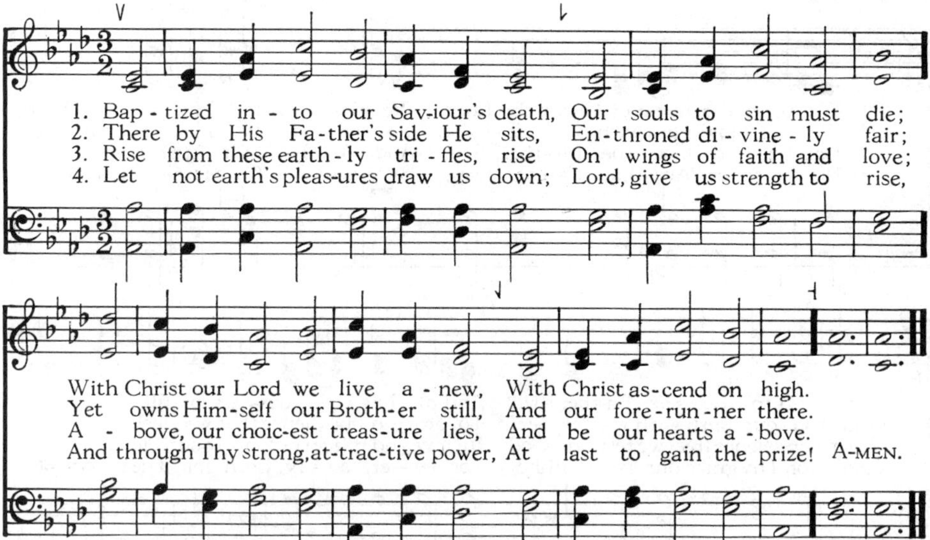
1. Bap - tized in - to our Sav-iour's death, Our souls to sin must die;
2. There by His Fa-ther's side He sits, En-throned di - vine - ly fair;
3. Rise from these earth - ly tri - fles, rise On wings of faith and love;
4. Let not earth's pleas-ures draw us down; Lord, give us strength to rise,
With Christ our Lord we live a - new, With Christ as-cend on high.
Yet owns Him-self our Broth-er still, And our fore - run - ner there.
A - bove, our choic-est treas-ure lies, And be our hearts a - bove.
And through Thy strong, at-trac-tive power, At last to gain the prize!
A-MEN.

Dear Master, in Thy Way 425

. . . we also should walk in newness of life. Rom. 6:4

TRENTHAM S.M.

John Thomas, 1839-1922

Robert Jackson, 1842-1914

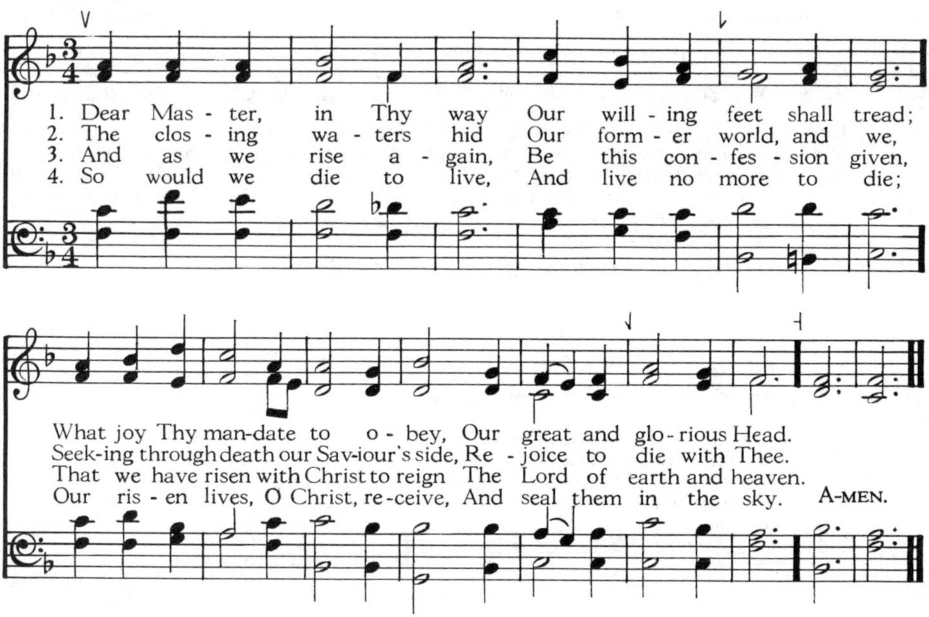
1. Dear Mas - ter, in Thy way Our will - ing feet shall tread;
2. The clos - ing wa - ters hid Our form - er world, and we,
3. And as we rise a - gain, Be this con - fes - sion given,
4. So would we die to live, And live no more to die;
What joy Thy man-date to o - bey, Our great and glo - rious Head.
Seek-ing through death our Sav-iour's side, Re - joice to die with Thee.
That we have risen with Christ to reign The Lord of earth and heaven.
Our ris - en lives, O Christ, re-ceive, And seal them in the sky.
A-MEN.

426 We Bless the Name of Christ the Lord

... it becometh us to fulfil all righteousness. ... Matt. 3:15

RETREAT L.M.

Samuel F. Coffman, 1872-1954 — Thomas Hastings, 1784-1872

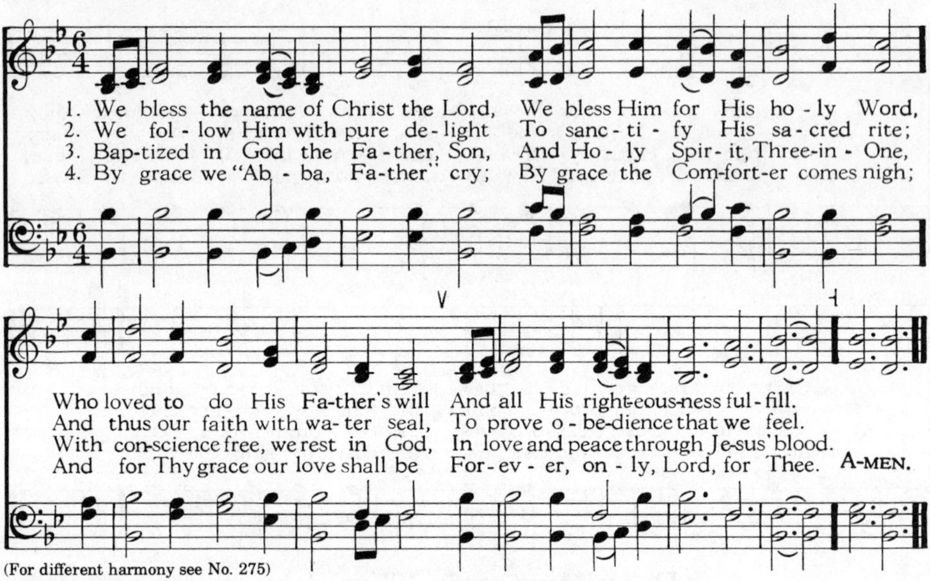
1. We bless the name of Christ the Lord, We bless Him for His ho - ly Word,
2. We fol - low Him with pure de - light To sanc - ti - fy His sa - cred rite;
3. Bap - tized in God the Fa - ther, Son, And Ho - ly Spir - it, Three-in - One,
4. By grace we "Ab - ba, Fa - ther" cry; By grace the Com - fort - er comes nigh;
Who loved to do His Fa - ther's will And all His right - eous - ness ful - fill.
And thus our faith with wa - ter seal, To prove o - be - dience that we feel.
With con - science free, we rest in God, In love and peace through Je - sus' blood.
And for Thy grace our love shall be For - ev - er, on - ly, Lord, for Thee.
A - MEN.

(For different harmony see No. 275)

427 Come, Holy Spirit, Dove Divine

... arise, and be baptized ... Acts 22:16

MARYTON L.M.

Attributed to Adoniram Judson, 1788-1850 — Henry P. Smith, 1825-1898

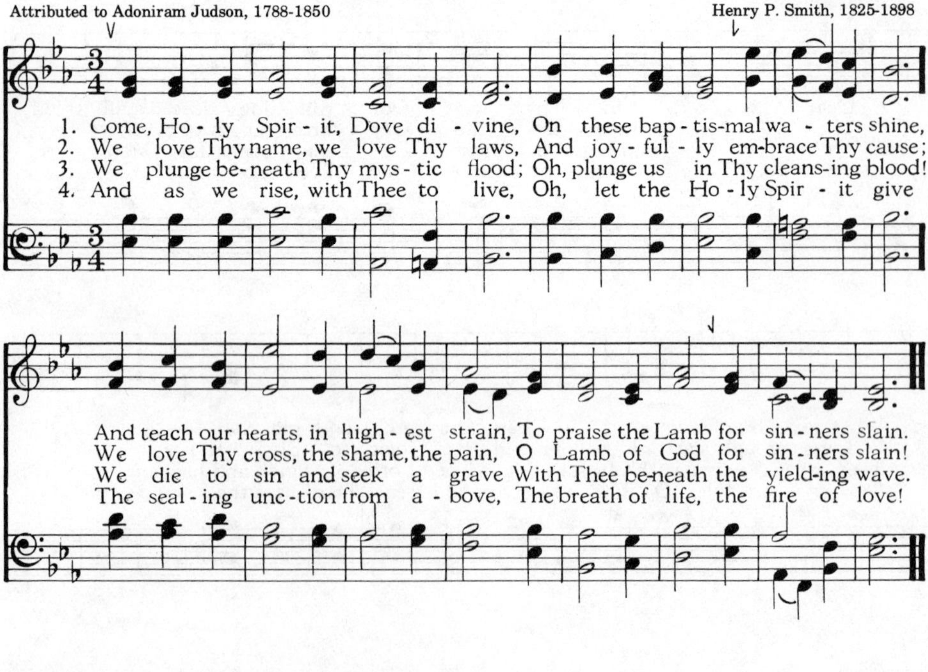
1. Come, Ho - ly Spir - it, Dove di - vine, On these bap - tis - mal wa - ters shine,
2. We love Thy name, we love Thy laws, And joy - ful - ly em - brace Thy cause;
3. We plunge be - neath Thy mys - tic flood; Oh, plunge us in Thy cleans - ing blood!
4. And as we rise, with Thee to live, Oh, let the Ho - ly Spir - it give
And teach our hearts, in high - est strain, To praise the Lamb for sin - ners slain.
We love Thy cross, the shame, the pain, O Lamb of God for sin - ners slain!
We die to sin and seek a grave With Thee be - neath the yield - ing wave.
The seal - ing unc - tion from a - bove, The breath of life, the fire of love!

Let All Mortal Flesh Keep Silence 428

But the Lord is in his holy temple . . . Hab. 2:20

PICARDY 8.7.8.7.8.7.

From the Liturgy of St. James, circa 6th century
Translated by Gerard Moultrie, 1829-1885

French carol melody, 17th century
Hymn version, 1906

UNISON
1. Let all mor - tal flesh keep si - lence, And with fear and trem - bling stand;
2. King of kings, yet born of wo - man, As of old on earth He stood,
3. Rank on rank the host of heav - en Spreads its van-guard on the way,
4. At His feet the six - winged ser - aph; Cher - u - bim, with sleep - less eye,
Pon - der noth - ing earth - ly - mind - ed, For with bless-ing in His hand,
Lord of lords, in hu - man ves - ture— In the bod - y and the blood—
As the Light of light de - scend - eth From the realms of end - less day,
Veil their fac - es in God's pres - ence, As with cease-less voice they cry,
Christ our God to earth de - scend - eth, Our full hom-age to de - mand.
He will give to all the faith - ful His own self for heaven-ly food.
That the powers of hell may van - ish As the dark-ness clears a - way.
Al - le - lu - ia, Al - le - lu - ia, Al - le - lu - ia, Lord Most High! A-MEN.

429 Here, O My Lord

He that eateth my flesh, and drinketh my blood, dwelleth in me, and I in him. John 6:56

Horatius Bonar, 1808-1889

ST. AGNES (Langran) 10.10.10.10.
James Langran, 1835-1909

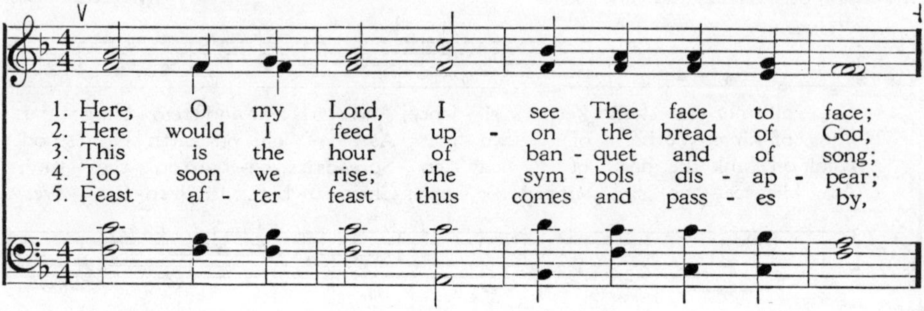
1. Here, O my Lord, I see Thee face to face;
2. Here would I feed up - on the bread of God,
3. This is the hour of ban - quet and of song;
4. Too soon we rise; the sym - bols dis - ap - pear;
5. Feast af - ter feast thus comes and pass - es by,

Here would I touch and han - dle things un - seen,
Here drink with Thee the roy - al wine of heaven;
This is the heaven - ly ta - ble spread for me;
The feast, though not the love, is past and gone;
Yet, pass - ing, points to the glad feast a - bove,

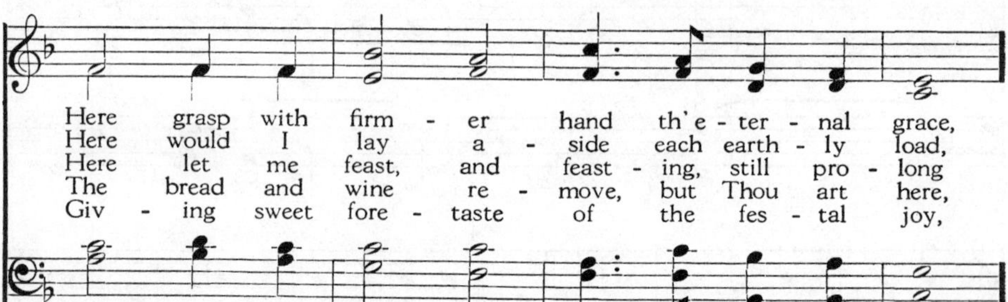
Here grasp with firm - er hand th' e - ter - nal grace,
Here would I lay a - side each earth - ly load,
Here let me feast, and feast - ing, still pro - long
The bread and wine re - move, but Thou art here,
Giv - ing sweet fore - taste of the fes - tal joy,

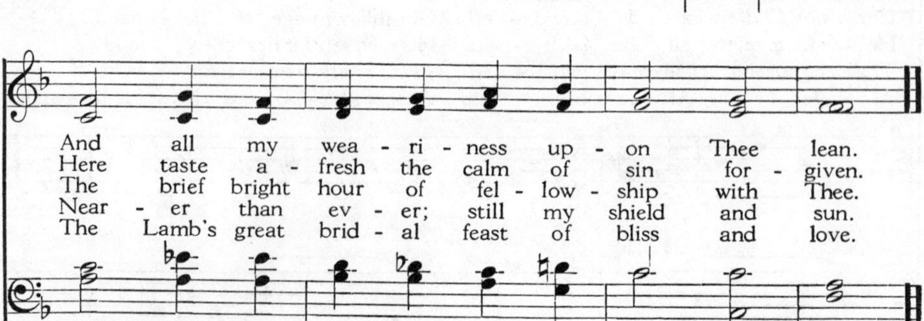
And all my wea - ri - ness up - on Thee lean.
Here taste a - fresh the calm of sin for - given.
The brief bright hour of fel - low - ship with Thee.
Near - er than ev - er; still my shield and sun.
The Lamb's great brid - al feast of bliss and love.

My God, and Is Thy Table Spread? 430

Thou preparest a table before me . . . Psa. 23:5

HURSLEY L.M.
Austrian melody, 18th century
From *Hymns Ancient and Modern,* 1861

Philip Doddridge, 1702-1751

1. My God, and is Thy ta - ble spread? And does Thy
2. Hail, sa - cred feast, which Je - sus makes, Rich ban - quet
3. Let all ap - proach with hearts pre - pared, With hearts in -
4. Oh, let Thy ta - ble hon - ored be And fur - nished
cup with love o'er - flow? Thith - er be all Thy chil - dren
of His flesh and blood! Thrice hap - py he who here par -
flamed let all at - tend; Nor, when we leave our Fa - ther's
well with joy - ful guests; And may each soul sal - va - tion
led And let them all its sweet - ness know.
takes That sa - cred stream, that heaven - ly food!
board, The pleas - ure or the prof - it end.
see That here its sa - cred pledg - es tastes. A - MEN.

431 According to Thy Gracious Word

... this do in remembrance of me. Luke 22:19

MANOAH C.M.

James Montgomery, 1771-1854

From Henry W. Greatorex's *Collection*, 1851

1. According to Thy gracious Word, In meek humility,
2. Thy body, broken for my sake, My bread from heaven shall be;
3. Gethsemane can I forget? Or there Thy conflict see,
4. When to the cross I turn mine eyes And rest on Calvary,
5. And when these failing lips grow dumb And mind and memory flee,

This will I do, my dying Lord, I will remember Thee.
Thy testamental cup I take, And thus remember Thee.
Thine agony and bloody sweat, And not remember Thee?
O Lamb of God, my sacrifice, I must remember Thee.
When Thou shalt in Thy kingdom come, Jesus, remember me.

A-MEN.

(For lower key see No. 281)

432 Forever Here My Rest Shall Be

... I will give thee rest. Exod. 33:14

MARTYRDOM C.M.

Charles Wesley, 1707-1788

Hugh Wilson, 1764-1824

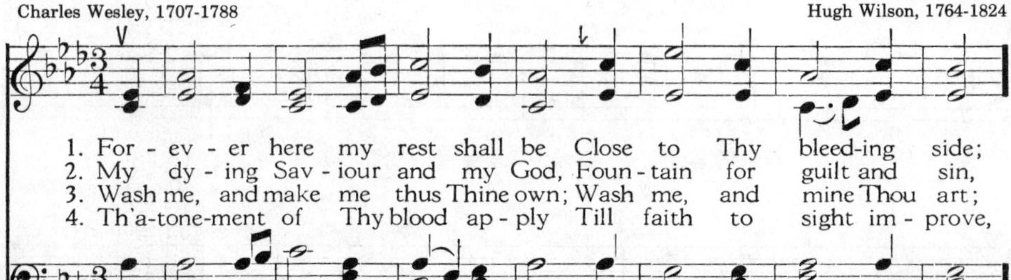

1. Forever here my rest shall be Close to Thy bleeding side;
2. My dying Saviour and my God, Fountain for guilt and sin,
3. Wash me, and make me thus Thine own; Wash me, and mine Thou art;
4. Th'atonement of Thy blood apply Till faith to sight improve,

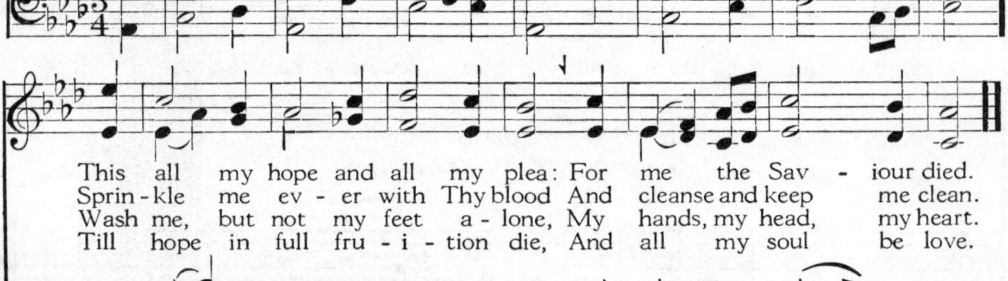

This all my hope and all my plea: For me the Saviour died.
Sprinkle me ever with Thy blood And cleanse and keep me clean.
Wash me, but not my feet alone, My hands, my head, my heart.
Till hope in full fruition die, And all my soul be love.

(For different harmony and lower key see No. 407)

In Remembrance of Thee 433

. . . this do in remembrance of me. 1 Cor. 11:24

Doris Miller, b. 1918 Doris Miller, b. 1918

1. In re - mem-brance of Thee do we gath - er to - day, 'Round Thy
2. Here a ta - ble is spread of for - give - ness and grace, Here our
3. There He drank of the cup of our sin and our death, Let us
4. When He comes for His church what a joy it will be To par -
ta - ble of mer - cy so free; For as oft as we eat, and as
needs and our wants He doth meet; He took bread and gave thanks, and He
come and for - give - ness re - ceive Thru' His blood which was shed for re -
take of the cup from His hand. We will sit at His feet as we
oft as we drink, Do we come in re - mem - brance of Thee.
broke it for them. He said: "Take of my bod - y and eat."
mis - sion of sin, Let us come, eat and drink and be - lieve.
wor - ship our Lord, From all tongues and all tribes and all lands.
CODA
In re-mem-brance of Thee, We do show the Lord's death 'til He come.

434 Till He Come—Oh, Let the Words

. . . ye do shew the Lord's death till he come. 1 Cor. 11:26

ST. PETERSBURG 7.7.7.7.7.7.

Edward H. Bickersteth, 1825-1906 — Dmitri S. Bortnianski, 1751-1825 (adapted)

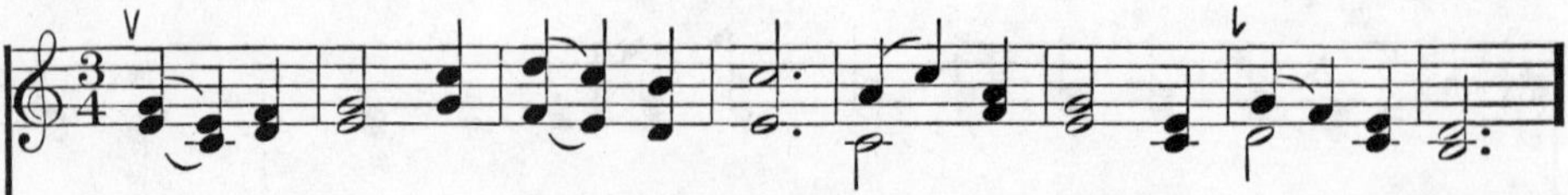

1. Till He come—oh, let the words Lin - ger on the trem-bling chords;
2. When the wea - ry ones we love En - ter on their rest a - bove,
3. Clouds and con-flicts round us press— Would we have one sor - row less?
4. See, the feast of love is spread, Drink the wine, and break the bread;

Let the lit - tle while be - tween In their gold - en light be seen;
Seems the earth so poor and vast, All our life— joy o - ver - cast?
All the sharp - ness of the cross, All that tells the world is loss,
Sweet me - mo - rials—till the Lord Call us round His heaven-ly board;

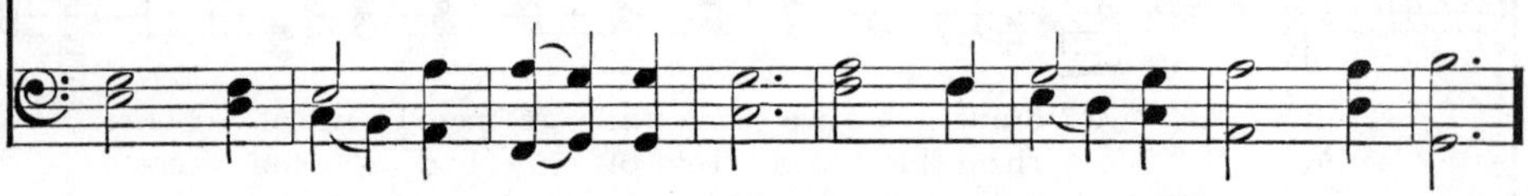

Let us think how heaven and home Lie be - yond that "Till He come."
Hush, be ev - ery mur - mur dumb— It is on - ly till He come.
Death and dark - ness, and the tomb, On - ly whis - per "Till He come."
Some from earth, from glo - ry some, Sev - ered on - ly till He come.

O Perfect Love **435**

Let love be without dissimulation. . . . Rom. 12:9

Dorothy F.B. Gurney, 1858-1932

O PERFECT LOVE 11.10.11.10.
Joseph Barnby, 1838-1896

1. O per - fect Love, all hu - man thought tran - scend - ing,
2. O per - fect Life, be Thou their full as - sur - ance
3. Grant them the joy which bright - ens earth - ly sor - row;
4. Hear us, O Fa - ther, gra - cious and for - giv - ing,
Low - ly we kneel in prayer be - fore Thy throne,
Of ten - der char - i - ty and stead - fast faith,
Grant them the peace which calms all earth - ly strife,
Through Je - sus Christ, Thy co - e - ter - nal Word,
That theirs may be the love that has no end - ing,
Of pa - tient hope, and qui - et, brave en - dur - ance,
And to life's day the glo - rious, un - known mor - row
Who, with the Ho - ly Ghost, by all things liv - ing
Whom Thou for - ev - er - more dost join in one.
With child - like trust that fears nor pain nor death.
That dawns up - on e - ter - nal love and life.
Now and to end - less a - ges art a - dored. A - MEN.

436 O Happy Home

. . . as for me and my house, we will serve the Lord. Josh. 24:15

Carl J.P. Spitta, 1801-1859
Translated by Sarah B. Findlater, 1823-1907

CONSOLATION (Mendelssohn) 11.10.11.10.
Adapted from Felix Mendelssohn, 1809-1847

1. O hap - py home, where Thou art loved the dear - est,
2. O hap - py home, whose lit - tle ones are giv - en
3. O hap - py home, where each one serves Thee, low - ly,
4. O hap - py home, where Thou art not for - got - ten
5. Un - til at last, when earth's day's - work is end - ed,
Thou lov - ing Friend and Sav - iour of our race;
Ear - ly to Thee, in hum - ble faith and prayer,
What - ev - er his ap - point - ed work may be,
When joy is o - ver - flow - ing, full and free;
All meet Thee in the bless - ed home a - bove,
And where a - mong the guests there nev - er com - eth
To Thee, their friend, who from the heights of heav - en
Till ev - ery com - mon task seems great and ho - ly,
O hap - py home, where ev - ery wound - ed spir - it
From whence Thou cam - est, where Thou hast as - cend - ed,
One who can hold such high and hon - ored place.
Guides them and guards with more than moth - er's care.
When it is done, O Lord, as un - to Thee.
Is brought, Phy - si - cian, Com - fort - er, to Thee;
Thy ev - er - last - ing home of peace and love.

(For different harmony see No. 308)

O Lord, May Church and Home 437

. . . they shall keep my laws . . . in all mine assemblies . . . Ezek. 44:24

LAND OF REST C.M.
American melody
Carlton C. Buck, 1907-1961
Harmony by Annabel M. Buchanan, b. 1888

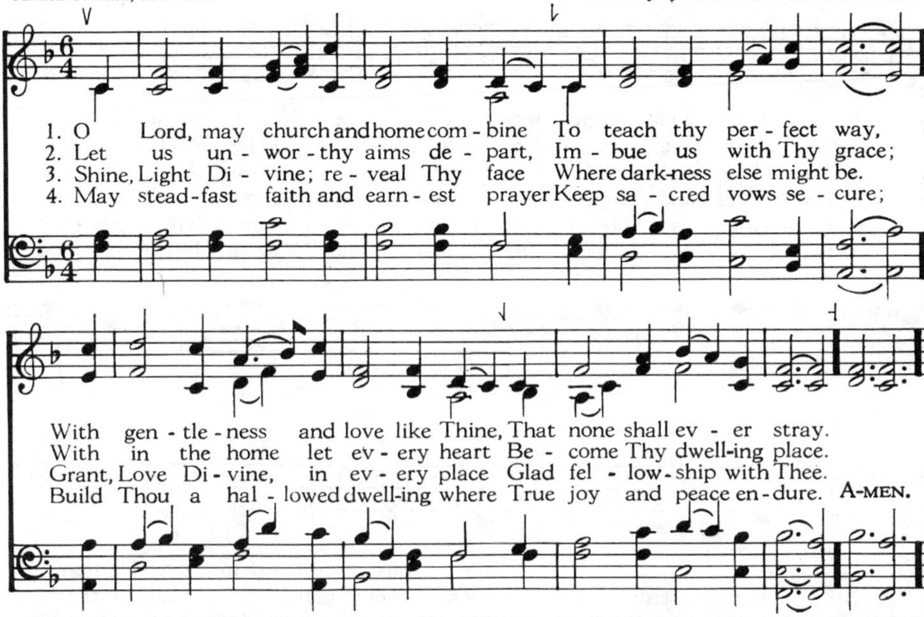
1. O Lord, may church and home com - bine To teach thy per - fect way,
2. Let us un - wor - thy aims de - part, Im - bue us with Thy grace;
3. Shine, Light Di - vine; re - veal Thy face Where dark-ness else might be.
4. May stead-fast faith and earn - est prayer Keep sa - cred vows se - cure;
With gen - tle - ness and love like Thine, That none shall ev - er stray.
With in the home let ev - ery heart Be - come Thy dwell-ing place.
Grant, Love Di - vine, in ev - ery place Glad fel - low - ship with Thee.
Build Thou a hal - lowed dwell-ing where True joy and peace en - dure. A-MEN.

Happy the Home When God Is There 438

. . . This day is salvation come to this house . . . Luke 19:9

BEATITUDO C.M.
Henry Ware, Jr., 1794-1843
John B. Dykes, 1823-1876

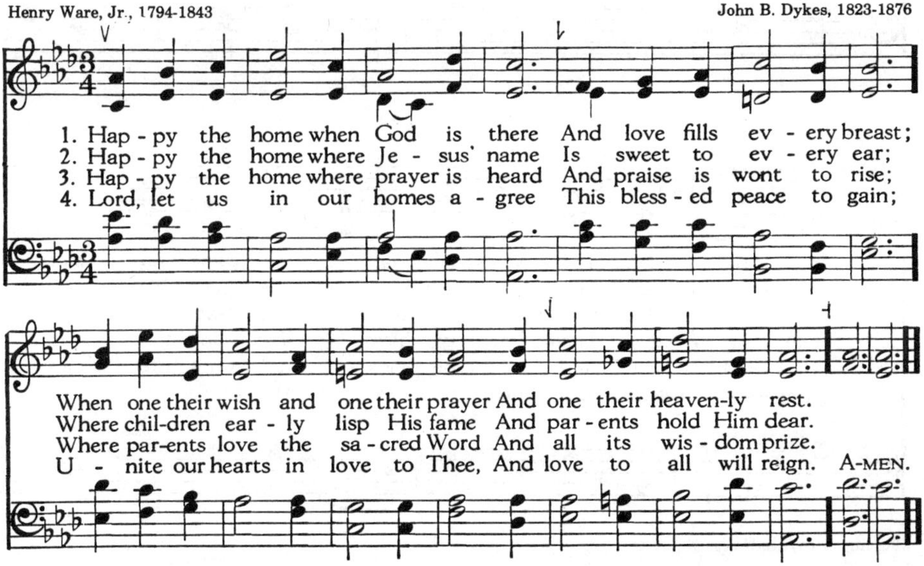
1. Hap - py the home when God is there And love fills ev - ery breast;
2. Hap - py the home where Je - sus' name Is sweet to ev - ery ear;
3. Hap - py the home where prayer is heard And praise is wont to rise;
4. Lord, let us in our homes a - gree This bless - ed peace to gain;
When one their wish and one their prayer And one their heaven-ly rest.
Where chil-dren ear - ly lisp His fame And par - ents hold Him dear.
Where par-ents love the sa - cred Word And all its wis - dom prize.
U - nite our hearts in love to Thee, And love to all will reign. A-MEN.

439 Jesus Shall Reign

. . . and he shall reign forever and ever. Rev. 11:15

DUKE STREET L.M.

Isaac Watts, 1674-1748

John Hatton, circa 1710-1793

1. Je - sus shall reign wher - e'er the sun Doth his suc -
2. Be - hold, the is - lands with their kings And Eur - ope
3. To Him shall end - less prayer be made, And prais - es
4. Peo - ples and realms of ev - ery tongue Dwell on His
5. Bless - ings a - bound wher - e'er He reigns; The pris - oner
6. Let ev - ery crea - ture rise and bring Pe - cu - liar
ces - sive jour - neys run; His king - dom stretch from
her best trib - ute brings; From north to south the
throng to crown His head. His name like sweet per -
love with sweet - est song, And in - fant voic - es
leaps to loose his chains; The wea - ry find e -
hon - ors to our King. An - gels de - scend with
shore to shore, Till moons shall wax and wane no more.
princ - es meet To pay their hom - age at His feet.
fume shall rise With ev - ery morn - ing sac - ri - fice.
shall pro - claim Their ear - ly bless - ings on His name.
ter - nal rest And all the sons of want are blest.
songs a - gain And earth re - peat the long A - men.

(For higher key see No. 588)

Lord of the Living Harvest

440

Pray . . . that he will send forth labourers into his harvest. Matt. 9:38

LANCASHIRE 7.6.7.6.D.

John S.B. Monsell, 1811-1875

Henry T. Smart, 1813-1879

1. Lord of the liv - ing har - vest That whit - ens o'er the plain,
2. As la - borers in Thy vine - yard, Send them out, Christ, to be
3. Be with them, God the Fa - ther; Be with them, God the Son;
Where an - gels soon shall gath - er Their sheaves of gold - en grain,
Con - tent to bear the bur - den Of wea - ry days for Thee,
Be with them, God the Spir - it, E - ter - nal Three - in - One!
Ac - cept fresh hands to la - bor, Fresh hearts to trust and love,
Con - tent to ask no wag - es When Thou shalt call them home,
Make them a roy - al priest-hood, Thee right - ly to a - dore,
And deign with them to has - ten Thy king-dom from a - bove.
But to have shared the trav - ail That makes Thy king-dom come.
And fill them with Thy full - ness Now and for - ev - er - more. A-MEN.

(For lower key see No. 451)

441 Thou Whose Almighty Word

. . . who commanded the light to shine out of darkness, hath shined in our hearts . . . 2 Cor. 4:6

ITALIAN HYMN 6.6.4.6.6.6.4.

John Marriott, 1780-1825 — Felice de Giardini, 1716-1796

1. Thou whose al - might - y word Cha - os and dark - ness heard
2. Thou who didst come to bring On Thy re - deem - ing wing
3. Spir - it of truth and love, Life - giv - er from a - bove,
4. Ho - ly and bless - ed Three, Glo - ri - ous Trin - i - ty,

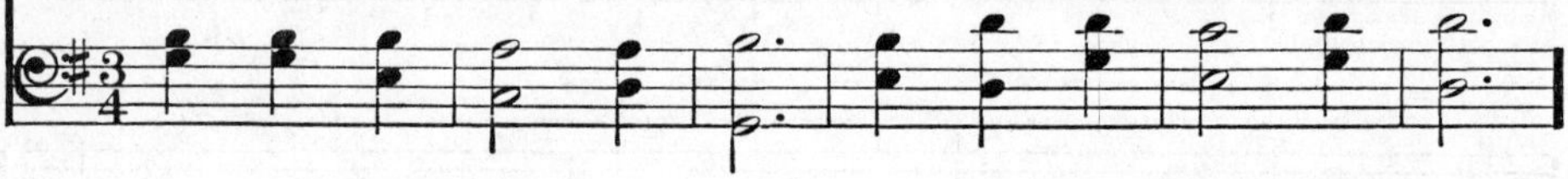

And took their flight, Hear us, we hum - bly pray, And, where the
Heal - ing and sight, Health to the sick in mind, Sight to the
Speed forth Thy flight, Move on the wa - ters' face, Bear - ing the
Wis - dom, Love, Might, Bound-less as o - cean tide, Roll - ing in

gos - pel - day Sheds not its glo - rious ray, Let there be light.
in - ly blind, Oh now, to all man-kind, Let there be light.
lamp of grace, And in earth's dark - est place Let there be light.
full - est pride, Through the world, far and wide, Let there be light. A-MEN.

(For different version of tune see No. 3)

Hark, the Voice of Jesus Calling 442

. . . The harvest truly is plenteous, but the labourers are few. Matt. 9:37

HYFRYDOL 8.7.8.7.D.

Daniel March, 1816-1909

Melody by Rowland H. Prichard, 1811-1887

1. Hark, the voice of Je - sus call - ing–"Who will go and work to - day?
2. If you can - not cross the o - cean And the hea - then lands ex - plore,
3. If you can - not speak like an - gels, If you can - not preach like Paul,
4. Let none hear you i - dly say - ing, "There is noth - ing I can do,"
Fields are white and har - vests wait - ing, Who will bear the sheaves a-way?"
You can find the hea - then near - er, You can help them at your door;
You can tell the love of Je - sus, You can say He died for all.
While the souls of men are dy - ing And the Mas - ter calls for you.
Loud and long the Mas - ter call - eth, Rich re - ward He of - fers free;
If you can - not give your thou-sands, You can give the wid - ow's mite,
If you can - not rouse the wick - ed With the judg-ment's dread a - larms,
Take the task He gives you glad - ly; Let His work your pleas-ure be;
Who will an - swer, glad - ly say - ing, "Here am I; send me, send me"?
And the least you give for Je - sus Will be pre - cious in His sight.
You can lead the lit - tle chil - dren To the Sav-iour's wait - ing arms.
An - swer quick - ly when He call - eth, "Here am I; send me, send me."

(For different harmony and higher key see No. 335)

443 He Was Not Willing

The Lord is . . . not willing that any should perish . . . 2 Pet. 3:9

Lucy R. Meyer, 19th century

Lucy R. Meyer, 19th century

1. He was not will - ing that an - y should per - ish;
2. He was not will - ing that an - y should per - ish:
3. Plen - ty for pleas - ure, but lit - tle for Je - sus:
4. He was not will - ing that an - y should per - ish;
Je - sus en - throned in the glo - ry a - bove,
Clothed in our flesh with its sor - row and pain,
Time for the world, with its trou - bles and toys,
Am I His fol - low - er, and can I live
Saw our poor fall - en world, pit - ied our sor - rows,
Came He to seek the lost, com - fort the mourn - er,
No time for Je - sus' work, feed - ing the hun - gry,
Long - er at ease with a soul go - ing down - ward,
Poured out His life for us— won - der - ful love!
Heal the heart bro - ken by sor - row and shame.
Lift - ing lost souls to e - ter - ni - ty's joys.
Lost for the lack of the help I might give?

He Was Not Willing

Per - ish - ing, per - ish - ing! Throng - ing our path - way,
Per - ish - ing, per - ish - ing! Har - vest is pass - ing,
Per - ish - ing, per - ish - ing! Hark, how they call us:
Per - ish - ing, per - ish - ing! Thou wast not will - ing;
Hearts break with bur - dens too heav - y to bear,
Reap - ers are few and the night draw - ing near,
"Bring us your Sav - iour, oh, tell us of Him!
Mas - ter, for - give, and in - spire us a - new;
Je - sus would save, but there's no one to tell them,
Je - sus is call - ing thee, haste to the reap - ing;
We are so wea - ry, so heav - i - ly la - den,
Ban - ish our world - li - ness! Oh, may we ev - er
No one to lift them from sin and de - spair.
Thou shalt have souls, pre - cious souls for thy hire.
And with long weep - ing our eyes have grown dim."
Live with e - ter - ni - ty's val - ues in view.

444 The Call for Reapers

Pray . . . that he will send forth labourers into his harvest. Matt. 9:38

HARVESTTIME 8.7.8.7. with Refrain

John O. Thompson, 1782-1818

J.B.O. Clemm, 19th century

1. Far and near the fields are teem-ing With the waves of ri-pened grain;
2. Send them forth with morn's first beam-ing; Send them in the noon-tide's glare;
3. O thou, whom thy Lord is send-ing, Gath-er now the sheaves of gold;
Far and near their gold is gleam-ing O'er the sun-ny slope and plain.
When the sun's last rays are gleam-ing, Bid them gath-er ev-ery-where.
Heaven-ward then at eve-ning wend-ing, Thou shalt come with joy un-told.
REFRAIN
Lord of har-vest, send forth reap-ers! Hear us, Lord, to Thee we cry;
Send them now the sheaves to gath-er, Ere the har-vest-time pass by.

Soldiers of Christ, Arise 445

Put on the whole armour of God . . . Eph. 6:11

Charles Wesley, 1707-1788

DIADEMATA S.M.D.
George J. Elvey, 1816-1893

1. Sol - diers of Christ, a - rise And put your ar - mor on,
2. Stand, then, in His great might, With all His strength en - dued;
3. Leave no un - guard - ed place, No weak - ness of the soul;

Strong in the strength which God sup - plies, Through His e - ter - nal Son.
And take, to arm you for the fight, The pan - o - ply of God.
Take ev - ery vir - tue, ev - ery grace And for - ti - fy the whole.

Strong in the Lord of Hosts, And in His might - y power,
That, hav - ing all things done And all your con - flicts past,
From strength to strength go on; Wres - tle, and fight, and pray;

Who in the strength of Je - sus trusts Is more than con - quer - or.
Ye may o'er - come through Christ a - lone And stand com - plete at last.
Tread all the powers of dark - ness down And win the well - fought day.

446 Ye Servants of God, Your Master Proclaim

Give unto the Lord the glory due unto his name . . . Psa. 96:8

HANOVER 10.10.11.11.

Charles Wesley, 1707-1788

Attributed to William Croft, 1678-1727

1. Ye ser - vants of God, your Mas - ter pro - claim,
2. God rul - eth on high, al - might - y to save;
3. "Sal - va - tion to God, who sits on the throne,"
4. Then let us a - dore, and give Him His right,
And pub - lish a - broad His won - der - ful Name;
And still He is nigh— His pres - ence we have;
Let all cry a - loud and hon - or the Son;
All glo - ry and power, all wis - dom and might;
The Name all vic - to - rious of Je - sus ex - tol;
The great con - gre - ga - tion His tri - umph shall sing,
The prais - es of Je - sus the an - gels pro - claim,
All hon - or and bless - ing, with an - gels a - bove,
His King - dom is glo - rious, He rules o - ver all.
As - crib - ing sal - va - tion to Je - sus our King.
Fall down on their fac - es, and wor - ship the Lamb.
And thanks nev - er ceas - ing, and in - fi - nite love. A - MEN.

Lift Up Your Heads, Ye Gates of Brass 447

. . . I will break in pieces the gates of brass . . . Isa. 45:2

ELLACOMBE C.M.D.
German melody, 18th century
From *Hymns Ancient and Modern,* 1868

James Montgomery, 1771-1854

1. Lift up your heads, ye gates of brass, Ye bars of i - ron, yield,
2. A ho - ly war those ser-vants wage; In that mys - ter - ious strife,
3. Though few and small and weak your bands, Strong in your Cap-tain's strength,
4. Then fear not, faint not, halt not now! Quit you like men, be strong!
And let the King of glo - ry pass; The cross is in the field.
The powers of heaven and hell en - gage For more than death or life.
Go to the con-quest of all lands– All must be His at length.
To Christ shall all the na - tions bow And sing the tri - umph song.
That ban - ner, bright - er than the star That leads the train of night,
Ye ar - mies of the liv - ing God, Sworn war-riors of Christ's host,
Those spoils at His vic - to - rious feet You shall re - joice to lay,
Up - lift - ed are the gates of brass, The bars of i - ron yield;
Shines on the march and guides from far His ser - vants to the fight.
Where hal - lowed foot-steps nev - er trod, Take your ap - point - ed post.
And lay your-selves as tro - phies meet In His great judg - ment day.
Be - hold the King of glo - ry pass; The cross has won the field.

(For different harmony and higher key see No. 98)

448 Hail to the Brightness

And the Gentiles shall come to thy light, and kings to the brightness of thy rising. Isa. 60:3

WESLEY 11.10.11.10.

Thomas Hastings, 1784-1872

Lowell Mason, 1792-1872

1. Hail to the bright-ness of Zi - on's glad morn - ing!
2. Hail to the bright-ness of Zi - on's glad morn - ing,
3. Lo, in the des - ert rich flow - ers are spring - ing,
4. See, from all lands, from the isles of the o - cean,
Joy to the lands that in dark - ness have lain!
Long by the proph - ets of Is - rael fore - told!
Streams ev - er cop - ious are glid - ing a - long;
Praise to Je - ho - vah as - cend - ing on high;
Hushed be the ac - cents of sor - row and mourn - ing;
Hail to the mil - lions from bond - age re - turn - ing!
Loud from the moun - tain - tops ech - oes are ring - ing,
Fallen are the en - gines of war and com - mo - tion,
Zi - on in tri - umph be - gins her mild reign.
Gen - tiles and Jews the blest vis - ion be - hold.
Wastes rise in ver - dure and min - gle in song.
Shouts of sal - va - tion are rend - ing the sky.

The Son of God Goes Forth to War 449

. . . they loved not their lives unto the death. Rev. 12:11

Reginald Heber, 1783-1826

ALL SAINTS NEW C.M.D.
Henry S. Cutler, 1824-1902

1. The Son of God goes forth to war, A king - ly crown to gain;
2. The mar - tyr first, whose ea - gle eye Could pierce be - yond the grave,
3. A glo - rious band, the cho - sen few On whom the Spir - it came,
4. A no - ble ar - my, men and boys, The ma - tron and the maid,
His blood - red ban - ner streams a - far: Who fol - lows in His train?
Who saw his Mas - ter in the sky And called on Him to save—
Twelve val - iant saints, their hope they knew And mocked the cross and flame.
A - round the Sav - iour's throne re - joice In robes of light ar - rayed.
Who best can drink his cup of woe, Tri - umph - ant o - ver pain;
Like Him, with par - don on his tongue, In midst of mor - tal pain,
They met the ty - rant's brand - ished steel, The li - on's go - ry mane;
They climbed the steep as - cent of heaven Through per - il, toil, and pain.
Who pa - tient bears his cross be - low— He fol - lows in His train.
He prayed for them that did the wrong— Who fol - lows in his train?
They bowed their necks the death to feel. Who fol - lows in their train?
O God, to us may grace be given To fol - low in their train! A-MEN.

450 The Battle Is the Lord's!

. . . he will give you into our hands. 1 Sam. 17:47

LEONI (Yigdal) 6.6.8.4.D.
Hebrew melody
Adapted by Meyer Lyon, 1751-1797

E. Margaret Clarkson, b. 1915

1. The battle is the Lord's! The harvest fields are white:
How few the reaping hands appear, Their strength how slight!
Yet victory is sure— We face a vanquished foe:
Then forward with the risen Christ To battle go!
2. The battle is the Lord's! Not ours is strength or skill,
But His alone, in sovereign grace, To work His will.
Ours, counting not the cost, Unflinching, to obey;
And in His time His holy arm Shall win the day.
3. The battle is the Lord's! The Victor crucified
Must with the travail of His soul Be satisfied.
The powers of hell shall fail, And all God's will be done
Till every soul whom He hath given To Christ be won.
4. The battle is the Lord's! Stand still, my soul, and see
The great salvation God hath wrought Revealed for thee.
Then, resting in His might, Lift high His triumph song,
For power, dominion, kingdom, strength To Christ belong!

(For different harmony and higher key see No. 30)

Lead On, O King Eternal

451

. . . I am the Lord thy God which . . . leadeth thee . . . Isa. 48:17

LANCASHIRE 7.6.7.6.D.

Ernest W. Shurtleff, 1862-1917

Henry T. Smart, 1813-1879

1. Lead on, O King e - ter - nal, The day of march has come;
2. Lead on, O King e - ter - nal, To lands of deep - est night;
3. Lead on, O King e - ter - nal; We fol - low not with fears,
Hence-forth in fields of con - quest Thy tents shall be our home.
We fol - low where Thou lead - est As her - alds of the light.
For glad - ness breaks like morn - ing Wher - e'er Thy face ap - pears.
Through days of prep - a - ra - tion Thy grace has made us strong,
May we to souls im - mor - tal Thy Word of life con - vey
Thy cross is lift - ed o'er us; We jour - ney in its light;
And now, O King e - ter - nal, We lift our bat - tle song.
And o - pen heav - en's por - tal Through Christ, the truth, the way.
The crown a - waits the con - quest; Lead on, O God of might.

(For higher key see No. 440)

452 From Greenland's Icy Mountains

. . . Come over into Macedonia, and help us. Acts 16:9

MISSIONARY HYMN 7.6.7.6.D.

Reginald Heber, 1783-1826 — Lowell Mason, 1792-1872

1. From Green-land's i - cy moun - tains, From In - dia's cor - al strand,
2. What though the spi - cy breez - es Blow soft o'er Cey - lon's isle;
3. Shall we, whose souls are light - ed With wis - dom from on high,
4. Waft, waft, ye winds, His sto - ry, And you, ye wa - ters, roll,
Where Af - ric's sun - ny foun - tains Roll down their gold - en sand,
Though ev - ery pros - pect pleas - es, And on - ly man is vile?
Shall we to men be - night - ed The lamp of life de - ny?
Till, like a sea of glo - ry, It spreads from pole to pole;
From man - y an an - cient riv - er, From man - y a palm - y plain,
In vain with lav - ish kind - ness The gifts of God are strown;
Sal - va - tion! Oh, sal - va - tion! The joy - ful sound pro - claim,
Till o'er our ran - somed na - ture The Lamb for sin - ners slain,
They call us to de - liv - er Their land from er - ror's chain.
The hea - then in his blind - ness Bows down to wood and stone.
Till earth's re - mot - est na - tion Has learned Mes - si - ah's name.
Re - deem - er, King, Cre - a - tor, In bliss re - turns to reign. A-MEN.

O Zion, Haste

453

And we declare unto you glad tidings . . . Acts 13:32

Mary A. Thomson, 1834-1923

TIDINGS 11.10.11.10. with Refrain
James Walch, 1837-1901

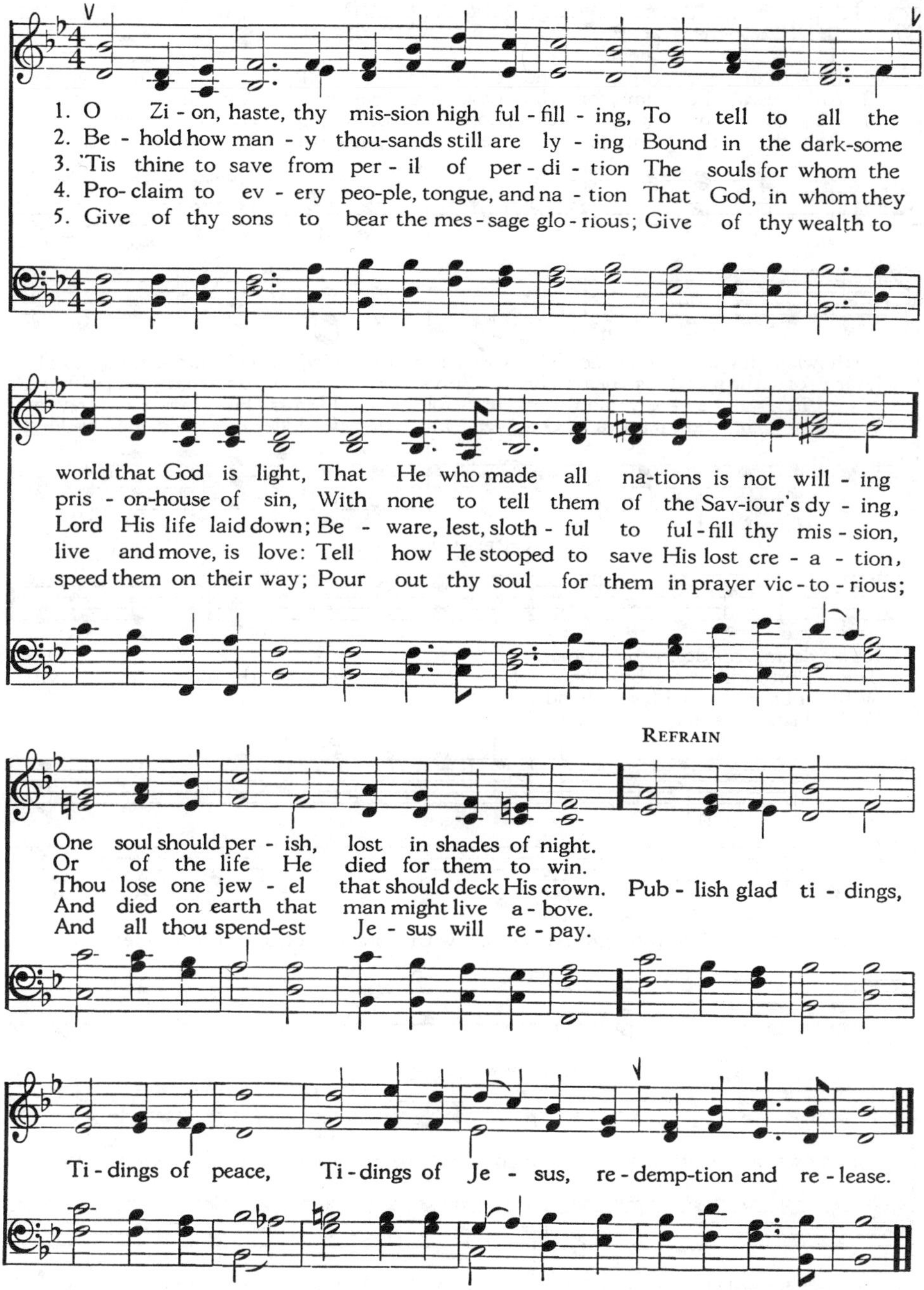
1. O Zi - on, haste, thy mis-sion high ful - fill - ing, To tell to all the
2. Be - hold how man - y thou-sands still are ly - ing Bound in the dark-some
3. 'Tis thine to save from per - il of per - di - tion The souls for whom the
4. Pro- claim to ev - ery peo-ple, tongue, and na - tion That God, in whom they
5. Give of thy sons to bear the mes - sage glo - rious; Give of thy wealth to
world that God is light, That He who made all na-tions is not will - ing
pris - on-house of sin, With none to tell them of the Sav-iour's dy - ing,
Lord His life laid down; Be - ware, lest, sloth - ful to ful - fill thy mis - sion,
live and move, is love: Tell how He stooped to save His lost cre - a - tion,
speed them on their way; Pour out thy soul for them in prayer vic - to - rious;
One soul should per - ish, lost in shades of night.
Or of the life He died for them to win.
Thou lose one jew - el that should deck His crown.
And died on earth that man might live a - bove.
And all thou spend-est Je - sus will re - pay.
Refrain
Pub - lish glad ti - dings,
Ti - dings of peace, Ti - dings of Je - sus, re - demp-tion and re - lease.

454 Redeem the Time

. . . because the days are evil. Eph. 5:16

Albert B. Simpson, 1843-1919

Melody by Margaret M. Simpson, 1876-1958

1. Re - deem the time, for the days are e - vil! It rings o'er the
2. Re - deem the time, for the days are sol - emn, And the cri - sis
3. Re - deem the time, for the Lord is work - ing By His might-y
4. Re - deem the time, let us send the gos - pel To the far - thest
earth with its notes sub-lime; 'Tis the voice of God to His slum-bering peo-ple;
hour of the world is near; The mys - tic scroll is un - fold - ing swift - ly,
power in ev - ery land; Let us fol - low Him as He leads His ser-vants
bounds of the hu - man race; O - ver all the world let us spread the ti-dings,
Re - deem, re - deem the time;
The Lord will soon be here.
With His al - might-y hand.
While lasts our day of grace.
REFRAIN
Re - deem the time, for the days are e - vil!
Let it ring through the world with its notes sub - lime; The
shad-ows are length-ening, the night is near, Re - deem, re - deem the time.

Send the Light

O send out thy light and thy truth . . . Psa. 43:3

MCCABE 11.6.11.6. with Refrain

Charles H. Gabriel, 1856-1932 | Charles H. Gabriel, 1856-1932

1. There's a call comes ring - ing o'er the rest-less wave, "Send the light!
2. We have heard the Mac - e - do - nian call to - day, "Send the light!
3. Let us not grow wea - ry in the work of love, Send the light!
Send the light!
Send the light!" There are souls to res - cue, there are souls to save;
Send the light!" And a gold - en of - fering at the cross we lay;
Send the light! Let us gath - er jew - els for a crown a - bove,
Refrain
Send the light! Send the light! Send the light, the bless - ed
Send the light!
gos - pel light; Let it shine from shore to shore; Send the light,
the bless - ed gos - pel light; Let it shine for - ev - er - more.

456 Speed the Light

. . . to them that sit in darkness . . . Luke 1:79

Elisha A. Hoffman, 1839-1929 | Melody by Elisha A. Hoffman, 1839-1929

1. To the mil-lions liv-ing o'er the deep, deep sea, Speed the light,
2. There in an-guish mil-lions for the gos-pel wait, Speed the light,
3. Je-sus bids us bear to them the gos-pel news, Speed the light,
4. We will go, and in our bless-ed Mas-ter's name Speed the light,
Speed the light,
speed the light; To their cry of pit-y dare we heed-less be?
speed the light; Go and seek their res-cue ere it is too late,
speed the light; Can the souls He ran-somed His re-quest re-fuse?
speed the light; We will His sal-va-tion and His love pro-claim,
speed the light;
Speed the light, Oh, speed the light!
Speed the light, Oh, speed the light!
Refrain
Speed the light, the bless-ed gos-pel light, To the lands

Speed the Light

which are in gloom and night; Souls are wait - ing, and the

fields are white; Speed the light, Oh, speed the light!
Speed the light,

How Beauteous Are Their Feet 457

. . . that bringeth good tidings, that publisheth peace . . . Isa. 52:7

ST. THOMAS S.M.

Isaac Watts, 1674-1748

From Aaron Williams' *Psalmody*, 1770

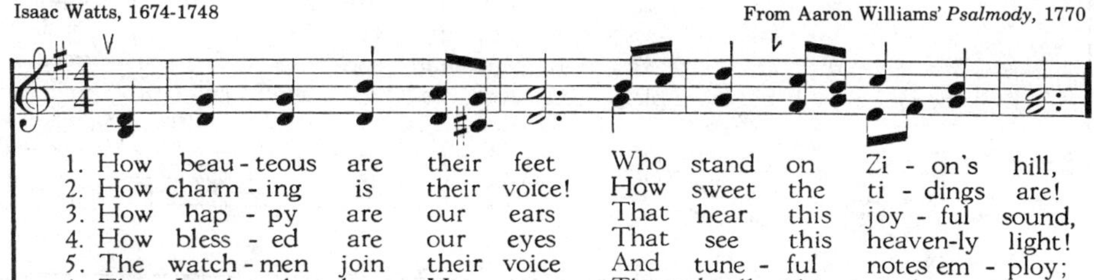
1. How beau - teous are their feet Who stand on Zi - on's hill,
2. How charm - ing is their voice! How sweet the ti - dings are!
3. How hap - py are our ears That hear this joy - ful sound,
4. How bless - ed are our eyes That see this heaven-ly light!
5. The watch - men join their voice And tune - ful notes em - ploy;
6. The Lord makes bare His arm Through all the earth a - broad;

Who bring sal - va - tion on their tongues, And words of peace in - still!
Zi - on, be - hold thy Sav - iour King; He reigns and tri - umphs here.
Which kings and proph - ets wait - ed for, And sought, but nev - er found!
Proph - ets and kings de - sired it long, But died with-out the sight.
Je - ru - sa - lem breaks forth in songs, And des - erts learn the joy.
Let all the na - tions now be - hold Their Sav - iour and their God.

458 Go and Tell Them

... go thou and preach the kingdom of God. Luke 9:60

Albert B. Simpson, 1843-1919

Melody by Albert B. Simpson, 1843-1919
Harmony by J. Buchanan MacMillan, b. 1915

1. Send the gos-pel of sal - va - tion To a world of dy - ing men;
2. 'Tis the Church's great com - mis - sion, 'Tis the Mas-ter's last com - mand;
3. Tell it out to Chi-na's mil - lions, Tell it out in fair Ja - pan;
4. 'Mid the lone Ti - bet - an moun - tains, By the O - ri - no - co's strand,
5. Christ is gath-ering out a peo - ple To His name from ev - ery race;
6. Give the gos - pel as a wit - ness To a world of sin - ful men,
Tell it out to ev - ery na - tion Till the Lord shall come a - gain.
Christ has died for ev - ery crea - ture, Tell it out in ev - ery land.
Tell it by the might - y Zai - re Tell it in the dark Su - dan.
O'er the burn - ing plains of In - dia— Tell it out in ev - ery land.
Haste to give the in - vi - ta - tion Ere shall end the day of grace.
Till the Bride shall be com - plet - ed And the Lord shall come a - gain.
REFRAIN
Go and tell them, go and tell them Je - sus died for sin - ful men;
Go and tell them, go and tell them He is com - ing back a - gain.

Go Ye into All the World 459

. . . and preach the gospel to every creature. Mark 16:15

GO YE 11.10.11.10. with Refrain

James McGranahan, 1840-1907 | James McGranahan, 1840-1907

1. Far, far a - way, in hea-then dark-ness dwell-ing, Mil - lions of souls for - ev - er may be lost; Who, who will go, sal - va-tion's sto - ry tell - ing, Look - ing to Je - sus, count-ing not the cost?
2. See o'er the world wide - o - pen doors in - vit - ing; Sol - diers of Christ, a - rise and en - ter in! Chris-tians, a-wake! Your forc - es all u - nit - ing, Send forth the gos-pel, break the chains of sin.
3. "Why will ye die?" the voice of God is call - ing, "Why will ye die?" re - ech - o in His name; Je - sus hath died to save from death ap-pall - ing, Life and sal - va-tion there-fore go pro-claim.
4. God speed the day when those of ev - ery na - tion "Glo - ry to God!" tri - um-phant - ly shall sing; Ran - somed, re-deemed, re - joic - ing in sal - va - tion, Shout "Hal - le - lu - jah, for the Lord is King."
REFRAIN
"All power is giv - en un - to Me, All power is giv - en un - to Me, Go ye in - to all the world and preach the gos - pel, And lo, I am with you al - way."

460 The Regions Beyond

Go ye therefore, and teach all nations . . . Matt. 28:19

Albert B. Simpson, 1843-1919

Margaret M. Simpson, 1876-1958

1. To the re - gions be-yond I must go, I must go, Where the sto - ry has
2. To the hard - est of plac - es He calls me to go, Not think-ing of
3. O ye that are spend-ing your lei - sure and powers In pleas-ures so
4. There are oth - er lost sheep that the Mas - ter must bring, And to them must the
nev - er been told; To the mil - lions that nev - er have heard of His love,
com-fort or ease; The world may pro-nounce me a dream-er, a fool—
fool - ish and fond, A - wake from your self - ish-ness, fol - ly, and sin
mes - sage be told. He sends me to gath - er them out of all lands
I must tell the sweet sto - ry of old.
E - nough if the Mas-ter I please.
And go to the re - gions be - yond.
And wel-come them back to His fold.
REFRAIN
To the re - gions be - I must go,
yond, I must go, I must go, Till the
I must go, To the re-gions be - yond I must go,
world, all the world, His sal - va - tion shall know.
Till the world, all the world, His sal - va-tion shall know.

We've a Story to Tell to the Nations 461

... this gospel ... shall be preached ... for a witness unto all nations ... Matt. 24:14

MESSAGE 10.8.8.7.7. with Refrain

Henry E. Nichol, 1862-1928 | Henry E. Nichol, 1862-1928

1. We've a sto - ry to tell to the na - tions That shall turn their
2. We've a song to be sung to the na - tions That shall lift their
3. We've a mes - sage to give to the na - tions That the Lord who
4. We've a Sav - iour to show to the na - tions Who the path of
hearts to the right, A sto - ry of truth and mer - cy, A
hearts to the Lord, A song that shall con - quer e - vil And
reign - eth a - bove Hath sent us His Son to save us And
sor - row hath trod, That all of the world's great peo - ples Might
sto - ry of peace and light, A sto - ry of peace and light.
shat - ter the spear and sword, And shat - ter the spear and sword.
show us that God is love, And show us that God is love.
come to the truth of God, Might come to the truth of God.
REFRAIN
For the dark-ness shall turn to dawn-ing, And the dawn-ing to noon-day bright,
And Christ's great king-dom shall come to earth, The king-dom of love and light.

462 A Missionary Cry

Multitudes, multitudes in the valley of decision . . . Joel 3:14

Albert B. Simpson, 1843-1919

Melody by J.H. Burke, 19th century

1. A hun - dred thou - sand souls a day Are pass - ing one by
2. O Ho - ly Ghost, Thy peo - ple move, Bap - tize their hearts with
3. The Mas - ter's com - ing draw - eth near; The Son of Man will
4. Oh, let us then His com - ing haste, Oh, let us end this
5. They're pass - ing, pass - ing fast a - way, A hun - dred thou - sand
one a - way In Christ - less guilt and gloom; With - out one ray of
faith and love And con - se - crate their gold. At Je - sus' feet their
soon ap - pear; His king - dom is at hand. But ere that glo - rious
aw - ful waste Of souls that nev - er die. A thou-sand mil - lions
souls a day In Christ - less guilt and gloom. O Church of Christ, what
hope or light, With fu - ture dark as end - less night,
mil - lions pour, And all their ranks u - nite once more,
day can be, This gos - pel of the king - dom we
still are lost; A Sav - iour's blood has paid the cost,
wilt thou say When, in the aw - ful judg - ment day,
They're pass - ing to their doom, They're pass - ing to their doom.
As in the days of old, As in the days of old.
Must preach in ev - ery land, Must preach in ev - ery land.
Oh, hear their dy - ing cry, Oh, hear their dy - ing cry.
They charge thee with their doom, They charge thee with their doom?

A Missionary Cry

REFRAIN
They're pass - ing, pass - ing fast a - way In thou - sands day by
day; They're pass - ing to their doom, They're pass - ing to their doom.

Speed Thy Servants, Saviour 463

... The harvest truly is great ... Luke 10:2

Thomas Kelly, 1769-1854

DISMISSAL 8.7.8.7.8.7.
William L. Viner, 1790-1867

1. Speed Thy ser - vants, Sav - iour, speed them; Thou art Lord of winds and waves;
2 Friends, and home, and all for - sak - ing, Lord, they go at Thy com - mand,
3. Where no fruit ap - pears to cheer them And they seem to toil in vain,
4. In the midst of op - po - si - tion Let them trust, O Lord, in Thee;
They were bound, but Thou hast freed them; Now they go to free the slaves:
As their stay Thy prom - ise tak - ing While they trav - erse sea and land:
Then in mer - cy, Lord, draw near them, Then their sink - ing hopes sus - tain:
When suc - cess at - tends their mis - sion, Let Thy ser - vants hum - bler be:
Be Thou with them, Be Thou with them; 'Tis Thy arm a - lone that saves!
Oh, be with them, Oh, be with them; Lead them safe - ly by the hand!
Thus sup - port - ed, Thus sup - port - ed, Let their zeal re - vive a - gain!
Nev - er leave them! Nev - er leave them Till Thy face in heaven they see!

464 Macedonia

. . . Lift up your eyes, and look on the fields; for they are white . . . to harvest. John 4:35

Anne Ortlund, b. 1923

ALL SAINTS, NEW C.M.D.
Henry S. Cutler, 1824-1902

1. The vi - sion of a dy - ing world Is vast be - fore our eyes;
2. The sav - age hugs his god of stone And fears de - scent of night;
3. To - day, as un - der-stand-ing's bounds Are stretched on ev - ery hand,
4. The warn - ing bell of judg-ment tolls, A - bove us looms the cross;
We feel the heart-beat of its need, We hear its fee - ble cries:
The cit - y dwell - er cring - es lone A - mid the gar - ish light:
Oh, clothe Thy Word in bright, new sounds, And speed it o'er the land;
A - round are ev - er - dy - ing souls— How great, how great the loss!
Lord Je - sus Christ, re - vive Thy Church In this, her cru - cial hour!
Lord Je - sus Christ, a - rouse Thy Church To see their mute dis - tress!
Lord Je - sus Christ, em - pow - er us To preach by ev - ery means!
O Lord, con-strain and move Thy Church The glad news to im - part!
Lord Je - sus Christ, a-wake Thy Church With Spir - it giv - en power.
Lord Je - sus Christ, e - quip Thy Church With love and ten - der - ness.
Lord Je - sus Christ, em-bold - en us In near and dis - tant scenes.
And Lord, as Thou dost stir Thy Church, Be - gin with - in my heart.
A-MEN.

Ready

... *I am ready to preach the gospel* ... Rom. 1:15

A.C. Palmer, 1845-1882
From *Hymns of Consecration and Faith* (altered)

TILLMAN 8.6.8.6. with Refrain
Melody by Charles D. Tillman, 1861-1943

1. Read-y to suf-fer grief or pain, Read-y to stand the test;
2. Read-y to go, read-y to bear, Read-y to watch and pray;
3. Read-y to speak, read-y to think, Read-y with heart and brain;
4. Read-y to speak, read-y to warn, Read-y o'er souls to yearn;
Read-y to stay at home and send Oth-ers if He sees best.
Read-y to stand a-side and give Till He shall clear the way.
Read-y to stand where He sees fit, Read-y to bear the strain.
Read-y in life, read-y in death, Read-y for His re-turn.
Refrain
Read-y to go, read-y to stay, Read-y my place to fill;
Read-y for serv-ice, low-ly or great, Read-y to do His will.

466 Master, Use Me

. . . Then said I, Here am I; send me. Isa. 6:8

Elisha A. Hoffman, 1839-1929

Melody by Elisha A. Hoffman, 1839-1929

1. Send me forth, O bless - ed Mas - ter, where are souls in
2. There are lives that may be bright - ened by a word of
3. There is work with - in the vine - yard, there is serv - ice
4. Oh, I would not be an i - dler in the vine - yard
sor - row bowed, Send me forth to homes of want and homes of care,
hope and cheer, There are souls with whom life's bless - ings I should share;
to be done, There's a mes - sage of sal - va - tion to de - clare;
of the Lord; With the Christ the vine - yard la - bor I would share;
And with joy I will o - bey the call, and in Thy pre-cious name
There are hearts that may be light-ened of the bur - dens which they bear;
Send me forth to tell the sto - ry in the homes of sin - ful men;
In - to hearts that know not Je - sus I would speak the sav - ing Word;
I will take the bless - ed light of the gos - pel there.
Let me take the bless - ed hope of the gos - pel there.
Let me take the bless - ed Christ of the gos - pel there.
Let me take the bless - ed joy of the gos - pel there.

Master, Use Me

Refrain
Call me forth to ac - tive serv - ice, And my
call me forth
prompt re - sponse shall be, "Here am I! Send me." I am
read - y to re - port for or - ders, Mas - ter, sum - mon me,
And I'll go on an - y er - rand of love for Thee.

467 So Send I You

. . . as my Father hath sent me, even so send I you. John 20:21

SO SEND I YOU 11.10.11.10. with Refrain

E. Margaret Clarkson, b. 1915

John W. Peterson, b. 1921

1. So send I you, by grace made strong to tri - umph O'er hosts of
2. So send I you to take to souls in bond - age The Word of
3. So send I you, My strength to know in weak - ness, My joy in
4. So send I you to bear My cross with pa - tience, And then one
hell, o'er dark - ness, death and sin, My name to bear, and in that
truth that sets the cap - tive free, To break the bonds of sin, to
grief, My per - fect peace in pain, To prove My power, My grace, My
day with joy to lay it down, To hear My voice, "Well done, My
name to con - quer. So send I you, My vic - to - ry to win.
loose death's fet - ters. So send I you, to bring the lost to Me.
prom - ised pres - ence. So send I you, e - ter - nal fruit to gain.
faith - ful ser - vant. Come, share My throne, My king - dom and My crown!"
CODA
"As the Fa - ther hath sent Me, So send I you."

Saving and Serving 468

. . . by love serve one another. Gal. 5:13

Albert B. Simpson, 1843-1919

Melody by Margaret M. Simpson, 1876-1958

1. Sav - ing and serv - ing our watch-word shall be; Liv - ing for oth - ers and
2. Serv - ing a Mas - ter so good and so true; Find - ing some serv - ice in
3. Sav - ing the lost ones wher - ev - er they roam; Seek - ing the wan-derers and
4. Sav - ing and serv - ing, oh, bless - ed em - ploy! Heav - en it - self has no
liv - ing for Thee; Help us, dear Lord, to be true to our trust, Serv-ing the
all that we do; Seek - ing His glo - ry and do - ing His will; Wait-ing or
bring-ing them home; Go - ing where dark-ness and sor - row are found; Seek-ing the
ho - li - er joy; Thus we shall win heav-en's rich-est re - ward–Sav - ing the
REFRAIN
Mas - ter and sav - ing the lost.
work - ing but serv - ing Him still. Serv - ing the Lord and sav - ing the lost,
lost to earth's ut - ter-most bounds.
lost ones and serv - ing the Lord.
Shrink-ing not from dan - ger, count - ing not the cost, Keep us, bless - ed
Mas - ter, true to our trust— Serv - ing the Lord and sav - ing the lost.

469 Jesus Saves

... all the ends of the earth shall see the salvation of our God. Isa. 52:10

JESUS SAVES 7.6.7.6.7.7.7.6.

Priscilla J. Owens, 1829-1907

William J. Kirkpatrick, 1838-1921

1. We have heard the joy - ful sound: Je - sus saves! Je - sus saves!
2. Waft it on the roll - ing tide; Je - sus saves! Je - sus saves!
3. Sing a - bove the bat - tle's strife, Je - sus saves! Je - sus saves!
4. Give the winds a might - y voice, Je - sus saves! Je - sus saves!
Spread the ti - dings all a - round: Je - sus saves! Je - sus saves!
Tell to sin - ners far and wide: Je - sus saves! Je - sus saves!
By His death and end - less life, Je - sus saves! Je - sus saves!
Let the na - tions now re - joice, Je - sus saves! Je - sus saves!
Bear the news to ev - ery land, Climb the steeps and cross the waves;
Sing, ye is - lands of the sea; Ech - o back, ye o - cean caves;
Sing it soft - ly through the gloom, When the heart for mer - cy craves;
Shout sal - va - tion full and free, To each shore that o - cean laves—
On - ward—'tis our Lord's com - mand. Je - sus saves! Je - sus saves!
Earth shall keep her ju - bi - lee— Je - sus saves! Je - sus saves!
Sing in tri - umph o'er the tomb, Je - sus saves! Je - sus saves!
This our song of vic - to - ry: Je - sus saves! Je - sus saves!

Rescue the Perishing 470

For the Son of man is come to seek and to save that which was lost. Luke 19:10

RESCUE 11.10.11.10. with Refrain

Fanny J. Crosby, 1820-1915

William H. Doane, 1832-1915

1. Res - cue the per - ish - ing, Care for the dy - ing, Snatch them in pit - y from
2. Though they are slight - ing Him, Still He is wait - ing, Wait - ing the pen - i - tent
3. Down in the hu - man heart, Crushed by the tempt - er, Feel - ings lie bur - ied that
4. Res - cue the per - ish - ing, Du - ty de - mands it; Strength for thy la - bor the
sin and the grave; Weep o'er the err - ing one, Lift up the fall - en,
child to re - ceive; Plead with them ear - nest - ly, Plead with them gent - ly,
grace can re - store; Touched by a lov - ing heart, Wak - ened by kind - ness,
Lord will pro - vide. Back to the nar - row way Pa - tient - ly win them;
Tell them of Je - sus the might - y to save.
He will for - give if they on - ly be - lieve.
Chords that were bro - ken will vi - brate once more.
Tell the poor wan - derer a Sav - iour has died.
Refrain
Res - cue the per - ish - ing,
Care for the dy - ing; Je - sus is mer - ci - ful, Je - sus will save.

471 The Breaking of the Bread

. . . he blessed, and brake, and gave the loaves to his disciples . . . Matt. 14:19

Beatrice B. Bixler, b. 1916

Beatrice B. Bixler, b. 1916
Arranged by Helen I. Young, b. 1931

1. A - long the shores of Gal - i - lee, When Christ five thou - sand fed
2. Long years have passed and few have heard That Je - sus Christ has bled, That
3. Great God, Who gave Thine on - ly Son, Help us, now Spir - it led, To
Not one was o - mit - ted In the break-ing of the bread. To -
they might feed on Him Who died To be that Liv - ing Bread. To
tell the sto - ry of Thy love To those who ask for bread. Then
day they die in hea-then lands, They die in want and dread, For
gods of stone and wood they cry, Yet they are nev - er fed For
glad - ly will we go or send, Till this blest news has spread, And
they have been o - mit - ted in the break-ing of the Bread.
they have been o - mit - ted in the break-ing of the Bread.
they have been in - clud - ed in the break-ing of the Bread.

The Breaking of the Bread

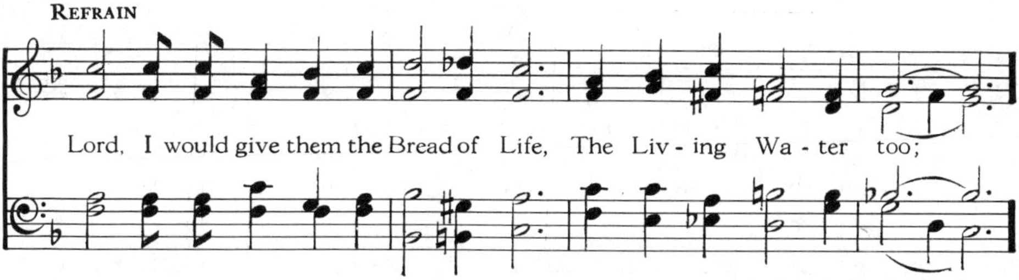
Refrain
Lord, I would give them the Bread of Life, The Liv - ing Wa - ter too;

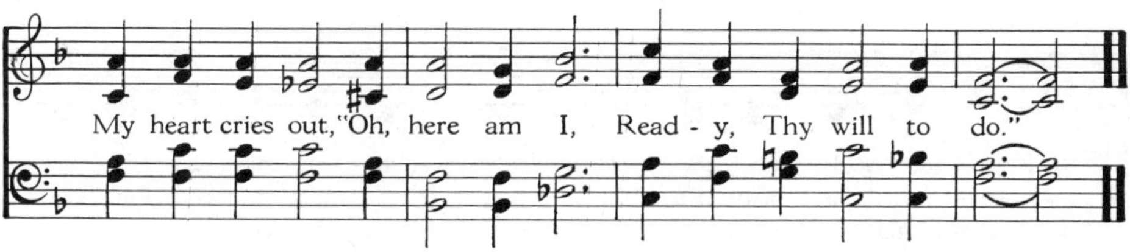
My heart cries out,"Oh, here am I, Read - y, Thy will to do."

Thy Kingdom Come 472

. . . Thy will be done in earth, as it is in heaven. Matt. 6:10

Albert B. Simpson, 1843-1919

PAROUSIA 6.6.6.4. with repeat
Melody by Albert B. Simpson, 1843-1919

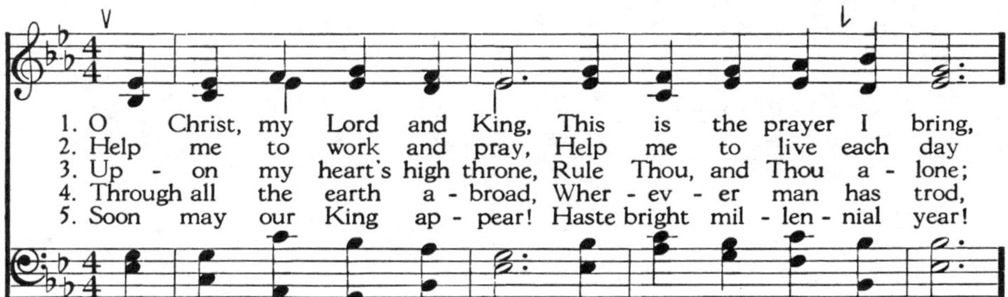
1. O Christ, my Lord and King, This is the prayer I bring,
2. Help me to work and pray, Help me to live each day
3. Up - on my heart's high throne, Rule Thou, and Thou a - lone;
4. Through all the earth a - broad, Wher - ev - er man has trod,
5. Soon may our King ap - pear! Haste bright mil - len - nial year!

This is the song I sing: Thy king-dom come, Thy king-dom come.
That all I do may say, Thy king-dom come, Thy king-dom come.
Let me be all Thine own! Thy king-dom come, Thy king-dom come.
Send forth Thy Word, O God— Thy king-dom come, Thy king-dom come.
We live to bring it near. Thy king-dom come, Thy king-dom come. A-men.

473 Bringing in the Sheaves!

He that goeth forth . . . shall . . . come . . . with . . . his sheaves . . . Psa. 126:6

Knowles Shaw, 1834-1878

Arranged from George A. Minor, 1845-1904

1. Sow - ing in the morn - ing, sow - ing seeds of kind - ness, Sow - ing
2. Sow - ing in the sun - shine, sow - ing in the shad - ows, Fear - ing
3. Go then, ev - er weep - ing, sow - ing for the Mas - ter, Though the
in the noon - tide and the dew - y eves: Wait - ing for the har - vest
nei - ther clouds nor win - ter's chill - ing breeze: By and by the har - vest
loss sus - tained our spir - it of - ten grieves: When our weep - ing's o - ver,
and the time of reap - ing, We shall come re - joic - ing, bring - ing in the sheaves!
and the la - bor end - ed, We shall come re - joic - ing, bring - ing in the sheaves!
He will bid us wel - come, We shall come re - joic - ing, bring - ing in the sheaves!
REFRAIN
Bring - ing in the sheaves! Bring - ing in the sheaves! We shall come re -
joic - ing, bring - ing in the sheaves! Bring - ing in the sheaves! Bring - ing

Bringing in the Sheaves!

in the sheaves! We shall come re - joic - ing, bring - ing in the sheaves!

Come, Labor On! 474

. . . always abounding in the work of the Lord . . . 1 Cor. 15:58

NYACK 4.10.10.10.4.

Jane L. Borthwick, 1813-1897 | J. Buchanan MacMillan, b. 1915

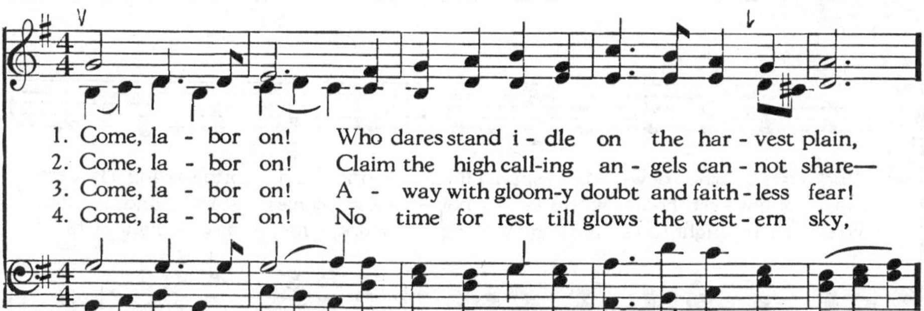
1. Come, la - bor on! Who dares stand i - dle on the har - vest plain,
2. Come, la - bor on! Claim the high call-ing an - gels can - not share—
3. Come, la - bor on! A - way with gloom-y doubt and faith - less fear!
4. Come, la - bor on! No time for rest till glows the west - ern sky,

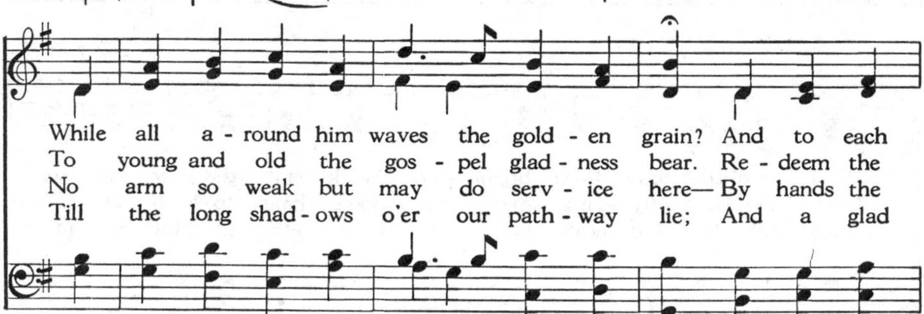
While all a - round him waves the gold - en grain? And to each
To young and old the gos - pel glad - ness bear. Re - deem the
No arm so weak but may do serv - ice here— By hands the
Till the long shad - ows o'er our path - way lie; And a glad

ser - vant doth the Mas - ter say, "Go, work to - day."
time; its hours too swift - ly fly; The night draws nigh.
fee - blest can our God ful - fill His per - fect will.
sound comes with the set - ting sun, "Ser - vant, well done!"

475 Work, for the Night Is Coming

. . . the night cometh, when no man can work. John 9:4

DILIGENCE 7.6.7.5.D.

Anna L. Coghill, 1836-1907 (altered) | Lowell Mason, 1792-1872

1. Work, for the night is com - ing, Work through the morn - ing hours;
2. Work, for the night is com - ing, Work through the sun - ny noon;
3. Work, for the night is com - ing, Un - der the sun - set skies;
Work while the dew is spark - ling, Work 'mid spring - ing flowers;
Fill bright - est hours with la - bor— Rest comes sure and soon.
While their bright tints are glow - ing, Work, for day - light flies;
Work when the day grows bright - er, Work in the glow - ing sun;
Give ev - ery fly - ing min - ute Some - thing to keep in store;
Work till the last beam fad - eth, Fad - eth to shine no more;
Work, for the night is com - ing When man's work is done.
Work, for the night is com - ing When man works no more.
Work while the night is dark-ening, When man's work is o'er.
A-MEN.

The Cleansing Wave

476

. . . there shall be a fountain opened . . . for sin and for uncleanness. Zech. 13:1

Phoebe P. Knapp, 1839-1908 | Phoebe P. Knapp, 1839-1908

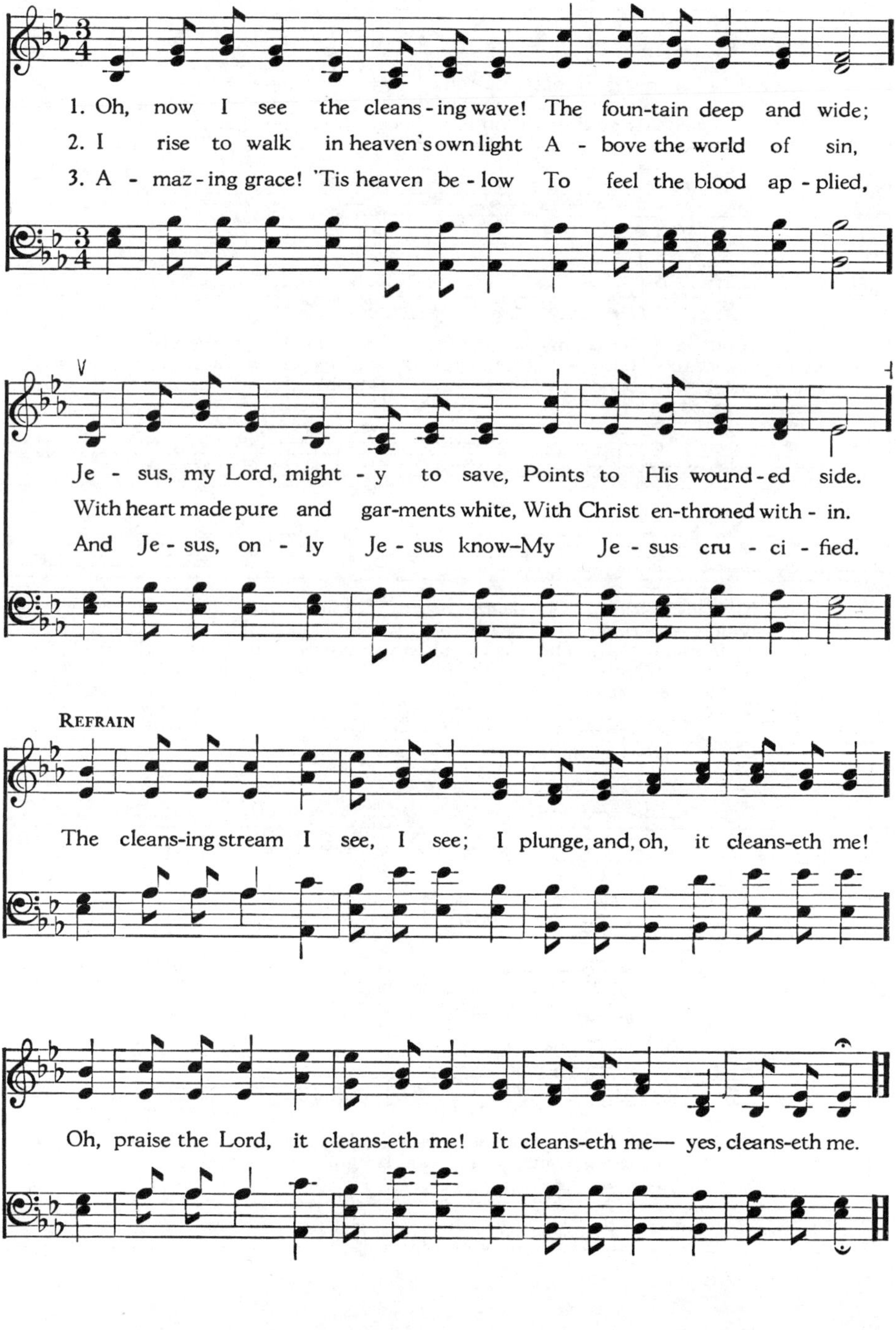
1. Oh, now I see the cleans-ing wave! The foun-tain deep and wide;
2. I rise to walk in heaven's own light A - bove the world of sin,
3. A - maz-ing grace! 'Tis heaven be - low To feel the blood ap - plied,
Je - sus, my Lord, might - y to save, Points to His wound-ed side.
With heart made pure and gar-ments white, With Christ en-throned with - in.
And Je - sus, on - ly Je - sus know–My Je - sus cru - ci - fied.
REFRAIN
The cleans-ing stream I see, I see; I plunge, and, oh, it cleans-eth me!
Oh, praise the Lord, it cleans-eth me! It cleans-eth me— yes, cleans-eth me.

477 Nor Silver Nor Gold

. . . ye were not redeemed with . . . silver and gold . . . 1 Pet. 1:18

PRICELESS 12.11.12.11. with Refrain

James M. Gray, 1851-1935

Daniel B. Towner, 1850-1919

1. Nor sil - ver nor gold hath ob-tained my re-demp-tion; No rich - es of
2. Nor sil - ver nor gold hath ob-tained my re-demp-tion; The guilt on my
3. Nor sil - ver nor gold hath ob-tained my re-demp-tion; The ho - ly com -
4. Nor sil - ver nor gold hath ob-tained my re-demp-tion; The way in - to
earth could have saved my poor soul. The blood of the cross is my
con - science too heav - y had grown. The blood of the cross is my
mand - ment for - bade me draw near. The blood of the cross is my
heav - en could not thus be bought. The blood of the cross is my
on - ly foun-da - tion; The death of my Sav-iour now mak - eth me whole.
on - ly foun-da - tion; The death of my Sav-iour could on - ly a - tone.
on - ly foun-da - tion; The death of my Sav-iour re - mov - eth my fear.
on - ly foun-da - tion; The death of my Sav-iour re-demp-tion hath wrought.
REFRAIN
I am re - deemed, but not with sil - ver;
I am re-deemed, I am re - deemed, but not with sil - ver;
I am bought, but not with gold; Bought with a
I am bought, I am bought, but not with gold;

Nor Silver Nor Gold

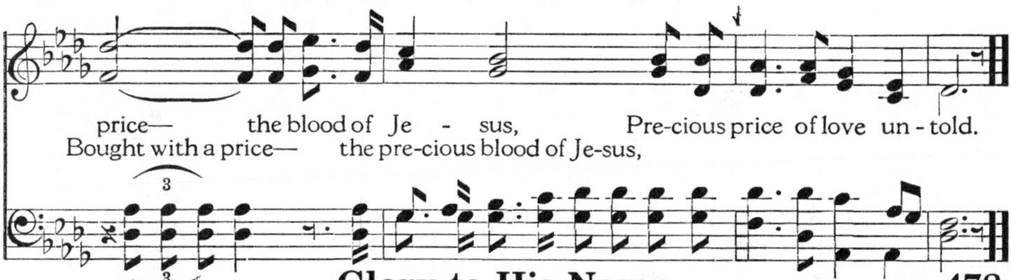
price— the blood of Je - sus, Pre-cious price of love un - told.
Bought with a price— the pre-cious blood of Je-sus,
3
3

Glory to His Name 478

. . . unto thy name give glory . . . Psa. 115:1

GLORY TO HIS NAME 9.9.9.5. with Refrain

Elisha A. Hoffman, 1839-1929

John H. Stockton, 1813-1877

1. Down at the cross where my Sav - iour died, Down where for cleans-ing from sin I cried–There to my heart was the blood ap - plied; Glo-ry to His name!
2. I am so won-drous - ly saved from sin; Je - sus so sweet - ly a - bides with - in, There at the cross where He took me in; Glo-ry to His name!
3. Oh, pre-cious foun - tain that saves from sin! I am so glad I have en - tered in; There Je - sus saves me and keeps me clean; Glo-ry to His name!
4. Come to this foun - tain so rich and sweet; Cast thy poor soul at the Sav-iour's feet; Plunge in to - day and be made com-plete; Glo-ry to His name!
REFRAIN
Glo - ry to His name, Glo - ry to His name;
There to my heart was the blood ap - plied; Glo - ry to His name!

479 At Calvary

. . . Calvary, there they crucified him . . . Luke 23:33

CALVARY 9.9.9.4. with Refrain

William R. Newell, 1868-1956

Daniel B. Towner, 1850-1919

1. Years I spent in van - i - ty and pride, Car - ing
2. By God's Word at last my sin I learned; Then I
3. Now I've given to Je - sus ev - ery - thing; Now I
4. Oh, the love that drew sal - va - tion's plan! Oh, the
not my Lord was cru - ci - fied, Know - ing not it was for
trem - bled at the law I'd spurned Till my guilt - y soul im -
glad - ly own Him as my King; Now my rap - tured soul can
grace that brought it down to man! Oh, the might - y gulf that
me He died On Cal - va - ry.
plor - ing turned To Cal - va - ry.
on - ly sing Of Cal - va - ry.
God did span At Cal - va - ry!
REFRAIN
Mer - cy there was great, and
grace was free; Par - don there was mul - ti - plied to me;
There my bur - dened soul found lib - er - ty— At Cal - va - ry.

Burdens Are Lifted at Calvary

480

Cast thy burden upon the Lord . . . Psa. 55:22

John M. Moore, b. 1925

John M. Moore, b. 1925

1. Days are filled with sor - row and care, Hearts are lone - ly and drear;
2. Cast your care on Je - sus to - day, Leave your wor - ry and fear;
3. Trou - bled soul, the Sav - iour can see Ev - ery heart-ache and tear;
Bur - dens are lift - ed at Cal - va - ry, Je - sus is ver - y near.
Bur - dens are lift - ed at Cal - va - ry, Je - sus is ver - y near.
Bur - dens are lift - ed at Cal - va - ry, Je - sus is ver - y near.
REFRAIN
Bur - dens are lift - ed at Cal - va - ry, Cal - va - ry, Cal - va - ry;
Bur - dens are lift - ed at Cal - va - ry, Je - sus is ver - y near.

481 Saved by the Blood

. . . by his own blood he . . . obtained eternal redemption for us. Heb. 9:12

GLORY I'M SAVED 10.11.11.10. with Refrain
Melody by Daniel B. Towner, 1850-1919

S.J. Henderson, 19th century

1. Saved by the blood of the cru - ci - fied One! Now ran - somed from
2. Saved by the blood of the cru - ci - fied One! The an - gels re -
3. Saved by the blood of the cru - ci - fied One! The Fa - ther He
4. Saved by the blood of the cru - ci - fied One! All hail to the
sin and a new work be - gun, Sing praise to the Fa - ther and
joic - ing be - cause it is done; A child of the Fa - ther, joint
spake, and His will it was done; Great price of my par - don, His
Fa - ther, all hail to the Son, All hail to the Spir - it— the
praise to the Son, Saved by the blood of the cru - ci - fied One!
heir with the Son, Saved by the blood of the cru - ci - fied One!
own pre - cious Son; Saved by the blood of the cru - ci - fied One!
great Three - in - One! Saved by the blood of the cru - ci - fied One!
REFRAIN
Saved! Saved! My sins are all par - doned, my guilt is all gone!
Glo - ry, I'm saved! Glo - ry I'm saved!
Saved! Saved! I am saved by the blood of the cru - ci - fied One!
Glo - ry, I'm saved! Glo - ry, I'm saved!

Is My Name Written There? 482

And whosoever was not found written in the book of life was cast into the lake of fire. Rev. 20:15

Mary A. Kidder, 1820-1905

Frank M. Davis, 1839-1896

1. Lord, I care not for rich - es, Nei - ther sil - ver nor gold; I would
2. Lord, my sins they are man - y Like the sands of the sea, But Thy
3. Oh, that beau - ti - ful cit - y With its man-sions of light, With its
make sure of heav - en, I would en - ter the fold. In the book of Thy
blood, O my Sav - iour, Is suf - fi - cient for me; For Thy prom-ise is
glo - ri - fied be - ings In pure gar-ments of white! Where no e - vil thing
king-dom With its pa - ges so fair, Tell me, Je - sus, my Sav-iour, Is my
writ - ten In bright let-ters that glow, "Though your sins be as scar - let, I will
com-eth To de - spoil what is fair, Where the an - gels are watch-ing! Yes, my
name writ - ten there?
make them like snow." Is my name writ - ten there, On the page white and fair?
name's writ-ten there. (3) Yes, my name's writ-ten there, On the page white and fair!
REFRAIN
In the book of Thy king - dom, Is my name writ - ten there?
In the book of Thy king - dom, Yes, my name's writ - ten there.

483 The King's Business

. . . we are ambassadors for Christ . . . 2 Cor. 5:20

E. Taylor Cassel, 1849-1930

Flora H. Cassel, 1852-1911

1. I am a stran - ger here with - in a for - eign land, My home is
2. This is the King's com - mand, that all men ev - ery - where Re - pent and
3. My home is bright - er far than Shar - on's ros - y plain, E - ter - nal
far a - way up - on a gold - en strand; Am - bas - sa - dor to be of
turn a - way from sin's se - duc - tive snare; That all who will o - bey with
life and joy through - out its vast do - main; My Sov - ereign bids me tell how
realms be - yond the sea, I'm here on busi - ness for my King.
Him shall reign for aye, And that's my busi - ness for my King.
mor - tals there may dwell, And that's my busi - ness for my King.
REFRAIN
This is the mes - sage that I bring, A mes - sage an - gels fain would sing; "Oh, be ye
rec - on - ciled," Thus saith my Lord and King, "Oh, be ye rec - on - ciled to God."

The Lion of Judah

... the Root of David, hath prevailed ... Rev. 5:5

Anonymous

From *Sacred Songs and Solos*

1. 'Twas Je - sus, my Sav - iour, who died on the tree To
2. And when I was will - ing with all things to part, He
3. Though round me the storms of ad - ver - si - ty roll, And the
4. And when with the ran-somed, by Je - sus, my Head, From
o - pen a foun-tain for sin - ners like me; His blood is that
gave me His bless - ing, His love in my heart; So now I am
waves of de - struc-tion en - com - pass my soul, In vain this frail
foun-tain to foun-tain I then shall be led, I'll fall at His
foun - tain which par - don be - stows And cleans - es the foul - est wher -
joined with the con-quer - ing band Who are march - ing to glo - ry at
ves - sel the tem-pest shall toss— My hope is se - cure through the
feet and His mer - cy a - dore, And sing Hal - le - lu - jah to
ev - er it flows.
Je - sus' com-mand.
blood of the cross.
God ev - er - more.
REFRAIN
For the Li - on of Ju - dah shall break ev - ery
chain And give us the vic - tory a - gain and a - gain.

485 The Lily of the Valley

I am the rose of Sharon, and the lily of the valleys. Song of Sol. 2:1

SALVATIONIST Irregular with Refrain

Attributed to Charles W. Fry, 1837-1882

William S. Hays, 1837-1907

1. I have found a friend in Je - sus, He's ev - ery - thing to me,
2. He all my griefs has tak - en and all my sor - rows borne;
3. He will nev - er, nev - er leave me nor yet for - sake me here,
He's the fair - est of ten thou - sand to my soul; The
In temp - ta - tion He's my strong and might - y tower; I have
While I live by faith and do His bless - ed will; A
Li - ly of the Val - ley, in Him a - lone I see
all for Him for - sak - en and all my i - dols torn
wall of fire a - bout me, I've noth - ing now to fear;
All I need to cleanse and make me ful - ly whole.
From my heart, and now He keeps me by His power.
With His man - na He my hun - gry soul shall fill;

The Lily of the Valley

In sor - row He's my com - fort, in trou - ble He's my stay;
Though all the world for - sake me and Sa - tan tempt me sore,
Then sweep - ing up to glo - ry to see His bless - ed face,
He tells me ev - ery care on Him to roll.
Through Je - sus I shall safe - ly reach the goal.
Where riv - ers of de - light shall ev - er roll.
Refrain
He's the Li - ly of the Val - ley, the bright and Morn - ing Star,
He's the fair - est of ten thou - sand to my soul.

486 My Redeemer

Who gave himself for us, that he might redeem us . . . Titus 2:14

MY REDEEMER 8.7.8.7. with Refrain

Philip P. Bliss, 1838-1876

James McGranahan, 1840-1907

1. I will sing of my Re-deem-er And His won-drous love to me;
2. I will tell the won-drous sto - ry, How my lost es - tate to save,
3. I will sing of my Re-deem-er, And His heaven-ly love for me;
On the cru - el cross He suf - fered, From the curse to set me free.
In His bound-less love and mer - cy, He the ran - som free - ly gave.
He from death to life hath brought me, Son of God with Him to be.
REFRAIN
Sing, oh, sing of my Re - deem - er,
of my Re-deem-er, Sing, oh, sing of my Re-deem-er,
With His blood He pur-chased me,
He pur-chased me, With His blood He pur-chased me,
On the cross He sealed my par - don,
He sealed my par - don, On the cross He sealed my par - don,

My Redeemer

Paid the debt, and made me free.
and made me free, and made me free.

I Will Sing of My Redeemer 487

. . . they shall sing to thy name. . . . Psa. 66:4

Philip P. Bliss, 1838-1876

HYFRYDOL 8.7.8.7. with Refrain
Melody by Rowland H. Prichard, 1811-1887

1. I will sing of my Re-deem-er And His won-drous love to me;
2. I will tell the won-drous sto-ry, How my lost es-tate to save,
3. I will praise my dear Re-deem-er, His tri-um-phant power I'll tell,
4. I will sing of my Re-deem-er And His heaven-ly love for me;
On the cru-el cross He suf-fered, From the curse to set me free.
In His bound-less love and mer-cy, He the ran-som free-ly gave.
How the vic-to-ry He giv-eth O-ver sin, and death, and hell.
He from death to life hath brought me, Son of God with Him to be.
REFRAIN
Sing, oh, sing of my Re-deem-er, With His blood He pur-chased me,
On the cross He sealed my par-don, Paid the debt, and made me free.

(For different harmony and higher key see No. 335; for alternate tune see No. 504)

488 Redeemed

Let the redeemed of the Lord say so . . . Psa. 107:2

Fanny J. Crosby, 1820-1915

William J. Kirkpatrick, 1838-1921

1. Re-deemed–how I love to pro-claim it! Re-deemed by the blood of the Lamb;
2. Re-deemed and so hap-py in Je - sus; No lan-guage my rap - ture can tell.
3. I think of my bless-ed Re-deem - er, I think of Him all the day long;
4. I know I shall see in His beau - ty The King in whose law I de - light,
Re-deemed through His in - fi - nite mer - cy, His child, and for - ev - er, I am.
I know that the light of His pres - ence With me doth con - tin - ual - ly dwell.
I sing, for I can-not be si - lent; His love is the theme of my song.
Who lov - ing - ly guard-eth my foot - steps And giv - eth me songs in the night.
REFRAIN
Re - deemed, re - deemed, Re-deemed by the blood of the Lamb;
re-deemed, re-deemed,
Re - deemed, re - deemed, His child, and for - ev - er, I am.
re-deemed, re-deemed,

Since I Have Been Redeemed

489

. . . I will exalt thee, I will praise thy name . . . Isa. 25:1

OTHELLO C.M. with Refrain

Edwin O. Excell, 1851-1921

Melody by Edwin O. Excell, 1851-1921

1. I have a song I love to sing, Since I have been re - deemed,
2. I have a Christ that sat - is - fies, Since I have been re - deemed,
3. I have a wit - ness bright and clear, Since I have been re - deemed,
4. I have a joy I can't ex - press, Since I have been re - deemed,
5. I have a home pre - pared for me, Since I have been re - deemed,
Of my Re - deem-er, Sav-iour, King– Since I have been re - deemed.
To do His will my high-est prize– Since I have been re - deemed.
Dis - pell - ing ev - ery doubt and fear– Since I have been re - deemed.
All through His blood and right-eous-ness– Since I have been re - deemed.
Where I shall dwell e - ter - nal - ly– Since I have been re - deemed.
Refrain
Since I have been re - deemed, Since I have been re-deemed,
Since I have been re-deemed, since I have been re-deemed,
I will glo - ry in His name; Since I have been re -
Since I have been re-deemed, since
deemed, I will glo - ry in the Sav - iour's name.
I have been re-deemed,

490 I'm Redeemed

. . . they sung as it were a new song before the throne . . . Rev. 14:3

Russell K. Carter, 1849-1928 | Russell K. Carter, 1849-1928

1. I can sing now the song Of the blood-ran-somed throng; In my soul there is peace, rest, and calm; I am free from all doubt And I join in the shout— I'm re-deemed by the blood of the Lamb.
2. I have grace for the day, I have help by the way; There is heal-ing and com-fort-ing balm. For my sick-ness there's health, For my pov-er-ty wealth— I'm re-deemed by the blood of the Lamb.
3. In the storm and the night, In the midst of the fight Je-sus puts in my hand vic-tory's palm; O-ver-com-ing all foes, In the Lord I re-pose— I'm re-deemed by the blood of the Lamb.
REFRAIN
I'm re-deemed, I'm re-deemed, Jesus saves me and
I'm re-deemed, I'm re-deemed,
keeps me just now, Hal-le-lu-jah, And I join with the throng

I'm Redeemed

round the throne in the song—I'm re-deemed by the blood of the Lamb.

Jesus Paid It All

491

. . . your sins . . . they shall be as white as snow . . . Isa. 1:18

ALL TO CHRIST 6.6.7.7. with Refrain

Elvina M. Hall, 1820-1889

John T. Grape, 1835-1915

1. I hear the Sav - iour say, "Thy strength in - deed is small;
2. Lord, now in - deed I find Thy power, and Thine a - lone,
3. For noth - ing good have I Where - by Thy grace to claim—
4. And when, be - fore the throne, I stand in Him com - plete,
Child of weak - ness, watch and pray, Find in Me thine all in all."
Can change the lep - er's spots And melt the heart of stone.
I'll wash my gar - ments white In the blood of Cal - vary's Lamb.
"Je - sus died my soul to save," My lips shall still re - peat.
REFRAIN
Je - sus paid it all, All to Him I owe;
Sin had left a crim - son stain, He washed it white as snow.

492 In Tenderness He Sought Me

Rejoice . . . for I have found my sheep . . . Luke 15:6

CLARENDON 7.6.7.6.8.8. with Refrain

W. Spencer Walton, 1850-1906

Adoniram J. Gordon, 1836-1895

1. In ten - der - ness He sought me, Wea - ry and sick with sin, And
2. He washed the bleed-ing sin wounds And poured in oil and wine; He
3. He point - ed to the nail prints, For me His blood was shed; A
4. I'm sit - ting in His pres - ence, The sun-shine of His face, While
5. So while the hours are pass - ing, All now is per - fect rest; I'm
on His shoul - ders brought me Back to His fold a - gain, While
whis - pered to as - sure me, "I've found thee, thou art Mine." I
mock - ing crown so thorn - y Was placed up - on His head: I
with a - dor - ing won - der His bless - ings I re - trace. It
wait - ing for the morn - ing, The bright - est and the best, When
an - gels in His pres-ence sang Un - til the courts of heav - en rang.
nev - er heard a sweet - er voice; It made my ach - ing heart re - joice!
won-dered what He saw in me To suf - fer such deep ag - o - ny.
seems as if e - ter - nal days Are far too short to sound His praise.
He will call us to His side To be with Him, His spot - less Bride.
REFRAIN
Oh, the love that sought me! Oh, the blood that bought me! Oh, the grace that
brought me to the fold— Won-drous grace that brought me to the fold!

The Haven of Rest

493

For we which have believed do enter into rest . . . Heb. 4:3

Henry L. Gilmour, 1837-1920

George D. Moore, 19th century

1. My soul, in sad ex - ile, was out on life's sea, So bur-dened with
2. I yield - ed my - self to His ten - der em-brace, And, faith tak - ing
3. The song of my soul, since the Lord made me whole, Has been the old
sin and dis - tressed, Till I heard a sweet voice say-ing, "Make me your choice,"
hold of the Word, My fet - ters fell off, and I an-chored my soul—
sto - ry so blest Of Je - sus, who'll save who - so - ev - er will have
And I en-tered the ha - ven of rest.
A home in the ha - ven of rest.
REFRAIN
The ha - ven of rest is my Lord. I've an-chored my soul in the
ha - ven of rest, I'll sail the wide seas no more; The tem-pest may
sweep o'er the wild, storm-y deep— In Je - sus I'm safe ev - er - more.

494 Saved, Saved, Saved

... according to his mercy he saved us ... Titus 3:5

Oswald J. Smith, b. 1890

HICKMAN 9.9.9.9. with Refrain
Roger M. Hickman, 1888-1968

1. Saved! saved! saved! my sins are all for - given; Christ is
2. Saved! saved! saved! by grace and grace a - lone; Oh, what
3. Saved! saved! saved! O joy be - yond com - pare! Christ my
mine! I'm on my way to heaven; Once a guilt - y
won - drous love to me was shown, In my stead Christ
life and I His con - stant care; Yield - ing all and
sin - ner, lost, un - done, Now a child of God, saved through His Son.
Je - sus bled and died, Bore my sins, for me was cru - ci - fied.
trust-ing Him a - lone, Liv - ing now each mo - ment as His own.
REFRAIN
Saved! I'm saved through Christ, my all in all; Saved! I'm saved, what-
my all in all;
ev - er may be - fall; He died up - on the cross for me, He bore the aw - ful

Saved, Saved, Saved

pen-al-ty; And now I'm saved e-ter-nal-ly, I'm saved! saved! saved!

Satisfied

495

For he satisfieth the longing soul . . . Psa. 107:9

SATISFIED 8.7.8.7. with Refrain

Clara T. Williams, 1858-1937

Ralph E. Hudson, 1843-1901

1. All my life long I had pant-ed For a drink from some cool spring
2. Feed-ing on the husks a-round me Till my strength was al-most gone,
3. Poor I was, and sought for rich-es, Some-thing that would sat-is-fy;
4. Well of wa-ter, ev-er spring-ing, Bread of life, so rich and free.
That I hoped would quench the burn-ing Of the thirst I felt with-in.
Longed my soul for some-thing bet-ter, On-ly still to hun-ger on.
But the dust I gath-ered round me On-ly mocked my soul's sad cry.
Un-told wealth that nev-er fail-eth, My Re-deem-er is to me.
REFRAIN
Hal-le-lu-jah! I have found Him Whom my soul so long has craved!
Je-sus sat-is-fies my long-ings; Through His blood I now am saved.

496 My Faith Has Found a Resting Place

. . . in that, while we were yet sinners, Christ died for us. Rom. 5:8

LANDAS C.M. with Refrain
Norse Air
Arranged by William J. Kirkpatrick, 1838-1921

Lidie H. Edmunds, 19th century

1. My faith has found a rest-ing place, Not in de-vice nor creed;
2. E-nough for me that Je-sus saves–This ends my fear and doubt;
3. My heart is lean-ing on the Word, The writ-ten Word of God,
4. My great Phy-si-cian heals the sick, The lost He came to save;
I trust the ev-er-liv-ing One, His wounds for me shall plead.
A sin-ful soul I come to Him, He'll nev-er cast me out.
Sal-va-tion by my Sav-iour's name, Sal-va-tion through His blood.
For me His pre-cious blood He shed, For me His life He gave.
REFRAIN
I need no oth-er ar-gu-ment, I need no oth-er plea;
It is e-nough that Je-sus died, And that He died for me.

Trusting Jesus

. . . blessed is the man that trusteth in him. Psa. 34:8

TRUSTING JESUS 7.7.7.7. with Refrain
Ira D. Sankey, 1840-1908

Edgar P. Stites, 1836-1921

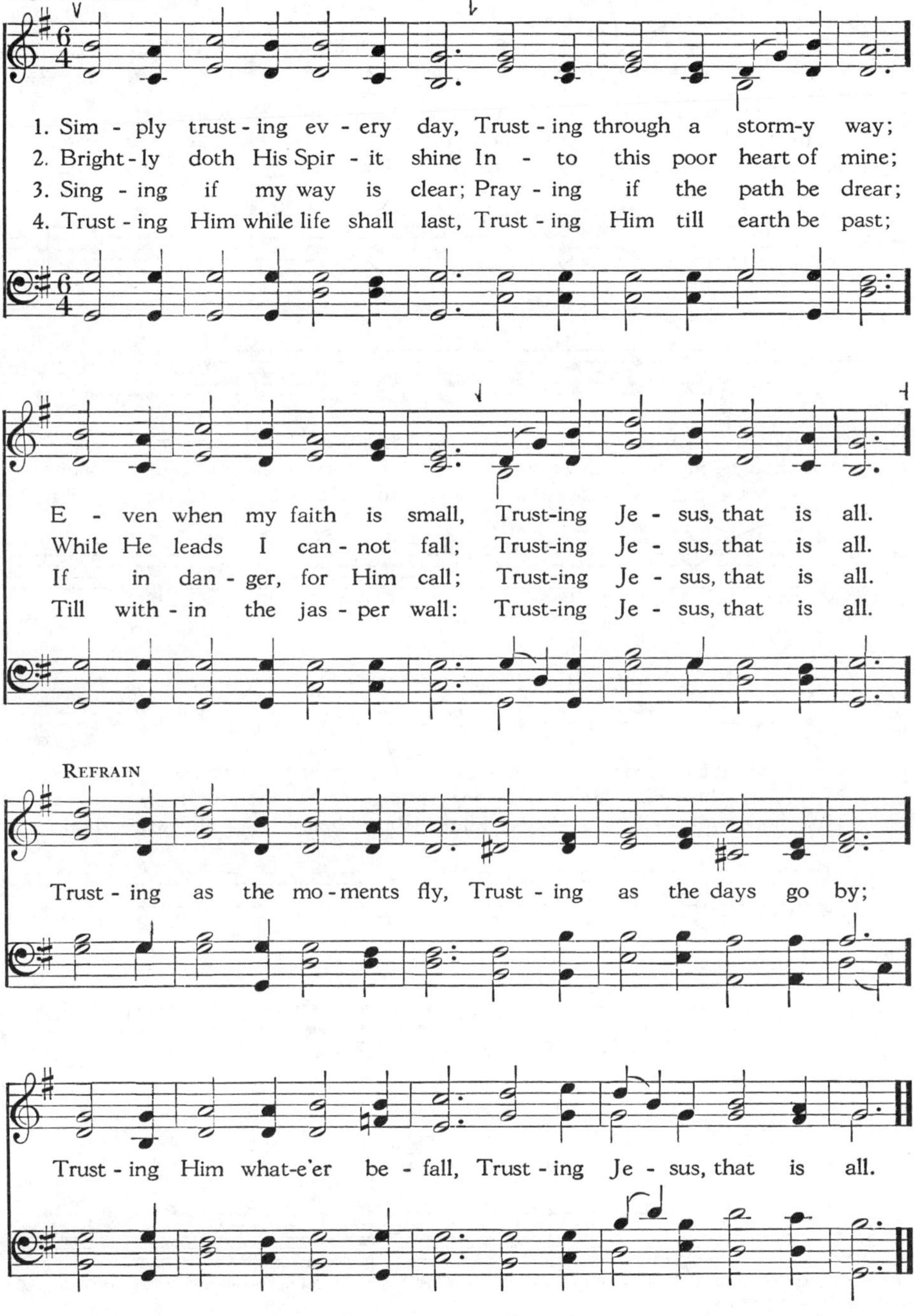
1. Sim - ply trust - ing ev - ery day, Trust - ing through a storm-y way;
2. Bright - ly doth His Spir - it shine In - to this poor heart of mine;
3. Sing - ing if my way is clear; Pray - ing if the path be drear;
4. Trust - ing Him while life shall last, Trust - ing Him till earth be past;
E - ven when my faith is small, Trust-ing Je - sus, that is all.
While He leads I can - not fall; Trust-ing Je - sus, that is all.
If in dan - ger, for Him call; Trust-ing Je - sus, that is all.
Till with - in the jas - per wall: Trust-ing Je - sus, that is all.
REFRAIN
Trust - ing as the mo - ments fly, Trust - ing as the days go by;
Trust - ing Him what-e'er be - fall, Trust - ing Je - sus, that is all.

498 He Lives

. . . he is risen; he is not here . . . Mark 16:6

Alfred H. Ackley, 1887-1960

ACKLEY Irregular with Refrain
Alfred H. Ackley, 1887-1960

1. I serve a ris - en Sav - iour, He's in the world to - day;
2. In all the world a - round me I see His lov - ing care,
3. Re - joice, re - joice, O Chris - tian, lift up your voice and sing
I know that He is liv - ing, what - ev - er men may say;
And though my heart grows wea - ry, I nev - er will de - spair;
E - ter - nal hal - le - lu - jahs to Je - sus Christ the King!
I see His hand of mer - cy, I hear His voice of cheer;
I know that He is lead - ing through all the storm - y blast;
The hope of all who seek Him, the help of all who find,
And just the time I need Him He's al - ways near.
The day of His ap - pear - ing will come at last.
None oth - er is so lov - ing, so good and kind.

He Lives

REFRAIN
He lives, He lives, Christ Je - sus lives to - day!
He lives, He lives,
He walks with me and talks with me a - long life's nar - row way.
He lives, He lives, sal - va - tion to im - part!
He lives, He lives,
You ask me how I know He lives? He lives with - in my heart.

499 Since Jesus Came into My Heart

. . . behold, all things are become new. 2 Cor. 5:17

MCDANIEL 12.8.12.8. with Refrain

Rufus H. McDaniel, 1850-1940

Charles H. Gabriel, 1856-1932

1. What a won-der-ful change in my life has been wrought Since Je-sus came in-to my heart! I have light in my soul for which long I have sought,
2. I have ceased from my wan-dering and go-ing a-stray, Since Je-sus came in-to my heart! And my sins, which were man-y, are all washed a-way,
3. I shall go there to dwell in that Cit-y, I know, Since Je-sus came in-to my heart! And I'm hap-py, so hap-py, as on-ward I go,
Since Je-sus came in-to my heart!
REFRAIN
Since Je-sus came in-to my heart, Since Je-sus came in-to my heart, Floods of joy o'er my soul like the sea bil-lows roll, Since Je-sus came in-to my heart.

Christ Liveth in Me 500

. . . and the life which I now live in the flesh I live by the faith of the Son of God . . . Gal. 2:20

CHRIST LIVETH IN ME C.M. with Refrain

Daniel W. Whittle, 1840-1901

James McGranahan, 1840-1907

1. Once far from God and dead in sin, No light my heart could see;
2. As rays of light from yon - der sun The flowers of earth set free,
3. As lives the flower with - in the seed, As in the cone the tree,
4. With long - ing all my heart is filled That like Him I may be,
But in God's Word the light I found, Now Christ liv - eth in me.
So life and light and love came forth From Christ liv - ing in me.
So, praise the God of truth and grace, His Spir-it dwell-eth in me.
As on the won-drous thought I dwell, That Christ liv - eth in me.
REFRAIN
Christ liv - eth in me, Christ liv - eth in me;
Oh, what a sal - va - tion this, That Christ liv - eth in me!

501 'Twas a Glad Day When Jesus Found Me

. . . we also joy in God through our Lord Jesus Christ . . . Rom. 5:11

Albert S. Reitz, b. 1879 — Albert S. Reitz, b. 1879

1. I was lost in sin when Je - sus found me, But He
2. Oh, the bells of heav - en now are ring - ing, For I
3. Oh, the joy when we shall meet in glo - ry, In the

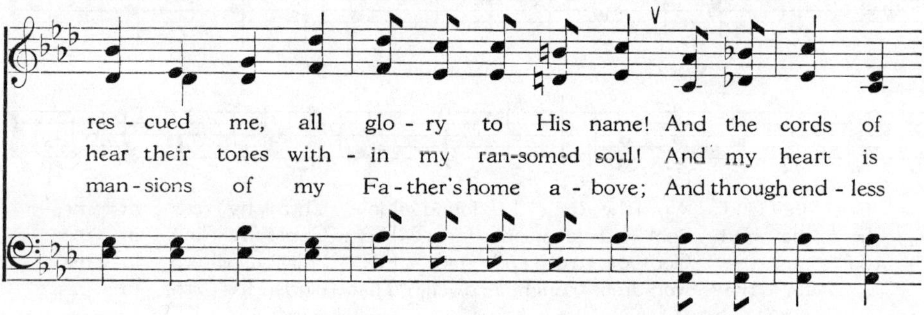
res - cued me, all glo - ry to His name! And the cords of
hear their tones with - in my ran-somed soul! And my heart is
man - sions of my Fa - ther's home a - bove; And through end - less

world - ly pleas - ure bound me Till He saved me from sin and shame.
filled with joy - ful sing - ing Since the Sav-iour hath made me whole.
a - ges tell the sto - ry Of the Sav-iour's re - deem - ing love.

REFRAIN
'Twas a glad day when Je - sus found me, When His strong arms were

'Twas a Glad Day When Jesus Found Me

thrown a - round me, When my sins He bur - ied in the deep - est sea,
And my soul He filled with joy and vic - to - ry; 'Twas a
glad day, Oh, hal - le - lu - jah! 'Twas a glad day He
claimed His own. I will shout a glad ho - san - na in
glo - ry When I see Him up - on His throne.

502 Hallelujah, 'Tis Done!

. . . I will joy in the God of my salvation. Hab. 3:18

Philip P. Bliss, 1838-1876 | Philip P. Bliss, 1838-1876

1. 'Tis the prom - ise of God, full sal - va - tion to give
2. Though the path - way be lone - ly and dan - ger - ous too,
3. Man - y loved ones have I in yon heav - en - ly throng;
4. There's a part in that cho - rus for you and for me,
Un - to him who on Je - sus, His Son, will be - lieve.
Sure - ly Je - sus is a - ble to car - ry me through.
They are safe now in glo - ry, and this is their song:
And the theme of our prais - es for - ev - er will be:
Refrain
Hal - le - lu - jah, 'tis done! I be - lieve on the Son; I am
saved by the blood of the Cru - ci - fied One; Cru - ci - fied One.
1.
2.

Fill My Cup, Lord 503

. . . the fulness of him that filleth all in all. Eph. 1:23

FILL MY CUP 11.8.9.9. with Refrain

Richard Blanchard, 20th century — Richard Blanchard, 20th century

1. Like the wom-an at the well I was seek-ing For things that
2. There are mil-lions in this world who are crav-ing The pleas-ure
3. So, my broth-er, if the things this world gave you Leave hun-gers
could not sat-is-fy; And then I heard my Sav-iour speak-ing: "Draw
earth-ly things af-ford; But none can match the won-drous treas-ure
that won't pass a-way, My bless-ed Lord will come and save you,
from My well that nev-er shall run dry."
That I find in Je-sus Christ my Lord.
If you kneel to Him and hum-bly pray:
REFRAIN
Fill my cup, Lord, I lift it
up, Lord! Come and quench this thirst-ing of my soul; Bread of heav-en,
feed me till I want no more, Fill my cup, fill it up and make me whole!

504 I Will Sing the Wondrous Story

Sing . . . of all his wondrous works. 1 Chron. 16:9

WONDROUS STORY 8.7.8.7. with Refrain

Francis H. Rowley, 1854-1952

Peter P. Bilhorn, 1861-1936

1. I will sing the won-drous sto - ry Of the Christ who died for me,
2. I was lost, but Je - sus found me, Found the sheep that went a - stray,
3. I was bruised, but Je - sus healed me; Faint was I from many a fall;
4. Days of dark - ness still come o'er me, Sor - row's paths I of - ten tread,
5. He will keep me till the riv - er Rolls its wa - ters at my feet;
How He left His home in glo - ry For the cross of Cal - va - ry.
Threw His lov - ing arms a - round me, Drew me back in - to His way.
Sight was gone, and fears pos - sessed me, But He freed me from them all.
But the Sav - iour still is with me; By His hand I'm safe - ly led.
Then He'll bear me safe - ly o - ver Where the loved ones I shall meet.
REFRAIN
Yes, I'll sing the won-drous sto - ry Of the
Yes, I'll sing the won-drous sto - ry, won-drous sto - ry
Christ who died for me, Sing it with the saints in
Of the Christ Sing it with the saints in
glo - ry Gath - ered by the crys - tal sea.
glo - ry, saints in glo - ry Gath - ered by

(For alternate tune see No. 487)

Sunshine in My Soul 505

For God . . . hath shined in our hearts . . . 2 Cor. 4:6

SUNSHINE 9.6.8.6. with Refrain

Eliza E. Hewitt, 1851-1920 John R. Sweney, 1837-1899

1. There is sun-shine in my soul to-day, More glo-ri-ous and bright
2. There is mu-sic in my soul to-day, A car-ol to my King;
3. There is spring-time in my soul to-day, For, when the Lord is near,
4. There is glad-ness in my soul to-day And hope and praise and love
Than glows in an-y earth-ly sky, For Je-sus is my light.
And Je-sus, lis-ten-ing, can hear The songs I can-not sing.
The dove of peace sings in my heart, The flowers of grace ap-pear.
For bless-ings which He gives me now, For joys laid up a-bove.
REFRAIN
Oh, there's sun - shine, bless-ed sun - shine,
Oh, there's sun-shine in my soul, bless-ed sun-shine in my soul,
While the peace-ful, hap-py mo-ments roll; When
hap-py mo-ments roll;
Je-sus shows His smil-ing face, There is sun-shine in my soul.

506 Love Found a Way

For God so loved the world, that he gave his only begotten Son . . . John 3:16

Avis M.B. Christiansen, 1895-1966 — Harry D. Loes, 1892-1965

1. Won - der - ful love that res - cued me, Sunk deep in sin,
2. Love brought my Sav - iour here to die, On Cal - va - ry
3. Love o - pened wide the gates of light To heaven's do - main,
Guilt - y and vile as I could be— No hope with - in;
For such a sin - ful wretch as I— How can it be?
Where in e - ter - nal power and might Je - sus shall reign;
When ev - ery ray of light had fled— Oh, glo - rious day!
Love bridged the gulf twixt me and heaven, Taught me to pray;
Love lift - ed me from depths of woe To end - less day;
Rais - ing my soul from out the dead, Love found a way.
I am re-deemed, set free, for - given— Love found a way.
There was no help in earth be - low— Love found a way.
Refrain
Love found a way to re - deem my soul, Love found a
a way to re-deem my soul,

Love Found a Way

way that could make me whole; Love sent my Lord to the
a way could make me whole; my Lord
cross of shame, Love found a way– Oh, praise His ho - ly name!
to the cross of shame,

I Am Not Skilled to Understand 507

. . . the Lord give thee understanding in all things. 2 Tim. 2:7

Dora Greenwell, 1821-1882

GREENWELL 8.8.8.7.
William J. Kirkpatrick, 1838-1921

1. I am not skilled to un - der - stand What God hath willed, what God hath planned; I on - ly know at His right hand Is One who is my Sav - iour!
2. I take Him at His Word in - deed: "Christ died for sin - ners"—this I read; For in my heart I find a need Of Him to be my Sav - iour!
3. That He should leave His place on high And come for sin - ful man to die, You count it strange? So once did I Be - fore I knew my Sav - iour!
4. And, oh, that He ful - filled may see The trav - ail of His soul in me, And with His work con - tent - ed be, As I with my dear Sav - iour!
5. Yes, liv - ing, dy - ing, let me bring My strength, my sol - ace from this spring— That He who lives to be my King Once died to be my Sav - iour!

508 Love Lifted Me

. . . perfect love casteth out fear . . . 1 John 4:18

LOVE LIFTED ME 7.6.7.6.7.6.7.4. with Refrain

James Rowe, 1865-1933

Howard E. Smith, 1863-1918

1. I was sink - ing deep in sin, Far from the peace - ful shore, Ver - y deep - ly
2. All my heart to Him I give; Ev - er to Him I'll cling, In His bless - ed
3. Souls in dan - ger, look a - bove; Je - sus com - plete - ly saves. He will lift you
stained with - in, Sink - ing to rise no more. But the Mas - ter of the sea
pres - ence live, Ev - er His prais - es sing. Love so might - y and so true
by His love Out of the an - gry waves. He's the Mas - ter of the sea;
Heard my de - spair - ing cry, From the wa - ters lift - ed me; Now safe am I.
Mer - its my soul's best songs; Faith - ful, lov - ing serv - ice, too, To Him be - longs.
Bil - lows His will o - bey. He your Sav - iour wants to be— Be saved to - day.
Refrain
Love lift - ed me! Love lift - ed me! When noth - ing
e - ven me! e - ven me!
else could help, Love lift - ed me. Love lift - ed me.
1.
2.

There Is Power in the Blood 509

. . . we have redemption through his blood . . . Col. 1:14

POWER IN THE BLOOD 10.9.10.8. with Refrain

Lewis E. Jones, 1865-1936 | Lewis E. Jones, 1865-1936

1. Would you be free from the bur - den of sin? There's power in the blood, power in the blood; Would you o'er e - vil a vic - to - ry win? There's wonderful power in the blood.
2. Would you be free from your pas - sion and pride? There's power in the blood, power in the blood; Come for a cleans - ing to Cal - va - ry's tide; There's wonderful power in the blood.
3. Would you be whit - er, much whit - er than snow? There's power in the blood, power in the blood; Sin - stains are lost in its life - giv - ing flow; There's wonderful power in the blood.
4. Would you do serv - ice for Je - sus, your King? There's power in the blood, power in the blood; Would you live dai - ly His prais - es to sing? There's wonderful power in the blood.
REFRAIN
There is power, power, Won-der-work-ing power
there is
In the blood of the Lamb;
In the blood of the Lamb;
There is power, power,
there is
Won - der - work - ing power In the pre - cious blood of the Lamb.

510 The Precious Blood

. . . of Christ, as of a lamb without blemish and without spot. 1 Pet. 1:19

William McDonald, 1820-1901

John H. Stockton, 1813-1877

1. The cross, the cross, the blood-stained cross, The hal-lowed cross I see!
2. A thou-sand, thou-sand foun-tains spring Up from the throne of God;
3. That price-less blood my ran-som paid While I in bond-age stood;
4. By faith that blood now sweeps a-way My sins, as like a flood;
5. This won-drous theme will best em-ploy My harp be-fore my God,
Re-mind-ing me of pre-cious blood That once was shed for me.
But none to me such bless-ings bring As Je-sus' pre-cious blood.
On Je-sus all my sins were laid, He saved me with His blood.
Nor lets one guilt-y blem-ish stay: All praise to Je-sus' blood.
And make all heaven re-sound with joy For Je-sus' cleans-ing blood.
REFRAIN
Oh, the blood, the pre-cious blood That Je-sus shed for me!
Up-on the cross, in crim-son flood, Just now by faith I see.

When I See the Blood

511

. . . I will pass over you . . . Exod. 12:13

John G. Foote, 19th century

John G. Foote, 19th century

1. Christ, our Re-deem-er, died on the cross, Died for the sin-ner, paid all his due; Sprin-kle your soul with the blood of the Lamb,
2. Chief-est of sin-ners, Je-sus will save; All He has prom-ised, that He will do; Wash in the foun-tain o-pened for sin,
3. Judg-ment is com-ing, all will be there, Each one re-ceiv-ing just-ly his due; Hide in the sav-ing, sin-cleans-ing blood,
4. Oh, great com-pas-sion! Oh, bound-less love! Oh, lov-ing-kind-ness, faith-ful and true! Find peace and shel-ter un-der the blood,
And I will pass, will pass o-ver you.
REFRAIN
When I see the blood, When I see the blood, When I see the blood, I will pass, I will pass o-ver you.
When I see the blood, When I see the blood, When I see the blood, o-ver you.

512 Nothing But the Blood

. . . being now justified by his blood, we shall be saved . . . Rom. 5:9

PLAINFIELD 7.8.7.8. with Refrain

Robert Lowry, 1826-1899

Robert Lowry, 1826-1899

1. What can wash a - way my sin? Noth-ing but the blood of Je - sus;
2. For my par-don this I see— Noth-ing but the blood of Je - sus;
3. Noth-ing can for sin a - tone— Noth-ing but the blood of Je - sus;
4. This is all my hope and peace—Noth-ing but the blood of Je - sus;
What can make me whole a - gain? Noth-ing but the blood of Je - sus.
For my cleans-ing, this my plea— Noth-ing but the blood of Je - sus.
Naught of good that I have done— Noth-ing but the blood of Je - sus.
This is all my right-eous-ness— Noth-ing but the blood of Je - sus.
Refrain
Oh, pre - cious is the flow That makes me white as snow;
No oth - er fount I know, Noth-ing but the blood of Je - sus.

Washed in the Blood of the Lamb

. . . the blood of Jesus Christ his Son cleanseth us from all sin. 1 John 1:7

WASHED IN THE BLOOD 11.9.11.9. with Refrain

Elisha A. Hoffman, 1839-1929 | Elisha A. Hoffman, 1839-1929

1. Have you been to Je - sus for the cleans-ing power? Are you washed in the
2. Are you walk - ing dai - ly by the Sav-iour's side? Are you washed in the
3. When the Bride-groom com - eth, will your robes be white, Pure and white in the
4. Lay a - side the gar-ments that are stained with sin And be washed in the
blood of the Lamb? Are you ful - ly trust-ing in His grace this hour? Are you
blood of the Lamb? Do you rest each mo-ment in the Cru - ci - fied? Are you
blood of the Lamb? Will your souls be read - y for the man-sions bright And be
blood of the Lamb; There's a foun-tain flow-ing for the soul un - clean; Oh, be
washed in the blood of the Lamb?
washed in the blood of the Lamb? Are you washed in the blood,
washed in the blood of the Lamb?
washed in the blood of the Lamb.
REFRAIN
Are you washed in the blood,
In the soul-cleans-ing blood of the Lamb? Are your gar-ments spot-less?
of the Lamb?
Are they white as snow? Are you washed in the blood of the Lamb?

514 The Way of the Cross Leads Home

. . . narrow is the way, which leadeth unto life . . . Matt. 7:14

Jessie B. Pounds, 1861-1921

Charles H. Gabriel, 1856-1932

1. I must needs go home by the way of the cross, There's no oth - er
2. I must needs go on in the blood-sprin - kled way, The path that the
3. Then I bid fare - well to the way of the world To walk in it
way but this; I shall ne'er get sight of the gates of light,
Sav - iour trod, If I ev - er climb to the heights sub - lime,
nev - er - more; For my Lord says, "Come," and I seek my home
REFRAIN
If the way of the cross I miss.
Where the soul is at home with God. The way of the cross leads
Where He waits at the o - pen door.
home, The way of the cross leads home; It is
leads home, leads home;
sweet to know, as I on - ward go, The way of the cross leads home.

Hallelujah for the Cross

515

But God forbid that I should glory, save in the cross . . . Gal. 6:14

KINSMAN 6.8.6.8.6.6.6.7. with Refrain

Horatius Bonar, 1808-1889

James McGranahan, 1840-1907

1. The cross it stand-eth fast, Hal - le - lu - jah! Hal - le - lu - jah! De - fy - ing
2. It is the old cross still, Hal - le - lu - jah! Hal - le - lu - jah! Its tri - umph
3. 'Twas here the debt was paid, Hal - le - lu - jah! Hal - le - lu - jah! Our sins on
ev - ery blast, Hal-le - lu - jah! Hal - le - lu - jah! The winds of hell have blown, The
let us tell, Hal-le - lu - jah! Hal - le - lu - jah! The grace of God here shone Through
Je - sus laid, Hal-le - lu - jah! Hal - le - lu - jah! So round the cross we sing Of
world its hate hath shown, Yet it is not o-ver-thrown, Hal-le - lu - jah for the cross!
Christ the bless - ed Son, Who did for sin a - tone, Hal-le - lu - jah for the cross!
Christ, our of - fer - ing, Of Christ, our liv - ing King, Hal-le - lu - jah for the cross!
REFRAIN
Hal - le - lu - jah, hal - le - lu - jah, hal - le - lu - jah for the cross;
Hal - le - lu - jah, hal - le - lu - jah, it shall nev - er suf - fer loss!

516 Never Thirst Again

. . . whosoever drinketh of the water that I shall give him shall never thirst . . . John 4:14

May A. Stephens, 1865-1935
Refrain, anonymous

Stanza by May A. Stephens, 1865-1935
Refrain, anonymous

1. There flows from Cal - va - ry a stream For ev - ery sin - ner's pain,
2. Earth's foun-tains fair but mock our souls, Like des - ert phan - toms lure,
3. This stream from Cal - va - ry still flows To bless and cleanse and heal,
4. Oh, bless - ed stream of pure de - light! Oh, balm for ev - ery pain!
And he that drink - eth, Je - sus said, Shall nev - er thirst a - gain.
And they that drink, the faint - er grow, The keen - er thirst en - dure.
And he that drink - eth, Je - sus said, New life and rest shall feel.
To thee I haste, for Je - sus said, I'll nev - er thirst a - gain.
REFRAIN
What, nev - er thirst a - gain? No, nev - er thirst a - gain; What,
nev - er thirst a - gain? No, nev - er thirst a - gain; For
he that drink - eth, Je - sus said, Shall nev - er, nev - er thirst a - gain.

Jesus Is Victor

Thine, O Lord, is the . . . victory . . . 1 Chron. 29:11

Russell K. Carter, 1849-1928 — Russell K. Carter, 1849-1928

1. Je - sus is Vic - tor! His work is com-plete, Crush-ing all en - e - mies
2. Je - sus is Vic - tor! The bat - tle is won; We can do noth - ing, for
3. Je - sus is Vic - tor! With-out and with - in, Sav - ing and cleans-ing and
4. Je - sus is Vic - tor! Ef - fects of the fall, Tri - als and weak-ness, Him -
5. Je - sus is Vic - tor! The heav-ens shall ring; Dread king of ter - rors, oh,
un - der His feet; Je - sus is Vic - tor! He died not in vain;
all has been done; Je - sus is Vic - tor! The foe from the dust
keep - ing from sin; Je - sus is Vic - tor! O heav - en - ly Dove,
self bears them all; Je - sus is Vic - tor! Though sick - ness as - sail,
where is thy sting? Je - sus is Vic - tor! We'll shout o'er the grave—
Ris - en and glo - ri - fied, Je - sus doth reign.
Nev - er can rise a - gain, if we but trust.
Come to a - bide and make per - fect in love.
He's the Phy - si - cian that nev - er can fail.
Glo - ry to God! He is might - y to save.
REFRAIN
Je - sus is Vic - tor!
Vic - tor! Vic - tor! Ev - er - more His flag's un - furled; Je - sus hath
con-quered! Con-quered! Con-quered The dev - il, the flesh, and the world.

518 Victory in Jesus

But thanks be to God, which giveth us the victory . . . 1 Cor. 15:57

HARTFORD 15.15.15.14. with Refrain

Eugene M. Bartlett, 1885-1941

Eugene M. Bartlett, 1885-1941

1. I heard an old, old sto - ry, how a Sav - iour came from glo - ry,
2. I heard a - bout His heal - ing, of His cleans-ing power re - veal - ing,
3. I heard a - bout a man - sion He has built for me in glo - ry,
How He gave His life on Cal - va - ry to save a wretch like me.
How He made the lame to walk a - gain and caused the blind to see.
And I heard a - bout the streets of gold be - yond the crys - tal sea,
I heard a - bout His groan - ing, of His pre - cious blood's a - ton - ing.
And then I cried, "Dear Je - sus, come and heal my bro - ken spir - it";
A - bout the an - gels sing - ing, and the old re - demp - tion sto - ry;
Then I re - pent - ed of my sins and won the vic - to - ry.
And some - how Je - sus came and brought to me the vic - to - ry.
And some sweet day I'll sing up there the song of vic - to - ry.
REFRAIN
Oh, vic - to - ry in Je - sus, my Sav - iour, for - ev - er! He sought me and

Victory in Jesus

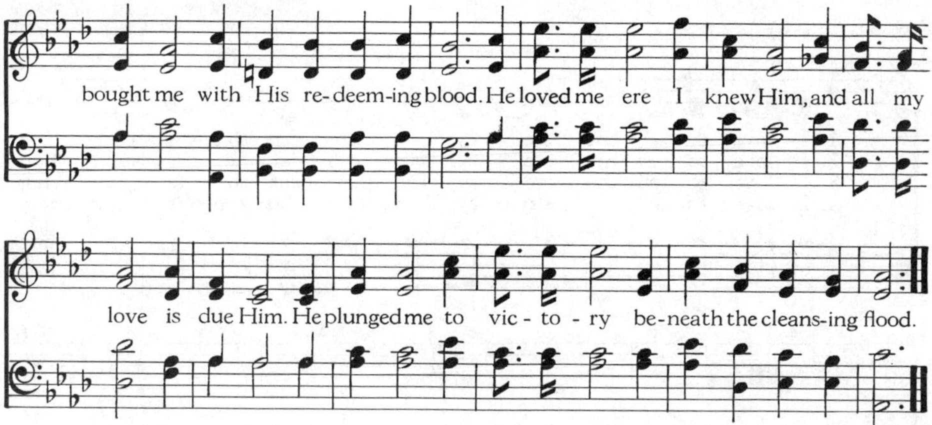
bought me with His re-deem-ing blood. He loved me ere I knew Him, and all my
love is due Him. He plunged me to vic - to - ry be-neath the cleans-ing flood.

Jesus Never Fails 519

. . . the same yesterday, and today, and forever. Heb. 13:8

Arthur A. Luther, 1891-1960 — Arthur A. Luther, 1891-1960

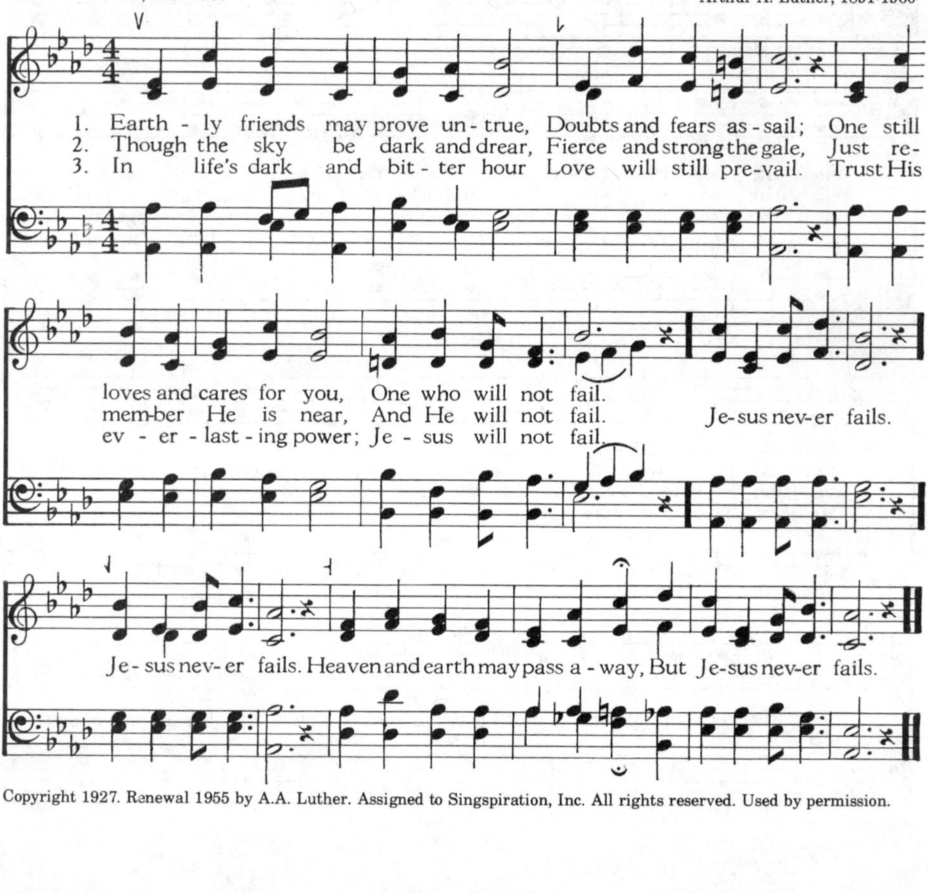
1. Earth - ly friends may prove un - true, Doubts and fears as - sail; One still
2. Though the sky be dark and drear, Fierce and strong the gale, Just re-
3. In life's dark and bit - ter hour Love will still pre-vail. Trust His
loves and cares for you, One who will not fail.
mem-ber He is near, And He will not fail.
ev - er - last - ing power; Je - sus will not fail.
Je-sus nev-er fails.
Je - sus nev- er fails. Heaven and earth may pass a - way, But Je-sus nev-er fails.

520 I Love to Tell the Story

. . . I will declare what he hath done for my soul. Psa. 66:16

HANKEY 7.6.7.6.D. with Refrain

Arabella C. Hankey, 1834-1911

William G. Fischer, 1835-1912

1. I love to tell the sto - ry Of un - seen things a - bove, Of
2. I love to tell the sto - ry, More won - der - ful it seems Than
3. I love to tell the sto - ry, 'Tis pleas - ant to re - peat What
4. I love to tell the sto - ry, For those who know it best Seem
Je - sus and His glo - ry, Of Je - sus and His love. I love to
all the gold - en fan - cies Of all our gold - en dreams. I love to
seems, each time I tell it, More won - der - ful - ly sweet. I love to
hun - ger - ing and thirst - ing To hear it like the rest. And when, in
tell the sto - ry Be - cause I know 'tis true; It sat - is - fies my
tell the sto - ry, It did so much for me; And that is just the
tell the sto - ry, For some have nev - er heard The mes - sage of sal-
scenes of glo - ry, I sing the new, new song, 'Twill be the old, old
Refrain
long - ings As noth - ing else can do.
rea - son I tell it now to thee. I love to tell the sto - ry, 'Twill
va - tion From God's own ho - ly Word.
sto - ry That I have loved so long.
be my theme in glo - ry To tell the old, old sto - ry Of Je - sus and His love.

Tell Me the Old, Old Story

521

... the prophets ... prophesied of the grace that should come ... 1 Pet. 1:10

EVANGEL 7.6.7.6.D. with Refrain

Arabella C. Hankey, 1834-1911

Melody by William H. Doane, 1832-1915

1. Tell me the old, old sto - ry Of un - seen things a - bove, Of Je - sus
2. Tell me the sto - ry slow - ly That I may take it in— That won - der -
3. Tell me the sto - ry soft - ly With ear - nest tones and grave; Re - mem - ber
4. Tell me the same old sto - ry When you have cause to fear That this world's
and His glo - ry, Of Je - sus and His love; Tell me the sto - ry
ful re - demp-tion, God's rem - e - dy for sin; Tell me the sto - ry
I'm the sin - ner Whom Je - sus came to save; Tell me the sto - ry
emp-ty glo - ry Is cost - ing me too dear; Yes, and when that world's
sim-ply As to a lit - tle child, For I am weak and wea - ry,
oft - en, For I for - get so soon; The ear - ly dew of morn - ing
al-ways, If you would real-ly be, In an - y kind of trou - ble,
glo - ry Is dawn-ing on my soul, Tell me the old, old sto - ry:
And help - less and de - filed.
Has passed a - way at noon.
A com - fort - er to me.
"Christ Je - sus makes thee whole."
REFRAIN
Tell me the old, old sto - ry, Tell me the
old, old sto - ry, Tell me the old, old sto - ry Of Je - sus and His love.

522 Tell Me the Story of Jesus

. . . tell them how great things the Lord hath done for thee . . . Mark 5:19

STORY OF JESUS 8.7.8.7. with Refrain
Melody by John R. Sweney, 1837-1899

Fanny J. Crosby, 1820-1915

1. Tell me the sto - ry of Je - sus, Write on my heart ev - ery word;
2. Fast - ing a - lone in the des - ert, Tell of the days that are passed,
3. Tell of the cross where they nailed Him, Writh - ing in an - guish and pain;
Tell me the sto - ry most pre - cious, Sweet - est that ev - er was heard.
How for our sins He was tempt - ed, Yet was tri - um - phant at last.
Tell of the grave where they laid Him, Tell how He liv - eth a - gain.
Tell how the an - gels, in cho - rus, Sang as they wel - comed His birth,
Tell of the years of His la - bor, Tell of the sor - row He bore;
Love in that sto - ry so ten - der Clear - er than ev - er I see;
"Glo - ry to God in the high - est! Peace and good ti - dings to earth."
He was de - spised and af - flict - ed, Home - less, re - ject - ed, and poor.
Stay, let me weep while you whis - per, Love paid the ran - som for me.
Refrain
Tell me the sto - ry of Je - sus, Write on my heart ev - ery word;

Tell Me the Story of Jesus

Tell me the sto - ry most pre - cious, Sweet-est that ev - er was heard.

Healing at the Fountain

523

. . . with thee is the fountain of life . . . Psa. 36:9

Fanny J. Crosby, 1820-1915

William J. Kirkpatrick, 1838-1921

1. There is heal - ing at the foun - tain, Come, be - hold the crim-son tide,
2. There is heal - ing at the foun - tain, Come and find it, wea - ry soul,
3. There is heal - ing at the foun - tain, Look to Je - sus now and live,
4. There is heal - ing at the foun - tain, Pre - cious foun-tain filled with blood;
Flow - ing down from Cal-vary's moun-tain, Where the Prince of Glo - ry died.
There your sins may all be cov - ered; Je - sus waits to make you whole.
At the cross lay down thy bur - den; All thy wan-derings He'll for - give.
Come, oh come, the Sav - iour calls you, Come and plunge be-neath its flood.
REFRAIN
Oh, the foun-tain! Bless-ed heal-ing foun-tain! I am glad 'tis flow - ing free;
Oh, the foun-tain! Pre-cious, cleans-ing foun-tain! Praise the Lord, it cleans-eth me.

524 The Great Physician

Who forgiveth all thine iniquities; who healeth all thy diseases. Psa. 103:3

William Hunter, 1811-1877

GREAT PHYSICIAN 8.7.8.7. with Refrain
Melody by John H. Stockton, 1813-1877

1. The great Phy-si-cian now is near, The sym-pa-thiz-ing Je-sus;
2. Your man-y sins are all for-given—Oh, hear the voice of Je-sus;
3. All glo-ry to the dy-ing Lamb, I now be-lieve in Je-sus;
4. His name dis-pels my guilt and fear, No oth-er name but Je-sus;
He speaks the droop-ing heart to cheer—Oh, hear the voice of Je-sus.
Go on your way in peace to heaven And wear a crown with Je-sus.
I love the bless-ed Sav-iour's name, I love the name of Je-sus.
Oh, how my soul de-lights to hear The charm-ing name of Je-sus.
REFRAIN
Sweet-est note in ser-aph song, Sweet-est name on mor-tal tongue,
Sweet-est car-ol ev-er sung— Je-sus, bless-ed Je-sus.

He Is Able to Deliver Thee 525

. . . our God . . . is able to deliver us . . . Dan. 3:17

William A. Ogden, 1841-1897 | William A. Ogden, 1841-1897

1. 'Tis the grand-est theme through the a - ges rung; 'Tis the grand-est theme for a
2. 'Tis the grand-est theme in the earth or main; 'Tis the grand-est theme for a
3. 'Tis the grand-est theme, let the ti-dings roll To the guilt - y heart, to the
mor-tal tongue; 'Tis the grand-est theme that the world e'er sung—"Our God is
mor-tal strain; 'Tis the grand-est theme, tell the world a - gain—"Our God is
sin - ful soul; Look to God in faith, He will make thee whole—"Our God is
a - ble to de - liv - er thee." He is a - ble to de - liv - er thee,
REFRAIN
He is a - ble to de - liv - er thee; Though by sin op-pressed,
Go to Him for rest—"Our God is a - ble to de - liv - er thee."

526 Jesus Is Mighty to Save

. . . he is able also to save them to the uttermost . . . Heb. 7:25

Annie Wittenmyer, 19th century — William G. Fischer, 1835-1912

1. All glo - ry to Je - sus be given That life and sal - va - tion are free!
2. From dark-ness of sin and de - spair Out in - to the light of His love,
3. The rap - tur-ous heights of His love! The meas-ure-less depths of His grace!
4. In Him all my wants are sup - plied; In Him is my heav-en be - low.
Now all may be washed and for - given; Yes, Je - sus can save e - ven me!
He has brought me and made me an heir To king-doms and man-sions a - bove.
My soul all His full-ness would prove And live in His lov-ing em - brace.
And free - ly to me is ap - plied His blood that makes whit-er than snow!
REFRAIN
Yes, Je - sus is might - y to save! And all His sal -
va - tion may know; On His bos - om I lean, And His
blood makes me clean— For His blood wash - es whit - er than snow!

What a Wonderful Saviour

. . . who is the Saviour of all men, specially of those that believe. 1 Tim. 4:10

Elisha A. Hoffman, 1839-1929 | Elisha A. Hoffman, 1839-1929

1. Christ has for sin a - tone-ment made, What a won - der - ful Sav - iour!
2. I praise Him for the cleans-ing blood, What a won - der - ful Sav - iour!
3. He cleansed my heart from all its sin, What a won - der - ful Sav - iour!
4. He walks be - side me all the way, What a won - der - ful Sav - iour!
5. He gives me o - ver - com-ing power, What a won - der - ful Sav - iour!
6. To Him I've giv - en all my heart, What a won - der - ful Sav - iour!
We are re-deemed! The price is paid! What a won - der - ful Sav - iour!
That rec - on - ciled my soul to God; What a won - der - ful Sav - iour!
And now He reigns and rules there - in; What a won - der - ful Sav - iour!
And keeps me faith - ful day by day; What a won - der - ful Sav - iour!
And tri - umph in each try - ing hour; What a won - der - ful Sav - iour!
The world shall nev - er share a part; What a won - der - ful Sav - iour!
REFRAIN
What a won - der - ful Sav - iour is Je - sus, my Je - sus!
What a won - der - ful Sav - iour is Je - sus, my Lord!

528 Wonderful, Wonderful Jesus

... and his name shall be called Wonderful ... Isa. 9:6

Anna B. Russell, 1862-1954

Ernest O. Sellers, 1869-1952

1. There is nev - er a day so drear - y, There is nev - er a
2. There is nev - er a cross so heav - y, There is nev - er a
3. There is nev - er a care or bur - den, There is nev - er a
4. There is nev - er a guilt - y sin - ner, There is nev - er a
night so long (so long), But the soul that is trust - ing Je - sus Will
weight of woe (of woe), But that Je - sus will help to car - ry Be -
grief or loss (or loss), But that Je - sus in love will light - en When
wan - dering one (not one), But that God can in mer - cy par - don Through
some-where find a song (a song).
cause He lov - eth so (loves so).
car - ried to the cross (the cross).
Je - sus Christ, His Son (His Son).
REFRAIN
Won - der - ful, won - der - ful Je - sus,
In the heart He im-plant-eth a song; A song of de - liv-erance, of
He plant-eth a song,
cour - age, of strength, In the heart He im - plant-eth a song (a song).

The Light of the World 529

Then spake Jesus again unto them, saying, I am the light of the world . . . John 8:12

LIGHT OF THE WORLD 11.8.11.8. with Refrain

Philip P. Bliss, 1838-1876

Philip P. Bliss, 1838-1876

1. The whole world was lost in the dark-ness of sin; The Light of the world is Je - sus; Like sun-shine at noon-day His glo - ry shone in,
2. No dark-ness have we who in Je - sus a - bide, The Light of the world is Je - sus; We walk in the light when we fol - low our guide,
3. Ye dwell - ers in dark-ness with sin - blind - ed eyes, The Light of the world is Je - sus; Go, wash at His bid-ding, and light will a - rise,
4. No need of the sun-light in heav - en, we're told, The Light of the world is Je - sus; The Lamb is the Light in the cit - y of gold,
The Light of the world is Je - sus.
REFRAIN
Come to the Light, 'tis shin - ing for thee; Sweet - ly the Light has dawned up - on me; Once I was blind, but now I can see; The Light of the world is Je - sus.

530 Verily, I Say unto You

. . . He that . . . believeth . . . hath everlasting life . . . John 5:24

VERILY 10.10.10.6. with Refrain

James McGranahan, 1840-1907 James McGranahan, 1840-1907

1. Oh, what a Sav - iour that He died for me! From con - dem -
2. All my in - i - qui - ties on Him were laid, All my in -
3. Though poor and need - y, I can trust my Lord; Though weak and
4. Though all un - wor - thy, yet I will not doubt; For him that
na - tion He hath made me free; "He that be - liev - eth on the
debt - ed - ness by Him was paid; All who be - lieve on Him, the
sin - ful, I be - lieve His Word; Oh, glad mes - sage! Ev - ery
com - eth He will not cast out: "He that be - liev - eth," oh, the
Son," saith He, "Hath ev - er - last - ing life."
Lord hath said, "Have ev - er - last - ing life."
child of God "Hath ev - er - last - ing life."
good news shout! "Hath ev - er - last - ing life."
Refrain
"Ver - i - ly, ver - i - ly,
I say un - to you; Ver - i - ly, ver - i - ly," mes - sage ev - er new!

Verily, I Say unto You

"He that be - liev - eth on the Son"–'tis true!–"Hath ev - er - last - ing life!"

Revive Us Again 531

. . . that thy people may rejoice . . . Psa. 85:6

William P. Mackay, 1839-1885

REVIVE US AGAIN 11.11. with Refrain
John J. Husband, 1760-1825

1. We praise Thee, O God, for the Son of Thy love, For Je - sus who died and is now gone a - bove.
2. We praise Thee, O God, for Thy Spir - it of light, Who has shown us our Sav - iour and scat-tered our night.
3. All glo - ry and praise to the Lamb that was slain, Who has borne all our sins and has cleansed ev - ery stain.
4. Re - vive us a - gain, fill each heart with Thy love; May each soul be re - kin - dled with fire from a - bove.
REFRAIN
Hal - le - lu - jah! Thine the glo - ry, Hal-le - lu - jah! A - men; Hal - le - lu - jah! Thine the glo - ry; Re - vive us a - gain.

532 A Revival Hymn

. . . O Lord, revive thy work . . . Hab. 3:2

Oswald J. Smith, b. 1890

Bentley D. Ackley, 1872-1958

1. Re - vive Thy work, O Lord! And man - i - fest Thy power;
2. Re - vive Thy work, O Lord! And ev - ery soul in - spire;
3. Re - vive Thy work, O Lord! And give a - bound - ing joy;
4. Re - vive Thy work, O Lord! And make Thy ser - vants bold;
5. Re - vive Thy work, O Lord! Ful - fill Thy prom - ise true;
Thy work, O Lord!
Oh, come up - on Thy church and give A pen - i - ten - tial shower!
Oh, kin - dle in each heart, we pray, The Pen - te - cos - tal fire!
Oh, fill our hearts with per - fect love And burn out all al - loy!
Con - vict of sin and work once more As in the days of old.
Let Je - sus Christ be glo - ri - fied And great things for us do.
Refrain
Re - vive Thy work, O Lord, Come now and an - swer prayer;
an-swer prayer;
Oh, come in Ho - ly Spir - it power And save men ev - ery - where.

Ye Must Be Born Again 533

Jesus . . . said . . . be born again . . . John 3:3

BORN AGAIN Irregular with Refrain

William T. Sleeper, 1819-1904

George C. Stebbins, 1846-1945

1. A rul-er once came to Je-sus by night To ask Him the
2. Ye chil-dren of men, at-tend to the word So sol-emn-ly
3. Oh, ye who would en-ter that glo-ri-ous rest And sing with the
4. A dear one in heav-en thy heart yearns to see At the beau-ti-ful
way of sal-va-tion and light; The Mas-ter made an-swer in
ut-tered by Je-sus, the Lord; And let not this mes-sage to
ran-somed the song of the blest, The life ev-er-last-ing if
gate may be watch-ing for thee; Then list to the note of this
words true and plain, "Ye must be born a-gain."
you be in vain, "Ye must be born a-gain."
ye would ob-tain, "Ye must be born a-gain."
sol-emn re-frain, "Ye must be born a-gain."
REFRAIN
"Ye must be born a-gain, Ye must be born a-gain, I ver-i-ly,
ver-i-ly say un-to you, Ye must be born a-gain."

534 Ring the Bells of Heaven

. . . joy shall be in heaven over one sinner that repenteth . . . Luke 15:7

William O. Cushing, 1823-1902 George F. Root, 1820-1895

1. Ring the bells of heav - en! There is joy to - day For a soul re -
2. Ring the bells of heav - en! There is joy to - day For the wan-derer
3. Ring the bells of heav - en! Spread the feast to - day! An - gels, swell the
turn-ing from the wild! See, the Fa - ther meets him out up - on the way,
now is rec - on - ciled: Yes, a soul is res - cued from his sin - ful way
glad, tri-um-phant strain! Tell the joy - ful ti - dings, bear it far a - way,
Wel - com-ing His wea - ry, wan-dering child.
And is born a - new a ran-somed child.
For a pre-cious soul is born a - gain.
REFRAIN
Glo - ry! Glo - ry! How the
an - gels sing; Glo - ry! Glo - ry! How the loud harps ring! 'Tis the ran-somed
ar - my, like a might - y sea, Peal - ing forth the an-them of the free.

There Shall Be Showers of Blessing

. . . I will cause the shower to come down in his season . . . Ezek. 34:26

SHOWERS OF BLESSING 8.7.8.7. with Refrain

Daniel W. Whittle, 1840-1901

James McGranahan, 1840-1907

1. There shall be show - ers of bless - ing— This is the prom-ise of love;
2. There shall be show - ers of bless - ing— Pre - cious, re - viv - ing a - gain;
3. There shall be show - ers of bless - ing— Send them up - on us, O Lord!
4. There shall be show - ers of bless - ing— Oh, that to - day they might fall,
5. There shall be show - ers of bless - ing, If we but trust and o - bey;
There shall be sea - sons re - fresh - ing Sent from the Sav-iour a - bove.
O - ver the hills and the val - leys Sound of a - bun-dance of rain.
Grant to us now a re - fresh - ing; Come, and now hon - or Thy Word.
Now as to God we're con - fess - ing, Now as on Je - sus we call!
There shall be sea - sons re - fresh - ing, If we let God have His way.
REFRAIN
Show - - ers of bless - ing,
Show - ers, show - ers of bless - ing, Show - ers of bless - ing we need;
Mer - cy drops round us are fall - ing, But for the show-ers we plead.

536 The Ninety and Nine

. . . he rejoiceth more of that sheep, than of the ninety and nine . . . Matt. 18:13

Elizabeth C. Clephane, 1830-1869

Melody by Ira D. Sankey, 1840-1908

1. There were nine - ty and nine that safe - ly lay In the
2. "Lord, Thou hast here Thy nine - ty and nine— Are
3. But none of the ran - somed ev - er knew How
4. "Lord, whence are those blood - drops all the way That
5. And all through the moun - tains, thun - der riven, And
shel - ter of the fold; But one was out on the
they not e - nough for Thee?" But the Shep - herd made an - swer,
deep were the wa - ters crossed; Nor how dark was the night that the
mark out the moun - tain's track?" "They were shed for one who had
up from the rock - y steep, There rose a cry to the
hills a - way, Far off from the gates of gold, A -
"This of Mine Has wan - dered a - way from Me; And al -
Lord passed through Ere He found His sheep that was lost.
gone a - stray, Ere the Shep - herd could bring him back." "Lord,
gate of heaven, "Re - joice, I have found My sheep!" And the
way on the moun - tains wild and bare, A - way from the ten - der
though the road be rough and steep, I go to the des - ert to
Out in the des - ert He heard its cry, Sick and help - less and
whence are Thy hands so rent and torn?" "They are pierced to - night by
an - gels ech - oed a - round the throne, "Re - joice, for the Lord brings

The Ninety and Nine

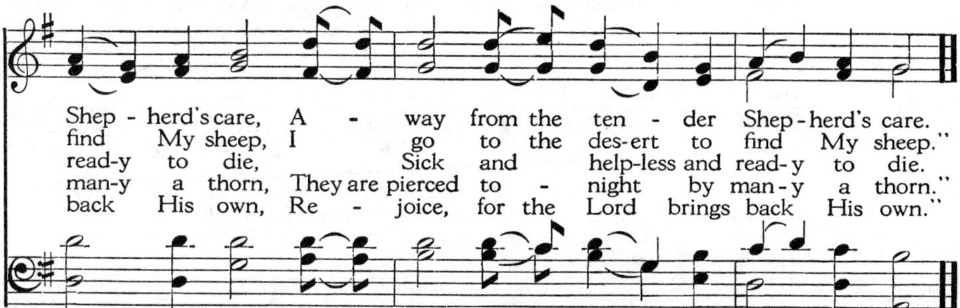
Shep - herd's care, A - way from the ten - der Shep - herd's care.
find My sheep, I go to the des - ert to find My sheep."
read - y to die, Sick and help - less and read - y to die.
man - y a thorn, They are pierced to - night by man - y a thorn."
back His own, Re - joice, for the Lord brings back His own."

Jesus Only, Let Me See 537

... they saw no man, save Jesus only. Matt. 17:8

Oswald J. Smith, b. 1890

Daniel B. Towner, 1850-1919

1. For sal - va - tion full and free, Pur - chased once on Cal - va - ry,
2. He my guide from day to day As I jour - ney on life's way;
3. May my mod - el ev - er be Christ the Lord, and none save He,
4. He shall reign from shore to shore; His the glo - ry ev - er - more.
Christ a - lone shall be my plea— Je - sus! Je - sus on - ly!
Close be - side Him let me stay— Je - sus! Je - sus on - ly!
That the world may see in me— Je - sus! Je - sus on - ly!
Heaven and earth shall bow be - fore— Je - sus! Je - sus on - ly!
REFRAIN
Je - sus on - ly, let me see, Je - sus on - ly, none save He;
Then my song shall ev - er be— Je - sus! Je - sus on - ly!

538 Wonderful Words of Life

. . . the words that I speak unto you . . . they are life. John 6:63

WORDS OF LIFE 8.6.8.6.6.6. with Refrain

Philip P. Bliss, 1838-1876

Melody by Philip P. Bliss, 1838-1876

1. Sing them o-ver a-gain to me, Won-der-ful words of life!
Let me more of their beau-ty see, Won-der-ful words of life!
Words of life and beau-ty, Teach me faith and du-ty!
2. Christ, the bless-ed One, gives to all Won-der-ful words of life!
Sin-ner, list to the lov-ing call, Won-der-ful words of life!
All so free-ly giv-en, Woo-ing us to heav-en!
3. Sweet-ly ech-o the gos-pel call, Won-der-ful words of life!
Of-fer par-don and peace to all, Won-der-ful words of life!
Je-sus, on-ly Sav-iour, Sanc-ti-fy for-ev-er!
Refrain
Beau-ti-ful words! Won-der-ful words! Won-der-ful words of life!
Beau-ti-ful words! Won-der-ful words! Won-der-ful words of life!

We Have an Anchor 539

Which hope we have as an anchor of the soul . . . Heb. 6:19

ANCHOR 10.9.10.9. with Refrain

Priscilla J. Owens, 1829-1907

William J. Kirkpatrick, 1838-1921

1. Will your an - chor hold in the storms of life, When the clouds un - fold
2. It is safe - ly moored, 'twill the storm with-stand, For 'tis well se - cured
3. It will firm - ly hold in the straits of fear, When the break-ers have told
4. When our eyes be - hold through the gath - ering night The cit - y of gold,
their wings of strife? When the strong tides lift and the ca - bles strain,
by the Sav - iour's hand; And the ca - bles, passed from His heart to mine,
the reef is near; Though the tem - pest rave and the wild winds blow,
our har - bor bright, We shall an - chor fast by the heaven-ly shore,
Will your an - chor drift or firm re - main?
Can de - fy that blast through strength di - vine.
Not an an - gry wave shall our bark o'er - flow.
With the storms all past for - ev - er - more.
REFRAIN
We have an an - chor that
keeps the soul Stead - fast and sure while the bil - lows roll, Fas-tened to the
Rock which can - not move, Ground-ed firm and deep in the Sav-iour's love.

540 Christ Receiveth Sinful Men

... This man receiveth sinners, and eateth with them. Luke 15:2

Erdmann Neumeister, 1671-1756
Translated by Emma F. Bevan, 1827-1909

NEUMEISTER 7.7.7.7. with Refrain
James McGranahan, 1840-1907

1. Sin - ners Je - sus will re - ceive; Sound this word of grace to all
2. Come, and He will give you rest; Trust Him, for His Word is plain;
3. Now my heart con-demns me not; Pure be - fore the law I stand;
4. Christ re - ceiv - eth sin - ful men, E - ven me with all my sin;
Who the heaven - ly path - way leave, All who lin - ger, all who fall.
He will take the sin - ful - est; Christ re - ceiv - eth sin - ful men.
He who cleansed me from all spot Sat - is - fied its last de - mand.
Purged from ev - ery spot and stain, Heaven with Him I en - ter in.
Refrain
Sing it o'er and o'er a - gain; Christ re -
Sing it o'er a - gain, sing it o'er a - gain; Christ re -
ceiv - eth sin - ful men; Make the mes sage
ceiv-eth sin-ful men, Christ re - ceiv-eth sin-ful men; Make the mes-sage plain,
clear and plain: Christ re - ceiv - eth sin - ful men.
make the mes-sage plain:

Jesus Is Able

541

. . . what he had promised, he was able also to perform. Rom 4:21

Albert B. Simpson, 1843-1919 — Margaret M. Simpson, 1876-1958

1. Je-sus is a-ble to save you Though you have gone a-stray;
2. Je-sus is a-ble to cleanse you Whit-er than wool or snow,
3. Je-sus is a-ble to keep you Safe from the tempt-er's power;
4. Je-sus is a-ble to make you Hap-py the whole day long,
5. Je-sus is a-ble to take you Home when your life is done,
He will for-give you free-ly, Wash all your sins a-way.
A-ble to save you from sin-ning, Guide you wher-ev-er you go.
Je-sus is a-ble to give you Strength for the try-ing hour.
Fill-ing your heart with sun-shine, Fill-ing your mouth with song.
Home to a crown and king-dom Bright-er than star or sun.
Refrain
A-ble to save, yes, a-ble to save, Je-sus is a-ble and
will-ing to save; Once His own life for your ran-som He gave,
And He is a-ble and will-ing to save.

542 Once for All

. . . the offering of the body of Jesus Christ once for all. Heb. 10:10

ONCE FOR ALL 10.10.9.8. with Refrain
Melody by Philip P. Bliss, 1838-1876

Philip P. Bliss, 1838-1876

1. Free from the law— oh, hap-py con-di-tion! Je - sus hath bled, and
2. There on the cross your bur-den up-bear-ing, Thorns on His brow your
3. Now are we free–there's no con-dem-na-tion; Je - sus pro-vides a
4. Chil-dren of God— oh, glo-ri-ous call-ing, Sure-ly His grace will
there is re-mis-sion; Cursed by the law and bruised by the fall,
Sav-iour is wear-ing; Nev-er a-gain your sin need ap-pall,
per-fect sal-va-tion: "Come un-to Me," oh, hear His sweet call,
keep us from fall-ing; Pass-ing from death to life at His call,
REFRAIN
Grace hath re-deemed us once for all.
You have been par-doned once for all.
Come, and He saves us once for all.
Bless-ed sal-va-tion once for all.
Once for all— oh, sin-ner, re-
ceive it; Once for all— oh, doubt-er, be-lieve it; Cling to the
cross, the bur-den will fall, Christ hath re-deemed us once for all.

The Saviour Can Solve Every Problem 543

Ah Lord God! . . . there is nothing too hard for thee. Jer. 32:17

Oswald J. Smith, b. 1890 — Bentley D. Ackley, 1872-1958

1. The Sav - iour can lift ev-ery bur - den, The heav - y as well as the light;
2. The Sav - iour can bear ev-ery sor - row, In Him there is com-fort and rest:
3. The Sav - iour can strength-en the wea - ry, His grace is suf - fi - cient for all;
4. The Sav - iour can break sin's do - min - ion, The vic - tory He won long a - go;
5. The Sav - iour can sat - is - fy ful - ly The heart that the world can-not fill;
His strength is made per - fect in weak-ness, In Him there is pow - er and might.
No mat - ter how great the af - flic - tion, He on - ly per-mits what is best.
He knows ev - ery step of the path-way And lis - tens to hear when we call.
In Him there is free-dom from bond-age, He's a - ble to con-quer the foe.
His pres - ence will sanc - ti - fy whol - ly The soul that is yield - ed and still.
REFRAIN
The Sav-iour can solve ev-ery prob-lem, The tan-gles of life can un - do;
He can un-do;
There is noth-ing too hard for Je - sus, There is noth-ing that He can-not do.

544 Whosoever Will May Come

. . . whosoever will, let him take the water of life freely. Rev. 22:17

WHOSOEVER Irregular with Refrain

Philip P. Bliss, 1838-1876 | Philip P. Bliss, 1838-1876

1. "Who - so - ev - er hear - eth," shout, shout the sound! Spread the bless-ed ti - dings
2. Who - so - ev - er com - eth need not de - lay, Now the door is o - pen,
3. "Who - so - ev - er will," the prom - ise is se - cure; "Who - so - ev - er will," for -
all the world a - round; Tell the joy - ful news wher - ev - er man is found,
en - ter while you may; Je - sus is the true, the on - ly liv - ing Way:
ev - er must en - dure; "Who - so - ev - er will," 'tis life for - ev - er-more;
REFRAIN
"Who - so - ev - er will may come." "Who - so - ev - er will, who - so - ev - er will!"
Send the proc - la - ma - tion o - ver vale and hill; 'Tis a lov - ing
Fa - ther calls the wan-derer home: "Who - so - ev - er will may come."

Grace Greater Than Our Sin

545

. . . where sin abounded, grace did much more abound. Rom. 5:20

Julia H. Johnston, 1849-1919

MOODY 9.9.9.9. with Refrain
Daniel B. Towner, 1850-1919

1. Mar - vel - ous grace of our lov - ing Lord, Grace that ex - ceeds our
2. Sin and de - spair, like the sea waves cold, Threat-en the soul with
3. Dark is the stain that we can - not hide, What can a - vail to
4. Mar - vel - ous, in - fi - nite, match - less grace Free - ly be - stowed on
sin and our guilt, Yon - der on Cal - va - ry's mount out - poured,
in - fi - nite loss; Grace that is great - er, yes, grace un - told,
wash it a - way? Look! There is flow - ing a crim - son tide;
all who be - lieve; You that are long - ing to see His face,
There where the blood of the Lamb was spilt.
Points to the ref - uge, the might - y cross.
Whit - er than snow you may be to - day.
Will you this mo - ment His grace re - ceive?
REFRAIN
Grace, grace,
Mar - vel - ous grace,
God's grace, Grace that will par - don and cleanse with - in; Grace,
in - fi - nite grace,
Mar - vel - ous
grace, God's grace, Grace that is great - er than all our sin.
grace, in - fi - nite grace,

546 Trust and Obey

. . . if ye will obey . . . ye shall be a peculiar treasure unto me . . . Exod. 19:5

TRUST AND OBEY 6.6.9.D. with Refrain

John H. Sammis, 1846-1919

Daniel B. Towner, 1850-1919

1. When we walk with the Lord In the light of His Word, What a glo - ry He
2. Not a shad - ow can rise, Not a cloud in the skies, But His smile quick-ly
3. But we nev - er can prove The de - lights of His love Un - til all on the
4. Then in fel - low - ship sweet We will sit at His feet, Or we'll walk by His
sheds on our way! While we do His good will, He a - bides with us still
drives it a - way; Not a doubt nor a fear, Not a sigh nor a tear
al - tar we lay; For the fa - vor He shows And the joy He be-stows
side in the way; What He says we will do, Where He sends we will go—
And with all who will trust and o - bey.
Can a - bide while we trust and o - bey.
Are for them who will trust and o - bey.
Nev - er fear, on - ly trust and o - bey.
REFRAIN
Trust and o - bey, for there's no oth - er
way To be hap - py in Je - sus, But to trust and o - bey.

'Tis Better Far to Follow Jesus 547

. . . Christ also suffered for us . . . that ye should follow his steps. 1 Pet. 2:21

May A. Stephens, 1865-1935

Anonymous
Arranged by May A. Stephens, 1865-1935

1. 'Tis bet - ter far to fol - low Je - sus, No mat - ter where His hand may lead,
2. What mat - ter if the way be thorn - y Or if dark waves of sor-row roll?
3. What mat - ter while I walk with Je - sus If to Geth-sem - a - ne I go,
4. What mat - ter if I stand at Cal-vary And lay my life down for the lost?
Than with the world's vain fleet-ing pleas-ures Our souls' im - mor - tal long-ings feed;
Be - side me walks my lov - ing Sav - iour And I shall safe - ly reach the goal;
And in the dark-ness of its shad-ows The full - est cup of an-guish know?
'Twas on - ly what He did be - fore me—I'll fol - low Him at an - y cost;
For He has made us for His glo - ry And His are joys that nev - er die;
For me He bore the thorns and scoff-ing, It was for me He bled and died;
For me shall be the af - ter sweet-ness Of an - gels' min - is-try and strength,
Then from the pain, and shame, and dy - ing, In glo-rious power I'll rise a - gain
'Tis sweet - er far to fol - low Je - sus, For He a - lone can sat - is - fy.
'Tis sweet that I may share His sor - row And walk for - ev - er at His side.
And though the wa - ters may be bit - ter, In heav - en's peace I'll rest at length.
To share the glo - ry of His king - dom And ev - er-more with Je - sus reign.

548 Take the Name of Jesus with You

... do all in the name of the Lord Jesus ... Col. 3:17

PRECIOUS NAME 8.7.8.7. with Refrain

Lydia Baxter, 1809-1874

William H. Doane, 1832-1915

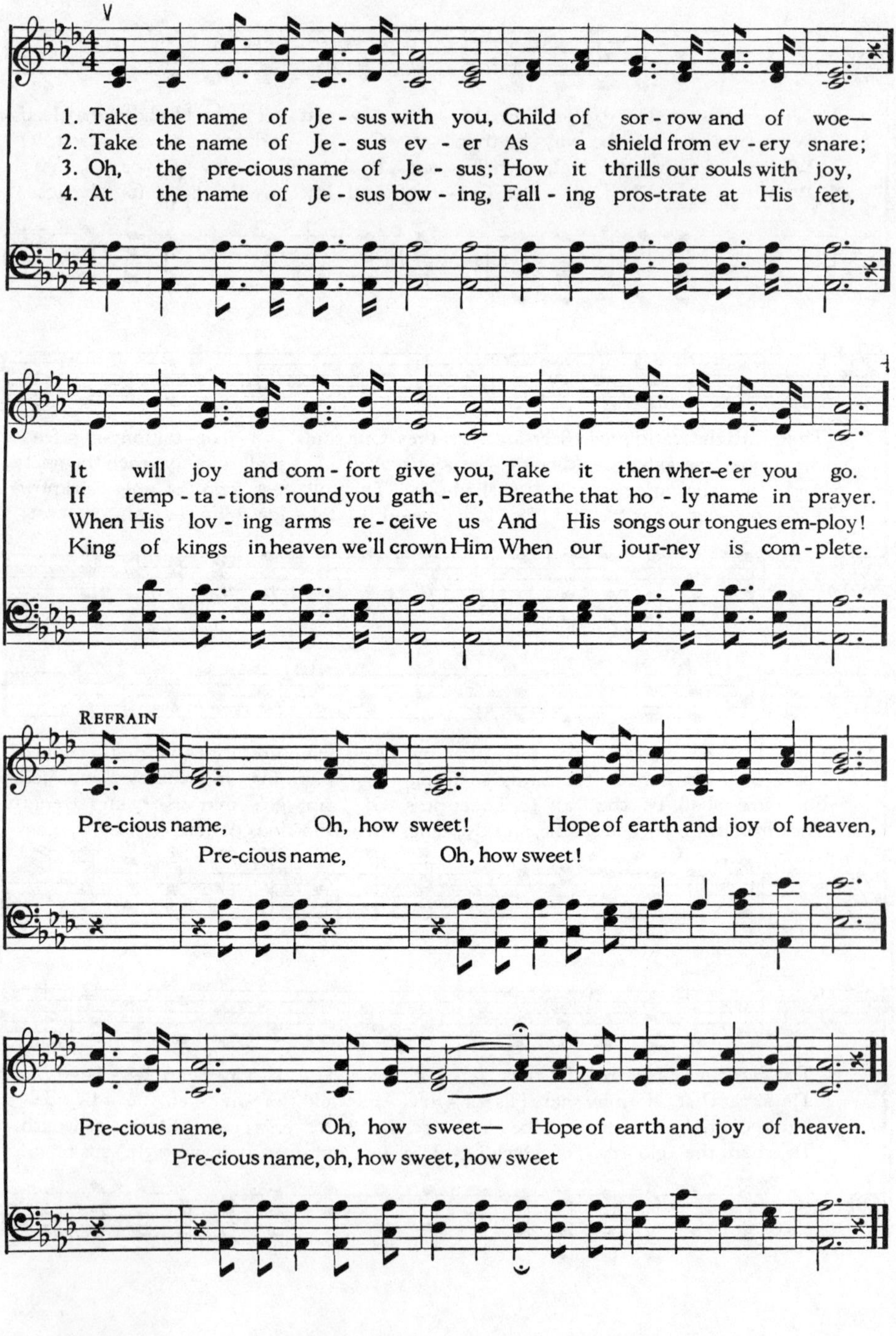
1. Take the name of Je - sus with you, Child of sor - row and of woe—
2. Take the name of Je - sus ev - er As a shield from ev - ery snare;
3. Oh, the pre-cious name of Je - sus; How it thrills our souls with joy,
4. At the name of Je - sus bow - ing, Fall - ing pros-trate at His feet,
It will joy and com - fort give you, Take it then wher-e'er you go.
If temp - ta - tions 'round you gath - er, Breathe that ho - ly name in prayer.
When His lov - ing arms re - ceive us And His songs our tongues em-ploy!
King of kings in heaven we'll crown Him When our jour-ney is com - plete.
REFRAIN
Pre-cious name, Oh, how sweet! Hope of earth and joy of heaven,
Pre-cious name, Oh, how sweet!
Pre-cious name, Oh, how sweet— Hope of earth and joy of heaven.
Pre-cious name, oh, how sweet, how sweet

Him That Cometh unto Me 549

. . . I will in no wise cast out. John 6:37

Eliza Edmunds Hewitt, 1851-1920 William J. Kirkpatrick, 1838-1921

1. Lis - ten to the bless - ed in - vi - ta - tion, Sweet - er than the notes of an - gel - song, Chim-ing soft - ly with a heaven - ly ca - dence, Call - ing to the pass - ing throng.
2. Wea - ry toil - er, sad and heav - y - la - den, Joy - ful - ly the great sal - va - tion see; Close be - side thee stands the Bur - den Bear - er, Strong to bear thy load and thee.
3. Come, ye thirst - y, to the liv - ing wa - ters, Hun - gry, come and on His boun - ty feed; Not thy fit - ness is the plea to bring Him, But thy press - ing ut - most need.
4. Him that com - eth, blind or maimed or sin - ful, Com - ing for His heal - ing touch di - vine, For the cleans-ing of the blood so pre - cious, Prove a - new this gra - cious line.
5. Com - ing hum - bly, dai - ly to this Sav - iour, Breath-ing all the heart to Him in prayer; Com - ing some day to the heaven - ly man - sions, He will give thee wel - come there.
Refrain
Him that com - eth un - to Me, un - to Me, Him that com - eth un - to Me, un - to Me, Him that com - eth un - to Me, un - to Me, I will in no wise cast out.

550 Softly and Tenderly

Come unto me, all ye that . . . are heavy laden . . . Matt. 11:28

Will L. Thompson, 1847-1909

THOMPSON 11.7.11.7. with Refrain
Will L. Thompson, 1847-1909

1. Soft - ly and ten - der - ly Je - sus is call - ing, Call - ing for
2. Why should we tar - ry when Je - sus is plead - ing, Plead - ing for
3. Time is now fleet - ing, the mo - ments are pass - ing, Pass - ing from
4. Oh, for the won - der - ful love He has prom - ised, Prom - ised for
you and for me; See on the por - tals He's wait - ing and
you and for me? Why should we lin - ger and heed not His
you and from me; Shad - ows are gath - er - ing, death - beds are
you and for me! Though we have sinned, He has mer - cy and
watch - ing, Watch - ing for you and for me.
mer - cies, Mer - cies for you and for me?
com - ing, Com - ing for you and for me.
par - don, Par - don for you and for me.
REFRAIN
Come home, come home, come home,
Ye who are wea - ry, come home,
Ear - nest - ly, ten - der - ly Je - sus is call - ing,
Call - ing, O sin - ner, come home!

Jesus Is Tenderly Calling Thee Home 551

. . . *Today if ye will hear his voice, harden not your hearts.* Heb. 4:7

CALLING TODAY Irregular with Refrain

Fanny J. Crosby, 1820-1915

George C. Stebbins, 1846-1945

1. Je-sus is ten-der-ly call-ing thee home–Call-ing to-day, call-ing to-day;
2. Je-sus is call-ing the wea-ry to rest– Call-ing to-day, call-ing to-day;
3. Je-sus is wait-ing, oh, come to Him now– Wait-ing to-day, wait-ing to-day;
4. Je-sus is plead-ing, oh, list to His voice–Hear Him to-day, hear Him to-day;
Why from the sun-shine of love wilt thou roam Far-ther and far-ther a-way?
Bring Him thy bur-den, and thou shalt be blest; He will not turn thee a-way.
Come with thy sins, at His feet low-ly bow; Come, and no long-er de-lay.
They who be-lieve on His name shall re-joice; Quick-ly a-rise and a-way.
Refrain
Call - ing to-day! Call - ing to-day!
Call-ing, call-ing to-day, to-day! Call-ing, call-ing to-day, to-day!
Je - sus is call - ing, Is ten-der-ly call-ing to-day.
Je-sus is ten-der-ly call-ing to-day,

552 Don't Turn Him Away

. . . if any man . . . open the door, I will come in to him . . . Rev. 3:20

Haldor Lillenas, 1885-1959 | Haldor Lillenas, 1885-1959

1. Be - hold, the lov - ing Sav - iour stands Out - side your bolt - ed door,
2. He stood there when in child - ish play Your heart was free from care,
3. He stood there when your heart was filled With sor - row, grief, and pain,
4. The blood-stained hands of Christ some day Their gen - tle knocks will cease,
There knock - ing with His nail-pierced hands As of - ten-times be - fore.
And now when locks are sil - ver gray He still is stand - ing there.
And when your life with joy was thrilled He stood there all in vain.
When you at last have grieved a - way The bless - ed Prince of Peace.
REFRAIN
Don't turn Him a - way, Don't turn Him a - way, He has come
back to your heart a - gain Al - though you've gone a - stray; Oh, how you
need Him to plead your cause On that e - ter - nal day!

Don't Turn Him Away

Don't turn the Sav - iour a - way from your heart, Don't turn Him a - way.

God Calling Yet 553

Seek ye the Lord while he may be found . . . Isa. 55:6

Gerhard Tersteegen, 1697-1769
Translated by Jane L. Borthwick, 1813-1897

FEDERAL STREET L.M.
Henry K. Oliver, 1800-1885

1. God call - ing yet! Shall I not hear? Earth's pleas - ures
2. God call - ing yet! Shall I not rise? Can I His
3. God call - ing yet! And shall He knock And I my
4. God call - ing yet! I can - not stay; My heart I
shall I still hold dear? Shall life's sweet pass - ing
lov - ing voice de - spise, And base - ly His kind
heart the clos - er lock? He still is wait - ing
yield with - out de - lay: Vain world, fare - well! From
years all fly And still my soul in slum - bers lie?
care re - pay? He calls me still; can I de - lay?
to re - ceive, And shall I dare His Spir - it grieve?
thee I part; The voice of God hath reached my heart.

554 Come, Sinner, Come

. . . I am not come to call the righteous, but sinners to repentance. Matt. 9:13

Will E. Witter, b. 1854

Melody by Horatio R. Palmer, 1834-1907

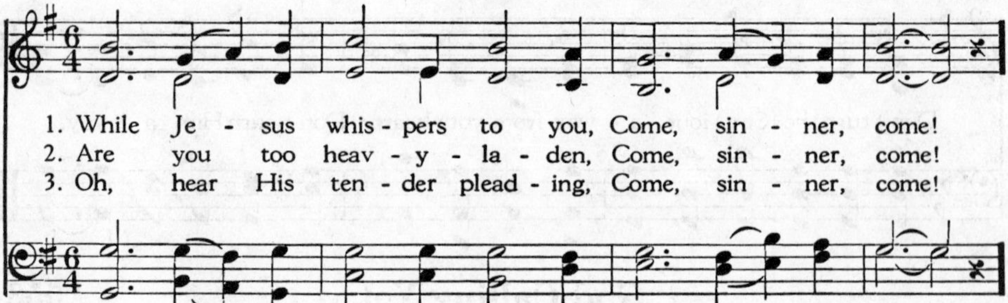
1. While Je - sus whis - pers to you, Come, sin - ner, come!
2. Are you too heav - y - la - den, Come, sin - ner, come!
3. Oh, hear His ten - der plead - ing, Come, sin - ner, come!

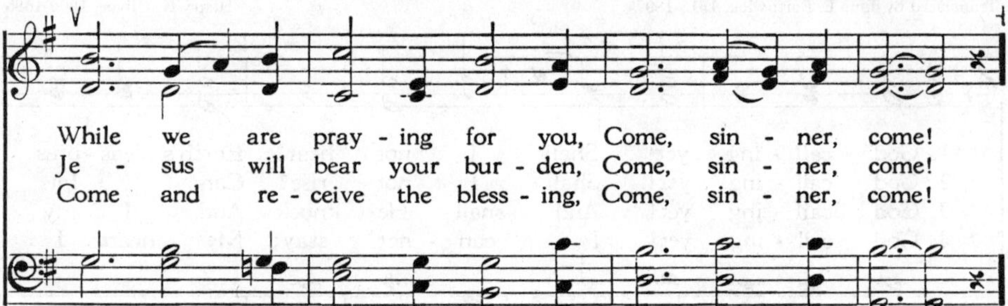
While we are pray - ing for you, Come, sin - ner, come!
Je - sus will bear your bur - den, Come, sin - ner, come!
Come and re - ceive the bless - ing, Come, sin - ner, come!

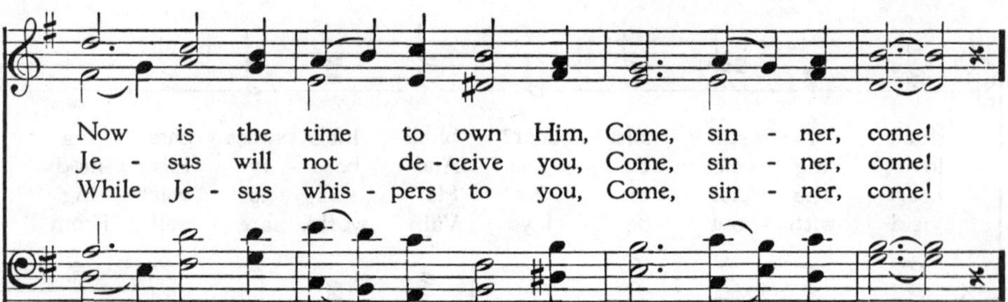
Now is the time to own Him, Come, sin - ner, come!
Je - sus will not de - ceive you, Come, sin - ner, come!
While Je - sus whis - pers to you, Come, sin - ner, come!

Now is the time to know Him, Come, sin - ner, come!
Je - sus can now re - deem you, Come, sin - ner, come!
While we are pray - ing for you, Come, sin - ner, come!

Come, Ye Sinners, Poor and Needy 555

. . . him that cometh to me I will in no wise cast out. John 6:37

BRYN CALFARIA 8.7.8.7.4.7. with repeats

Joseph Hart, 1712-1768

Melody by William Owen, 1814-1893

1. Come, ye sin - ners, poor and need - y, Weak and wound-ed, sick and sore;
2. Now, ye need - y, come and wel-come; God's free boun - ty glo - ri - fy:
3. Come, ye wea - ry, heav - y - la - den, Bruised and ru - ined by the fall;
4. Let not con-science make you lin - ger, Nor of fit - ness fond - ly dream;
5. Lo, th'in-car - nate God as - cend - ed, Pleads the mer - it of His blood;
Je - sus read - y stands to save you, Full of pit - y, love, and power:
True be - lief and true re - pent-ance—Ev - ery grace that brings you nigh—
If you tar - ry till you're bet - ter, You will nev - er come at all:
All the fit - ness He re - quir - eth Is to feel your need of Him:
Ven - ture on Him, ven-ture whol - ly, Let no oth - er trust in - trude;
He is a - ble, He is a - ble, He is a - ble;
With - out mon - ey, With - out mon - ey, With - out mon - ey,
Not the right - eous, Not the right - eous, Not the right - eous—
This He gives you, This He gives you, This He gives you—
None but Je - sus, None but Je - sus, None but Je - sus
He is will-ing; doubt no more! He is will - ing; doubt no more!
Come to Je - sus Christ and buy, Come to Je - sus Christ and buy.
Sin-ners, Je - sus came to call, Sin - ners, Je - sus came to call.
'Tis the Spir-it's ris - ing beam, 'Tis the Spir - it's ris - ing beam.
Can do help-less sin - ners good, Can do help - less sin - ners good.

556 Jesus, I Come

In the day of my trouble I sought the Lord . . . Psa. 77:2

JESUS, I COME Irregular

William T. Sleeper, 1819-1904

George C. Stebbins, 1846-1945

1. Out of my bond-age, sor-row, and night, Je-sus, I come, Je-sus, I come;
2. Out of my shame-ful fail-ure and loss, Je-sus, I come, Je-sus, I come;
3. Out of un-rest and ar-ro-gant pride, Je-sus, I come, Je-sus, I come;
4. Out of the fear and dread of the tomb, Je-sus, I come, Je-sus, I come;
In-to Thy free-dom, glad-ness, and light, Je-sus, I come to Thee;
In-to the glo-rious gain of Thy cross, Je-sus, I come to Thee;
In-to Thy bless-ed will to a-bide, Je-sus, I come to Thee;
In-to the joy and light of my home, Je-sus, I come to Thee;
Out of my sick-ness in-to Thy health, Out of my want and in-to Thy wealth,
Out of earth's sor-rows in-to Thy balm, Out of life's storms and in-to Thy calm,
Out of my-self to dwell in Thy love, Out of de-spair in-to rap-tures a-bove,
Out of the depths of ru-in un-told, In-to the peace of Thy shel-ter-ing fold,
Out of my sin and in-to Thy-self, Je-sus, I come to Thee.
Out of dis-tress to ju-bi-lant psalm, Je-sus, I come to Thee.
Up-ward for aye on wings like a dove, Je-sus, I come to Thee.
Ev-er Thy glo-rious face to be-hold, Je-sus, I come to Thee.

Lord, I'm Coming Home

If we confess our sins, he is faithful and just to forgive us our sins . . . 1 John 1:9

COMING HOME 8.5.8.5. with Refrain

William J. Kirkpatrick, 1838-1921 — William J. Kirkpatrick, 1838-1921

1. I've wan-dered far a - way from God, Now I'm com-ing home;
2. I've wast - ed man - y pre - cious years, Now I'm com-ing home;
3. I'm tired of sin and stray - ing, Lord, Now I'm com-ing home;
4. My soul is sick, my heart is sore, Now I'm com-ing home;
5. My on - ly hope, my on - ly plea, Now I'm com-ing home;
6. I need His cleans-ing blood, I know, Now I'm com-ing home;
The paths of sin too long I've trod; Lord, I'm com-ing home.
I now re - pent with bit - ter tears; Lord, I'm com-ing home.
I'll trust Thy love, be - lieve Thy Word; Lord, I'm com-ing home.
My strength re - new, my hope re - store; Lord, I'm com-ing home.
That Je - sus died, and died for me; Lord, I'm com-ing home.
Oh, wash me whit - er than the snow; Lord, I'm com-ing home.
REFRAIN
Com - ing home, com - ing home, Nev - er - more to roam,
O - pen wide Thine arms of love; Lord, I'm com-ing home.

558 Just As I Am, without One Plea

. . . come . . . without money and without price. Isa. 55:1

WOODWORTH 8.8.8.6.2.

Charlotte Elliott, 1789-1871

William B. Bradbury, 1816-1868

1. Just as I am, with - out one plea, But
2. Just as I am and wait - ing not To
3. Just as I am, though tossed a - bout With
4. Just as I am, Thou wilt re - ceive, Wilt
5. Just as I am, Thy love un - known Hath

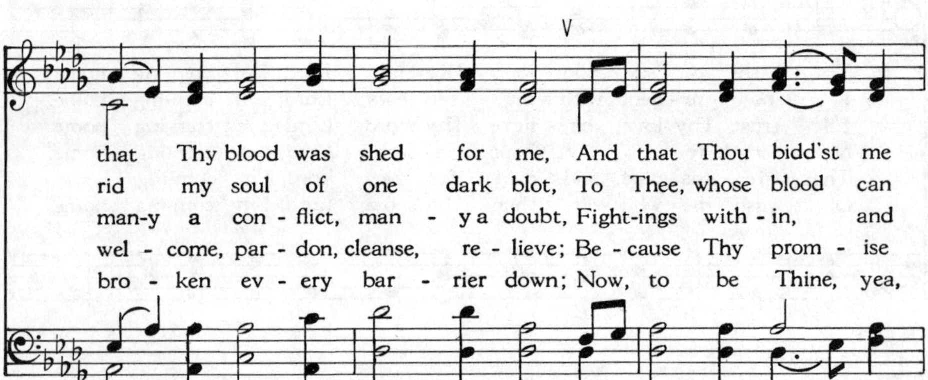
that Thy blood was shed for me, And that Thou bidd'st me
rid my soul of one dark blot, To Thee, whose blood can
man-y a con - flict, man - y a doubt, Fight-ings with - in, and
wel - come, par - don, cleanse, re - lieve; Be - cause Thy prom - ise
bro - ken ev - ery bar - rier down; Now, to be Thine, yea,

come to Thee, O Lamb of God, I come, I come!
cleanse each spot, O Lamb of God, I come, I come!
fears with - out, O Lamb of God, I come, I come!
I be - lieve, O Lamb of God, I come, I come!
Thine a - lone, O Lamb of God, I come, I come!

The Saviour Is Waiting

559

. . . that he may be gracious unto you . . . Isa. 30:18

CARMICHAEL 11.7.11.7. with Refrain

Ralph R. Carmichael, b. 1927

Ralph R. Carmichael, b. 1927

1. The Sav-iour is wait-ing to en-ter your heart, Why don't you let Him come in? There's noth-ing in this world to keep you a-part, What is your an-swer to Him?
2. If you'll take one step toward the Sav-iour, my friend, You'll find His arms o-pen wide; Re-ceive Him, and all of your dark-ness will end, With-in your heart He'll a-bide.
Refrain
Time af-ter time He has wait-ed be-fore, And now He is wait-ing a-gain To see if you're will-ing to o-pen the door, Oh, how He wants to come in.

560 Pass Me Not

. . . let thine ears be attentive to the voice of my supplications. Psa. 130:2

PASS ME NOT 8.5.8.5. with Refrain

Fanny J. Crosby, 1820-1915

William H. Doane, 1832-1915

1. Pass me not, O gen - tle Sav - iour, Hear my hum - ble cry;
2. Let me at the throne of mer - cy Find a sweet re - lief;
3. Trust - ing on - ly in Thy mer - it, Would I seek Thy face;
4. Thou, the Spring of all my com - fort, More than life to me,
While on oth - ers Thou art call - ing, Do not pass me by.
Kneel - ing there in deep con - tri - tion, Help my un - be - lief.
Heal my wound - ed, bro - ken spir - it, Save me by Thy grace.
Whom have I on earth be - side Thee? Whom in heaven but Thee?
Refrain
Sav - iour, Sav - iour, Hear my hum - ble cry; While on
oth - ers Thou art call - ing, Do not pass me by.

Only Trust Him

561

Blessed is that man that maketh the Lord his trust . . . Psa. 40:4

MINERVA C.M. with Refrain

John H. Stockton, 1813-1877

John H. Stockton, 1813-1877

1. Come, ev - ery soul by sin op-pressed, There's mer - cy with the Lord,
2. For Je - sus shed His pre - cious blood, Rich bless - ings to be - stow;
3. Yes, Je - sus is the truth, the way That leads you in - to rest;
4. Come, then, and join this ho - ly band And on to glo - ry go,
And He will sure - ly give you rest By trust - ing in His Word.
Plunge now in - to the crim - son flood That wash - es white as snow.
Be - lieve in Him with - out de - lay And you are ful - ly blest.
To dwell in that ce - les - tial land Where joys im - mor - tal flow.
REFRAIN
On - ly trust Him, on - ly trust Him, On - ly trust Him now;
He will save you, He will save you, He will save you now.

562 Though Your Sins Be as Scarlet

. . . they shall be as white as snow . . . Isa. 1:18

Fanny J. Crosby, 1820-1915

Melody by William H. Doane, 1832-1915

1. Though your sins be as scar - let, They shall be as white as snow;
2. Hear the voice that en-treats you: Oh, re-turn ye un - to God!
3. He'll for - give your trans-gres-sions And re-mem-ber them no more;
Though your sins be as scar - let, They shall be as white as snow;
Hear the voice that en - treats you: Oh, re - turn ye un - to God!
He'll for - give your trans - gres - sions And re - mem - ber them no more;
UNISON
Though they be red, yes red like crim - son, They shall be as wool.
He is of great, so great com - pas - sion, And of won - drous love;
"Look un - to Me, to Me, ye peo - ple," Saith the Lord, your God;
Though your sins be as scar - let, Though your sins be as scar - let,
Hear the voice that en - treats you, Hear the voice that en - treats you:
He'll for - give your trans-gres-sions, He'll for - give your trans-gres - sions

Though Your Sins Be as Scarlet

They shall be as white as snow, They shall be as white as snow.
Oh, re - turn ye un - to God! Oh, re - turn ye un - to God!
And re - mem - ber them no more, And re - mem-ber them no more.

Almost Persuaded 563

. . . Almost thou persuadest me to be a Christian. Acts 26:28

Philip P. Bliss, 1838-1876 Philip P. Bliss, 1838-1876

1. Al - most per - suad - ed, now to be - lieve; Al - most per - suad - ed,
2. Al - most per - suad - ed, come, come to - day; Al - most per - suad - ed,
3. Al - most per - suad - ed, har - vest is past! Al - most per - suad - ed,
Christ to re - ceive; Seems now some soul to say: "Go, Spir - it,
turn not a - way; Je - sus in - vites you here, An - gels are
doom comes at last! Al - most can - not a - vail; Al - most is
go Thy way, Some more con - ven - ient day On Thee I'll call."
lin - gering near, Prayers rise from hearts so dear— O wan-derer, come.
but to fail! Sad, sad, that bit - ter wail— Al - most, but lost.

564 I Am Praying for You

I pray for them . . . John 17:9

Samuel O. Clough, 1837-1910

Ira D. Sankey, 1840-1908

1. I have a Sav - iour, He's plead - ing in glo - ry, A dear, lov - ing
2. I have a Fa - ther: to me He has giv - en A hope for e -
3. I have a robe—'tis re - splend - ent in white - ness–A wait - ing in
4. I have a peace: it is calm as a riv - er– A peace that the
5. When He has found you, tell oth - ers the sto - ry That my lov - ing
Sav - iour, though earth-friends be few; And now He is watch - ing in
ter - ni - ty, bless - ed and true; And soon He will call me to
glo - ry my won - der - ing view; Oh, when I re - ceive it all
friends of this world nev - er knew: My Sav - iour a - lone is its
Sav - iour is your Sav - iour too; Then pray that your Sav - iour may
ten - der-ness o'er me, And, oh, that my Sav - iour were your Sav-iour too!
meet Him in heav - en, But, oh, that He'd let me bring you with me too!
shin - ing in bright-ness, Dear friend, could I see you re - ceiv - ing one too!
au - thor and giv - er, And, oh, could I know it was giv - en for you!
bring them to glo - ry, And prayer will be an-swered–'twas an-swered for you!
Refrain
For you I am pray - ing, For you I am pray - ing,
For you I am pray - ing, I'm pray - ing for you.

Is Thy Heart Right with God? 565

Search me, O God, and know my heart . . . Psa. 139:23

Elisha A. Hoffman, 1839-1929 | Elisha A. Hoffman, 1839-1929

1. Have thine af - fec - tions been nailed to the cross? Is thy heart
2. Hast thou do - min - ion o'er self and o'er sin? Is thy heart
3. Is there no more con - dem - na - tion for sin? Is thy heart
4. Are all thy powers un - der Je - sus' con - trol? Is thy heart
5. Art thou now walk - ing in heav - en's pure light? Is thy heart
right with God? Dost thou count all things for Je - sus but loss?
right with God? O - ver all e - vil with - out and with - in?
right with God? Does Je - sus rule in the tem - ple with - in?
right with God? Does He each mo - ment a - bide in thy soul?
right with God? Is thy soul wear - ing the gar - ment of white?
Is thy heart right with God?
Refrain
Is thy heart right with God?
Washed in the crim - son flood, Cleansed and made ho - ly,
hum - ble and low - ly, Right in the sight of God?

566 What Will You Do with Jesus?

. . . What shall I do then with Jesus . . . Matt. 27:22

Albert B. Simpson, 1843-1919

Mary L. Stocks, 1863-1934

1. Je - sus is stand-ing in Pi-late's hall–Friend-less, for-sak-en, be-trayed by all:
2. Je - sus is stand-ing on tri - al still, You can be false to Him if you will,
3. Will you e-vade Him as Pi-late tried? Or will you choose Him, what-e'er be-tide?
4. Will you, like Pe-ter, your Lord de - ny? Or will you scorn from His foes to fly,
5. "Je - sus, I give Thee my heart to-day! Je - sus, I'll fol-low Thee all the way,
Hark-en! What mean-eth the sud-den call? What will you do with Je - sus?
You can be faith-ful through good or ill: What will you do with Je - sus?
Vain-ly you strug-gle from Him to hide: What will you do with Je - sus?
Dar-ing for Je-sus to live or die? What will you do with Je - sus?
Glad-ly o-bey-ing Thee!" will you say: "This will I do with Je - sus!"
Refrain
What will you do with Je - sus? Neu-tral you can-not be;
Some day your heart will be ask - ing, "What will He do with me?"

Abide with Me 567

But they constrained him, saying, Abide with us . . . Luke 24:29

Henry F. Lyte, 1793-1847

EVENTIDE 10.10.10.10.
William H. Monk, 1823-1889

1. A - bide with me— fast falls the e - ven - tide;
2. Swift to its close ebbs out life's lit - tle day;
3. I need Thy pres - ence ev - ery pass - ing hour;
4. I fear no foe with Thee at hand to bless;
5. Hold Thou Thy cross be - fore my clos - ing eyes;
The dark - ness deep - ens— Lord, with me a - bide!
Earth's joys grow dim, its glo - ries pass a - way;
What but Thy grace can foil the tempt - er's power?
Ills have no weight, and tears no bit - ter - ness;
Shine through the gloom, and point me to the skies;
When oth - er help - ers fail and com - forts flee,
Change and de - cay in all a - round I see;
Who, like Thy - self, my guide and stay can be?
Where is death's sting? Where, grave, thy vic - to - ry?
Heaven's morn - ing breaks and earth's vain shad - ows flee!
Help of the help - less, oh, a - bide with me!
O Thou, who chang - est not, a - bide with me!
Through cloud and sun - shine, oh, a - bide with me!
I tri - umph still if Thou a - bide with me!
In life, in death, O Lord, a - bide with me!

568 Saviour, Again to Thy Dear Name

Peace I leave with you, my peace I give unto you . . . John 14:27

John Ellerton, 1826-1893

ELLERS 10.10.10.10.
Edward J. Hopkins, 1818-1901

1. Sav - iour, a - gain to Thy dear name we raise
2. Grant us Thy peace up - on our home - ward way;
3. Grant us Thy peace, Lord, through the com - ing night;
4. Grant us Thy peace through - out our earth - ly life,
With one ac - cord our part - ing hymn of praise:
With Thee be - gan, with Thee shall end the day;
Turn Thou for us its dark - ness in - to light:
Our balm in sor - row, and our stay in strife;
We stand to bless Thee ere our wor - ship cease;
Guard Thou the lips from sin, the hearts from shame,
From harm and dan - ger keep Thy chil - dren free,
Then, when Thy voice shall bid our con - flict cease,
Then, low - ly kneel - ing, wait Thy word of peace.
That in this house have called up - on Thy name.
For dark and light are both a - like to Thee.
Call us, O Lord, to Thine e - ter - nal peace. A - MEN.

Sun of My Soul, Thou Saviour Dear 569

. . . the darkness hideth not from thee; but the night shineth as the day . . . Psa. 139:12

John Keble, 1792-1866

HURSLEY L.M.
Austrian melody, 18th century
From *Hymns Ancient and Modern*, 1861

1. Sun of my soul, Thou Sav - iour dear, It is not
2. When the soft dews of kind - ly sleep My wea - ried
3. A - bide with me from morn till eve, For with - out
4. Watch by the sick; en - rich the poor With bless - ings
5. Come near and bless us when we wake, Ere through the

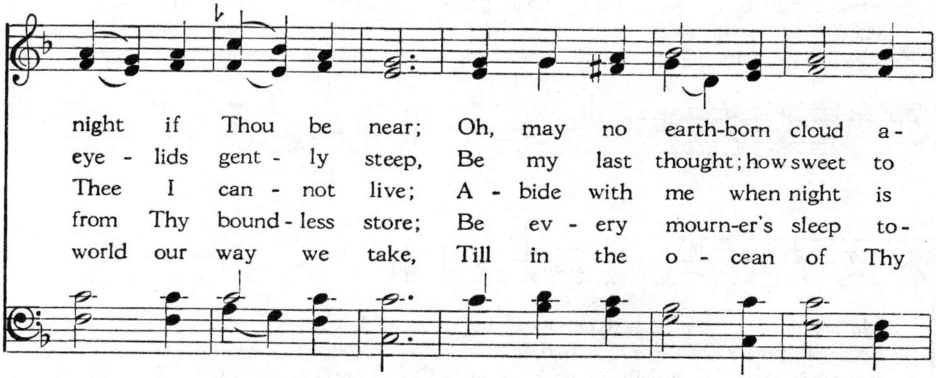
night if Thou be near; Oh, may no earth-born cloud a-
eye - lids gent - ly steep, Be my last thought; how sweet to
Thee I can - not live; A - bide with me when night is
from Thy bound - less store; Be ev - ery mourn-er's sleep to-
world our way we take, Till in the o - cean of Thy

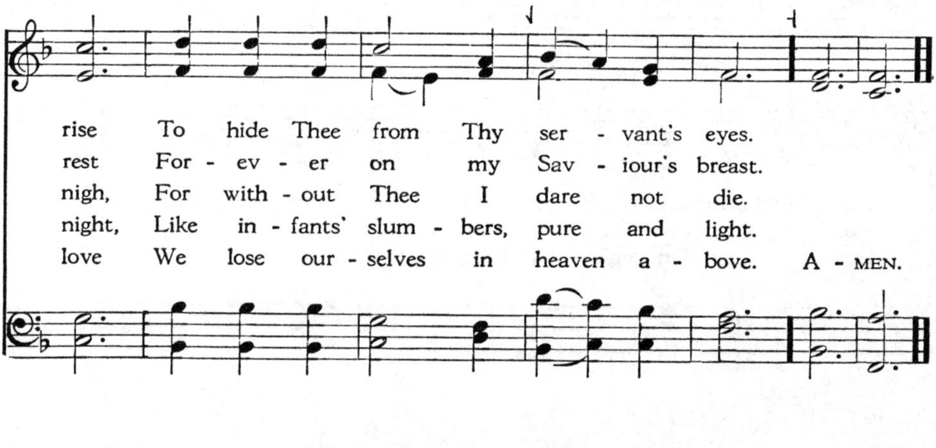
rise To hide Thee from Thy ser - vant's eyes.
rest For - ev - er on my Sav - iour's breast.
nigh, For with - out Thee I dare not die.
night, Like in - fants' slum - bers, pure and light.
love We lose our - selves in heaven a - bove. A - MEN.

570 God, That Madest Earth and Heaven

He hath made every thing beautiful in his time . . . Eccles. 3:11

Reginald Heber, 1783-1826
Stanza 2 by William Mercer, 1811-1873
Stanza 3 by Richard Whately, 1787-1863

AR HYD Y NOS 8.4.8.4.8.8.8.4.
Welsh melody, 18th century
Harmony by L.O. Emerson, 1820-1915

1. God, that mad - est earth and heav - en, Dark - ness and light;
2. And when morn a - gain shall call us To run life's way,
3. Guard us wak - ing, guard us sleep - ing, And when we die,
Who the day for toil hast giv - en, For rest the night;
May we still, what - e'er be - fall us, Thy will o - bey.
May we in Thy might - y keep - ing All peace - ful lie;
May Thy an - gel guards de - fend us, Slum - ber sweet Thy mer - cy send us;
From the power of e - vil hide us, In the nar - row path-way guide us,
When the last dread call shall wake us, Do not Thou, our God, for - sake us,
Ho - ly dreams and hopes at - tend us This live - long night.
Nor Thy smile be e'er de - nied us The live - long day.
But to reign in glo - ry take us With Thee on high. A-MEN.

Day Is Dying in the West 571

. . . Holy, holy, holy, is the Lord of hosts: the whole earth is full of his glory. Isa. 6:3

Mary A. Lathbury, 1841-1913

CHAUTAUQUA 7.7.7.7.4. with Refrain
William F. Sherwin, 1826-1888

1. Day is dy - ing in the west, Heaven is touch - ing earth with rest;
2. Lord of life, be - neath the dome Of the u - ni - verse, Thy home,
3. While the deep-ening shad-ows fall, Heart of love, en - fold - ing all,
4. When for - ev - er from our sight Pass the stars, the day, the night,
Wait and wor - ship while the night Sets her eve - ning lamps a - light
Gath - er us, who seek Thy face, To the fold of Thy em-brace,
Through the glo - ry and the grace Of the stars that veil Thy face,
Lord of an - gels, on our eyes Let e - ter - nal morn - ing rise
Through all the sky.
For Thou art nigh.
Our hearts as - cend.
And shad-ows end.
Refrain
Ho - ly, ho - ly, ho - ly, Lord God of hosts! Heaven and
earth are full of Thee; Heaven and earth are prais-ing Thee, O Lord most high!

572 We Gather Together

The Lord hath been mindful of us: he will bless us . . . Psa. 115:12

KREMSER 12.11.12.11.
Dutch melody
From *Nederlandtsch Gedenckclanck,* 1626
Arranged by Edward Kremser, 1838-1914

Dutch, 16th century
Translated by Theodore Baker, 1851-1934

1. We gath - er to - geth - er to ask the Lord's bless - ing;
2. Be - side us to guide us, our God with us join - ing,
3. We all do ex - tol Thee, Thou Lead - er tri - um - phant,
He chas - tens and has - tens His will to make known;
Or - dain - ing, main - tain - ing His king - dom di - vine;
And pray that Thou still our de - fend - er wilt be.
The wick - ed op - press - ing now cease from dis - tress - ing,
So from the be - gin - ning the fight we were win - ning:
Let Thy con - gre - ga - tion es - cape trib - u - la - tion:
Sing prais - es to His name: He for - gets not His own.
Thou, Lord, wast at our side, all glo - ry be Thine!
Thy name be ev - er praised! O Lord, make us free! A-MEN.

Come, Ye Thankful People, Come 573

Let us come before his presence with thanksgiving . . . Psa. 95:2

ST. GEORGE'S, WINDSOR 7.7.7.7.D.

Henry Alford, 1810-1871

George J. Elvey, 1816-1893

1. Come, ye thank - ful peo - ple, come, Raise the song of har - vest home:
2. All the world is God's own field, Fruit un - to His praise to yield;
3. For the Lord our God shall come And shall take His har - vest home;
4. E - ven so, Lord, quick - ly come To Thy fi - nal har - vest home;
All is safe - ly gath - ered in, Ere the win - ter storms be - gin;
Wheat and tares to - geth - er sown, Un - to joy or sor - row grown:
From His field shall in that day All of - fen - ses purge a - way;
Gath - er Thou Thy peo - ple in, Free from sor - row, free from sin;
God, our Mak - er, doth pro - vide For our wants to be sup - plied:
First the blade, and then the ear, Then the full corn shall ap - pear:
Give His an - gels charge at last In the fire the tares to cast,
There, for - ev - er pu - ri - fied, In Thy pres - ence to a - bide:
Come to God's own tem - ple, come, Raise the song of har - vest home.
Lord of har - vest, grant that we Whole-some grain and pure may be.
But the fruit - ful ears to store In His gar - ner ev - er - more.
Come, with all Thine an - gels come, Raise the glo - rious har - vest home. A-MEN.

574 We Plow the Fields and Scatter

Every good gift and every perfect gift is from above . . . James 1:17

Matthias Claudius, 1740-1815
Translated by Jane M. Campbell, 1817-1878

WIR PFLÜGEN (Dresden) 7.6.7.6.D. with Refrain
Johann A.P. Schulz, 1747-1800

1. We plow the fields and scat - ter The good seed on the land, But it is
2. He on - ly is the mak - er Of all things near and far, He paints the
3. We thank Thee, then, O Fa - ther, For all things bright and good, The seed-time
fed and wa - tered By God's al-might - y hand; He sends the snow in
way-side flow - er, He lights the eve - ning star; The winds and waves o -
and the har - vest, Our life, our health, our food; Ac - cept the gifts we
win - ter, The warmth to swell the grain, The breez - es and the sun - shine, And
bey Him, By Him the birds are fed; Much more to us, His chil - dren, He
of - fer, For all Thy love im-parts, And what Thou most de - sir - est, Our
soft re - fresh-ing rain.
gives our dai - ly bread.
hum-ble, thank-ful hearts.
REFRAIN
All good gifts a - round us Are sent from heaven a -

We Plow the Fields and Scatter

bove; Then thank the Lord, Oh, thank the Lord For all His love. A-MEN.

Rejoice, Ye Pure in Heart 575

Rejoice evermore. . . . In everything give thanks . . . 1 Thess. 5:16, 18

Edward H. Plumptre, 1821-1891

MARION S.M. with Refrain
Arthur H. Messiter, 1834-1916

1. Re - joice, ye pure in heart, Re - joice, give thanks, and sing;
2. Bright youth and snow-crowned age, Strong men and maid - ens fair,
3. With all the an - gel choirs, With all the saints on earth,
4. Yes, on through life's long path, Still chant - ing as ye go;
5. Still lift your stand - ard high, Still march in firm ar - ray;
Your fes - tal ban - ner wave on high, The cross of Christ your King.
Raise high your free, ex - ult - ing song, God's won-drous praise de - clare.
Pour out the strains of joy and bliss, True rap-ture, no-blest mirth!
From youth to age, by night and day, In glad-ness and in woe.
As war - riors through the dark - ness toil Till dawns the gold - en day.
REFRAIN
Re-joice, re - joice, Re - joice, give thanks, and sing! A - MEN.
Re - joice, re - joice,

576 Great Is Thy Faithfulness

. . . his compassions fail not. They are new every morning . . . Lam. 3:22-23

FAITHFULNESS 11.10.11.10. with Refrain

Thomas O. Chisholm, 1866-1960

William M. Runyan, 1870-1957

1. Great is Thy faith - ful - ness, O God my Fa - ther,
2. Sum - mer and win - ter, and spring - time and har - vest,
3. Par - don for sin and a peace that en - dur - eth,
There is no shad - ow of turn - ing with Thee;
Sun, moon, and stars in their cours - es a - bove
Thy own dear pres - ence to cheer and to guide,
Thou chang - est not, Thy com - pas - sions they fail not;
Join with all na - ture in man - i - fold wit - ness
Strength for to - day and bright hope for to - mor - row—
As Thou hast been Thou for - ev - er wilt be.
To Thy great faith - ful - ness, mer - cy, and love.
Bless - ings all mine, with ten thou - sand be - side!

Great Is Thy Faithfulness

Refrain
Great is Thy faith - ful - ness! Great is Thy faith - ful - ness!
Morn - ing by morn - ing new mer - cies I see;
All I have need - ed Thy hand hath pro - vid - ed—
Great is Thy faith - ful - ness, Lord, un - to me!

577 Sing to the Lord of Harvest

Sing unto him, sing psalms unto him . . . 1 Chron. 16:9

WIE LIEBLICH IST DER MAIEN 7.6.7.6.D.
Melody by Johann Steurlein, 1546-1613
Harmony by Healey Willan, 1880-1968

John S.B. Monsell, 1811-1875

1. Sing to the Lord of har - vest, Sing songs of love and praise;
2. By Him the clouds drop rich - ness, The des - erts bloom and spring,
3. Heap on His sa - cred al - tar The gifts His good-ness gave,
With joy - ful hearts and voic - es Your al - le - lu - ias raise:
The hills leap up in glad - ness, The val - leys laugh and sing:
The gold - en sheaves of har - vest, The souls He died to save:
By Him the roll - ing sea - sons In fruit - ful or - der move;
He fill - eth with His full - ness All things with large in - crease;
Your hearts lay down be - fore Him When at His feet ye fall,
Sing to the Lord of har - vest A song of hap - py love.
He crowns the year with good - ness, With plen - ty, and with peace.
And with your lives a - dore Him, Who gave His life for all.

Now Thank We All Our God 578

. . . our God, we thank thee, and praise thy glorious name. 1 Chron. 29:13

NUN DANKET 6.7.6.7.6.6.6.6.

Martin Rinkart, 1586-1649
Translated by Catherine Winkworth, 1827-1878

Johann Crüger, 1598-1662
Harmony by Felix Mendelssohn, 1809-1847

1. Now thank we all our God With heart and hands and voic - es,
2. Oh, may this boun - teous God, Through all our life be near us,
3. All praise and thanks to God The Fa - ther now be giv - en,
Who won - drous things hath done, In whom His world re - joic - es;
With ev - er joy - ful hearts And bless - ed peace to cheer us;
The Son, and Him who reigns With them in high - est heav - en,
Who, from our moth - er's arms, Hath blessed us on our way
And keep us in His grace, And guide us when per - plexed,
The one e - ter - nal God, Whom earth and heaven a - dore;
With count - less gifts of love, And still is ours to - day.
And free us from all ills In this world and the next.
For thus it was, is now, And shall be ev - er - more. A - MEN.

579 Standing at the Portal

. . . Behold, I make all things new . . . Rev. 21:5

Frances R. Havergal, 1836-1879

ST. ALBAN 6.5.6.5.D. with Refrain
Adapted from Franz Joseph Haydn, 1732-1809

1. Stand-ing at the por - tal Of the o-pening year, Words of com-fort
2. "I, the Lord, am with thee, Be thou not a - fraid; I will help and
3. For the year be - fore us, Oh, what rich sup - plies! For the poor and
4. He will nev - er fail us, He will not for - sake; His e - ter - nal
meet us Hush-ing ev - ery fear, Spo-ken through the si - lence By our
strength-en, Be thou not dis-mayed: Yea, I will up - hold thee With My
need - y Liv - ing streams shall rise; For the sad and sin - ful Shall His
cov - enant He will nev - er break. Rest-ing on His prom - ise What have
Fa - ther's voice, Ten - der, strong, and faith - ful, Mak - ing us re - joice.
own right hand; Thou art called and cho - sen In My sight to stand."
grace a - bound; For the faint and fee - ble Per - fect strength be found.
we to fear? God is all suf - fi - cient For the com-ing year.
Refrain
On - ward, then, and fear not, Chil - dren of the day,

Standing at the Portal

For His Word shall nev - er, Nev - er pass a - way. A-MEN.

Great God, We Sing That Mighty Hand 580

. . . The hand of our God is upon all them for good that seek him . . . Ezra 8:22

WALTON L.M.

Philip Doddridge, 1702-1751

From William Gardiner's *Sacred Melodies*, 1815

1. Great God, we sing that might - y hand By
2. By day, by night, at home, a - broad, Still
3. With grate - ful hearts the past we own; The
4. In scenes ex - alt - ed or de - pressed, Thou
which sup - port - ed still we stand; The o-pening year Thy
are we guard - ed by our God, By His in - ces - sant
fu - ture, all to us un - known, We to Thy guard - ian
art our joy, and Thou our rest; Thy good-ness all our
mer - cy shows, That mer - cy crowns it till it close.
boun - ty fed, By His un - err - ing coun - sel led.
care com - mit And peace-ful leave be - fore Thy feet.
hopes shall raise, A - dored through all our chang-ing days. A-MEN.

(For different harmony see No. 157)

581 Days of Heaven

So teach us to number our days, that we may apply our hearts unto wisdom. Psa. 90:12

Albert B. Simpson, 1843-1919 — A. Verne Westlake, 1884-1939

1. The days of heaven are peace-ful days, Still as yon glass-y sea;
2. The days of heaven are ho-ly days, From sin for-ev-er free;
3. The days of heaven are hap-py days, Sor-row they nev-er see;
4. The days of heaven are health-ful days, They feed on life's fair tree;
So calm, so still in God, our days As days of heaven would be.
So cleansed and kept our days, O Lord, As days of heaven would be.
So full of glad-ness all our days As days of heaven would be.
So feed-ing on Thy strength, O Christ, Our days as heaven may be.
Refrain
Walk with us, Lord, through all the days, And let us walk with Thee
Till as Thy will is done in heaven, On earth so shall it be.

God Be with You Till We Meet Again 582

. . . The Lord watch between me and thee, when we are absent one from another. Gen. 31:49

GOD BE WITH YOU Irregular with Refrain

Jeremiah E. Rankin, 1828-1904

William G. Tomer, 1833-1896

1. God be with you till we meet a-gain, By His coun-sels guide, up-hold you,
2. God be with you till we meet a-gain, 'Neath His wings pro-tect-ing hide you,
3. God be with you till we meet a-gain, When life's per-ils thick con-found you,
4. God be with you till we meet a-gain, Keep love's ban-ner float-ing o'er you,
With His sheep se-cure-ly fold you, God be with you till we meet a-gain.
Dai-ly man-na still pro-vide you, God be with you till we meet a-gain.
Put His arms un-fail-ing round you, God be with you till we meet a-gain.
Smite death's threat-ening wave be-fore you, God be with you till we meet a-gain.
REFRAIN
Till we meet, till we meet, Till we meet at Je-sus' feet;
Till we meet, till we meet, God be with you till we meet a-gain.

583 My Trust

. . . it is required in stewards, that a man be found faithful. 1 Cor. 4:2

Albert B. Simpson, 1843-1919 | Albert B. Simpson, 1843-1919

1. Lord, Thou hast given to me a trust, A high and ho - ly
2. Thou hast com - mand - ed us to go; Oh, nev - er let our
3. We all are debt - ors to our race; God holds us bound to
dis - pen - sa - tion, To tell the world, and tell I must, The
hearts be - tray Thee; And Thou hast left an aw - ful woe On
one an - oth - er; The gifts and bless - ings of His grace Were
sto - ry of Thy great sal - va - tion; Thou might'st have sent from
all who light - ly dis - o - bey Thee; Oh, let us feel and
giv - en thee to give thy broth - er; We owe to ev - ery
heaven a - bove An - gel - ic hosts to tell the sto - ry, But, in Thy
fear that woe As we would guard our own sal - va - tion, And let us
child of sin One chance, at least, for hope of heav - en; Oh, by the

My Trust

con - de-scend-ing love, On men Thou hast con-ferred the glo - ry.
an - swer to that "Go," As wit - ness - es in ev - ery na - tion.
love that brought us in, Let help and hope to them be giv - en.
REFRAIN
Let me be faith - ful to my trust, Tell - ing the world the sto - ry;
Press on my heart the woe; Put in my feet the go;
Let me be faith - ful to my trust And use me for Thy glo - ry.

584 Be True

. . . be thou faithful unto death . . . Rev. 2:10

Albert B. Simpson, 1843-1919 | Albert B. Simpson, 1843-1919

1. We are go - ing forth from the school of Je - sus, We have sat at His
2. We are go - ing forth from the up - per cham-ber, From the days of our
3. We are go - ing forth with a trust so sa - cred And a truth so di-
4. We are go - ing forth with a glo - rious mis-sion As am - bas - sa -
5. We are go - ing forth with the bless - ed Spir - it And the Mas - ter
6. We are go - ing forth with a hope, su - per - nal, 'Tis the hope of our
bless - ed feet, We have drunk from truth's ce - les - tial foun - tain, We have
Pen - te - cost, We have given our-selves in a full sur - ren - der And been
vine and deep, With a mes - sage clear and a work so glo - rious And a
dors for God, We are sent with heav - en's last word of mer - cy O - ver
al - ways near: He has told us, "Lo, I am with you al - ways," And we
heaven-ly home; We shall not have gone o - ver all the cit - ies Till the
tast - ed its hon - ey sweet. We are wit - ness - es for our bless - ed
filled with the Ho - ly Ghost. We are go - ing forth as e - pis - tles
charge, such a charge to keep. Let it be our great - est joy, my
all the world a - broad. We are sent to save from the blight of
need not faint or fear. With the Mas - ter's pres - ence al - ways
Son of man be come. We are call - ing out the guests to the
Mas - ter In a world where friends are few; And He sends us
ho - ly And to live as Christ would do; Let us al - ways
broth - er, That the Lord can de - pend on you, And if all be -
sor - row, And the curse of sin un - do; With a work so
near us, Shall we not both dare and do, With the might - y
mar - riage, We are hast - ening to meet Him, too; May He find us

Be True

forth with the watch-word ho - ly, What - so - ev - er it costs, be true.
rep - re - sent our Mas - ter, Let our life be al - ways true.
sides should fail and fal - ter, To your trust be al - ways true.
grand and a trust so ho - ly, Oh, what heart would not be true?
Ho - ly Ghost with - in us, Shall we not be al - ways true?
watch - ing and robed and read - y; May He say, "Thou hast been true."
REFRAIN
Be true! Be true! Let the ho - ly watch-word ring;
We'll be true, we'll be true, we'll be true,
Be true to your trust, Be true to your glo-rious King;
We'll be true to our trust We'll be true,
yes,
Be true! Be true! Wheth-er friends be false or few;
We'll be true, we'll be true, we'll be true, we'll be true,
we'll be true,
What-so-e'er be - tide, ev - er at His side, Let Him al - ways find you true.

584

585 America, the Beautiful

Blessed is the nation whose God is the Lord . . . Psa. 33:12

MATERNA C.M.D.

Katherine L. Bates, 1859-1929 | Samuel A. Ward, 1847-1903

1. O beau - ti - ful for spa - cious skies, For am - ber waves of grain,
2. O beau - ti - ful for pil - grim feet, Whose stern, im - pas-sioned stress
3. O beau - ti - ful for he - roes proved In lib - er - at - ing strife,
4. O beau - ti - ful for pa - triot dream That sees be - yond the years
For pur - ple moun-tain maj - es - ties A - bove the fruit - ed plain!
A thor - ough-fare for free - dom beat A - cross the wil - der - ness!
Who more than self their coun - try loved, And mer - cy more than life!
Thine al - a - bas - ter cit - ies gleam, Un-dimmed by hu - man tears!
A - mer - i - ca! A - mer - i - ca! God shed His grace on thee,
A - mer - i - ca! A - mer - i - ca! God mend thine ev - ery flaw,
A - mer - i - ca! A - mer - i - ca! May God thy gold re - fine
A - mer - i - ca! A - mer - i - ca! God shed His grace on thee
And crown thy good with broth - er - hood From sea to shin - ing sea!
Con - firm thy soul in self - con-trol, Thy lib - er - ty in law!
Till all suc - cess be no - ble-ness And ev - ery gain di - vine!
And crown thy good with broth - er - hood From sea to shin - ing sea! A-MEN.

America

Righteousness exalteth a nation: but sin is a reproach to any people. Prov. 14:34

AMERICA 6.6.4.6.6.6.4.

Samuel F. Smith, 1808-1895

From *Thesaurus Musicus,* circa 1740

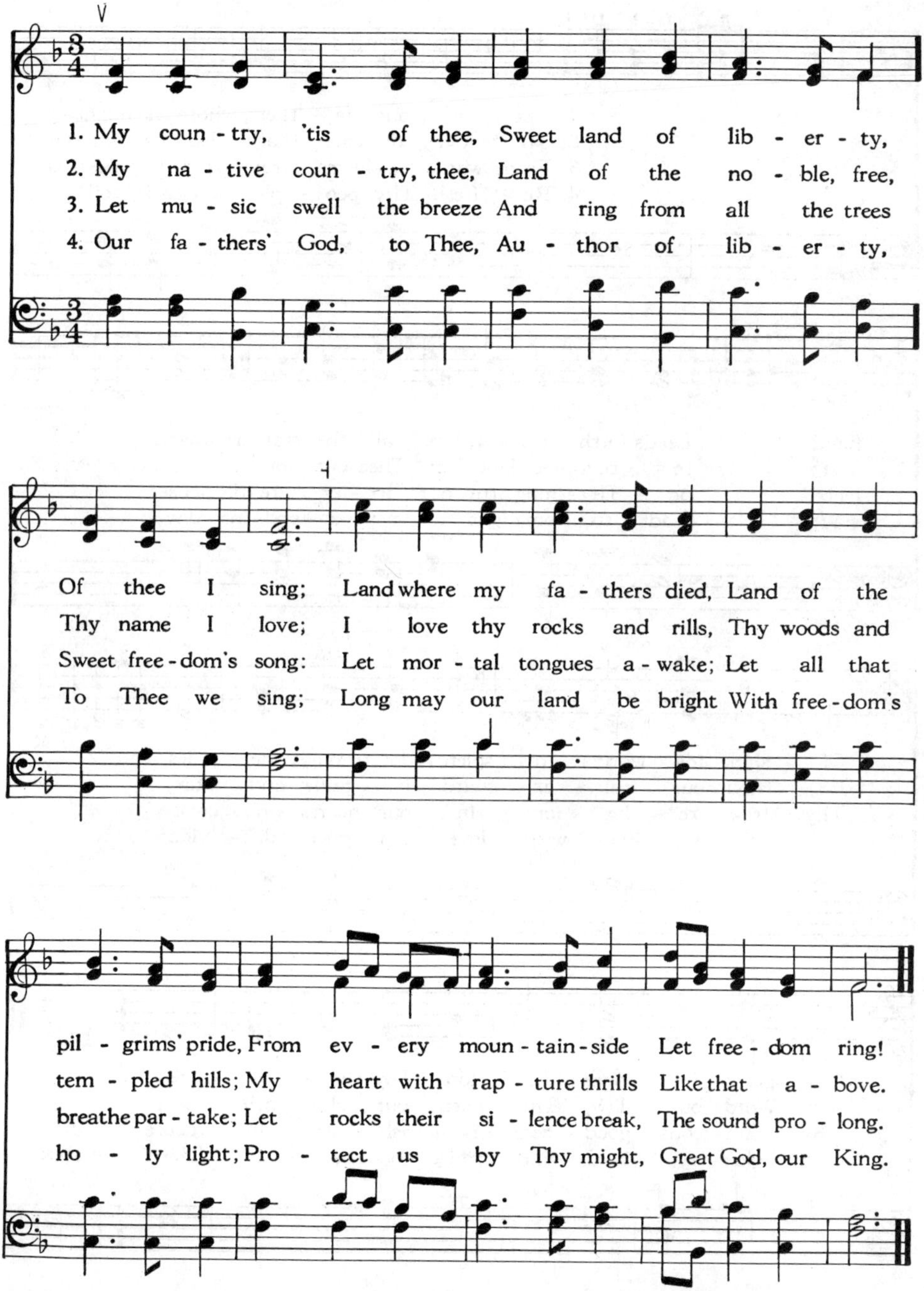
1. My coun - try, 'tis of thee, Sweet land of lib - er - ty,
2. My na - tive coun - try, thee, Land of the no - ble, free,
3. Let mu - sic swell the breeze And ring from all the trees
4. Our fa - thers' God, to Thee, Au - thor of lib - er - ty,
Of thee I sing; Land where my fa - thers died, Land of the
Thy name I love; I love thy rocks and rills, Thy woods and
Sweet free - dom's song: Let mor - tal tongues a - wake; Let all that
To Thee we sing; Long may our land be bright With free - dom's
pil - grims' pride, From ev - ery moun - tain - side Let free - dom ring!
tem - pled hills; My heart with rap - ture thrills Like that a - bove.
breathe par - take; Let rocks their si - lence break, The sound pro - long.
ho - ly light; Pro - tect us by Thy might, Great God, our King.

587 God of Our Fathers

. . . The Lord strong and mighty, the Lord mighty in battle. Psa. 24:8

NATIONAL HYMN 10.10.10.10.

Daniel C. Roberts, 1841-1907

George W. Warren, 1828-1902

1. God of our fa - thers, whose al - might - y
2. Thy love di - vine hath led us in the
3. From war's a - larms, from dead - ly pes - ti -
4. Re - fresh Thy peo - ple on their toil-some
hand Leads forth in beau - ty all the star - ry band
past; In this free land by Thee our lot is cast;
lence, Be Thy strong arm our ev - er sure de - fense;
way; Lead us from night to nev - er - end - ing day;
Of shin - ing worlds in splen - dor through the skies,
Be Thou our rul - er, guard - ian, guide, and stay,
Thy true re - lig - ion in our hearts in - crease,
Fill all our lives with love and grace di - vine;
Our grate - ful songs be - fore Thy throne a - rise.
Thy Word our law, Thy paths our cho - sen way.
Thy boun - teous good - ness nour - ish us in peace.
And glo - ry, laud, and praise be ev - er Thine. A-MEN.

O God, Beneath Thy Guiding Hand 588

... thou shalt judge the people righteously, and govern the nations upon earth.... Psa. 67:4

DUKE STREET L.M.

Leonard Bacon, 1802-1881

John Hatton, circa 1710-1793

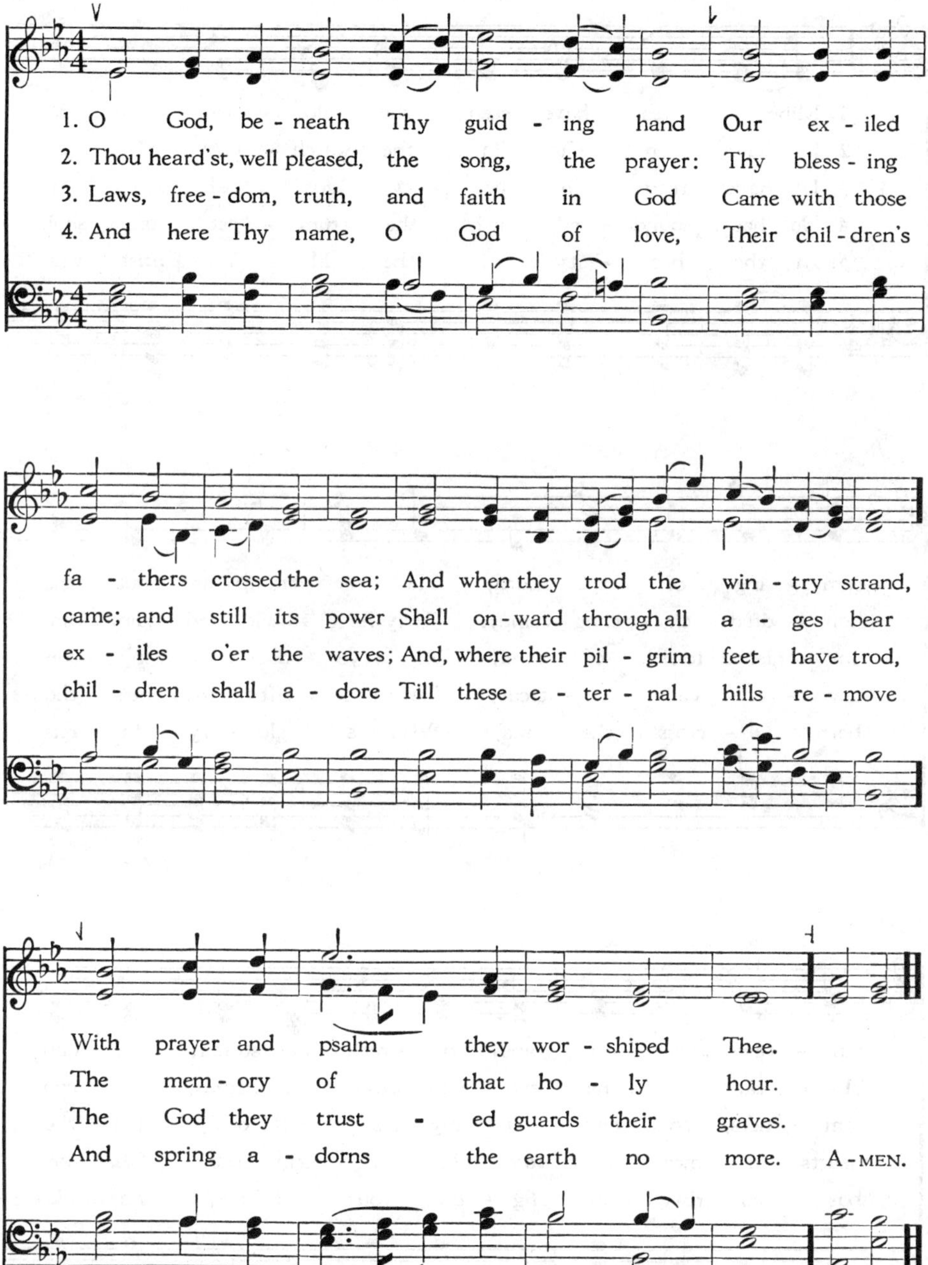
1. O God, be - neath Thy guid - ing hand Our ex - iled
2. Thou heard'st, well pleased, the song, the prayer: Thy bless - ing
3. Laws, free - dom, truth, and faith in God Came with those
4. And here Thy name, O God of love, Their chil - dren's
fa - thers crossed the sea; And when they trod the win - try strand,
came; and still its power Shall on - ward through all a - ges bear
ex - iles o'er the waves; And, where their pil - grim feet have trod,
chil - dren shall a - dore Till these e - ter - nal hills re - move
With prayer and psalm they wor - shiped Thee.
The mem - ory of that ho - ly hour.
The God they trust - ed guards their graves.
And spring a - dorns the earth no more. A - MEN.

(For lower key see No. 439)

589 Battle Hymn of the Republic

. . . the truth of the Lord endureth forever. . . . Psa. 117:2

Julia W. Howe, 1819-1910

BATTLE HYMN 15.15.15.6. with Refrain
American melody

1. Mine eyes have seen the glo - ry of the
2. I have seen Him in the watch - fires of a
3. I have read a fier - y gos - pel, writ in
4. He has sound - ed forth the trum - pet that shall
5. In the beau - ty of the lil - ies, Christ was
com - ing of the Lord; He is tramp - ling out the
hun - dred cir - cling camps; They have build - ed Him an
bur - nished rows of steel; "As ye deal with my con -
nev - er call re - treat; He is sift - ing out the
born a - cross the sea, With a glo - ry in His
vin - tage where the grapes of wrath are stored; He hath
al - tar in the eve - ning dews and damps; I can
tem - ners, so with you my grace shall deal; Let the
hearts of men be - fore His judg - ment seat; Oh, be
bos - om that trans - fig - ures you and me; As He

Battle Hymn of the Republic

loosed the fate-ful light-ning of His ter-ri-ble swift sword,
read His right-eous sen-tence by the dim and flar-ing lamps.
He-ro, born of wo-man, crush the ser-pent with His heel
swift, my soul, to an-swer Him! Be ju-bi-lant, my feet!
died to make men ho-ly, let us die to make men free
REFRAIN
His truth is march-ing on.
His day is march-ing on.
Since God is march-ing on." Glo-ry! Glo-ry! Hal-le-
Our God is march-ing on.
While God is march-ing on.
lu-jah! Glo-ry! Glo-ry! Hal-le-lu-jah! Glo-ry!
Glo-ry! Hal-le-lu-jah! His truth is march-ing on.

590 The Star-Spangled Banner

Through God we shall do valiantly: for he it is that shall tread down our enemies. Psa. 60:12

NATIONAL ANTHEM Irregular

Francis Scott Key, 1779-1843

Attributed to John S. Smith, 1750-1836

1. O— say! Can you see by the dawn's ear - ly light,
2. On the shore, dim - ly seen through the mists of the deep,
3. O— thus be it ev - er when free men shall stand
What so proud - ly we hailed at the twi - light's last gleam - ing?
Where the foe's haugh - ty host in dread si - lence re - pos - es,
Be - tween their loved homes and the war's des - o - la - tion!
Whose broad stripes and bright stars through the per - il - ous fight,
What is that which the breeze, o'er the tow - er - ing steep,
Blest with vic - tory and peace, may the heaven - res - cued land
O'er the ram - parts we watched were so gal - lant - ly stream - ing?
As it fit - ful - ly blows half con - ceals, half dis - clos - es?
Praise the Power that hath made and pre - served us a na - tion!

The Star-Spangled Banner

And the rock - et's red glare, the bomb burst - ing in air
Now it catch - es the gleam of the morn - ing's first beam,
Then con - quer we must, when our cause it is just,
Gave proof through the night that our flag was still there.
In full glo - ry re - flect - ed now shines on the stream,
And this be our mot - to: "In God is our trust!"
O— say, does that Star - Span-gled Ban - ner yet wave
'Tis the Star - Span - gled Ban - ner— O long may it wave
And the Star - Span - gled Ban - ner in tri - umph shall wave
O'er the land of the free and the home of the brave?
O'er the land of the free and the home of the brave!
O'er the land of the free and the home of the brave!

591 O Canada

Blessed is the nation whose God is the Lord . . . Psa. 33:12

R. Stanley Weir, 1856-1926

Melody by Calixa Lavallée, 1842-1891

1. O Can - a - da! Our home and na - tive land! True pa - triot
2. O Can - a - da! Where pines and ma - ples grow, Great prair - ies
3. O Can - a - da, be-neath thy shin - ing skies May stal - wart
4. Rul - er Su - preme, who hear - est hum-ble prayer, Hold our Do -
love in all thy sons com - mand. With glow - ing hearts we
spread and lord - ly riv - ers flow, How dear to us Thy
sons and gen - tle maid - ens rise To keep thee stead - fast
min - ion in thy lov - ing care; Help us to find, O
see thee rise, The True North, strong and free, From far and
broad do - main, From East to West - ern Sea Thou land of
through the years From East to West - ern Sea, Our own be -
God, in Thee A last - ing, rich re - ward, As, wait - ing
wide, O Can - a - da, We stand on guard for thee.
hope for all who toil! Thou True North, strong and free.
lov - ed na - tive land, Our True North, strong and free.
for the bet - ter day, We ev - er stand on guard.

O Canada

REFRAIN
God keep our land, glo - rious and free! O Can - a - da, we
stand on guard for thee. O Can - a - da, we stand on guard for thee.

God Save the Queen 592

Remember them which have the rule over you . . . Heb. 13:7

Anonymous, 18th century

NATIONAL ANTHEM 6.6.4.6.6.6.4.
From *Thesaurus Musicus*, circa 1740

1. God save our gra - cious Queen! Long live our no - ble Queen!
2. Thy choic - est gifts in store, On her be pleased to pour,
God save the Queen! Send her vic - to - ri - ous, Hap - py and
Long may she reign. May she de - fend our laws, And ev - er
glo - ri - ous, Long to reign o - ver us, God save the Queen!
give us cause To sing with heart and voice, God save the Queen!

593 Not Alone for Mighty Empire

Some trust in chariots, and some in horses: but we will remember . . . our God. Psa. 20:7

HYMN TO JOY 8.7.8.7.D.
Melody from *9th Symphony,* Ludwig van Beethoven, 1770-1827
William P. Merrill, 1867-1954 — Harmony by J. Buchanan MacMillan, b. 1915

1. Not a - lone for might - y em - pire, Stretch-ing far o'er land and sea;
2. Not for bat - tle - ship and for - tress, Not for con - quests of the sword;
3. For the ar - mies of the faith - ful, Souls that passed and left no name;
4. God of jus - tice, save the peo - ple From the clash of race and creed,
Not a - lone for boun - teous har - vests, Lift we up our hearts to Thee.
But for con - quests of the spir - it Give we thanks to Thee, O Lord;
For the glo - ry that il - lu - mines Pa - triot lives of death - less fame;
From the strife of class and fac - tion: Make our na - tion free in - deed.
Stand-ing in the liv - ing pres - ent, Mem - o - ry and hope be - tween,
For the her - it - age of free - dom, For the home, the church, the school;
For our proph-ets and a - pos - tles, Loy - al to the liv - ing Word;
Keep her faith in sim - ple man - hood Strong as when her life be - gan,
Lord, we would with deep thanks - giv - ing Praise Thee most for things un - seen.
For the o - pen door to man - hood In a land the peo - ple rule.
For all he - roes of the Spir - it, Give we thanks to Thee, O Lord.
Till it find its full fru - i - tion In sal - va - tion's glo - rious plan.

We Have Come to Worship Thee

John W. Peterson, b. 1921
From the cantata, *Night of Miracles*

John W. Peterson, b. 1921
From the cantata, *Night of Miracles*

We have come to wor - ship Thee, Sav - iour of Is - ra - el,
Grate - ful - ly now do we bow at Thy feet;
We have come to wor - ship Thee, Son of the High - est,
Glad hearts we raise, Lord, Thy praise to re - peat. A-MEN.
3
3

595 The Lord Is in His Holy Temple

QUAM DILECTA Irregular
Habakkuk 2:20
George F. Root, 1820-1895

The Lord is in His ho - ly tem - ple, The Lord is in His ho - ly
tem - ple; Let all the earth keep si - lence, Let all the earth keep si - lence be -
fore Him, Keep si - lence, keep si - lence be - fore Him. A-MEN.

596 He Is Lord

HE IS LORD Irregular
From Philippians 2:10-11
Anonymous

He is Lord, He is Lord! He is ris - en from the dead, and He is Lord!
Ev - ery knee shall bow, ev - ery tongue con - fess that Je - sus Christ is Lord.

The Doxology 597

OLD HUNDREDTH L.M.
Melody from *Genevan Psalter,* 1551
Attributed to Louis Bourgeois, circa 1510-1561

Thomas Ken, 1637-1711

Praise God from whom all bless-ings flow; Praise Him, all crea-tures here be-low;
Praise Him a-bove, ye heaven-ly host; Praise Fa-ther, Son, and Ho-ly Ghost. A-MEN.

Glory Be to the Father 598

GLORIA PATRI Irregular
Henry W. Greatorex, 1813-1858

Latin

Glo-ry be to the Fa-ther, and to the Son, and to the
Ho-ly Ghost; As it was in the be-gin-ning, is now and
ev-er shall be, world with-out end. A-men, A-men.

599 Thou Art Worthy

Revelation 4:11

Pauline M. Mills, 20th century

Thou art wor-thy, Thou art wor-thy, Thou art wor-thy, O
Lord, To re-ceive glo-ry, glo-ry and hon-or, glo-ry and
hon-or and power. For Thou hast cre-a-ted, hast all things cre-
a-ted. Thou hast cre-a-ted all things. And for Thy
plea-sure they are cre-a-ted, for Thou art wor-thy, O Lord.

Holy, Holy 600

HOLY, HOLY Irregular

Jimmy Owens, 20th century

Jimmy Owens, 20th century

1. Ho - ly, ho - ly, ho - ly, ho - ly, Ho - ly, ho - ly Lord God Al - might - y; And we lift our hearts be - fore You as a tok - en of our love, Ho - ly, ho - ly, ho - ly ho - ly.
2. Gra - cious Fa - ther, gra - cious Fa - ther, We're so blest to be Your chil - dren, gra - cious Fa - ther; And we lift our heads be - fore You as a tok - en of our love, Gra - cious Fa - ther, gra - cious Fa - ther.
3. Pre - cious Je - sus, pre - cious Je - sus, We're so glad that You've re - deemed us, pre - cious Je - sus; And we lift our hands be - fore You as a tok - en of our love, Pre - cious Je - sus, pre - cious Je - sus.
4. Ho - ly Spir - it, Ho - ly Spir - it Come and fill our hearts a - new, Ho - ly Spir - it; And we lift our voice be - fore You as a tok - en of our love, Ho - ly Spir - it, Ho - ly Spir - it.
5. Hal - le - lu - jah, hal - le - lu - jah, Hal - le - lu - jah, hal - le - lu - jah; And we lift our hearts be - fore You as a tok - en of our love, Hal - le - lu - jah, hal - le - lu - jah.

Father, I Adore You 601

Terrye Coelho, 20th century

Terrye Coelho, 20th century

1
2
3
Three part round (in unison)
1. Fa - ther, I a - dore You, Lay my life be - fore You, How I love You.
2. Je - sus, I a - dore You, Lay my life be - fore You, How I love You.
3. Spir - it, I a - dore You, Lay my life be - fore You, How I love You.

602 Spirit of the Living God

LIVING GOD 7.4.7.4.4.4.7.4.
Daniel Iverson, b. 1890

Daniel Iverson, b. 1890

Spir - it of the Liv - ing God, Fall fresh on me,
Spir - it of the Liv - ing God, Fall fresh on me.
Melt me, Mold me, Fill me, use me.
Spir - it of the Liv - ing God, Fall fresh on me.

603 Where the Spirit of the Lord Is

THERE IS PEACE Irregular
Stephen R. Adams, 20th century

Stephen R. Adams, 20th century

Where the Spir - it of the Lord is, there is peace;
Where the Spir - it of the Lord is, there is love.

Where the Spirit of the Lord Is

There is com-fort in life's dark-est hour, there is light and life; There is
help and pow-er in the Spir-it, in the Spir-it of the Lord.

Thy Loving Kindness 604

Psalm 63:3-4

Anonymous

1. Thy lov-ing kind-ness is bet-ter than life. Thy lov-ing
2. I lift my hands, Lord, un-to Thy name. I lift my
kind-ness is bet-ter than life. My lips shall praise Thee, thus will I
hands, Lord, un-to Thy name. My lips shall praise Thee, thus will I
bless Thee. I will lift up my hands un-to Thy name.
bless Thee. I will lift up my hands un-to Thy name.

605 Alleluia

Jerry Sinclair, 20th century

1. Al - le - lu - ia, al - le - lu - ia, Al - le - lu - ia, al - le - lu - ia,
Al - le - lu - ia, al - le - lu - ia, Al - le - lu - ia, al - le - lu - ia.

2. Lord, I love you, 3. I will serve Him, 4. He is coming.

606 Let the Beauty of Jesus

Albert Orsborn, 1886-1967

Arranged by Richard Hainsworth, 1885-1959

Let the beau - ty of Je - sus be seen in me, All His won - der - ful
pas - sion and pu - ri - ty; O Thou Spir - it di - vine, All my
na - ture re - fine Till the beau - ty of Je - sus be seen in me.

God Is So Good 607

Anonymous | African Christian folk song

1. God is so good, God is so good,
2. Je - sus is real, Je - sus is real,
3. He saved my soul, He saved my soul,
4. I praise His name, I praise His name,
God is so good, He's so good to me!
Je - sus is real, He's so real to me!
He saved my soul And He made me whole!
I praise His name, He's so good to me!

5. I love Him so. 6. Com-ing a-gain.

Make Them a Blessing Today 608

Henry J. Zelley, 1859-1942 | Henry L. Gilmour, 1837-1920

Bless them, Lord, and make them a bless-ing, They'll glad-ly Thy mes-sage con-vey;
Use them to help a great man-y souls, And make them a bless-ing each day.

609 The Lord Reigns! Tell the Nations!

Beatrice B. Bixler, b. 1916

Beatrice B. Bixler, b. 1916
Harmony by Helen I. Young, b. 1931

The Lord reigns! Tell the na-tions! Tell how He rules up-on His throne.
He is the God of all cre-a-tion. He is God a-lone!
Tell how He loved the world and gave His on-ly Son that
world to save. The Lord reigns! Tell the na-tions! He is Lord of
all! He is Lord of all! Christ is Lord of all!

The Lord Bless You and Keep You 610

BENEDICTION Irregular

Numbers 6:24-26

Peter C. Lutkin, 1858-1931

The Lord bless you and keep you. The Lord lift His
coun-te-nance up - on you, and give you peace,
and give you peace, and give you
The Lord make His face to shine up - on you,
and give you peace. The Lord make His face to shine up - on you,
peace.
and be gra - cious un-to you, be gra-cious.
and be gra-cious, and be gra-cious. The Lord be
gra-cious, gra-cious un - to you. A - MEN.

611 Lord, Dismiss Us with Thy Blessing

Attributed to John Fawcett, 1740-1817
Altered by Godfrey Thring, 1823-1903

SICILIAN MARINERS' HYMN 8.7.8.7.8.7.
From William D. Tattersall's *Psalmody*, 1794

1. Lord, dis - miss us with Thy bless - ing, Fill our hearts with joy and peace;
2. Thanks we give and ad - o - ra - tion For Thy gos - pel's joy - ful sound;
3. So that when Thy love shall call us, Sav - iour from the world a - way,
Let us each, Thy love pos - sess - ing, Tri - umph in re - deem - ing grace:
May the fruits of Thy sal - va - tion In our hearts and lives a - bound:
Fear of death shall not ap - pall us; Glad Thy sum - mons to o - bey,
Oh, re - fresh us, Oh, re - fresh us, Trav - eling through this wil - der - ness.
Ev - er faith - ful, ev - er faith - ful To the truth may we be found—
May we ev - er, may we ev - er, Reign with Thee in end - less day.

612 Sevenfold Amen

John Stainer, 1840-1901

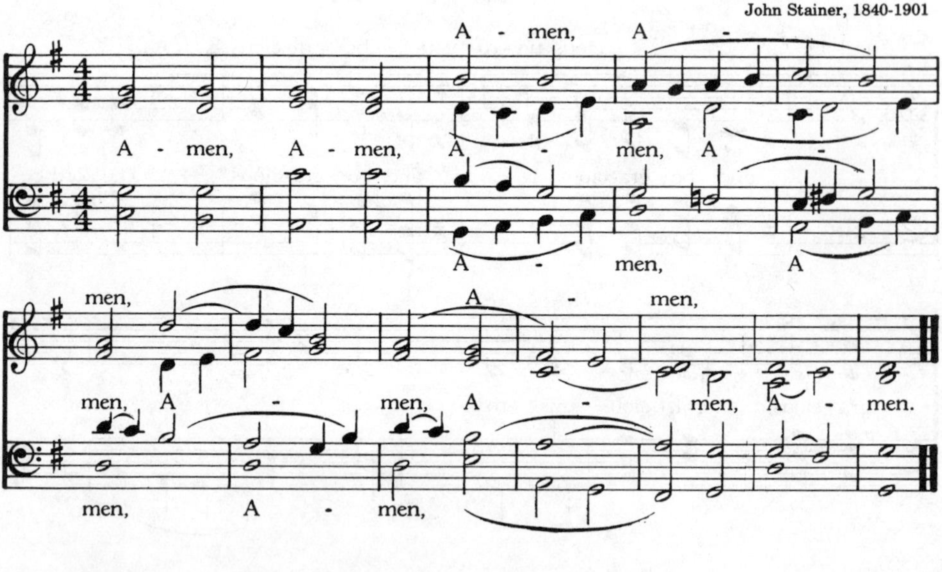
A - men, A - men,
A - men, A - men, A - men, A - men, A - men, A - men.
A - men, A - men, A - men,
men, A - men,

SCRIPTURE READINGS

An integral part of worship, whether private or on the levels of the family circle or the public convocation, is the reading of the Word of God. The section that follows contains a number of Bible readings relevant to the major themes of Scripture. These readings are not intended to take the place of the lesson material used in conjunction with the sermon, but their inclusion is designed to afford an opportunity for wider personal participation in the worship of God.

This section of readings includes three divisions. The first is composed of passages from the Psalms given in Biblical sequence. Historically the entire collection of Psalms made up a manual of praise and worship for the temple service. In the synagogue the Psalter was considered the "Hymnal of the Temple" and was utilized for participation in worship. The early church service was largely patterned after that of the synagogue. The Scripture portions appear here in responsory form and hence should be read responsively. Verse numbers have been included for those who prefer to read responsively by verse rather than by the original poetic structure of the Psalter. The lines printed in Roman letter are to be read by the minister; the lines in italic by the people.

The second division is a compilation of Scripture Readings arranged for responsive use and listed according to subject and themes. The third division is a topical listing of passages of Scripture that are suitable for use as unison readings in worship.

SCRIPTURE READINGS

613

Psalm 1

1 **Blessed is the man that walketh not in the counsel of the ungodly,**

Nor standeth in the way of sinners,
Nor sitteth in the seat of the scornful.

2 **But his delight is in the law of the Lord;**

And in his law doth he meditate day and night.

3 **And he shall be like a tree planted by the rivers of water,**

That bringeth forth his fruit in his season;

His leaf also shall not wither;

And whatsoever he doeth shall prosper.

4 **The ungodly are not so:**

But are like the chaff which the wind driveth away.

5 **Therefore the ungodly shall not stand in the judgment,**

Nor sinners in the congregation of the righteous.

6 **For the Lord knoweth the way of the righteous:**

But the way of the ungodly shall perish.

614

Psalm 2

1 **Why do the heathen rage,**

And the people imagine a vain thing?

2 **The kings of the earth set themselves,**

And the rulers take counsel together,
Against the Lord, and against his anointed, saying,

3 **Let us break their bands asunder,**

And cast away their cords from us.

4 **He that sitteth in the heavens shall laugh:**

The Lord shall have them in derision.

5 **Then shall he speak unto them in his wrath,**

And vex them in his sore displeasure.

6 **Yet have I set my king**

Upon my holy hill of Zion.

7 **I will declare the decree:**
The Lord hath said unto me,
Thou art my Son;

This day have I begotten thee.

8 **Ask of me, and I shall give thee the heathen for thine inheritance,**

And the uttermost parts of the earth for thy possession.

9 **Thou shalt break them with a rod of iron;**

Thou shalt dash them in pieces like a potter's vessel.

10 **Be wise now therefore, O ye kings:**

Be instructed, ye judges of the earth.

11 **Serve the Lord with fear,**

And rejoice with trembling.

12 **Kiss the Son, lest he be angry, and ye perish from the way,**
When his wrath is kindled but a little.

Blessed are all they that put their trust in him.

615

Psalm 8

1 **O Lord, our Lord,**
How excellent is thy name in all the earth!

Who hast set thy glory above the heavens.

2 **Out of the mouth of babes and sucklings hast thou ordained strength because of thine enemies,**

That thou mightest still the enemy and the avenger.

3 **When I consider thy heavens, the work of thy fingers,**

The moon and the stars, which thou hast ordained;

4 **What is man, that thou art mindful of him?**

And the son of man, that thou visitest him?

5 **For thou hast made him a little lower than the angels,**

And hast crowned him with glory and honor.

6 **Thou madest him to have dominion over the works of thy hands;**

Thou hast put all things under his feet:

7 **All sheep and oxen,**

Yea, and the beasts of the field;

8 **The fowl of the air, and the fish of the sea,**

And whatsoever passeth through the paths of the seas.

9 **O Lord our Lord,**

How excellent is thy name in all the earth!

616

Psalm 13

1 **How long wilt thou forget me, O Lord? for ever?**

How long wilt thou hide thy face from me?

2 **How long shall I take counsel in my soul, having sorrow in my heart daily?**

How long shall mine enemy be exalted over me?

3 **Consider and hear me, O Lord my God:**

Lighten mine eyes, lest I sleep the sleep of death:

4 **Lest mine enemy say, I have prevailed against him;**

And those that trouble me rejoice when I am moved.

5 **But I have trusted in thy mercy;**

My heart shall rejoice in thy salvation.

6 **I will sing unto the Lord,**

Because he hath dealt bountifully with me.

Psalm 15

1 **Lord, who shall abide in thy tabernacle?**

Who shall dwell in thy holy hill?

2 **He that walketh uprightly, and worketh righteousness,**

And speaketh the truth in his heart.

3 **He that backbiteth not with his tongue,**
Nor doeth evil to his neighbor,

Nor taketh up a reproach against his neighbor.

4 **In whose eyes a vile person is contemned;**

But he honoreth them that fear the Lord.

He that sweareth to his own hurt, and changeth not.

5 *He that putteth not out his money to usury,*

Nor taketh reward against the innocent.

He that doeth these things shall never be moved.

617

Psalm 16

1 **Preserve me, O God:**

For in thee do I put my trust.

2 **O my soul, thou hast said unto the Lord, Thou art my Lord:**

My goodness extendeth not to thee;

3 **But to the saints that are in the earth,**

And to the excellent, in whom is all my delight.

4 **Their sorrows shall be multiplied that hasten after another God:**
Their drink offerings of blood will I not offer,

Nor take up their names into my lips.

5 **The Lord is the portion of mine inheritance and of my cup:**

Thou maintainest my lot.

6 **The lines are fallen unto me in pleasant places:**

Yea, I have a goodly heritage.

7 **I will bless the Lord, who hath given me counsel:**

My reins also instruct me in the night seasons.

8 **I have set the Lord always before me:**

Because he is at my right hand, I shall not be moved.

9 **Therefore my heart is glad, and my glory rejoiceth:**

My flesh also shall rest in hope.

10 **For thou wilt not leave my soul in hell;**

Neither wilt thou suffer thine Holy One to see corruption.

11 **Thou wilt show me the path of life:**
In thy presence is fulness of joy;

At thy right hand there are pleasures for evermore.

618

Psalm 19

1 **The heavens declare the glory of God;**

And the firmament showeth his handiwork.

2 **Day unto day uttereth speech,**

And night unto night showeth knowledge.

3 **There is no speech nor language,**

Where their voice is not heard.

4 **Their line is gone out through all the earth,**

And their words to the end of the world.
In them hath he set a tabernacle for the sun,

5 **Which is as a bridegroom coming out of his chamber,**

And rejoiceth as a strong man to run a race.

6 **His going forth is from the end of the heaven,**
And his circuit unto the ends of it:

And there is nothing hid from the heat thereof.

7 **The law of the Lord is perfect, converting the soul:**

The testimony of the Lord is sure, making wise the simple.

8 **The statutes of the Lord are right, rejoicing the heart:**

The commandment of the Lord is pure, enlightening the eyes.

9 **The fear of the Lord is clean, enduring forever:**

The judgments of the Lord are true and righteous altogether.

10 **More to be desired are they than gold, yea, than much fine gold:**

Sweeter also than honey and the honeycomb.

11 **Moreover by them is thy servant warned:**
And in keeping of them there is great reward.

12 *Who can understand his errors? Cleanse thou me from secret faults.*

13 **Keep back thy servant also from presumptuous sins;**
Let them not have dominion over me:

Then shall I be upright, and I shall be innocent from the great transgression.

14 **Let the words of my mouth, and the meditation of my heart, be acceptable in thy sight,**

O Lord, my strength, and my redeemer.

619

Psalm 23

1 **The Lord is my shepherd;**

I shall not want.

2 **He maketh me to lie down in green pastures:**

He leadeth me beside the still waters.

3 **He restoreth my soul:**

He leadeth me in the paths of righteousness for his name's sake.

4 **Yea, though I walk through the valley of the shadow of death, I will fear no evil: for thou art with me;**

Thy rod and thy staff they comfort me.

5 **Thou preparest a table before me in the presence of mine enemies:**

Thou anointest my head with oil; my cup runneth over.

6 **Surely goodness and mercy shall follow me all the days of my life:**

And I will dwell in the house of the Lord for ever.

620

Psalm 24

1 **The earth is the Lord's, and the fulness thereof:**

The world, and they that dwell therein.

2 **For he hath founded it upon the seas,**

And established it upon the floods.

3 **Who shall ascend into the hill of the Lord?**

Or who shall stand in his holy place?

4 **He that hath clean hands, and a pure heart;**

Who hath not lifted up his soul unto vanity, nor sworn deceitfully.

5 **He shall receive the blessing from the Lord,**

And righteousness from the God of his salvation.

6 **This is the generation of them that seek him,**

That seek thy face, O Jacob.

7 **Lift up your heads, O ye gates; and be ye lift up, ye everlasting doors;**

And the King of glory shall come in.

8 **Who is this King of glory?**

The Lord strong and mighty, the Lord mighty in battle.

9 **Lift up your heads, O ye gates; even lift them up, ye everlasting doors;**

And the King of glory shall come in.

10 **Who is this King of glory?**

The Lord of hosts, he is the King of glory.

621

Psalm 25

1 **Unto thee, O Lord, do I lift up my soul.**

2 **O my God, I trust in thee:**

Let me not be ashamed, let not mine enemies triumph over me.

3 **Yea, let none that wait on thee be ashamed:**

Let them be ashamed which transgress without cause.

4 **Show me thy ways, O Lord;**

Teach me thy paths.

5 **Lead me in thy truth, and teach me; for thou art the God of my salvation;**

On thee do I wait all the day.

6 **Remember, O Lord, thy tender mercies and thy lovingkindnesses;**

For they have been ever of old.

7 **Remember not the sins of my youth, nor my transgressions:**

According to thy mercy remember thou me, for thy goodness' sake, O Lord.

8 **Good and upright is the Lord:**

Therefore will he teach sinners in the way.

9 **The meek will he guide in judgment;**

And the meek will he teach his way.

10 **All the paths of the Lord are mercy and truth**

Unto such as keep his covenant and his testimonies.

11 **For thy name's sake, O Lord, pardon mine iniquity;**

For it is great.

12 **What man is he that feareth the Lord?**

Him shall he teach in the way that he shall choose.

13 **His soul shall dwell at ease;**

And his seed shall inherit the earth.

14 **The secret of the Lord is with them that fear him;**

And he will show them his covenant.

15 **Mine eyes are ever toward the Lord;**

For he shall pluck my feet out of the net.

16 **Turn thee unto me, and have mercy upon me;**

For I am desolate and afflicted.

17 **The troubles of my heart are enlarged:**

O bring thou me out of my distresses.

18 **Look upon mine affliction and my pain;**

And forgive all my sins.

19 **Consider mine enemies; for they are many;**

And they hate me with cruel hatred.

20 **O keep my soul and deliver me: let me not be ashamed;**

For I put my trust in thee.

21 **Let integrity and uprightness preserve me; for I wait on thee.**

22 *Redeem Israel, O God, out of all his troubles.*

622

Psalm 27

1 **The Lord is my light and my salvation; whom shall I fear?**

The Lord is the strength of my life; of whom shall I be afraid?

2 **When the wicked, even mine enemies and my foes, came upon me to eat up my flesh,**

They stumbled and fell.

3 **Though an host should encamp against me, my heart shall not fear:**

Though war should rise against me, in this will I be confident.

4 **One thing have I desired of the Lord, that will I seek after; That I may dwell in the house of the Lord all the days of my life,**

To behold the beauty of the Lord, and to inquire in his temple.

5 **For in the time of trouble he shall hide me in his pavilion: In the secret of his tabernacle shall he hide me;**

He shall set me up upon a rock.

6 **And now shall mine head be lifted up above mine enemies round about me: Therefore will I offer in his tabernacle sacrifices of joy;**

I will sing, yea, I will sing praises unto the Lord.

7 **Hear, O Lord, when I cry with my voice:**

Have mercy also upon me, and answer me.

8 **When thou saidst, Seek ye my face;**

My heart said unto thee, Thy face, Lord, will I seek.

9 **Hide not thy face far from me; put not thy servant away in anger:**

Thou hast been my help; leave me not, neither forsake me, O God of my salvation.

10 **When my father and my mother forsake me,**

Then the Lord will take me up.

11 **Teach me thy way, O Lord,**

And lead me in a plain path, because of mine enemies.

12 **Deliver me not over unto the will of mine enemies:**

For false witnesses are risen up against me, and such as breathe out cruelty.

13 **I had fainted, unless I had believed to see the goodness of the Lord in the land of the living.**

14 *Wait on the Lord:*

Be of good courage, and he shall strengthen thine heart:

Wait, I say, on the Lord.

623

Psalm 30

1 **I will extol thee, O Lord; for thou hast lifted me up,**

And hast not made my foes to rejoice over me.

2 **O Lord my God, I cried unto thee,**

And thou hast healed me.

3 **O Lord, thou hast brought up my soul from the grave:**

Thou hast kept me alive, that I should not go down to the pit.

4 **Sing unto the Lord, O ye saints of his,**

And give thanks at the remembrance of his holiness.

5 **For his anger endureth but a moment;**
In his favor is life:

Weeping may endure for a night, but joy cometh in the morning.

6 **And in my prosperity I said,**

I shall never be moved.

7 **Lord, by thy favor thou hast made my mountain to stand strong:**

Thou didst hide thy face, and I was troubled.

8 **I cried to thee, O Lord;**

And unto the Lord I made supplication.

9 **What profit is there in my blood, when I go down to the pit?**

Shall the dust praise thee? shall it declare thy truth?

10 **Hear, O Lord, and have mercy upon me:**

Lord, be thou my helper.

11 **Thou hast turned for me my mourning into dancing:**

Thou hast put off my sackcloth, and girded me with gladness;

12 **To the end that my glory may sing praise to thee, and not be silent.**

O Lord, my God, I will give thanks unto thee for ever.

624

Psalm 31

1 **In thee, O Lord, do I put my trust; let me never be ashamed:**

Deliver me in thy righteousness.

2 **Bow down thine ear to me; deliver me speedily:**

Be thou my strong rock, for an house of defence to save me.

3 **For thou art my rock and my fortress;**

Therefore for thy name's sake lead me, and guide me.

4 **Pull me out of the net that they have laid privily for me:**

For thou art my strength.

5 **Into thine hand I commit my spirit:**

Thou hast redeemed me, O Lord God of truth.

15 **My times are in thy hand: deliver me from the hand of mine enemies,**

And from them that persecute me.

16 **Make thy face to shine upon thy servant:**

Save me for thy mercies' sake.

19 **Oh how great is thy goodness, which thou hast laid up for them that fear thee;**

Which thou hast wrought for them that trust in thee before the sons of men!

20 **Thou shalt hide them in the secret of thy presence from the pride of man:**

Thou shalt keep them secretly in a pavilion from the strife of tongues.

21 **Blessed be the Lord:**

For he hath showed me his marvelous kindness in a strong city.

22 **For I said in my haste, I am cut off from before thine eyes:**

Nevertheless thou heardest the voice of my supplications when I cried unto thee.

23 **O love the Lord, all ye his saints: for the Lord preserveth the faithful,**

And plentifully rewardeth the proud doer.

24 **Be of good courage, and he shall strengthen your heart,**

All ye that hope in the Lord.

625

Psalm 32

1 **Blessed is he whose transgression is forgiven,**

Whose sin is covered.

2 **Blessed is the man unto whom the Lord imputeth not iniquity,**

And in whose spirit there is no guile.

3 **When I kept silence, my bones waxed old through my roaring all the day long.**

4 *For day and night thy hand was heavy upon me:*

My moisture is turned into the drought of summer.

5 *I acknowledged my sin unto thee, and mine iniquity have I not hid.*

I said, I will confess my transgressions unto the Lord;

And thou forgavest the iniquity of my sin.

6 **For this shall every one that is godly pray unto thee in a time when thou mayest be found:**

Surely in the floods of great waters they shall not come nigh unto him.

7 **Thou art my hiding place; thou shalt preserve me from trouble;**

Thou shalt compass me about with songs of deliverance.

8 **I will instruct thee and teach thee in the way which thou shalt go:**

I will guide thee with mine eye.

9 **Be ye not as the horse, or as the mule, which have no understanding:**

Whose mouth must be held in with bit and bridle, lest they come near unto thee.

10 **Many sorrows shall be to the wicked:**

But he that trusteth in the Lord, mercy shall compass him about.

11 **Be glad in the Lord, and rejoice, ye righteous:**

And shout for joy, all ye that are upright in heart.

626

Psalm 33

1 **Rejoice in the Lord, O ye righteous:**

For praise is comely for the upright.

2 **Praise the Lord with harp:**

Sing unto him with the psaltery and an instrument of ten strings.

3 **Sing unto him a new song:**

Play skilfully with a loud noise.

4 **For the word of the Lord is right;**

And all his works are done in truth.

5 **He loveth righteousness and judgment:**

The earth is full of the goodness of the Lord.

6 **By the word of the Lord were the heavens made;**

And all the hosts of them by breath of his mouth.

7 **He gathereth the waters of the sea together as an heap:**

He layeth up the depth in storehouses.

8 **Let all the earth fear the Lord:**

Let all the inhabitants of the world stand in awe of him.

9 **For he spake, and it was done:**

He commanded, and it stood fast.

10 **The Lord bringeth the counsel of the heathen to nought:**

He maketh the devices of the people of none effect.

11 **The counsel of the Lord standeth for ever,**

The thoughts of his heart to all generations.

12 **Blessed is the nation whose God is the Lord;**

And the people whom he hath chosen for his own inheritance.

13 **The Lord looketh from heaven;**

He beholdeth all the sons of men.

14 **From the place of his habitation he looketh**

Upon all the inhabitants of the earth.

15 **He fashioneth their hearts alike;**

He considereth all their works.

16 **There is no king saved by the multitude of an host:**

A mighty man is not delivered by much strength.

17 **An horse is a vain thing for safety:**

Neither shall he deliver any by his great strength.

18 **Behold, the eye of the Lord is upon them that fear him,**

Upon them that hope in his mercy;

19 **To deliver their soul from death,**

And to keep them alive in famine.

20 **Our soul waiteth for the Lord:**

He is our help and our shield.

21 **For our heart shall rejoice in him,**

Because we have trusted in his holy name.

22 **Let thy mercy, O Lord, be upon us,**

According as we hope in thee.

627

Psalm 34

1 **I will bless the Lord at all times:**

His praise shall continually be in my mouth.

2 **My soul shall make her boast in the Lord:**

The humble shall hear thereof, and be glad.

3 **O magnify the Lord with me,**

And let us exalt his name together.

4 **I sought the Lord, and he heard me,**

And delivered me from all my fears.

5 **They looked unto him, and were lightened:**

And their faces were not ashamed.

6 **This poor man cried, and the Lord heard him,**

And saved him out of all his troubles.

7 **The angel of the Lord encampeth round about them that fear him,**

And delivereth them.

8 **O taste and see that the Lord is good:**

Blessed is the man that trusteth in him.

9 **O fear the Lord, ye his saints:**

For there is no want to them that fear him.

10 **The young lions do lack, and suffer hunger:**

But they that seek the Lord shall not want any good thing.

11 **Come, ye children, hearken unto me:**

I will teach you the fear of the Lord.

12 **What man is he that desireth life.**

And loveth many days, that he may see good?

13 **Keep thy tongue from evil,**

And thy lips from speaking guile.

14 **Depart from evil, and do good;**

Seek peace, and pursue it.

15 **The eyes of the Lord are upon the righteous,**

And his ears are open unto their cry.

16 **The face of the Lord is against them that do evil,**

To cut off the remembrance of them from the earth.

17 **The righteous cry, and the Lord heareth,**

And delivereth them out of all their troubles.

18 **The Lord is nigh unto them that are of a broken heart:**

And saveth such as be of a contrite spirit.

628

Psalm 37

1 **Fret not thyself because of evil-doers,**

Neither be thou envious against the workers of iniquity.

2 **For they shall soon be cut down like the grass,**

And wither as the green herb.

3 **Trust in the Lord and do good:**

So shalt thou dwell in the land, and verily thou shalt be fed.

4 **Delight thyself also in the Lord;**

And he shall give thee the desires of thine heart.

5 **Commit thy way unto the Lord;**

Trust also in him; and he shall bring it to pass.

6 **And he shall bring forth thy righteousness as the light,**

And thy judgment as the noonday.

7 **Rest in the Lord and wait patiently for him:**

Fret not thyself because of him who prospereth in his way,
Because of the man who bringeth wicked devices to pass.

8 **Cease from anger, and forsake wrath:**

Fret not thyself in any wise to do evil.

23 **The steps of a good man are ordered by the Lord:**

And he delighteth in his way.

24 **Though he fall, he shall not be utterly cast down:**

For the Lord upholdeth him with his hand.

25 **I have been young, and now am old;**

Yet have I not seen the righteous forsaken, nor his seed begging bread.

26 **He is ever merciful, and lendeth;**

And his seed is blessed.

27 **Depart from evil, and do good;**

And dwell for evermore.

28 **For the Lord loveth judgment,**

And forsaketh not his saints;

They are preserved for ever:

But the seed of the wicked shall be cut off.

29 **The righteous shall inherit the land,**

And dwell therein for ever.

30 **The mouth of the righteous speaketh wisdom,**

And his tongue talketh of judgment.

31 **The law of his God is in his heart;**

None of his steps shall slide.

37 **Mark the perfect man, and behold the upright;**

For the end of that man is peace.

629

Psalm 40

1 **I waited patiently for the Lord;**

And he inclined unto me, and heard my cry.

2 **He brought me up also out of a horrible pit, out of the miry clay,**

And set my feet upon a rock, and established my goings.

3 **And he hath put a new song in my mouth, even praise unto our God:**

Many shall see it, and fear, and shall trust in the Lord.

4 **Blessed is the man that maketh the Lord his trust,**

And respecteth not the proud, nor such as turn aside to lies.

5 **Many, O Lord my God, are thy wonderful works which thou hast done,**

And thy thoughts which are to us-ward:

They cannot be reckoned up in order unto thee:

If I would declare and speak of them, they are more than can be numbered.

6 **Sacrifice and offering thou didst not desire; mine ears hast thou opened:**

Burnt offering and sin offering hast thou not required.

7 **Then said I, Lo, I come:**

In the volume of the book it is written of me,

8 **I delight to do thy will, O my God:**

Yea, thy law is within my heart.

9 **I have preached righteousness in the great congregation:**

Lo, I have not refrained my lips, O Lord, thou knowest.

10 **I have not hid thy righteousness within my heart;**
I have declared thy faithfulness and thy salvation:

I have not concealed thy lovingkindness and thy truth from the great congregation.

11 **Withhold not thou thy tender mercies from me, O Lord:**

Let thy lovingkindness and thy truth continually preserve me.

12 **For innumerable evils have compassed me about:**

Mine iniquities have taken hold upon me, so that I am not able to look up;

They are more than the hairs of mine head:

Therefore my heart faileth me.

13 **Be pleased, O Lord, to deliver me:**

O Lord, make haste to help me.
16 *Let all those that seek thee rejoice and be glad in thee:*

Let such as love thy salvation say continually,

The Lord be magnified.

17 **But I am poor and needy;**

Yet the Lord thinketh upon me:

Thou art my help and my deliverer:

Make no tarrying, O my God.

630

Psalm 42

1 **As the hart panteth after the water brooks,**

So panteth my soul after thee, O God.

2 **My soul thirsteth for God, for the living God:**

When shall I come and appear before God?

3 **My tears have been my meat day and night,**

While they continually say unto me, Where is thy God?

4 **When I remember these things I pour out my soul in me:**
For I had gone with the multitude, I went with them to the house of God,

With the voice of joy and praise, with a multitude that kept holyday.

5 **Why art thou cast down, O my soul? and why art thou disquieted in me?**

Hope thou in God: for I shall yet praise him, for the help of his countenance.

7 **Deep calleth unto deep at the noise of thy waterspouts:**

All thy waves and thy billows are gone over me.

8 **Yet the Lord will command his lovingkindness in the daytime,**

And in the night his song shall be with me, and my prayer unto the God of my life.

9 **I will say unto God, my rock, Why hast thou forgotten me?**

Why go I mourning, because of the oppression of the enemy?

10 **As with a sword in my bones, mine enemies reproach me;**

While they say daily unto me, Where is thy God?

11 **Why art thou cast down, O my soul? and why art thou disquieted within me?**

Hope thou in God: for I shall yet praise him,
Who is the health of my countenance, and my God.

631

Psalm 46

1 **God is our refuge and strength,**

A very present help in trouble.

2 **Therefore will not we fear, though the earth be removed,**

And though the mountains be carried into the midst of the sea;

3 **Though the waters thereof roar and be troubled,**

Though the mountains shake with the swelling thereof.

4 **There is a river, the streams whereof shall make glad the city of God;**

The holy place of the tabernacles of the most High.

5 **God is in the midst of her; she shall not be moved:**

God shall help her, and that right early.

6 **The heathen raged, the kingdoms were moved:**

He uttered his voice, the earth melted.

7 **The Lord of hosts is with us;**

The God of Jacob is our refuge.

8 **Come, behold the works of the Lord,**

What desolations he hath made in the earth.

9 **He maketh wars to cease unto the end of the earth:**

He breaketh the bow, and cutteth the spear in sunder; he burneth the chariot in the fire.

10 **Be still, and know that I am God:**

I will be exalted among the heathen, I will be exalted in the earth.

11 **The Lord of hosts is with us;**

The God of Jacob is our refuge.

632

Psalm 51

1 **Have mercy upon me, O God, according to thy lovingkindness:**

According unto the multitude of thy tender mercies, blot out my transgressions.

2 **Wash me thoroughly from mine iniquity,**

And cleanse me from my sin.

3 **For I acknowledge my transgressions:**

And my sin is ever before me.

4 **Against thee, thee only, have I sinned,**

And done this evil in thy sight:

That thou mightest be justified when thou speakest,

And be clear when thou judgest.

5 **Behold, I was shapen in iniquity;**

And in sin did my mother conceive me.

6 **Behold, thou desirest truth in the inward parts:**

And in the hidden part thou shalt make me to know wisdom.

7 **Purge me with hyssop, and I shall be clean:**

Wash me, and I shall be whiter than snow.

8 **Make me to hear joy and gladness;**

That the bones which thou hast broken may rejoice.

9 **Hide thy face from my sins,**

And blot out all mine iniquities.

10 **Create in me a clean heart, O God;**

And renew a right spirit within me.

11 **Cast me not away from thy presence;**

And take not thy holy spirit from me.

12 **Restore unto me the joy of thy salvation;**

And uphold me with thy free spirit.

13 **Then will I teach transgressors thy ways;**

And sinners shall be converted unto thee.

14 **Deliver me from bloodguiltiness, O God, thou God of my salvation;**

And my tongue shall sing aloud of thy righteousness.

15 **O Lord, open thou my lips;**

And my mouth shall show forth thy praise.

16 **For thou desirest not sacrifice; else would I give it:**

Thou delightest not in burnt offering.

17 **The sacrifices of God are a broken spirit:**

A broken and a contrite heart, O God, thou wilt not despise.

633

Psalm 57

1 **Be merciful unto me, O God, be merciful unto me:**

For my soul trusteth in thee:

Yea, in the shadow of thy wings will I make my refuge,

Until these calamities be overpast.

2 **I will cry unto God most high;**

Unto God that performeth all things for me.

3 **He shall send from heaven, and save me from the reproach of him that would swallow me up.**

God shall send forth his mercy and his truth.

4 **My soul is among lions:**

And I lie even among them that are set on fire,

Even the sons of men, whose teeth are spears and arrows,

And their tongue a sharp sword.

5 **Be thou exalted, O God, above the heavens;**

Let thy glory be above all the earth.

6 **They have prepared a net for my steps;**

My soul is bowed down:

They have digged a pit before me,

Into the midst whereof they are fallen themselves.

7 **My heart is fixed, O God, my heart is fixed:**

I will sing and give praise.

8 **Awake up, my glory; awake, psaltery and harp:**

I myself will awake early.

9 **I will praise thee, O Lord, among the people:**

I will sing unto thee among the nations.

10 **For thy mercy is great unto the heavens,**

And thy truth unto the clouds.

11 **Be thou exalted, O God, above the heavens:**

Let thy glory be above all the earth.

634

Psalm 65

1 **Praise waiteth for thee, O God, in Zion:**

And unto thee shall the vow be performed.

2 **O thou that hearest prayer, unto thee shall all flesh come.**

3 *Iniquities prevail against me: as for our transgressions, thou shalt purge them away.*

4 **Blessed is the man whom thou choosest,**
And causest to approach unto thee, that he may dwell in thy courts:

We shall be satisfied with the goodness of thy house, even of thy holy temple.

5 **By terrible things in righteousness wilt thou answer us, O God of our salvation;**

Who art the confidence of all the ends of the earth, and of them that are afar off upon the sea:

6 **Which by his strength setteth fast the mountains; being girded with power:**

7 *Which stilleth the noise of the seas, the noise of their waves, and the tumult of the people.*

8 **They also that dwell in the uttermost parts are afraid at thy tokens:**

Thou makest the outgoings of the morning and evening to rejoice.

9 **Thou visitest the earth, and waterest it:**

Thou greatly enrichest it with the river of God,

Which is full of water:

Thou preparest them corn, when thou hast so provided for it.

10 **Thou waterest the ridges thereof abundantly;**
Thou settlest the furrows thereof:

Thou makest it soft with showers; thou blessest the springing thereof.

11 **Thou crownest the year with thy goodness;**

And thy paths drop fatness.

12 **They drop upon the pastures of the wilderness;**

And the little hills rejoice on every side.

13 **The pastures are clothed with flocks;**

The valleys also are covered over with corn; they shout for joy, they also sing.

635

Psalm 66

1 **Make a joyful noise unto God, all ye lands.**

2 *Sing forth the honor of his name; make his praise glorious.*

3 **Say unto God, How terrible art thou in thy works!**

Through the greatness of thy power shall thine enemies submit themselves unto thee.

4 **All the earth shall worship thee, and shall sing unto thee;**

They shall sing to thy name.

5 **Come and see the works of God:**

He is terrible in his doing toward the children of men.

6 **He turned the sea into dry land: they went through the flood on foot:**

There did we rejoice in him.

7 **He ruleth by his power for ever; His eyes behold the nations:**

Let not the rebellious exalt themselves.

8 **O bless our God, ye people,**

And make the voice of his praise to be heard:

9 **Which holdeth our soul in life,**

And suffereth not our feet to be moved.

16 **Come and hear, all ye that fear God,**

And I will declare what he hath done for my soul.

17 **I cried unto him with my mouth,**

And he was extolled with my tongue.

18 **If I regard iniquity in my heart,**

The Lord will not hear me:

19 **But verily God hath heard me;**

He hath attended to the voice of my prayer.

20 **Blessed be God, which hath not turned away my prayer,**

Nor his mercy from me.

636

Psalm 67

1 **God be merciful unto us, and bless us:**

And cause his face to shine upon us;

2 **That thy way may be known upon earth,**

Thy saving health among all nations.

3 **Let the people praise thee, O God,**

Let all the people praise thee.

4 **O let the nations be glad and sing for joy: for thou shalt judge the people righteously,**

And govern the nations upon earth.

5 **Let the people praise thee, O God,**

Let all the people praise thee.

6 **Then shall the earth yield her increase;**

And God, even our own God, shall bless us.

7 *God shall bless us; and all the ends of the earth shall fear him.*

637

Psalm 71

1 **In thee, O Lord, do I put my trust:**

Let me never be put to confusion.

2 **Deliver me in thy righteousness, and cause me to escape:**

Incline thine ear unto me, and save me.

3 **Be thou my strong habitation, whereunto I may continually resort:**
Thou hast given commandment to save me:

For thou art my rock and my fortress.

4 **Deliver me, O my God, out of the hand of the wicked,**

Out of the hand of the unrighteous and cruel man.

5 **For thou art my hope, O Lord God:**

Thou art my trust from my youth.

6 **By thee have I been holden up from the womb: Thou art he that took me out of my mother's bowels:**

My praise shall be continually of thee.

17 **O God, thou hast taught me from my youth:**

And hitherto have I declared thy wondrous works.

18 **Now also when I am old and grayheaded, O God, forsake me not; Until I have showed thy strength unto this generation,**

And thy power to every one that is to come.

19 **Thy righteousness also, O**

God, is very high, who hast done great things;

O God, who is like unto thee!

20 **Thou, which hast showed me great and sore troubles, shalt quicken me again,**

And shalt bring me up again from the depths of the earth.

21 **Thou shalt increase my greatness,**

And comfort me on every side.

22 **I will also praise thee with the psaltery; even thy truth, O my God:**

Unto thee will I sing with the harp, O thou Holy One of Israel.

23 **My lips shall greatly rejoice when I sing unto thee;**

And my soul, which thou hast redeemed.

24 **My tongue also shall talk of thy righteousness all the day long:**

For they are confounded, for they are brought unto shame, that seek my hurt.

638

Psalm 84

1 **How amiable are thy tabernacles,**

O Lord of hosts!

2 **My soul longeth, yea, even fainteth for the courts of the Lord:**

My heart and my flesh crieth out for the living God.

3 **Yea, the sparrow hath found a house,**

And the swallow a nest for herself, where she may lay her young,

Even thine altars, O Lord of hosts,

My King and my God.

4 **Blessed are they that dwell in thy house:**

They will be still praising thee.

5 **Blessed is the man whose strength is in thee;**

In whose heart are the ways of them;

6 **Who passing through the valley of Baca make it a well:**

The rain also filleth the pools.

7 **They go from strength to strength,**

Every one of them in Zion appeareth before God.

8 **O Lord God of hosts, hear my prayer:**

Give ear, O God of Jacob.

9 **Behold, O God our shield,**

And look upon the face of thine anointed.

10 **For a day in thy courts is better than a thousand.**

I had rather be a doorkeeper in the house of my God, than to dwell in the tents of wickedness.

11 **For the Lord God is a sun and shield: the Lord will give grace and glory:**

No good thing will he withhold

from them that walk uprightly.

12 *O Lord of hosts, blessed is the man that trusteth in thee.*

639

Psalm 86

1 **Bow down thine ear, O Lord, hear me:**

For I am poor and needy.

2 **Preserve my soul; for I am holy:**

O thou my God, save thy servant that trusteth in thee.

3 **Be merciful unto me, O Lord:**

For I cry unto thee daily.

4 **Rejoice the soul of thy servant:**

For unto thee, O Lord, do I lift up my soul.

5 **For thou, Lord, art good, and ready to forgive;**

And plenteous in mercy unto all them that call upon thee.

6 **Give ear, O Lord, unto my prayer,**

And attend to the voice of my supplications.

7 **In the day of my trouble I will call upon thee:**

For thou wilt answer me.

8 **Among the gods there is none like unto thee, O Lord;**

Neither are there any works like unto thy works.

9 **All nations whom thou hast made shall come and worship before thee, O Lord;**

And shall glorify thy name.

10 **For thou art great, and doest wondrous things:**

Thou art God alone.

11 **Teach me thy way, O Lord; I will walk in thy truth:**

Unite my heart to fear thy name.

12 **I will praise thee, O Lord my God, with all my heart:**

And I will glorify thy name for evermore.

13 **For great is thy mercy toward me:**

And thou hast delivered my soul from the lowest hell.

14 **O God, the proud are risen against me, and the assemblies of violent men have sought after my soul;**

And have not set thee before them.

15 **But thou, O Lord, art a God full of compassion, and gracious,**

Long-suffering, and plenteous in mercy and truth.

16 **O turn unto me, and have mercy upon me;**

Give thy strength unto thy servant, and save the son of thine handmaid.

17 **Show me a token for good: that they which hate me may see it, and be ashamed:**

Because thou, Lord, hast holpen me, and comforted me.

640

Psalm 91

1 **He that dwelleth in the secret place of the most High**

Shall abide under the shadow of the Almighty.

2 **I will say of the Lord, he is my refuge and my fortress:**

My God; in him will I trust.

3 **Surely he shall deliver thee from the snare of the fowler,**

And from the noisome pestilence.

4 **He shall cover thee with his feathers, and under his wings shalt thou trust:**

His truth shall be thy shield and buckler.

5 **Thou shalt not be afraid for the terror by night,**

Nor for the arrow that flieth by day,

6 **Nor for the pestilence that walketh in darkness,**

Nor for the destruction that wasteth at noonday.

7 **A thousand shall fall at thy side, and ten thousand at thy right hand;**

But it shall not come nigh thee.

8 **Only with thine eyes shalt thou behold**

And see the reward of the wicked.

9 **Because thou hast made the Lord, which is my refuge,**

Even the most High, thy habitation,

10 **There shall no evil befall thee,**

Neither shall any plague come nigh thy dwelling.

11 **For he shall give his angels charge over thee,**

To keep thee in all thy ways.

12 **They shall bear thee up in their hands,**

Lest thou dash thy foot against a stone.

13 **Thou shalt tread upon the lion and adder:**

The young lion and the dragon shalt thou trample under feet.

14 **Because he hath set his love upon me, therefore will I deliver him:**

I will set him on high, because he hath known my name.

15 **He shall call upon me, and I will answer him: I will be with him in trouble;**

I will deliver him, and honor him.

16 **With long life will I satisfy him,**

And show him my salvation.

641

Psalm 95

1 **O come, let us sing unto the Lord:**

Let us make a joyful noise to the rock of our salvation.

2 **Let us come before his presence with thanksgiving,**

And make a joyful noise unto him with psalms.

3 **For the Lord is a great God,**

And a great King above all gods.

4 **In his hands are the deep places of the earth:**

The strength of the hills is his also.

5 **The sea is his, and he made it:**

And his hands formed the dry land.

6 **O come, let us worship and bow down:**

Let us kneel before the Lord our maker.

7 **For he is our God;**

And we are the people of his pasture, and the sheep of his hand.

To day if ye will hear his voice,
8 **Harden not your heart, as in the provocation,**

And as in the day of temptation in the wilderness:

9 **When your fathers tempted me,**

Proved me, and saw my work.

10 **Forty years long was I grieved with this generation, and said, It is a people that do err in their heart,**

And they have not known my ways:

11 **Unto whom I sware in my wrath,**

That they should not enter into my rest.

642

Psalm 96

1 **O sing unto the Lord a new song:**

Sing unto the Lord, all the earth.

2 **Sing unto the Lord, bless his name;**

Show forth his salvation from day to day.

3 **Declare his glory among the heathen,**

His wonders among all people.

4 **For the Lord is great, and greatly to be praised:**

He is to be feared above all gods.

5 **For all the gods of the nations are idols:**

But the Lord made the heavens.

6 **Honor and majesty are before him:**

Strength and beauty are in his sanctuary.

7 **Give unto the Lord, O ye kindreds of the people,**

Give unto the Lord glory and strength.

8 **Give unto the Lord the glory due unto his name:**

Bring an offering, and come into his courts.

9 **O worship the Lord in the beauty of holiness:**

Fear before him, all the earth.

10 **Say among the heathen that the Lord reigneth; The world also shall be established that it shall not be moved:**

He shall judge the people righteously.

11 **Let the heavens rejoice, and let the earth be glad;**

Let the sea roar, and the fulness thereof.

12 **Let the field be joyful, and all that is therein:**

Then shall all the trees of the wood rejoice

13 **Before the Lord: for he cometh,**

For he cometh to judge the earth:

He shall judge the world with righteousness,

And the people with his truth.

643

Psalm 98

1 **O sing unto the Lord a new song: for he hath done marvelous things:**

His right hand and his holy arm hath gotten him the victory.

2 **The Lord hath made known his salvation:**

His righteousness hath he openly showed in the sight of the heathen.

3 **He hath remembered his mercy and his truth toward the house of Israel:**

All the ends of the earth have seen the salvation of our God.

4 **Make a joyful noise unto the Lord, all the earth:**

Make a loud noise, and rejoice, and sing praise.

5 **Sing unto the Lord with the harp:**

With the harp, and the voice of a psalm.

6 **With trumpets and sound of cornet**

Make a joyful noise before the Lord, the King.

7 **Let the sea roar, and the fulness thereof;**

The world, and they that dwell therein.

8 **Let the floods clap their hands:**

Let the hills be joyful together

9 **Before the Lord; for he cometh to judge the earth;**

With righteousness shall he judge the world, and the people with equity.

Psalm 100

1 **Make a joyful noise unto the Lord, all ye lands.**

2 *Serve the Lord with gladness: come before his presence with singing.*

3 **Know ye that the Lord he is God: it is he that hath made us, and not we ourselves;**

We are his people, and the sheep of his pasture.

4 **Enter into his gates with thanksgiving, and into his courts with praise:**

Be thankful unto him, and bless his name.

5 **For the Lord is good; his mercy is everlasting;**

And his truth endureth to all generations.

644

Psalm 103

1 **Bless the Lord, O my soul:**

And all that is within me, bless his holy name.

2 **Bless the Lord, O my soul,**

And forget not all his benefits:

3 **Who forgiveth all thine iniquities;**

Who healeth all thy diseases;

4 **Who redeemeth thy life from destruction;**

Who crowneth thee with lovingkindness and tender mercies;

5 **Who satisfieth thy mouth with good things;**

So that thy youth is renewed like the eagle's.

6 **The Lord executeth righteousness**

And judgment for all that are oppressed.

7 **He made known his ways unto Moses,**

His acts unto the children of Israel.

8 **The Lord is merciful and gracious,**

Slow to anger and plenteous in mercy.

9 **He will not always chide:**

Neither will he keep his anger for ever.

10 **He hath not dealt with us after our sins;**

Nor rewarded us according to our iniquities.

11 **For as the heaven is high above the earth,**

So great is his mercy toward them that fear him.

12 **As far as the east is from the west,**

So far hath he removed our transgressions from us.

13 **Like as a father pitieth his children,**

So the Lord pitieth them that fear him.

14 **For he knoweth our frame;**

He remembereth that we are dust.

15 **As for man, his days are as grass:**

As a flower of the field, so he flourisheth.

16 **For the wind passeth over it and it is gone;**

And the place thereof shall know it no more.

17 **But the mercy of the Lord is from everlasting to everlasting upon them that fear him,**

And his righteousness unto children's children;

18 **To such as keep his covenant,**

And to those that remember his commandments to do them.

19 **The Lord hath prepared his throne in the heavens:**

And his kingdom ruleth over all.

20 **Bless the Lord, ye his angels, that excel in strength,**

That do his commandments, hearkening unto the voice of his word.

21 **Bless ye the Lord, all ye his hosts;**

Ye ministers of his, that do his pleasure.

22 **Bless the Lord, all his works in all places of his dominion:**

Bless the Lord, O my soul.

645

Psalm 104

1 **Bless the Lord, O my soul. O Lord my God, thou art very great;**

Thou art clothed with honor and majesty.

2 **Who coverest thyself with light as with a garment:**

Who stretchest out the heavens like a curtain:

3 **Who layeth the beams of his chambers in the waters: Who maketh the clouds his chariot:**

Who walketh upon the wings of the wind:

4 **Who maketh his angels spirits;**

His ministers a flaming fire:

5 **Who laid the foundations of the earth,**

That it should not be removed for ever.

6 **Thou coveredst it with the deep as with a garment:**

The waters stood above the mountains.

7 **At thy rebuke they fled;**

At the voice of thy thunder they hasted away.

8 **They go up by the mountains; they go down by the valleys**

Unto the place which thou hast founded for them.

9 **Thou hast set a bound that they may not pass over;**

That they turn not again to cover the earth.

10 **He sendeth the springs into the valleys,**

Which run among the hills.

24 **O Lord, how manifold are thy works! in wisdom hast thou made them all:**

The earth is full of thy riches.

25 **So is this great and wide sea, wherein are things creeping innumerable,**

Both small and great beasts.

27 **These wait all upon thee:**

That thou mayest give them their meat in due season.

28 **That thou givest them they gather:**

Thou openest thine hand, they are filled with good.

29 **Thou hidest thy face, they are troubled:**

Thou takest away their breath,

they die, and return to their dust.

30 **Thou sendest forth thy spirit, they are created:**

And thou renewest the face of the earth.

31 **The glory of the Lord shall endure for ever:**

The Lord shall rejoice in his works.

32 **He looketh on the earth, and it trembleth:**

He toucheth the hills, and they smoke.

33 **I will sing unto the Lord as long as I live:**

I will sing praise to my God while I have my being.

34 **My meditation of him shall be sweet:**

I will be glad in the Lord.

646

Psalm 107

1 **O give thanks unto the Lord, for he is good:**

For his mercy endureth for ever.

2 **Let the redeemed of the Lord say so,**

Whom he hath redeemed from the hand of the enemy;

3 **And gathered them out of the lands,**

From the east, and from the west, from the north, and from the south.

4 **They wandered in the wilderness in a solitary way;**

They found no city to dwell in.

5 **Hungry and thirsty,**

Their soul fainted in them.

6 **Then they cried unto the Lord in their trouble,**

And he delivered them out of their distresses.

7 **And he led them forth by the right way,**

That they might go to a city of habitation.

8 **Oh that men would praise the Lord for his goodness,**

And for his wonderful works to the children of men!

9 **For he satisfieth the longing soul,**

And filleth the hungry soul with goodness.

10 **Such as sit in darkness and in the shadow of death,**

Being bound in affliction and iron;

11 **Because they rebelled against the words of God,**

And contemned the counsel of the most High:

12 **Therefore he brought down their heart with labor;**

They fell down, and there was none to help.

13 **Then they cried unto the Lord in their trouble,**

And he saved them out of their distresses.

14 **He brought them out of darkness and the shadow of death,**

And brake their bands in sunder.

15 **Oh that men would praise the Lord for his goodness,**

And for his wonderful works to the children of men!

16 **For he hath broken the gates of brass,**

And cut the bars of iron in sunder.

17 **Fools because of their transgression,**

And because of their iniquities, are afflicted.

18 **Their soul abhorreth all manner of meat;**

And they draw near unto the gates of death.

19 **Then they cry unto the Lord in their trouble,**

And he saveth them out of their distresses.

20 **He sent his word, and healed them,**

And delivered them from their destructions.

21 **Oh that men would praise the Lord for his goodness,**

And for his wonderful works to the children of men!

22 **And let them sacrifice the sacrifices of thanksgiving,**

And declare his works with rejoicing.

647

Psalm 115

1 **Not unto us, O Lord, not unto us, but unto thy name give glory,**

For thy mercy, and for thy truth's sake.

2 **Wherefore should the heathen say,**

Where is now their God?

3 **But our God is in the heavens:**

He hath done whatsoever he hath pleased.

4 **Their idols are silver and gold,**

The work of men's hands.

5 **They have mouths, but they speak not:**

Eyes have they, but they see not:

6 **They have ears, but they hear not:**

Noses have they, but they smell not:

7 **They have hands, but they handle not:**

Feet have they, but they walk not: neither speak they through their throat.

8 **They that make them are like unto them;**

So is every one that trusteth in them.

9 **O Israel, trust thou in the Lord:**

He is their help and their shield.

10 **O house of Aaron, trust in the Lord:**

He is their help and their shield.

11 **Ye that fear the Lord, trust in the Lord:**

He is their help and their shield.

12 **The Lord hath been mindful of us: he will bless us; he will bless the house of Israel;**

He will bless the house of Aaron.

13 **He will bless them that fear the Lord,**

Both small and great.

14 **The Lord shall increase you more and more,**

You and your children.

15 **Ye are blessed of the Lord,**

Which made heaven and earth.

16 **The heaven, even the heavens, are the Lord's:**

But the earth hath he given to the children of men.

17 **The dead praise not the Lord,**

Neither any that go down into silence.

18 **But we will bless the Lord**

From this time forth and for evermore.
Praise the Lord.

648

Psalm 116

1 **I love the Lord,**

Because he hath heard my voice and my supplications.

2 **Because he hath inclined his ear unto me,**

Therefore will I call upon him as long as I live.

3 **The sorrows of death compassed me, and the pains of hell gat hold upon me:**

I found trouble and sorrow.

4 **Then called I upon the name of the Lord:**

O Lord, I beseech thee, deliver my soul.

5 **Gracious is the Lord, and righteous:**

Yea, our God is merciful.

6 **The Lord preserveth the simple:**

I was brought low, and he helped me.

7 **Return unto thy rest, O my soul;**

For the Lord hath dealt bountifully with thee.

8 **For thou hast delivered my soul from death,**

Mine eyes from tears, and my feet from falling.

9 **I will walk before the Lord**

In the land of the living.

12 **What shall I render unto the Lord**

For all his benefits toward me?

13 **I will take the cup of salvation,**

And call upon the name of the Lord.

14 **I will pay my vows unto the Lord**

Now in the presence of all his people.

15 **Precious in the sight of the Lord**

Is the death of his saints.

16 **O Lord, truly I am thy servant; I am thy servant, and the son of thine handmaid:**

Thou hast loosed my bonds.

17 **I will offer to thee the sacrifice of thanksgiving,**

And will call upon the name of the Lord.

18 **I will pay my vows unto the Lord**

Now in the presence of all his people,

19 **In the courts of the Lord's house,**

In the midst of thee, O Jerusalem.
Praise ye the Lord.

649

Psalm 119

1 **Blessed are the undefiled in the way,**

Who walk in the law of the Lord.

2 **Blessed are they that keep his testimonies,**

And that seek him with the whole heart.

3 **They also do no iniquity:**

They walk in his ways.

4 **Thou hast commanded us to keep thy precepts diligently.**

5 *O that my ways were directed to keep thy statutes!*

6 **Then shall I not be ashamed,**

When I have respect unto all thy commandments.

7 **I will praise thee with uprightness of heart,**

When I shall have learned thy righteous judgments.

8 **I will keep thy statutes:**

O forsake me not utterly.

9 **Wherewithal shall a young man cleanse his way?**

By taking heed thereto according to thy word.

10 **With my whole heart have I sought thee:**

O let me not wander from thy commandments.

11 **Thy word have I hid in mine heart,**

That I might not sin against thee.

12 **Blessed art thou, O Lord:**

Teach me thy statutes.

13 **With my lips have I declared**

All the judgments of thy mouth.

14 **I have rejoiced in the way of thy testimonies,**

As much as in all riches.

15 **I will meditate in thy precepts,**

And have respect unto thy ways.

16 **I will delight myself in thy statutes:**

I will not forget thy word.

650

Psalm 119

89 **For ever, O Lord, thy word is settled in heaven.**

90 **Thy faithfulness is unto all generations:**

Thou hast established the earth, and it abideth.

91 **They continue this day according to thine ordinances:**

For all are thy servants.

92 **Unless thy law had been my delights,**

I should then have perished in mine affliction.

93 **I will never forget thy precepts:**

For with them thou hast quickened me.

94 **I am thine, save me;**

For I have sought thy precepts.

95 **The wicked have waited for me to destroy me:**

But I will consider thy testimonies.

96 **I have seen an end of all perfection:**

But thy commandment is exceeding broad.

97 **O how love I thy law!**

It is my meditation all the day.

98 **Thou, through thy commandments, hast made me wiser than mine enemies:**

For they are ever with me.

99 **I have more understanding than all my teachers:**

For thy testimonies are my meditation.

100 **I understand more than the ancients,**

Because I keep thy precepts.

101 **I have refrained my feet from every evil way,**

That I might keep thy word.

102 **I have not departed from thy judgments:**

For thou hast taught me.

103 **How sweet are thy words unto my taste!**

Yea, sweeter than honey to my mouth.

104 **Through thy precepts I get understanding:**

Therefore I hate every false way.

105 **Thy word is a lamp unto my feet,**

And a light unto my path.

106 **I have sworn, and I will perform it,**

That I will keep thy righteous judgments.

107 **I am afflicted very much:**

Quicken me, O Lord, according unto thy word.

108 **Accept, I beseech thee, the freewill offerings of my mouth, O Lord,**

And teach me thy judgments.

651

Psalm 121

1 **I will lift up mine eyes unto the hills,**

From whence cometh my help.

2 **My help cometh from the Lord,**

Which made heaven and earth.

3 **He will not suffer thy foot to be moved:**

He that keepeth thee will not slumber.

4 **Behold, he that keepeth Israel**

Shall neither slumber nor sleep.

5 **The Lord is thy keeper:**

The Lord is thy shade upon thy right hand.

6 **The sun shall not smite thee by day,**

Nor the moon by night.

7 **The Lord shall preserve thee from all evil:**

He shall preserve thy soul.

8 **The Lord shall preserve thy going out and thy coming in**

From this time forth, and even for evermore.

Psalm 122

1 **I was glad when they said unto me,**

Let us go into the house of the Lord.

2 **Our feet shall stand within thy gates, O Jerusalem,**

3 *Jerusalem is builded as a city that is compact together:*

4 **Whither the tribes go up, the tribes of the Lord,**

Unto the testimony of Israel, to give thanks unto the name of the Lord.

5 **For there are set thrones of judgment,**

The thrones of the house of David.

6 **Pray for the peace of Jerusalem:**

They shall prosper that love thee.

7 **Peace be within thy walls,**

And prosperity within thy palaces.

8 **For my brethren and companions' sakes,**

I will now say, Peace be within thee.

9 **Because of the house of the Lord our God,**

I will seek thy good.

652

Psalm 127

1 **Except the Lord build the house, they labor in vain that build it:**

Except the Lord keep the city, the watchman waketh but in vain.

2 **It is vain for you to rise up early, to sit up late, to eat the bread of sorrows:**

For so he giveth his beloved sleep.

3 **Lo, children are an heritage of the Lord:**

And the fruit of the womb is his reward.

4 **As arrows are in the hand of a mighty man;**

So are children of the youth.

5 **Happy is the man that hath his quiver full of them:**

They shall not be ashamed, but they shall speak with the enemies in the gate.

Psalm 128

1 **Blessed is every one that feareth the Lord,**

That walketh in his ways.

2 **For thou shalt eat the labor of thine hands:**

Happy shalt thou be, and it shall be well with thee.

3 **Thy wife shall be as a fruitful vine by the sides of thine house;**

Thy children like olive plants round about thy table.

4 **Behold, that thus shall the man be blessed**

That feareth the Lord.

5 **The Lord shall bless thee out of Zion:**

And thou shalt see the good of Jerusalem all the days of thy life.

6 **Yea, thou shalt see thy children's children,**

And peace upon Israel.

653

Psalm 130

1 **Out of the depths have I cried unto thee, O Lord.**

2 *Lord, hear my voice: let thine ears be attentive to the voice of my supplications.*

3 **If thou, Lord, shouldest mark iniquities,**

O Lord, who shall stand?

4 **But there is forgiveness with thee,**

That thou mayest be feared.

5 **I wait for the Lord, my soul doth wait,**

And in his word do I hope.

6 **My soul waiteth for the Lord more than they that watch for the morning:**

I say, more than they that watch for the morning.

7 **Let Israel hope in the Lord: for with the Lord there is mercy,**

And with him is plenteous redemption.

8 *And he shall redeem Israel from all his iniquities.*

Psalm 133

1 **Behold, how good and how pleasant it is**

For brethren to dwell together in unity!

2 **It is like the precious ointment upon the head, that ran down upon the beard, even Aaron's beard:**

That went down to the skirts of his garments;

3 **As the dew of Hermon, and as the dew that descended upon the mountains of Zion:**

For there the Lord commanded the blessing, even life for evermore.

Psalm 134

1 **Behold, bless ye the Lord, all ye servants of the Lord,**

Which by night stand in the house of the Lord.

2 **Lift up your hands in the sanctuary,**

And bless the Lord.

3 **The Lord, that made heaven and earth,**

Bless thee out of Zion.

654

Psalm 139

1 **O Lord, thou hast searched me, and known me.**

2 **Thou knowest my downsitting and mine uprising,**

Thou understandest my thought afar off.

3 **Thou compassest my path and my lying down,**

And art acquainted with all my ways.

4 **For there is not a word in my tongue,**

But lo, O Lord, thou knowest it altogether.

5 **Thou hast beset me behind and before,**

And laid thine hand upon me.

6 **Such knowledge is too wonderful for me;**

It is high, I cannot attain unto it.

7 **Whither shall I go from thy spirit?**

Or whither shall I flee from thy presence?

8 **If I ascend up into heaven, thou art there:**

If I make my bed in hell, behold, thou art there.

9 **If I take the wings of the morning,**

And dwell in the uttermost parts of the sea;

10 **Even there shall thy hand lead me,**

And thy right hand shall hold me.

11 **If I say, Surely the darkness shall cover me;**

Even the night shall be light about me.

12 **Yea, the darkness hideth not from thee; but the night shineth as the day:**

The darkness and the light are both alike to thee.

17 **How precious also are thy thoughts unto me, O God!**

How great is the sum of them!

18 **If I should count them, they are more in number than the sand:**

When I awake, I am still with thee.

23 **Search me, O God, and know my heart:**

Try me and know my thoughts:

24 **And see if there be any wicked way in me,**

And lead me in the way everlasting.

655

Psalm 142

1 **I cried unto the Lord with my voice;**

With my voice unto the Lord did I make my supplication.

2 **I poured out my complaint before him;**

I showed before him my trouble.

3 **When my spirit was overwhelmed within me, then thou knewest my path.**

In the way wherein I walked have they privily laid a snare for me.

4 **I looked on my right hand, and beheld, but there was no man that would know me:**

Refuge failed me; no man cared for my soul.

5 **I cried unto thee, O Lord: I said, Thou art my refuge.**

And my portion in the land of the living.

Psalm 143

1 **Hear my prayer, O Lord; give ear to my supplications:**

In thy faithfulness answer me, and in thy righteousness.

2 **And enter not into judgment with thy servant:**

For in thy sight shall no man living be justified.

3 **For the enemy hath persecuted my soul;**

He hath smitten my life down to the ground;

He hath made me to dwell in darkness,

As those that have been long dead.

4 **Therefore is my spirit overwhelmed within me:**

My heart within me is desolate.

5 **I remember the days of old; I meditate on all thy works;**

I muse on the work of thy hands.

6 **I stretch forth my hands unto thee:**

My soul thirsteth after thee, as a thirsty land.

7 **Hear me speedily, O Lord; my spirit faileth:**

Hide not thy face from me, lest I be like unto them that go down into the pit.

8 **Cause me to hear thy lovingkindness in the morning;**

For in thee do I trust:

Cause me to know the way wherein I should walk;

For I lift up my soul unto thee.

9 **Deliver me, O Lord, from mine enemies:**

I flee unto thee to hide me.

10 **Teach me to do thy will; for thou art my God.**

Thy spirit is good; lead me into the land of uprightness.

11 **Quicken me, O Lord, for thy name's sake:**

For thy righteousness' sake bring my soul out of trouble.

656

Psalm 145

1 **I will extol thee, my God, O King;**

And I will bless thy name for ever and ever.

2 **Every day will I bless thee;**

And I will praise thy name for ever and ever.

3 **Great is the Lord, and greatly to be praised;**

And his greatness is unsearchable.

4 **One generation shall praise thy works to another,**

And shall declare thy mighty acts.

5 **I will speak of the glorious honor of thy majesty,**

And of thy wondrous works.

6 **And men shall speak of the might of thy terrible acts:**

And I will declare thy greatness.

7 **They shall abundantly utter the memory of thy great goodness,**

And shall sing of thy righteousness.

8 **The Lord is gracious and full of compassion;**

Slow to anger, and of great mercy.

9 **The Lord is good to all:**

And his tender mercies are over all his works.

10 **All thy works shall praise thee, O Lord;**

And thy saints shall bless thee.

11 **They shall speak of the glory of thy kingdom,**

And talk of thy power;

12 **To make known to the sons of men his mighty acts,**

And the glorious majesty of his kingdom.

13 **Thy kingdom is an everlasting kingdom,**

And thy dominion endureth throughout all generations.

14 **The Lord upholdeth all that fall,**

And raiseth up all those that be bowed down.

15 **The eyes of all wait upon thee;**

And thou givest them their meat in due season.

16 **Thou openest thine hand,**

And satisfiest the desire of every living thing.

17 **The Lord is righteous in all his ways,**

And holy in all his works.

18 **The Lord is nigh unto all them that call upon him,**

To all that call upon him in truth.

19 **He will fulfil the desire of them that fear him;**

He also will hear their cry, and will save them.

20 **The Lord preserveth all them that love him:**

But all the wicked will he destroy.

21 **My mouth shall speak the praise of the Lord:**

And let all flesh bless his holy name for ever and ever.

657

Psalm 146

1 **Praise ye the Lord.**

Praise the Lord, O my soul.

2 **While I live will I praise the Lord:**

I will sing praises unto my God while I have any being.

3 **Put not your trust in princes,**

Nor in the son of man, in whom there is no help.

4 **His breath goeth forth, he returneth to his earth;**

In that very day his thoughts perish.

5 **Happy is he that hath the God of Jacob for his help,**

Whose hope is in the Lord his God:

6 **Which made heaven, and earth, the sea, and all that therein is:**

Which keepeth truth for ever:

7 **Which executeth judgment for the oppressed:**

Which giveth food to the hungry.

The Lord looseth the prisoners:

8 *The Lord openeth the eyes of the blind:*

The Lord raiseth them that are bowed down:

The Lord loveth the righteous:

9 **The Lord preserveth the strangers; he relieveth the fatherless and widow;**

But the way of the wicked he turneth upside down.

10 **The Lord shall reign for ever,**

Even thy God, O Zion, unto all generations.
Praise ye the Lord.

Psalm 147

1 **Praise ye the Lord: for it is good to sing praises unto our God:**

For it is pleasant, and praise is comely.

2 **The Lord doth build up Jerusalem:**

He gathereth together the outcasts of Israel.

3 **He healeth the broken in heart**

And bindeth up their wounds.

4 **He telleth the number of the stars;**

He calleth them all by their names.

5 **Great is our Lord, and of great power:**

His understanding is infinite.

6 **The Lord lifteth up the meek:**

He casteth the wicked down to the ground.

7 **Sing unto the Lord with thanksgiving;**

Sing praise upon the harp unto our God.

658

Psalm 150

1 **Praise ye the Lord. Praise God in his sanctuary:**

Praise him in the firmament of his power.

2 **Praise him for his mighty acts:**

Praise him according to his excellent greatness.

3 **Praise him with the sound of the trumpet:**

Praise him with the psaltery and harp.

4 **Praise him with the timbrel and dance:**

Praise him with stringed instruments and organs.

5 **Praise him upon the loud cymbals:**

Praise him upon the high sounding cymbals.

6 **Let everything that hath breath praise the Lord.**

Praise ye the Lord.

---

659 COMFORT IN AFFLICTION

Blessed be God, even the Father of our Lord Jesus Christ, the Father of mercies, and the God of all comfort;

Who comforteth us in all our tribulation, that we may be able to comfort them which are in any trouble, by the comfort wherewith we ourselves are comforted of God.

For as the sufferings of Christ abound in us, so our consolation also aboundeth by Christ.

And whether we be afflicted, it is for your consolation and salvation, which is effectual in the enduring of the same sufferings which we also suffer:

Or whether we be comforted, it is for your consolation and salvation.

And our hope of you is stedfast, knowing, that as ye are partakers of the sufferings, so shall ye be also of the consolation.

2 Corinthians 1:3-7

Beloved, think it not strange concerning the fiery trial which is to try you, as though some strange thing happened unto you:

But rejoice, inasmuch as ye are partakers of Christ's sufferings; that, when his glory shall be revealed, ye may be glad also with exceeding joy.

Yet if any man suffer as a Christian, let him not be ashamed; but let him glorify God on this behalf.

Wherefore let them that suffer according to the will of God commit the keeping of their souls to him in well doing, as unto a faithful Creator.

1 Peter 4:12-13, 16, 19

660 FAITH

Now faith is the substance of things hoped for, the evidence of things not seen.

For by it the elders obtained a good report.

Through faith we understand that the worlds were framed by the word of God, so that things which are seen were not made of things which do appear.

By faith Abel offered unto God a more excellent sacrifice than Cain, by which he obtained witness that he was righteous, God testifying of his gifts: and by it he being dead yet speaketh.

By faith Enoch was translated that he should not see death; and was not found, because God had translated him: for before his translation he had this testimony, that he pleased God.

But without faith it is impossible to please him: for he that cometh to God must believe that he is, and that he is a rewarder of them that diligently seek him.

By faith Noah, being warned of God of things not seen as yet, moved with fear, prepared an ark to the saving of his house; by the which he condemned the world, and became heir of the righteousness which is by faith.

By faith Abraham, when he was called to go out into a place which he should after receive for an inheritance, obeyed; and he went out, not knowing whither he went.

By faith he sojourned in the land of promise, as in a strange country, dwelling in tabernacles with Isaac and Jacob, the heirs with him of the same promise:

For he looked for a city which hath foundations, whose builder and maker is God.

Through faith also Sara herself received strength to conceive seed, and was delivered of a child when she was past age, because she judged him faithful who had promised.

Therefore sprang there even of one, and him as good as dead, so many as the stars of the sky in multitude, and as the sand which is by the sea shore innumerable.

These all died in faith, not having received the promises, but having seen them afar off, and were persuaded of them, and embraced them, and confessed that they were strangers and pilgrims on the earth.

For they that say such things declare plainly that they seek a country.

And truly, if they had been mindful of that country from whence they came out, they might have had opportunity to have returned.

But now they desire a better country, that is, an heavenly: wherefore God is not ashamed to be called their God: for he hath prepared for them a city.

And these all, having obtained a good report through faith, received not the promise:

God having provided some better thing for us, that they without us should not be made perfect.

Hebrews 11:1-16, 39-40

661 PRAYER

Ask, and it shall be given you; seek, and ye shall find; knock, and it shall be opened unto you:

For every one that asketh receiveth; and he that seeketh findeth; and to him that knocketh it shall be opened.

Or what man is there of you, whom if his son ask bread, will he give him a stone?

Or if he ask a fish, will he give him a serpent?

If ye then, being evil, know how to give good gifts unto your children, how much more shall your Father which is in heaven give good things to them that ask him?

Matthew 7:7-11

But thou, when thou prayest, enter into thy closet, and when thou hast shut thy door, pray to thy Father which is in secret; and thy Father which seeth in secret shall reward thee openly.

Matthew 6:6

Bow down thine ear, O Lord, hear me: for I am poor and needy.

Rejoice the soul of thy servant: for unto thee, O Lord, do I lift up my soul.

For thou, Lord, art good, and ready to forgive; and plenteous in mercy unto all them that call upon thee.

Give ear, O Lord, unto my prayer; and attend to the voice of my supplications.

In the day of my trouble I will call upon thee: for thou wilt answer me.

Among the gods there is none like unto thee, O Lord; neither are there any works like unto thy works.

All nations whom thou hast made shall come and worship before thee, O Lord; and shall glorify thy name.

For thou art great, and doest wondrous things: thou art God alone.

Shew me a token for good; that they which hate me may see it, and be ashamed: because thou, Lord, hast holpen me, and comforted me.

Psalm 86:1, 4-10, 17

The Lord hath heard my supplication; the Lord will receive my prayer.

Psalm 6:9

662 THE WORD OF GOD

The law of the Lord is perfect, converting the soul: the testimony of the Lord is sure, making wise the simple.

The statutes of the Lord are right, rejoicing the heart: the commandment of the Lord is pure, enlightening the eyes.

The fear of the Lord is clean, enduring for ever: the judgments of the Lord are true and righteous altogether.

More to be desired are they than gold, yea, than much fine gold: sweeter also than honey and the honeycomb.

Moreover by them is thy servant warned: and in keeping of them there is great reward.

Psalm 19:7-11

Wherewithal shall a young man cleanse his way? by taking heed thereto according to thy word.

With my whole heart have I sought thee: O let me not wander from thy commandments.

Thy word have I hid in mine heart, that I might not sin against thee.

Psalm 119:9-11

But continue thou in the things which thou hast learned and hast been assured of, knowing of whom thou hast learned them;

And that from a child thou hast known the holy scriptures, which are able to make thee wise unto salvation through faith which is in Christ Jesus.

All scripture is given by inspiration of God, and is profitable for doctrine, for reproof, for correction, for instruction in righteousness:

That the man of God may be perfect, throughly furnished unto all good works.

2 Timothy 3:14-17

663 THE COMMANDMENTS

And God spake all these words, saying,

I am the Lord thy God, which have brought thee out of the land of Egypt, out of the house of bondage.

Thou shalt have no other gods before me.

Thou shalt not make unto thee any graven image, or any likeness of any thing that is in heaven above, or that is in the earth beneath, or that is in the water under the earth.

Thou shalt not bow down thyself to them, nor serve them: for I the Lord thy God am a jealous God, visiting the iniquity of the fathers upon the children unto the third and fourth generation of them that hate me;

And shewing mercy unto thousands of them that love me, and keep my commandments.

Thou shalt not take the name of the Lord thy God in vain; for the Lord will not hold him guiltless that taketh his name in vain.

Remember the sabbath day, to keep it holy.

Six days shalt thou labour, and do all thy work:

But the seventh day is the sabbath of the Lord thy God: in it thou shalt not do any work, thou, nor thy son, nor thy daughter, thy manservant, nor thy maidservant, nor thy cattle, nor thy stranger that is within thy gates:

For in six days the Lord made heaven and earth, the sea, and all that in them is, and rested the seventh day: wherefore the Lord blessed the sabbath day, and hallowed it.

Honour thy father and thy mother: that thy days may be long upon the land which the Lord thy God giveth thee.

Thou shalt not kill.

Thou shalt not commit adultery.

Thou shalt not steal.

Thou shalt not bear false witness against thy neighbour.

Thou shalt not covet thy neighbour's house, thou shalt not covet thy neighbour's wife, nor his manservant, nor his maidservant, nor his ox, nor his ass, nor anything that is thy neighbour's.

Exodus 20:1-17

664 THE BEATITUDES

And seeing the multitudes, he went up into a mountain: and when he was set, his disciples came unto him:

And he opened his mouth, and taught them, saying,

Blessed are the poor in spirit: for their's is the kingdom of heaven.

Blessed are they that mourn: for they shall be comforted.

Blessed are the meek: for they shall inherit the earth.

Blessed are they which do hunger and thirst after righteousness: for they shall be filled.

Blessed are the merciful: for they shall obtain mercy.

Blessed are the pure in heart: for they shall see God.

Blessed are the peacemakers: for they shall be called the children of God.

Blessed are they which are persecuted for righteousness' sake: for their's is the kingdom of heaven.

Blessed are ye, when men shall revile you, and persecute you, and shall say all manner of evil against you falsely, for my sake.

Rejoice, and be exceeding glad: for great is your reward in heaven: for so persecuted they the prophets which were before you.

Ye are the salt of the earth: but if the salt have lost his savour, wherewith shall it be salted? it is thenceforth good for nothing, but to be cast out, and to be trodden under foot of men.

Ye are the light of the world. A city that is set on an hill cannot be hid.

Neither do men light a candle, and put it under a bushel, but on a candlestick; and it giveth light unto all that are in the house.

Let your light so shine before men, that they may see your good works, and glorify your Father which is in heaven.

Matthew 5:1-16

665 THE SAVIOUR'S BIRTH

And it came to pass in those days, that there went out a decree from Caesar Augustus, that all the world should be taxed.

(And this taxing was first made when Cyrenius was governor of Syria.)

And all went to be taxed, every one into his own city.

And Joseph also went up from Galilee, out of the city of Nazareth, into Judea, unto the city of David, which is called Bethlehem; (because he was of the house and lineage of David:)

To be taxed with Mary his espoused wife, being great with child.

And so it was, that, while they were there, the days were accomplished that she should be delivered.

And she brought forth her firstborn son, and wrapped him in swaddling clothes, and laid him in a manger; because there was no room for them in the inn.

And there were in the same country shepherds abiding in the field, keeping watch over their flock by night.

And, lo, the angel of the Lord came upon them, and the glory of the Lord shone round about them: and they were sore afraid.

And the angel said unto them, Fear not: for, behold, I bring you good tidings of great joy, which shall be to all people.

For unto you is born this day in the city of David a Saviour, which is Christ the Lord.

And this shall be a sign unto you; Ye shall find the babe wrapped in swaddling clothes, lying in a manger.

And suddenly there was with the angel a multitude of the heavenly host praising God, and saying,

Glory to God in the highest, and on earth peace, good will toward men.

And it came to pass, as the angels were gone away from them into heaven, the shepherds said one to another, Let us now go even unto Bethlehem, and see this thing which is come to pass, which the Lord hath made known unto us.

And they came with haste, and found Mary, and Joseph, and the babe lying in a manger.

And when they had seen it, they made known abroad the saying which was told them concerning this child.

And all they that heard it wondered at those things which were told them by the shepherds.

But Mary kept all these things, and pondered them in her heart.

And the shepherds returned, glorifying and praising God for all the things that they had heard and seen, as it was told unto them.

Luke 2:1-20

666 CHRIST INCARNATE

In the beginning was the Word, and the Word was with God, and the Word was God.

The same was in the beginning with God.

All things were made by him; and without him was not any thing made that was made.

In him was life; and the life was the light of men.

And the light shineth in darkness; and the darkness comprehended it not.

There was a man sent from God, whose name was John.

The same came for a witness, to bear witness of the Light, that all men through him might believe.

He was not that Light, but was sent to bear witness of that Light.

That was the true Light, which lighteth every man that cometh into the world.

He was in the world, and the world was made by him, and the world knew him not.

He came unto his own, and his own received him not.

But as many as received him, to them gave he power to become the sons of God, even to them that believe on his name:

Which were born, not of blood, nor of the will of the flesh, nor of the will of man, but of God.

And the Word was made flesh, and dwelt among us, (and we beheld his glory, the glory as of the only begotten of the Father,) full of grace and truth.

John 1:1-14

667 THE SUFFERING LAMB

Who hath believed our report? and to whom is the arm of the Lord revealed?

For he shall grow up before him as a tender plant, and as a root out of a dry ground: he hath no form nor comeliness; and when we shall see him, there is no beauty that we should desire him.

He is despised and rejected of men; a man of sorrows, and acquainted with grief: and we hid as it were our faces from him; he was despised, and we esteemed him not.

Surely he hath borne our griefs, and carried our sorrows: yet we did esteem him stricken, smitten of God, and afflicted.

But he was wounded for our transgressions, he was bruised for our iniquities: the chastisement of our peace was upon him; and with his stripes we are healed.

All we like sheep have gone astray; we have turned every one to his own way; and the Lord hath laid on him the iniquity of us all.

He was oppressed, and he was afflicted, yet he opened not his mouth: he is brought as a lamb to the slaughter, and as a sheep before her shearers is dumb, so he openeth not his mouth.

He was taken from prison and from judgment: and who shall declare his generation? for he was cut off out of the land of the living: for the transgression of my people was he stricken.

And he made his grave with the wicked, and with the rich in his death; because he had done no violence, neither was any deceit in his mouth.

Yet it pleased the Lord to bruise him; he hath put him to grief: when thou shalt make his soul an offering for sin, he shall see his seed, he shall prolong his days, and the pleasure of the Lord shall prosper in his hand.

He shall see of the travail of his soul, and shall be satisfied: by his knowledge shall my righteous servant justify many; for he shall bear their iniquities.

Therefore will I divide him a portion with the great, and he shall divide the spoil with the strong; because he hath poured out his soul unto death: and he was numbered with the transgressors; and he bare the sin of many, and made intercession for the transgressors.

Isaiah 53:1-12

668 THE TRIUMPHAL ENTRY

And when they came nigh to Jerusalem, unto Bethphage and Bethany, at the mount of Olives, he sendeth forth two of his disciples,

And saith unto them, Go your way into the village over against you: and as soon as ye be entered into it, ye shall find a colt tied, whereon never man sat; loose him, and bring him.

And if any man say unto you, Why do ye this? say ye that the Lord hath need of him; and straightway he will send him hither.

And they went their way, and found the colt tied by the door without in a place where two ways met; and they loose him.

And certain of them that stood there said unto them, What do ye, loosing the colt?

And they said unto them even as Jesus had commanded: and they let them go.

And they brought the colt to Jesus, and cast their garments on him; and he sat upon him.

And many spread their garments in the way: and others cut down branches off the trees, and strawed them in the way.

And they that went before, and they that followed, cried, saying, Hosanna; Blessed is he that cometh in the name of the Lord:

Blessed be the kingdom of our father David, that cometh in the name of the Lord: Hosanna in the highest.

And Jesus entered into Jerusalem, and into the temple: and when he had looked round about upon all things, and now the eventide was come, he went out unto Bethany with the twelve.

Mark 11:1-11

669 THE CRUCIFIXION

Then delivered he him therefore unto them to be crucified. And they took Jesus, and led him away.

And he bearing his cross went forth into a place called the place of a skull, which is called in the Hebrew Golgotha:

Where they crucified him, and two other with him, on either side one, and Jesus in the midst.

And Pilate wrote a title, and put it on the cross. And the writing was, JESUS OF NAZARETH THE KING OF THE JEWS.

This title then read many of the Jews: for the place where Jesus was crucified was nigh to the city: and it was written in Hebrew, and Greek, and Latin.

Then said the chief priests of the Jews to Pilate, Write not, The King of the Jews; but that he said, I am King of the Jews.

Pilate answered, What I have written I have written.

Then the soldiers, when they had crucified Jesus, took his garments, and made four parts, to every soldier a part; and also his coat: now the coat was without seam, woven from the top throughout.

They said therefore among themselves, Let us not rend it, but cast lots for it, whose it shall be: that the scripture might be fulfilled, which saith, They parted my raiment among them, and for my vesture they did cast lots. These things therefore the soldiers did.

Now there stood by the cross of Jesus his mother, and his mother's sister, Mary the wife of Cleophas, and Mary Magdalene.

When Jesus therefore saw his mother, and the disciple standing by, whom he loved, he saith unto his mother, Woman, behold thy son!

Then saith he to the disciple, Behold thy mother! And from that hour that disciple took her unto his own home.

After this, Jesus knowing that all things were now accomplished, that the scripture might be fulfilled, saith, I thirst.

Now there was set a vessel full of vinegar: and they filled a spunge with vinegar, and put it upon hyssop, and put it to his mouth.

When Jesus therefore had received the vinegar, he said, It is finished: and he bowed his head, and gave up the ghost.

John 19:16-30

670 THE RISEN SAVIOUR

In the end of the sabbath, as it began to dawn toward the first day of the week, came Mary Magdalene and the other Mary to see the sepulchre.

And, behold, there was a great earthquake: for the angel of the Lord descended from heaven, and came and rolled back the stone from the door, and sat upon it.

His countenance was like lightning, and his raiment white as snow:

And for fear of him the keepers did shake, and became as dead men.

And the angel answered and said unto the women, Fear not ye: for I know that ye seek Jesus, which was crucified.

He is not here: for he is risen, as he said. Come, see the place where the Lord lay.

And go quickly, and tell his disciples that he is risen from the dead; and, behold, he goeth before you into Galilee; there shall ye see him: lo, I have told you.

And they departed quickly from the sepulchre with fear and great joy; and did run to bring his disciples word.

And as they went to tell his disciples, behold, Jesus met them, saying, All hail. And they came and held him by the feet, and worshipped him.

Then said Jesus unto them, Be not afraid: go tell my brethren that they go into Galilee, and there shall they see me.

Matthew 28:1-10

Then the same day at evening, being the first day of the week, when the doors were shut where

the disciples were assembled for fear of the Jews, came Jesus and stood in the midst, and saith unto them, Peace be unto you.

And when he had so said, he shewed unto them his hands and his side. Then were the disciples glad, when they saw the Lord.

And after eight days again his disciples were within, and Thomas with them: then came Jesus, the doors being shut, and stood in the midst, and said, Peace be unto you.

Then saith he to Thomas, Reach hither thy finger, and behold my hands; and reach hither thy hand, and thrust it into my side: and be not faithless, but believing.

And Thomas answered and said unto him, My Lord and my God.

Jesus saith unto him, Thomas, because thou hast seen me, thou hast believed: blessed are they that have not seen, and yet have believed.

John 20:19-20, 26-29

I am he that liveth, and was dead; and, behold, I am alive for evermore, Amen; and have the keys of hell and of death.

Revelation 1:18

671 THE RESURRECTION

And if Christ be not raised, your faith is vain; ye are yet in your sins.

Then they also which are fallen asleep in Christ are perished.

If in this life only we have hope in Christ, we are of all men most miserable.

But now is Christ risen from the dead, and become the firstfruits of them that slept.

For since by man came death, by man came also the resurrection of the dead.

For as in Adam all die, even so in Christ shall all be made alive.

But every man in his own order: Christ the firstfruits; afterward they that are Christ's at his coming.

Then cometh the end, when he shall have delivered up the kingdom to God, even the Father; when he shall have put down all rule and all authority and power.

For he must reign, till he hath put all enemies under his feet.

The last enemy that shall be destroyed is death.

1 Corinthians 15:17-26

Behold, I shew you a mystery; We shall not all sleep, but we shall all be changed,

In a moment, in the twinkling of an eye, at the last trump: for the trumpet shall sound, and the dead shall be raised incorruptible, and we shall be changed.

For this corruptible must put on incorruption, and this mortal must put on immortality.

So when this corruptible shall have put on incorruption, and this mortal shall have put on immortality, then shall be brought to pass the saying that is written, Death is swallowed up in victory.

O death, where is thy sting? O grave, where is thy victory?

The sting of death is sin; and the strength of sin is the law.

But thanks be to God, which giveth us the victory through our Lord Jesus Christ.

Therefore, my beloved brethren, be ye stedfast, unmoveable, always abounding in the work of the Lord, forasmuch as ye know that your labour is not in vain in the Lord.
1 Corinthians 15:51-58

672 THE ASCENSION

And as they thus spake, Jesus himself stood in the midst of them, and saith unto them, Peace be unto you.

But they were terrified and affrighted, and supposed that they had seen a spirit.

And he said unto them, Why are ye troubled? and why do thoughts arise in your hearts?

Behold my hands and my feet, that it is I myself: handle me, and see; for a spirit hath not flesh and bones, as ye see me have.

And when he had thus spoken, he shewed them his hands and his feet.

And while they yet believed not for joy, and wondered, he saith unto them, Have ye here any meat?

And they gave him a piece of a broiled fish, and of an honeycomb.

And he took it, and did eat before them.

And he said unto them, These are the words which I spake unto you, while I was yet with you, that all things must be fulfilled, which were written in the law of Moses, and in the prophets, and in the psalms, concerning me.

Then opened he their understanding, that they might understand the scriptures,

And said unto them, Thus it is written, and thus it behoved Christ to suffer, and to rise from the dead the third day:

And that repentance and remission of sins should be preached in his name among all nations, beginning at Jerusalem.

And ye are witnesses of these things.

And, behold, I send the promise of my Father upon you: but tarry ye in the city of Jerusalem, until ye be endued with power from on high.

And he led them out as far as to Bethany, and he lifted up his hands, and blessed them.

And it came to pass, while he blessed them, he was parted from them, and carried up into heaven.

And they worshipped him, and returned to Jerusalem with great joy:

And were continually in the temple, praising and blessing God. Amen.
Luke 24:36-53

673 THE PROMISED COMFORTER

A new heart also will I give you, and a new spirit will I put within you: and I will take away the stony heart out of your flesh, and

I will give you an heart of flesh.

And I will put my spirit within you, and cause you to walk in my statutes, and ye shall keep my judgments, and do them.

Ezekiel 36:26-27

And I will pray the Father, and he shall give you another Comforter, that he may abide with you for ever;

Even the Spirit of truth; whom the world cannot receive, because it seeth him not, neither knoweth him: but ye know him; for he dwelleth with you, and shall be in you.

I will not leave you comfortless: I will come to you.

Yet a little while, and the world seeth me no more; but ye see me: because I live, ye shall live also.

At that day ye shall know that I am in my Father, and ye in me, and I in you.

He that hath my commandments, and keepeth them, he it is that loveth me: and he that loveth me shall be loved of my Father, and I will love him, and will manifest myself to him.

Judas saith unto him, not Iscariot, Lord, how is it that thou wilt manifest thyself unto us, and not unto the world?

Jesus answered and said unto him, If a man love me, he will keep my words: and my Father will love him, and we will come unto him, and make our abode with him.

He that loveth me not keepeth not my sayings: and the word which ye hear is not mine, but the Father's which sent me.

These things have I spoken unto you, being yet present with you.

But the Comforter, which is the Holy Ghost, whom the Father will send in my name, he shall teach you all things, and bring all things to your remembrance, whatsoever I have said unto you.

John 14:16-26

674 HOLY SPIRIT POWER

The former treatise have I made, O Theophilus, of all that Jesus began both to do and teach,

Until the day in which he was taken up, after that he through the Holy Ghost had given commandments unto the apostles whom he had chosen:

To whom also he shewed himself alive after his passion by many infallible proofs, being seen of them forty days, and speaking of the things pertaining to the kingdom of God:

And, being assembled together with them, commanded them that they should not depart from Jerusalem, but wait for the promise of the Father, which, saith he, ye have heard of me.

For John truly baptized with water; but ye shall be baptized with the Holy Ghost not many days hence.

When they therefore were come together, they asked of him, saying, Lord, wilt thou at this time restore again the kingdom to Israel?

And he said unto them, It is not

for you to know the times or the seasons, which the Father hath put in his own power.

But ye shall receive power, after that the Holy Ghost is come upon you: and ye shall be witnesses unto me both in Jerusalem, and in all Judaea, and in Samaria, and unto the uttermost part of the earth.

And when he had spoken these things, while they beheld, he was taken up; and a cloud received him out of their sight.

And while they looked stedfastly toward heaven as he went up, behold, two men stood by them in white apparel;

Which also said, Ye men of Galilee, why stand ye gazing up into heaven? this same Jesus, which is taken up from you into heaven, shall so come in like manner as ye have seen him go into heaven.

Acts 1:1-11

675 HOLY SPIRIT FILLED (PENTECOST)

And when the day of Pentecost was fully come, they were all with one accord in one place.

And suddenly there came a sound from heaven as of a rushing mighty wind, and it filled all the house where they were sitting.

And there appeared unto them cloven tongues like as of fire, and it sat upon each of them.

And they were all filled with the Holy Ghost, and began to speak with other tongues, as the Spirit gave them utterance.

And there were dwelling at Jerusalem Jews, devout men, out of every nation under heaven.

Now when this was noised abroad, the multitude came together, and were confounded, because that every man heard them speak in his own language.

And they were all amazed and marvelled, saying one to another, Behold, are not all these which speak Galileans?

And how hear we every man in our own tongue, wherein we were born?

Parthians, and Medes, and Elamites, and the dwellers in Mesopotamia, and in Judaea, and Cappadocia, in Pontus, and Asia,

Phrygia, and Pamphylia, in Egypt, and in the parts of Libya about Cyrene, and strangers of Rome, Jews and proselytes,

Cretes and Arabians, we do hear them speak in our tongues the wonderful works of God.

And they were all amazed, and were in doubt, saying one to another, What meaneth this?

Others mocking said, These men are full of new wine.

But Peter, standing up with the eleven, lifted up his voice, and said unto them, Ye men of Judaea, and all ye that dwell at Jerusalem, be this known unto you, and hearken to my words:

For these are not drunken, as ye suppose, seeing it is but the third hour of the day.

But this is that which was spoken by the prophet Joel;

And it shall come to pass in the last days, saith God, I will pour out of my Spirit upon all flesh: and your sons and your daughters shall prophesy, and your young men shall see visions, and your old men shall dream dreams:

And on my servants and on my handmaidens I will pour out in those days of my Spirit; and they shall prophesy.

Acts 2:1-18

676 HOLY SPIRIT LED

There is therefore now no condemnation to them which are in Christ Jesus, who walk not after the flesh, but after the Spirit.

For the law of the Spirit of life in Christ Jesus hath made me free from the law of sin and death.

For what the law could not do, in that it was weak through the flesh, God sending his own Son in the likeness of sinful flesh, and for sin, condemned sin in the flesh:

That the righteousness of the law might be fulfilled in us, who walk not after the flesh, but after the Spirit.

For they that are after the flesh do mind the things of the flesh; but they that are after the Spirit the things of the Spirit.

For to be carnally minded is death; but to be spiritually minded is life and peace.

Because the carnal mind is enmity against God: for it is not subject to the law of God, neither indeed can be.

So then they that are in the flesh cannot please God.

But ye are not in the flesh, but in the Spirit, if so be that the Spirit of God dwell in you. Now if any man have not the Spirit of Christ, he is none of his.

And if Christ be in you, the body is dead because of sin; but the Spirit is life because of righteousness.

But if the Spirit of him that raised up Jesus from the dead dwell in you, he that raised up Christ from the dead shall also quicken your mortal bodies by his Spirit that dwelleth in you.

Therefore, brethren, we are debtors, not to the flesh, to live after the flesh.

For if ye live after the flesh, ye shall die: but if ye through the Spirit do mortify the deeds of the body, ye shall live.

For as many as are led by the Spirit of God, they are the sons of God.

For ye have not received the spirit of bondage again to fear; but ye have received the Spirit of adoption, whereby we cry, Abba, Father.

The Spirit itself beareth witness with our spirit, that we are the children of God:

And if children, then heirs; heirs of God, and joint-heirs with Christ; if so be that we suffer with him, that we may be also glorified together.

For I reckon that the sufferings of this present time are not worthy to be compared with the glory which shall be revealed in us.

Romans 8:1-18

677 HOLY SPIRIT FRUIT

This I say then, Walk in the Spirit, and ye shall not fulfill the lust of the flesh.

For the flesh lusteth against the Spirit, and the Spirit against the flesh: and these are contrary the one to the other: so that ye cannot do the things that ye would.

But if ye be led of the Spirit, ye are not under the law.

Now the works of the flesh are manifest, which are these; Adultery, fornication, uncleanness, lasciviousness,

Idolatry, witchcraft, hatred, variance, emulations, wrath, strife, seditions, heresies,

Envyings, murders, drunkenness, revellings, and such like: of the which I tell you before, as I have also told you in time past, that they which do such things shall not inherit the kingdom of God.

But the fruit of the Spirit is love, joy, peace, longsuffering, gentleness, goodness, faith,

Meekness, temperance: against such there is no law.

And they that are Christ's have crucified the flesh with the affections and lusts.

If we live in the Spirit, let us also walk in the Spirit.

Let us not be desirous of vain glory, provoking one another, envying one another.

Galatians 5:16-26

678 THE CHRISTIAN WALK

I therefore, the prisoner of the Lord, beseech you that ye walk worthy of the vocation wherewith ye are called,

With all lowliness and meekness, with longsuffering, forbearing one another in love;

Endeavouring to keep the unity of the Spirit in the bond of peace.

There is one body, and one Spirit, even as ye are called in one hope of your calling;

One Lord, one faith, one baptism,

One God and Father of all, who is above all, and through all, and in you all.

But unto every one of us is given grace according to the measure of the gift of Christ.

Wherefore he saith, When he ascended up on high, he led captivity captive, and gave gifts unto men.

(Now that he ascended, what is it but that he also descended first into the lower parts of the earth?

He that descended is the same also that ascended up far above all heavens, that he might fill all things.)

And he gave some, apostles; and some, prophets; and some, evangelists; and some, pastors and teachers;

For the perfecting of the saints, for

the work of the ministry, for the edifying of the body of Christ:

Till we all come in the unity of the faith, and of the knowledge of the Son of God, unto a perfect man, unto the measure of the stature of the fulness of Christ:

That we henceforth be no more children, tossed to and fro, and carried about with every wind of doctrine, by the sleight of men, and cunning craftiness, whereby they lie in wait to deceive;

But speaking the truth in love, may grow up into him in all things, which is the head, even Christ.

Ephesians 4:1-15

679 SERVICE

Therefore, my beloved brethren, be ye stedfast, unmoveable, always abounding in the work of the Lord, forasmuch as ye know that your labour is not in vain in the Lord.

1 Corinthians 15:58

Wherefore we labour, that, whether present or absent, we may be accepted of him.

2 Corinthians 5:9

Remembering without ceasing your work of faith, and labour of love, and patience of hope in our Lord Jesus Christ, in the sight of God and our Father.

1 Thessalonians 1:3

For the love of Christ constraineth us; because we thus judge, that if one died for all, then were all dead:

And that he died for all, that they which live should not henceforth live unto themselves, but unto him which died for them, and rose again.

Now then we are ambassadors for Christ, as though God did beseech you by us: we pray you in Christ's stead, be ye reconciled to God.

2 Corinthians 5:14-15, 20

Now he that planteth and he that watereth are one: and every man shall receive his own reward according to his own labour.

For we are labourers together with God: ye are God's husbandry, ye are God's building.

According to the grace of God which is given unto me, as a wise masterbuilder, I have laid the foundation, and another buildeth thereon. But let every man take heed how he buildeth thereupon.

For other foundation can no man lay than that is laid, which is Jesus Christ.

Now if any man build upon this foundation gold, silver, precious stones, wood, hay, stubble;

Every man's work shall be made manifest: for the day shall declare it, because it shall be revealed by fire; and the fire shall try every man's work of what sort it is.

If any man's work abide which he hath built thereupon, he shall receive a reward.

If any man's work shall be burned, he shall suffer loss: but he himself shall be saved; yet so as by fire.

1 Corinthians 3:8-15

680 THE CHURCH

Paul, an apostle of Jesus Christ,

by the will of God, to the saints which are at Ephesus, and to the faithful in Christ Jesus:

Grace be to you, and peace, from God our Father, and from the Lord Jesus Christ.

Blessed be the God and Father of our Lord Jesus Christ, who hath blessed us with all spiritual blessings in heavenly places in Christ:

According as he hath chosen us in him before the foundation of the world, that we should be holy and without blame before him in love:

Having predestinated us unto the adoption of children by Jesus Christ to himself, according to the good pleasure of his will,

To the praise of the glory of his grace, wherein he hath made us accepted in the beloved.

In whom we have redemption through his blood, the forgiveness of sins, according to the riches of his grace;

Wherein he hath abounded toward us in all wisdom and prudence;

Having made known unto us the mystery of his will, according to his good pleasure which he hath purposed in himself:

That in the dispensation of the fulness of times he might gather together in one all things in Christ, both which are in heaven, and which are on earth; even in him.

Ephesians 1:1-10

Now therefore ye are no more strangers and foreigners, but fellowcitizens with the saints, and of the household of God;

And are built upon the foundation of the apostles and prophets, Jesus Christ himself being the chief corner stone;

In whom all the building fitly framed together groweth unto an holy temple in the Lord:

In whom ye also are builded together for an habitation of God through the Spirit.

Ephesians 2:19-22

681 THE NEW BIRTH

There was a man of the Pharisees, named Nicodemus, a ruler of the Jews:

The same came to Jesus by night, and said unto him, Rabbi, we know that thou art a teacher come from God: for no man can do these miracles that thou doest, except God be with him.

Jesus answered and said unto him, Verily, verily, I say unto thee, Except a man be born again, he cannot see the kingdom of God.

Nicodemus saith unto him, How can a man be born when he is old? can he enter the second time into his mother's womb, and be born?

Jesus answered, Verily, verily, I say unto thee, Except a man be born of water and of the Spirit, he cannot enter into the kingdom of God.

That which is born of the flesh is flesh; and that which is born of the Spirit is spirit.

Marvel not that I said unto thee, Ye must be born again.

The wind bloweth where it listeth, and thou hearest the sound thereof, but canst not tell whence it cometh, and whither it goeth: so is every one that is born of the Spirit.

Nicodemus answered and said unto him, How can these things be?

Jesus answered and said unto him, Art thou a master of Israel, and knowest not these things?

Verily, verily, I say unto thee, We speak that we do know, and testify that we have seen; and ye receive not our witness.

If I have told you earthly things, and ye believe not, how shall ye believe, if I tell you of heavenly things?

And no man hath ascended up to heaven, but he that came down from heaven, even the Son of man which is in heaven.

And as Moses lifted up the serpent in the wilderness, even so must the Son of man be lifted up:

That whosoever believeth in him should not perish, but have eternal life.

For God so loved the world, that he gave his only begotten Son, that whosoever believeth in him should not perish, but have everlasting life.

John 3:1-16

682 CONSECRATION

I beseech you therefore, brethren, by the mercies of God, that ye present your bodies a living sacrifice, holy, acceptable unto God, which is your reasonable service.

And be not conformed to this world: but be ye transformed by the renewing of your mind, that ye may prove what is that good, and acceptable, and perfect, will of God.

Romans 12:1-2

If ye then be risen with Christ, seek those things which are above, where Christ sitteth on the right hand of God.

Set your affection on things above, not on things on the earth.

For ye are dead, and your life is hid with Christ in God.

When Christ, who is our life, shall appear, then shall ye also appear with him in glory.

Put on therefore, as the elect of God, holy and beloved, bowels of mercies, kindness, humbleness of mind, meekness, longsuffering;

Forbearing one another, and forgiving one another, if any man have a quarrel against any: even as Christ forgave you, so also do ye.

And above all these things put on charity, which is the bond of perfectness.

And let the peace of God rule in your hearts, to the which also ye are called in one body; and be ye thankful.

Let the word of Christ dwell in you richly in all wisdom; teaching and admonishing one another in psalms and hymns and spiritual songs, singing with grace in your hearts to the Lord.

And whatsoever ye do in word or deed, do all in the name of the Lord

Jesus, giving thanks to God and the Father by him.

Colossians 3:1-4, 12-17

683 REVIVAL

Then Peter said unto them, Repent, and be baptized every one of you in the name of Jesus Christ for the remission of sins, and ye shall receive the gift of the Holy Ghost.

For the promise is unto you, and to your children, and to all that are afar off, even as many as the Lord our God shall call.

And with many other words did he testify and exhort, saying, Save yourselves from this untoward generation.

Then they that gladly received his word were baptized: and the same day there were added unto them about three thousand souls.

And they continued stedfastly in the apostles' doctrine and fellowship, and in breaking of bread, and in prayers.

And fear came upon every soul: and many wonders and signs were done by the apostles.

And all that believed were together, and had all things common;

And sold their possessions and goods, and parted them to all men, as every man had need.

And they, continuing daily with one accord in the temple, and breaking bread from house to house, did eat their meat with gladness and singleness of heart,

Praising God, and having favour with all the people. And the Lord added to the church daily such as should be saved.

Acts 2:38-47

Then Philip went down to the city of Samaria, and preached Christ unto them.

And the people with one accord gave heed unto those things which Philip spake, hearing and seeing the miracles which he did.

For unclean spirits, crying with loud voice, came out of many that were possessed with them: and many taken with palsies, and that were lame, were healed.

And there was great joy in that city.

Acts 8:5-8

684 MISSIONS

Brethren, my heart's desire and prayer to God for Israel is, that they might be saved.

For I bear them record that they have a zeal of God, but not according to knowledge.

For they being ignorant of God's righteousness, and going about to establish their own righteousness, have not submitted themselves unto the righteousness of God.

For Christ is the end of the law for righteousness to every one that believeth.

For Moses describeth the righteousness which is of the law, That the man which doeth those things shall live by them.

But the righteousness which is of

faith speaketh on this wise, Say not in thine heart, Who shall ascend into heaven? (that is, to bring Christ down from above:)

Or, Who shall descend into the deep? (that is, to bring up Christ again from the dead.)

But what saith it? The word is nigh thee, even in thy mouth, and in thy heart: that is, the word of faith, which we preach;

That if thou shalt confess with thy mouth the Lord Jesus, and shalt believe in thine heart that God hath raised him from the dead, thou shalt be saved.

For with the heart man believeth unto righteousness; and with the mouth confession is made unto salvation.

For the scripture saith, Whosoever believeth on him shall not be ashamed.

For there is no difference between the Jew and the Greek: for the same Lord over all is rich unto all that call upon him.

For whosoever shall call upon the name of the Lord shall be saved.

How then shall they call on him in whom they have not believed? and how shall they believe in him of whom they have not heard? and how shall they hear without a preacher?

And how shall they preach, except they be sent?

Romans 10:1-15a

And Jesus came and spake unto them, saying, All power is given unto me in heaven and in earth.

Go ye therefore, and teach all nations, baptizing them in the name of the Father, and of the Son, and of the Holy Ghost:

Teaching them to observe all things whatsoever I have commanded you: and, lo, I am with you alway, even unto the end of the world. Amen.

Matthew 28:18-20

Then saith he unto his disciples, The harvest truly is plenteous, but the labourers are few;

Pray ye therefore the Lord of the harvest, that he will send forth labourers into his harvest.

Matthew 9:37-38

685 STEWARDSHIP

Honour the Lord with thy substance, and with the firstfruits of all thine increase:

So shall thy barns be filled with plenty, and thy presses shall burst out with new wine.

Proverbs 3:9-10

Bring ye all the tithes into the storehouse, that there may be meat in mine house, and prove me now herewith, saith the Lord of hosts, if I will not open you the windows of heaven, and pour you out a blessing, that there shall not be room enough to receive it.

Malachi 3:10

This I say, He which soweth sparingly shall reap also sparingly; and he which soweth bountifully shall reap also bountifully.

Every man according as he purposeth in his heart, so let him give; not grudgingly, or of necessity: for God loveth a cheerful giver.

And God is able to make all grace abound toward you; that ye, always having all sufficiency in all things, may abound to every good work.

2 Corinthians 9:6-8

Above all things have fervent charity among yourselves: for charity shall cover the multitude of sins.

Use hospitality one to another without grudging.

As every man hath received the gift, even so minister the same one to another, as good stewards of the manifold grace of God.

1 Peter 4:8-10

686 CHRIST AND THE CHILDREN

At the same time came the disciples unto Jesus, saying, Who is the greatest in the kingdom of heaven?

And Jesus called a little child unto him, and set him in the midst of them,

And said, Verily I say unto you, Except ye be converted, and become as little children, ye shall not enter into the kingdom of heaven.

Whosoever therefore shall humble himself as this little child, the same is greatest in the kingdom of heaven.

And whoso shall receive one such little child in my name receiveth me.

But whoso shall offend one of these little ones which believe in me, it were better for him that a millstone were hanged about his neck, and that he were drowned in the depth of the sea.

Matthew 18:1-6

And they brought young children to him, that he should touch them: and his disciples rebuked those that brought them.

But when Jesus saw it, he was much displeased, and said unto them, Suffer the little children to come unto me, and forbid them not: for of such is the kingdom of God.

Verily I say unto you, Whosoever shall not receive the kingdom of God as a little child, he shall not enter therein.

And he took them up in his arms, put his hands upon them, and blessed them.

Mark 10:13-16

687 HEALING

When he was come down from the mountain, great multitudes followed him.

And, behold, there came a leper and worshipped him, saying, Lord, if thou wilt, thou canst make me clean.

And Jesus put forth his hand, and touched him, saying, I will; be thou clean. And immediately his leprosy was cleansed.

And Jesus saith unto him, See thou tell no man; but go thy way, shew thyself to the priest, and offer the gift that Moses commanded, for a testimony unto them.

And when Jesus was entered into Capernaum, there came unto him a centurion, beseeching him,

And saying, Lord, my servant lieth at home sick of the palsy, grievously tormented.

And Jesus saith unto him, I will come and heal him.

The centurion answered and said, Lord, I am not worthy that thou shouldest come under my roof: but speak the word only, and my servant shall be healed.

For I am a man under authority, having soldiers under me: and I say to this man, Go, and he goeth; and to another, Come, and he cometh; and to my servant, Do this, and he doeth it.

When Jesus heard it, he marvelled, and said to them that followed, Verily I say unto you, I have not found so great faith, no, not in Israel.

And I say unto you, That many shall come from the east and west, and shall sit down with Abraham, and Isaac, and Jacob, in the kingdom of heaven.

But the children of the kingdom shall be cast out into outer darkness: there shall be weeping and gnashing of teeth.

And Jesus said unto the centurion, Go thy way; and as thou hast believed, so be it done unto thee. And his servant was healed in the selfsame hour.

When the even was come, they brought unto him many that were possessed with devils: and he cast out the spirits with his word, and healed all that were sick:

That it might be fulfilled which was spoken by Esaias the prophet, saying, Himself took our infirmities, and bare our sicknesses.

Matthew 8:1-13, 16-17

Is any sick among you? let him call for the elders of the church; and let them pray over him, anointing him with oil in the name of the Lord:

And the prayer of faith shall save the sick, and the Lord shall raise him up; and if he have committed sins, they shall be forgiven him.

Confess your faults one to another, and pray one for another, that ye may be healed.

James 5:14-16a

688 THANKSGIVING

Therefore thou shalt keep the commandments of the Lord thy God, to walk in his ways, and to fear him.

For the Lord thy God bringeth thee into a good land, a land of brooks of water, of fountains and depths that spring out of valleys and hills;

A land of wheat, and barley, and vines, and fig trees, and pomegranates; a land of oil olive, and honey;

A land wherein thou shalt eat bread without scarceness, thou shalt not lack any thing in it; a land whose stones are iron, and out of whose hills thou mayest dig brass.

When thou hast eaten and art full, then thou shalt bless the Lord thy God for the good land which he hath given thee.

Beware that thou forget not the Lord thy God, in not keeping his commandments, and his judg-

ments, and his statutes, which I command thee this day:

Lest when thou hast eaten and art full, and hast built goodly houses, and dwelt therein;

And when thy herds and thy flocks multiply, and thy silver and thy gold is multiplied, and all that thou hast is multiplied;

Then thine heart be lifted up, and thou forget the Lord thy God, which brought thee forth out of the land of Egypt, from the house of bondage;

Who led thee through that great and terrible wilderness, wherein were fiery serpents, and scorpions, and drought, where there was no water; who brought thee forth water out of the rock of flint;

Who fed thee in the wilderness with manna, which thy fathers knew not, that he might humble thee, and that he might prove thee, to do thee good at thy latter end;

And thou say in thine heart, My power and the might of mine hand hath gotten me this wealth.

But thou shalt remember the Lord thy God: for it is he that giveth thee power to get wealth, that he may establish his covenant which he sware unto thy fathers, as it is this day.

Deuteronomy 8:6-18

689 PRAISE

Sing unto the Lord, all the earth; shew forth from day to day his salvation.

Declare his glory among the heathen; his marvellous works among all nations.

For great is the Lord, and greatly to be praised: he also is to be feared above all gods.

For all the gods of the people are idols: but the Lord made the heavens.

Glory and honour are in his presence; strength and gladness are in his place.

Give unto the Lord, ye kindreds of the people, give unto the Lord glory and strength.

Give unto the Lord the glory due unto his name: bring an offering, and come before him: worship the Lord in the beauty of holiness.

Fear before him, all the earth: the world also shall be stable, that it be not moved.

Let the heavens be glad, and let the earth rejoice: and let men say among the nations, The Lord reigneth.

Let the sea roar, and the fulness thereof: let the fields rejoice, and all that is therein.

Then shall the trees of the wood sing out at the presence of the Lord, because he cometh to judge the earth.

O give thanks unto the Lord; for he is good; for his mercy endureth for ever.

And say ye, Save us, O God of our salvation, and gather us together, and deliver us from the heathen, that we may give thanks to thy holy name, and glory in thy praise.

Blessed be the Lord God of Israel for ever and ever. And all the people said, Amen, and praised the Lord.
1 Chronicles 16:23-36

690 THE EXALTATION OF CHRIST

Let this mind be in you, which was also in Christ Jesus:

Who, being in the form of God, thought it not robbery to be equal with God:

But made himself of no reputation, and took upon him the form of a servant, and was made in the likeness of men:

And being found in fashion as a man, he humbled himself, and became obedient unto death, even the death of the cross.

Wherefore God also hath highly exalted him, and given him a name which is above every name:

That at the name of Jesus every knee should bow, of things in heaven, and things in earth, and things under the earth;

And that every tongue should confess that Jesus Christ is Lord, to the glory of God the Father.
Philippians 2:5-11

And I beheld, and I heard the voice of many angels round about the throne and the beasts and the elders: and the number of them was ten thousand times ten thousand, and thousands of thousands; saying with a loud voice,

Worthy is the Lamb that was slain to receive power, and riches, and wisdom, and strength, and honor, and glory, and blessing.

And every creature which is in heaven, and on the earth, and under the earth, and such as are in the sea, and all that are in them, heard I saying, Blessing, and honor, and glory, and power, be unto him that sitteth upon the throne, and unto the Lamb for ever and ever.

Revelation 5:11-13

691 THE LORD'S RETURN

And while they looked stedfastly toward heaven as he went up, behold, two men stood by them in white apparel;

Which also said, Ye men of Galilee, why stand ye gazing up into heaven? this same Jesus, which is taken up from you into heaven, shall so come in like manner as ye have seen him go into heaven.
Acts 1:10-11

For this we say unto you by the word of the Lord, that we which are alive and remain unto the coming of the Lord shall not prevent them which are asleep.

For the Lord himself shall descend from heaven with a shout, with the voice of the archangel, and with the trump of God: and the dead in Christ shall rise first:

Then we which are alive and remain shall be caught up together with them in the clouds, to meet the Lord in the air: and so shall we ever be with the Lord.

Wherefore comfort one another with these words.
1 Thessalonians 4:15-18

Therefore be ye also ready: for in

such an hour as ye think not the Son of man cometh.

Matthew 24:44

For our conversation is in heaven; from whence also we look for the Saviour, the Lord Jesus Christ.

Philippians 3:20

Seeing then that all these things shall be dissolved, what manner of persons ought ye to be in all holy conversation and godliness,

Looking for and hasting unto the coming of the day of God, wherein the heavens being on fire shall be dissolved, and the elements shall melt with fervent heat?

Nevertheless we, according to his promise, look for new heavens and a new earth, wherein dwelleth righteousness.

Wherefore, beloved, seeing that ye look for such things, be diligent that ye may be found of him in peace, without spot, and blameless.

2 Peter 3:11-14

692 HEAVEN

After this I looked, and, behold, a door was opened in heaven: and the first voice which I heard was as it were of a trumpet talking with me; which said, Come up hither, and I will shew thee things which must be hereafter.

And immediately I was in the spirit: and, behold, a throne was set in heaven, and one sat on the throne.

And he that sat was to look upon like a jasper and a sardine stone: and there was a rainbow round about the throne, in sight like unto an emerald.

And round about the throne were four and twenty seats: and upon the seats I saw four and twenty elders sitting, clothed in white raiment; and they had on their heads crowns of gold.

Revelation 4:1-4

And I saw a new heaven and a new earth: for the first heaven and the first earth were passed away; and there was no more sea.

And I John saw the holy city, new Jerusalem, coming down from God out of heaven, prepared as a bride adorned for her husband.

And I heard a great voice out of heaven saying, Behold, the tabernacle of God is with men, and he will dwell with them, and they shall be his people, and God himself shall be with them, and be their God.

And God shall wipe away all tears from their eyes; and there shall be no more death, neither sorrow, nor crying, neither shall there be any more pain: for the former things are passed away.

And he carried me away in the spirit to a great and high mountain, and shewed me that great city, the holy Jerusalem, descending out of heaven from God,

Having the glory of God: and her light was like unto a stone most precious, even like a jasper stone, clear as crystal.

And I saw no temple therein: for the Lord God Almighty and the Lamb are the temple of it.

And the city had no need of the sun, neither of the moon, to shine in it: for the glory of God did lighten it, and the Lamb is the light thereof.

And the nations of them which are saved shall walk in the light of it: and the kings of the earth do bring their glory and honour into it.

Revelation 21:1-4, 10-11, 22-24

And there shall be no more curse: but the throne of God and of the Lamb shall be in it; and his servants shall serve him:

And they shall see his face; and his name shall be in their foreheads.

And there shall be no night there; and they need no candle, neither light of the sun; for the Lord God giveth them light: and they shall reign for ever and ever.

Revelation 22:3-5

TOPICAL SELECTIONS FOR UNISON READING

The Commandments	Exodus 20:1-21
The Charge to Joshua	Joshua 1:1-18
Loyalty	Ruth 1:1-18
Solomon's Prayer	1 Kings 8:22-30
The Source of Wisdom	Job 28:12-28
A Father's Advice	Proverbs 3:1-12
Wisdom's Call	Proverbs 8:1-20
The Virtuous Woman	Proverbs 31:10-31
The Prophetic Call	Isaiah 6:1-8
The King and His Kingdom	Isaiah 11:1-9
The Greatness of God	Isaiah 40:1-13
God's Sovereignty	Isaiah 40:14-31
The Servant's Commission	Isaiah 42:1-12
The Suffering Servant	Isaiah 52:13—53:12
The Call to Salvation	Isaiah 55:1-13
The Prophetic Authority	Isaiah 61:1-9
Balm in Gilead	Jeremiah 8:18-22
Visions of God	Ezekiel 1:1-28
The Ancient of Days	Daniel 7:9-14
The Call to Repentance	Joel 2:12-20
The Temptation of Jesus	Matthew 4:1-11
The Beatitudes	Matthew 5:3-16
True Treasures	Matthew 6:19-34
The Teaching Christ	Matthew 7:13-29
The Healing Christ	Matthew 8:1-17
The Transfiguration	Matthew 17:1-9
Little Children	Matthew 18:1-11
The Second Coming	Matthew 24:27-42
Missions	Mark 16:14-20
The Magnificat	Luke 1:46-55
The Child Jesus	Luke 2:40-52
The Good Samaritan	Luke 10:25-37
Prayer	Luke 11:1-13
The Seeking Christ	Luke 15:1-10
The Responsibility of Opportunity	Luke 16:19-31
The Walk to Emmaus	Luke 24:13-35
The New Birth	John 3:1-21
The True Shepherd	John 10:1-18
Christian Humility	John 13:3-17
A Message of Comfort	John 14:1-14
The Promise of the Comforter	John 14:15-27

Topical Selections for Unison Reading

Topic	Reading
Abiding in Christ	John 15:1-16
The True High Priest	John 17:16-26
Missions	Romans 1:14-23
Justification by Faith	Romans 5:1-11
Christian Baptism	Romans 6:4-11
The Ministry of the Spirit	Romans 8:1-18
Missions	Romans 10:1-15
The Dedicated Life	Romans 12:1-21
The Mind of Christ	Romans 15:4-13
The Good Race	1 Corinthians 9:24—10:13
The Gifts of the Spirit	1 Corinthians 12:1-11
Love	1 Corinthians 12:31—13:13
The Resurrection	1 Corinthians 15:1-22
Christ's Sufficiency	2 Corinthians 3:4-11
Workers Together	2 Corinthians 6:1-10
The New Mediator	Galatians 3:15-22
The Fruit of the Spirit	Galatians 5:16-26
Living for His Glory	Ephesians 1:3-14
The Church	Ephesians 2:1-22
Followers of Christ	Ephesians 5:1-9
Wives, Husbands, Children	Ephesians 5:22—6:4
The Mind of Christ	Philippians 2:1-15
Jesus Christ Preeminent	Colossians 1:1-18
The Coming of Christ	1 Thessalonians 4:13-18
The Children of Light	1 Thessalonians 5:5-24
Godliness with Contentment	1 Timothy 6:6-16
A Beloved Brother	Philemon 4-18
The Excellency of Christ	Hebrews 1:1-12
The Promised Rest	Hebrews 4:1-16
Mediator of a Better Covenant	Hebrews 8:1-13
The Confession of Our Hope	Hebrews 10:19-36
Faith	Hebrews 11:1-16
The Race Set Before Us	Hebrews 12:1-29
Whence Comes Conflicts	James 4:1-10
Pray One for Another	James 5:13-20
The Ministry of Trial	1 Peter 4:12-19
The Certainty of God's Word	2 Peter 1:16-21
The Children of God	1 John 3:1-10
Brotherly Love	1 John 4:7-21
Born of God	1 John 5:4-12
The New Creation	Revelation 21:1-14

CALLS TO WORSHIP

Be still, and know that I am God: I will be exalted among the heathen, I will be exalted in the earth. Psalm 46:10

Exalt the Lord our God, and worship at his holy hill; for the Lord our God is holy. Psalm 99:9

O give thanks unto the Lord, for he is good: for his mercy endureth for ever. Let the redeemed of the Lord say so. Psalm 107:1-2

O praise the Lord, all ye nations: praise him, all ye people. For his merciful kindness is great toward us: and the truth of the Lord endureth for ever. Praise ye the Lord. Psalm 117

This is the day which the Lord hath made; we will rejoice and be glad in it. Psalm 118:24

I was glad when they said unto me, Let us go into the house of the Lord. Psalm 122:1

Praise ye the Lord. Praise God in his sanctuary: praise him in the firmament of his power. Let every thing that hath breath praise the Lord. Psalm 150:1, 6

The Lord is in his holy temple: let all the earth keep silence before him. Habakkuk 2:20

Come unto me, all ye that labour and are heavy laden, and I will give you rest. Matthew 11:28

The hour cometh, and now is, when the true worshippers shall worship the Father in spirit and in truth: for the Father seeketh such to worship him. John 4:23

God is a Spirit: and they that worship him must worship him in spirit and in truth. John 4:24

If ye then be risen with Christ, seek those things which are above, where Christ sitteth on the right hand of God. Set your affection on things above, not on things on the earth. Colossians 3:1-2

INVOCATIONS

I will come into thy house in the multitude of thy mercy: and in thy fear will I worship toward thy holy temple. Lead me, O Lord, in thy righteousness because of mine enemies; make thy way straight before my face. Psalm 5:7-8

Unto thee, O Lord, do I lift up my soul. O my God, I trust in thee: let me not be ashamed, let not mine enemies triumph over me. Yea, let none that wait on thee be ashamed: let them be ashamed which transgress without cause. Show me thy ways, O Lord; teach me thy paths. Lead me in thy truth, and teach me: for thou art the God of my salvation; on thee do I wait all the day. Psalm 25:1-5

Invocations

Lord, I have loved the habitation of thy house, and the place where thine honour dwelleth. I will walk in mine integrity; redeem me, and be merciful unto me. My foot standeth in an even place: in the congregations will I bless the Lord. Psalm 26:8, 11-12

I will praise thee, O Lord, among the people: I will sing unto thee among the nations. For thy mercy is great unto the heavens, and thy truth unto the clouds. Be thou exalted, O God, above the heavens: let thy glory be above all the earth. Psalm 57:9-11

O God, thou art my God; early will I seek thee: my soul thirsteth for thee, my flesh longeth for thee in a dry and thirsty land, where no water is; To see thy power and thy glory, so as I have seen thee in the sanctuary. Because thy lovingkindness is better than life, my lips shall praise thee. Psalm 63:1-3

How amiable are thy tabernacles, O Lord of hosts! My soul longeth, yea, even fainteth for the courts of the Lord: my heart and my flesh crieth out for the living God. Blessed are they that dwell in thy house: they will be still praising thee. Psalm 84:1-2, 4

Give ear, O Lord, unto my prayer; and attend to the voice of my supplications. In the day of my trouble I will call upon thee: for thou wilt answer me. Among the gods there is none like unto thee, O Lord; neither are there any works like unto thy works. All nations whom thou hast made shall come and worship before thee, O Lord; and shall glorify thy name. For thou art great, and doest wondrous things: thou art God alone. Psalm 86:6-10

Unto thee lift I up mine eyes, O thou that dwellest in the heavens. Behold, as the eyes of servants look unto the hand of their masters, and as the eyes of a maiden unto the hand of her mistress; so our eyes wait upon the Lord our God, until that he have mercy upon us. Have mercy upon us, O Lord, have mercy upon us. Psalm 123:1-3

OFFERTORY SENTENCES

Offer unto God thanksgiving; and pay thy vows unto the most High. Psalm 50:14

Give unto the Lord, O ye kindreds of the people, give unto the Lord glory and strength. Give unto the Lord the glory due unto his name: bring an offering, and come into his courts. Psalm 96:7-8

Honour the Lord with thy substance, and with the firstfruits of all thine increase. Proverbs 3:9

Bring ye all the tithes into the storehouse, that there may be meat in mine house, and prove me now herewith, saith the Lord of hosts, if I will not open you the windows of heaven, and pour you out a blessing, that there shall not be room enough to receive it. Malachi 3:10

Upon the first day of the week let every one of you lay by him in store, as God hath prospered him. I Corinthians 16:2

BENEDICTIONS

The Lord bless thee, and keep thee: The Lord make his face shine upon thee, and be gracious unto thee: The Lord lift up his countenance upon thee, and give thee peace. Numbers 6:24-26

Now to him that is of power to stablish you according to my gospel, and the preaching of Jesus Christ, according to the revelation of the mystery, which was kept secret since the world began, But now is made manifest, and by the scriptures of the prophets, according to the commandment of the everlasting God, made known to all nations for the obedience of faith: To God only wise, be glory through Jesus Christ for ever. Amen. Romans 16:25-27

The grace of the Lord Jesus Christ, and the love of God, and the communion of the Holy Ghost, be with you all. Amen. II Corinthians 13:14

Grace be to you and peace from God the Father, and from our Lord Jesus Christ, Who gave himself for our sins, that he might deliver us from this present evil world, according to the will of God and our Father: To whom be glory for ever and ever. Amen. Galatians 1:3-5

Now unto him that is able to do exceeding abundantly above all that we ask or think, according to the power that worketh in us, Unto him be glory in the church by Christ Jesus throughout all ages, world without end. Amen. Ephesians 3:20-21

And the very God of peace sanctify you wholly; and I pray God your whole spirit and soul and body be preserved blameless unto the coming of our Lord Jesus Christ. I Thessalonians 5:23

Now unto the King eternal, immortal, invisible, the only wise God, be honour and glory for ever and ever. Amen. I Timothy 1:17

Now the God of peace, that brought again from the dead our Lord Jesus, that great shepherd of the sheep, through the blood of the everlasting covenant, Make you perfect in every good work to do his will, working in you that which is wellpleasing in his sight, through Jesus Christ; to whom be glory for ever and ever. Amen. Hebrews 13:20-21

But the God of all grace, who hath called us unto his eternal glory by Christ Jesus, after that ye have suffered a while, make you perfect, stablish, strengthen, settle you. To him be glory and dominion for ever and ever. Amen. I Peter 5:10-11

Now unto him that is able to keep you from falling, and to present you faultless before the presence of his glory with exceeding joy, To the only wise God our Saviour, be glory and majesty, dominion and power, both now and ever. Amen. Jude 24-25

Unto him that loved us, and washed us from our sins in his own blood, And hath made us kings and priests unto God and his Father; to him be glory and dominion for ever and ever. Amen. Revelation 1:5-6

WORDS OF PARDON AND PROMISE

Let the wicked forsake his way, and the unrighteous man his thoughts: and let him return unto the Lord, and he will have mercy upon him; and to our God, for he will abundantly pardon. Isaiah 55:7

Call unto me, and I will answer thee, and show thee great and mighty things, which thou knowest not. Jeremiah 33:3

Come unto me, all ye that labour and are heavy laden, and I will give you rest. Matthew 11:28

But as many as received him, to them gave he power to become the sons of God, even to them that believe on his name. John 1:12

For God so loved the world, that he gave his only begotten Son, that whosoever believeth in him should not perish, but have everlasting life. John 3:16

I am come that they might have life, and that they might have it more abundantly. John 10:10

By grace are ye saved through faith; and that not of yourselves: it is the gift of God: not of works, lest any man should boast. Ephesians 2:8-9

Denying ungodliness and worldly lusts, we should live soberly, righteously, and godly, in this present world; Looking for that blessed hope, and the glorious appearing of the great God and our Saviour Jesus Christ. Titus 2:12-13

The prayer of faith shall save the sick, and the Lord shall raise him up; and if he have committed sins, they shall be forgiven him. James 5:15

The blood of Jesus Christ his Son cleanseth us from all sin. I John 1:7

Now are we the sons of God, and it doth not yet appear what we shall be: but we know that, when he shall appear, we shall be like him; for we shall see him as he is. I John 3:2

Behold, I stand at the door, and knock: if any man hear my voice, and open the door, I will come in to him, and will sup with him, and he with me. Revelation 3:20

THE APOSTLES' CREED

I believe in God the Father Almighty, Maker of heaven and earth:

And in Jesus Christ His only Son, our Lord, who was conceived by the Holy Ghost, born of the Virgin Mary, suffered under Pontius Pilate, was crucified, dead, and buried; He descended into hell; the third day He rose again from the dead; He ascended into heaven and sitteth on the right hand of God the Father Almighty; from thence He shall come to judge the quick and the dead.

I believe in the Holy Ghost, the holy catholic Church, the communion of saints, the forgiveness of sins, the resurrection of the body, and the life everlasting. Amen.

THE NICENE CREED

I believe in one God, the Father Almighty, Maker of heaven and earth, and of all things visible and invisible;

And in one Lord Jesus Christ, the only begotten Son of God, begotten of His Father before all worlds, God of God, Light of Light, very God of very God, begotten, not made, being of one substance with the Father, by whom all things were made: who, for us men and for our salvation, came down from heaven, and was incarnate by the Holy Ghost of the Virgin Mary, and was made man; and was crucified also for us under Pontius Pilate. He suffered and was buried; and the third day He rose again according to the Scriptures, and ascended into heaven, and sitteth on the right hand of the Father. And He shall come again with glory to judge both the quick and the dead: whose kingdom shall have no end.

And I believe in the Holy Ghost, the Lord and Giver of life, who proceedeth from the Father and the Son, who with the Father and the Son together is worshiped and glorified, who spake by the prophets. And I believe one holy catholic and apostolic Church. I acknowledge one baptism for the remission of sins; and I look for the resurrection of the dead, and the life of the world to come. Amen.

SCRIPTURAL ALLUSIONS AND QUOTATIONS IN HYMNS

Scriptural Allusions and Quotations in Hymns

Scriptural Allusions and Quotations in Hymns

ALPHABETICAL INDEX OF TUNES

Alphabetical Index of Tunes

Alphabetical Index of Tunes

METRICAL INDEX OF TUNES

Metrical Index of Tunes

Metrical Index of Tunes

Metrical Index of Tunes

INDEX OF AUTHORS, COMPOSERS, AND SOURCES

Index of Authors, Composers, and Sources

Index of Authors, Composers, and Sources

Index of Authors, Composers, and Sources

Index of Authors, Composers, and Sources

Index of Authors, Composers, and Sources

TOPICAL INDEX OF TITLES AND FIRST LINES

Title is given in **Bold Face**

ABIDING IN CHRIST

Topical Index of Titles and First Lines

Topical Index of Titles and First Lines

Topical Index of Titles and First Lines

Topical Index of Titles and First Lines

Topical Index of Titles and First Lines

Topical Index of Titles and First Lines

Topical Index of Titles and First Lines

Topical Index of Titles and First Lines

Topical Index of Titles and First Lines

Topical Index of Titles and First Lines

Topical Index of Titles and First Lines

INDEX OF TITLES AND FIRST LINES

Title is given in **Bold Face**

Index of Titles and First Lines

Index of Titles and First Lines

Index of Titles and First Lines

Index of Titles and First Lines

Index of Titles and First Lines

U

V

W